FOURTH EDITION

HUMAN RELATIONS
INTERPERSONAL, JOB-ORIENTED SKILLS

Andrew J. DuBrin
College of Business
Rochester Institute of Technology

Terri Geerinck
Sir Sandford Fleming College

PEARSON

Toronto

Vice-President, Editorial Director: Gary Bennett
Editor-in-Chief: Michelle Sartor
Acquisitions Editor: David Le Gallais
Sponsoring Editor: Joel Gladstone
Marketing Coordinator: Ariel Kroon
Supervising Developmental Editor: Madhu Ranadive
Developmental Editor: Louise MacKenzie
Project Manager: Richard di Santo
Production Editor: Rashmi Tickyani, Aptara®, Inc.
Copy Editor: Rodney Rawlings
Proofreader: Sally Glover
Compositor: Aptara®, Inc.
Photo Researcher: Caroline Mariya Vincent, PreMediaGlobal
Permissions Researcher: Jill C. Dougan, Electronic Publishing Services Inc.
Art Director: Jayne Conte
Cover Designer: Suzanne Duda
Cover Image: Andres Rodriguez/Fotolia

Credits and acknowledgments for material borrowed from other sources and reproduced, with permission, in this textbook appear on the appropriate page within the text.

Original edition published by Pearson Education, Inc., Upper Saddle River, New Jersey, USA. Copyright © 2013 Pearson Education, Inc. This edition is authorized for sale only in Canada.

If you purchased this book outside the United States or Canada, you should be aware that it has been imported without the approval of the publisher or the author.

Copyright © 2015, 2009, 2006, 2002 Pearson Canada Inc. All rights reserved. Manufactured in the United States of America. This publication is protected by copyright and permission should be obtained from the publisher prior to any prohibited reproduction, storage in a retrieval system, or transmission in any form or by any means, electronic, mechanical, photocopying, recording, or likewise. To obtain permission(s) to use material from this work, please submit a written request to Pearson Canada Inc., Permissions Department, 26 Prince Andrew Place, Don Mills, Ontario, M3C 2T8, or fax your request to 416-447-3126, or submit a request to Permissions Requests at www.pearsoncanada.ca.

Library and Archives Canada Cataloguing in Publication
DuBrin, Andrew J., author
Human relations : interpersonal, job-oriented skills / Andrew J. DuBrin,
College of Business, Rochester Institute of Technology, Terri Geerinck, Sir
Sandford Fleming College. — Fourth edition.

Includes bibliographical references and index.
ISBN 978-0-13-310530-8 (pbk.)

1. Interpersonal relations—Textbooks.   2. Success in business—Textbooks.
3. Personnel management—Textbooks.   4. Interpersonal communication—
Textbooks.   5. Self-management (Psychology)—Textbooks.   I. Geerinck, Terri,
1958-, author   II. Title.

HD6955.D823 2014   650.1'3   C2013-906187-8

9 2022

PEARSON

ISBN: 978-0-13-310530-8

BRIEF CONTENTS

Chapter 1   A Framework for Interpersonal Skill Development   2

Chapter 2   Understanding Individual Differences   18

Chapter 3   Building Self-Esteem and Self-Confidence   42

Chapter 4   Interpersonal Communication   62

Chapter 5   Interpersonal Skills for the Digital World   86

Chapter 6   Developing Teamwork Skills   108

Chapter 7   Group Problem Solving and Decision Making   136

Chapter 8   Cross-Cultural Relations and Diversity   154

Chapter 9   Resolving Conflicts with Others   174

Chapter 10   Becoming an Effective Leader   198

Chapter 11   Skills for Motivating and Helping Others   222

Chapter 12   Positive Political Skills   250

Chapter 13   Customer Satisfaction Skills   278

Chapter 14   Enhancing Ethical Behaviour   300

Chapter 15   Personal Productivity and Stress Management   324

Chapter 16   Job Search and Career Management Skills (Online)

CONTENTS

Preface xv
Supplemental Materials xviii
Acknowledgments xx

Chapter 1 A Framework for Interpersonal Skill Development 2

Plan of the Text 3
A Model for Improving Interpersonal Skills 5
   Goal or Desired State of Affairs 5
   Assessing Reality 7
   An Action Plan 7
   Feedback on Actions 8
   Frequent Practice 8
Identification of Developmental Needs 9
Universal Needs for Improving Interpersonal Relations 10
Developing Interpersonal Skills on the Job 12
   Informal Learning 13
   Specific Developmental Experiences 14
Developing Your Human Relations Skills and Reinforcing Concepts 15
Summary 15
Interpersonal Relations Case 1-1: Nobody Likes Me 15
Case Questions 16
Interpersonal Relations Case 1-2: Sumera Sets Some Goals 16
Case Questions 15
Questions for Discussion and Review 16
Multiple Choice 16
Short Answer 16
The Web Corner 17

Chapter 2 Understanding Individual Differences 18

Personality 19
   Eight Major Personality Factors and Traits 19
   The Eight Factors and Traits and Job Performance 22
Cognitive Styles and Personality Types 23
   Guidelines for Dealing with Different Personality Types 25
Cognitive Ability 27
   Traditional Intelligence 27

Practical Intelligence 28
Multiple Intelligences 29
Emotional Intelligence 30
Guidelines for Relating to People of Different Levels and Types of Intelligence 32

Values as a Source of Individual Differences 33
Classification of Values 33
Generational Differences in Values 33
How Values Are Learned 35
Clarifying Your Values 35
The Mesh between Individual and Job Values 36
Guidelines for Using Values to Improve Interpersonal Relations 37

Developing Your Human Relations Skills and Reinforcing Concepts 39
Summary 39
Interpersonal Relations Case 2-1: Capitalizing on Hidden Talent at Westmont Centre 39
Case Questions 40
Interpersonal Relations Case 2-2: "We've Got to Make Our Numbers" 40
Case Questions 40
Questions for Discussion and Review 41
Multiple Choice 41
Short Answer 41
The Web Corner 41

Chapter 3 Building Self-Esteem and Self-Confidence 42

The Meaning of Self-Esteem, Its Development and Consequences 43
How Self-Esteem Develops 45
The Consequences of High Self-Esteem 46

Enhancing Self-Esteem 47
Attain Legitimate Accomplishments 48
Be Aware of Personal Strengths 48
Rebut the Inner Critic 49
Practise Self-Nurturing 50
Minimize Settings and Interactions That Detract from Your Feelings of Competence 50
Get Help from Others 51
Model the Behaviour of People with High Self-Esteem 51
Create a High-Self-Esteem Living Space 51
How a Manager Helps Build the Self-Esteem of Group Members 52

The Importance of Self-Confidence and Self-Efficacy 52
Techniques for Developing and Enhancing Your Self-Confidence 54
Develop a Solid Knowledge Base 54
Use Positive Self-Talk 55
Avoid Negative Self-Talk 55
Use Positive Visual Imagery 56

Set High Expectations for Yourself (the Galatea Effect) 56
Develop the Explanatory Style of Optimists 56
Strive for Peak Performance 57
Bounce Back from Setbacks and Embarrassments 58

Developing Your Human Relations Skills and Reinforcing Concepts 59

Summary 59

Interpersonal Relations Case 3-1: The Confetti Man 59
Case Questions 60
Interpersonal Relations Case 3-2: Why Can't I Get a Job? 60
Case Questions 60
Questions for Discussion and Review 60
Multiple Choice 60
Short Answer 61
The Web Corner 61

Chapter 4 — Interpersonal Communication 62

Steps in the Communication Process 64
Relationship Building and Interpersonal Communication 65
Nonverbal Communication in Organizations 66
    Modes of Transmission of Nonverbal Communication 67
    Guidelines for Improving Nonverbal Communication 70

Guidelines for Overcoming Communication Problems and Barriers 71
Understand the Receiver 71
Minimize Defensive Communication 72
Repeat Your Message Using Multiple Channels (in Moderation) 72
Check Comprehension and Feelings through Verbal and Nonverbal Feedback 73
Display a Positive Attitude 73
Communicate Persuasively 74
Engage in Active Listening 75
Prepare for Stressful Conversations 78
Engage in Metacommunication 80
Recognize Gender Differences in Communication Style 80

Developing Your Human Relations Skills and Reinforcing Concepts 83

Summary 83

Interpersonal Relations Case 4-1: Why Am I Not Getting through to These People? 83
Case Questions 83
Interpersonal Relations Case 4-2: Karl Walks Around 84
Case Questions 84
Questions for Discussion and Review 84
Multiple Choice 84
Short Answer 85
The Web Corner 85

Chapter 5 Interpersonal Skills for the Digital World 86

Interpersonal Skills for One-on-One Interactions 89
- Cell Phones and Text Messaging 89
- Email Messages and Instant Messaging 92
- Webcam Job Interviews 93
- Interpersonal Aspects of Multitasking 96
- Harassment and Cyberbullying of Others 97

Interpersonal Skills for Small and Large Audiences 98
- Social Networking by Internet 98
- Laptop and Personal Digital Assistant Use during Meetings and Other Formal Settings 100
- Interpersonal Aspects of Presentation Technology 101
- Videoconferencing 101
- Interpersonal Skills Linked to Telecommuting 103
- Avoiding Damage to Your Online Reputation 103

Developing Your Human Relations Skills and Reinforcing Concepts 105

Summary 105

Interpersonal Relations Case 5-1: Unveiled on Facebook 105

Case Questions 105

Interpersonal Relations Case 5-2: Kevin, the Twitter Guy 106

Case Questions 106

Questions for Discussion and Review 106

Multiple Choice 106

Short Answer 107

The Web Corner 107

Chapter 6 Developing Teamwork Skills 108

Face-to-Face versus Virtual Teams 109
- Face-to-Face (Traditional) Teams 110
- Virtual Teams 111

Advantages and Disadvantages of Teams and Teamwork 112
- Advantages of Group Work and Teamwork 112
- Disadvantages of Group Work and Teamwork 113

Team Member Roles 117

Guidelines for the Interpersonal Aspects of Team Play 119
- Trust Team Members 121
- Display a High Level of Cooperation and Collaboration 121
- Recognize the Interests and Achievements of Others 122
- Give and Receive Helpful Criticism 122
- Share the Glory 123
- Take Care Not to Rain on Another Person's Parade 123

Guidelines for the Task Aspects of Team Play 123
- Provide Technical Expertise (or Knowledge of the Task) 124
- Assume Responsibility for Problems 124
- See the Big Picture 124
- Believe in Consensus 125
- Focus on Deadlines 125

CONTENTS vii

    Help Team Members Do Their Jobs Better 125
    Be a Good Organizational Citizen 125
Developing Team Leadership Skills 126
    Engage in Shared Leadership 128
    Build a Mission Statement 128
    Show Your Team Members That They Are Trusted 129
    Establish a Sense of Urgency and High Performance Standards 129
    Hold Question-and-Answer Sessions with the Team 129
    Encourage Team Members to Recognize Each Other's Accomplishments 130
    Encourage Honest Criticism 130
    Use Peer Evaluations 131
    Help Team Members See the Big Picture 131
    Minimize Formation of In-Groups and Out-Groups 131
Developing Your Human Relations Skills and Reinforcing Concepts 133
Summary 133
Interpersonal Relations Case 6-1: Leah Puts on Her Team-Player Face 133
Case Questions 134
Interpersonal Relations Case 6-2: Ruth Waves a Red Flag 134
Case Questions 134
Questions for Discussion and Review 134
Multiple Choice 134
Short Answer 135
The Web Corner 135

Chapter 7 Group Problem Solving and Decision Making 136

Rational versus Political Decision Making in Groups 137
Guidelines for Using General Problem-Solving Groups 139
    Working through the Group Problem-Solving Steps 139
    Managing Disagreement about Group Decision Making 142
    Aiming for Inquiry versus Advocacy in Group Decision Making 143
Guidelines for Brainstorming 143
Guidelines for the Nominal Group Technique 145
Using Standup Meetings to Facilitate Problem Solving 147
Using Email and Groupware to Facilitate Group Decision Making 148
    Using Email to Facilitate Meetings 148
    Using Groupware to Facilitate Group Problem Solving 149
Suggestions for Being an Effective Meeting Participant 150
Developing Your Human Relations Skills and Reinforcing Concepts 151
Summary 151
Interpersonal Relations Case 7-1: Pet Groomers on Wheels Get into a Huddle 151
Case Questions 152

Interpersonal Relations Case 7-2: The Torpedoed Submarine
Rolls   152
Case Questions   152
Questions for Discussion and Review   152
Multiple Choice   152
Short Answer   153
The Web Corner   153

Chapter 8   Cross-Cultural Relations and Diversity   154

The Diversity Umbrella   155
Understanding Cultural Differences   158
   Cultural Sensitivity and Political Correctness   158
   Cultural Intelligence   159
   Respect for All Workers and Cultures   160
   Cultural Fluency   161
   Dimensions of Differences in Cultural Values   161
   Cultural Bloopers   164
Overcoming Cross-Cultural Barriers   164
Techniques for Improving Cross-Cultural Relations   166
   Cultural Training   167
   Cultural Intelligence Training   167
   Language Training   168
   Diversity Training   168
   Cross-Cultural and Cross-Gender Mentoring
     Programs   169
Developing Your Human Relations Skills and Reinforcing
  Concepts   171
Summary   171
Interpersonal Relations Case 8-1: What to Do with
  Shabana?   171
Case Questions   172
Interpersonal Relations Case 8-2: Akiak Wants to Fit In   172
Case Questions   172
Questions for Discussion and Review   172
Multiple Choice   172
Short Answer   173
The Web Corner   173

Chapter 9   Resolving Conflicts with Others   174

Sources of Interpersonal Conflict in Organizations   175
   Competition for Limited Resources   176
   Role Conflict   176
   Competing Work and Family Demands   177
   Personality Clashes   178
   Bullies in the Workplace   178
   Incivility and Rudeness   179
   Cross-Generational Conflict   180
   Workplace Violence (A Cause and Effect of Conflict)   180
Conflict Management Styles   181
   Competitive Style   181

      Accommodative Style   181
      Sharing Style   182
      Collaborative Style   182
      Avoidant Style   182
  Guidelines and Techniques for Resolving Conflicts   183
      Confrontation and Problem Solving   183
      Constructive Handling of Criticism   184
      Reframing   185
      Negotiating and Bargaining   186
  Combatting Sexual Harassment: A Special Type of Conflict   190
      The Adverse Effects of Sexual Harassment   192
      Guidelines for Preventing and Dealing with Sexual Harassment   192
  Developing Your Human Relations Skills and Reinforcing Concepts   195
  Summary   195
  Interpersonal Relations Case 9-1: The Apprehensive Sales Trainee   195
  Case Questions   195
  Interpersonal Relations Case 9-2: The Refrigerator Caper   196
  Case Questions   196
  Questions for Discussion and Review   196
  Multiple Choice   196
  Short Answer   197
  The Web Corner   197

Chapter 10   Becoming an Effective Leader   198

  Key Leadership Traits to Develop   200
      Self-Confidence and Leadership Efficacy   200
      Positive Core Self-Evaluation   201
      Assertiveness   201
      Trustworthiness and Morality   202
      Sense of Humour   204
      Self-Awareness and Self-Objectivity   205
      Cognitive Skills Including Critical Assessments   205
      Emotional Intelligence   206
      Passion and Enthusiasm   207
      Self-Sacrificing Personality   208
  Suggestions for Developing Charisma   208
  Coaching and Training Others   210
      Coaching Skills and Techniques   211
      Training Others   214
  Developing Your Leadership Potential   217
  Developing Your Human Relations Skills and Reinforcing Concepts   219
  Summary   219
  Interpersonal Relations Case 10-1: So Is This How You Learn Leadership?   219
  Case Questions   220

Interpersonal Relations Case 10-2: The Reality Coach   220
Case Questions   220
Questions for Discussion and Review   221
Multiple Choice   221
Short Answer   221
The Web Corner   221

Chapter 11   Skills for Motivating and Helping Others   222

Motivation Skill Based on the Principle of "What's in It for Me?"   223
Using Positive Reinforcement to Motivate Others   226
Using Recognition to Motivate Others   229
  Why Recognition Is a Strong Motivator   229
  Approaches to Giving Recognition   230
  Fine Points about Using Recognition to Motivate Others   231
Using Expectancy Theory to Motivate Others   231
  Capsule Overview of Expectancy Theory   231
  Basic Components of Expectancy Theory   232
  How Moods Influence Expectancy Theory   233
  Diagnosing Motivation with Expectancy Theory   234
  Guidelines for Applying Expectancy Theory   234
Motivating Others by Nurturing and Mentoring   235
  Being a Nurturing, Positive Person   235
  Being a Mentor to Co-Workers   237
  Characteristics and Types of Mentoring   238
  Specific Mentoring Behaviours   238
  Helping Difficult People   240
  Types of Difficult People   240
  Tactics for Dealing with Difficult People   242
Developing Your Human Relations Skills and Reinforcing Concepts   246
Summary   246
Interpersonal Relations Case Problem 11-1: On Time at Prime Time   246
Case Questions   247
Interpersonal Relations Case 11-2: The Nightmare in the Logistics Department   247
Case Questions   248
Questions for Discussion and Review   248
Multiple Choice   248
Short Answer   248
The Web Corner   249

Chapter 12   Positive Political Skills   250

Political Skill and Other Human Relations Skills   253
  Sensitivity to Your Surroundings   253
  Emotional Intelligence and Social Intelligence   254
  Relationship Building with the Leader   254
  Overcoming the Effects of Injustice   255

Impression Management and Etiquette 255
Tactics of Impression Management 255
Business Etiquette 258

Building Relationships with Managers and Other Key People 261
Network with Influential People 261
Help Your Manager Succeed 263
Understand Unwritten Boundaries 263
Volunteer for Assignments 264
Flatter Influential People Sensibly 264
Use Information Power 264
Appear Cool under Pressure 265
Laugh at Your Manager's Humour 265
Express Constructive Disagreement 265
Present a Clear Picture of Your Accomplishments 266

Building Relationships with Co-workers and Other Work Associates 266
Maintain Honest and Open Relationships 266
Make Others Feel Important 267
Be Diplomatic 268
Exchange Favours 269
Ask Advice 269
Share Constructive Gossip 269
Minimize Microinequities 270
Follow Group Norms 270

Avoiding Political Blunders 271

Developing Your Human Relations Skills and Reinforcing Concepts 274

Summary 274

Interpersonal Relations Case Problem 12-1: What Do My Table Manners Have to Do with the Job? 274

Case Questions 275

Interpersonal Relations Case Problem 12-2: Passed-Over Pete 275

Case Questions 276

Questions for Discussion and Review 276

Multiple Choice 276

Short Answer 276

The Web Corner 277

Chapter 13 Customer Satisfaction Skills 278

The Three Components of Customer Experience (Service) 280

Following the General Principles of Customer Satisfaction 281
Be Satisfied So You Can Provide Better Customer Service 282
Receive Emotional Support from Co-workers to Give Better Customer Service 283
Understand Customer Needs and Put Them First 284
Focus on Solving Problems, Not Just Taking Orders 285
Respond Positively to Moments of Truth 285
Be Ready to Accept Empowerment 286

Enhance Customer Service through Information Technology 287
Avoid Rudeness and Hostility toward Customers 288

Creating a Bond with Your Customer 289
Create a Welcoming Attitude, Including a Smile 290
Provide Exceptional Service 290
Show Care and Concern 290
Make the Buyer (Customer) Feel Good 291
Build a Personal Relationship 291
Invite the Customer Back 292

Dealing with Customer Dissatisfaction 292
Deal Constructively with Customer Complaints and Anger 294
Involve the Customer in Working Out the Problem 295
Anticipate How to Handle an Unreasonable Request 295
Maintain a Realistic Customer Retention Attitude 296

Developing Your Human Relations Skills and Reinforcing Concepts 297

Summary 297

Interpersonal Relations Case 13-1: The Rumpled Claims Forms 297

Case Questions 297

Interpersonal Relations Case 13-2: The Troublesome Big Screen 298

Case Questions 298

Questions for Discussion and Review 298

Multiple Choice 298

Short Answer 299

The Web Corner 299

Chapter 14 Enhancing Ethical Behaviour 300

Why Be Concerned about Business Ethics? 301

Common Ethical Problems 303
Why Being Ethical Isn't Easy 303
A Survey of the Extent of Ethical Problems 304
Frequent Ethical Dilemmas 305
Choosing between Two Rights: Dealing with Defining Moments 308

Guidelines for Behaving Ethically 310
Developing Virtuousness 310
Following a Guide to Ethical Decision-Making 311
Developing Closer Relationships with Work Associates 314
Using Corporate Ethics Programs 314
Being Environmentally Conscious 316
Following an Applicable Professional Code of Conduct 318
Be Ready to Exert Upward Ethical Leadership 319

Developing Your Human Relations Skills and Reinforcing Concepts 321

Summary 321

Interpersonal Relations Case 14-1: The Highly Rated, but Expendable Marsha 321

Case Questions   321
Interpersonal Relations Case 14-2: Am I Paid to Be My Manager's TV Repair Technician?   322
Case Questions   322
Questions for Discussion and Review   322
Multiple Choice   322
Short Answer   323
The Web Corner   323

Chapter 15   Personal Productivity and Stress Management   324

Increasing Personal Productivity   325
  Dealing with Procrastination   325
  Attitudes and Values That Increase Personal Productivity   327
  Work Habits and Skills That Increase Personal Productivity   330
  Overcoming Time Wasters   333
Understanding and Managing Stress   335
  Symptoms and Consequences of Stress   336
  Personality and Job Factors Contributing to Stress   338
  Methods and Techniques for Managing Stress   343
Developing Your Human Relations Skills and Reinforcing Concepts   348
Summary   348
Interpersonal Relations Case 15-1: Rachel Runs the Treadmill   348
Case Questions   349
Interpersonal Relations Case 15-2: Stress-Busting at the Agriculture and Markets Group   349
Case Questions   350
Questions for Discussion and Review   350
Multiple Choice   350
Short Answer   350
The Web Corner   351

Glossary   353

Notes   357

Index   369

PREFACE

Welcome to the fourth Canadian edition of *Human Relations: Interpersonal, Job-Oriented Skills*. Success in any position involving interaction with people requires two broad sets of competencies: functional skills and generic skills. The term *functional skills* refers to knowledge of one's discipline (or organizational function), technical skills, specialty skills, or simply details of the job. *Generic skills* (often referred to as *employability* or *soft skills*) refers to competencies important in a variety of jobs. Among these generic skills are good work habits and time management, computer skills, high ethical standards, and interpersonal skills.

Our purpose in writing this book is to help readers improve their interpersonal skills in the workplace. By improving interpersonal skills, a person has a better chance of capitalizing upon his or her other skills. Two primary approaches are used in this text to achieve this lofty goal. First, basic concepts are introduced to enhance understanding of key topics in interpersonal relations in organizations. Second, skill-building suggestions, exercises, and cases are designed to improve interpersonal skills related to the topic. Chapter 6, for example, presents general information about the nature of teamwork, followed by suggestions for improving teamwork. The chapter also includes several exercises or experiential activities and two case problems—all designed to improve teamwork skills.

Third, examples and opening scenarios provide insight into how a particular skill is applied on the job. For example, in Chapter 3, we describe a successful Canadian entrepreneur who had enough confidence and self-esteem to make collecting junk a successful business.

AUDIENCE

The primary audience for this book is people taking courses that emphasize the development of interpersonal skills. Such courses typically include the term *human relations*. Because interpersonal relations contribute so heavily to effective leadership, the text is suited to participants in leadership and supervisory training courses that emphasize interpersonal skills rather than leadership theory and research.

FRAMEWORK

The information is organized into chapters, all emphasizing interpersonal relations between two or more people. Chapter 1, "A Framework for Interpersonal Skill Development," sets the stage for improving one's interpersonal skills on the job. Chapter 2, "Understanding Individual Differences," presents information that is the foundation of effective interpersonal relations. Chapter 3, "Building Self-Esteem and Self-Confidence," describes how to develop self-esteem and self-confidence both for oneself and to improve relationships with others. Chapter 4, "Interpersonal Communication," deals with skills in sending and receiving messages.

Chapter 5, "Interpersonal Skills for the Digital World," describes how interpersonal skills can enhance the use of digital devices, as well as how these devices lend themselves to poor interpersonal skills, such as cellphone abuse. Chapter 6, "Developing Teamwork Skills," sensitizes the reader to a vital set of skills in the workplace. Chapter 7, "Group Problem Solving and Decision Making," provides additional skill in collaborative effort.

Chapter 8, "Cross-Cultural Relations and Diversity," is about developing cross-cultural skills in a diverse workforce. Chapter 9, "Resolving Conflicts with Others," helps the reader develop skills in finding constructive solutions to differences of opinion and disputes with others.

Three consecutive chapters deal with exerting influence over others: Chapter 10, "Becoming an Effective Leader," presents information relevant to exercising leadership in the workplace; Chapter 11, "Skills for Motivating and Helping Others," emphasizes skills required in encouraging others to work hard to achieve goals and how to work with difficult people; and Chapter 12, "Positive Political Skills," describes how to use power and influence for constructive purposes.

Chapter 13, "Customer Satisfaction Skills," describes several approaches to enhancing skills required for satisfying customers. Chapter 14, "Enhancing Ethical Behaviour," translates ethical principles into usable skills. The rationale here is that an ethical base is important for achieving career-long effectiveness in interpersonal relations. Chapter 15, "Personal Productivity and Stress Management," supports the development of interpersonal skills by showing that productive people who have stress under control can relate more effectively to others. Chapter 16, "Job Search and Career Management Skills," includes information about the application of interpersonal skills (such as networking) in advancing one's career.

CHANGES IN THE NEW EDITION

The new edition of *Human Relations* adds several new features and content, most notably two chapters: one about the development of self-esteem and self-confidence (Chapter 3) and one about interpersonal skills for the digital age (Chapter 5). In many places throughout the text, we have added a third level of heading to better organize the information for the student. We have added many new skill-building exercises and new self-assessment quizzes as well as some role-playing exercises. New questions or statements are added to several of the self-quizzes. New information, research findings, and examples appear throughout the text. Most chapters have new case openers with many featuring notable Canadians and Canadian businesses. Material that may have lost some of its relevance has been selectively pruned.

The new topics in the text are as follows:

- Description of personality types and cognitive styles as measured by the Golden Personality Type Profiler (Chapter 2)
- New system of classifying values and associated goals (Chapter 3)
- How a manager builds the self-esteem of group members (Chapter 4)
- More information about active listening (Chapter 4)
- New chapter that includes information from previous edition about etiquette in relation to the use of electronic devices in the workplace (Chapter 5)
- New section on face-to-face versus virtual teams, replacing the previous edition's section "Types of Teams" (Chapter 6)
- More information about the advantages of group work and teamwork (Chapter 6)
- The importance of collective efficacy for group problem solving (Chapter 7)
- Cultural factors and group decision making (Chapter 7)
- New dimension of differences in cultural values, social-support-seeking (Chapter 8)
- Work-to-family conflict and family-to-work conflict (Chapter 9)
- The issue of work–life choices (Chapter 9)
- More about bullies in the workplace (Chapter 9)
- More about workplace violence (Chapter 9)
- Cross-generational conflict (Chapter 9)
- Workplace violence (Chapter 9)
- Conflict-resolution technique of allowing for face-saving (Chapter 9)

- A type of self-confidence specifically for leaders—leadership efficacy (Chapter 10)
- Group of personality traits associated with leadership effectiveness—positive core evaluation (Chapter 10)
- Making critical assessments as a leadership skill (Chapter 10)
- Self-sacrificing personality and leadership effectiveness (Chapter 10)
- Techniques for self-motivation (Chapter 11)
- Expansion of discussion of types of difficult people (Chapter 11)
- New section on political skills and other human relations skills (Chapter 12)
- Organizational citizenship behaviour as part of impression management (Chapter 12)
- Customer-centric sales process (Chapter 13)
- New survey on the extent of ethical problems (Chapter 14)
- Wasting company time as an ethical dilemma (Chapter 14)
- More strategies to enhance ethical behaviour at work (Chapter 14)
- Figure listing representative suggestions for helping a company contribute to a sustainable environment (Chapter 14)
- Adverse interaction with customers and emotional labour in relation to stress (Chapter 15)
- Job loss as a source of stress (Chapter 15)
- Cognitive behavioural approach to stress management (Chapter 15)
- Salary discussion during a job interview (Chapter 16)
- Career-advancement strategy of pursuing fields and industries many others overlook (Chapter 16)

This fourth Canadian edition features an increased presence of Canadian examples, research, and statistics. As well, whenever possible, Canadian businesses and organizations, or those with Canadian locations, are used to provide better examples of practices in Canada. Many companies are international with global locations, so not all were replaced.

SUPPLEMENTAL MATERIALS

RESOURCES FOR INSTRUCTORS

The following instructor supplements are available for downloading from a password-protected section of Pearson Canada's online catalogue. Navigate to your book's catalogue page to view a list of those supplements that are available. See your local sales representative for details and access.

Instructor's Manual

The Instructor's Manual for this text contains chapter outlines and lecture notes, answers to discussion questions and case problems, and comments about the exercises.

Test Item File

The Test Item File includes 800 questions in multiple choice and true/false format. Each question is accompanied by the correct answer.

PowerPoint Lecture Presentation Package

This supplement provides a comprehensive selection of slides highlighting key concepts featured in the text. The slides have been specifically developed for clear and easy communication of themes, ideas, and definitions.

RESOURCES FOR STUDENTS

MySearchLab with eText

MySearchLab with eText provides access to an online interactive version of the text and contains writing, grammar, and research tools, access to a variety of academic journals, Associated Press news feeds, and discipline-specific readings to help you hone your writing and research skills. Just like the printed text, you can highlight and add notes to the eText online. You can also access the eText on your iPad or Android tablet by downloading the free Pearson eText app. For more information and to redeem or purchase an access code please visit www.mysearchlab.com.

CourseSmart

CourseSmart goes beyond traditional expectations, providing instant, online access to the textbooks and course materials you need at a lower cost for students. And even as students save money, you can save time and hassle with a digital eText that allows you to search for the most relevant content at the very moment you need it. Whether it's evaluating textbooks or creating lecture notes to help students with difficult concepts, CourseSmart can make life a little easier. See how when you visit www.coursesmart.com/instructors.

Technology Specialists

Pearson's Technology Specialists work with faculty and campus course designers to ensure that Pearson technology products, assessment tools, and online course materials are tailored to meet your specific needs. This highly qualified team is dedicated to helping schools take full advantage of a wide range of educational resources, by assisting in the integration of a variety of instructional materials and media formats. Your local Pearson sales representative can provide you with more details on this service program.

Pearson Custom Library

For enrollments of at least 25 students, you can create your own textbook by choosing the chapters that best suit your own course needs. To begin building your custom text, visit **www.pearsoncustomlibrary.com**. You may also work with a dedicated Pearson Custom editor to create your ideal text—publishing your own original content or mixing and matching Pearson content. Contact your local Pearson representative to get started.

ACKNOWLEDGMENTS

My appreciation goes to the many people who contributed to the development and production of this book. Special thanks to Robert A. Herring III at Winston–Salem State University and Nancy Kriscenski at Manchester Community College for their insightful comments on this revision. Appreciation is also expressed to the outside reviewers who made suggestions for shaping this and previous editions of the text: Abhirjun Dutta, Bainbridge College; Robert G. DelCampo, University of New Mexico; David W. Robinson, Malaspina University College; Tim Blood, Lane Community College; Jane Bowerman, University of Oklahoma; John Adamski II, Ivy Tech State College; Patricia Lynn Anderson, Valdosta State University; Judy Bowie, DeVry Institute of Technology; Robert A. Herring III, Winston–Salem State University; H. Frederick Holmes, Ogeechee Technical Institute; Ruth V. Kellar, Ivy Tech State College; Diane Paul, TVI Community College; Lou Jean Peace, Valdosta Technical Institute; Gary W. Piggrem, Ph.D., DeVry Institute of Technology; Dean Weeden, Utah Career College; and James E. Wetz, Central Florida Community College.

My family members give me an additional reason for writing, so I extend my appreciation to Drew, Douglas, Melanie, Gizella, Will, Rosie, Clare, Camila, Sofia, Eliana, Julian, and Carson. I thank Stefanie, the woman in my life, for her contribution to my well-being.

Andrew J. DuBrin
Rochester, New York

My sincere appreciation goes to the many people who contributed to the development and production of this book. My primary thanks are extended to the editorial and production team at Pearson Education Canada. A special thanks to the outside reviewers who provided valuable insights and ideas: Christine Doody, Algonquin College; Karen Katsedemas, Fanshawe College; Teresa Kisilevich, Okanagan College; Fran Jeffrey, Durham College; Michelle Jordan, Humber College; Shauna Moore, Durham College; and Cheryl Veinotte, Nova Scotia Community College.

I would also like to thank my co-workers and friends for their support and encouragement. And last, but never least, thanks to my wonderful family and partner, who tolerate my writing binges and continue to be my best inspiration.

Terri Geerinck
Peterborough, Ontario

HUMAN RELATIONS
INTERPERSONAL, JOB-ORIENTED SKILLS

CHAPTER 1

A Framework for Interpersonal Skill Development

less business downtown

Dominique was one of several receptionists at a large hotel located not far from the airport in Vancouver. Two of the hotel executives were discussing which receptionist should be promoted to assistant hotel manager, a vacancy created because the current assistant manager was being promoted to manager of one of the company's suburban hotels.

One manager said to the other, "I think that Dominique is the strongest candidate for the assistant manager position. She has a little less experience than the other three receptionists, but I think she would make a wonderful assistant manager."

The other manager replied, "But take Todd, for example; he has a much better knowledge of hotel operations and our computer system than Dominique does. So maybe Todd should get the promotion this time." The first manager pointed out that Dominique's superior skills with people

Pressmaster/Shutterstock

LEARNING Objectives

After reading and studying this chapter and doing the exercises, you should be able to

1. Explain how interpersonal skills are learned.
2. Explain the model for interpersonal skill improvement.
3. Pinpoint your needs for improvement in interpersonal relations.
4. Describe potential opportunities for developing interpersonal skills on the job.

made her the best candidate for the position. "I think that in time Dominique can learn more about our operations, including the new computer system. We can't forget that hotels are a people business, and Dominique gets along well with people. I've seen her resolve tough problems with both guests and other members of the hotel staff. And what a warm smile she has. While Todd has a better knowledge of operations and the computing system, several guests have described him as rather cold or aloof. He often appears not to care about the guests and he rarely smiles. He has also had some issues with co-workers and he is not always a good team player."

After thinking for a few moments, the second manager said, "You've got a good point. Let's offer the promotion to Dominique, with Todd as a strong second choice. We'll also coach Todd on his people skills so he can be promoted in the future. At that time we would offer him the promotion, assuming he were interested."

Scenes like this one are common in the workplace. Many people are promoted to a supervisory position because they have good human relations skills combined with adequate technical skills. As the Dale Carnegie organization states, "To achieve success in today's work world—with its emphasis on collaboration, teamwork, motivation, and leadership—you need to perfect your interpersonal skills."[1] Effective interpersonal relations must be combined with technical knowledge and good work habits to achieve success in any job involving interaction with people. Workers at all levels are expected not only to solve problems and improve processes (how work is performed), but also to interact effectively with other employees.[2] Furthermore, the lack of good interpersonal skills can adversely affect a person's career. A study found that 90 percent of firings result from poor attitudes, inappropriate behaviour, and problems in interpersonal relationships.[3]

This chapter explains how people develop interpersonal skills and how the workplace can be a natural setting for that development. It also presents a model that can serve as a foundation for improving your interpersonal skills.

Steve Gorton/Dorling Kindersley

interpersonal relations
The technical term for relationships with people.

LEARNING OBJECTIVE 1

PLAN OF THE TEXT

This entire text is devoted to the many different ways of improving interpersonal relations in organizations. A three-part strategy is presented for achieving the high level of effectiveness in interpersonal relations required in today's workplace. First, each chapter presents

A FRAMEWORK FOR INTERPERSONAL SKILL DEVELOPMENT

FIGURE 1-1   Plan for Achieving Effectiveness in Interpersonal Relation

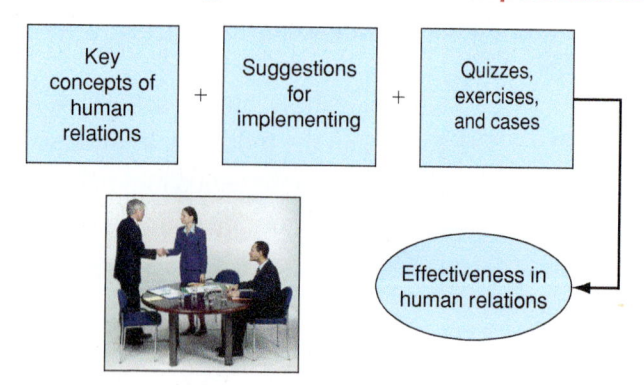

key concepts required for understanding a particular aspect of interpersonal relations, such as resolving conflict. Second, the chapter provides specific suggestions or behavioural guidelines for improvement in that aspect of interpersonal relations. Third, a variety of exercises gives you the opportunity to work on and improve your skills. Among these exercises are self-assessment quizzes, skill-building exercises, and cases for analysis. In addition, the questions at the end of each chapter give you an opportunity to think through and apply that chapter's key ideas. Weblinks are also provided at the end of each chapter to enable you to explore areas of interest in more depth. Figure 1-1 illustrates the plan of the text.

Much of this text is concerned with **interpersonal skills training**, the teaching of skills in dealing with others, so those skills can be put into practice. Interpersonal skills training is referred to as *soft-skill* training to differentiate it from technical training. (Technical skills are referred to as *hard skills*.) Soft-skill training builds interpersonal skills, including communication, listening, group problem solving, cross-cultural relations, and customer service. Several specific competencies related to soft skills are as follows:

interpersonal skills training
The teaching of skills in dealing with others.

- Effectively translating and conveying information
- Being able to accurately interpret other people's emotions
- Being sensitive to other people's feelings
- Calmly arriving at resolutions to conflicts
- Avoiding negative gossip
- Being polite[4]
- Being able to cooperate with others to meet objectives (teamwork)

Soft-skill training is more important than ever as organizations realize that a combination of human effort and technology is needed to produce results. Multiple studies have shown that soft skills can compensate for more traditional cognitive (or analytical) intelligence. For example, a supervisor with good interpersonal skills might perform well even if he or she is not outstandingly intelligent. The statement does not mean, however, that outstanding soft skills will compensate for high cognitive intelligence when doing highly analytical work such as analyzing the value of an investment or a company. Findings from the Conference Board of Canada, in its Employability Skills 2000+ report, indicate the increased need for soft skills in this economy, including communication skills, positive attitudes and behaviours, working with others, thinking critically, goal setting, and adaptability.[5]

Soft skills are often the differentiating factor between adequate and outstanding performance, because dealing with people is part of so many jobs.[6] Assume that a company establishes an elaborate intranet system to enable employees to exchange work-related information with each other. The system will not achieve its potential unless employees are motivated to use it properly and they develop a spirit of cooperation. The employees must also be willing to share some of their best ideas with each other. Consider this example:

Sara, a newly hired intake receptionist in a cardiac clinic, notices that too often the patients present incomplete or inaccurate information, such as omitting data about their next of kin. Sara spends considerable amounts of time reworking forms with the patients, until she begins using soft skills more effectively. With coaching from her supervisor, Sara learns that if she attempts to calm down a patient first, the patient is more likely to complete the intake form accurately.

Well-known executive coach Marshall Goldsmith reminds us that building relationships with people is important for workers at every level in the organization, including the CEO. An example of an interpersonal skill that would help build relationships would be demanding good results from others yet showing them respect at the same time.[7]

A MODEL FOR IMPROVING INTERPERSONAL SKILLS

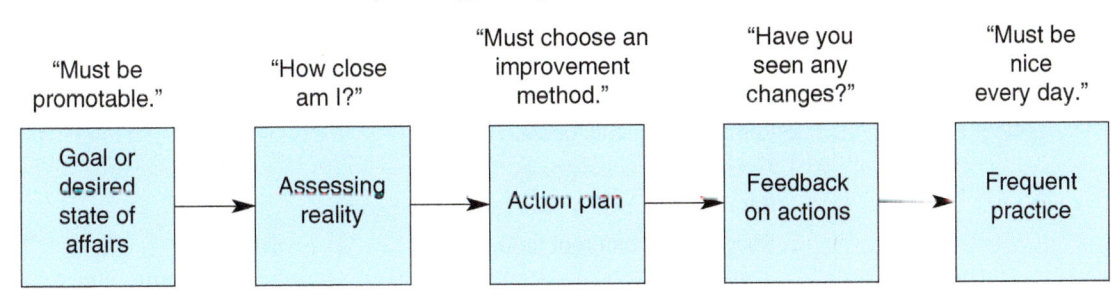

Acquiring and improving interpersonal skills is facilitated by following a basic model of learning as it applies to changing your behaviour. Following a basic model of learning as it applies to changing your behaviour causes you to acquire and improve interpersonal skills. Learning is a complex subject, yet its fundamentals follow a five-part sequence, as shown in Figure 1-2. To change your behaviour, and therefore improve, you need a goal and a way to measure your current reality (behaviours or actions) against this goal. You also need a way to assess your reality, and a way to obtain feedback on the impact of your new actions.[8]

LEARNING OBJECTIVE 2

Goal or Desired State of Affairs

Changing your behaviour, including improving your interpersonal relations, requires a clear goal or desired state of affairs. Your goal can also be regarded as what you want to accomplish as a result of your effort. A major reason why a goal is important is that having a specific goal improves performance. With a goal in mind, a person will usually not be satisfied until the goal is attained. So he or she keeps plugging away until the goal is attained, thereby increasing both personal satisfaction and performance on the task. Goals are also important because where people perceive that they have not attained their goal, they typically increase their effort or modify their strategy to reach the goal.[9]

As a concrete example, let us take the common problem of a person who nibbles his fingernails during tense situations, such as being called on in a meeting. The nibbler might say, "My hope [a goal] is to be able to sit in a meeting and not bite my nails, even though I know I might be called upon." This man's desired state of affairs (his goal) is to avoid putting his nails in his mouth so that he can appear calm and professional. Having a goal helps provide motivation and makes it possible to exercise the self-discipline necessary to follow through on your plans. In short, the goal focuses your effort on making the behavioural improvements you seek.

Here we turn to Sean, a credit analyst who is being blocked from promotion because his manager perceives him as having poor interpersonal skills. After a discussion with his manager, Sean recognizes that he must improve his interpersonal relations if he wants to become a team leader.

Sean's goal is to be considered promotable to a leadership position. To achieve his goal, he will have to achieve the general goal of improving his interpersonal relations. By conferring with the human resources director, Sean learns that his broad goal of "improving my

FIGURE 1-2 A Model for Improving Interpersonal Skills

"Must be promotable."	"How close am I?"	"Must choose an improvement method."	"Have you seen any changes?"	"Must be nice every day."
Goal or desired state of affairs	→ Assessing reality	→ Action plan	→ Feedback on actions	→ Frequent practice

interpersonal relations" will have to be supported by more specific goals. Having poor interpersonal relations or "rubbing people the wrong way" includes many different behaviours. To begin, Sean selects one counterproductive behaviour to improve: He is exceptionally intolerant of others and does not hide his intolerance. Sean's goal is to become less intolerant and more patient in his dealings with others on the job.

Fine Points about Goal Setting. So far we have made goal setting seem easy. A truer description of goal setting is that it involves several fine points to increase the probability that the goal will be achieved. Key points about setting effective goals are outlined in Figure 1-3, and described next.

1. **State each goal as a positive statement.** Expressing your goals in positive statements is likely to be more energizing than focusing on the negative.[10] An example of a positive statement would be, "During the next year when I am attending networking events, I will create a positive, professional impression on everybody I meet." The negative counterpart would be, "During the next year, I will avoid making a fool of myself when I am attending networking events." Despite this suggestion, there are times when a negative goal is useful, such as in reducing errors.

2. **Formulate specific goals.** A goal such as "attain success" is too vague to serve as a guide to daily action. A more useful goal would be to state specifically what you mean by success and when you expect to achieve it. For example, "I want to be the manager of patient services at a large medical clinic by January 1, 2015, and receive above-average performance reviews."

3. **Formulate concise goals.** A useful goal can usually be expressed in a short, punchy statement—for example, "Decrease input errors in bank statements so that customer complaints are decreased by 25 percent by September 30 of this year." People new to goal setting typically commit the error of formulating lengthy, rambling goal statements. These lengthy goals involve so many different activities that they fail to serve as specific guides to action.

4. **Set realistic as well as stretch goals.** A realistic goal is one that represents the right amount of challenge for the person pursuing the goal. On the one hand, easy goals are not very motivational—they may not spring you into action. On the other hand, goals that are too far beyond your capabilities may lead to frustration and despair because there is a good chance you will fail to reach them. The extent to which a goal is realistic depends on a person's capabilities.

An easy goal for an experienced person might be a realistic goal for a beginner. **Self-efficacy** is also a factor in deciding whether a goal is realistic. (The term refers to the confidence in your ability to carry out a specific task.) The higher your self-efficacy, the more likely you are to think that a particular goal is realistic. A person with high self-efficacy for learning Chinese might say, "I think learning two new Chinese words a day is realistic."

Several goals that stretch your capability might be included in your list of goals. An extreme stretch goal might be for a store manager trainee to become the vice-president of merchandising for Target within four years. Another type of stretch goal is striving for a noble cause. A Home Hardware supervisor might not get excited about having the store associates load lumber onto the steel shelves.

self-efficacy
Confidence in one's ability to carry out a specific task.

FIGURE 1-3 **Guidelines for Goal Setting**

1. State each goal as a positive statement.
2. Formulate specific goals.
3. Formulate concise goals.
4. Set realistic goals as well as stretch goals.
5. Set goals for different time periods.

However, she might get excited about the lumber being used to build homes, schools, and hospitals.

5. **Set goals for different time periods.** Goals are best set for different time periods, such as daily, short-range, medium-range, and long-range. Daily goals are essentially a to-do list. Short-range goals cover the period from approximately one week to one year into the future. Finding a new job, for example, is typically a short-range goal. Medium-range goals relate to events that will take place within approximately two to five years. They concern such things as the type of education or training you plan to undertake and the next step in your career.

    Long-range goals refer to events taking place five years into the future and beyond. As such, they relate to the overall lifestyle you wish to achieve, including the type of work and family situation you hope to have. Although every person should have a general idea of a desirable lifestyle, long-range goals should be flexible. You might, for example, plan to stay single until age 40. But while on vacation next summer, you just might happen to meet the right partner for you.

    Short-range goals make an important contribution to attaining goals of longer duration. If a one-year career goal is to add 25 worthwhile contacts to your social network, a good way to motivate yourself is to search for two contacts per month for 11 months, and three for one month. Progress toward a larger goal is self-rewarding.

Assessing Reality

The second major requirement for changing behaviour is to assess the current reality. Sean needs a way to estimate how far he is from his goal of being eligible for promotion, and how intolerant he is perceived as being. Sean has already heard from his manager, Alison, that he is not currently eligible for promotion. Sean might want to dig for more information by finding answers to the following questions:

"If I were more tolerant, would I be promoted now?"
"How bad are my interpersonal relations in the office?"
"How many people in the office think I rub them the wrong way?"
"How many deficiencies do my manager and co-workers perceive me to have?"

One starting point in answering these questions might be for Sean to confer with Alison about his behaviour. To be more thorough, however, Sean might ask a friend in the office to help him answer the questions. Sometimes a co-worker is in an excellent position to provide feedback on how one is perceived by others in the office. Sean could also ask a confidant outside the office about his intolerance. He could ask a parent, a significant other, or both about the extent of his intolerance.

An Action Plan

The learning model needs some mechanism to change the relationship between the person and his or her environment. An **action plan** is a series of steps necessary to achieve a goal. Without an action plan, a personal goal will be elusive. The person who sets the goal may not initiate steps to make his or her dream (a high-level goal) come true. If your goal is to someday become a self-employed business owner, your action plan should include saving money, establishing a good credit rating, and developing dozens of contacts.

Sean has to take action to improve his interpersonal relations, especially his intolerance. The changes should ultimately lead to the promotion he desires. Sean's action plan for becoming more tolerant includes the following:

- Pausing to attempt to understand why a person is acting the way he or she is. An example would be trying to understand why a sales representative wants to extend credit to a customer with a poor credit rating.
- Learning to control his own behaviour so he does not make intolerant statements simply because he is experiencing pressure.
- Taking a course in interpersonal or human relations.

action plan
A series of steps designed to achieve a goal.

- Asking Alison to give him a quick reminder whenever she directly observes or hears of him being intolerant toward customers or workmates.

In addition to formulating these action plans, Sean must have the self-discipline to implement them. For example, he should keep a log of situations in which he was intolerant and those in which he was tolerant. He might also make a mental note to attempt to be cooperative and flexible in most of his dealings at work. When a customer does not provide all the information he needs to assess his or her creditworthiness, Sean should remind himself to say, "I want to process your credit application as quickly as possible. To do this, I need some important additional information." Sean's habitual reflex in the same situation had been to snap: "I can't read your mind. If you want to do business with us, you've got to stop hiding the truth."

Feedback on Actions

The fourth step in the learning model is to measure the effects of one's actions against reality—you obtain feedback on the consequences of your actions. When your skill-improvement goal is complex, such as becoming more effective at resolving conflict, you will usually need to measure your progress in several different ways. You will also need both short- and long-term measures of the effectiveness of your actions. Long-term measures are important because skill-development activities of major consequence have long-range implications.

To obtain short-range feedback, Sean can consult with Alison to see whether she has observed any changes in his tolerance levels. Alison can also collect any feedback she hears from others in the office. Sean will also profit from feedback over a prolonged period of time, perhaps one or two years. He will be looking to see if he has become more tolerant by being polite in his interactions instead of snapping at others or being impatient.

Frequent Practice

The final step in the learning model makes true skill development possible. Implementing the new behaviour and using feedback for fine-tuning is an excellent start in acquiring a new interpersonal skill. For the skill to be long-lasting, however, it must be integrated into your usual way of conducting yourself. In Sean's case, he will have to practise being tolerant regularly until it becomes habitual.

Once a skill has been programmed into your repertoire, it becomes a habit. This is important, because a skill involves many habits. For example, good customer service skills include the habits of smiling and listening carefully. After you attempt the new interpersonal skills described in this text, you will need to practise them frequently to make a noticeable difference in your behaviour.

A sports analogy is appropriate here. Assume that Marty, a tennis player, takes a lesson to learn how to hit the ball with greater force. The instructor points out that the reason Marty is not hitting with much force is that he is relying on his arm too much and not enough on his leg and body strength. To hit the ball with more force, Marty is told that he must put one foot out in front of him when he strikes the ball.

Under the watchful eye of the coach, Marty does indeed put a foot out in front of him when he strikes the ball. Marty is excited about the good results. But if Marty fails to make the same manoeuvre with his feet during matches, he will persist in hitting weakly. If Marty makes the effort to make better use of his legs on almost every shot, he will soon integrate the new movement into his game.

In summary, a model for learning skills comprises five steps: (1) choosing a goal, (2) assessing the current reality, (3) deciding on an action plan, (4) gathering feedback on actions, and (5) frequently practising the new behaviour. Skill-Building Exercise 1-1 will give you an opportunity to apply this model to improve interpersonal skills.

BACK TO THE OPENING CASE

If Todd wishes to be promoted, he will need to work on his interpersonal (soft) skills. While his technical skills are good, he lacks some of the skills required to be effective in a more senior position. With feedback from his supervisor, Todd can set goals, make an action plan, practise, and solicit feedback to improve how he comes across to customers. He may also want to work on team skills such as cooperation. With improvement in these areas, he is more likely to earn a promotion.

SKILL-BUILDING EXERCISE 1-1

Applying the Model for Improving Interpersonal Skills

The model for improving interpersonal skills is aimed at developing skills. At the same time, becoming effective in applying the model is a valuable skill within itself. You will need to apply the model perhaps a few times before you can become effective at developing an interpersonal skill when you want to. To get started with the model, attempt to develop an important, yet basic, interpersonal skill. For illustrative purposes, begin with enhancing your ability to give recognition to others for actions and words you consider meritorious. If you are already good at giving recognition, you can enhance your skill even further. For additional information you might want to refer to the discussion about giving recognition in Chapter 11. The exercise under discussion should take a few minutes here and there to spread out over several weeks.

Step 1: Goal or Desired State of Affairs.

Your goal here is to learn how to give recognition, or to enhance further your skill in giving recognition. You want to recognize others in such a way that they are encouraged to keep up the good work. (Or perhaps you have another, related goal.)

Step 2: Assessing Reality.

Ask a few confidants how good you already are in giving recognition. Ask questions such as, "How good have I been in saying thank you?" "When you have done something nice for me, how did I react to you?" "How many thank-you emails have I sent you since you've known me?" Also, reflect on your own behaviour in such matters as giving a server a big tip for exceptional service, or explaining to a tech specialist how much he or she has helped you. Ask yourself whether you have ever thanked a teacher for an outstanding course, or explained to a coach how much his or her advice helped you.

Step 3: Action Plan.

What are you going to do in the next few weeks to recognize the meritorious behaviour of others? Will you be sending thank-you emails, text messages, and warmly worded postcards; offering smiles and handshakes to people who help you; or giving larger-than-usual tips for excellent service with an explanation of why the tip is so large? Part of the action plan will be *who* you will recognize, *where* you will recognize them, *when* you will be giving the recognition, and *how* (in what form) you will be giving the recognition.

Step 4: Feedback on Actions.

Observe carefully how people react to your recognition. Do they smile? Do they shrug off your form of recognition? It is especially important to observe how the person reacts to you during your next interaction. For example, does the server you tipped so generously give you a big welcome? Does the bank teller you thanked so sincerely seem eager to cash your next cheque? If you do not get the intended result from your recognition efforts, you might need to fine-tune your sincerity. Perhaps when you sent a recognition email or text message, you did not mention the person's name, and just wrote, "Hey." Perhaps you did not combine a thank-you with a smile. Analyze carefully the feedback you receive.

Step 5: Frequent Practice.

For this exercise, perhaps you can only practise giving recognition in one or two settings. Yet if this exercise appears promising, you might continue to practise in the future. Should you continue to practise, you will be taking personal steps to making the world a better place.

IDENTIFICATION OF DEVELOPMENTAL NEEDS

LEARNING OBJECTIVE 3

An important concept in skill development is that people are most likely to develop new skills when they feel the need for change. The importance of the perceived need for change is reflected in a variation of an old joke:

Question: How many psychologists does it take to change a light bulb?

Answer: None, if the light bulb wants to change.

As you read this text and do the experiential exercises, you will probably be more highly motivated to follow through with skill development in areas in which you think you need improvement. A specific area in which a person needs to change is referred to as a **developmental need**. For instance, some people are too shy or too abrasive. Some do not give others the encouragement they need.

To improve interpersonal skills, we must first be aware of how we are perceived by other people who interact with us.[11] Developmental needs related to interpersonal skills can be identified in several ways. First, if you are candid with yourself, you can probably point

developmental need
A specific area in which a person needs to change or improve.

to areas in which change is needed. You might reflect on your experiences and realize that you have repeatedly encountered problems in resolving conflict. A second, related approach is to think of feedback you have received. If you have been consistently asked to improve in a particular area, you could assume that the feedback has merit. If five different people have told you that you are not a good team player, you should probably list "becoming a better team player" as one of your developmental needs.

A third approach to assessing developmental needs is to solicit feedback. Ask the people who know you well to help you identify areas for improvement with respect to interpersonal skills. Present and previous managers are a valuable source of this type of feedback.

A fourth approach to pinpointing developmental needs is closely related to the previous three: feedback from performance appraisals or evaluations. If you have worked for a firm that conducts performance appraisals, you may have already received constructive suggestions that you can revisit now.

For example, one manager advised his assistant: "You need to project more self-confidence when you talk on the telephone. You tend to sound unsure and vague. I have noticed this, and several customers have joked about it." The recipient of this feedback was prompted to participate in assertiveness training, where she learned how to express herself more positively.

Self-Assessment Quiz 1-1 provides you with an opportunity to identify your developmental needs. The same exercise is a first step in improving your interpersonal relations on the job, because identification of a problem is the first—and most important—step toward change. For example, if you cite improving your relations with people from cultures different than your own, you have planted the seeds for change. You are then more likely to seek out people from other cultures in the workplace or at school and cultivate their friendship.

Now that you (and perhaps another person) have identified specific behaviours that may require change, you need to draw up an action plan. Proceed with your action plan even though you have just begun studying this text, but peek ahead to relevant chapters if you wish. For each checked statement, briefly describe a plan of attack for bringing about the change you hope to achieve. Ideas for your action plan can come from information presented anywhere in this text, from outside reading, or from talking to a person experienced in dealing with people. A basic example: If you check "I feel awkward dealing with a customer," you might study materials about customer service or observe an effective model.

UNIVERSAL NEEDS FOR IMPROVING INTERPERSONAL RELATIONS

LEARNING OBJECTIVE 4

universal training needs
Areas for improvement common to most people.

We have just described how understanding your unique developmental needs makes improving your interpersonal skills possible. There are also areas for skill improvement in interpersonal relations that are shared by most managerial, professional, technical, and sales personnel. We refer to these common areas as **universal training needs**. Almost any professional person, for example, could profit from improving his or her negotiating and listening skills.

This text provides opportunities for skill development in a number of these common areas. In working through these universal training needs, be aware that many will also fit your specific developmental needs; a given universal training need can be an individual's developmental need at the same time. It is reasonable to expect that you will be more strongly motivated to improve skills that relate closely to your developmental needs.

The following major universal training needs are covered in this text:

1. **Understanding individual differences.** To deal effectively with others in the workplace, it is necessary to recognize that people have different capabilities, needs, and interests.
2. **Self-esteem and self-confidence.** To function effectively with people in most work and personal situations, people need to feel good about themselves and believe that they can accomplish important tasks. Although self-esteem and self-confidence are essentially attitudes about the self, they also involve skills such as attaining legitimate accomplishments and using positive self-talk.

SELF-ASSESSMENT QUIZ 1-1

What Are Your Developmental Needs?

This exercise is designed to heighten your awareness of areas in which you could profit from personal improvement. It is not a test and there is no scoring, but your answers to the checklist may prove helpful to you in mapping out a program to improve your interpersonal relations.

Directions: Below are a number of statements reflecting specific problems in interpersonal relations. Check each statement that is generally true for you. To get a more accurate picture of your developmental needs, consider asking one or two other people who know you well to select the statements they think describe you, and compare their answers with yours.

		Place check in this column
1.	I'm too shy.	
2.	I'm overbearing and obnoxious.	
3.	I intimidate too many people.	
4.	I have trouble expressing my feelings.	✓
5.	I make negative comments about people too readily.	✓
6.	I have a difficult time solving problems when working in a group.	
7.	I'm a poor team player.	✓
8.	Very few people listen to me.	
9.	My temper is too often out of control.	
10.	I am a poor listener.	
11.	When I'm in conflict with another person, I usually lose.	
12.	I hog too much time in meetings or in class.	
13.	I'm very poor at office politics.	
14.	People find me boring.	✓
15.	It is difficult for me to criticize others.	
16.	I'm too serious most of the time.	
17.	I feel awkward working with a person from a culture quite different from mine.	
18.	I avoid controversy in dealing with others.	
19.	It is difficult for me to find things to talk about with others.	
20.	I don't get my point across well.	
21.	I feel awkward dealing with a customer.	
22.	I don't get the point of the importance of ethics in business. *moral*	
23.	My attempts to lead others have failed. *try*	
24.	I rarely smile when I am with other people.	
25.	*I lose confidence* (Fill in your own statement.) *when I have to communicate with many ppl*	

3. **Interpersonal communication.** Effective communication with people is essential for carrying out more than 50 percent of the work conducted by most professional and managerial staff.

4. **Behaving appropriately when using digital devices.** Digital devices are integrated into most facets of our work and personal lives. Knowing how to use various electronic devices including email, cell phones, and smart phones in a positive, constructive way instead of being uncivil and unproductive can be a major contributor to your interpersonal relationships.

5. **Developing teamwork skills.** The most sweeping change in the organization of work in recent years has been a shift to teams and away from conventional departments. Knowing how to be an effective team player therefore increases your chances for success in the modern organization.

6. **Group problem solving and decision making.** As part of the same movement that emphasizes work teams, organizations now rely heavily on group problem solving. As a consequence, being an above-average contributor to group problem

solving is a key component of effective interpersonal relations on the job. In addition to solving the problem, a decision must be made.

7. **Cross-cultural relations.** The modern workplace has greater cultural diversity than ever before. Being able to deal effectively with people from different cultures, from both within and outside Canada, is therefore an important requirement for success.

8. **Resolving conflicts with others.** Conflict in the workplace is almost inevitable as people compete for limited resources. Effective interpersonal relations therefore depend on knowing how to resolve conflict successfully.

9. **Becoming an effective leader.** In today's organizations, a large number of people have the opportunity to practise leadership, even if only through temporary assignments. Improving one's leadership skills is therefore almost a universal requirement.

10. **Motivating others.** Whether you have the title of manager or leader or are working alone, you need to know how to motivate people on whom you depend to get your work accomplished. Given that few people are gifted motivators, most people can profit from skill development in motivation.

11. **Helping others develop and grow.** As power is shared in organizations among managers and individual contributors (non-managers) alike, more people are required to help each other grow and develop. To carry out this role, most of us need skill development in coaching and mentoring.

12. **Positive political skills.** Whether you work in a small firm or a large one, part of having effective interpersonal relations is being able to influence others so your interests are satisfied. Positive political skills help you satisfy your interests without being unethical or devious.

13. **Customer service skills.** The current emphasis on customer satisfaction dictates that every worker should know how to provide good service to customers. Most people can benefit from strengthening their skills in serving both external and internal customers. (**Internal customers** are the people within your company for whom you perform a service as a part of your job.)

14. **Enhancing ethical behaviour.** Although in their hearts most workers know right from wrong, we can all sharpen our ability to make ethical decisions. By consistently making highly ethical decisions, people can improve their interpersonal relations.

15. **Personal productivity and stress management.** Even though they are not interpersonal skills themselves, having good work habits and time-management skills contributes to relating well to others. By being efficient and productive and having your stress under control, you are in a better position to relate comfortably to others. Co-workers enjoy relating to a person who does not procrastinate and who is not visibly stressed.

16. **Job search and career-management skills.** Finding an outstanding job for yourself, holding on to it, and moving ahead are not specifically interpersonal skills. However, both finding the right job and managing your career rely heavily on good interpersonal skills. Two basic examples are conducting yourself well in an interview and developing a network of contacts through which you can advance.

internal customers
The people within an individual's own company for whom the person performs a service in the course of doing his or her job.

apops/Fotolia

DEVELOPING INTERPERSONAL SKILLS ON THE JOB

The primary thrust of this text is to teach interpersonal skills that can be applied to the job. As part of your effort to enhance these skills, you should be aware that learning opportunities exist both inside and outside the workplace. This dual environment for learning soft skills mirrors the way hard skills are learned. For example, studying a text and doing laboratory exercises will help you learn useful information technology skills. On the job one day, you might be asked to establish your company's presence on Facebook. Having never performed this task before, you may search a computer manual, ask questions of co-workers, and use trial and error. Within an hour, you will have acquired a valuable new skill. The information technology skills you learned facilitated learning new computer tasks, yet the actual learning of how to set up a Facebook presence for your company was done on the job.

We now look at two related aspects of learning interpersonal skills on the job—informal learning and specific developmental experiences.

Informal Learning

Business firms, as well as nonprofit organizations, invest an enormous amount of money and time in teaching interpersonal skills. Teaching methods include sending employees to courses off-site, conducting training on company premises, videoconferencing, and web-based courses. Workers also develop interpersonal skills by interacting with work associates and observing how others confront interpersonal challenges. Figure 1-4 presents a summary of how people learn on the job. Observe that the learning experiences are a mixture of formal learning, such as company-provided training, and informal learning, such as interaction with co-workers. Much of the learning shown in Figure 1-4 refers to technical skills and knowledge, but learning about interpersonal skills is also included.

Informal learning is the acquisition of knowledge and skills that takes place naturally outside a structured learning environment. In the context of the workplace, informal learning occurs without direct supervision by the organization. A study of more than 1000 employees at seven companies found that up to 70 percent of learning takes place informally. Another researcher reported about the same figure more recently.[12] The director of the first study emphasizes that formal training includes both a goal stated by the organization and a defined method or process. Informal learning can take place whether or not a goal is stated or the method defined.

A more recent study also found that informal learning is part of how employees learn. Nearly one-half of the 1104 respondents said that informal learning is occurring to a high or very high extent in their organizations. Email emerged as the top-ranked informal learning tool, with accessing information from an intranet being a close second.[13]

Employees can learn interpersonal skills informally through such means as observing a co-worker, manager, or team leader deal with a situation. A newly hired assistant store manager could not help seeing and overhearing a customer screaming at the store manager about a defective space heater. The manager said calmly, "I can see you are pretty upset that your heater caused a short-circuit in your house. What can I do to help you?" The customer's anger was released like air from a balloon. The assistant store manager

informal learning
The acquisition of knowledge and skills that takes place naturally outside a structured learning environment.

FIGURE 1-4 Sources of Learning on the Job

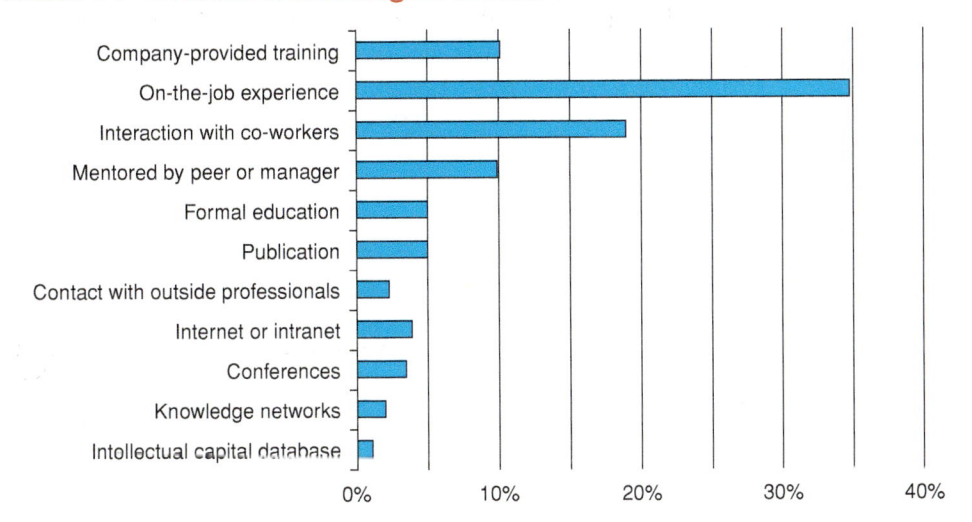

Source: Learning on the Job, MaciaConner.com © 2007–2014. Reprinted with permission of Marcia Conner.

thought to herself, "Now I know how to handle a customer who has gone ballistic. I'll state what the customer is probably feeling and then offer to help."

Informal learning can also occur when another person shows you how to handle a situation. The store manager might have said to the new assistant manager, "Let me tell you what to do when you encounter customers who lose their temper. Summarize in a few words what they are probably feeling and then offer to help. The effect can be remarkable." (This incident is classified as informal learning because it takes place outside a classroom.)

Formal and informal learning of interpersonal skills supplement each other naturally. If you are formally studying interpersonal skills, your level of awareness about them will increase. You are therefore more likely to pick up new ideas about dealing effectively with people at work. You may have noticed that if you are taking lessons in a sport, you become much more observant of the techniques of outstanding athletes you watch in person or on television.

Specific Developmental Experiences

Another perspective on developing interpersonal skills in the workplace is that certain experiences are particularly suited to such development. Coping with a difficult customer, as suggested above, would be one such experience. Morgan W. McCall Jr., an industrial psychologist, has for many years studied ways in which leaders develop on the job. Contending with certain challenges is at the heart of these key learning experiences. Several of the powerful learning experiences McCall has identified are particularly geared to developing better interpersonal skills:[14]

- **Unfamiliar responsibilities.** The person has to handle responsibilities that are new, very different, or much broader than previous ones. Dealing with these unfamiliar responsibilities necessitates asking others for help and gaining their cooperation. For example, being assigned to supervise a group doing work unfamiliar to you would put you in the position of needing to gain the cooperation of group members who know more about the work than you do.
- **Proving yourself.** If you feel added pressure to show others that you can deal effectively with responsibilities, you are likely to develop skills in projecting self-confidence and persuading others.
- **Problems with employees.** If you supervise employees or have co-workers who lack adequate experience, competence, or motivation, you need to practise such skills as effective listening and conflict resolution to be able to work smoothly with them.
- **Influencing without authority.** An excellent opportunity for practising influence skills is being forced to influence co-workers, higher management, company outsiders, and other key people over whom you have no control. Team leaders typically face the challenge of needing to influence workers whom they lack the authority to discipline or grant raises to. (A team leader usually does not have as much formal authority as a traditional manager.)
- **Difficult manager.** If you and your manager have different opinions on how to approach problems, or if your manager has serious shortcomings, you will need to use your best human relations skills to survive. You will need to develop such subtle skills as using diplomacy to explain to your manager that his or her suggestion is completely unworkable.

The general point to be derived from these scenarios is that certain on-the-job challenges require a high level of interpersonal skills. Faced with such challenges, you will be prompted to use the best interpersonal skills you have. Formal training can be a big help at these times, because you might remember a skill that could be effective. Assume, for instance, that you are faced with an overbearing manager who belittles you in front of others. You might be prompted to try a conflict-resolution technique you acquired in class. Thus the formal training you have experienced will assist you in using a new technique to confront this person.

Access the eText in MySearchLab to learn more about this chapter's self-assessment quizzes.

To Watch ✻ Explore ✓ Practice ✓ Study and Review, visit MySearchLab

Developing Your Human Relations Skills and Reinforcing Concepts

Summary ✓ Practice Glossary Flashcards

- Effective interpersonal relations can be learned using a three-part strategy; each chapter presents concepts related to an area of interpersonal skills, as well as behavioural guidelines and experiential exercises.
- A five-part model of learning can be applied to improving interpersonal skills. The steps include stating a goal; assessing the reality of how far you are from your goal; developing an action plan; soliciting feedback to measure the effects of your actions against reality; and continuing your practice of the newly learned skill.
- Opportunities exist in the workplace to develop interpersonal skills through informal learning or formal training.

Interpersonal Relations Case 1-1

Nobody Likes Me

Marge Caitlin, the supervisor of inventory control, was walking down the aisle, BlackBerry in hand, thinking about the major inventory-reduction program taking place at the company. She thought to herself, "The CEO is putting a lot of pressure on us to trim inventory to the bone. Yet the manufacturing and sales groups want enough inventory available so they can do their job. We really have to get focused and creative to satisfy everybody."

As Caitlin hurried down the aisle thinking about the inventory challenge, she still kept a watchful eye on her staff working in their cubicles. She noticed that Phil Baxter, one of the inventory control analysts, was looking even more discouraged than usual. Caitlin put aside her BlackBerry, and tapped on the entrance to Baxter's cubicle. "Can we talk?" said Caitlin with a reassuring smile on her face.

"Sure," said Baxter. "Did I screw up again?"

"Phil, there you go putting yourself down again," said Caitlin. "I just noticed that you look a little glum today. I want to know if you are having a problem that I could help with."

"Thanks, Marge, for being interested in my problems. It's really nothing new—just the same old problem that I have had in school and on the job. Nobody likes me. Nobody wants me. It gets sickening after a while."

"What makes you so sure that nobody likes you and that nobody wants you?" asked Caitlin.

Baxter responded, "First of all, almost nobody asks me to go out to lunch with him or her. Second, when you asked us to form our own teams, no team invited me to join them. I was finally chosen to be on one of the three teams because I was the last person not assigned."

"What do you think is your problem?" asked Caitlin.

"Maybe you could tell me. I think people see me as kind of a nerd. Maybe I'm just not likeable. I don't think I'm special in any way."

"Just hang in there," said Caitlin. "After this big inventory overhaul is completed, I will get back to you with some suggestions."

"I'll be waiting for your magic bullet," said Baxter with a dejected look.

Case Questions

1. What developmental needs does Phil Baxter appear to have?
2. If you were Marge Caitlin, what would you recommend that Baxter do?
3. From the little evidence that you have, what is your opinion of Caitlin's interpersonal skills?

Interpersonal Relations Case 1-2

Sumera Sets Some Goals

Sumera is a marketing specialist at Pasta Mucho, the biggest pasta maker in her region. Two years in the position, she contributed to the success of the Pasta Mucho product line. Although Sumera admits that a recession has contributed to the upswing in pasta sales nationwide, she believes that more than luck is involved. "After all," she says," "I contributed to the marketing campaign that preparing pasta at home makes you cool."

Sumera's boss, Garth, is pleased with her job performance; but as part of the performance evaluation process, he has encouraged Sumera to prepare a goal sheet, mapping out her plans for the upcoming year. "Make it impressive," said Garth, "because my boss will be reviewing your goals also." Three days later, Sumera sent Garth an email setting out her goals as follows:

1. Help make Pasta Mucho one of the great brands on the planet, much like Coca-Cola, Mercedes, and Microsoft.
2. Become the best marketing executive I can be.
3. Help the company develop some other wildly successful brands.
4. Get in good with more buyers at supermarket chains.
5. Get Pasta Mucho all over Facebook and Twitter.

Case Questions

1. If you were Garth, what would you tell Sumera about her goals without hurting her feelings?
2. What suggestions can you offer Sumera to improve her goal statement?
3. How might interpersonal skills contribute to Sumera attaining her goals?

Questions for Discussion and Review

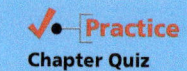

✓ Practice
Chapter Quiz

Multiple Choice

1. Interpersonal skills can also be referred to as
   a. hard skills.
   b. technical skills.
   c. soft skills.
   d. none of the above
2. An effective goal should be
   a. specific.
   b. short-range rather than long-range.
   c. worded negatively.
   d. easily obtainable.
3. According to the text, a developmental need is
   a. the same as a goal.
   b. a specific area a person needs to change.
   c. a growth stage.
   d. a communication stage.
4. Sitting beside a co-worker to learn a function in a spreadsheet that you are unfamiliar with would be an example of
   a. formal learning.
   b. informal learning.
   c. enhancing teamwork skills.
   d. a developmental need.
5. Universal training needs can be defined as
   a. training opportunities that teach diversity.
   b. company goals included in their mission statements.
   c. global challenges within the new economy.
   d. common areas for improvement that almost everyone could benefit from in training.

Short Answer

6. Why do people need soft skills in an era of high technology?
7. How could doing a thorough job with Self-Assessment Quiz 1-1 have a major impact on a person's career?
8. Based on what you have learned so far in this text, and your own intuition, how would you respond to the statement, "You can't learn how to get along with people from reading a book"?
9. Give an example of a skill you might have learned informally at any point in your life.
10. Open your MySearchLab. Along the left sidebar, there is a personality profile test, the Golden Personality Type Profiler. While you will be asked to formally do it in Chapter 2, this might also be a good time to take that test. Your results will show your preferred learning style, your communication style, your approach to working on teams, your motivation, your leadership style, and how you manage stress. Print your results to refer to them as you read this text. You can use the results to set several goals to improve your interpersonal skills.

Answers to multiple-choice questions: 1. c. 2. a. 3. b. 4. b. 5. d.

The Web Corner

www.conferenceboard.ca
The Conference Board of Canada website contains information about job skills and has links to related sites.

www.impactfactory.com
Interpersonal skill development

www.winsportcanada.ca/cop
Developing interpersonal skills through a challenge course

Internet Skill Builder: The Importance of Interpersonal Skills

One of the themes of this chapter and the entire text is that interpersonal skills are important for success in business. But what do employers really think? To find out, visit the websites of five of your favourite companies, such as www.timhortons.com or www.apple.com. Go to the employment section and search for a job that you might qualify for now or in the future. Investigate which interpersonal or human relations skills the employer mentions as a requirement, such as "Must have superior spoken communication skills." Make up a list of the interpersonal skills you find mentioned. What conclusion or conclusions do you reach from this exercise?

MySearchLab

Visit **MySearchLab** to find self-grading review quizzes in the eText, discipline-specific media and readings, access to a variety of academic journals, and Associated Press news feeds, along with a wide range of writing, grammar, and research tools and to help hone writing and research skills.

CHAPTER 2
Understanding Individual Differences

On August 27, 2001, Captain Robert Piché was piloting Air Transat flight 236 en route to Lisbon, when the Airbus 330 lost much of its fuel due to a faulty engine part. Loss of fuel meant eventually losing engine power. At more than 30,000 feet above the Atlantic and with less than 70 percent of the aircraft's flight instruments working, the crew knew they were in serious trouble. The 293 passengers and 13 crew members were preparing to die. Piché decided to head for Lajes airport in the Azores archipelago, 1500 kilometres west of Lisbon. Once the plane was completely without engine power, Piché had to pilot the plane as if it were a glider for some 20 minutes. Piché managed to land the aircraft safely at the airport. "Had I not done time in prison, I would never have been able to land the plane." says Piché.

michaeljung /Shutterstock

Upon his return to Canada, he received a hero's welcome but he was sure that things would change rather quickly. Two days later, he contacted his employers at Air Transat to let them know that he expected the issue of his criminal record to pop up in the media. Air Transat authorities were aware of that troubling episode and his past imprisonment. Indeed, in 1983, he had been sentenced to a 10-year prison term in the United States for drug trafficking. After serving 16 months in a Georgia prison, he had come back to Canada to pursue a career as a pilot. After five attempts at getting a job at Air Transat, he was eventually hired in 1996. Twenty years after his release from prison, Robert Piché has come to realize the full impact that his prison experiences (including one assassination attempt) had on his ability to land the aircraft. "I understood that prison and an aircraft in distress are pretty much the same. You have no choice but to deal with the situation if you want to come out in one piece." While he does not talk about why he was flying an airplane with drugs aboard, prison did change him: He is better able to deal with crises.

Despite his having saved over 300 lives, Piché has always maintained that he is not a hero; however, he does admit that he enjoys being in the public eye. He has resumed his duties as captain and has lost track of the number of awards he has received and the number of invitations to speak publicly about his experiences.[1]

LEARNING Objectives

After reading and studying this chapter and doing the exercises, you should be able to

1. Make adjustments for the individual differences among people when dealing with them on the job.
2. Develop insight into how your personality, mental ability, emotional intelligence, and values differ from those of others.
3. Respond to personality differences among people.
4. Respond to differences in mental ability among people.
5. Respond to differences in values among people.

The story about the hero pilot Piché illustrates several of the key topics about differences among people to be described in this chapter. Native intelligence, including the capacity to memorize details; practical intelligence (wisdom and common sense); and emotional control all play an important role in job performance. The major theme of this chapter is how people vary on a wide range of personal factors. **Individual differences** exert a profound effect on job performance and behaviour. Such differences refer to variations in how people respond to the same situation based on personal characteristics. One of hundreds of possible examples is that some people can concentrate longer and harder on their work, producing more and higher-quality work, than others.

This chapter describes several of the major sources of individual differences on the job. It also gives you the opportunity to measure your standing on several key dimensions of behaviour and helps you develop skill in responding to individual differences. Knowing how to respond to such differences is the cornerstone of effective interpersonal relations.

individual differences
Variations in how people respond to the same situation based on personal characteristics.

PERSONALITY

"We're not going to promote you to department head," said the manager to the analyst. "Although you are a great troubleshooter, you've alienated too many people in the company. You're too blunt and insensitive." As this implies, successes and failures in people-contact jobs are largely attributable to interpersonal, or human relations, skills. Among the most important contributors to these skills are personality traits. The subject of individual differences in personality must therefore be given consideration in any serious study of interpersonal relations in the workplace.

LEARNING OBJECTIVE 1

LEARNING OBJECTIVE 2

Personality refers to those persistent and enduring behaviour patterns that tend to be expressed in a wide variety of situations. A person who is brash and insensitive in one situation is likely to behave similarly in many other situations. Your personality is what makes you unique. Your walk, your talk, your appearance, your speech, and your inner values and conflicts all contribute to your personality. Have you ever noticed that when you know people well, you can identify them by their footsteps? This is true because most people have a distinctive gait.

personality
Persistent and enduring behaviour patterns that tend to be expressed in a wide variety of situations.

We will illustrate the importance of personality to interpersonal relations in organizations by describing eight key personality traits and psychological types related to cognitive styles. In addition, you will be given guidelines for dealing effectively with individuals with different personality types.

Eight Major Personality Factors and Traits

Many psychologists believe that the basic structure of human personality is represented by five broad factors, known as the Five Factor Model (or Big Five): extraversion (the

FIGURE 2-1 Eight Major Personality Factors Related to Interpersonal Skills

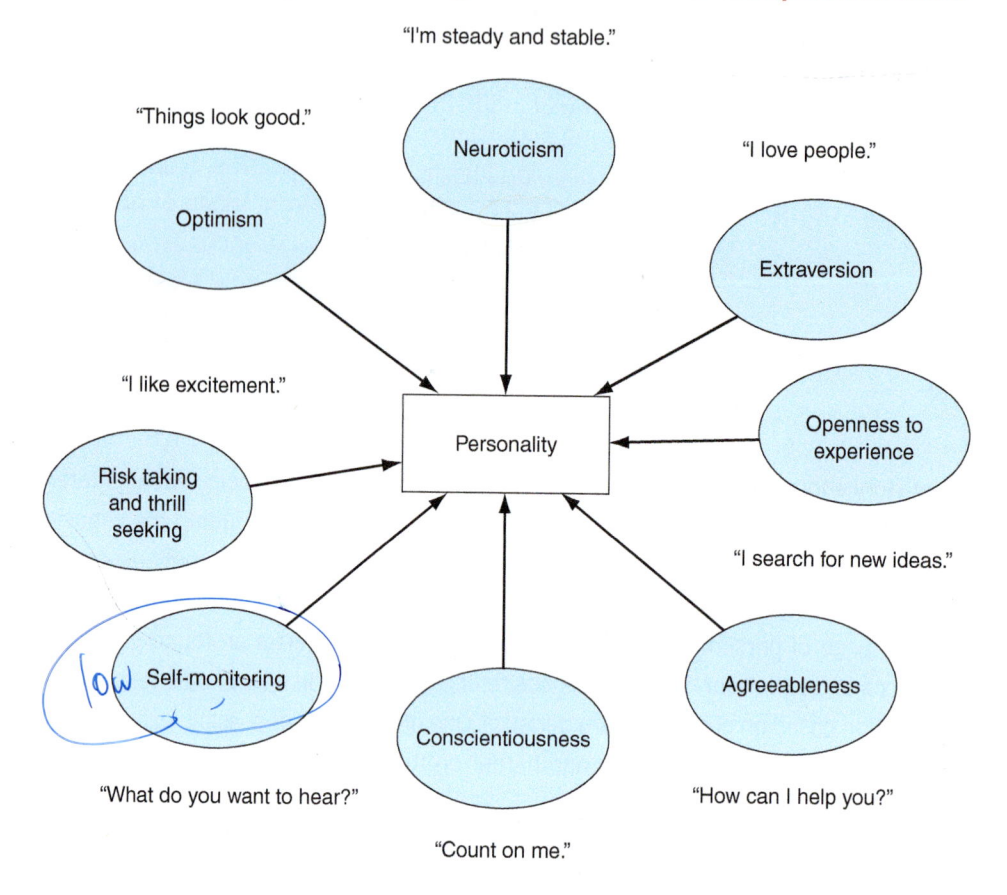

- "I'm steady and stable." — Neuroticism
- "Things look good." — Optimism
- "I love people." — Extraversion
- "I like excitement." — Risk taking and thrill seeking
- "Openness to experience"
- "What do you want to hear?" — Self-monitoring
- "I search for new ideas." — Agreeableness
- "Count on me." — Conscientiousness
- "How can I help you?"

scientific spelling of *extroversion*), emotional stability, agreeableness, conscientiousness, and openness to experience. Three other factors—self-monitoring of behaviour, risk taking and thrill seeking, and optimism—are also included here.

All eight personality factors have a substantial impact on interpersonal relations and job performance. The interpretation and meaning of these factors provides useful information, enabling you to pinpoint important areas for personal development. Although these factors are partially inherited, most people can improve upon them, providing they exert much conscious effort over a period of time. For example, it usually takes a minimum of three months of effort before a person is perceived to be more agreeable. The eight personality factors, also shown in Figure 2-1, are described in detail in the following list.

1. **Extraversion.** Traits associated with the extraversion factor include being social, gregarious, assertive, talkative, and active. An outgoing person is often described as extraverted, while a shy person is described as being introverted.
2. **Emotional stability (low neuroticism).** A person with a high degree of emotional stability or low neuroticism is calm, confident, and usually in control. Traits associated with low emotional stability or higher neuroticism include being anxious, depressed, angry, embarrassed, emotional, and worried. Thus, a person with low emotional stability is often referred to as neurotic or emotionally unstable.
3. **Agreeableness.** An agreeable person is friendly and cooperative. Traits associated with the agreeableness factor include being courteous, flexible, trusting, good-natured, cooperative, forgiving, soft-hearted, and tolerant.
4. **Conscientiousness.** A variety of meanings have been attached to the conscientiousness factor, but it generally signifies dependability. Traits associated with conscientiousness include being careful, thorough, responsible, organized, and purposeful. Honesty is also closely related to conscientiousness. Other related

SELF-ASSESSMENT QUIZ 2-1

Practice
The Risk-Taking Scale

The Risk-Taking Scale

Directions: Answer "True" or "False" to the following questions to obtain an approximate idea of your tendency to take risks, or your desire to do so:

		True	False
1.	I eat sushi or other raw fish.	☑	☐
2.	I think that amusement park roller coasters should be abolished.	☐	☑
3.	I don't like trying foods from other cultures.	☐	☑
4.	I would choose bonds over growth stocks.	☑	☐
5.	I like to challenge people in positions of power.	☐	☑
6.	I don't always wear a seat belt while driving.	☑	☐
7.	I sometimes talk on my cell phone while driving at highway speeds.	☑	☐
8.	I would love to be an entrepreneur (or I love being one).	☑	☐
9.	I would like helping out in a crisis such as a product recall.	☐	☑
10.	I would like to go cave exploring (or already have done so).	☐	☑
11.	I would be willing to have at least one-third of my compensation based on a bonus for good performance.	☑	☐
12.	I would be willing to visit a maximum-security prison on a job assignment.	☐	☑

Scoring and Interpretation: Give yourself one point each time your answer agrees with the key. If you score 10–12, you are probably a high risk taker; 6–9, you are a moderate risk taker; 3–5, you are cautious; 0–2, you are a very low risk taker.

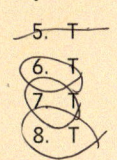

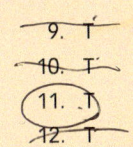

1. T	5. T	9. T
2. F	6. T	10. T
3. F	7. T	11. T
4. F	8. T	12. T

Source: The idea of a test about risk-taking comfort, as well as several of the statements on the quiz, comes from psychologist Frank Farley.

---

traits include being hard-working, achievement-oriented, and persevering. The person low in conscientiousness is lazy, disorganized, and unreliable.

5. **Openness to experience.** People who score high on the openness-to-experience factor have well-developed intellects. Traits commonly associated with this factor include being imaginative, cultured, curious, original, broad-minded, intelligent, and artistically sensitive. People low on this personality factor are practical, with narrow interests.

6. **Self-monitoring of behaviour.** The self-monitoring trait refers to the process of observing and controlling how we are perceived by others. High self-monitors are pragmatic and even chameleon-like actors in social groups. They often say what others want to hear. Low self-monitors avoid situations that require them to adopt different outer images. In this way, their outer behaviour adheres to their inner values. Low self-monitoring can often lead to inflexibility.

7. **Risk taking and thrill seeking.** People with high risk-taking and thrill-seeking propensities tend to be sensation seekers who pursue novel, intense, and complex sensations. They are willing to take risks for the sake of such experiences. The search for giant payoffs and daily thrills motivates people with an intense need for risk taking and thrill seeking.[2] Take Self-Assessment Quiz 2-1 to measure your propensity for risk taking and thrill seeking.

8. **Optimism.** *Optimism* is a tendency to experience positive emotional states, and to typically believe that positive outcomes will be forthcoming from most activities. The other end of the scale is *pessimism*—a tendency to experience negative

UNDERSTANDING INDIVIDUAL DIFFERENCES 21

emotional states, and to typically believe that negative outcomes will be forthcoming from most activities. Optimism versus pessimism is also referred to in more technical terms as positive affectivity versus negative affectivity, and is considered a major personality trait. A person's tendency toward having positive affectivity (optimism) versus negative affectivity (pessimism) also influences job satisfaction. Being optimistic, as you would suspect, tends to enhance job satisfaction.[3] A potential downside of optimism is that a person may not fear risks, such as the risk of being fired for poor performance.

Evidence for the relevance of the Five Factor Model (factors 1 through 5 of the previous list) in understanding human behaviour comes from a cross-cultural study involving 7134 individuals. The five-factor structure of the North-American (both American and Canadian) personality was also found to hold true for German, Portuguese, Hebrew, Chinese, Korean, and Japanese samples when the personality test questions were translated into each of these languages. Based on this extensive study, it was concluded that personality structure is universal,[4] much like the structure of the brain or the body.

Another reason the Big Five model is useful in understanding individual differences is that the five factors included contribute heavily to what is being measured by most personality tests. The evidence for these factors has been corroborated by people's own self-ratings, which match the test results.[5]

As already suggested, a high standing on a given trait is not always an advantage, and a low standing is not always a disadvantage.[6] For example, a person who is highly extraverted might spend so much time interacting with co-workers that he or she does not spend enough time on analytical work. Also, a person who is a low self-monitor might give people such honest feedback—rather than telling them what they want to hear—that he or she helps others grow and develop.

The Eight Factors and Traits and Job Performance

Depending on the job, any one of the preceding personality factors can be important for success. One explanation for personality being tied to performance is that a particular personality trait gives a **bias** or positive spin to certain actions.[7] A person high in conscientiousness, for example, believes that if people are diligent they will accomplish more work and receive just rewards. Conscientiousness relates to job performance for many different occupations, and has proven to be the personality trait most consistently related to success. As explained in the discussion above, each of the Big Five factors is composed of more narrow or specific traits. With respect to conscientiousness, the specific trait of *dependability* may be the most important contributor to job performance.[8]

Extraversion and Self-Monitoring.
Another important research finding is that extraversion is associated with success for managers and sales representatives. The explanation is that managers and salespeople are required to interact extensively with other people.[9] For people who want to advance in their careers, being a high self-monitor is important. An analysis was made of the self-monitoring personality by combining 136 studies involving 23,101 people. A major finding was that high self-monitors tend to receive better performance ratings than low self-monitors. High self-monitors were also more likely to emerge as leaders and work their way into top management positions.[10] Another advantage to being a high self-monitor is that the individual is more likely to help out other workers, even when not required. An example would be helping a worker outside your department with a currency exchange problem even though this was not your responsibility. Self-monitors are also much more likely to "click" with other workers and to succeed in the workplace. This may lead to good relationships which facilitate performing well.[11]

Organizational Citizenship Behaviour.
The willingness to go beyond one's job description without a specific reward

---

bias

A prejudgment about something, not usually based on fact.

apparent is referred to as **organizational citizenship behaviour**. (We mention organizational citizenship behaviour here because it is linked to other traits, particularly agreeableness and conscientiousness.) Good organizational citizens are highly valued by employers. An analysis of studies based on a total of more than 50,000 employees highlights the importance of organizational citizenship behaviour in understanding how a willingness to help others contributes to both individual and organizational success. Among the findings were that being a good organizational citizen leads to better performance ratings by supervisors, higher salary increases, and less turnover and absenteeism. Organizational citizenship behaviour also contributes to higher productivity, reduced costs, and better customer satisfaction.[12]

Another perspective on organizational citizenship behaviour is that an employee will make a short-term sacrifice, which can lead to long-term benefits to the organization.[13] For example, an employee voluntarily works on her own time to deal with customer confusion about a product recall. This can lead to more loyal and appreciative customers.

organizational citizenship behaviour
The willingness to go beyond one's job description.

Turnover and Personality. A recent synthesis of studies suggests that personality can be linked to turnover. Employees who are emotionally stable are less likely to plan to quit, or to actually quit. Employees who score higher on the traits of conscientiousness and agreeableness are less likely to leave voluntarily. Another finding of note is that workers who are low on agreeableness and high on openness to experience are likely to quit spontaneously.[14] (Maybe the grouchy, intellectually curious employee may jump on a sudden opportunity for another job.)

Optimism and Pessimism. Optimism and pessimism also can be linked to job performance. Optimism can be quite helpful when attempting such tasks as selling a product or service or motivating a group of people. Yet psychologist Julie Normen has gathered considerable evidence that pessimism can sometimes enhance job performance. Pessimists usually assume that something will go wrong, and will carefully prepare to prevent botches and bad luck. A pessimist, for example, will carefully back up computer files or plan for emergencies that might shut down operations.[15]

Combination of Standing on Several Personality Traits. A combination of personality factors will sometimes be more closely associated with job success than one factor alone. A study about personality and job performance ratings was conducted with diverse occupations including clerical workers and wholesale appliance sales representatives. A key finding was that conscientious workers who also scored high on agreeableness performed better than conscientious workers who were less agreeable.[16] (Being agreeable toward your manager helps elevate performance evaluations!) A study with experienced pharmaceutical sales representatives found that the combination of extraversion and conscientiousness was associated with higher sales. However, being conscientious was the personality factor most closely associated with growth in sales over several years for the experienced sales representatives.[17]

COGNITIVE STYLES AND PERSONALITY TYPES

People go about solving problems in various ways. You may have observed, for example, that some people are more analytical and systematic, while others are more intuitive. Modes of problem solving are referred to as **cognitive styles**. According to this method of understanding problem-solving styles, your personality traits influence strongly how you approach problems, such as being introverted makes you lean toward dealing with concepts and ideas. Knowledge of these cognitive styles can help you relate better to people because you can better appreciate how they make decisions.

cognitive styles
Mental processes used to perceive and make judgments from situations.

The most widely used method of classifying problem-solving styles is the Myers-Briggs Type Indicator (MBTI), a self-report questionnaire designed to make the theory of psychological types developed by psychoanalyst Carl Jung applicable to everyday life.[18] Another leading method of measuring types is the Golden Personality Type Profiler.[19] This is an excellent time to open your MySearchLab and take the Golden Personality Type Profiler. Like the Myers-Briggs Type Inventory, the Golden Personality Type Profiler asks

UNDERSTANDING INDIVIDUAL DIFFERENCES

you to rate a series of statements as to how much they apply to you. Once you have completed the profile, look carefully at your results as you read the rest of the chapter. (Also, keep your results handy as you read other chapters.) The results of this assessment will help you understand your different preferences and reactions to a number of life events including stress and work style.

As measured by the Golden Profiler, four separate dichotomies direct the typical use of perception and judgment by an individual. The four dichotomies can also be considered a person's cognitive style.[20]

1. **Energy flow: Extraversion versus introversion.** Extraverts direct their energy primarily toward the outer world of people and objects. In contrast, introverts direct their energy primarily toward the inner world of experiences and ideas. In the workplace, extraverts may contribute more on teams (or at least participate more). If there is an introvert on one of your teams, ask for ideas as introverts may also have good ideas to contribute to achieving team goals.

2. **Information gathering: Sensation versus intuition.** People who rely on sensing focus primarily on what can be perceived by the five primary senses of touch, sight, sound, smell, and taste. People who rely on intuition focus primarily on perceiving patterns and interrelationships. People who score high on intuition look for relationships and may make decisions based on their "gut" feeling rather than what they can see or hear. Making a decision to hire a new employee based on feeling rather than the tight facts of a résumé would more likely be done by someone who scores high in intuition.

3. **Decision making: Thinking versus feeling.** People who rely primarily on thinking base conclusions on logical analysis and emphasize objectivity and detachment. People who rely on feelings base conclusions on personal or social values, and focus on understanding and harmony. For example, a thinker may be more objective and readily agree with the money savings that layoffs will provide, while the feeling type is concerned about how the stress of layoffs will affect those who are given notice.

4. **Lifestyle orientation: Judging versus perceiving.** Individuals high on judging tend to orient their lives in a deliberate and planned manner. Individuals high on perceiving tend to orient their lives in a spontaneous and open-ended manner. At work, someone who is more of a judging type prefers to plan long in advance of a meeting whereas someone who is more of a perceiver may arrive with few notes and just "go with the flow."

Combining the four types with each other results in 16 personality types, such as the ESFP, or "The Entertainer." ESFP refers to extraverted/sensing/feeling/perceiving. It is believed that approximately 13 percent of the population can be classified as the ESFP type. People of this type are optimistic, and are skilled at living joyfully and entertaining others. ESFPs are effective at communicating their good-natured realism to others.

Here our concern is with how your personality influences your learning style. Figure 2-2 presents 4 of the 16 personality types along with the implications for each one with respect to cognitive style.

Far too many people perceive personality types as being definitive indicators of an individual's personality and therefore think they know exactly how to classify that person in terms of personality. The developers of the Golden Profiler point out that the instrument is an accurate and dependable measure of the aspects of personality measured. However, it is up to the person taking the Golden to determine if the report's description of him or her is accurate.[21] If the results completely disagree with what you believe to be true about yourself, or what others have told you about your personality, the results of the Golden (or other type of indicator) should not be a cause for concern.

An interpersonal skills application of understanding the Golden personality types is to help people get along better within a work group. All the group members have their types assessed using the Golden instrument, and all members would be made aware of each other's type or working style. Knowing your type among the 16 types and the types of the other group members would give you some clues for working smoothly together.

FIGURE 2-2 Four Cognitive Styles of the Golden Personality Types

Personality Type	Highlights of Type
ENFP (The Proponent) Extraverted/iNtuitive/Feeling/Perceiving	Lives continually in the realm of the possible. When absorbed in their latest project, they think of little else. Filled with energy, they are tireless in their pursuit of goals. Have an almost magnetic quality that enables them to have fun in almost any setting. The combination of Extraversion, Intuition, and Perceiving is well suited for leadership.
ENFJ (The Communicator) Extraverted/iNtuitive/Feeling/Judging	Chief concern is fostering harmony and cooperation between self and others. Has strong ideals and a potent sense of loyalty, whether to a mate, a school, a hometown, or a favourite cause. Usually good at organizing people to get things done while keeping everyone happy. At work, well armed to deal with both variety and action. Typically patient and conscientious, make a concerted effort of sticking with a job until finished.
INFP (The Advocate) Introverted/iNtuitive/Feeling/Perceiving	Capable of immense sensitivity and has an enormous emotional capacity that is guarded closely. Has to know people well before letting down the guard and displaying warmth. Interpersonal relationships are a crucial focus. Has powerful sense of faithfulness, duty, and commitment to the people and causes he or she is attracted to. Able to express emotion and move people through his or her communication. A perfectionist on the job. Prefers a quiet working environment and, despite attraction for human companionship, will often work best alone. Will work at best only in job he or she truly believes in.
INFJ (The Foreseer) Introverted/iNtuitive/Feeling/Judging	Imaginative, inspired, tenacious, creative, and inward-looking. Also stubborn, easily bored by routine work, and often pays little attention to obstacles. Makes decisions easily. Lives in a world of ideas, and will have a unique vision. Pours all own energy into achieving his or her goal. Trusts own intuition. Can express emotion and move people through written communication. Although cherishes the companionship of people, prefers a quiet working environment, and working alone. Perfectionist about quality. Creativity is his or her hallmark.

Code: E = Extraverted, N = Intuitive, F = Feeling, P = Perceiving, I = Introverted, J = Judging
Source: From *Boundless Diversity: An Introduction to the Golden Personality Type Profiler* by Karen A. Deitz and John P. Golden, (San Antonio, Texas: Pearson TalentLens, 2004). Reprinted with permission from Pearson Education, Inc.

To illustrate, let us use a couple of the types shown in Figure 2-2. Visualize yourself as a member of a work group. You know that Nick is a foreseer (INFJ). The group has an assignment that calls for creating something new, so you consult with Nick to capitalize on his imaginative thinking, determination to attain goals, and fine written communication skills. Yet you know that you and Margot are proponents (ENFP), so you two will play a heavy role in helping translate Nick's plan into action. And you, Nick, and Margot know that Jason is an advocate (INFP), so you will have to work slowly with him to get him to believe in the new project so that he can make good use of his tendency toward perfectionism. You will also not discourage Jason from spending some time working alone, so he can be at his best.

Guidelines for Dealing with Different Personality Types

A key purpose in presenting information about a sampling of various personality types is to provide guidelines for individualizing your approach to people. As a basic example, if you wanted to score points with an introvert, you would approach that person in a restrained, laid-back fashion. In contrast, a more gregarious, lighthearted approach might be more effective with an extravert. The purpose of individualizing your approach is to build a better working relationship or establish rapport with the other person. To match your approach to dealing with a person of a given personality type, you must first arrive

LEARNING OBJECTIVE 3

at an approximate idea of the individual's personality. The following suggestions are therefore restricted to readily observable aspects of personality:

1. When relating to a person who appears to be neurotic, based on symptoms of worry and tension, be laid-back and reassuring. Attempt not to project your own anxiety and fears. Be a good listener. If possible, minimize the emphasis on deadlines and the dire consequences of a project's failing. Show concern and interest in the person's welfare.

2. When relating to an *extraverted* individual, emphasize friendliness and warmth, and maintain a stream of chatter. Talk about people more than ideas, things, or data. Express an interest in a continuing working relationship.

3. When relating to an *introverted* individual, move slowly in forming a working relationship. Do not confuse quietness with a lack of interest. Tolerate moments of silence. Emphasize ideas, things, and data more heavily than people.

4. When relating to a person who is open to experience, emphasize information sharing, idea generation, and creative approaches to problems. Appeal to his or her intellect by discussing topics of substance rather than ordinary chatter and gossip.

5. When relating to a person who is *closed to experience*, stick closely to the facts of the situation at hand. Recognize that the person prefers to think small and deal with the here and now.

6. When relating to an *agreeable* person, just relax and be yourself. Reciprocate with kindness to sustain a potentially excellent working relationship.

7. When relating to a *disagreeable* person, be patient and tolerant. At the same time, set limits on how much mistreatment you will take. Disagreeable people sometimes secretly want others to put brakes on their antisocial behaviour.

8. When relating to a *conscientious* person, give him or her freedom and do not nag. The person will probably honour commitments without prompting. Conscientious people are often taken for granted, so remember to acknowledge the person's dependability.

9. When relating to a person who lacks *conscientiousness*, keep close tabs on him or her, especially if you need that person's output to do your job. Do not assume that the person's honest face and pleasing smile mean he or she will deliver as promised. Frequently follow up on your requests, and impose deadlines if you have the authority. Express deep appreciation when the person does follow through.

10. When dealing with a person you suspect is a *high self-monitor*, be cautious in thinking that the person genuinely supports your position. The person could just be following his or her natural tendency to appear to please others, without really being supportive.

11. When relating to a person with a *high propensity for risk taking and thrill seeking*, emphasize the risky and daring aspects of activities familiar to you. Talk about a new product introduction in a highly competitive market, stock options, investing in high technology start-up firms, bungee jumping, and racecar driving.

12. When relating to a person with a *low propensity for risk taking and thrill seeking*, emphasize the safe and secure aspects of activities familiar to you. Talk about the success of an established product in a stable market (like pencils and paperclips), or talk about investing in government bonds, buying life insurance, camping, and gardening.

13. When dealing with a *sensing-type* person, emphasize facts, figures, and conventional thinking without sacrificing your own values. To convince the sensation type, emphasize logic more than emotional appeal. Focus on details more than on the big picture.

14. When dealing with an *intuiting-type* individual, emphasize feelings, judgments, playing with ideas, imagination, and creativity. Focus more on the big picture than on details.

SKILL-BUILDING EXERCISE 2-1

Personality Role-Plays

The Extravert: One student assumes the role of a successful outside sales representative who has just signed a $3 million order for the company. The sales rep comes back to the office elated. The other student assumes the role of a member of the office support staff. He or she decides this is a splendid opportunity to build a good relationship with the triumphant sales rep. Run the role-play for about 10 minutes. The people not involved will observe and then provide feedback when the role-play is completed. (These directions regarding time, observation, and feedback also apply to the two other role-plays in this exercise and throughout the text).

The Open-to-Experience Type: One student plays the role of an experienced worker in the department who is told to spend some time orienting a new co-op student. Another student plays the role of the co-op student, who is open to experience and eager to be successful in this new position.

The Organizational Citizen: One student plays the role of a strong organizational citizen who wants to help other people, going beyond what is found in his or her job description. The strong organizational citizen is thinking, "What can I do today to help somebody?" As the student walks down the row of cubicles, he or she spots a person who is staring at the computer with an agonized, perplexed look. The good organizational citizen thinks, "Maybe here is a good opening to be useful today." The other student plays the role of the perplexed worker who might need help with a specific problem facing him or her at the moment.

For the three scenarios, observers rate the role players on two dimensions, using a 1-to-5 scale from Very Poor to Very Good. One dimension is "effective use of human relations techniques"; the other is "acting ability." A few observers might voluntarily provide feedback to the role players in terms of sharing their ratings and observations. The course instructor might also provide feedback.

To start putting these guidelines into practice, do the role-plays in Skill-Building Exercise 2-1. Remember that a role player is an extemporaneous actor. Put yourself in the shoes of the character you play and visualize how he or she would act. Because you are given only the general idea of a script, use your imagination to fill in the details.

COGNITIVE ABILITY

Cognitive ability (also referred to as mental ability or intelligence) is one of the major sources of individual differences affecting job performance and behaviour. **Intelligence** is the capacity to acquire and apply knowledge, including solving problems. Intelligent workers best solve abstract problems. In a very simple or rote job, such as packing shoes into boxes, having below-average intelligence is not a problem, as the employee can master the components of the job without difficulty.

Understanding the nature of intelligence contributes to effective interpersonal relations in organizations. Your evaluation of a person's intelligence can influence how you relate to that person. For example, if you think a person is intelligent, you will tend to seek his or her input on a difficult problem. If you realize that different types of intelligence exist, you are more likely to appreciate people's strengths regardless of their level of intelligence. You are thus less likely to judge others as being either good or poor problem-solvers.

Here we describe four important aspects of cognitive ability: (1) the components of traditional intelligence; (2) practical intelligence; (3) multiple intelligences; and (4) emotional intelligence. Knowledge of these four aspects will enrich your understanding of other workers and yourself.

intelligence
The capacity to acquire and apply knowledge, including solving problems.

Traditional Intelligence

Intelligence consists of more than one component. A component of intelligence is much like a separate mental aptitude. Evidence suggests that intelligence consists of a **g (general) factor** and **s (special) factors** that contribute to problem-solving ability. Scores of tests of almost any type (such as math, aptitude for computer programming, or reading skill) are somewhat influenced by the *g* factor. The *g* factor helps explain why some people perform well in so many different mental tasks. Substantial evidence has accumulated over the years that workers with high intelligence tend to perform better. The relationship between *g* and job performance is likely to be strongest for those aspects of jobs involving thinking and knowledge, such as problem solving and technical expertise.[22]

g (general) factor
A factor in intelligence that contributes to the ability to perform well in many tasks.

s (special) factors
Specific components of intelligence that contribute to problem-solving ability.

Over the years, various investigators have arrived at different special factors contributing to overall mental aptitude. The following seven factors have been consistently identified:

1. **Verbal comprehension.** The ability to understand the meaning of words and their relationship to each other and to comprehend written and spoken information.
2. **Word fluency.** The ability to use words quickly and easily, without an emphasis on verbal comprehension.
3. **Numerical acuity.** The ability to handle numbers, engage in mathematical analysis, and do arithmetic calculations.
4. **Spatial perception.** The ability to visualize forms in space and manipulate objects mentally, particularly in three dimensions.
5. **Memory.** Having a good rote memory for symbols, words, and lists of numbers, along with other associations.
6. **Perceptual speed.** The ability to perceive visual details, to pick out similarities and differences, and to perform tasks requiring visual perception.
7. **Inductive reasoning.** The ability to discover a rule or principle and apply it in solving a problem and to make judgments and decisions that are logically sound.

Being strong in any of the preceding mental aptitudes often leads to an enjoyment of work associated with that aptitude. The reverse can also be true: Enjoying a type of mental activity might lead to the development of an aptitude for the activity.

Attempts to improve cognitive skills, or intelligence, have become an entire industry, including both brain-stimulating exercises and food supplements. Common wisdom suggests that staying in shape mentally by doing activities such as crossword puzzles, surfing the Internet, or studying a foreign language can slow the decline of an aging brain. Brain-imaging studies support the idea that mental workouts help preserve **cognitive fitness**, a state of optimized ability to remember, learn, plan, and adapt to changing circumstances. Acquiring expertise in such diverse areas as playing a cello, juggling, speaking a foreign language, and playing video games and computer games expands your neural systems and helps them communicate with one another. This means that by learning new skills, you can alter the physical makeup of the brain even in later life. Engaging in play also enhances brain functioning that helps explain the link between creativity and play.[23]

cognitive fitness
A state of optimized ability to remember, learn, plan, and adapt to changing circumstances.

Practical Intelligence

Many people, including psychologists, are concerned that the traditional way of understanding intelligence inadequately describes mental ability. An unfortunate implication of intelligence testing is that intelligence as traditionally calculated is based largely upon the ability to perform tasks related to scholastic work. Thus a person who scores very high on an intelligence test could follow a complicated instruction manual but might not be street smart.

To overcome the limited idea that intelligence mostly involves the ability to solve abstract problems, the **triarchic theory of intelligence** has been proposed. (See Figure 2-3.) The theory holds that intelligence is composed of three different subtypes: analytical, creative, and practical. The *analytical* subtype is the traditional intelligence needed for solving difficult problems. Analytical intelligence is required to perform well in most school subjects. The *creative* subtype is the type of intelligence required for imagination and combining things in novel ways. The *practical* subtype is the type of intelligence required for adapting your environment to suit your needs.[24]

triarchic theory of intelligence
An explanation of mental ability, holding that intelligence is composed of three different subtypes: analytical, creative, and practical.

The idea of practical intelligence helps explain why a person who has a difficult time getting through school can still be a successful business person, politician, or athlete. Practical intelligence incorporates the ideas of common sense, wisdom, and street smarts.

A person with high practical intelligence would also have good **intuition**, an experience-based way of knowing or reasoning in which the weighing and balancing of evidence are done automatically. Examples of good intuition include a merchandiser who develops a hunch that a particular style will be hot next season, a basketball coach who sees the possibilities in a gangly youngster, and a supervisor who has a hunch that a neighbour would be a great fit for her department. Intuition is also required for creative intelligence.

intuition
An experience-based way of knowing or reasoning in which the weighing and balancing of evidence are done automatically.

FIGURE 2-3   The Triarchic Theory of Intelligence

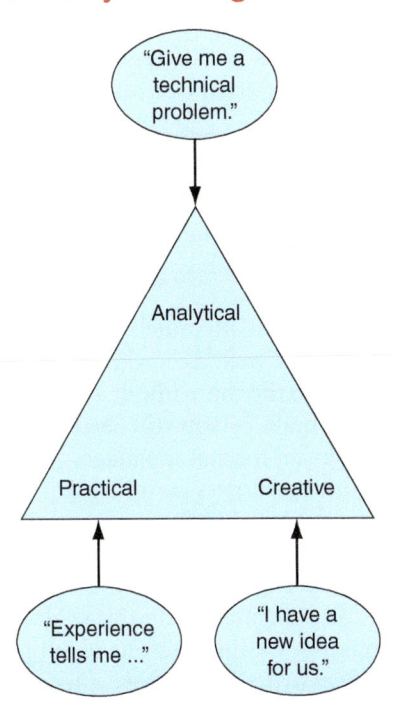

```
                    ┌─────────────┐
                    │ "Give me a  │
                    │  technical  │
                    │  problem."  │
                    └──────┬──────┘
                           │
                           ▼
                         ╱╲
                        ╱  ╲
                       ╱    ╲
                      ╱Analyt╲
                     ╱ ical   ╲
                    ╱          ╲
                   ╱            ╲
                  ╱Practical Creat╲
                 ╱_____ive___╲
                      ▲        ▲
                      │        │
              ┌───────┴──┐ ┌───┴──────┐
              │"Experience│ │"I have a │
              │ tells me..│ │new idea  │
              │     ."   │ │ for us." │
              └──────────┘ └──────────┘
```

An important implication of practical intelligence is that experience is helpful in developing intellectual skills and judgment. At younger ages, raw intellectual ability such as required for learning information technology skills may be strongest. However, judgment and wisdom are likely to be stronger with accumulated experience. This is why people in their forties and older are more likely to be chosen for position such as the CEO of a large business or a commercial airline pilot. Poor judgment is *sometimes* associated with inexperience and youth, and the frequent impulsiveness of young people is often referred to as the *teenage brain*. One major reservation some have about practical intelligence is the implication that people who are highly intelligent in the traditional sense are not practical thinkers. In truth, most executives and other high-level workers score quite well on tests of mental ability. These tests usually measure analytical intelligence.

Multiple Intelligences

Another approach to understanding the diverse nature of mental ability is the theory of **multiple intelligences**. According to Howard Gardner, people know and understand the world in distinctly different ways and learn in different ways. Individuals possess the following eight intelligences, or faculties, in varying degrees:

1. **Linguistic.** Enables people to communicate through language, including reading, writing, and speaking.
2. **Logical-mathematical.** Enables individuals to see relationships between objects and solve problems, as in calculus and statistics.
3. **Musical.** Gives people the capacity to create and understand meanings conveyed through sounds and to enjoy different types of music.
4. **Spatial.** Enables people to perceive and manipulate images in the brain and to recreate them from memory, as is required in making graphic designs.
5. **Bodily/kinesthetic.** Enables people to use their body and perceptual and motor systems in skilled ways such as in dancing, playing sports, and expressing emotion through facial expressions.
6. **Intrapersonal.** Enables people to perceive their own feelings and acquire accurate self-knowledge.

multiple intelligences
A theory of intelligence contending that people know and understand the world in distinctly different ways and learn in different ways.

7. **Interpersonal.** Enables people to discern and respond appropriately to the moods, temperaments, motivations, needs, and desires of other people.
8. **Naturalist.** Enables individuals to differentiate among, classify, and utilize various features of the physical external environment.

Your profile of intelligences influences how you learn best and to which types of jobs you are best suited. Gardner believes that it is possible to develop these separate intelligences through concentrated effort. However, any of these intelligences might fade if not used.[25] These separate types of intelligence might also be perceived as different talents or abilities. Having high general problem-solving ability (g) would contribute to high standing on each of the eight intelligences.

While natural abilities can account for much of a person's ability, hard work also develops these abilities and talents as well. According to the 10,000-hour rule proposed by Malcolm Gladwell, no one gets to the top without 10,000 hours of practice in a field.[26] Guided practice does indeed help, but a person still needs some basic talent to attain high-level success in such fields as finance, foreign languages, and sports. Recognize also that many teenagers achieve outstanding success in information technology, science, sports, and music without having practised 1000 hours per year for 10 years.

The three types of intelligence mentioned so far (traditional, practical, and multiple) all contribute to but do not guarantee our ability to think critically. Critical thinking is the process of evaluating evidence, and then based on this evaluation, making judgments and decisions. Through critical thinking, we find reasons to support or reject an argument.[27] Personality factors contribute heavily to whether we choose to use these types of intelligence. For example, the personality factor of openness facilitates critical thinking, because the individual enjoys gathering evidence to support or refute an idea. Conscientiousness also facilitates critical thinking, because the individual feels compelled to gather more facts and think harder.[28]

Emotional Intelligence

emotional intelligence
Qualities such as understanding one's own feelings, empathy for others, and the regulation of emotion to one's own benefit.

How people use their emotions has a major impact on their success. **Emotional intelligence** refers to qualities such as understanding one's own feelings, having empathy for others, and regulating one's emotions to one's own benefit. A person with high emotional intelligence would be able to engage in such behaviours as assessing people, pleasing others, and influencing them. In recent years, several different versions of emotional intelligence have been proposed. Four key factors included in a well-accepted analysis of emotional intelligence are as follows:[29]

1. **Self-awareness.** The ability to understand your moods, emotions, and needs, as well as their impact on others. Self-awareness also includes using intuition to make decisions you can live with happily. A person with good self-awareness knows whether he or she is pushing other people too far. Imagine that Amanda is an assistant to the food service manager at a financial services company. Amanda believes strongly that the cafeteria should ensure that no food served on company premises contains trans fats. However, the food services manager seems lukewarm to the idea. So instead of badgering the manager, Amanda decides to fight her battle bit by bit by presenting facts and reminders in a friendly way. Eventually, the manager agrees to have a meeting on the subject with a nutritionist invited. So Amanda's self-awareness has paid off.
2. **Self-management.** The ability to control one's emotions and act with honesty and integrity in a consistent and acceptable manner. The right degree of self-management helps prevent a person from throwing tantrums when activities do not go as planned. Effective workers do not let their occasional bad moods ruin their day. If they cannot overcome the bad mood, they let co-workers know of their problem and how long it might last. A person with low self-management would suddenly decide to drop a project because the work was frustrating.
    Imagine that Jack is an assistant to the export sales manager, and today is a big day because a company in Russia appears ready to make a giant purchase.

The export sales manager says, "Today we need peak performance from everybody. If we nail down this sale, we will exceed our sales quota for the year." Unfortunately, Jack is in a grim mood. His favourite NHL team was eliminated from the playoffs the night before, and his dog has been diagnosed as having a torn abdominal muscle. Jack would like to lash out in anger against everybody he meets today, but instead he focuses his energy on getting the job done, and does not let his personal problems show through.

3. **Social awareness.** Includes having empathy for others and having intuition about work problems. A team leader with social awareness, or empathy, would be able to assess whether a team member has enough enthusiasm for a project to assign him to that project. Another facet of social skill is the ability to interpret nonverbal communication, such as frowns and types of smiles.[30] A supervisor with social awareness, or empathy, would take into account the most likely reaction of group members before making a decision affecting them.

   Imagine that Cindy has been working as an assistant purchasing manager for six months. Company policy prohibits accepting "lavish" gifts from vendors or potential vendors attempting to sell the company goods or services. Cindy has been put in charge of purchasing all paper towelling for the company. Although most of the purchasing is made over the Internet, sales representatives still make the occasional call. The representative from the paper-towel company asks Cindy if she would like an iPhone as a token gift for even considering his company. Cindy badly wants an iPhone, and it is not yet in her budget. After thinking through the potential gift for five minutes, Cindy decides to refuse. Perhaps an iPhone is not really a lavish gift, but her intuition tells her it would look to be a conflict of interest if she accepted the iPhone.

4. **Relationship management.** Includes the interpersonal skills of being able to communicate clearly and convincingly, disarm conflicts, and build strong personal bonds. Effective workers use relationship management skills to spread their enthusiasm and solve disagreements, often with kindness and humour. A worker with relationship management skill would use a method of persuasion that is likely to work well with a particular group or individual. A study showed that emotional intelligence is closely related to the evaluation by a superior of a manager's interpersonal behaviours. The specific skills noted were "guides, mentors, and develops people," and "someone who communicates clearly."[31]

Emotional intelligence thus incorporates many of the skills and attitudes necessary to achieve effective interpersonal relations in organizations. Most of the human relations tasks dealt with in this text, such as resolving conflict, helping others develop, and deploying positive political skills, require emotional intelligence. It is therefore reasonable to regard emotional intelligence as being a mixture of cognitive skills and personality. Emotional intelligence can be measured in a way similar to IQ and is referred to as your **EQ**, or *emotional intelligence quotient*. One relevant Canadian study underscores the need for a high EQ to be more successful on the job.[32]

EQ
Abbreviation for emotional intelligence, or emotional intelligence quotient, assessed by a variety of tests.

BACK TO THE OPENING CASE

The heroics of Captain Piché have been widely reported as he continues to speak publicly about his experience. He has come to realize that his experiences in prison helped him perform what he needed to do in a crisis that meant life or death to him, his crew, and passengers. Here we want to emphasize that one of his traits must be high emotional stability, enabling him to prevent a terrible disaster.

SKILL-BUILDING EXERCISE 2-2

Adapting to People of Different Mental Ability

The Cognitively Skilled Co-Worker: One person plays the role of a worker who needs to load a new software package onto the hard drive of his or her computer. He or she wants to approach a particular co-worker known for having a sharp mind, but wonders whether this highly intelligent person will be interested in the problem. The other person plays the role of the computer whiz who ordinarily does not like to solve problems for people that they should be able to solve themselves. The first worker meets with the second to discuss loading the software.

The Cognitively Average Team Member: One student plays the role of a supervisor who needs to explain to a team member how to calculate discounts for customers. To the supervisor's knowledge, the team member does not know how to calculate discounts, although it will be an important part of the team member's new job. The supervisor and the team member get together for a session on calculating discounts.

Guidelines for Relating to People of Different Levels and Types of Intelligence

LEARNING OBJECTIVE 4

Certainly, you cannot expect to administer mental ability and emotional intelligence tests to all of your work associates, gather their scores, and then relate to associates differently based on their scores. Yet it is possible to intuitively develop a sense for the mental quickness of people and the types of mental tasks they perform best. For example, managers must make judgments about mental ability in selecting people for jobs and assigning them to tasks. Following are several guidelines worth considering to improve your working relationships with others:

1. If you perceive another worker (your manager included) to have high cognitive skill in a specific area, present your ideas in depth. Incorporate difficult words into your conversation and reports. Ask the person challenging questions.

2. If you perceive another worker to have lower cognitive skill in a specific area, present your ideas with a minimum of technical depth. Use a basic vocabulary, without being patronizing. Ask for frequent feedback about having been clear.

3. If you perceive a workmate to enjoy crunching numbers, use quantitative information when attempting to persuade that person. Instead of using phrases such as "most people," say "about 65 percent."

4. If you perceive a work associate to have high creative intelligence, solicit his or her input on problems requiring a creative solution. Use statements such as "Here's a problem that requires a sharp, creative mind, so I've come to you."

5. If you perceive a work associate to have a lower emotional intelligence, explain your feelings and attitudes clearly. The person may not catch hints and indirect expressions. Make an occasional statement such as "How I feel about his situation is quite important" to emphasize the emotional aspect. The person may not get the point of hints and indirect expressions.

To start putting these guidelines into practice, do the role-plays in Skill-Building Exercises 2-2 and 2-3.

SKILL-BUILDING EXERCISE 2-3

Helping an Intellectually Challenged Worker Get Started

You are an order-fulfillment supervisor at the distribution centre for a large online store. Your area of responsibility is the order fulfillment of games, toys, and sports. Part of top-level management's human resources philosophy is "Give a break to those who need a break." One way of implementing this is to hire the occasional job applicant who is well below average in cognitive (traditional) intelligence. Under this program, you are assigned Jimmy, an amiable, physically able, and energetic 20-year-old who has substantially below-average problem-solving ability (such as measured by IQ). Your manager instructs you to assign Jimmy to a job you think he can handle. You decide that packing orders for video games would be a starting point. It is day one on the job, and you want to get Jimmy to feel useful right away. Jimmy also wants to feel useful, yet he is apprehensive about the situation.

Demonstrate how you will reassure Jimmy, and show him how to get started packing the box and attaching the shipping label. Another student plays the role of Jimmy.

VALUES AS A SOURCE OF INDIVIDUAL DIFFERENCES

Another group of factors influencing how a person behaves on the job is that person's values and beliefs. A **value** refers to the importance a person attaches to something. Values are tied to the enduring belief that some modes of conduct are better than others. If you believe that good interpersonal relations are the most important part of your life, your humanistic values are strong. Similarly, you may think that people who are not highly concerned about interpersonal relations have poor values.

Values are closely related to **ethics**, or the moral choices a person makes. A person's values influence which kinds of behaviours he or she believes are ethical. An executive who strongly values profits might not find it unethical to raise prices higher than needed to cover additional costs. Another executive who strongly values family life might suggest that the company invest money in an on-premises daycare centre. Ethics is such an important topic in interpersonal relations in organizations that it receives separate attention in Chapter 14.

value
The importance a person attaches to something.

ethics
The moral choices a person makes.

Classification of Values

An almost automatic response to classifying values is that people have either good or bad values, with bad values meaning those that are quite different than yours. To the person with a strong work ethic, an individual who took a casual approach to work might have "bad values." To the person with a weak work ethic, the person who was work-obsessed might have "bad values." Shalom H. Schwartz, a professor from the Hebrew University of Jerusalem, has developed a method of classifying values that is particularly useful because it points up how we establish goals to fit our values.[33] For example, as shown in Table 2-1, people who value power are likely to set the goals of attaining power, strength, and control. And those who value benevolence are likely to establish the goals of being kind, charitable, and showing respect for others. The link between values and goals has extensive research support.

Generational Differences in Values

Differences in values among people often stem from age, or generational, differences. Workers over the age of 50, in general, may have values that are quite different from

TABLE 2-1 A Classification of Values and Associated Goals

Value	Goals Associated with Each Value
Power	Power, strength, control
Achievement	Achievement, ambition, success
Hedonism	Luxury, pleasure, delight
Stimulation	Excitement, novelty, thrill
Self-direction	Independence, freedom, liberty
Universalism	Unity, justice, equality
Benevolence	Kindness, charity, mercy
Tradition	Tradition, custom, respect
Conformity	Restraint, regard, consideration
Security	Security, safety, protection

Source: Anat Bardi, Rachel M. Calogero, and Brian Mullen, "A New Archival Approach to the Study of Values and Value-Behavior Relations: Validation of the Value Lexicon," *Journal of Applied Psychology*, May 2008, pp. 483–497.

those of people much younger. These differences in values based on age have often been seen as a clash between Baby Boomers and members of Generation X and Generation Y. The category of the Boomers is so broad that part of that generation is said to include Generation Jones, the younger boomers born between 1954 and 1964. Boomers make up a large portion of the Canadian population. Members of Generation Jones are typically entering the peak of their careers, and are not yet thinking much about retirement.[34]

According to the stereotype, Boomers see Generation X and Generation Y as being disrespectful of rules, unwilling to pay their dues, and disloyal to employers. Generation X and Generation Y see Boomers as worshipping hierarchy (layers of authority), being overcautious, and wanting to preserve the status quo.

Table 2-2 summarizes these stereotypes, but keep in mind that massive group stereotypes like this are only partially accurate, because there are literally millions of exceptions.

TABLE 2-2 Value Stereotypes for Several Generations of Workers

Baby Boomers (1946–1964) Including Generation Jones (1954–1965)	Generation X (1961–1980)	Generation Y (1981–2002) Millennials
Uses technology as a necessary tool, but not obsessed with technology for its own sake	Techno-savvy	Techno-savvy, and even questions the value of standard IT techniques such as email, with a preference for communications on a website
Appreciates hierarchy	Teamwork very important	Teamwork very important, highly team-focused
Tolerates teams but values independent work	Dislikes hierarchy	Dislikes hierarchy, prefers participation
Strong career orientation	Strives for work–life balance but will work long hours for now; prefers flexible work schedule	Strives for work–life balance, and may object to work interfering with personal life; expects flexible work schedule
More loyalty to organization	Loyalty to own career and profession	Loyalty to own career and profession and feels entitled to career goals
Favours diplomacy and tact	Candid in conversation	Quite direct in conversation
Seeks long-term employment	Will accept long-term employment if situation is right	Looks upon each company as a stepping stone to a better job in another
Believes that issues should be formally discussed	Believes that feedback can be administered informally, and welcomes feedback	Believes that feedback can be given informally, even on the fly, and craves feedback
Somewhat willing to accept orders and suggestions	Often questions why things should be done in certain way	Often asks why things should be done in a certain way, and asks loads of questions
Willing to take initiative to establish starting and completion dates for projects	Slight preference for a manager to provide structure about project dates	Prefers structure on dates and other activities based on childhood of structured activities
Regards rewards as a positive consequence of good performance and seniority	Expects frequent rewards	Feels strong sense of entitlement to rewards, including promotions
Will multitask in front of work associates when it seems necessary	Feels comfortable in multitasking while interacting with work associates	Assumes that multitasking, including listening to music on earphones while dealing with work associates, is acceptable behaviour

Note: Disagreement exists about which age brackets Baby Boomers, Generation X, and Generation Y each fit into, with both professional publications and dictionaries showing slight differences.

Source: The majority of ideas in this table are from Sommer Kehrli and Trudy Sopp, "Managing Generation Y: Stop Resisting and Start Embracing the Challenges Generation Y Brings to the Workplace," *HR Magazine*, May 2006, pp. 113–119; Ron Alsop, *The Trophy Kids Grow Up: How the Millennial Generation Is Shaking Up the Workforce* (San Francisco: Jossey-Bass/Wiley, 2008); Ronald Alsop, "Schools, Recruiters Try to Define Traits for Future Students," *The Wall Street Journal*, February 14, 2006, p. B6; Kathryn Tyler, "Generation Gaps: Millennials May Be out of Touch with the Basics of Workplace Behavior," *HR Magazine*, January 2008, pp. 69–72; Lindsay Holloway, "Stick Together," *Entrepreneur*, March 2008, p. 30; Martha Irvine, "Recession Intensifies Gen X Discontent at Work," *The Detroit News* (www.detnews.com), November 16, 2009; Chris Penttila, "Talking about My Generation," *Entrepreneur*, March 2009, pp. 53–55.

For example, many Baby Boomers are fascinated with technology, and many members of Generation Y like hierarchy.

How Values Are Learned

People acquire values in the process of growing up, and many values are learned by the age of four. Whereas in the past the family was the most important environment for shaping values, attitudes, and beliefs, today children are exposed via television and the Internet to many more role models, values, ways of thinking, and choices than ever before.[35] Models can be teachers, friends, brothers, sisters, and even public figures. If we identify with a particular person, the probability is high that we will develop some of his or her major values. For example, if a parent valued helping less fortunate people, the child might put a high value on helping people in need later in life.

Another major way values are learned is through the communication of attitudes. The attitudes that we hear expressed directly or indirectly help shape our values. Assume that using credit to purchase goods and services was considered a very foolish practice among your family and friends. You might therefore hold negative values about installment purchases. Unstated but implied attitudes may also shape your values. If key people in your life showed no enthusiasm when you talked about work accomplishments, you might not put such a high value on achieving outstanding results. If, on the other hand, your family and friends centred their lives on their careers, you might develop similar values. (Or you might rebel against such a value because it interfered with a more relaxed lifestyle.) Many key values are also learned through religion, and thus become the basis for society's morals. For example, most religions emphasize treating other people fairly and kindly. To "stab somebody in the back" is considered immoral both on and off the job.

Although many core values are learned early in life, our values continue to be shaped by events later in life. The media, including the dissemination of information about popular culture, influence the values of many people throughout their lives. The aftermath of the 2011 Japanese tsunami intensified a belief in the value of helping less fortunate people around the world. Many organizations such as the Canadian Red Cross and World Vision Canada sent volunteers, and, only hours after the tsunami hit Japan, Canadians had already donated over $77,000 in emergency funds.[36] The outpouring of private donations made on websites underscores that, in addition to volunteering, making donations is a value shared by many people.

The media, particularly advertisements, can also encourage the development of values that are harmful to a person intent on developing a professional career. People featured in advertisements for consumer products, including snack food, beer, and vehicles, are often rude and use flagrantly incorrect grammar. This sends the message that such behaviour is associated with success.

Changes in technology can also change our values. As the world has become increasingly digitized, more and more people come to value a *digital lifestyle* as the normal way of life. Many people would not think of spending time away from the house, even while participating in sports, or watching sports without taking their electronic gadgets with them. Being part of the digital lifestyle is therefore an important value for many people.

Clarifying Your Values

The values that you develop early in life are directly related to the kind of person you are and to the quality of the relationships you form.[37] A recognition of this fact has led to exercises designed to help people clarify and understand some of their own values. Almost all of these values-clarification exercises ask you, in one way or another, to compare the relative importance you attach to different objects and activities. Self-Assessment Quiz 2-2 provides you with an opportunity to clarify your values.

SELF-ASSESSMENT QUIZ 2-2

Clarifying Your Values

Directions: Examine the list of 19 values below. If there is another value that you would like to add, do so under a heading "Other." Now rank them from 1 to 19 (or 1 to 20 if you filled out the extra one) according to the importance of these values to you as a person. The most important value on the list receives a rank of 1.

_____ Having my own place to live
_____ Having one or more children
_____ Having an interesting job and career
_____ Owning a car
_____ Having a good relationship with co-workers
_____ Having good health
_____ Spending time on my favourite social networking sites
_____ Staying in frequent contact with friends by cell phone and texting
_____ Watching my favourite television shows
_____ Participating in sports or other pastimes
_____ Following a sports team, athlete, music group, or other entertainer
_____ Being a religious person
_____ Helping people less fortunate than myself
_____ Loving and being loved by another person
_____ Having physical intimacy with another person
_____ Making an above-average income
_____ Being in good physical condition
_____ Being a knowledgeable, informed person
_____ Completing my formal education
_____ Other:

1. Discuss and compare your ranking of these values with the person next to you.
2. Perhaps your class, assisted by your instructor, can arrive at a class average on each of these values. How does your ranking compare with the class ranking?
3. Look back at your own ranking. Does it surprise you?
4. Any surprises in the class ranking? Which values did you think would be highest and lowest?

The Mesh between Individual and Job Values

Under the best of circumstances, the values of employees mesh with those required by the job. When this state of congruence exists, job performance is likely to be higher. Suppose that Jacquelyn strongly values giving people with limited formal education an opportunity to work and thus avoid being placed on welfare. So she takes a job as a manager of a dollar store that employs many people who would ordinarily have limited opportunity for employment. Jacquelyn is satisfied because her employer and she share a similar value.

A group of researchers attempted to discover why congruence between individual and organizational values leads to positive outcomes such as low turnover and high performance. The major factor creating positive outcomes appears to be employees trusting managers based on the congruence. Communication also plays a role because when communication is regular, open, and consistent, trust is enhanced. For example, trust is enhanced when management explains the reasons behind major decisions. Good communication also enhanced interpersonal attraction between managers and employees. Goal congruence also came about to a lesser extent because employees liked the managers. Liking, in turn, was enhanced by managers communicating well with employees.[38]

A person suffers **person–role conflict** when personal values clash with demands made by the organization. The individual wants to obey orders but does not want to perform an act that seems inconsistent with his or her values. A situation such as this might occur when an employee is asked to produce a product that he or she feels is unsafe or of no value to society. Consider the following scenario:

> *A manager of a commercial weight-reduction centre resigned after two years of service. The owners pleaded with her to stay, based on her excellent performance. The manager replied, "Sorry, I think my job is immoral. We sign up all these people with great expectations of losing weight permanently. Most of them do achieve short-term weight reduction. My conflict is that over 90 percent of our clientele regain the weight they lost once they go back to eating normal food. I think we are deceiving them by not telling them upfront that they will most likely gain back the weight they lose."*

person–role conflict

The situation that occurs when the demands made by the organization clash with the basic values of the individual.

Guidelines for Using Values to Improve Interpersonal Relations

Values are intangible and abstract, and thus not easy to manipulate to help improve your interpersonal relations on the job. Despite their vagueness, values are an important driver of interpersonal effectiveness. Consider the following guidelines:

LEARNING OBJECTIVE 5

1. Establish the values you will use in your relationships with others on the job, and then use those values as firm guidelines in working with others. For example, following the Golden Rule, you might establish the value of treating others as you want to be treated. You would not then lie to others to gain personal advantage and would not backstab your rivals.

2. Establish the values that will guide you as an employee. When you believe that your values are being compromised, express your concern to your manager in a tactful and constructive manner. You might say to your manager, "Sorry, I choose not to tell our customers that our competitor's product is inferior just to make a sale. I choose not to say this because our competitor makes a fine product. But what I will say is that our service is exceptional."

3. Remember that many values are a question of opinion, not a statement of being right versus wrong. If you believe that your values are right, and anybody who disagrees is wrong, you will have frequent conflict. For example, you may believe that the most important value top managers should have is to bring shareholders a high return on their investment. Another worker believes that profits are important, but providing jobs for as many people as possible is an equally important value. Both of you have a good point, but neither is right or wrong. So it is better to discuss these differences rather than hold grudges because of them.

4. Respect differences in values and make appropriate adjustment when the value clash is reasonable. If you are an older person recognize that you may have to win the respect of a younger co-worker rather than assume that because you are more exprienced, or a manager, that respect will come automatically.[39] If you are a younger person, recognize that an older person might be looking for respect, so search for something you can respect right away, such as his or her many valuable contacts in the company.

5. Recognize that many people today are idealistic about their jobs, and want to have an impact on the lives of others.[40] In the meantime, you might feel that you need that person's cooperation to get an important task done right now, such as fulfilling a larger order. Invest a couple of minutes in helping that person understand how an ordinary task might be having an impact on the lives of others—such as earning money to feed a hungry baby at home!

To help you put the above guidelines into practice, do Skill-Building Exercise 2-4. Remember, however, that being skilled at using your values requires day-by-day monitoring.

SKILL-BUILDING EXERCISE 2-4

The Value-Conflict Role-Play

One student plays the role of a company president who is announcing to the group that the company must soon lay off 10 percent of the workforce to remain profitable. The president also points out that the company has a policy against laying off good performers. He or she then asks four of the company managers to purposely give below-average performance ratings to 10 percent of employees. In this way, laying them off will fit company policy.

Four other students play the role of the company managers who receive this directive. If such manipulation of performance evaluations clashes with your values, engage in a dialogue with your manager expressing your conflict. Remember, however, that you may not want to jeopardize your job.

Conduct this group role-play for about 10 minutes, with other class members observing and preparing to offer feedback.

Access the eText in MySearchLab to learn more about this chapter's self-assessment quizzes.

To Watch Explore Practice Study and Review, visit **MySearchLab**

Developing Your Human Relations Skills and Reinforcing Concepts

Summary ✓ Practice / Glossary Flashcards

- There are eight personality factors that are major sources of individual differences: extraversion, emotional stability, agreeableness, conscientiousness, openness to experience, self-monitoring of behaviour, risk taking and thrill seeking, and optimism.
- Personality also influences a person's cognitive style, or modes of problem solving, and the mental processes used to perceive and make judgments from information. According to the Myers-Briggs Type Indicator (MBTI) and the Golden Personality Type Profiler, four dimensions of psychological functioning are energy flow: introverted versus extraverted; information gathering: thinking versus feeling; sensing versus intuiting; decision making: thinking versus feeling; and lifestyle orientation: judging versus perceiving.
- There are several theories of intelligence, including traditional intelligence, practical intelligence, multiple intelligences, and emotional intelligence.
- Values and beliefs are another set of factors that influence behaviour on the job, including interpersonal relations. The values a person develops early in life are directly related to the kind of adult he or she becomes and to the quality of relationships formed.

Interpersonal Relations Case 2-1

Capitalizing on Hidden Talent at Westmont Centre

Ginette Gagnon is the director of Westmont Centre, a residential centre for older persons who require assisted living, such as being served meals, help with taking baths, and supervision for taking daily medication. Many of the residents also need readily available professional health care provided by physicians or nurses. Westmont takes care of an average of 125 guests on a given month.

At a recent meeting with the Westmont board of directors, Gagnon addressed the Centre's most critical problem. She explained, "We are in good shape financially. Because of the aging population in the area we serve, there is a never-ending supply of people who want entrance to Westmont. I say with pride that the good reputation of our staff, and our comfortable physical facilities have enhanced our reputation.

"Our biggest need is for to attract staff who will stick around long enough after they are trained and experienced. You will recall that we used to emphasize hiring young people. We still hire young people, but they tend not to stay very long. Many of them see taking care of older people as a stepping stone to other work. Our program of recruiting young retirees has worked somewhat. The older folks usually have developed nurturing skills, and that is exactly what our residents need. The big problem is that we cannot find enough retirees who want to take care of people not much older than themselves."

"Ginette, please get to the point," said Karl Adams, one of the board members.

"Okay, here is what I am proposing. I would like to start a pilot program of hiring about five workers with developmental disabilities to work on our staff. Our local community college has a program of preparing people with mild intellectual deficiencies for the workforce. The people in the program are not college students, but individuals whose parents or guardians have enrolled them in this cooperative program between the General Arts and Science department and a community agency.

"We would assign these workers to basic jobs like baking bread and muffins, folding laundry, and bringing meals to residents. Running the dishwashing machine would be another possibility, as would be trimming bushes. We would make sure that the workers in the pilot program perform the same tasks every day. McDonald's has had a program like this for years, and both the workers and the restaurants have benefited quite well."

"Hold on," said Jean Weiss. "When the word gets out that we are staffing our Centre with mentally unstable people, we will be in big trouble. I can imagine headlines in the newspapers and the blogs."

Ginette responded with a tone of anger. "I must say, Jean, you do not understand the meaning of an intellectual deficiency, or I am not making myself clear. A developmental disability such as having difficulty learning has nothing to do with mental instability, which refers to emotional problems. Emotional stability and IQ are not particularly related."

The discussion with the board lasted another hour. Ralph Goodwin, the chairperson of the board, concluded the meeting in these words: "I think we see advantages and disadvantages in hiring about five people with intellectual deficiencies to work at Westmont. We would be doing a social good; we would have a new source of dependable workers. Yet we have some concerns about hiring people who might not be able to think well in emergencies. Also, maybe some of our constituents would think that we are hiring mentally unstable people."

"I am disappointed that we could not reach an approval of my plan today," said Gagnon. "However, with more study, I think the board will see the merit in my plan of hiring a group of workers who have mild intellectual deficiencies."

Case Questions

1. What do you recommend that the board should do in terms of approving Gagnon's plan for hiring about five people with intellectual deficiencies to work at Westmont?
2. Assuming that the workers with mild intellectual deficiencies are hired, what recommendations can you make to the supervisors for their training and supervision?
3. Gagnon mentioned a few potential jobs at the Centre for workers with light intellectual deficiencies. What other tasks would you recommend?

Interpersonal Relations Case 2-2

"We've Got to Make Our Numbers"

Bruce Malone works as an account manager for an office-supply company with branches in most major cities in Canada. The company has two lines of business, retail and commercial. Among the many products the company sells are computers and related equipment, office furniture, copy paper, and other basic office supplies.

The retail trade is served by customers walking directly into the store or ordering online. Many of the customers are small-business owners or corporate employees who work at home for part of their work week. The commercial trade also does some walk-in purchasing and online ordering. However, each large customer is also assigned an account manager, who calls on them periodically to discuss their needs for larger purchases such as office furniture and multiple copiers and desktop computers.

Malone is meeting his sales targets for the year despite a flat economy in the city where the office supplier is located. Shortly before Thanksgiving, Malone was analyzing his sales to estimate his performance for the year. According to his projections, his total sales would be 1 percent beyond his quota, giving him a satisfactory year. Making his quota would qualify him for a year-end bonus.

The Friday after Thanksgiving, Malone received an email message from his boss, Lucille Whitman, requesting that the two meet Monday morning before Bruce began working with his customers. At the start of the meeting, Whitman told Malone that she had something very important to discuss with him. "Bruce, we are getting a lot of heat from corporate headquarters," Whitman began. "If we don't make our numbers [attaining the sales goals] the stock price could dip big time, and the home office executives will be in trouble. Even their bonuses will be at risk."

"I've done what I can," responded Malone. "I'm going to make my quota for the year plus a little extra margin. So I guess I'm covered. There isn't much I can do about the company as a whole."

"Let me be a little more specific," replied Whitman. "The company is in trouble, so we all have to pitch in and show better numbers for the year. What we need our account managers to do is to pump up the sales figures a little. Maybe you could count as December sales a few of the purchases your customers have planned for early January. Or maybe you could ship extra-large orders at a discount, and tell your customers they can pay as late as February or March.

"You're smart, Bruce. Beef up your sales figures for the year a little because we have got to make our numbers."

"Lucille, maybe I could work extra hard to pull in a few more sales in the next eight weeks. But I would feel rotten faking my sales figures for December. I'm a professional."

With an angry tone, Whitman responded, "I don't care what you call yourself; we have got to make our numbers. Get back to me soon with your plan for increasing your numbers before the end of December."

Case Questions

1. What is the nature of the conflict Bruce Malone is facing?
2. What type of values is Lucille Whitman demonstrating?
3. What do you recommend Bruce should have done to work his way out of the problem he was facing?
4. Is Bruce too naïve for a career in business?

Questions for Discussion and Review

Practice Chapter Quiz

Multiple Choice

1. The personality factor of agreeableness is associated with the traits of
   a. creativity and curiosity.
   b. courteous and cooperative.
   c. emotional instability and anxiousness.
   d. competiveness.

2. Individuals who score high in self-monitoring are more likely to
   a. dislike being the centre of attention.
   b. adjust their behaviour to gain positive reactions from others.
   c. be insensitive to others' reactions.
   d. adhere to their inner values across situations.

3. The theory of multiple intelligences proposes that
   a. most people score the same across several types of intelligences.
   b. musical intelligence should be disregarded in the workplace.
   c. people learn in different ways and thus have different strengths.
   d. linguistic intelligence is the most relevant of all the intelligences.

4. Which of the following is *not* a component of emotional intelligence?
   a. introversion
   b. self-awareness
   c. self-management
   d. social awareness

5. Person–role conflict occurs when
   a. personal values conflict with the values and demands of an organization.
   b. personal values are better than those of an organization.
   c. an individual does not have values.
   d. there is high consistency between personal and organizational values.

Short Answer

6. Why is responding to individual differences considered the cornerstone of effective interpersonal relations?
7. How can knowledge of major personality factors help a person form better interpersonal relations on the job?
8. Suppose a highly self-monitoring person is attending a company-sponsored social event and that person dislikes such events. How is he or she likely to behave?
9. How can you use information about a person's values to help you relate more effectively to him or her?
10. When you examined your results from the Golden Personality Type Profiler, were you surprised by the results? In what ways was the assessment very typical of you? If you disagree with the results, how are you different from the profile and assessment?

Answers to multiple choice questions: 1. b, 2. b, 3. c, 4. a, 5. a.

The Web Corner

www.queendom.com/tests
This site contains literally hundreds of tests, quizzes, and assessments, including locus-of-control tests, a conflict-management styles test, intelligence tests, and other personality assessments.

http://myskillprofile.com
This site provides many self-quizzes, including emotional intelligence, sports mental skills, and spiritual intelligence. Several of the tests are free.

Internet Skill Builder: Boosting Your Mental Ability

Do you want to be smarter? Thousands of specialists think they have developed intelligent ways of making people more intelligent. You will find at least 2 million websites that provide information about improving brain functioning through such methods as practice in problem solving and taking food supplements. Try out one of these sites. Evaluate the suggestions for plausibility. You might even try the exercises for a couple of weeks and observe if you become smarter. Ask somebody close to you if have become smarter. You might also see if you do better on tests with the same amount of study and classroom attentiveness.

MySearchLab

Visit **MySearchLab** to find self-grading review quizzes in the eText, discipline-specific media and readings, access to a variety of academic journals, and Associated Press news feeds, along with a wide range of writing, grammar, and research tools and to help hone writing and research skills.

CHAPTER 3

Building Self-Esteem and Self-Confidence

Have you heard of the business 1-800-GOT-JUNK? You may have seen their blue-and-green trucks with the catchy phone number on its sides. Who would have thought that you could become a millionaire by picking up others' unwanted items? Brian Scudamore, the founder and CEO of the company, thought that he could make a living doing just that. He started the Vancouver-based business in 1989 after finishing high school with a $700 investment. That summer he earned the $1700 he needed to pay for his first year of college. Later he dropped out of his fourth year from a commerce program at the University of British Columbia to pursue his junk business. By 1997, his company earnings hit the million-dollar mark. Since its humble

Inti St. Clair/Digital Vision/
Getty Images

LEARNING Objectives

After reading and studying this chapter and doing the exercises, you should be able to

1. Describe the nature, development, and consequences of self-esteem.
2. Explain how to enhance self-esteem.
3. Describe the importance of self-confidence and self-efficacy.
4. Pinpoint methods of enhancing and developing your self-confidence.

beginnings, the company has grown to more than 200 franchises across North America as well as Australia. In 2012, the company made more than $100 million. Scudamore expects Got Junk to double its revenues to $200 million by 2016.

The concept was simple: Offer on-time service, uniformed and polite drivers, and up-front pricing. He states that there are several keys to his success, but one key is discussed in this chapter: Scudamore sets high goals for himself and he knows exactly where he wants to go. "Have a clear vision for the company. People who know me, and who work along with me, know that when I set a goal, we get there. That becomes the challenge; it becomes the game."

What is his next venture? Stay tuned for 1-888-WOW-1DAY, his one-day painting service.[1]

THE MEANING OF SELF-ESTEEM, ITS DEVELOPMENT AND CONSEQUENCES

Understanding the self from various perspectives is important because who you are and what you think of you influence many different facets of your life both on and off the job. A particularly important role is played by self-esteem, the overall evaluation people make about themselves, whether positive or negative.[2] A useful distinction is that our **self-concept** is what we *think* about ourselves whereas self-esteem is what we *feel* about ourselves.[3] People with positive self-esteem have a deep-down, inside-the-self feeling of their own worth. Consequently, they develop a positive self-concept. Before reading further, you are invited to measure your current level of self-esteem by doing Self-Assessment Quiz 3-1. We look next at the development of self-esteem and many of its consequences.

LEARNING OBJECTIVE 1

self-concept
What we think about ourselves and who we are.

✓ Practice
The Self-Esteem Checklist

SELF-ASSESSMENT QUIZ 3-1

The Self-Esteem Checklist
Indicate whether each of the following statements is Mostly True or Mostly False as it applies to you.

	Mostly True	Mostly False
1. I am excited about starting each day.	_____	_____
2. Most of any progress I have made in my work or school can be attributed to luck.	_____	_____
3. I often ask myself, "Why can't I be more successful?"	_____	_____
4. When my manager or team leader gives me a challenging assignment, I usually dive in with confidence.	_____	_____

(Continued)

5. I believe that I am working up to my potential.
6. I am able to set limits to what I will do for others without feeling anxious.
7. I regularly make excuses for my mistakes.
8. Negative feedback crushes me.
9. I care very much how much money other people make, especially when they are working in my field.
10. I feel like a failure when I do not achieve my goals.
11. Hard work gives me an emotional lift.
12. When others compliment me, I doubt their sincerity.
13. Complimenting others makes me feel uncomfortable.
14. I find it comfortable to say, "I'm sorry."
15. It is difficult for me to face up to my mistakes.
16. My co-workers think I am not worthy of promotion.
17. People who want to become my friends usually do not have much to offer.
18. If my manager praised me, I would have a difficult time believing it was deserved.
19. I'm just an ordinary person.
20. Having to face change really disturbs me.
21. When I make a mistake, I have no fear owning up to it in public.
22. When I look in the mirror, I typically see someone who is attractive and confident.
23. When I think about the greater purpose in my life, I feel like I am drifting.
24. When I make a mistake, I tend to feel ashamed and embarrassed.
25. When I make a commitment to myself, I usually stick to it with conviction and await the rewards that I believe will come from it.

Scoring and Interpretation: The answers in the high self-esteem direction are as follows:

1. Mostly True
2. Mostly False
3. Mostly False
4. Mostly True
5. Mostly True
6. Mostly True
7. Mostly False
8. Mostly False
9. Mostly False
10. Mostly False
11. Mostly True
12. Mostly False
13. Mostly False
14. Mostly True
15. Mostly False
16. Mostly False
17. Mostly False
18. Mostly False
19. Mostly False
20. Mostly False
21. Mostly True
22. Mostly True
23. Mostly False
24. Mostly False
25. Mostly True

20–25 You have very high self-esteem. Yet if your score is 25, it could be that you are denying any self-doubts.

14–19 Your self-esteem is in the average range. It would probably be worthwhile for you to implement strategies to boost your self-esteem (described in this chapter) so that you can develop a greater feeling of well-being.

0–13 Your self-esteem needs bolstering. Talk over your feelings about yourself with a trusted friend or with a mental health professional. At the same time, attempt to implement several tactics for boosting self-esteem described in this chapter.

Questions

1. How does your score on this quiz match your evaluation of your self-esteem?
2. What would it be like being married to somebody who scored 0 on this quiz?

Source: Statements 21–25 are based on information in the National Association for Self-Esteem, "Self-Esteem Self-Guided Tour—Rate Your Self-Esteem," http://www.self-esteem-nase.org/jssurvey.shtml, accessed May 6, 2005, pp. 1–4.

How Self-Esteem Develops

Part of understanding the nature of self-esteem is to know how it develops. Self-esteem develops and evolves throughout our lives based on interactions with people, events, and things.[4] As an adolescent or adult, your self-esteem might be boosted by a key accomplishment. A 44-year-old woman who was studying to become registered practical nurse (RPN) said that her self-esteem increased when she received an A in a pharmacology course. Self-esteem can also go down in adulthood by means of a negative event such as being laid off, and not being able to find new employment.

Early life experiences have a major impact on self-esteem. People who were encouraged to feel good about themselves and their accomplishments by family members, friends, and teachers are more likely to enjoy high self-esteem. Early life experiences play a key role in the development of both healthy self-esteem and low self-esteem, according to research synthesized at the Counseling and Mental Health Centre of the University of Texas.[5] Childhood experiences that lead to healthy self-esteem include

- being praised.
- being listened to.
- being spoken to respectfully.
- getting attention and hugs.
- experiencing success in sports or school.

In contrast, childhood experiences that lead to low self-esteem include

- being harshly criticized.
- being yelled at or beaten.
- being ignored, ridiculed, or teased.
- being expected to be "perfect" all the time.
- experience failures in sports or school.
- often being given messages that failed experiences (losing a game, getting a poor grade, and so forth) were failures of their whole self.

A widespread explanation of self-esteem development is that compliments, praise, and hugs alone build self-esteem. Yet many developmental psychologists seriously question this perspective. Instead, they believe that self-esteem results from accomplishing worthwhile activities and then feeling proud of these accomplishments. Receiving encouragement, however, can help the person accomplish activities that build self-esteem.

Leading psychologist Martin Seligman argues that self-esteem is caused by a variety of successes and failures. To develop self-esteem, people need to improve their skills for dealing with the world.[6] Self-esteem therefore comes about by genuine accomplishments, followed by praise and recognition. Heaping undeserved praise and recognition on people may lead to a temporary high, but it does not produce genuine self-esteem. The child develops self-esteem not from being told he or she can score a goal in soccer but from scoring that goal.

In attempting to build the self-esteem of children and students, many parents and teachers give children too many undeserved compliments. Researchers suggest that inappropriate compliments are turning too many adults into narcissistic praise-junkies. As a result, many young adults feel insecure if they do not receive compliments regularly.[7]

As mentioned above, experiences in adult life can influence the development of self-esteem. David De Cremer of the Tilburg University (Netherlands) and his associates conducted two studies with Dutch college students about how the behaviour of leaders and fair procedures influence self-esteem. The focus of the leaders' behaviour was whether he or she motivated the workers/students to reward *themselves* for a job well done, such as a self-compliment. Procedural fairness was measured in terms of whether the study participants were given a voice in making decisions. Self-esteem was measured by a questionnaire somewhat similar to Self-Assessment Quiz 3-1 in this chapter. The study questionnaire reflected the self-perceived value that individuals have of themselves as organizational members.

TABLE 3-1 Several Consequences of High Self-Esteem

1. Career success, including a high income
2. Good mental health
3. Profiting from feedback
4. Organizational success
5. Negative consequences, such as trying too hard to preserve one's status

The study found that self-esteem was related to procedural fairness and leadership that encourages self-rewards. When leadership that encouraged rewards was high, procedural fairness was more strongly related to self-esteem. The interpretation given of the findings is that a leader/supervisor can facilitate self-esteem when he or she encourages self-rewards and uses fair procedures. Furthermore, fair procedures have a stronger impact on self-esteem when the leader encourages self-rewards.[8] A takeaway from this study would that rewarding yourself for a job well done, even in adult life, can boost your self-esteem a little.

The Consequences of High Self-Esteem

High self-esteem has many positive consequences for people, as well as a few potential negative ones. Table 3-1 outlines these consequences, and they are described in the following paragraphs. Low self-esteem would typically have a negative impact on the first three factors. People with low self-esteem are likely to have less career success, poorer mental health, and profitless from feedback. Also, an organization populated with low self-esteem workers would be less successful. Yet on the positive side of low self-esteem, it would not lead to trying too hard to preserve one's status.

Career Success. No single factor is as important to career success as self-esteem, as observed by psychologist Eugene Raudsepp. People with positive self-esteem understand their own competence and worth, and have a positive perception of their ability to cope with problems and adversity.[9]

As part of a larger study of personal characteristics and career success, psychology professors Timothy A. Judge, Chalice Hurst, and Lauren S. Simon studied the impact of *core self-evaluation*. Core self-evaluation is a personality trait representing the favourability of a person's overall self-concept. The self-evaluation includes self-esteem, belief in self-control of events in one's life, self-confidence, and emotional stability. Three hundred participants were studied over a 10-year period. One of the many findings in the study was that people with a higher core self-evaluation tended to have higher incomes. Two other factors studied, general mental ability and physical attractiveness, were also found to have a positive relationship with income from employment. A partial explanation of these findings was that being smart and physically attractive contributed to having high self-esteem.[10]

Good Mental Health. One of the major consequences of high self-esteem is good mental health. People with high self-esteem feel good about themselves and have a positive outlook on life. One of the links between good mental health and self-esteem is that high self-esteem helps prevent many situations from being stressful. Few negative comments from others are likely to bother you when your self-esteem is high. A person with low self-esteem might crumble if somebody insulted his or her appearance, posted something negative on Facebook, or received a poor job evaluation. A person with high self-esteem might shrug off an insult as simply being the other person's point of view. If faced with an everyday setback, such as losing keys, the high self-esteem person might think, "I have so much going for me, why fall apart over this incident?"

Positive self-esteem also contributes to good mental health because it helps us ward off being troubled by feelings of jealousy, and acting aggressively toward others because of our jealousy. Particularly with adolescents, lower self-worth leads to jealousy about friends liking other people better.[11]

Profiting from Feedback. Although people with high self-esteem can readily shrug off undeserved insults, they still profit well from negative feedback. Because they are secure, they can profit from the developmental opportunities suggested by negative feedback.

Organizational Success. Workers with high self-esteem develop and maintain favourable work attitudes and perform at a high level. These positive consequences take place because such attitudes and behaviour are consistent with the personal belief that they are competent individuals. Mary Kay Ash, the legendary founder of a beauty products company, put it this way: "It never occurred to me I couldn't do it. I always knew that if I worked hard enough, I could." Furthermore, research has shown that high-self-esteem individuals value reaching work goals more than do low-self-esteem individuals.[12]

Monkey Business Images/Fotolia

The combined effect of workers having high self-esteem helps a company prosper. Long-term research by Nathaniel Branden, as well as more recent studies, suggests that self-esteem is a critical source of competitive advantage in an information society. Companies gain the edge when, in addition to having an educated workforce, employees have high self-esteem, as shown by such behaviours as the following:

- Being creative and innovative
- Taking personal responsibility for problems
- A feeling of independence (yet still wanting to work cooperatively with others)
- Trusting one's own capabilities
- Taking the initiative to solve problems[13]

Behaviours such as these help workers cope with the challenges of a rapidly changing workplace where products and ideas often become obsolete quickly. Workers with high self-esteem are more likely to be able to cope with new challenges regularly because they are confident that they can master their environment.

Potential Negative Consequences. High self-esteem can sometimes have negative consequences, particularly because individuals with high self-esteem work hard to preserve their high status relative to others. When people with high self-esteem are placed in a situation where undermining others helps them maintain their status, they will engage in behaviours that diminish others. In one study, it was shown that high-self-esteem individuals who are also a little neurotic (somewhat emotionally unstable) will often engage in the following undermining behaviours: criticizing group members in front of others, intentionally ignoring others, talking down to other group members, going back on their word, giving others the silent treatment, belittling others, and not listening to people.[14]

According to economist Robert H. Frank of Cornell University, our own reference group has the biggest impact on self-esteem. He writes: "When you see Bill Gates's mansion, you don't actually aspire to have one like it. It's who is local, who is near you physically and who is most like you—your family members, co-workers and old high school classmates—with whom you compare yourself. If someone in your reference group has a little more, you get a little anxious."[15]

ENHANCING SELF-ESTEEM

Improving self-esteem is a lifelong process because self-esteem is related to the success of your activities and interactions with people. Self-esteem can be viewed as a continuum from low to high; even if you have good self-esteem, you may want to continue to enhance your self-esteem as part of self-development and self-improvement. The following suggestions are approaches to enhancing self-esteem that are related to how self-esteem develops.

LEARNING OBJECTIVE 2

BUILDING SELF-ESTEEM AND SELF-CONFIDENCE

FIGURE 3-1 Methods of Enhancing Self-Esteem

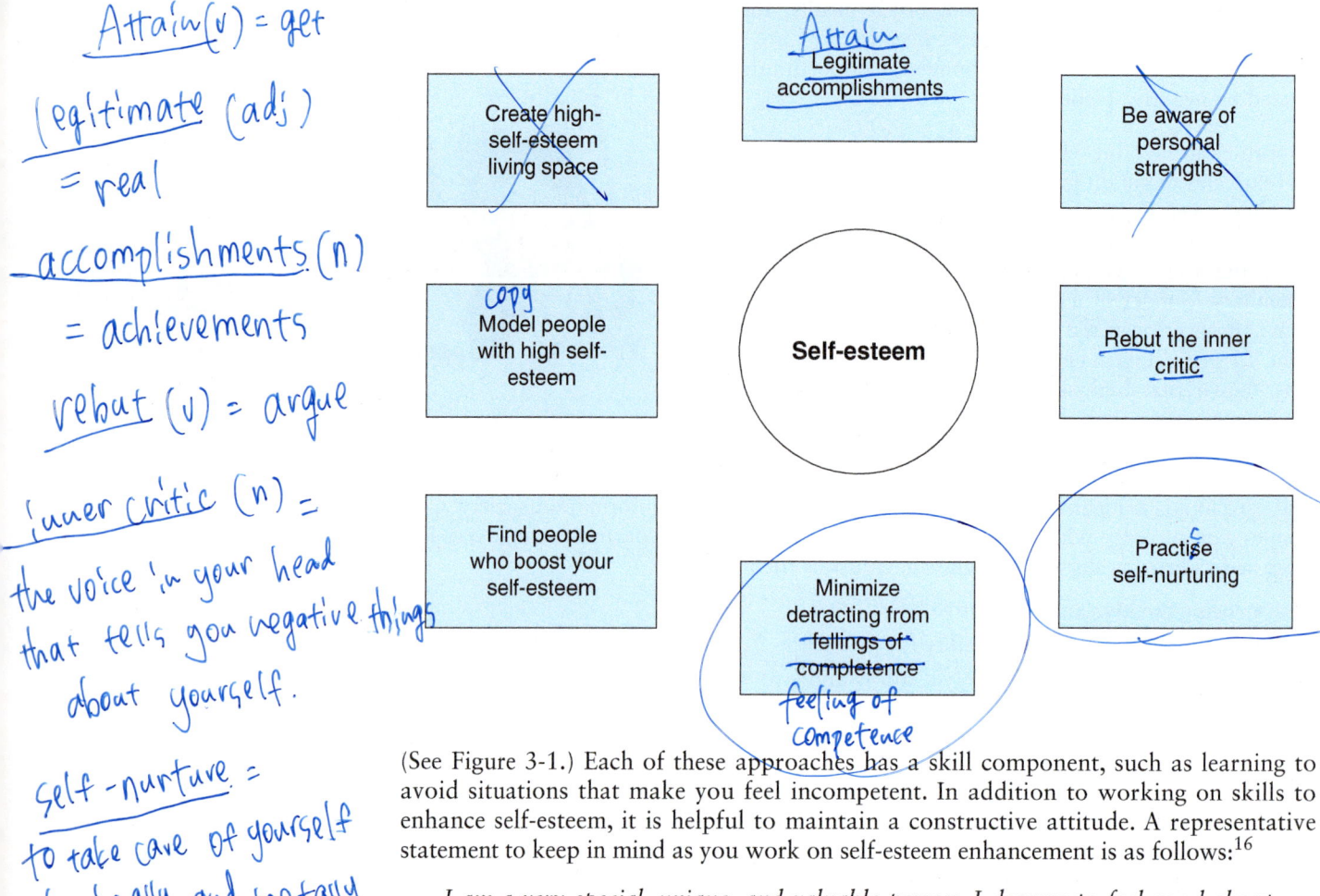

- Create high-self-esteem living space
- Legitimate accomplishments
- Be aware of personal strengths
- Model people with high self-esteem
- **Self-esteem**
- Rebut the inner critic
- Find people who boost your self-esteem
- Minimize detracting from feelings of competence
- Practise self-nurturing

(See Figure 3-1.) Each of these approaches has a skill component, such as learning to avoid situations that make you feel incompetent. In addition to working on skills to enhance self-esteem, it is helpful to maintain a constructive attitude. A representative statement to keep in mind as you work on self-esteem enhancement is as follows:[16]

I am a very special, unique, and valuable person. I deserve to feel good about myself.

Attain Legitimate Accomplishments

To emphasize again, accomplishing worthwhile activities is a major contributor to self-esteem (as well as self-confidence) in both children and adults. Social science research suggests this sequence of events: Person establishes a goal; person pursues the goal; person achieves the goal; person develops esteem-like feelings.[17] The opposite point of view is this sequence: Person develops esteem-like feelings; person establishes a goal; person pursues the goal; person achieves the goal. Similarly, giving people large trophies for mundane accomplishments is unlikely to raise self-esteem. More likely, the person will see through the transparent attempt to build his or her self-esteem and develop negative feelings about the self. What about you? Would your self-esteem receive a bigger boost by

1. receiving an A in a course in which 10 percent of the class received an A, or by
2. receiving an A in a class in which everybody received the same grade?

Be Aware of Personal Strengths

Another method of improving your self-esteem is to develop an appreciation of your strengths and accomplishments. A good starting point is to list your strengths and accomplishments on a word processing document or paper. This list is likely to be more impressive than you expected.

You can sometimes develop an appreciation of your strengths by participating in a group exercise designed for such purposes. A group of about seven people meet to

CHAPTER 3

SKILL-BUILDING EXERCISE 3-1

Reinforcing a Positive Self-Image

To do this exercise, you will need a piece of paper and a pencil or pen or a word processor, and a timer or clock. Set a timer for 10 minutes or note the time on your watch, your cell phone, or a clock. Write your name across the top of the document. Then write everything positive and good you can think of about yourself. Include special attributes, talents, and achievements. You can use single words or sentences. You can write the same things over and over if you want to emphasize them. Your ideas do not have to be well organized. Write down whatever comes to mind. You are the only one who will see this document. Avoid using any negative words. Use only positive ones.

When the 10 minutes are up, read the document over to yourself. You may feel sad when you read it over because it is a new, different, and positive way of thinking about yourself. Your document will contradict some of the negative thoughts you have had about yourself. Those feelings will diminish as you reread this document. Read the document over again several times. Print the document if written by computer, and put it in a convenient place, such as in your pocket, purse, wallet, or bedside table. Read it over at least once a day to keep reminding yourself of how great you are! Find a private space and read it aloud. If you have a good friend or family member who is supportive, read it to that person. Maybe your confidant can think of a positive attribute that you have missed.

Source: Based on "Building Self-Esteem: A Self-Help Guide," http://mentalhealth.samhsa.gov, accessed September 7, 2007.

---

form a support group. All group members first spend about 10 minutes answering the question, "What are my three strongest points, attributes, or skills?" After each group member records his or her three strengths, the person discusses them with the other group members.

Each group member then comments on the list. Other group members sometimes add to your list of strengths or reinforce what you have to say. Sometimes you may find disagreement. One member told the group, "I'm handsome, intelligent, reliable, athletic, self-confident, and very moral. I also have a good sense of humour." Another group member retorted, "And I might add that you're unbearably conceited."

Skill-Building Exercises 3-1 and 3-2 provide additional ways of developing self-esteem, both of which focus on appreciation of strengths.

Rebut the Inner Critic

Another early step in attaining better self-esteem is to rebut your inner critic—the voice inside you that sends negative messages about your capabilities. Rebutting critical

SKILL-BUILDING EXERCISE 3-2

The Self-Esteem Building Club

You and your classmates are invited to participate in one of the most humane and productive possible human relations skill-building exercises, membership in the "self-esteem building club." Your assignment is for three consecutive weeks to help build the self-esteem of one person. Before embarking upon the exercise, review the information about self-esteem development in the chapter. One of the most effective tactics would be to find somebody who had a legitimate accomplishment, and give that person a reward or thank-you. Record carefully what the person did, what you did, and any behavioural reactions of the person whose self-esteem you attempted to build. Here is an example, written by a 46-year-old student of human relations:

Thursday night two weeks ago, I went to the athletic club to play racquetball. Differently than usual, I had a date after the club. I wanted to look good, so I decided to wear my high school class ring. The ring doesn't have much resale value, but I was emotionally attached to it, having worn it for special occasions for 28 years. I stuffed the ring along with my watch and wallet in my athletic bag.

When I was through with racquetball, I showered, and got dressed. My ring was missing from my bag even though my wallet and watch were there. I kind of freaked out because I hate to lose a prized possession. Very discouraged, I left my name, telephone number, and email address at the front desk just in case somebody turned in the ring. I kept thinking that I must have lost the ring when I stopped at the desk to check in.

The next morning before going to class, I got a phone call from a front-desk clerk at the club. The clerk told me that Karl, from the housekeeping staff, heard a strange noise while he was vacuuming near the front desk. He shut off the vacuum cleaner immediately, and pulled out my ring. To me Karl was a hero. I made a special trip to the club that night to meet with Karl. I shook his hand, and gave him a 10-dollar bill as a reward. I told him that honest, hardworking people like him who take pride in their work make this world a better place. It made my day when Karl smiled and told me it was a pleasure to be helpful.

Your instructor might organize a sharing of self-esteem building episodes in the class. If the sharing does take place, look for patterns in terms of what seemed to work in terms of self-esteem building. Also, listen for any patterns in failed attempts at self-esteem building.

statements about you might also be considered another way of appreciating your strengths. Two examples of rebutting your inner critic follow:[18]

1. **Your unfairly harsh inner critic says:** "People said they liked my presentation, but it was nowhere as good as it should have been. I can't believe no one noticed all the places I messed up. I'm such an imposter."

   Your reassuring rebuttal: "Wow, they really liked it. Maybe it wasn't perfect, but I worked hard on that presentation and did a good job. I'm proud of myself. This was a great success."

2. **Your harsh inner critic makes leaps of illogic:** "He is frowning. He didn't say anything, but I know it means that he doesn't like me!"

   Your rebuttal that challenges the illogic: "Okay, he's frowning, but I don't know why. It could have nothing to do with me. Maybe I should ask."

The above are but two examples of the type of putdowns we often hear from our inner critic. To boost your self-esteem in spite of such criticism, you need to develop the skill of rebuttal by rebutting your inner critic frequently.

Practise Self-Nurturing

Although you may be successful at pointing to your strengths and rebutting the inner voice that puts you down, it is also helpful to treat yourself as a worthwhile person. Start to challenge negative experiences and messages from the past by nurturing and caring for yourself in ways that show how valuable, competent, deserving, and lovable you really are. Self-nurturing is often referred to as treating yourself well or spoiling yourself. Here are two suggestions for self-nurturing, both of which involve a modest amount of skill development:

- **Administer self-rewards for a job well done.** When you have carried out an activity especially well in relation to your typical performance, reward yourself in a small, constructive way. You might dine at a favourite restaurant, take an afternoon off to go for a nature walk, or spend an hour on a website you usually do not have the time to visit.
- **Take good care of yourself mentally and physically.** Make sure that you get enough sleep and rest, eat nutritious foods, avoid high-bacteria environments such as a public keyboard unless you use a bacteria spray, and participate in moderate physical exercise. Even taking an extra shower or bath can give you a physical and mental boost. The suggestions just mentioned are also part of stress management.

Real estate agent Laura provides a helpful example of how self-nurturing can help bolster self-esteem. While watching her son play soccer at four in the afternoon, she was asked by another soccer parent, "How's business?" Laura replied, "I haven't made a deal in two weeks, but I know times will get better. So for now, I'm enjoying myself watching Todd [her son] play his little heart out. Afterwards we are going for pizza, and a few video games. My soul will be energized again."

Minimize Settings and Interactions That Detract from Your Feelings of Competence

Most of us have situations in work and personal life that make us feel less than our best. If you can minimize exposure to those situations, you will have fewer feelings of incompetence. The problem with feeling incompetent is that it lowers your self-esteem. Suppose, for example, Sally is a very poor golf player, and intensely dislikes the sport. She is better off excusing herself from a small group of people at the office who invite her to a golf outing. A problem with avoiding all situations in which you feel lowly competent is that it might prevent you from acquiring needed skills. Also, it boosts your self-confidence and self-esteem to become comfortable in a previously uncomfortable situation. In Sally's case perhaps she can eventually learn to play golf better, and then she will be mentally prepared to participate in golf outings.

Get Help from Others

Self-esteem is strongly shaped by how others perceive us, so getting help from others is major step a person can take to improve his or her self-esteem. However, getting help from others can be difficult. People with low self-esteem often do not ask for help because they may not think they are worthy of receiving it. Yet help from others is effective in overcoming the negative messages received in the past.

Asking for support from friends can include such basic steps as these: (1) Ask friends to tell you what they like about you or think that you do well. (2) Ask someone who cares about you to listen to you complain about something without offering a solution to your problem. (3) Ask for a hug. (4) Ask someone who loves you to remind you that he or she does.

Getting help from teachers and other helps can include these steps: (1) Ask professors or tutors for help with work you find challenging. (2) If you lack self-confidence in certain areas, take classes or attempt new activities to increase your competence. An increasing number of retired people today are taking classes in such subjects as computer utilization and digital photography to help catch up with younger people whose skills have challenged their self-esteem.[19]

Another way of getting help from others is to talk and socialize frequently with people who can boost your self-esteem. Psychologist Barbara Ilardie says that the people who can raise your self-esteem are usually those with high self-esteem themselves. They are the people who give honest feedback because they respect others and themselves. Such high-self-esteem individuals should not be confused with yes-people, who agree with others just to be liked. The point is that you typically receive more from strong people than weak ones. Weak people will flatter you but will not give you the honest feedback you need to build self-esteem.[20]

For many people with low self-esteem, casual help from others will not increase self-esteem. In these situations, discussing low self-esteem with a mental health specialist might be the most effective measure.

Model the Behaviour of People with High Self-Esteem

Observe the way people who you believe to have high self-esteem stand, walk, speak, and act. Even if you are not feeling so secure inside, you will project a high self-esteem image if you act assured. Raudsepp recommends, "Stand tall, speak clearly and with confidence, shake hands firmly, look people in the eye and smile frequently. Your self-esteem will increase as you notice encouraging reactions from others."[21] (Notice here that self-esteem is considered to be about the same idea as self-confidence.)

Choose your models of high self-esteem from people you know personally, as well as celebrities you might watch on television news and interview shows. Observing actors on the large or small screen is a little less useful because they are guaranteed to be playing a role. Identifying a teacher or professor as a self-esteem model is widely practised, as is observing successful family members and friends. Twitter and other Internet tools can also allow you to follow your models and observe how they interact with others and share their views on a daily basis.

Create a High-Self-Esteem Living Space

A panel of mental health specialists recommends that to enhance your self-esteem you should make your living space into one that honours the person you are.[22] Whether you live in a single room, a small apartment, or a large house, make that space comfortable and attractive for you. If you have a clean, inviting living space, others are likely to treat you with more respect, which will contribute to your self-esteem. If you share your living space with others, dedicate some space just for you—a place where you can keep your things and know that they will not be disturbed and that you can decorate any way you choose. One author's daughter lived in a very ugly residence room in university for her first year and was very homesick, which reduced her self-esteem. Decorating the room with pictures of friends and family, putting up her art, and buying colourful bedding reduced homesickness and helped her gain enough self-confidence to be so far away from home.

> ## SKILL-BUILDING EXERCISE 3-3
>
> ### The Self-Esteem Calendar
>
> Find a calendar or daily planner on paper or on the computer, with large blank spaces for each day. Schedule into each day a small activity you enjoy doing, such as "watching YouTube to look for videos about people I know personally," "jogging through my neighbourhood," "texting a few people I care about," "reading the classified ads in the *Globe and Mail*," or "hugging somebody I love." Now make a commitment to check your enjoy-life calendar every day, and follow through to make sure that you engaged in the activity you entered into the calendar. The accumulation of small, enjoyable activities should boost your self-esteem a little because you will feel better about yourself.
>
> **Source:** Based on "Building Self-Esteem: A Self-Help Guide," *Health* (http://athealth.com/Consumer/disorder/self-esteem.html, p. 7).

Your living space is part of your self-image, so you may want to ask yourself if your living space projects the right self-image. Also, if you arrange your living space to fit your preferences you will feel better about yourself.

How a Manager Helps Build the Self-Esteem of Group Members

Above we mentioned that leaders who are fair and who encourage self-rewards contribute to the self-esteem of subordinates. There are many other actions and attitudes of managers that help group members enhance their self-esteem. Many of these approaches are related to suggestions for enhancing self-esteem just mentioned. For example, a manager who provides subordinates with an opportunity to accomplish challenging tasks, and then rewards them appropriately, will help bolster their self-esteem. Also, if the manager has high self-esteem, he or she can be your person to model.

Giving subordinates positive feedback about legitimate accomplishments is a powerful approach to enhancing their self-esteem. When accomplishments are out of the ordinary, they can be celebrated through such means as public recognition electronically or during a face-to-face meeting. Accurately assessing the strengths and skill sets of subordinates will often point them in the direction of accomplishing tasks that will boost self-esteem. Helping subordinates develop new skills by coaching can be quite useful as well.

Skill-Building Exercise 3-3 presents an easy, non-time-consuming activity for enhancing your self-esteem. Should the exercise not have a remarkable impact, at least it will have no damaging emotional consequences.

THE IMPORTANCE OF SELF-CONFIDENCE AND SELF-EFFICACY

LEARNING OBJECTIVE 3

self-efficacy
Confidence in one's ability to carry out a specific task.

Although self-confidence can be considered part of self-esteem (or almost its equivalent), it is important enough to study separately. **Self-efficacy** is confidence in your ability to carry out a specific task, in contrast to generalized self-confidence. Various studies have shown that people with a high sense of self-efficacy tend to have good job performance, so being self-confident is important for your career. They also set relatively high goals for themselves.[23] Self-confidence has also long been recognized as a trait of effective leaders. A straightforward implication of self-efficacy is that people who think they can perform well on a task do better than those who think they will do poorly.

Research by college professors and psychological consultants George P. Hollenbeck and Douglas T. Hall suggests that our feelings of self-confidence stem from five sources of information.[24] The first source is the *actual experience, or things we have done*. Having done something before and succeeded is the most powerful way to build self-confidence. If you successfully inserted a replacement battery into your watch without destroying the watch, you will be confident to make another replacement.

The second source of self-confidence is the *experiences of others, or modelling*. You can gain some self-confidence if you have carefully observed others perform a task, such as resolving conflict with a customer. You might say to yourself, "I've seen Tracy calm down the customer by listening and showing sympathy, and I'm confident I could do the same thing." The third source of self-confidence is *social comparison, or comparing yourself to others*. If you see other people with capabilities similar to your own perform a task well, your will gain in confidence. A person might say to himself or herself, "If that person can learn how to work with enterprise software, I can do it also. I'm just as smart."

The fourth source of self-confidence is *social persuasion, the process of convincing another person*. If a credible person convinces you that you can accomplish a particular task, you will often receive a large enough boost in self-confidence to give the task a try. If the encouragement is coupled with guidance on how to perform the task, your self-confidence gain will be higher. So the boss or teacher who says, "I know you can do it, and I'm here to help you," knows how to build self-confidence.

The fifth source of information for making a self-confidence judgment is *emotional arousal, or how we feel about events around us and manage our emotions*. We rely somewhat on our inner feelings to know if we are self-confident enough to perform the task. Imagine a person standing on top of a high mountain ready to ski down. However, he or she is trembling and nauseous with fear. Contrast this beginner to another person who simply feels mildly excited and challenged. Skier number one has a self-confidence problem, whereas skier number two has enough confidence to start the descent. (Have your emotional sensations ever influenced your self-confidence?)

The more these five sources of self-confidence are positive for you, the more likely your self-confidence will be positive. A subtle point about self-confidence is that while being too low in self-confidence is a problem, being too high is also a problem. The overly self-confident person might not listen carefully to the suggestions of others, and may be blind to criticism.

Self-Assessment Quiz 3-2 provides some insight into your level of self-confidence.

SELF-ASSESSMENT QUIZ 3-2

How Self-Confident Are You?

Indicate the extent to which you agree with each of the following statements. Use a 1-to-5 scale: (1) Disagree Strongly; (2) Disagree; (3) Neutral; (4) Agree; (5) Agree Strongly.

		DS	D	N	A	AS
1.	I frequently say to people, "I'm not sure."	5	4	3	(2)	1
2.	I perform well in most situations in life.	1	(2)	3	4	5
3.	I willingly offer advice to others.	1	(2)	3	4	5
4.	Before making even a minor decision, I usually consult with several people.	5	4	(3)	2	1
5.	I am generally willing to attempt new activities for which I have very little related skill or experience.	1	2	3	(4)	5
6.	Speaking in front of the class or other group is a frightening experience for me.	5	4	3	(2)	1
7.	I experience stress when people challenge me or put me on the spot.	5	4	3	2	(1)
8.	I feel comfortable attending a social event by myself.	1	(2)	3	4	5
9.	I'm much more of a winner than a loser.	1	2	3	(4)	5
10.	I am cautious about making any substantial change in my life.	5	4	(3)	2	1

Total score: 25

Scoring and Interpretation: Calculate your total score by adding the numbers circled. A tentative interpretation of the scoring is as follows:

- **45–50** Very high self-confidence with perhaps a tendency toward arrogance
- **38–44** A high, desirable level of self-confidence
- **30–37** Moderate, or average, self-confidence
- **10–29** Self-confidence needs strengthening

Questions:

1. How does your score on this test fit with your evaluation of your self-confidence?
2. What would it be like working for a manager who scored 10 on this quiz?

TECHNIQUES FOR DEVELOPING AND ENHANCING YOUR SELF-CONFIDENCE

LEARNING OBJECTIVE 4

Self-confidence is generally achieved by succeeding in a variety of situations. A confident civil engineering technician may not be generally self-confident unless he or she also achieves success in activities such as forming good personal relationships, navigating complex software, writing a letter, learning a second language, and displaying athletic skills.

Although this general approach to self-confidence building makes sense, it does not work for everyone. Some people who seem to succeed at everything still have lingering self-doubt. Low self-confidence is so deeply ingrained in this type of personality that success in later life is not sufficient to change things. Following are eight specific strategies and tactics for building and elevating self-confidence, as outlined in Figure 3-2. They will generally work unless the person has deep-rooted feelings of inferiority. The tactics and strategies are arranged approximately in the order in which they should be tried to achieve best results.

Develop a Solid Knowledge Base

A bedrock strategy for projecting self-confidence is to develop a knowledge base that enables you to provide sensible alternative solutions to problems. Intuition is very important, but working from a base of facts helps you project a confident image. Formal education is an obvious and important source of information for your knowledge base. Day-by-day absorption of information directly and indirectly related to your career is equally important. A major purpose of formal education is to get you in the right frame of mind to continue your quest for knowledge. In your quest for developing a solid knowledge base to project self-confidence, be sensitive to abusing this technique. If you bombard people with quotes, facts, and figures, you are likely to be perceived as an annoying know-it-all.

A solid knowledge base contributes to self-confidence also because the knowledge facilitates engaging in conversation with intelligent people. A weak counterargument is that having information stored in your brain is no longer important because information is so accessible online. When in a gathering of people, you could then use a smart phone

FIGURE 3-2 Boosting Your Self-Confidence

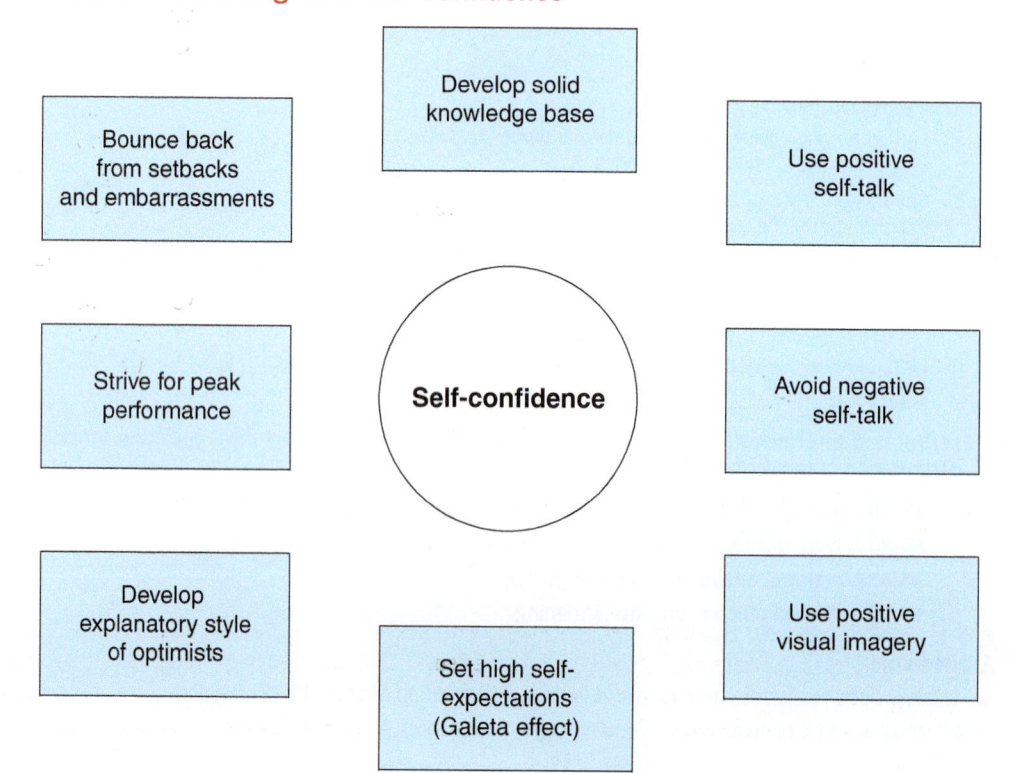

- Develop solid knowledge base
- Use positive self-talk
- Avoid negative self-talk
- Use positive visual imagery
- Set high self-expectations (Galeta effect)
- Develop explanatory style of optimists
- Strive for peak performance
- Bounce back from setbacks and embarrassments

→ Self-confidence

54 CHAPTER 3

to access some facts to talk about. Such behaviour is unlikely to help a person project a confident, intelligent image.

> ### BACK TO THE OPENING CASE
>
> Mark Scudamore used his self-confidence to go from one truck collecting "junk" to an enterprise. Believing in himself, it was easier to get others to also believe in his vision for the business. And he is gaining ground with a new business venture, 1-888-WOW-1DAY. To be this kind of business person, you need more than business acumen (business smarts). You also need a very healthy dose of self-confidence.

Use Positive Self-Talk

A basic method of building self-confidence is to engage in **positive self-talk**, saying positive things about yourself. The first step in using positive self-talk is to objectively state the incident that is casting doubt about self-worth.[25] The key word here is *objectively*. Terry, who is fearful of poorly executing a report-writing assignment, might say, "I've been asked to write a report for the company, and I'm not a good writer."

The next step is to objectively interpret what the incident *does not* mean. Terry might say, "Not being a skilled writer doesn't mean that I can't figure out a way to write a good report or that I'm an ineffective employee."

Next, the person should objectively state what the incident *does* mean. In doing this, the person should avoid put-down labels, such as "incompetent," "stupid," "dumb," "jerk," or "airhead." All these terms are forms of negative self-talk. Terry should state what the incident does mean: "I have a problem with one small aspect of this job."

The fourth step is to objectively account for the cause of the incident. Terry would say, "I'm really worried about writing a good report because I have very little experience in writing along these lines."

The fifth step is to identify some positive ways to prevent the incident from happening again. Terry might say, "I'll get out my textbook on business communications and review the chapter on report writing" or "I'll enroll in a course or seminar on business report writing."

The final step is to use positive self-talk. Terry imagines his boss saying, "This report is really good. I'm proud of my decision to select you to prepare this important report."

Positive self-talk builds self-confidence and self-esteem because it programs the mind with positive messages. Making frequent positive statements or affirmations about the self creates a more confident person. An example would be, "I know I can learn this new equipment rapidly enough to increase my productivity within five days."

Business coach Gary Lockwood emphasizes that positive self-talk is also useful for getting people past difficult times. "It's all in your head," he says. "Remember you are in charge of your feelings. You are in control of your attitude." Instead of berating yourself after making a mistake, learn from the experience and move on. Say to yourself, "Everyone makes mistakes," "Tomorrow is another day," or "What can I learn from this?"[26]

Despite the many advantages of positive self-talk, as with optimism there can be times when thinking too positively can create problems. Negative thoughts are often useful in alerting us to potential problems, and prompting us to develop a plan of correction. Imagine that Lisa is job hunting, and that she has urgent need of employment. She has a promising interview, and her positive thinking prompts her to think, "There is no doubt that I will receive an offer very soon." Her positive thinking blocks her from continuing her job search. When the offer in question does not come through, Lisa has lost momentum in her job search. In the words of author John Derbyshire, we must be "vigilantly realistic" toward the potential dangers of positive thinking.[27]

Avoid Negative Self-Talk

As implied, you should minimize negative statements about yourself to bolster self-confidence. A lack of self-confidence is reflected in statements such as "I may be stupid but . . ." "Nobody asked my opinion," "I know I'm usually wrong, but . . ." and "I know I don't have as much education as some people, but. . ." Self-effacing statements like these serve to reinforce low self-confidence.

positive self-talk
Saying positive things about yourself.

It is also important not to attribute to yourself negative, irreversible traits, such as "idiotic," "ugly," "dull," "loser," and "hopeless." Instead, look on your weak points as areas for possible self-improvement. Negative self-labelling can do long-term damage to your self-confidence. If a person stops that practice today, his or her self-confidence may begin to increase.

Use Positive Visual Imagery

Assume you have a situation in mind in which you would like to appear confident and in control. An example would be a meeting with a major customer who has told you by email that he is considering switching suppliers. Your intuitive reaction is that if you cannot handle his concerns without fumbling or appearing desperate, you will lose the account. An important technique in this situation is **positive visual imagery**, or picturing a positive outcome in your mind. To apply this technique in this situation, imagine yourself engaging in a convincing argument about why your customer should retain your company as the primary supplier. Imagine yourself talking in positive terms about the good service your company offers and how you can rectify any problems.

Visualize yourself listening patiently to your customer's concerns and then talking confidently about how your company can handle these concerns. As you rehearse this moment of truth, create a mental picture of you and the customer shaking hands over the fact that the account is still yours.

Positive visual imagery helps you appear self-confident because your mental rehearsal of the situation has helped you prepare for battle. If imagery works for you once, you will be even more effective in subsequent uses of the technique.

Set High Expectations for Yourself (the Galatea Effect)

If you set high expectations for yourself and you succeed, you are likely to experience a temporary or permanent boost in self-confidence. The **Galatea effect** is a type of self-fulfilling prophecy in which high expectations lead to high performance. Similar to positive self-talk, if you believe in yourself you are more likely to succeed. You expect to win, so you do. The Galatea effect may not work all the time, but it does work some of the time for many people.

Workplace behaviour researchers D. Brian McNatt and Timothy A. Judge studied the Galatea effect with 72 auditors in three offices of a major accounting firm over a three-month period. The auditors were given letters of encouragement to strengthen their feelings of self-efficacy. Information in the letters was based on facts about the auditors, such as information derived from their résumés and company records. The results of the experiment showed that creating a Galatea effect bolstered self-efficacy, motivation, and performance. However, the performance improvement was temporary, suggesting that self-expectations need to be boosted regularly.[28]

Develop the Explanatory Style of Optimists

According to the research and observations of consultant and trainer Price Pritchett, optimism is linked to self-confidence. Explaining events in an optimistic way can help preserve self-confidence and self-esteem. When experiencing trouble, optimists tend to explain the problems to themselves as temporary. Bad events are expected to be short-lived, and optimists look to the future when times will be better. Another aspect of optimists' explanatory style protects their self-confidence. Rather than condemn themselves for failures, they look for how other factors or circumstances have contributed to the problem. Optimists, then, do not take all the blame for a problem, but look to external factors to help explain what went wrong.

---

positive visual imagery
Picturing a positive outcome in your mind.

Galatea effect
A type of self-fulfilling prophecy in which high expectations lead to high performance.

Nyul/Fotolia

Interpreting difficulties in this way gives the optimists a sense of control. Instead of looking at the unfortunate situation as hopeless, they have faith in their ability to deal with it.[29] Suppose an optimist purchases a computer workstation that comes packed in a box with many parts along with directions. A problem arises in that some of the screws and dowels do not fit, and the directions are unclear. A pessimist might suffer a drop in self-confidence and self-esteem, saying, "What a fool I am. I can't even assemble a piece of office furniture." In contrast, the optimist might say, "I'm doing something wrong here, and I will get a buddy to help show me my mistake. But the manufacturer can also be blamed. The instructions are terrible, and all the parts may not fit together." In this way, the optimist does not take such a big hit to self-confidence and self-esteem.

Strive for Peak Performance

A key strategy for projecting self-confidence is to display peak performance, or exceptional accomplishment in a given task. The experience is transient but exceptionally meaningful. Peak performance refers to much more than attempting to do your best. Experiencing peak performance in various tasks over a long period of time would move a person toward self-actualization.[30] To achieve peak performance, you must be totally focused on what you are doing. When you are in the state of peak performance, you are mentally calm and physically at ease. Intense concentration is required to achieve this state. You are so focused on the task at hand that you are not distracted by extraneous events or thoughts. To use an athletic analogy, you are *in the zone* while you are performing the task. In fact, many sports psychologists and other sports trainers work with athletes to help them attain peak performance.

The mental state achieved during peak performance is akin to a person's sense of deep concentration when immersed in a sport or hobby. On days when tennis players perform way above their usual game, they typically comment, "The ball looked so large, I could read the label as I hit it." On the job, focus and concentration allow the person to sense and respond to relevant information coming both from within the mind and from outside stimuli. When you are at your peak, you impress others by responding intelligently to their input. While turning in peak performance, you are experiencing a mental state referred to as *flow*.

Although you are concentrating on an object or sometimes on another person during peak performance, you still have an awareness of the self. You develop a strong sense of the self, similar to self-confidence and self-efficacy, while you are concentrating the task. Peak performance is related to self-confidence in another important way. Achieving peak performance in many situations helps you develop self-confidence.

Skill-Building Exercise 3-4 gives you the opportunity to work on enhancing your self-confidence.

SKILL-BUILDING EXERCISE 3-4

Building Your Self-Confidence and Self-Efficacy

Most people could use a boost to their self-confidence. Even if you are a highly confident individual, perhaps there is room for building your feelings of self-efficacy in a particular area, such as a proud and successful business owner learning a new skill like editing digital photos or speaking a foreign language.

This skill-building exercise enhances your self-confidence or self-efficacy in the next two weeks by trying out one of the many suggestions for self-confidence building described in the text.

As part of planning the implementation of this exercise, think about any area in which your self-confidence could use a boost.

A candid human relations student, who was also a confident cheerleader, said, "Face it. I'm terrible at PowerPoint presentations. I put up so many details on my slides that the audience is trying to read my slides instead of looking at me. I have to admit that my PowerPoint presentation consists mostly of my reading my slides to the audience. I'm much better at cheerleading." So this student studied information in her human relations text about making better graphic presentations. She revamped her approach to using her slides as headlines and talking points.

She tried out one presentation in class, and one at her church. She received so many compliments about her presentations that now she has much higher self-efficacy with respect to PowerPoint presentations.

Your instructor might organize a sharing of self-confidence-building episodes in the class. If the sharing does take place, look for patterns in terms of what seemed to work in terms of self-confidence or self-efficacy building. Also, listen for any patterns in failed attempts at self-confidence building.

Explore
Simulation: Self-Esteem

Bounce Back from Setbacks and Embarrassments

Resilience is a major contributor to personal effectiveness. Overcoming setbacks also builds self-confidence, as implied from the description of the explanatory style of optimists. An effective self-confidence builder is to convince yourself that you can conquer adversity such as setbacks and embarrassments, thus being resilient. The vast majority of successful leaders have dealt successfully with at least one significant setback in their careers, such as being fired or demoted. In contrast, crumbling after a setback or series of setbacks will usually lower self-confidence. Two major suggestions for bouncing back from setbacks and embarrassments are presented next.

Get Past the Emotional Turmoil. Adversity has enormous emotional consequences. The emotional impact of severe job adversity can rival the loss of a personal relationship. The stress from adversity leads to a cycle of adversity followed by stress, followed by more adversity. A starting point in dealing with the emotional aspects of adversity is to *accept the reality of your problem*. Admit that your problems are real and that you are hurting inside.

A second step is *not to take the setback personally*. Remember that setbacks are inevitable so long as you are taking some risks in your career. Not personalizing setbacks helps reduce some of the emotional sting. If possible, *do not panic*. Recognize that you are in difficult circumstances under which many others panic. Convince yourself to remain calm enough to deal with the severe problem or crisis. Also, *get help from your support network*. Getting emotional support from family members and friends helps overcome the emotional turmoil associated with adversity.

Find a Creative Solution to Your Problem. An inescapable part of planning a comeback is to solve your problem. You often need to search for creative solutions. Suppose a person faced the adversity of not having enough money for educational expenses. The person might search through standard alternatives, such as applying for financial aid, looking for more lucrative part-time work, and borrowing from family members. Several students have solved their problem more creatively by asking strangers to lend them money as intermediate-term investments. An option the investors have is to receive a payback based on the future earnings of the students.

A useful approach to finding a creative solution to your problem is to use response-oriented thinking that focuses on finding answers. A resilience program developed by Joshua D. Margolis of the Harvard Business School and Paul G. Stoltz, the founder of a global research and consulting firm, includes finding answers to the four following questions:

1. What features can I improve or potentially improve?
2. What sort of positive impact can I personally have on what happens next?
3. How can I contain the negatives of the situation and generate currently unseen positives?
4. What can I do to begin addressing the problem now?[31]

It is highly recommended that you write down answers to these questions rather than merely thinking about them. Writing offers people more command over an adverse situation than does mere reflection. A plausible reason is that writing down something is an early step in developing an action plan. Getting back to the person concerned about educational expenses, he or she might write down in response to question 4, "What do I or my family members own that I might be able to sell over eBay that would raise a little cash to get me started?"

Access the eText in MySearchLab to learn more about this chapter's self-assessment quizzes.

To **Watch** **Explore** **Practice** **Study** and **Review**, visit MySearchLab

Developing Your Human Relations Skills and Reinforcing Concepts

Summary

- Self-esteem refers to the overall evaluation people make about themselves and has many important consequences: career success, including a high income; good mental health; profiting from feedback, and organizational success.
- Self-esteem can be enhanced in many ways: (a) Attain legitimate accomplishments; (b) be aware of your personal strengths; (c) rebut the inner critic; (d) practise self-nurturing; (e) minimize settings and interactions that detract from your feelings of competence; (f) get help from others, including talking and socializing frequently with people who boost your self-esteem; (g) model the behaviour of people with high self-esteem; and (h) create a high-self-esteem living space.
- Self-confidence and self-efficacy enhance job performance. Self-efficacy refers to your confidence in being able to accomplish a task.
- Specific methods for building self-confidence are: (a) Develop a solid knowledge base; (b) use positive self-talk; (c) avoid negative self-talk; (d) use positive visual imagery; (e) set high expectations for yourself (the Galatea effect); (f) develop the explanatory style of optimists; (e) strive for peak performance; and (f) bounce back from setbacks and embarrassments.

Interpersonal Relations Case 3-1

The Confetti Man

Nick Jablonski works for a manufacturer of property maintenance and recreational vehicles such as lawnmowers, snowblowers, and all-terrain vehicles. The company prospers even during downturns in the economy. This is true because when economic conditions are worrisome many people invest more money in taking care of their property and enjoying themselves close to home instead of travelling. Nick holds the job title of "Celebrations Assistant." The more traditional part of his job is to organize company events like picnics, sales meetings, and shareholder meetings.

When asked to explain the celebrations assistant part of his job in more detail, Nick, with a smile, replied:

> My job is to help workers throughout the company celebrate accomplishments that help the company reach its goals. I'll give you a couple of examples. Suppose I learn that a production technician has exceeded quota on inserting dashboards on riding mowers, I will visit the factory floor and help the technician celebrate. Sometimes I will attach a smiley face to his or her work area. I might shake his or her hand or pat the person on the back. Or to be more dramatic, I might shower the person with confetti.
>
> Just last week I was told by her supervisor that one of our customer service reps was working on the phone with a woman suffering from arthritis. The customer was having a difficult time starting one of our lawnmowers. The rep stayed on the phone twenty minutes with the lady until she could pull the start cord correctly. The customer was so pleased that she wrote a letter to the CEO praising the helpfulness of the rep.
>
> My response was to visit the customer service rep's area and have a little celebration. Not only did I throw two bags of confetti, I blew a foghorn. I could tell the rep became a little embarrassed because she blushed. Yet I knew that I really boosted her self-esteem.

When Jablonski was asked why his work boosted worker self-esteem, he answered as follows:

> My job is to make our employees feel good about themselves. My smiley faces, my encouraging message, and especially my confetti-throwing make people feel great.

If people feel great about themselves and their accomplishments, their self-esteem heads north. It's that simple.

Case Questions

1. To what extent do you think that the celebrations assistant is really boosting the self-esteem of workers?
2. Assume that Nick is successful in boosting worker self-esteem. How might this help the company?
3. Advise the CEO of the company in question as to whether having a celebrations assistant on the payroll is a good investment of company money.

Source: Several facts in this case are based on Jeffrey Zaslow, "The Most-Praised Generation Goes to Work," *The Wall Street Journal*, April 20, 2007, pp. W1, W7.

Interpersonal Relations Case 3-2

Why Can't I Get a Job?

Laura graduated with a diploma in General Business almost a year ago and has been actively seeking employment as an entry-level office assistant since then. While she has had several interviews, she never heard back from the employer and was getting very discouraged. She was starting to feel anxious all the time and spending more time alone. A friend, Michelle, who had been in the same program, was working two months after college and lived about two hours away from Laura's town. To cheer herself up a bit, Laura went to visit Michelle, and while there decided to ask her for job-hunting advice.

She explained to her friend, "I don't know what's wrong with me. I'm such a loser. I likely don't have enough education for these jobs. You're lucky. You were so much smarter than me and your grades were always better. I was a waitress before so maybe I should just give up on this business stuff and go back to waiting tables. Why did I ever think I could be an office assistant?"

Michelle was quite shocked to hear her friend talk this way. "Laura, you shouldn't put yourself down like that. Your grades were good and you were one of the best people to do homework with. We had lots of fun and you were always smiling. Don't let this set you back. I know you can get a good job. You just have to start believing in yourself again."

Case Questions

1. What advice would you give Laura to regain her self-confidence and to start feeling better about herself?
2. What is Laura doing right that will help her regain her confidence?
3. What suggestions should Michelle make to help her friend?

Questions for Discussion and Review

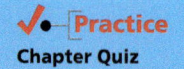

Practice Chapter Quiz

Multiple Choice

1. Many childhood experiences contribute to building high self-esteem, including
   a. getting attention and hugs.
   b. ignoring sports and concentrating on academics.
   c. being ridiculed.
   d. being judged.
2. A positive consequence of high self-esteem includes all but
   a. good mental health.
   b. career success.
   c. not requiring feedback.
   d. high work performance.
3. An example of a negative consequence of high self-esteem would be
   a. working hard to gain favourable reviews from your supervisor.
   b. the development of healthy work attitudes.
   c. talking down to your team members.
   d. being innovative and creative in your job.
4. An individual with high self-efficacy would
   a. belittle co-workers if he or she thought they would learn from it.
   b. make a poor manager as he or she is self-absorbed.
   c. jump from job to job as he or she is unable to work well with others.
   d. likely set high goals for himself or herself.
5. Picturing yourself competently handling a conflict with a co-worker is an example of
   a. self-efficacy.
   b. peak performance.
   c. setting high expectations.
   d. positive visual imagery.

Answers to multiple choice questions: 1. a,   2. c,   3. c,   4. d,   5. b.

Short Answer

6. A study by economists indicated that workers with higher levels of self-esteem tended to be more productive. What would be an explanation for this finding?

7. Exercises to boost self-esteem and self-confidence often emphasize focusing on your positive qualities. Why might it also be important to be aware of your weak points to develop self-esteem?

8. When you meet another person, on what basis do you conclude that he or she is self-confident?

9. In what way does your program of studies contribute to building your self-esteem and self-confidence?

10. Open up MySearchLab and select the Self-Esteem simulation. Work through the simulation about James. What other advice would you give James?

The Web Corner

www.athealth.com/Consumer/disorders/self-esteem.html
Measuring and building your self-esteem

www.self-confidence.co.uk
Developing your self-confidence

www.cmha.ca
Canadian Mental Health Association; many articles on mental health, including self-esteem

Internet Skill Builder: Learning More about Your Self-Esteem

The checklist in Self-Assessment Quiz 3-1 gave you one opportunity to assess your self-esteem. To gain additional insights into your self-esteem, visit www.more-selfesteem.com. Go to "quizzes" under Free Resources, and take the self-esteem test. How does your score on this quiz compare to your score on the checklist? If your level of self-esteem as measured by the two quizzes is quite different (such as high versus low), explain why this discrepancy might occur.

MySearchLab

Visit **MySearchLab** to find self-grading review quizzes in the eText, discipline-specific media and readings, access to a variety of academic journals, and Associated Press news feeds, along with a wide range of writing, grammar, and research tools and to help hone writing and research skills.

CHAPTER 4

Interpersonal Communication

Maria is the director of e-commerce for a company in Hamilton, Ontario, that is a reseller of a variety of specialty machines used in manufacturing. Many of the machines the company sells are new, and many are refurbished. Competition from overseas manufacturers, particularly in China, is making the sales of machines more difficult. Almost all of Maria's contacts with customers and prospective customers are over the Internet, including email as well as Facebook and LinkedIn.

Maria noticed one year ago that she had not received an order from one of the company's largest customers, a successful machine tool company in Montreal, Quebec. Maria wrote a few emails to her contact at the company, Larry, the chief operating officer, asking if there was any way her company could help his company. Larry basically ignored the email messages, except for one response that his company was in good shape with respect to machinery.

BananaStock/Thinkstock

LEARNING Objectives

After reading and studying this chapter and doing the exercises, you should be able to

1. Explain the basic steps in the communication process.
2. Explain the relationship-building aspect of interpersonal communication.
3. Recognize nonverbal communication and improve your nonverbal communication skills.
4. Identify barriers to communication, including gender differences, and know how to overcome them.
5. Enhance your listening skills.

Maria decided to telephone Larry and ask if she could visit him at his office. Larry responded, "We've done everything over the Internet so far. I had never thought of seeing you in person. But if you think the trip is worth your time and money, let's schedule a date." Maria did visit her customer in Montreal, and her visit lasted two hours. Larry proudly showed Maria how his company was expanding, and how her company's machines were being deployed. Larry also went into detail what he liked and did not like about the machines he had bought from Maria's company.

Within three months after the visit, Maria's company received two orders for machines that would help the Montreal company expand on a new product line. Larry also wrote Maria explaining that it was refreshing to see an e-commerce manager in person.

The story about the e-commerce manager actually making an in-person visit to a customer illustrates that in this era of high technology, face-to-face communication still plays an important role in business. **Communication** is the sending, receiving, and understanding of messages. It is also the basic process by which managers, customer-contact workers, and professionals accomplish their work. For example, a customer service representative cannot resolve a thorny customer problem without carefully receiving and sending information. Communication skills are a success factor for workers in a wide variety of jobs.

communication
The sending, receiving, and understanding of messages.

The subject of this chapter is interpersonal, or face-to-face, communication rather than electronic communication, such as email, instant messaging, text messaging, and videoconferencing. However, almost all principles of interpersonal communication also apply to electronic communication. Chapter 5 deals with the interpersonal aspects of communication in the digital world. Chapter 8 includes a section about coping with cross-cultural communication barriers and discusses some of the communication differences between cultures.

The importance of face-to-face communication has increased in the age of electronic communication. Many companies have discovered that the subtle aspects of communication possible in face-to-face communication can help productivity. A key example would be talking to a person to help build a good working relationship. As illustrated in the case opener, there is yet no good substitute for face-to-face contact in building relationships. Entrepreneurship consultant Jim Blasingame reports, "There is a comfort level that is achieved when you've met the person you're doing business with."[1]

The information in this chapter is aimed at reducing communication problems among people and helping you enhance your communication effectiveness. The chapter approaches these ends in two ways. First, it explains the nature of a few key facets of interpersonal communication. Second, it presents guidelines for improving your effectiveness, along with skill-building exercises. We place particular emphasis on listening as part of achieving good

INTERPERSONAL COMMUNICATION

communication. Keep in mind that communication underlies almost every human relations activity, as much as running supports almost every sport. You need good communication skills to get through job interviews, perform well on the job, and get promoted.

STEPS IN THE COMMUNICATION PROCESS

LEARNING OBJECTIVE 1

One way to understand how people communicate is to examine the steps involved in transmitting and receiving a message, illustrated in Figure 4-1. For effective communication to take place, six components must be present: a sender, a message, a channel, a receiver, feedback, and the environment. In addition, the entire communication process is affected by a seventh component—noise.

To help understand the communication process, assume that a production manager in a bicycle factory wants to inform a team leader that quality in her department slipped last month.

1. **Sender (or source).** The sender in a communication event is usually a person (in this case the production manager) attempting to send a spoken, written, sign-language, or nonverbal message to another person or persons. The perceived authority and credibility of the sender are important factors in influencing how much attention the message will receive.

2. **Message.** The heart of the communication event is the **message**, a purpose or idea to be conveyed. Many factors influence how a message is received. Among them are clarity, the alertness of the receiver, the complexity and length of the message, and how the information is organized. The production manager's message will most likely get across if he says directly, "I need to talk to you about last month's below-average quality figures."

3. **Channel (medium).** Several communication channels, or media, are usually available for sending messages in organizations. Typically, messages are written (usually electronically), spoken, or communicated as a combination of the two. Some kind of nonverbal signal such as a smile or hand gesture accompanies most spoken messages. In the production manager's case, he has chosen to drop by the team leader's office and deliver his message in a serious tone.

4. **Receiver.** A communication event can be complete only when another party receives the message and understands it properly. In the present example, the team leader is the receiver. Perceptual distortions of various types act as filters that can prevent a message from being received as intended by the sender. If the team leader is worried that her job is at stake, she might get defensive when she hears the production manager's message.

message
A purpose or idea to be conveyed.

FIGURE 4-1 A Basic Model of the Communication Process

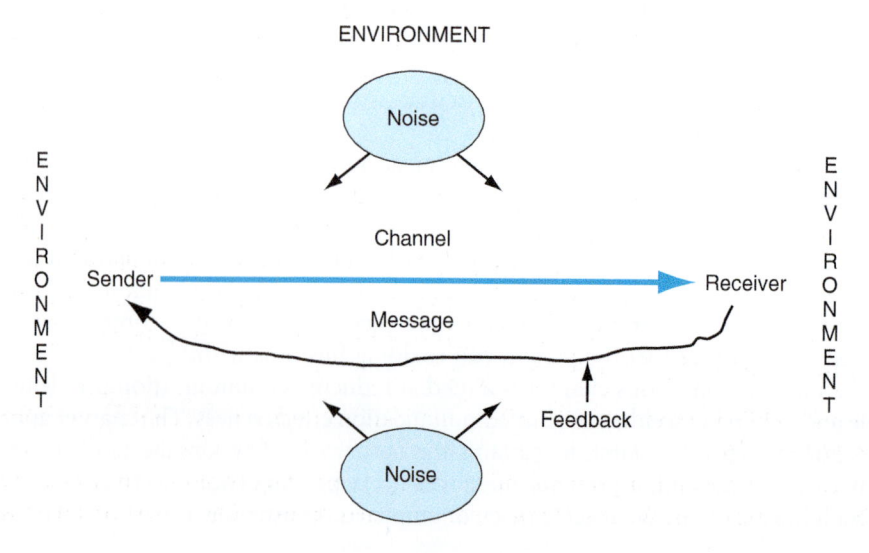

5. **Feedback.** Messages sent back from the receiver to the sender are referred to as **feedback**. Without feedback it is difficult to know whether a message has been received and understood. Feedback includes the *reactions* of the receiver. If the receiver takes action as intended by the sender, the message has been received satisfactorily. The production manager will know his message got across if the team leader says, "Okay, when would you like to review last month's quality reports?" Effective interpersonal communication therefore involves an exchange of messages between two people. The two communicators take turns being receivers and senders.

6. **Environment.** A full understanding of communication requires knowledge of the environment in which messages are transmitted and received. The organizational culture (attitudes and atmosphere) is a key environmental factor influencing communication. It is easier to transmit controversial messages when trust and respect are high than when they are low.

7. **Noise.** Distractions have a pervasive influence on the components of the communication process. In this context, **noise** is anything that disrupts communication, including the attitudes, biases, and emotions of the receiver and the sender. For example, Natalie wants to make a case for new software for her computer. When she explains her need to her supervisor, her supervisor has already made up her mind that she is not going to spend any money on software updates. It does not matter how eloquent or persuasive Natalie is with her argument as her supervisor has already made a decision. In this case, the supervisor's bias gets in the way of listening to Natalie. Noise also includes such factors as stress, fear, negative attitudes, and low motivation.

> **feedback**
> In communication, messages sent back from the receiver to the sender.

> **noise**
> Anything that disrupts communication, including the attitudes and emotions of the receiver.

RELATIONSHIP BUILDING AND INTERPERSONAL COMMUNICATION

Another way of understanding the process of interpersonal communication is to examine how communication is a vehicle for building relationships. According to Ritch Sorenson, Grace DeBord, and Ida Ramirez, we establish relationships along two primary dimensions: dominate–subordinate and cold–warm. In the process of communicating we attempt to dominate or subordinate. When we dominate, we attempt to control communication. When we subordinate we attempt to yield control, or think first of the wishes and needs of the other person. Dominators expect the receiver of messages to be submit to them; subordinate people send a signal that they expect the other person to dominate.[2]

LEARNING OBJECTIVE 2

We indicate whether we want to dominate or subordinate by the way we speak and write, or by the nonverbal signals we send. The dominator might speak loudly or enthusiastically, write forceful messages filled with exclamation points, or gesture with exaggerated, rapid hand movements. He or she might write a harsh email message such as, "It's about time you started taking your job seriously and put in some real effort."

In the subordinate mode, we might speak quietly and hesitantly, in a meek tone, and apologetically. A subordinate person might ask, "I know you have better things on your mind than to worry about me, but I was wondering when I can expect my reimbursement for travel expenses?" In a work setting we ordinarily expect people with more formal authority to have the dominant role in conversations. However, in more democratic, informal companies, workers with more authority are less likely to feel the need to dominate conversations.

The cold–warm dimension also shapes communication because we invite the same behaviour that we send. Cold, impersonal, negative messages evoke similar messages from others. In contrast, warm verbal and nonverbal messages evoke similar behaviour in others. Getting back to the inquiry about the travel-expense cheque, here is a colder-versus-warmer response by the manager:

Colder: Travel vouchers really aren't my responsibility. You'll just have to wait like everybody else.

Warmer: I understand your problem. Not getting reimbursed on time is a bummer. I'll follow up on the status of your expense cheque sometime today or tomorrow.

FIGURE 4-2   Communication Dimensions of Establishing a Relationship

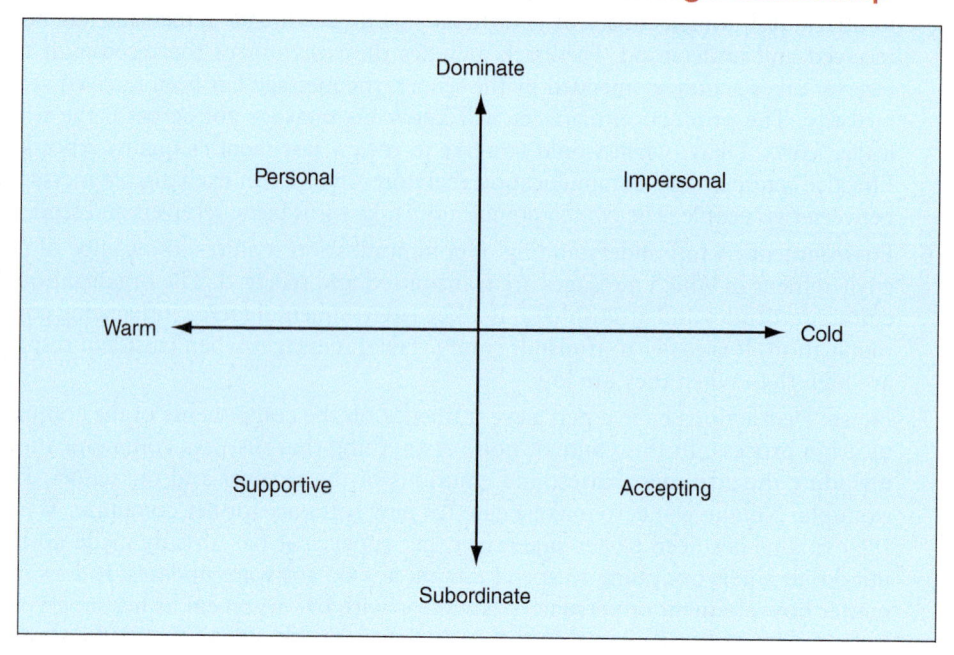

```
                       Dominate
                          ↑
          Personal        |       Impersonal
                          |
   Warm  ←───────────────┼───────────────→  Cold
                          |
          Supportive      |       Accepting
                          |
                          ↓
                       Subordinate
```

Source: Sorenson, Ritch; Debord, Grace; Ramirez, Ida, *Business and Management Communication: A Guide Book*, 4th Edition, © 2001. Adapted by permission of Pearson Education, Inc. Upper Saddle River, NJ.

The combination of dominant and cold communication sends the signal that the sender of the message wants to control and limit, or even withdraw from a personal relationship. A team leader might say that she cannot attend a Saturday morning meeting because she has to go out of town for her brother's wedding. A dominant and cold manager might say, "I don't want to hear about your personal life. Everyone in this department has to attend our Saturday meeting."

Subordinate actions combined with warm communication signal a desire to maintain or build the relationship while yielding to the other person. A manager communicating in a warm and subordinate manner in relation to the wedding request might say, "We'll miss you on Saturday morning because you are a key player in our department. However, I recognize that major events in personal life sometimes take priority over a business meeting."

Figure 4-2 summarizes how the dual dimensions of dominate–subordinate and cold–warm influence the relationship-building aspects of communication. Rather than regarding these four quadrants of relationships as good or bad, think of your purposes. In some situations you might want to dominate and be cold, yet in most situations you might want to submit a little and be warm in order to build a relationship. For example, being dominant and cold might be necessary for a security officer who is trying to control an unruly crowd at a sporting event.

Observe that the person in the quadrant *dominant–cold* has an impersonal relationship with the receiver, and the person in the *subordinate–warm* quadrant has a supportive relationship with the receiver. Being *dominant and warm* leads to a personal relationship, whereas being *submissive and cold* leads to an accepting relationship. The combinations of *dominant–cold* and *subordinate–warm* are more likely to produce the results indicated.

NONVERBAL COMMUNICATION IN ORGANIZATIONS

LEARNING OBJECTIVE 3

nonverbal communication
The transmission of messages through means other than words.

A substantial amount of communication between people, however, takes place at the nonverbal level. **Nonverbal communication** refers to the transmission of messages through means other than words. These messages accompany verbal messages, or sometimes stand alone. The general purpose of nonverbal communication is to communicate the feeling behind a message. For instance, you can say no with either a clenched fist or a smile, to communicate the intensity of your negative or positive feelings.

CHAPTER 4

The following paragraphs summarize the major modes of transmission of nonverbal communication and provide guidelines for improving it. Cultural differences in nonverbal communication are discussed in Chapter 8.

Modes of Transmission of Nonverbal Communication

Nonverbal communication can be transmitted in many modes. You may be surprised that certain factors, such as dress and appearance, are considered part of nonverbal communication.

Environment. The environment, or setting, in which you send a message can influence how that message is received. Assume that your manager invites you out to lunch at a fine restaurant to discuss a problem. You will think it is a more important topic under these circumstances than you would if the manager had lunch with you in the company cafeteria.

Other important silent environmental messages include room colour, temperature, lighting, and furniture arrangement. A person who sits behind a large, uncluttered desk, for example, appears more powerful than a person who sits behind a small, messy desk. A manager who has a comfortable chair arrangement in her office for meetings is perceived as less formal and authoritative than a manager who sits behind a large desk for a meeting. Even office location gives us some clues about organizational politics and structure. A manager with a large corner office with a wide expanse of windows is perceived as being higher in the organization than a manager with a small, windowless office.

Interpersonal Distance. The positioning of one's body in relation to someone else (*proxemics*) is widely used to transmit messages (see Figure 4-3). In general, getting physically close to another person conveys a positive attitude toward that person. Putting your arm around someone is generally interpreted as a friendly act. (Some people, however, recoil when touched by someone other than a close friend. Touching others on the job can also be interpreted as sexual harassment.) Also be aware that different cultures may have rules that govern touching and personal distance that may be very different from your own.

Closely related to interpersonal distance is where and how you sit in relation to another person during a meeting. Sitting across the table from a person during a negotiation session creates a defensive, competitive atmosphere, often leading each party to take a firm stand

FIGURE 4-3 Four Circles of Intimacy

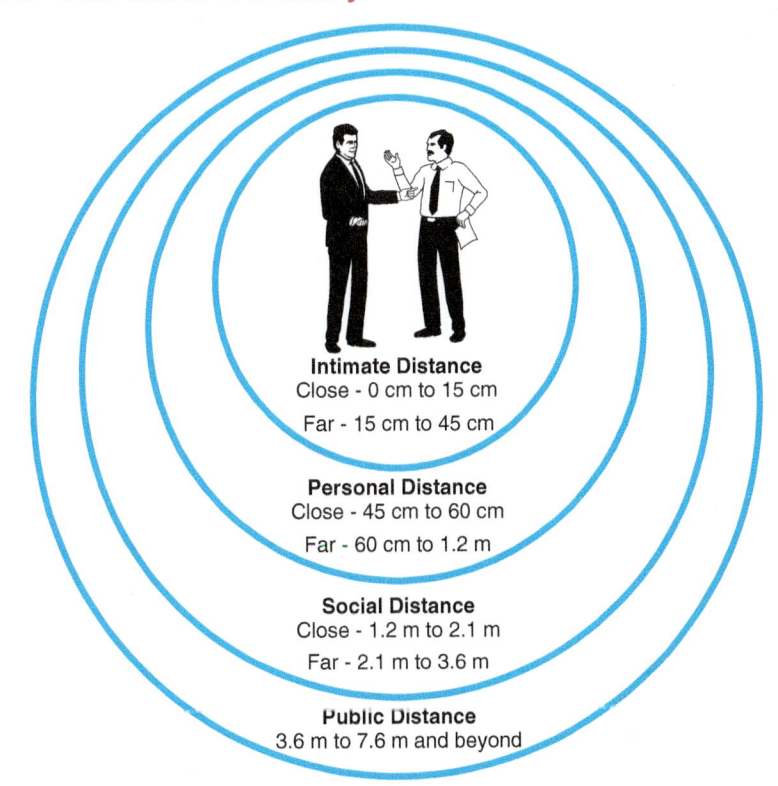

Intimate Distance
Close - 0 cm to 15 cm
Far - 15 cm to 45 cm

Personal Distance
Close - 45 cm to 60 cm
Far - 60 cm to 1.2 m

Social Distance
Close - 1.2 m to 2.1 m
Far - 2.1 m to 3.6 m

Public Distance
3.6 m to 7.6 m and beyond

on his or her point of view. The table becomes a tangible and psychological barrier between both parties. Recognition of this observation leads many managers and salespeople to sit down with another person with either no table or a coffee table between them. Even when seated on separate chairs instead of a sofa, removal of a large table or desk separating the two parties leads to a friendlier, more open negotiation or sales discussion.[3]

Posture. Posture communicates a variety of messages. Standing erect usually conveys the message that the person is self-confident and experiencing positive emotion. Slumping makes a person appear to be lacking in self-confidence or feeling down. Another interpersonal message conveyed by posture involves the direction of leaning. Leaning toward the sender suggests that you are favourably disposed toward his or her message; leaning backward communicates the opposite. Openness of the arms or legs serves as an indicator of liking or caring. In general, people establish closed postures (arms folded and legs crossed) when speaking to people they dislike. Can you think of an aspect of your posture that conveys a specific message?

Hand Gestures. Positive attitudes toward another person are shown by frequent hand movements. In contrast, dislike or lack of interest usually produces few gestures. An important exception is that some people wave their hands furiously while arguing. Gestures are also said to provide clues to a person's levels of dominance and submission. The gestures of dominant people are typically directed outward toward the other person. Examples include a steady, unwavering gaze and touching one's conversational partner. Submissive gestures are usually protective, such as touching oneself or shrugging one's shoulders.

Facial Expressions and Eye Contact. Using your head, face, and eyes in combination provides the clearest indications of interpersonal attitudes. Looking at the ceiling (without tilting your head), combined with a serious expression, almost always communicates the message "I doubt what you're saying is true." Maintaining eye contact with another person improves communication. To maintain eye contact, it is usually necessary to move your face and eyes *with* the other person. Moving your face and eyes *away* from the other person is often interpreted as defensiveness or a lack of self-confidence.

The face is often used as a primary source of information about how we feel. We look for facial clues when we want to determine another person's attitude. You can often judge someone's current state of happiness by looking at his or her face. The term "sourpuss" attests to this observation. Happiness, apprehension, anger, resentment, sadness, contempt, enthusiasm, and embarrassment are but a few of the emotions that can be expressed through the face.

Voice Quality. Often more significance is attached to the *way* something is said than to *what* is said. A forceful voice, which includes a consistent tone without vocalized pauses (like "uh" and "um"), connotes power and control. Closely related to voice tone are volume, pitch, and rate of speaking. Anger, boredom, and joy can often be interpreted from voice quality. Anger is noted when the person speaks loudly, with a high pitch and at a fast rate. Boredom is indicated by a monotone. Joy is indicated by loud volume. Avoiding an annoying voice quality can make a positive impact on others. The research of voice coach Jeffrey Jacobi provides some useful suggestions. He surveyed a sample of 1000 men and women and asked, "Which irritating or unpleasant voice annoys you the most?" The most irritating was a whining, complaining, or nagging tone.

Jacobi notes that we are judged by the way we sound. He also notes that careers can be damaged by voice problems such as those indicated in the survey. "We think about how

> **SELF-ASSESSMENT QUIZ 4-1**
>
> **Voice-Quality Checkup**
>
> The voice-quality study cited in the text ranked voice quality in decreasing order of annoyance, as follows:
>
> - Whining, complaining, or nagging tone—44.0%
> - High-pitched, squeaky voice—15.9%
> - Mumbling—11.1%
> - Very fast talking—4.9%
> - Weak and wimpy voice—3.6%
> - Flat, monotonous tone—3.5%
> - Thick accent—2.4%
>
> **Directions:** Ask yourself and two other people familiar with your voice whether you have one or more of the preceding voice-quality problems. If your self-analysis and feedback from others does indicate a serious problem, get started on self-improvement. Record your voice on tape and attempt to modify the biggest problem. Another avenue of improvement is to consult with a speech coach or therapist.

we look and dress," says Jacobi, "and that gets most of the attention. But people judge our intelligence much more by how we sound than how we dress.[4] Do Self-Assessment Quiz 4-1 to see how Jacobi's findings might apply to your development.

Personal Appearance. Your external image plays an important role in communicating messages to others. A current analysis confirms what has been known for a long time: A favourable personal appearance enhances a person's ability to persuade others, whether you are dealing with an individual receiver or an audience.[5] Job seekers show recognition of the personal appearance aspect of nonverbal communication when they carefully groom themselves for a job interview. People pay more respect and grant more privileges to those they perceive as being well-dressed and neatly groomed. The meaning of being well-dressed depends heavily on the situation. In an information technology firm, neatly pressed jeans, a stylish T-shirt, and clean sport shoes might qualify as being well dressed. The same attire worn in a financial service firm would qualify as being poorly dressed.

A recent tendency is a return to more formal business attire, to suggest that a person is ambitious and successful. A recent analysis concluded that formal dress frequently makes a better impression than casual wear on customers and bosses.[6] The best advice for using appearance to communicate nonverbal messages is to size up the environment to figure out what type of appearance and dress connotes the image you want to project.

Attention Paid to Other Person. The more attention paid to the other person during face-to-face interaction, the more valued and important that person feels. Paying attention to another individual includes other modes of nonverbal communication such as eye contact, an interested facial expression, and moving toward the other person. In a society that increasingly accepts and values multitasking, a natural tendency is to divide your attention between the person you are communicating and a computer screen, cellphone message, or text message. Such multitasking is acceptable and natural to some people, yet makes many others feel unimportant and marginalized. Communication consultant Erick Krell writes, "A CEO who checks her BlackBerry during a meeting can give the impression that the session is unimportant."[7]

Recent research using electronic data supports the idea that the appropriate type of nonverbal communication has a positive impact on effectiveness. MIT professors Sandy Pentland and Daniel Olguín outfitted executives at a party with electronic devices that recorded data on their nonverbal signals, including tone of voice, gesticulation, and proximity to others. Five days later the same executives presented business plans to a panel of judges in a contest related to business plans. Without reading or hearing the presentations made to the judges, Pentland correctly predicted the winners, using only data collected at the party. The presence of a larger number of positive nonverbal signals was used to predict success in presenting a business plan.[8]

INTERPERSONAL COMMUNICATION

Guidelines for Improving Nonverbal Communication

Nonverbal communication, like verbal communication, can be improved. Here are six suggestions to consider:

1. **Obtain feedback on your body language by asking others to comment on the gestures and facial expressions you use in conversations.** Have yourself videotaped conferring with another individual. After studying your body language, attempt to eliminate those mannerisms and gestures you think detract from your effectiveness. Common examples include nervous gestures such as moving knees from side to side, cracking knuckles, rubbing the eyes or nose, head-scratching, and jingling coins.

2. **Learn to relax when communicating with others.** Take a deep breath and consciously allow your body muscles to loosen. Tension-reducing techniques should be helpful here. It is easier for other people to relax around a relaxed person. You are likely to elicit more useful information from other people when you are relaxed.

3. **Use facial, hand, and body gestures to supplement your speech, but don't overdo it.** A good starting point is to use hand gestures to express enthusiasm. You can increase the potency of enthusiastic comments by shaking the other person's hand, nodding approval, or smiling.

4. **Avoid using the same nonverbal gesture indiscriminately.** If you want to use nodding to convey approval, do not nod with approval when you dislike what somebody else is saying. Also, do not pat everybody on the back. Nonverbal gestures used indiscriminately lose their effectiveness.

5. **Use role-playing to practise various forms of nonverbal communication.** A good starting point would be to practise selling your ideas about an important project or concept to another person. During your interchange, supplement your spoken messages with appropriate nonverbal cues such as posture, voice intonation, gestures, and so on. Later, inquire about the other person's perception of the effectiveness of your nonverbal communication.

6. **Use mirroring to establish rapport.** Nonverbal communication can be improved through **mirroring**, or subtly imitating someone. The most successful mirroring technique is to imitate the breathing pattern of another person. If you adjust your own breathing rate to match someone else's, you will soon establish a rapport with that individual. Another effective mirroring technique is to adapt the voice speed of the person with whom you are communicating. If the other person speaks more slowly than you typically do, slow down to mirror him or her.

mirroring
Subtly imitating someone.

You can also use mirroring to win favour by imitating a manager. Many group members have a relentless tendency to copy the boss's mannerisms, gestures, way of speaking, and dress. As a consequence, without realizing why, your manager may think more favourably of you.

Caution: Do not use mirroring to the extent that you appear to be mocking another person, thereby adversely affecting rapport. To get started in developing your mirroring skills, do Skill-Building Exercise 4-1.

SKILL-BUILDING EXERCISE 4-1

The Mirroring Technique

To practise mirroring, during the next 10 days each class member schedules one mirroring session with an unsuspecting subject. An ideal opportunity would be an upcoming meeting at work. Another possibility would be to ask a friend if you could practise your interviewing techniques with him or her—but do not mention the mirroring technique. A third possibility would be to sit down with a friend and engage in a social conversation. Imitate the person's breathing pattern, rate of speech, hand movements, eye movements, leg movements, or any other noticeable aspect of behaviour.

Afterward, hold a class discussion about the results, focusing on these questions:

1. Did the other person notice the mirroring and comment on the behaviour of the person doing the mirroring?
2. Was rapport improved (or hindered) by the mirroring?
3. How many of the students intend to repeat the mirroring technique in the future?

GUIDELINES FOR OVERCOMING COMMUNICATION PROBLEMS AND BARRIERS

Communication problems are ever-present in organizations. Some interference usually takes place between idea formation and action, as suggested earlier by the noise factor in Figure 4-2. The type of message influences the amount of interference. Routine or neutral messages are the easiest to communicate. Interference is most likely to occur when a message is complex, emotionally arousing, or clashes with a receiver's mental set. Once you have finished reading this section, you may want to attempt to answer the questions in the Business Simulation Cases in MySearchLab.

An emotionally arousing message deals with topics such as money or a relationship between two people. A message that clashes with a receiver's mental set requires the person to change his or her typical pattern of receiving messages. Try this experiment. The next time you visit a restaurant, order dessert first and the entrée second. The server probably will not receive your dessert order, because it deviates from the normal sequence.

We will now describe strategies and tactics for overcoming some of the more frequently observed communication problems in workplaces and other settings. (See Figure 4-4.)

LEARNING OBJECTIVE 4

Understand the Receiver

Understanding the person you are trying to reach is fundamental to overcoming communication barriers. The more you know about your receiver, the more effectively you can deliver your message. Three important aspects of understanding the receiver are (1) developing empathy, (2) recognizing his or her motivational state, and (3) understanding the other person's frame of reference.

Developing **empathy** requires putting yourself in the receiver's shoes. To accomplish this, you need to imagine yourself in the other person's role and assume the viewpoints and emotions of that individual. For example, if a supervisor were trying to communicate the importance of customer service to her sales associates, she might ask herself, "If I were a part-time employee being paid close to the minimum wage, how receptive would I be to messages about high-quality customer service?" To empathize, you need to understand another person. (To *sympathize*, in contrast, means to understand and agree.)

Research suggests that subtle patterns of brain cells, called mirror neurons, help us empathize with others. These brain circuits reflect the actions and intentions of others as if they were our own. Neuroscientist Marco Iacoboni explains that the mirror system gives us an open-mindedness and a propensity to understand others and cultures.

empathy
In communication, imagining oneself in the receiver's role, and assuming the viewpoints and emotions of that individual.

FIGURE 4-4 **Overcoming Communication Problems and Barriers**

1. Understand the receiver.
2. Minimize defensive communication.
3. Repeat your message using multiple channels.
4. Check comprehension and feelings through verbal and nonverbal feedback.
5. Display a positive attitude.
6. Use persuasive communication.
7. Engage in active listening.
8. Prepare for stressful conversations.
9. Engage in metacommunications.
10. Recognize gender differences in communication styles.

The cells work in this manner: When another person smiles or wrinkles his or her nose in distaste, motor cells in your own brain linked to those expressions resonate in response like a tuning fork. As a result, you get a hint of the feeling itself. The more empathy you have, the stronger the motor neuron response.[9]

The biological component to empathy should not lead you to conclude that empathy is not a skill that can be acquired. It is conceivable that as you develop empathy, your mirror neurons grow in number or become better developed, just as your calf muscles become better defined if you run frequently.

The receiver's **motivational state** could include any active needs and interests operating at the time. People tend to listen attentively to messages that show promise of satisfying an active need. Management usually listens attentively to a suggestion framed in terms of cost savings or increased profits.

motivational state
Any active needs and interests operating at a given time.

People perceive words and concepts differently because their vantage points, and perspectives differ. Such differences in **frame of reference** create barriers to communication. A frame of reference can also be considered a lens through which we view the world. A manager attempted to chastise a team member by saying, "If you keep up your present level of performance, you'll be a repair technician all your life." The technician replied, "That's good news," because he was proud of being the first person in his family to hold a skilled job. Understanding another person's frame of reference requires empathy.

frame of reference
A person's individual vantage point that causes him or her to perceive words and concepts differently.

On a day-by-day basis, understanding another person's frame of reference often translates into figuring out his or her mindset. A woman telephoned a tech support centre with a sense of frustration in her voice. She said she was instructed by her computer to "press any key to continue," and was upset that her keyboard didn't have an "any" key. The caller's mindset was that she had to search for the "any" key.[10] Of course, a more perceptive person might have noticed that the instructions did not say, press *the any key* to continue, but *any key*.

Minimize Defensive Communication

Defensive communication—the tendency to receive messages in such a way that our self-esteem is protected—is an important general communication barrier. Defensive communication also accounts for people sending messages to make themselves look good. For example, when being criticized for low production, an investment banker might blame the advertising agency used by his firm.

defensive communication
The tendency to receive messages in such a way that self-esteem is protected.

Overcoming the barrier of defensive communication requires two steps. First, people need to recognize the existence of defensive communication. Second, they need to try not to be defensive when questioned or criticized. Such behaviour is not easy because of the unconscious or semiconscious process of **denial**—the suppression of information we find uncomfortable. For example, the investment banker just cited would find it uncomfortable to think of himself as being responsible for below-average performance.

denial
The suppression of information a person finds uncomfortable.

Repeat Your Message Using Multiple Channels (in Moderation)

Repetition improves communication, particularly when different channels are used to convey the same message. Effective communicators at many job levels follow spoken agreements with written documentation. Since most communication is subject to at least some distortion, the chances of a message being received as intended increase when two or more channels are used.

Many firms have a policy of using a multiple-channel approach to communicate the results of a performance appraisal. The group member receives an oral explanation from the manager of the results of the review. The group member is also required to read the form and indicate by signature that he or she has read and understands the meaning of the review. Another good use of multiple channels is following up a telephone call or in-person conversation with an email message summarizing key facts or agreements.

When repeating your message or using multiple channels, use moderation to avoid contributing to the problem of **information overload**—a phenomenon that occurs when people are so overloaded with information that they cannot respond effectively to messages. Current research suggests that the expanding volume of information can not only create stress but also affect decision making, innovation, and productivity.[11]

information overload
A phenomenon that occurs when people are so overloaded with information that they cannot respond effectively to messages.

Check Comprehension and Feelings through Verbal and Nonverbal Feedback

Ask for feedback to determine whether your message has been received as intended. A frequent managerial practice is to conclude a meeting with a question such as "Okay, what have we agreed upon?" Unless feedback of this nature is obtained, you will not know whether your message has been received until the receiver carries out your request. If the request is carried out improperly, or if no action is taken, you will know that the message was received poorly.

Obtaining feedback is important because it results in two-way communication in which people take turns being sender and receiver, thereby having a dialogue. Dialogues take time because they require people to speak more slowly and listen more carefully. The results of having employees engage in dialogue are said to include a deeper sense of community (a feeling of belongingness) and greater trust among employees.[12] You might relate this finding to your own experiences. Do you trust another person more when the two of you exchange ideas and listen to each other?

Feedback is also important because it provides reinforcement to the sender, and few people will continue to communicate without any reinforcement. The sender is reinforced when the receiver indicates understanding of the message. When the original receiver indicates that he or she understands the message, that person becomes the sender. A nod of approval would be an appropriate type of nonverbal reinforcement for the sender to receive.

In addition to looking for verbal comprehension and emotions when you deliver a message, check for feelings after you have received a message. When a person speaks, we too often listen to the facts and ignore the feelings. If feelings are ignored, the true meaning and intent of the message is likely to be missed, thus creating a communication barrier. Your boss might say to you, "You never seem to take work home." To clarify what your boss means by this statement, you might ask, "Is that good or bad?" Your boss's response will give you feedback on his or her feelings about getting all your work done during regular working hours.

When you send a message, it is also helpful to express your feelings in addition to conveying the facts. For example, "Our defects are up by 12 percent (fact), and I'm quite disappointed about those results (feelings)." Because feelings contribute strongly to comprehension, you will help overcome a potential communication barrier.

Display a Positive Attitude

Being perceived as having a positive attitude helps melt communication barriers. Most people prefer to communicate with a positive person. According to Sharon Lund O'Neil, you must establish credibility and trustworthiness if you expect others to listen, let alone get them to react positively to your communication.[13] Being positive helps make you appear more credible and trustworthy, whereas being consistently negative makes you seem less so. As one co-worker said about a chronic complainer in his office, "Why take Margot seriously? She finds something wrong with everybody and everything."

Communicate Persuasively

A powerful tactic for overcoming communication barriers is to communicate so persuasively, so convincingly, that obstacles disappear and the receiver "buys" the message. Persuasion thus involves selling messages. Hundreds of articles, books, and videos have been developed to help people learn to be more persuasive. Type in the words "persuasive communication" as a YouTube search and literally thousands of hits will appear. The following are representative suggestions for becoming a more persuasive communicator:[14]

1. **Know exactly what you want.** Your chances of selling an idea increase to the extent that you have clarified the idea in your own mind. The clearer and more committed you are at the outset of a selling or negotiating session, the stronger you are as a persuader.

2. **Never suggest an action without specifying its end benefit.** In asking for a raise, you might say, "If I get this raise, I'll be able to afford to stay in this job as long as the company likes. I will also increase my productivity because I won't be distracted by thinking about meeting my expenses."

3. **Get a "yes response" early on.** It is helpful to give the selling session a positive tone by establishing a "yes pattern" at the outset. Assume that an employee wanted to convince the boss to allow him or her to perform some work at home during normal working hours. The employee might begin the idea-selling questions with, "Is it important for the company to obtain maximum productivity from all its employees?"

4. **Use power words.** An expert tactic for being persuasive is to sprinkle your speech with power (meaning *powerful*) words. Power words stir emotion and bring forth images of exciting events. Examples of power words include *decimating* the competition, *bonding* with customers, *surpassing* previous profits, *capturing* customer loyalty, and *rebounding* from a downturn.

5. **Minimize raising your pitch at the end of sentences.** Part of being persuasive is to not sound unsure and apologetic. In English and several other languages, a convenient way to ask a question or express doubt is to raise the pitch of your voice at the end of a sentence or phrase. As a test, use the sentence "You like my ideas." First say *ideas* using approximately the same pitch and tone as with every other word. Then say the same sentence by pronouncing *ideas* with a higher pitch and louder tone. By saying *ideas* in this way, you sound much less certain and are less persuasive.

6. **Talk to your audience, not the screen.** Computer-graphic presentations have become standard practice even in small-group meetings. Many presenters rely so heavily on computer-generated slides and transparencies that they essentially read the slides and transparencies to the audience. Jean Mausehund and R. Neil Dortch remind us that in an oral presentation, the predominant means of connection between sender and receiver should be eye contact. When your audience is frequently distracted by movement on the screen, computer sounds, garish colours, or your looking at the screen, eye contact suffers. As a result, the message is weakened and you are less persuasive.[15]

7. **Back up conclusions with data.** You will be more persuasive if you support your spoken and written presentations with solid data. You can collect the data yourself or quote from a printed or electronic source. Relying too much on research has a potential disadvantage, however. Being too dependent on data could suggest that you have little faith in your intuition. For example, you might convey a weak impression if, when asked your opinion, you respond, "I can't answer until I collect some data."

8. **Minimize "wimp" phrases.** Persuasive communicators minimize statements that make them appear weak and indecisive. Such phrases convey the impression that they are not in control of their actions. Wimp phrases include: "It's

one of those days," "I'm not sure about that," "Don't quote me on that," and "I'll try my best to get it done." (It is better to commit yourself forcibly by saying, "I'll get it done.") Wimpy words include "sort of," "hopefully," and "maybe." Although wimp phrases and words should be minimized, there are times when they reflect honest communication, such as a team leader saying to the manager, "Maybe we can get this crash project completed by the end of the month."

Another problem with wimp words and phrases is that they can mark your image, or make you seem not in control of your work. Three examples follow:

- "I'm too busy/I don't have time/I'm just swamped."
- "I'm having one of those days/Things are crazy here/You have caught me at a bad time."
- "We'll see how it goes/I'll try my best."[16]

9. **Avoid or minimize common language errors.** You will be more persuasive if you minimize common language errors, because you will appear more articulate and informed. Here are several common language errors:

- "Just between you and I" is wrong. "Just between you and me" is correct.
- *Irregardless* is not a word; *regardless* is correct.
- Avoid double negatives (despite their increasing popularity). Common examples are "I didn't get *nothing* from my best customer this week" and "We don't have *no money* in the budget for travel." Double negatives make the sender appear so ill informed that they fail to persuade.
- "We are customer-oriented" is correct. "We are customer-orientated" is wrong.
- "Ask your guest what *they* want for lunch" is incorrect despite the widespread use of a plural pronoun instead of the singular. "Ask your guest what *he* (or *she*) wants" is correct. A caution here is that it appears about 90 percent of North Americans including the well-educated confuse the singular and plural today, so using "they" instead of "he" or "she" is not a dreadful error in grammar. However, using "themselves" instead of "him" or "her" is a dreadful error. An example of this misuse is, "I prefer a co-worker who can speak up for *themselves*."

10. **Avoid overuse of jargon and clichés.** To feel "in" and hip, many workers rely heavily on jargon and clichés, such as referring to their "fave" (for *favourite*) product, or saying that "At the end of the day" something counts, or that software is "scalable" (meaning it can get bigger). Add to the list "a seamless company" to mean various departments cooperate with one another. The caution is that if a person uses jargon and hip phrases too frequently, the person appears to be too contrived, and lacking in imagination.[17]

If you can learn to implement most of the preceding 10 suggestions, you are on your way to becoming a persuasive communicator. In addition, you will need solid facts behind you, and you will need to make skillful use of nonverbal communication. Skill-Building Exercise 4-2 provides you with an opportunity to practise persuasive communication.

Engage in Active Listening

Persuasion deals primarily with sending messages. Improving one's receiving of messages is another part of developing better communication skills. Unless you receive messages as they are intended, you cannot perform your job properly or be a good companion. A major challenge in developing good listening skills is that we process information much more quickly than most people speak. The average speaking rate is about 130 words per minute. In contrast, the average rate of processing information is about 300 words per minute.[18] So you have to slow down mentally to listen well. A related problem is that many people like to dominate conversations, making it difficult to listen. As expressed by investment banker Herb Allen, "It's tough to listen when you're talking."[19]

Explore

Mastering Business Communication: Listening Effectively

SKILL-BUILDING EXERCISE 4-2

I Want a Raise

The purpose of this exercise is to practise your persuasive skills using a topic of interest to many people—obtaining a salary increase. One by one, students make a presentation in front of the class, presenting a persuasive argument why they merit a salary increase. The instructor will decide whether to use a handful of volunteers or the entire class. The audience represents the boss. The student will first explain his or her job title and key responsibilities. (Use your imagination here.) Next, make a three-minute, convincing argument as to why you merit a salary increase, and perhaps indicate how much you want. You will probably have to spend about 15 minutes in preparation, inside or outside of class.

After the presentations, volunteers will offer feedback on the effectiveness of selected presentations. During the presentations of the other students, make a few notes about the presenter's effectiveness. You may need a couple of minutes between presenters to make your notes. Consider these factors:

- Overall, how convincing was the presenter? If you were the boss, would you give him or her the requested salary increase?
- Which techniques of persuasion did he or she use?
- What aspect of the presentation was unconvincing or negative?

What lessons did you take away from this exercise about persuasive communication?

Listening can be even more essential than talking when engaged in face-to-face communication. Listening is a particularly important skill for anybody whose job involves troubleshooting, because one needs to gather information in order to solve problems. Another reason that improving the listening skills of employees is important is that insufficient listening is extraordinarily costly. Listening mistakes lead to reprocessing letters, rescheduling appointments, reshipping orders, and recalling defective products. Effective listening also improves interpersonal relations because the people listened to feel understood and respected.

A major component of effective listening is to be an **active listener**. The active listener listens intensely, with the goal of empathizing with the speaker. Several important skills and behaviours associated with active listening are presented next.

active listener
A person who listens intently, with the goal of empathizing with the speaker.

Accept the Sender's Figure of Speech.
A useful way of showing empathy is to accept the sender's figure of speech. By so doing, the sender feels understood and accepted. Also, if you reject the person's figure of speech by rewording it, the sender may become defensive. Many people use the figure of speech "I'm stuck" when they cannot accomplish a task. You can facilitate smooth communication by a response such as, "What can I do to help you get unstuck?" If you respond with something like, "What can I do to help you think more clearly?" the person is forced to change mental channels and may become defensive.[20]

Paraphrase and Listen Reflectively.
As a result of listening actively, the listener can give feedback to the speaker what he or she thinks the speaker meant. Feedback of this type relies on both verbal and nonverbal communication. Feedback is also important because it facilitates two-way communication. To be an active listener, it is important to **paraphrase**, or repeat in your own words what the sender says, feels, and means. Paraphrasing is also referred to as reflective listening, because the listener reflects back what the sender said. You might feel awkward the first several times you paraphrase. Therefore, try it with a person with whom you feel comfortable. With some practice, it will become a natural part of your communication skill set. Here is an example of how you might use paraphrasing:

paraphrase
To repeat in your own words what the sender says, feels, and means.

> **Other Person:** I'm getting ticked off at working so hard around here. I wish somebody else would pitch in and do a fair day's work.
>
> **You:** You're saying that you do more than your fair share of the tough work in our department.
>
> **Other Person:** You bet. Here's what I think we should be doing about it. . . .

Life coach Sophronia Scott advises that, after you have paraphrased, it is sometimes helpful to ask the person you listened to whether your impression of what he or she said is correct. Your goal is not to make others repeat themselves but to extend the conversation so that you can obtain more useful details.[21]

Minimize Distractions.   If feasible, keep papers and your computer screen out of sight when listening to somebody else. Having distractions in sight creates the temptation to glance away from the message sender. Glancing away can signal a lack of interest to the sender and create a communication barrier. Avoid answering a cellphone call unless you are anticipating an emergency call. At the start of your conversation, notice the other person's eye colour to help you establish eye contact. (But don't keep staring at his or her eyes!)

Ask Questions.   A major technique of active listening is to ask questions rather than making conclusive statements. Asking questions provides more useful information. Suppose a teammate is late with data you need to complete your analysis. Instead of saying, "I must have your input by Thursday afternoon," try, "When will I get your input?"

Allow the Sender to Finish His or Her Sentence.   Be sure to let others speak until they have finished. Do not interrupt by talking about you, jumping in with advice, or offering solutions unless requested. Equally bad for careful listening is to finish the sentence of a receiver. Almost all people prefer to complete their own thoughts, even though there are two curious traditions that run counter to this idea. One is that business partners who have been working together for many years, and understand each other well, have a tendency to finish each other's sentences. Couples in personal life behave similarly. Also, have you noticed how when you start to enter a phrase into a major search engine, suddenly you are given about 10 choices that are not necessarily what you are planning to write? (Of course, this is responding to writing and not really listening, but the overtaking of your thinking is the same.)

Use Nonverbal Communication.   Another component to active listening is to indicate by your body language that you are listening intently. When a co-worker comes to you with a question or concern, focus on that person and exclude all else. If you tap your fingers on the desk or glance around the room, you send the message that the other person and his or her concerns do not warrant your full attention. Listening intently through nonverbal communication also facilitates active listening because it demonstrates respect for the receiver.

Observing nonverbal communication is another important part of active listening. Look to see if the speaker's verbal communication matches his or her nonverbal communication. Suppose you ask another person if he or she would like to join your committee. If the person says yes, but looks bored and defensive, he or she is probably not really interested in joining your committee. Quite often a person's nonverbal communication is more indicative of the truth than is verbal communication.

Minimize Words That Shut Down Discussion.   A key part of listening is to keep the conversation flowing. According to executive coach Marshall Goldsmith, an especially useful approach to keep conversation going in most work situations is for the listener to minimize certain negatively toned words that frequently shut down conversation. When you say "no," "but," or "however," you effectively shut down or limit the conversation. No matter what words follow, the sender receives a message to the effect, "You are wrong and I am right." Even if you say, "I agree, but . . ." the shutdown message still comes through. The other person is likely to get into the defensive mode.[22] Another way of shutting down conversation is to say, "I already know that."

After the person has finished talking, there are times it will be appropriate to say "no," "but," or "however." Assume, for example, that a worker says to the business owner that the company should donate one-third its profits to charity each year. The owner might then reply, "I hear you, but if we give away all that money our profits will be too slim to grow the business."

Avoid the Need to Lie or Fake When You Have Not Been Paying Attention.   A consequence of active listening is that you will avoid the need to pretend that you have been paying attention.

FIGURE 4-5 Suggestions for Active Listening

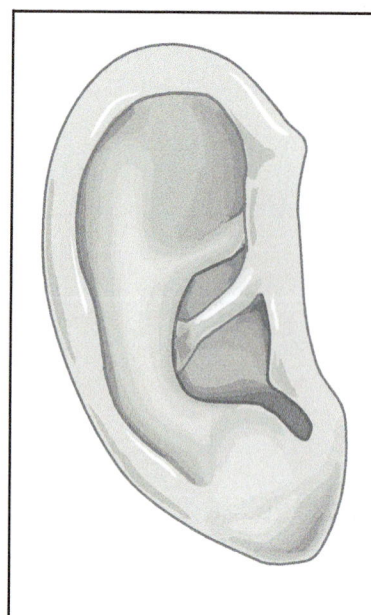

> 1. **While your target is talking, look at him or her intently.** At the same time, maintain steady eye contact.
> 2. **Be patient about your turn to speak.** A common barrier to effective listening is to mentally prepare an answer while another person is speaking.
> 3. **Nod your head in agreement from time to time.**
> 4. **Mutter "mmh" or "uh-huh" periodically but not incessantly.**
> 5. **Ask open-ended questions to encourage the other person to talk.** For example, you encourage more conversation by saying, "What do you think . . . of . . ." rather than asking, "Do you agree that . . . ?"
> 6. **Reflect your target's content or meaning.** Rephrase and summarize concisely what the other person is saying.
> 7. **Reflect the other person's feelings.** Reflection-of-feeling responses typically begin with "You feel that. . . ."
> 8. **Keep your ratio of talking to listening down to about 1 to 5.** In other words, spend 20 percent of your time talking, and 80 percent listening, to be perceived as a great listener.
> 9. **Ask yourself whether anything the other person is saying could benefit you.** Maintaining this perspective will enable you to benefit from most listening episodes and will motivate you to listen intently.

Specific suggestions for improving active listening skills are summarized in Figure 4-5. These suggestions relate to good listening in general, as well as active listening. Many suggestions reinforce what has already been described. As with any other suggestions for developing a new skill, considerable practice (with some supervision) is needed to bring about actual changes in behaviour. One of the problems a poor listener would encounter is the difficulty of breaking old habits in order to acquire new ones. Self-Assessment Quiz 4-2 gives you an opportunity to think about bad listening habits you may have acquired. To practise your listening skills, do Skill-Building Exercise 4-3.

BACK TO THE OPENING CASE

Much of Maria's success in expanding her business with the Montreal business firm can be attributed to the relationship building that took place based on face-to-face communication. Notice also that Maria engaged in active listening as she provided Larry an opportunity to describe what he liked and disliked about the machines he bought from her company. Maria listened carefully instead of becoming defensive when Larry described his concerns.

Prepare for Stressful Conversations

Communication barriers will frequently surface when two or more people are engaged in a conversation fraught with emotion, such as a highly negative performance review, a rejection of a person for membership in a team, or the firing of an employee. Giving praise is another exchange that can make both or either parties uncomfortable. The sender might feel that he or she is patronizing the receiver, and the receiver might feel unworthy of the praise. One technique for reducing the stress in potentially stressful conversations is to prepare for them in advance.

SELF-ASSESSMENT QUIZ 4-2

Practice
Listening Traps

Listening Traps

Communication specialists at Purdue University in the United States have identified certain behaviour patterns that interfere with effective hearing and listening. After thinking carefully about each trap, note whether it is "Not a Problem" for you or whether you "Need Improvement." To respond to the statements accurately, visualize how you acted when you were recently in a situation calling for listening.

	Not a Problem	Need Improvement
• **Mind reader.** You will receive limited information if you constantly think "What is this person really thinking or feeling?"	❏	❏
• **Rehearser.** Your mental rehearsals for "Here's what I'll say next" tune out the sender.	❏	❏
• **Filterer.** You engage in selective listening by hearing only what you want to hear. (Could be difficult to judge because the process is often unconscious.)	❏	❏
• **Dreamer.** You drift off during a face-to-face conversation, which often leads you to an embarrassing "What did you say?" or "Could you repeat that?"	❏	❏
• **Identifier.** If you refer everything you hear to your experience, you probably did not really listen to what was said.	❏	❏
• **Comparer.** When you get sidetracked sizing up the sender, you are sure to miss the message.	❏	❏
• **Derailer.** You change the subject too quickly, giving the impression that you are not interested in anything the sender has to say.	❏	❏
• **Sparrer.** You hear what is said, but quickly belittle or discount it, putting you in the same class as the derailer.	❏	❏
• **Placater.** You agree with everything you hear just to be nice or to avoid conflict. By behaving this way you miss out on the opportunity for authentic dialogue.	❏	❏

Interpretation: If you checked "Need improvement" for five or more of the above statements, you are correct—your listening needs improvement! If you checked only two or fewer of the above traps, you are probably an effective listener and a supportive person.

Source: Messages : The communication skills book by Mckay, Matthew; Davis, Martha; Fanning, Patrick. Reproduced with permission of New Harbinger Publications in the format Republish in a book via Copyright Clearance Center.

SKILL-BUILDING EXERCISE 4-3

Listening to a Co-worker

Before conducting the following role-plays, review the nine keys to effective listening presented in Figure 4-5. The sixth suggestion, about restating what you hear (summarization), is particularly important when listening to a person who is talking about an emotional topic.

The Elated Co-worker: One student plays the role of a worker who has just been offered a promotion to supervisor of another department. He or she will receive a 10 percent raise in pay and travel overseas twice a year for the company. This first worker is eager to describe full details of his or her good fortune to a co-worker, who is played by another student. The second worker decides to listen intently to the first worker. Other class members will rate the second student on his or her listening ability.

The Discouraged Co-worker: One student plays the role of an employee who has just been placed on probation for poor job performance. The employee's boss thinks that his or her performance is below standard and that his or her attendance and punctuality are poor. The worker is afraid that telling his or her spouse will end their relationship. The person is eager to tell this tale of woe to a co-worker, played by another student. The second worker decides to listen intently but is pressed for time. Other class members will rate the second student on listening ability.

A starting point in preparing for a stressful conversation is self-awareness about how you react to certain uncomfortable exchanges. For example, how do you feel when the receiver of the negative feedback reacts with hostility? Do you clam up, or do you become hostile yourself? If you anticipate a hostile reception to an upcoming conversation, rehearse the scenario with a neutral friend. Deliver the controversial content that you will be delivering during the real event. Practise the body language you will use when you deliver a message such as "As team leader, I must tell you that you have contributed almost nothing of value to our current project." Another part of the rehearsal is to practise delivering clear content—be explicit about what you mean. "You've contributed almost nothing of value to our current project" is much more explicit than "Your contribution has much room for improvement."

Also, practise *temperate phrasing*, or being tactful while delivering negative feedback. Communications specialist Holly Weeks suggests, for instance, that instead of snapping at someone by saying "Stop interrupting me," you could try this: "Can you hold on a minute? I want to finish before I lose my train of thought." Temperate phrasing will take some of the sting out of a stressful conversation.[23]

Engage in Metacommunication

When confronted with a communication problem, one response is to attempt to work around the barrier, perhaps by using one of the methods already described. A more typical response is to ignore the barrier by making no special effort to deal with the problem—a "take it or leave it" approach to communication. Another possibility is to **metacommunicate**, or communicate about your communication, to help overcome barriers or resolve a problem.[24] If you as a team leader were facing heavy deadline pressures, you might say to a team member, "I might appear brusque today and tomorrow. Please don't take it personally. It's just that I have to make heavy demands on you because the team is facing a gruelling deadline." A more common situation is when the person with whom you are attempting to communicate appears angry or indifferent. Instead of wasting the communication event, it would be better to say, "You do not seem receptive to listening to me now. Are we having a problem? Should I try again later?"

Recognize Gender Differences in Communication Style

A trend in organizations for many years has been to move toward gender equality. Despite this trend, substantial interest has arisen in identifying differences in communication styles between men and women.

People who are aware of these differences face fewer communication barriers between themselves and members of the opposite sex. As we describe these differences, recognize that they are group stereotypes. Please do not be offended by these stereotypes; they are exaggerations noticed by some researchers and observers. To cite one example that runs counter to the stereotype, some women dominate meetings whereas some men focus on listening to and supporting others during a meeting. Individual differences in communication style usually are more important than group (men versus women) differences. Here we will describe the major findings of gender differences in communication patterns. (Remember that these are stereotypes and do not represent all men or all women.)[25]

1. **Women prefer to use conversation for building rapport.** For most women, the intent of conversation is to build rapport and connections with people. Women are therefore more likely to emphasize similarities, to listen intently, and to be supportive.
2. **Men prefer to use talk as a means of preserving independence and status by displaying knowledge and skill.** When most men talk, they want to receive positive

---

metacommunicate

To communicate about your communication, to help overcome barriers or resolve a problem.

evaluation from others and maintain their hierarchical status within the group. Men are therefore more oriented to giving a *report* while women are more interested in establishing *rapport.*

3. **Women want empathy, not solutions.** When women share feelings of being stressed out, they seek empathy and understanding. If they feel they have been listened to carefully, they begin to relax. When listening to the woman, the man may feel blamed for her problems or that he has failed the woman in some way. To feel useful, the man might offer solutions to the woman's problems.

4. **Men prefer to work out their problems by themselves, whereas women prefer to talk out solutions with another person.** Women look upon having and sharing problems as an opportunity to build and deepen relationships. Men are more likely to look upon problems as challenges they must meet on their own. The communication consequence of these differences is that men may become uncommunicative when they have a problem.

5. **Women are more likely to compliment the work of a co-worker, whereas men are more likely to be critical.** A communication problem may occur when a woman compliments the work of a male co-worker and expects reciprocal praise.

6. **Men tend to be more directive in their conversation, whereas women emphasize politeness.** Women are therefore more likely to frequently use the phrases "I'm sorry" and "Thank you," even when there is no need to express apology or gratitude. For example, a supermarket manager notices that the store has suddenly become busy. She might say to a store clerk unpacking boxes, "I'm sorry, Jason, but we've become busy all of a sudden. Could you please open up a new lane up front? Thank you." A manager who is a stereotypical male might say, "Jason, we need you to open a line up front, pronto. Put down the boxes and get up there."

7. **Women tend to be more conciliatory when facing differences, whereas men become more intimidating.** Again, women are more interested in building relationships, whereas men are more concerned about coming out ahead.

8. **Men are more interested than women in calling attention to their accomplishments or in monopolizing recognition.** In one instance, a sales representative who had already made her sales quota for the month turned over an excellent prospect to a co-worker. She reasoned, "It's somebody else's turn. I've received more than my fair share of bonuses for the month."

9. **Men tend to dominate discussions during meetings.** One study of college faculty meetings found that women's longest turns at speaking were, on average, of shorter duration than men's shortest turns. A possible explanation is that women are still less assertive than men in the workplace.

How can the information just presented help overcome communication problems on the job? As a starting point, remember that these gender differences often exist. Understanding these differences will help you interpret the communication behaviour of people. For example, if a male co-worker is not as effusive with praise as you would like, remember that he is simply engaging in gender-typical behaviour; do not take it personally.

A woman can remind herself to speak up more in meetings because her natural tendency might be toward diffidence. A man might remind himself to be more complimentary and supportive toward co-workers, even though his natural tendency might be to skip the praise.

A woman should not take it personally when a male co-worker or subordinate is tight-lipped when faced with a problem. She should recognize that he needs more encouragement to talk about his problems than would a woman. If the man persists in

Access the eText in MySearchLab to learn more about this chapter's self-assessment quizzes.

not wanting to talk about the problem, the woman might say, "It looks like you want to work out this problem on your own. Go ahead. I'm available if you want to talk about it."

Men and women should recognize that when women talk over problems, they might not be seeking hard-hitting advice. Instead, they might simply be searching for a sympathetic ear so they can deal with the emotional aspect of the problem.

A general suggestion for overcoming gender-related communication barriers is for men to improve communication by becoming more empathetic listeners. Women can improve communication by becoming more direct.

To **Watch** **Explore** **Practice** **Study** and **Review**, visit MySearchLab

Developing Your Human Relations Skills and Reinforcing Concepts

Summary   ✓ Practice   Glossary Flashcards

- The communication process can be divided into six components: sender or source, message, channel (or medium), receiver, feedback, and environment. Noise, or interference, can disrupt communication within any of these components.
- Relationships are built through communication, including the dimensions of subordinate–dominate and cold–warm.
- Modes of nonverbal communication include the environment in which the message is sent, interpersonal distance, posture, gestures, facial expressions, voice quality, and personal appearance.
- Improve nonverbal communication by obtaining feedback, learning to relax, using gestures more discriminately, role-playing, and mirroring (which refers to subtly imitating someone).
- Overcome communication barriers by (1) understanding the receiver; (2) minimizing defensive communication; (3) repeating your message using multiple channels; (4) checking comprehension and feelings via verbal and nonverbal feedback; (5) displaying a positive attitude; (6) using persuasive communication; (7) engaging in active listening; (8) preparing for stressful conversations; (9) recognizing gender differences in communication styles; and (10) engaging in metacommunication (communicating about your communication).
- Active listening includes your ability to: (1) accept the sender's figure of speech; (2) paraphrase and listen reflectively; (3) minimize distractions; (4) allow the sender to finish his or her sentence; (5) use nonverbal communication; (6) minimize words that shut down discussion; and (7) avoid the need to lie or fake when you have not been paying attention.

Interpersonal Relations Case 4-1

Why Am I Not Getting through to These People?

A few years ago, Laura left her position as a supervisor in a health insurance company to start a lawn care, landscaping, and snow removal business. She started the business by taking care of the lawns and snow removal for a few relatives and friends. Laura charged them approximately half-price just so that she could establish the legitimacy of her business and get started seeking customers. Her first employees were a 16-year-old nephew, an 18-year-old niece, and an uncle.

After passing out hundreds of flyers in her neighbourhood and three adjoining neighbourhoods, Laura finally developed a big enough customer base to start obtaining referral business. Two years into running her firm, "Laura's Property Service," Laura was breaking even, including paying herself a modest salary. Her firm had grown to taking care of more than 100 customers, with three full-time and six part-time employees.

When asked about her biggest challenge in operating her business, Laura replied,

Getting through to my workers is my biggest headache, no doubt. A big money drain in my business is repairing the damage we do to people's lawns and driveways in the process of removing snow. Also, the fellows and gals sometimes bang into garages and drain pipes with our lawnmowers when they are cutting grass.

I keep telling the gang to be careful, but I am not making much of a dent in terms of reducing customer complaints about damage. The typical response I get when I deliver my message about being careful is "Yeah, yeah, I'll be careful."

Case Questions

1. What kind of communication problem does Laura appear to be facing?
2. What do you recommend Laura do so that her employees act positively in response to her message?

Interpersonal Relations Case 4-2

Karl Walks Around

Karl Bennett, a supervisor in a call centre located in Ontario, was urged by his manager to walk around the centre from time to time to chat informally with the call centre workers. His boss said to Karl, "It's always good to know what the call centre specialists are feeling and thinking. You might pick up some good ideas." Bennett had studied the technique of *management by walking around* in a human relations course, so he was enthused about the idea.

Karl chose a Tuesday evening to conduct his walkaround, and decided to stop by the cubicles of four call centre operators to test the technique. If it worked well, he would walk around again in another week.

Karl first stopped by the cubicle of Mandi, making sure first that she was not on the telephone with a customer. "I just dropped by to say hello and see how things are going," said Karl. "I take it everything is going fine, and that you have no problems," he continued. "Am I right?"

Mandi answered, "Yes, no real problems. Thanks for stopping by."

Next, Karl stopped by the cubicle of Pete, a relatively new operator. "How's it going Pete?" asked Karl. "What kind of problems might you be facing?"

Pete answered, "I'm having trouble understanding the accents of some of my customers. And some of the customers say I talk too fast. Other than that, the job is going well."

"That's interesting," said Karl. "But I see I have a couple of emails waiting for me on my BlackBerry. Maybe you do talk too fast. I'll get back to you later."

Karl thought to himself that the walkaround was going fine so far. He then dropped by Brittany's cubicle. "What's happening, Brittany?" asked Karl as Brittany was completing a customer inquiry about a defective piece of equipment. Brittany raised the palm of her right hand to signal that she was not quite finished with the call.

Karl then asked, "Are your wedding plans going along okay?"

Brittany replied, "Yes, Karl. Everything is fine; thanks for stopping by."

A few minutes later, Karl completed his walkaround by stopping to visit Derek, a rabid Toronto Maple Leafs fan. "Hey, Derek, how goes it?" said Karl. "I think the Leafs might make the playoffs this year. What do you think?"

Derek answered, "Oh yes, the Leafs are strong this season, and I'm optimistic. But so long as you have dropped by, I wanted to mention that our instruction manuals seem to be too complicated. People are calling in again and again with the most basic questions like how to find the serial number."

"Don't worry too much about that. A lot of our customers can hardly read these days. I think the term is functionally illiterate," said Karl with a smile.

Case Questions

1. How successful is Karl is using his walkaround to uncover useful information?
2. What can Karl do to increase his questioning effectiveness?
3. What can Karl do to increase his listening effectiveness?

Questions for Discussion and Review

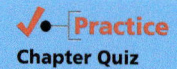

Practice Chapter Quiz

Multiple Choice

1. Mary is very upset about one of her children, who is ill at home, and she has to ask her office assistant several times to repeat herself. What step in the communication process is most likely being problematic for Mary?
   a. sender
   b. noise
   c. environment
   d. none of the above

2. Mirroring is a nonverbal technique that assists with
   a. establishing rapport.
   b. getting your point across more clearly.
   c. getting your way in an argument.
   d. annoying the speaker.

3. Active listening is a critical skill to learn in order to be
   a. well-liked and respected by your co-workers.
   b. persuasive.
   c. accurate with your understanding of other's messages.
   d. all of the above

4. In the workplace, gender differences in communication should always be
   a. ignored.
   b. recognized to avoid potential barriers in communication.
   c. pointed out bluntly so as to avoid these errors in judgment.
   d. recognized as stereotypes that are largely inaccurate and prone to bias.

5. Which of the following is *not* a suggestion in your text to improve your persuasive communication?
   a. get a yes response early on
   b. don't use power words
   c. back up conclusions with data
   d. avoid common language errors

Answers to multiple choice questions: 1. b, 2. a, 3. d, 4. b, 5. b.

Short Answer

6. Why are communication skills important in the field you are in or intend to enter?
7. How can knowing the steps in the communication process help a person become a more effective communicator?
8. How could watching television provide some useful ideas for improving your job-oriented communication skills?
9. Why does giving employees training in listening often lead to increased productivity and profits?
10. Log into your MySearchLab and watch the video on office communication. Keeping in mind that this video is rather exaggerated, write a list several mistakes that you can see in the scenarios. For one error, discuss how the person should have communicated to improve the relationship.

The Web Corner

www.optimalthinking.com/quiz-communication-skills.asp
Rate your level of communication.

www.queendom.com
Look for the Communication Skills Test.

http://nonverbal.ucsc.edu
Explore nonverbal communications, and test your ability to read nonverbal communication.

http://center-for-nonverbal-studies.org
Nonverbal dictionary of gestures, signs, and body-language cues

http://www.helpguide.org/mental/eq6_nonverbal_communication.htm
This site is devoted to improve your nonverbal skills, especially facial expressions and gestures. Lots of gestures and other nonverbal communication signals and their meanings can be found here.

www.listen.org
From the International Listening Association; a site all about listening, featuring tests, articles, and other information.

Internet Skill Builder: Practising Listening Skills

Infoplease offers some practical suggestions for improving your listening skills that both support and supplement the ideas offered in this chapter. The site divides listening into three basic steps: hearing, understanding, and judging. Visit the site at www.infoplease.com/homework/listeningskills1.html.

MySearchLab

Visit **MySearchLab** to find self-grading review quizzes in the eText, discipline-specific media and readings, access to a variety of academic journals, and Associated Press news feeds, along with a wide range of writing, grammar, and research tools and to help hone writing and research skills.

CHAPTER 5
Interpersonal Skills for the Digital World

Ron is a single father, recently divorced, with two young children. Having sole custody of his children after his separation, he was finding it a struggle to get the children ready, get them both to daycare, and drive to his demanding job as a product designer for Sensor Products. The company designs and manufactures electronic controls used in automobiles, trucks, and related vehicles. After work, he picks up the children from daycare and still has the house to look after as well as all of the responsibilities of trying to be a good father. He finds himself exhausted and frequently short-tempered with the children. At lunch, Ron was reading a business magazine that discussed the benefits of working from home (often referred telecommuting or

Roland IJdema/Shutterstock

LEARNING Objectives

After reading and studying this chapter and doing the exercises, you should be able to

1. Describe interpersonal skills related to one-on-one interactions in the digital world.
2. Describe interpersonal skills related to social networking.
3. Describe interpersonal skills related to working with small audiences with respect to digital devices.

teleworking) part of the time as a way to ease stress and yet still enjoy the benefits of full-time work. After much deliberation, Ron decides to go and see his manager to discuss the possibility of spending some of his week working from home, using the technology now available to stay connected with the office.

He explains his idea to his boss, Yakim, including many of the success stories he has read about. Yakim tells him he needs to think about this, as he is a trusted and valuable employee, and he will get back to him about his ideas.

About a week later, he calls Ron in and discusses his solution. As much of Ron's work is done using computer software, email, and other digital hardware, he proposes that he work from home two to three days per week and come in on the days on which he has meetings and other work that must be done at the plant with co-workers.

Three months after trying this arrangement, Ron feels that he is back in control of his newly single life. He uses his computer, Skypes into small meetings with his team, and keeps in touch by email and cell phone. On the days he works from home, he can also spend a bit of time doing laundry and other chores that were difficult to fit in during the week. By spending some of his time at the office, Ron also feels connected with co-workers, something that may have not been possible if he were to work from home full-time. He feels that he has the best of both worlds: connecting with his children at home and enjoying his job.

The story about the product designer illustrates one of the ways in which digital technology can help people accomplish their work in different ways than in the past, and how interpersonal skills continue to be important. Ron's ability to interact positively with others stimulates his own thinking—making her productive—and also contributes to his job satisfaction. Digital media have also changed *how* we work and communicate with others. In this chapter, we examine the interpersonal-skill aspects of working in the digital age, an often-neglected aspect of making good use of the communication and information technology surrounding us in the workplace. We organize this information into two broad categories. First, we describe interpersonal skills for using digital devices in one-on-one interaction. Second, we examine the interpersonal-skill aspects of using communication technology for social networking and small audiences.

To begin thinking through interpersonal skills in relation to the digital world, you are invited to take Self-Assessment Quiz 5-1. The statements in the quiz cover many of the behaviours relevant to digital interactions.

Practice
The Interpersonal Skills for the Digital World Checklist

SELF-ASSESSMENT QUIZ 5-1

The Interpersonal Skills for the Digital World Checklist

Indicate whether each of the following statements is Mostly True or Mostly False as it applies to you (or would apply to you if you were in the situation indicated by the statement). Even if your reaction to a particular statement is "duh," remember that all the statements reflect incidents of real behaviour.

Statement	Mostly True	Mostly False
1. I get really upset if I send a co-worker an instant message (IM), and I do not receive an answer within five minutes.	_____	_____
2. While being interviewed for a job, I receive and send text messages to a work associate or friend.	_____	_____
3. While working in a group, I regularly check my email and text messages.	_____	_____
4. I often check websites such as ESPN, Facebook, Twitter, or home shopping channels on my laptop while at a meeting.	_____	_____
5. I often eat while talking on my cell phone.	_____	_____
6. I typically check my email, text messages, or a website while talking on my cell phone.	_____	_____
7. If I made a webcam presentation for work purposes, I would make sure that my grooming was at its best.	_____	_____
8. I would bring a pet such as a cat, dog, or parrot along to a webcam conference for business purposes.	_____	_____
9. If I were giving a presentation at a business banquet, I would keep my personal digital assistant in my hand.	_____	_____
10. I keep my bottle of water in my hand at all times when making a PowerPoint presentation.	_____	_____
11. When making a PowerPoint presentation, I use the information on the slide as headlines for talking points rather than reading the slides to the audience.	_____	_____
12. If I attended a two-hour videoconference, I would see no problem in leaving the room from time to time just for a break.	_____	_____
13. I have posted, or would be willing to post, some outrageous videos of myself on Facebook, such as driving a vehicle with a bottle of beer in my hand.	_____	_____
14. I use, or would use, a social networking site to really blast a company whose product proved to be faulty.	_____	_____
15. For me, social networking sites are a useful place to post nasty things about people I do not like.	_____	_____
16. Older workers who are not savvy about information technology deserve nicknames like "Mr. Depends," or "Ms. Dinosaur."	_____	_____
17. I laugh when I see somebody doing something as old-fashioned as reading a newspaper.	_____	_____
18. I have received compliments about my ability to explain how to use technology to another worker.	_____	_____
19. I am patient and polite when a tech support person cannot resolve my technology problem right away.	_____	_____
20. I have sent handwritten thank-you notes to people even if they use email and text messaging.	_____	_____

Scoring and interpretation: Give yourself one point (+1) for each statement you gave in agreement with the keyed answer. The keyed answer indicates a positive interpersonal skill for the digital world.

1. Mostly false	6. Mostly false	11. Mostly true	16. Mostly false
2. Mostly false	7. Mostly true	12. Mostly false	17. Mostly false
3. Mostly false	8. Mostly false	13. Mostly false	18. Mostly true
4. Mostly false	9. Mostly false	14. Mostly false	19. Mostly true
5. Mostly false	10. Mostly false	15. Mostly false	20. Mostly true

> **15–20** If your answers are an accurate reflection of your behaviour, you have better-than-average interpersonal skills related specifically to digital technology.
>
> **6–14** If your answers are an accurate reflection of your behaviour, you have average interpersonal skills related specifically to digital technology.
>
> **1–5** If your answers are an accurate reflection of your behaviour, you have let the use of digital technology interfere with having good interpersonal skills. You need to think through carefully how you can blend the use of communication technology with solid human relations skills.

INTERPERSONAL SKILLS FOR ONE-ON-ONE INTERACTIONS

LEARNING OBJECTIVE 1

As with interpersonal skills in general, interactions with people one at a time create the majority of opportunities for displaying interpersonal skills related to the digital age. In this section, we describe four such settings or scenarios in which the communication is typically (not always) directed toward one person: cell phones and text messaging; email messages and instant messaging; webcam job interviews; and the interpersonal aspect of multitasking.

Cell Phones and Text Messaging

Cell phones have become such an integral part of life both on and off the job that many photographs in magazines and newspapers of business people show them using their phone. Television advertisements also often depict a worker using a cell phone even when the advertisement is not for phones. In the business districts of most cities, it appears that approximately two-thirds of the people in business attire are using a cell phone, smart phones, and personal digital assistants. Using cell phones, including sending text messages, therefore represents an enormous opportunity for displaying good, as well as poor, interpersonal skills. How often do use technology during a day? Open MySearchLab and do Web Exercise 2 to examine more carefully your technology usage.

Positive Interpersonal Skills While Using Cell Phones and Text Messaging. The many positive behaviours possible when using cell phones for one-on-one interaction usually are a question of doing the opposite of negative behaviours. The behaviours in the following list illustrate how positive interpersonal skills can be demonstrated while using cell phones and text messaging during one-on-one interactions.[1]

1. Use a standard ringtone instead of a loud, unusual tone. In this way if your phone rings in the presence of a work associate, your behaviour will not provoke surprise or laughter.
2. Inform the caller that you are receiving his or her call on a cell phone. If you let the caller know that you are on a cell phone, the caller will not be surprised when the reception fades in and out, or when you are interrupted by a honking horn or other background noises, including conversations of people walking by.
3. Inform work associates ahead of time if you are waiting for a call or a text message from a medical professional or in reference to an urgent home situation. Assume, for example, that you and a co-worker are discussing a customer problem. Let your co-worker know that your conversation might be interrupted by the type of urgent call just described. In this way, accepting a call will not be interpreted as rudeness.
4. Ask your work associate if he or she would like you to access an item of work-related information using your smart phone. Assume that sales rep Ashley is talking with customer Todd, and Todd wants to know if her company would have a large quantity of a specific product in stock. Ashley would be displaying good interpersonal skills by saying, "Todd, would you like me to access this

information on my iPhone? It will take just a minute." Todd will invariably agree, and he will also understand why Ashley is using her iPhone in the middle of their conversation.

5. Inform your co-worker that you are shutting off your cell phone or smart phone during your conversation. Because so many people do not think to, or refuse to, turn off their cell phone or smart phone, you can gain some psychological capital by mentioning your courteous behaviour. You tell your work associate, "Our meeting is important, so just one second. I want to turn off my cell phone and put it out of view."

6. For business purposes, use a fully functioning phone and stay current with your cellphone bill. You will appear much more professional to work associates when your cellphone call is not interrupted by a disappearing voice or reception much like you are in heavy traffic or a shower. Keeping current with your bill avoids the unprofessional image created by a message that your phone number is "temporarily out of service" or your inability to send an outgoing message.

7. When making calls from outside the office, search for a relatively quiet environment so that your message will be clearer, and you will not have to ask the receiver to repeat information. Even in a busy environment like an airport, it is possible to find a relatively quiet alcove from which to make a call. The interpersonal-skill link here is that you appear more professional when your communication is relatively free of environmental noise.

8. If absolutely necessary to take a cellphone call while interacting with a work associate, excuse yourself and move at least 15 feet (4.6 metres) away to process the call. Work associates who are themselves polite will appreciate your display of polite behaviour.

9. When you are the driver of the vehicle, explain to your work associate that for safety's sake you are putting your cell phone away. Point out that just as you would not be the driver when you are drunk, you will not use your cell phone for voice communication or text messaging while you are driving. Although many co-workers might think you are eccentric, the data are convincing about the dangers of cellphone use while driving. On balance, your concern for the safety of your passenger will be interpreted as a positive interpersonal skill.

10. When at work, make any cellphone calls on break, and away from your assigned physical location, for example outside the building or in an employee lounge (but not in the restroom!) Blocking your personal calls and making them outside your assigned work area shows you have enough interpersonal skills to care about the need of other workers for a tranquil work environment.

Negative Interpersonal Skills While Using Cell Phones and Text Messaging. Dissatisfaction and anger toward people who abuse cell phones in the workplace continue to be expressed in articles, books, blogs, and letters to the editor. All this negativity, however, must be placed in the proper context. If the person with whom you are interacting does not perceive a particular use of the cell phone as rudeness, then it is not rude. For example, if your co-worker smiles at you while you receive a phone call in his or her presence, you are probably not being perceived as displaying negative interpersonal behaviour. Following is a list of frequent cellphone and text-messaging behaviours that many (not all) people will interpret as rudeness and insensitivity. As a result, the person engaging in the act will be perceived as showing negative interpersonal skills.[2]

1. **Accepting a call during a work conversation.** You communicate the fact that your co-worker or other work associate is less important than the caller when you allow a call to interrupt your conversation. Some people interpret making a call

as even more insensitive than receiving a call, but both behaviours dismiss the importance of the work associate with whom you are interacting. Customers are likely to be irritated even more than co-workers if you interrupt your conversation to accept or make a phone call. CEOs who use their cell phones while talking to other workers are likely to be perceived as power abusers, and therefore as arrogant. In short, by accepting a call in the presence of others, you diminish the status of the person who is physically present—hardly an impressive interpersonal skill. Texting on your cell phone can also be perceived as accepting or making a call during a work conversation.

2. **Wearing a cellphone earpiece in the presence of a co-worker when not on the phone.** This suggests that you do not intend to remain fully engaged in your conversation. Also, when you are wearing an earpiece, the person in your physical presence is never sure whether you are listening to another call at the same time. Building rapport with an associate includes making him or her feel important. The fact that you appear to be ready to connect to the outside world trivializes that person.

3. **Making frequent personal calls in earshot of co-workers.** A major complaint of people who work in cubicles is that someone in an adjoining cubicle spends much of the day making calls loudly on a cell phone. The same practice would be possible on a landline, but many perceive using their cell phone for personal calls as more acceptable. Loud personal calls made throughout the day suggest lack of consideration for others, as well as a low work ethic and an unwillingness to do one's fair share of work.

4. **Talking loudly and shouting on the cell phone.** Whether in one-on-one interactions or in the middle of a group of work associates, talking loudly and shouting on the cell phone is widely disliked. Particularly annoying for many people is the compulsion many shouters have to repeatedly say "okay" in an especially loud voice. Talking so loudly on the cell phone suggests insensitivity to the feelings of others as well as being egocentric.

5. **Eating while making a call.** Eating with mouth open in a restaurant is a major violation of etiquette. Equally annoying and disgusting to many receivers of these messages is the sender eating while talking on the phone. Although this practice has become widespread, its vulgarity to many people has not diminished, and will not be tolerated by many customers. On display is the negative interpersonal skill of poor etiquette.

6. **Constant handling of or looking at the phone even when not in use.** Many workers have become so dependent on their cell phones and personal digital assistants that they handle them during conversations, and keep the phone in constant view. Workers have also been observed putting their cell phones on their laps while speaking with others. One manager frequently polishes his chrome-covered smart phone while talking to subordinates.

    The physical attachments just mentioned all suggest the negative trait of being so dependent on a physical device that it interferes with concentrating on others. The constant physical or visual contact with the cell phone also has the negative impact of making the worker look immature. An explanation offered for this physical attachment so many people have is that the phones have become "electronic pets." A technology reporter observed, "You constantly see people taking their little pets out and stroking the scroll wheel, coddling them basically petting them."[3]

7. **Driving a work associate while using a cell phone, including text messaging.** A positive interpersonal skill is not using your cell phone while driving a vehicle in which a work associate is present. A negative interpersonal skill is doing the opposite, even if you live in a province or country where cellphone use is permitted for drivers. A study published in a British medical journal reported

> **SKILL-BUILDING EXERCISE 5-1**
>
> **The Important Message**
>
> Two co-workers are discussing a joint assignment about preparing a spreadsheet related to product returns. The analysis needs to be completed by 5 p.m. One student plays the role of the worker who is intently focusing on the task. Another student plays the role of the worker who feels the cell phone attached to his or her belt vibrate. The worker notices a text message from the bank indicating that five cheques have bounced, which appears to be a bank mistake. The worker with the text message does not want to be totally rude, yet this is an urgent problem. Run the role-play for about four minutes. Observers might provide feedback on the quality of the interpersonal skills displayed in dealing with this text message challenge.

that talking on the cell phone while driving quadruples your risk of being in an accident. Using a hands-free device does little to reduce the risk of an accident.[4] Most provinces now have laws that prohibit the use of hand-held devices while driving, so it is not only dangerous, it is illegal and could lead to a ticket and hefty fine. While many work associates will accept driving while using a cell phone, including sending text messages, as typical and appropriate behaviour, others will interpret your behaviour as a propensity to engage in senseless risks.

8. **Accepting and sending phone messages from restrooms.** A widely reported form of cellphone rudeness is sending and receiving calls from public restrooms. Many receivers of these calls who hear water running from faucets or toilets flushing will be appalled and disgusted. The restroom cellphone user will therefore be perceived as insensitive and lacking in social graces—both quite negative interpersonal skills.

9. **Walking in a crowded corridor while text messaging.** While many people may feel skilled at this task, this behaviour leads to others trying to dodge the texter, who may be oblivious to the havoc this behaviour can cause. Stop and text, or wait until you have arrived at your destination.

Skill-Building Exercise 5-1 gives you an opportunity to practise a core skill with the use of a cell phone and text messaging in the office.

Email Messages and Instant Messaging

▶ Watch
Email Etiquette

Email messages and instant messages (IMs) provide another opportunity for displaying positive as well as negative interpersonal skills linked to the digital age. Many people believe that formality and careful use of language can be neglected when sending messages by email and IM, and when sending text messages. Remember, however, that how a message is sent tells something about the sender.

Email messages should be proofread, should be sent only when necessary, and should generally be no longer than one screen, not including attachments. Although many email users rely on a strikingly informal and casual writing style, such informality for business correspondence is poor etiquette. For example, avoid confirming a meeting with your CEO in these words: "C U LTR, 4 sure. ☺" Overloading the company system with attachments containing space-consuming graphics is often considered rude. Because of text messaging's limited space, the writing can be a bit more casual than in other electronic messages.

An email etiquette problem with legal implications is that company email messages are the property of the company, not the sender. So avoid sending insulting, vulgar, or inflammatory comments through email, because even deleted email messages can be retrieved. Be careful not to forward an email message that has negative comments about the recipient. For example, a customer service representative sent an email to a customer attempting to resolve a complaint. However, instead of beginning with a fresh email, the representative included an email from her boss that said, "Give this idiot what she wants to get her off our back." The customer later sued the company, and then agreed to a small financial settlement.

Instant messaging has created new challenges for email etiquette. Because instant messaging allows you to intrude on co-workers at any time—and them to drop in on you—the opportunities to be rude multiply. Managers should not intrude upon workers through instant messaging unless it is urgent. Think before you send, and make sure the message has real value to the recipient. Suggest politely to "buddies" taking up too much of your time with messages that they contact you after work.

Many companies are shifting from extensive use of email to having some of the written communication among people put on intranets, and internal websites similar to Facebook. For example, you can inform all your work associates at once that you are going on a business trip for three days and will not be able to respond to their messages. All of the comments about the polite use of language apply to these replacement technologies for email.

Figure 5-1 summarizes a large amount of information about etiquette related to emails and instant messaging. Following this accumulated wisdom will enhance your interpersonal skills linked to the digital age. In your MySearchLab, you can also view a video on email etiquette.

Webcam Job Interviews

Yet another interpersonal skill useful in the digital age is to perform well during a webcam interview. Performing well in such an interview combines interpersonal skills with those related to communication technology. On occasion, a hiring manager or human resources representative will request that an interview be conducted by webcam. The job candidate might have a webcam, or use one owned by a friend or the college placement office. (Skype is the leading webcam system.) A challenge in being interviewed via a webcam is that some job candidates do not come across as strongly as they believe.

As webcam technology continues to improve, and more managers are familiar with the technique, the number of these computer-based interviews is likely to increase. Some companies use webcam interviews to reduce travel costs, and this type of interview provides more data than a phone call.

Above all, a webcam interview is still an interview; so review the interview suggestions in Chapter 16 to appear at your best. In addition, keep in mind the following positive suggestions for this type of interview, all of which imply mistakes to avoid at the same time.[5]

1. **Use even lighting.** As with all forms of photography, lighting is a big part of making a successful webcam appearance. A bright light behind you is particularly poor, because your face will be in shadow. Lighting bounced off the ceiling works the best for a soft, even image, yet side-lighting will often suffice. Do not place a bright light on the computer in front of you, to avoid too much glare on your face, particularly if you are light-skinned.

2. **Wear appropriate clothing.** Dress as if you were having an in-person interview, and minimize how much of the colour white you wear because it comes across poorly on computer screens. Loud patterns are also distracting. Unless otherwise directed, it is best to wear a business suit or dress. Investigate what type of clothing job applicants typically wear. For example, if you were applying for a management training position at Home Hardware, business casual dress might be appropriate.

3. **Do your best to appear relaxed and not overly stressed.** Light exercise and a shower about 30 minutes before the interview will help give you a refreshed look. Use your favourite stress reduction technique shortly before the webcam interview. Familiarity with the webcam technology will help you feel relaxed.

FIGURE 5-1 Email and Messaging Etiquette

Observing the following tips will enhance your email etiquette and electronic communication effectiveness, as well as your interpersonal skills.

Address and sign your email messages. Many people neglect to mention a person's name in an email, or sign their own name. Giving your email a personal touch is a useful interpersonal micro-skill.

Keep it simple. Each message should have only one piece of information or request for action so that it's easier for the receiver to respond. However, avoid sending an email with an attachment without some type of greeting or explanation. Do not allow email threads longer than a couple of pages. Email messages longer than one screen are often filed instead of read. Brief emails show compassion for the recipient's workload.

Include an action step. Clearly outline what type of reply you're looking for as well as any applicable deadlines.

Use the subject line to your advantage. Generic terms such as "details" or "reminder" do not describe the contents of your message or whether it's time-sensitive. So the receiver may delay opening it. "Came In under Budget" illustrates a specific (and joyful) title. Do not forward a long chain of emails without changing the subject; otherwise, you might have a confusing subject line, such as "RE: FW: RE: FW: RE: FW."

Take care in writing emails. Clearly organize your thoughts to avoid sending emails with confusing, incomplete, or missing information. Use business writing style and check carefully for grammatical and typographical errors. (Also, generally avoid spelling "I" in lowercase.) When in doubt, use traditional fonts and black type rather than unusual fonts and brightly coloured type, because many people prefer them.

Inform receivers when sending emails from a mobile device. If you use a BlackBerry or comparable device, include a tagline informing people that you are using such a device. This will help explain your terseness. Without such an explanation, they might think you are rude or have limited writing skill.

Be considerate. Use "please" and "thank you" even in brief messages. Part of being considerate, or at least polite, is to begin your email with a warm salutation, such "Hello Gina," rather than jumping into the subject with no greeting. Avoid profane or harsh language. Another way of being considerate is to send emails only when necessary to help combat information overload. Sending copies to only recipients who need or want the information is part of being considerate. (Note that some people use the notation "cc" for copies, which really stands for "carbon copy." "Copy" is more precise, because you are sending an electronic copy.)

Don't include confidential information. The problem is that email is occasionally forwarded to unintended recipients. If your message is in any way sensitive or confidential, set up a meeting or leave a voice mail in which you request confidentiality. Also, avoid including gossip, including negative rumours, in email messages, because the subject of the gossip might accidentally receive the email, and might voice a major complaint.

Do not use email to blast a co-worker, and send copies to others. Criticizing another person with email is equivalent to blasting him or her during a large meeting.

Ask before sending huge attachments. Do not clog email systems without permission.

Encourage questions and requests for clarification. Email functions best when it is interactive, so ask receivers to send along questions they might have about your message, including any requests for clarification.

Consider the timing of email messages. An email that makes a major request should be sent earlier in the day so that the person has time to process the request. Good news can be sent almost anytime. For some recipients, bad news is best sent early in the day so that they can ask for your support in dealing with the problem. However, very bad news (such as being laid off) is best delivered in person. Some people prefer to receive bad news later in the day so that it will not disrupt their entire workday.

FIGURE 5-1 Continued

> **Avoid keeping a personal email account on the job unless welcomed by management.** An estimated one-quarter of emails received at work are for personal purposes.
>
> To resist the temptation of spending too much time with personal emails, it is best not to have a personal email account, such as Gmail, on the office computer. You will appear more professional if you avoid the temptation to spend a lot of work time sending and receiving personal email and instant messages.
>
> **Minimize "BIF" messages on evening and weekends.** In today's demanding workplace, it is easy to send "before I forget" messages in the evening, on weekends, and during holidays. Some people will regard you as insensitive to their lifestyle if you badger them outside of regular working hours with email messages. Save your urgent messages for the next workday—unless an immediate exchange of information is essential.
>
> Instant messaging requires a few additional considerations for practising good electronic etiquette:
>
> **Use instant messaging sparingly because it is interruptive.** Instant messages are likely to interrupt a person's concentration on an important task, so they should be sent infrequently. Be careful not to send an instant message to a co-worker who you know is working on an analytical task. However, if the company culture encourages the use of instant messaging, display good interpersonal skills by going with the flow.
>
> **Don't be Big Brother.** Some bosses use instant messaging to check up on others, to make sure that they are seated at their computer. Never intrude on workers unless it is urgent.
>
> **Take it offline.** When someone on your buddy list becomes too chatty, don't vent your frustration. By phone, in person, or through regular email, explain tactfully that you do not have time for processing so many instant messages. Suggest that the two of you might get together for lunch or coffee soon.
>
> **Set limits to avoid frustration.** To avoid constant interruptions, use a polite custom status message, such as "I will be dealing with customers today until 4:40."

Source: "Communicating Electronically: What Every Manager Needs to Know," *Communication Solutions*, Sample Issue, 2008, p. 2; Heinz Tschabitscher, "The Ten Most Important Rules of Email Etiquette," http://email.about.com/cs/netiquettetips/tp/core_netiquette.htm, accessed September 9, 2003; Monte Enbysk, "Bosses: 10 Tips for Better E-mails," *Microsoft Small Business Center*, http://www.microsoft.com/smallbusiness/resources/technology/communications/bossess_10, 2006; Nancy Flynn, "50% of Bosses Ban Personal E-mail Accounts," *Workplace Communication Examiner*, http://www.examiner.com, July 28, 2009; "5 Tactics to Curb E-mail Overload," *Manager's Edge*, June 2008, p. 6.

4. **Use or create an uncluttered area free of personal belongings, pets, and television sets.** Although your living quarters may be the locale of your interview, you still want to simulate the appearance of a professional office. Tidy up the interview area, and move away as much clutter as possible. Background noise, including a ringing telephone or a television set turned on, detracts from a professional image.

5. **Sit tall with good posture, and stay at approximately the same distance from the computer screen that you do for most of your computer work.** The worst posture mistake webcam interviewees typically make is to move the head to within a few centimetres of the screen. A close-up shot of this nature distorts the face and looks a little bizarre to most interviewers.

6. **Rehearse so that you will be better able to implement the previous five suggestions.** Collaborate with someone in your network of contacts to interview each other on webcam. The rehearsal will familiarize you with the technology, and

you can also get feedback on the adequacy of the lighting, and how natural and positive you appeared. As was often said in the early days of photography, "Smile, you're on camera."

A fundamental reason why rehearsal for a webcam interview is important is that people have a tendency to overrate the image they project on video. A webcam image is, of course, a kind of video image. Karen Friedman, a video presentation trainer, has this to say about the importance of getting an accurate feedback on the video image you project:

> People will tell you that they're perceived as dynamic, engaging, and interesting, with full command of the material. And when they see themselves on videotape or DVD and it's a rude awakening, because they see how other people really see them. You can pick up odd mannerisms you're not aware of. You may have the words down and the verbal techniques, but your body language might give away that you're nervous or unsure of yourself.[6]

Interpersonal Aspects of Multitasking

multitasking
(a) Having two or more projects that you are working on, but not working on them at the same time. (b) Doing two or more tasks simultaneously.

Multitasking has two meanings, and the difference is of major significance for interpersonal relationships. One meaning of multitasking is that you have two or more projects that you are working on, but you do not work on these projects at the same time. For example, today a person might be responsible for investigating customer complaints as well as purchasing new furniture for the office. In the morning she works on the complaints, and in the afternoon she negotiates a furniture purchase. The other type of multitasking can create more interpersonal problems. With this type of multitasking, the person does two or more things simultaneously, such as visiting an office-furniture website while talking on the phone with a dissatisfied customer.

Chapter 15 deals with the productivity problems often associated with multitasking. Also, the discussion of cellphone use described the insensitivity of accepting and sending cellphone calls while talking to another person (a frequent type of multitasking). Here we explain how multitasking can have both positive and negative influences on interpersonal relationships.

Multitasking and Positive Interpersonal Skills.

In some situations, performing two tasks at once can enhance interpersonal skills because you are helping another person. Imagine that Sally asks Jean-Guy for help in inserting accents into French words, such as converting "resume" into "résumé." Jean-Guy sits down next to Sally at her computer, and says, "Watch me, Sally. I am moving the cursor to the Insert tab in the word processing program. I click on the Symbol icon. Next, I scroll through the options until I find "é" and then click on it. You can find all the accented letters in this way."

Jean Guy is indeed doing two tasks at once—manipulating the keyboard and talking to Sally. If he had not multitasked, he would not have been a good tutor. Jean-Guy is also not being rude, because he has Sally's implicit permission to multitask. A lot of coaching and tutoring requires multitasking of the nature just described.

The scenario of Sally and Jean-Guy illustrates another key principle of using multitasking to enhance interpersonal skills. When two people are holding a conversation for purposes of joint problem solving, multitasking will sometimes enhance the problem solving, thereby creating a stronger interpersonal relationship. Visualize Mike and Tammy driving together on a business trip. Mike is driving, and his vehicle is not equipped with a GPS. Mike says to Tammy, "I think we may have missed the Confederation Road exit on this highway. It would be a nightmare to exit and find the way back. What should we do?"

"Hold on Mike," says Tammy. "I'll access the GPS app on my BlackBerry and get us centred in a minute." Fifty seconds later, Tammy says to Mike, while still looking at the screen on her BlackBerry, "We're okay. The Confederation Road exit is 5.6 kilometres down the road. We'll make a right turn off the exit ramp."

Multitasking and Negative Interpersonal Skills. The major negative interpersonal-skill aspect of multitasking is that it trivializes the person with whom you are interacting, as described with cellphone abuse. Imagine you are listening to a co-worker who is describing a proposed solution to a problem. You shift your gaze to your computer so that you can seek who just "poked" you on Facebook. This immediately sends the message that your "poker" is more important at the moment than your co-worker, who wanted to discuss a legitimate work problem.

Another negative interpersonal skill associated with multitasking is more subtle. When you respond to an electronic interruption, such as an IM message or an email alert, your attention is sapped for more time than it takes to read the message. You have to recover from the interruption and refocus your attention on your work associate. While you are in the recovery mode, perhaps even 30 seconds, you are paying less than full attention to the other person.[7] And this inattentiveness is obvious by the blank stare on your face, or recovery murmurs such as "yeah, yeah." Because of this issue, many organizations block access to social-media sites such as Facebook and disable IM on company computers.

Harassment and Cyberbullying of Others

A negative consequence of communication technology in the workplace is that it is easier to harass co-workers than in the analogue age. To harass co-workers in the past, it was necessary to say nasty things to them in person, telephone them in a menacing way, write them threatening notes, or send them upsetting words on paper or photographs. The Internet, including email and the web, has made it much easier to harass people.

A newer term, **cyberbullying**, includes harassment of others over the Internet as well as through social networking sites such as Facebook. Cyberbullying involves using information and communication technologies (ICT) to bully, embarrass, threaten or harass another person. It also includes engaging in conduct or behaviour that is derogatory, defamatory, degrading, illegal, and/or abusive.[8]

A CBC investigative report underscores the prevalence of bullying on the Internet: 14 percent of young Canadians reported having been threatened through instant messaging; 16 percent admitted to posting hateful comments.[9] A University of Calgary study found that more than 25 percent of students had been victims of cyberbullying.[10] In several instances such bullying has resulted in the victim committing suicide. While most studies are about young people, cyberbullying is experienced in the workplace through threatening emails, postings on social media sites, discussion boards, and instant messaging. Cyberbullying is subject to the same laws as other types of bullying and harassment, which will be discussed more fully in Chapter 11, "Skills for Motivating and Helping Others."

Creating a hostile environment by displaying pornography to co-workers who do not want to see it has become one of the most frequent forms of harassment. Aside from being rude, sexual harassment through pornography has frequently been ruled as illegal.

An employee can be accused of hostile environment harassment by simply leaving open a porn site on his or her desktop. Sending co-workers sexually oriented jokes by email can result in similar accusations. If you work for a company that distributes adult films, pornography would be part of your job, and you therefore might be excluded from the harassment accusation.

Harassment can also deal with a person's race or ethnicity, such as making insulting comments or jokes about a person's race. Age is another demographic factor that might lead to a person being harassed, such as continuous joking by email that a senior worker suffers from Alzheimer's disease.

Harassing others through communication technology is a negative interpersonal skill. A positive twist on this might be that the person who abstains 100 percent from any computer-related actions able to be interpreted as harassment is demonstrating a positive interpersonal skill. For example, if you receive an advertisement for adult videos that made its way past the company's spam filter, you might delete it without opening it.

cyberbullying
The use of information and communication technologies to bully, embarrass, threaten, or harass another person. It also includes the use of information and communications technology (ICT) to engage in conduct or behaviour that is derogatory, defamatory, degrading, illegal, and/or abusive.

INTERPERSONAL SKILLS FOR SMALL AND LARGE AUDIENCES

LEARNING OBJECTIVE 2

LEARNING OBJECTIVE 3

Since digital technologies are also used to interact with small or large groups, you also need interpersonal skills when using these technologies. You need good interpersonal skills for such things as social networking by Internet; using laptop computers and smart phones during meetings; making electronic presentations; videoconferencing; telecommuting; and preserving your online reputation. You will notice that in a couple of these situations, you may not actually be addressing a group; you may interacting with only one person. That is, you might send a message on a social networking site to one person rather than to a group.

Social Networking by Internet

Almost infinite knowledge exists about social networking, including its technology, application for building a personal network, and marketing.[11] Included in this abundance of information is how Twitter, Instagram, YouTube, and Facebook (and other applications that seem to be added daily) have completely transformed the way we live, and how email has now become obsolete because of social networking sites. While perhaps not classified as truly social networking, much work today is also done via online discussion boards, blogs, and wikis. Many online courses use discussion boards, and professors and teachers are often disappointed with the lack of etiquette and interpersonal skills displayed by some students. Our aim here is to simply list a few of the positive and negative interpersonal skills associated with the use of social networking sites, including a wide variety of online communication with others in small or perhaps even larger groups.

Fuse/Getty Images

Positive Interpersonal Skills and Social Networking. The use of Twitter, Facebook, LinkedIn, and the like provides the serious worker with several opportunities for displaying positive interpersonal skills, as follows:

1. **Demonstrate your loyalty by posting gracious comments about your employer.** Social networking sites often include blogs and discussion boards and therefore present an open forum for your ideas about the company. You can demonstrate empathy and compassion for the mission of your company by commenting on an action taken by the company that you perceive as positive. An example: "I'm proud to work for the Jeep division of Fiat/Chrysler. My wife and our three children were caught in a snowstorm. I put my Cherokee into four-wheel drive and made it through the storm until we could find a motel. There were dozens of overturned vehicles, but we made it to safety. The vehicle stabilization feature is really functional."

2. **Display your compassion for people in need.** Post on the company social networking site, and also a public site, that you want to help people in need in some specific way. For example, you might state that you have clothing you want to give to a needy family in any way associated with the company. Or explain that you have developed your language-tutoring skills and are willing to help for free any person who needs help in learning to read. Compassion might be considered a value, but it also translates into a skill in terms of helping people.

98   CHAPTER 5

3. **Demonstrate professional-level communication skills.** When making entries on Twitter in particular, many people feel compelled to write carelessly, foolishly, and viciously. Demonstrate your professionalism by writing in a style suited for a printed newspaper or a term paper. Remember that many influential people regard written communication skills as a subset of interpersonal skills.

4. **Pay deserved compliments to company personnel.** The ability to compliment others in a sensible way is an advanced interpersonal skill. Complimenting a person in private may be useful, but public compliments are welcome also. An example of a Facebook post of this nature: "I want everybody to know that Tom Barnes, our facilities manager, spearheaded the planting of a garden on the office building roof. We are saving the planet, one petunia at a time."

5. **Establish meaningful contact with workers far and wide.** The major purpose of social networking is to develop valuable contacts with many people with whom it would be difficult to maintain person-to-person or phone contact. Selective use of the social networking sites enables you to relate, at least on a written level, to a variety of people in your fields. You might be able to enhance your cross-cultural skills by interacting with professionals in different countries. (LinkedIn is particularly good for this purpose, because so many of its members have a professional intent.)

6. **Display a desire to help others grow and develop.** Social networking sites afford an easy opportunity to point others toward helpful information, such as referring friends to useful websites and books. You can also alert people to dangers, such as a new scam related to the sale of gold. Although the same type of alerts can be accomplished by email, social networking sites do not require long distribution lists. By pointing people in the direction of useful information, you will be demonstrating part of a useful interpersonal skill of helping others grow and develop. Instead of just writing about yourself on your post, include information that will help others.

Negative Interpersonal Skills and Social Networking. Social networking provides a setting for displaying negative as well as positive interpersonal skills. In general, all of the positive opportunities mentioned above could be reversed to become negative. For example, instead of helping others grow and develop with postings on your site or their site, you slam and demean these people, which can be classified as cyberbullying. The following list presents a few ways in which negative interpersonal skills are sometimes displayed on social networking sites.

1. **Using social networking sites to eliminate face-to-face interactions with work associates.** As with email, social networking sites provide an opportunity to avoid face-to-face interaction with co-workers, managers, and customers. However, the temptation is even greater with social networking sites because they tout the concept of being "friends" with people on your list of electronic contacts. A person might think consciously or subconsciously, "If my customer is already my friend, why should I have to talk to or personally visit him? Our relationship is already good." If all relationships could be built and maintained electronically, you would not need to be studying human relations.

2. **Posting confidential or derogatory information about your employer.** In the words of technology writer Bridget Carey, "Employees need to realize some conversations are privileged. Just because you're in a meeting about a new product, or worse, layoffs, doesn't mean you should be broadcasting to the world."[12] Posting negative information and insults about your employer demonstrates even lower emotional intelligence. Nasty comments about the employer, even if deserved, are often made out of uncontrolled anger. Hundreds of employees have been fired because of making inflammatory comments on social networking sites about their employers. Poor interpersonal skill is also displayed by joining a social networking group dedicated to destroying the reputation of your employer.

3. **Posting derogatory information and photos about a co-worker.** Social networking site administrators generally do not edit posts, so anybody registered on the site can post dreadful comments about another person as a mean prank or a deliberate effort to ruin the target's reputation. YouTube can serve a similar evil purpose. Some of these negative posts reflect backstabbing because another person encourages you to engage in embarrassing behaviour. He or she may quote you, or post a photo or video of you engaged in outrageous behaviour.

4. **Engaging in social networking at inappropriate times.** Many "Tweeters" (persons who post on Twitter) in particular are so habituated to visiting their favourite social networking site that they do so at inappropriate times, such as during work. Many office workers access their social networking sites during meetings. The interpersonal-skill deficiency of accessing a social network site for nonbusiness purposes during working hours is that it reflects insensitivity and immaturity. (Print-related distractions would also be unwelcome, such as doing crossword puzzles during a meeting.)

5. **Using discussion boards to vent feelings about a co-worker or fellow student.** While you may not always like the people with whom you work or study, discussion boards are not the places to make these feelings known. Calling someone's comments "stupid," "unlearned," or even "naïve," is not proper etiquette. While discussion boards do provide a place to discuss differing opinions, do so professionally. A rule of thumb is to start with a positive comment and then politely express your differing opinion. For example, "You have put a lot of thought into your argument Mary. However, I also think that . . . [and add your ideas here]." Keep your comments unbiased and non-personal.

Laptop and Personal Digital Assistant Use during Meetings and Other Formal Settings

Whether the use of laptop and netbook computers as well as personal digital assistants (smart phones) during meetings enhances your interpersonal skills depends on company custom and why you are using your computer. Some companies welcome computer use during meetings; in other companies, such a practice is considered distracting and inconsiderate.

At Ford Motor Company, CEO Alan Mulally is adamant about meetings not being interrupted by people using their BlackBerrys or laptop computers—as well as the interruption of side conversations.[13] Professors vary widely as to whether students should use their laptops and other devices during classes. One professor at a Canadian university welcomes students to use Twitter to tweet questions to her while she lectures, because it is less disruptive than asking questions out loud. Another college professor bans the use of all technology in the classroom, claiming that is rude and disruptive. While some students may use their devices to take notes, others may be on Facebook, playing games, or messaging others.

The practice of consulting a smart phone during a meeting has the potential to annoy, therefore detracting from the image of the smartphone user. For example, a vice-president who is continually messaging during important company meetings may be thought of as not caring about the company. As with cell phones, when laptop computers and smart phones are used at meetings to facilitate information gathering, and with permission, they can enhance interpersonal skills. If you contribute to the purpose of the meeting, and are not being rude or interruptive, you are displaying good interpersonal skills. Imagine you are present at a marketing meeting of a swimsuit designer and manufacturer. The head of marketing says, "We have been thinking of finding a distributor in the Yukon, but I wonder what percentage of people there own a swimsuit." You say, "If you would like, give me five minutes to search the Internet for a factual answer to your question." Particularly if you find a plausible answer, you will be perceived as constructive.

> ## SKILL-BUILDING EXERCISE 5-2
>
> **Justifying Laptop Use during a Meeting**
>
> Five students play the role of a group of workers who are developing a marketing campaign for a new energy drink, Vitalize27. Ideas are flying around the meeting room. One student plays the role of a member of the group, who suddenly opens a laptop computer, and begins watching the screen. By mistake the audio is turned on, and the other members of the group can easily hear that the laptop user has accessed a sports channel, ESPN.com. The laptop user gets a few frowns, also with some stern questioning from the team leader. The student playing the role of the laptop user must present a sensible and diplomatic excuse as to why he or she was tuned into ESPN during the meeting. Another student plays the role of the team leader who is disappointed with the behaviour he or she has observed. The other three role players might make any comments they deem to be appropriate.
>
> Observers rate the role players on two dimensions, using a 1-to-5 scale from Very Poor to Very Good. One dimension is "effective use of human relations techniques." The second dimension is "acting ability." A few observers might voluntarily provide feedback to the role players in terms of sharing their ratings and observations. The course instructor might also provide feedback.

The etiquette aspect of laptops, netbooks, and smart phones in meetings, classrooms, and other settings has created spirited debate. People with traditional attitudes about etiquette say the use of smart phones at meetings is as "gauche" (rude) as ordering out for pizza. In contrast, techno-evangelists insist that to ignore real-time text messages invites peril because so many people demand an immediate response to their email messages.[14] Again, to avoid being perceived as gauche, follow the corporate culture. Skill-Building Exercise 5-2 deals with this issue.

Interpersonal Aspects of Presentation Technology

Presentation technology has become almost synonymous with PowerPoint, Visio, and other computer software. However, presentation technology also includes laptops, data projectors, remote controls, and other presentation hardware. The use of presentation technology provides an exceptional opportunity to display interpersonal skills—good or poor.

The biggest challenge in using presentation technology is to maintain a human presence while still making effective use of the technology. Among the positive interpersonal skills during an electronic presentation are to maintain eye contact with the audience, smile, show a sense of humour, and interact with the audience. Among the negative interpersonal skills are reading detailed slides to the audience, not maintaining eye contact, and continually fiddling with your equipment thereby ignoring participants at the meeting.

All you have learned about making presentations (or public speaking) applies even though you might be tapping a key on your laptop computer while making a presentation. Self-Assessment Quiz 5-2 presents a list of behaviours that summarizes major points of demonstrating effective interpersonal skills during a presentation. Many people who are watching you make a presentation will be making judgments about your interpersonal and cognitive skills.

Videoconferencing

Videoconferencing especially requires making a good first impression, as well as demonstrating good interpersonal skills. Keep in mind the following considerations for this and for demonstrating sensitivity:[15]

1. **Choose your clothing carefully.** Some participants expect the screen to display only their upper torso, and therefore wear business attire above the waist, and perhaps shorts and sports shoes below. Busy patterns do not look good on camera. Clothing may be more superficial than interpersonal skill, but your choice of clothing reflects on your judgment and how seriously you take the conference.
2. **Speak in crisp, conversational tones, and pay close attention.** Maintain eye contact with live participants and remote viewers; this is as important interpersonal

Practice
The Presentation Technology Checklist of Interpersonal Behaviours

SELF-ASSESSMENT QUIZ 5-2

The Presentation Technology Checklist of Interpersonal Behaviours

Directions: Indicate whether each of the following statements is Mostly True or Mostly False as it applies to you (or would apply to you if you were in the situation indicated by the statement).

Statement Number	Mostly True	Mostly False
1. I make frequent eye contact with as many members of the audience as feasible.	_____	_____
2. I like to present a large number of slides in rapid sequence just to dazzle the audience.	_____	_____
3. I tend to get irritated if a member of the audience disagrees with one of my points.	_____	_____
4. I will often attempt to loosen up the audience by telling a joke related to nationality, age, or hair colour.	_____	_____
5. I attempt to pack as much information onto a slide as possible even it requires using a 10-point font.	_____	_____
6. If somebody in the audience complains about not being able to hear me, I like to retort with a negative comment like "Have you had your hearing checked lately?"	_____	_____
7. I smile frequently during my presentation.	_____	_____
8. I explain to the members of the audience that they can revisit my presentation on a specific website, or that I am willing to send them an email attachment of the presentation.	_____	_____
9. At the end of the presentation, I will typically thank the audience for having watched.	_____	_____
10. I will ask the audience an open-ended question like "What questions do you have?" rather than a close-ended question like "Any questions?"	_____	_____

Scoring and Interpretation: Give yourself one point (+1) for each statement you gave in agreement with the keyed answer. The keyed answer indicates a positive interpersonal skill for presentation technology.

1. Mostly true
2. Mostly false
3. Mostly false
4. Mostly false
5. Mostly false
6. Mostly false
7. Mostly true
8. Mostly true
9. Mostly true
10. Mostly true

9–10 You have good skills related to the interpersonal aspects of presentation technology.

1–8 You have much room for improvement in terms of your skills related to the interpersonal aspects of presentation technology.

---

skill as it is with presentation technologies. Getting up to leave the room looks particularly bad on camera.

3. **Never forget the powerful reach of the video camera.** Behaviour such as falling asleep or rolling the eyes in response to an executive's suggestions are readily seen by associates in the same and other locations. Such behaviour is likely to be interpreted as indicative of immaturity.

4. **Avoid culturally insensitive gestures.** For example, large hand and body motions make many Asians uncomfortable. Also, extreme behaviours sometimes appear magnified on video camera although they might be less distracting in person.

5. **Decrease nervousness about video interviews by rehearsing.** Use a camcorder to see how you appear and sound during a practice interview, engaging the help of a friend. Solicit his or her feedback about your performance. Appearing relaxed during a videoconference helps you project the important interpersonal skill of being self-confident.

Interpersonal Skills Linked to Telecommuting

As illustrated in the case introduction, people who work from home face challenges to their interpersonal skills related to communication. Telecommuters can communicate abundantly via electronic devices, but they miss out on the face-to-face interactions so vital for dealing with complex problems. Another communication problem telecommuters face is feeling isolated from activities at the main office and missing out on the encouragement and recognition that take place in face-to-face encounters. (Of course, many telecommuters prefer to avoid such contact.) Many telecommuters have another communications problem: Because they have very little face-to-face communication with key people in the organization, they believe that they are passed over for promotion. Most telecommuters spend some time in the traditional office, yet they miss the day-by-day contact.

Another communication problem with telecommuting is that it lacks a solid human connection. As one telecommuting marketing consultant put it, face time is critical for building empathy. "It's a human connection. It takes time, and human beings need visual cues, the symbols of being together and caring for one another."[16] To combat the problem of isolation, most companies schedule some face time with remote workers perhaps every few months. In the opening case, Rita enjoys working at home while still maintaining time at the office. At minimum, a supervisor might phone the teleworkers at least once a week, or hold a monthly videoconference.[17]

To display positive interpersonal skills as a worker from home or other remote location, the individual should make good use of the limited face-to-face contact he or she has with other workers. Display warmth toward and interest in work associates. Staying in touch online with a human relations twist is also important. Occasionally asking how the other person is doing is helpful, as is an occasional question about the person's interests or family life. Many telecommuters are asked to attend an occasional company meeting. On these occasions, it is important to display high enthusiasm. To keep interpersonal skills sharp, it is good to interact with store associates, and with service workers such as the postal service and package delivery workers.

Successful telecommuters also need the interpersonal skill of being able to work well without supervision. You also need to be able to work well in isolation, and not be dependent on frequent interaction with co-workers or a supervisor.[18] High-maintenance employees who need frequent praise and attention are much better suited for working in a traditional office than working from home.[19]

BACK TO THE OPENING CASE

Ron, the product designer, appears to have found the right balance between engaging in highly analytical tasks using his computer and interacting with other people with his part-time telecommuting. You will recall that he thought he might feel isolated working alone at home. By going into the office a couple of days per week and working from home the other days, he found balance between home life and career and had enough interaction with people to help him feel attached to the workforce.

Avoiding Damage to Your Online Reputation

Postings on the Internet, including newspaper articles, blogs, and video websites, can rapidly broadcast favourable or unfavourable data about your interpersonal skills and judgment. Based largely on the Internet, much more information about a person's private life has become public. Some aspects of your personal life therefore affect your professional reputation. If you recall the Vancouver riots after the Canucks lost the final game for the Stanley Cup in 2011, many people were identified and arrested via the Internet. The Vancouver Police Service set up an Internet site for people to post their videos and photos of the rioters. Some rioters even lost their jobs as a result of the postings. Companies do not want to have lawbreakers working for them, as this affects how they could be perceived by customers and clients.[20]

Matt Zimmerman, senior staff attorney for the Electronic Frontier Foundation, explains the importance of having a squeaky-clean reputation in these terms: "Now we have this giant megaphone of the Internet, where every little whisper about someone shows up in Google."[21]

A positive interpersonal and cognitive skill is therefore to avoid having embarrassing information or photographs linked to you accessible through search engines. Your reputation can also be damaged by posting extreme viewpoints on the web, because these might be frowned upon by employers. They want to avoid offending customers or potential customers. Two examples of extreme viewpoints are stating that all people who wear fur coats should be physically attacked, and that all investment bankers who earn more than $2 million in annual bonuses should be sent to jail.

Another aspect of your online reputation is that you might need to distance yourself from others who share your name. If you have a LinkedIn or Facebook profile, insert a clear photo of yourself. During a job search, when you send your résumé either by a hard copy or by online, provide a link to your profile.[22] Also, alert current or prospective employers if someone with the same name as yours has a negative online presence. A challenge in terms of job hunting is that an Internet search has become part of the employer's background investigation. Negative information about oneself on the web can sometimes be removed by request or by hiring a service to do it for you.

Access the eText in MySearchLab to learn more about this chapter's self-assessment quizzes.

To **Watch** **Explore** **Practice** **Study** and **Review**, visit MySearchLab

Developing Your Human Relations Skills and Reinforcing Concepts

Summary

Practice
Glossary Flashcards

- Display positive interactions with another person by appropriately using your cell phone, text messaging, and emailing, and during webcam interviews.
- Interpersonal skills are also required when social networking, as these will be viewed by others and could lead to negative consequences if not appropriate.
- These same positive skills also apply to using laptops and other digital technology during meetings, when giving presentations, and when videoconferencing.

Explore
Simulation: Business Communications

Interpersonal Relations Case 5-1

Unveiled on Facebook

Lisa works as tech support field representative in the digital printer division of a telecommunications company. The digital printers manufactured and sold by the company are designed for large, commercial printing companies. The starting price for these sophisticated and complex machines is $400,000. In addition to the machines, the company sells service contracts that include field visits by a tech support representative. These visits are necessary when there is a problem with the machine that cannot be resolved by telephone or computer to computer.

Lisa's company is located in Winnipeg. During a February cold spell there, a major customer in Miami was having trouble with a new digital printer. The problem could not be resolved by phone or through computer diagnostics, so Lisa was sent down. After Lisa arrived, she estimated that the job would take three days to accomplish.

At the end of the second day, Lisa received an urgent call from Barry, her boss, who told her to return home as quickly as possible because a customer in Toronto needed her expertise to solve a problem with its giant printing press. Lisa thought that because she had done such a great job fixing the Miami printing press, she deserved a day of vacation in Florida. So she explained to Barry that the customer needed one more day of hands-on support. As a result, she would be back to the office one day later than planned.

The next morning Lisa headed to South Beach in Miami along with two contacts she had made at the customer. One of the customer employees, Jessica, brought along a camcorder because, in her words, "I love to have souvenirs of good times." Without Lisa granting permission, Jessica then posted a video of her frolicking in the water at South Beach. She also sent a message to the Facebook account of Lisa's boss, alerting him to "check out my new video."

When Lisa arrived back in the office, Barry confronted her about the video and asked, "Explain to me clearly how you were helping our customer with their problem while you were in the water at South Beach. Our company cannot tolerate liars."

Lisa replied, "I was thinking about the customer's problem while I was at South Beach. Besides, after all that hard work I needed a little rest and relaxation."

Case Questions

1. What does this case have to do with interpersonal skills?
2. What would you advise Lisa to do so that she can resolve her problem with her employer? (You might want to glance at Chapter 9, which includes a discussion of conflict resolution.)
3. What advice would you offer Jessica, the work associate who posted a video of Lisa on Facebook?
4. If you were Barry, how would you handle this situation?

Interpersonal Relations Case 5-2

Kevin, the Twitter Guy

Kevin, a real estate agent specializing in low-priced homes in Vancouver, is an avid Twitter user. He spends approximately two hours per day checking out his Twitter feed. Kevin posts about six tweets a day with the hope of building his reputation as an intelligent professional, as well as obtaining referrals of potential homebuyers. The contents of 10 tweets Kevin posted last month are presented next.

1. The BC Lions might be good this season. Owing a home in downtown is a good investment. kevin@MetroRealty.com
2. My buddies love my barbeques. Get in touch to buy a house. kevin@MetroRealty.com
3. Looks like I have pink eye today. Send along your home-hunting friends. kevin@MetroRealty.com
4. I tried one of those electronic cigarettes. No thanks. Home ownership is a great investment. kevin@MetroRealty.com
5. My niece sent me a Valentine's Day card saying she loves me. kevin@MetroRealty.com
6. Just advised my folks to get a reverse mortgage. I told them home ownership is good. kevin@MetroRealty.com
7. Keep an eye on your BMI (body mass index). Did you know that I sell houses? kevin@MetroRealty.com
8. I may need a new transmission on my SUV. I'm waiting for a referral from you guys. kevin@MetroRealty.com
9. It's hot and my AC in the SUV is down. Home ownership is the Canadian Dream. kevin@MetroRealty.com
10. Did you know that Domino's has made its pizzas spicier and tastier? Pizza goes great with a house. kevin@MetroRealty.com

Case Questions

1. How well is Kevin doing in terms of projecting the image of an intelligent professional?
2. What advice might you give to Kevin so that his tweeting might lead to more referrals?
3. To what extent is Kevin just wasting time with his Twitter activity?

Questions for Discussion and Review

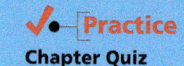

Practice Chapter Quiz

Multiple Choice

1. Which of the following would demonstrate a positive interpersonal skill while using a cell phone?
   a. Peek at your cell phone when a text message comes in rather than holding it up and making it obvious that you are checking your phone.
   b. Inform a co-worker that you are shutting off your phone for the duration of the conversation.
   c. Talk loudly if you are in traffic and need to make a call.
   d. Make personal cellphone calls quietly at your desk.
2. Which of the following is the *best* example of cyber-bullying?
   a. Phoning a person and insulting them over the phone
   b. Leaving an insulting voice mail
   c. Posting a mean comment about another person on their Facebook page
   d. Telling someone that she is a poor team member
3. What is the definition of multitasking?
   a. Having two or more projects that you are working on, but you do not work on these projects at the same time
   b. Doing two or more tasks at the same time
   c. Both a and b are correct.
   d. Neither a nor b is correct.
4. A positive interpersonal skill using social networking would be
   a. complimenting a co-worker for a job well done using Twitter.
   b. posting meeting information for everyone to read.
   c. using social networking in place of face-to-face communication with a co-worker.
   d. correcting another student on the discussion board when their opinion is obviously wrong.
5. When videoconferencing, participants should
   a. speak as you would normally.
   b. choose clothing carefully.
   c. not worry about their gestures.
   d. ignore the camera.

Answers to multiple choice questions: 1. b, 2. c, 3. c, 4. a, 5. b.

Short Answer

6. You and a co-worker are having a work-related conversation, seated on a bench outside the office building during lunch break. Your friend's cell phone rings; he notices from the number that the boss is calling, so he answers the call immediately. Explain whether your friend's answering the call is appropriate.

7. What should a person invited for a webcam job interview do if he or she does not feel telegenic (photogenic on TV) enough to perform well in such an interview?

8. What might you be able to do in the next several days to demonstrate on Facebook or Twitter a positive aspect of your interpersonal skills?

9. Give an example of one of the best displays of interpersonal skills you have seen in a PowerPoint presentation by one of your professors, showing that he or she has good interpersonal skills.

10. Log on to MySearchLab and view the video on email etiquette. How will the suggestions in this video assist you in writing more professional emails for the workplace?

The Web Corner

http://www.akdart.com/cell.html
Avoiding cellphone rudeness

http://www.inc.com/ss/video-conferencing-best-practices
Presenting yourself well during a videoconference

http://www.ikeepsafe.org/be-a-pro/reputation/social-networks-and-a-positive-online-reputation/
Developing a good online reputation

Internet Skill Builder: Finding Yourself on the Internet

Have you tried to search your name on the Internet? This can be a worthwhile activity and you may be surprised by the results. Often, people do not realize how much information about themselves is on the Internet. Give this a try and share your results with other classmates.

MySearchLab

Visit **MySearchLab** to find self-grading review quizzes in the eText, discipline-specific media and readings, access to a variety of academic journals, and Associated Press news feeds, along with a wide range of writing, grammar, and research tools and to help hone writing and research skills.

CHAPTER 6

Developing Teamwork Skills

Ann Livermore, head of Hewlett-Packard's storage and servers, software and services businesses, has faced decisions at her company that might have sent some executives heading for the door. But despite deals that cut into her territory, she keeps her focus on the big picture, on the challenges at hand, and on new opportunities for growth. It's all part of knowing that "business is a team sport," she says.

That sentiment isn't common among business leaders these days. Many senior executives are more focused on their individual well-being than on furthering their company goals. They're quick to jump to new employers when they don't feel appreciated.

Some outside HP had speculated that Livermore was unhappy about relinquishing part of her portfolio after the company announced plans to acquire Electronic Data Systems, an

Kzenon/Fotolia

LEARNING Objectives

After reading and studying this chapter and doing the exercises, you should be able to

1. Explain the difference between a traditional team and a virtual team.
2. Explain the strengths and weaknesses of teams.
3. Identify various team member roles.
4. Apply people-related tactics for effective team play.
5. Apply task-related tactics for effective team play.
6. Apply interpersonal skills to become an effective team leader.

IT outsourcing company. She says she's staying put. "This isn't about me," she said in an interview. "It's about what is best for HP. It makes sense to combine all outsourcing businesses—and with a merger this big for EDS to report directly to Mark [Mark Hurd, former CEO of HP]."[1]

The attitude of the executive just described illustrates a spirit of teamwork that can help a company prosper. The modern organization depends on teamwork throughout the company. Many firms rely more on teamwork than on individuals acting alone to accomplish work. To be successful in the modern organization, it is therefore necessary to be an effective team player. You have to work smoothly with other members of the team to accomplish your goals. Teamwork is more important as people work their way up through the organization. Executives, such as CEOs, preach teamwork but tend to dominate meetings and make more decisions by themselves.[2] (Ann Livermore might be an exception.)

The challenges a team member faces come to light when the true nature of a team is recognized. Two experts on the subject define a **team** as "a small number of people with complementary skills who are committed to a common purpose, set of performance goals, and approach for which they hold themselves mutually accountable."[3] In other words, members of a team work together smoothly and all pull in the same direction. A workplace team should be more like an effective athletic team than a group of people out for individual glory.

This chapter provides the information, insights, and preliminary practice necessary to develop effective teamwork skills, including those that make will make you a more effective team leader. Self-Assessment Quiz 6-1 will help you assess your current mental readiness to be a contributing team member.

team
A small number of people with complementary skills who are committed to a common purpose, set of performance goals, and approach for which they hold themselves mutually accountable.

FACE-TO-FACE VERSUS VIRTUAL TEAMS

All teams in the workplace have the common element of people working together cooperatively and possessing a mix of skills. No matter what label the team carries, its broad purpose is to contribute to a *collaborative workplace* in which people help each other achieve constructive goals. The idea is for workers to collaborate (a high level of cooperation) rather than to compete with or prevent others from getting their work done.

As teams have become more common in the workplace, effort has been directed toward specifying the skills and knowledge a person needs to function effectively on a team. Self-Assessment Quiz 6-2 presents a representative listing of team skills as perceived by employers.

LEARNING OBJECTIVE 1

DEVELOPING TEAMWORK SKILLS

> ### SELF-ASSESSMENT QUIZ 6-1
>
> #### Team Player Attitudes
>
> **Directions:** Describe how well you agree with each of the following statements, using the following scale: Disagree Strongly (DS); Disagree (D); Neutral (N); Agree (A); Agree Strongly (AS).
>
> | | | DS | D | N | A | AS |
> |----|--|----|---|---|---|----|
> | 1. | I am at my best when working alone. | 5 | 4 | 3 | 2 | (1)|
> | 2. | I have belonged to clubs and teams ever since I was a child. | (1)| 2 | 3 | 4 | 5 |
> | 3. | It takes far too long to get work accomplished within a group. | 5 | 4 | 3 | (2)| 1 |
> | 4. | I like the friendship of working in a group. | 1 | 2 | (3)| 4 | 5 |
> | 5. | I would prefer to run a one-person business than to be a member of a large firm. | 5 | 4 | 3 | 2 | (1)|
> | 6. | It's difficult to trust others in the group on key assignments. | 5 | 4 | 3 | (2)| 1 |
> | 7. | Encouraging others comes to me naturally. | 1 | (2)| 3 | 4 | 5 |
> | 8. | I like the give-and-take of ideas that is possible in a group. | 1 | (2)| 3 | 4 | 5 |
> | 9. | It is fun for me to share responsibility with other group members. | 1 | (2)| 3 | 4 | 5 |
> | 10.| Much more can be accomplished by a team than by the same number of people working alone. | 1 | (2)| 3 | 4 | 5 |
>
> **Total Score** 18
>
> **Scoring and Interpretation:** Add the numbers you circled to obtain your total score.
>
> **41–50** You have strong positive attitudes toward being a team member and working cooperatively with other members.
>
> **30–40** You have moderately favourable attitudes toward being a team member and working cooperatively with other members.
>
> **(10–29)** You much prefer working by yourself to being a team member. To work effectively in a company that emphasizes teamwork, you may need to develop more positive attitudes toward working jointly with others.

Although many different types of teams exist, a useful distinction is between the traditional teams, in which workers share the same physical space, and virtual teams, whereby the team members rarely see each other in person.

Face-to-Face (Traditional) Teams

The best-known workplace team is a group of workers who take some of the responsibility for managing their own work. Face-to-face teams are used in a wide variety of activities, including producing motorcycles, printing telephone directories, manufacturing a major component for a large computer, or launching a new product. Team members interact with other frequently rather than doing their work in isolation from one another.

Members of a traditional team typically work together on an ongoing, day-to-day basis, thus differentiating it from a task force or a committee. The team is often given total responsibility for or "ownership" of an entire product or service, such as producing a telephone directory. At other times, the team is given responsibility for a major chunk of a job, such as building an airplane engine (but not the entire airplane).

A major hurdle in forming a true team is to help employees overcome the attitude reflected in the statement "I'm not paid to think." Teams often rely less on supervisors and more on the workers assuming more responsibilities for managing their own activities.

As with all teams, mutual trust among members contributes to team effectiveness. A study conducted with business students, however, showed that if the members trust each other too much, they may not monitor (check up on) each other's work enough. As a result, group performance will suffer. This problem of too much trust surfaces primarily when the team members have individual assignments that do not bring them into frequent contact with each other.[4] An example of an individual, or autonomous, project would be preparing a statistical report that would later be given to the group.

SELF-ASSESSMENT QUIZ 6-2

Team Skills

A variety of skills are required to be an effective member of various types of teams. Several different business firms use the skill inventory below to help guide employees toward the competencies they need to become high-performing team members. Review each team skill listed and rate your skill level for each, using the following classification:

S = strong (capable and comfortable with effectively implementing the skill)
M = moderate (demonstrated skill in the past)
B = basic (minimal ability in this area)
N = not applicable (not relevant to the type of work I do)

Communication Skills	Skill Level (S, M, B, or N)
Speak effectively	_____
Foster open communications	_____
Listen to others	_____
Deliver presentations	_____
Prepare written communication	_____
Self-Management Skills	
Act with integrity	_____
Demonstrate adaptability	_____
Engage in personal development	_____
Strive for results	_____
Display a commitment to work	_____
Thought-Process Skills	
Find innovative solutions to problems	_____
Use sound judgment	_____
Analyze issues	_____
Think "outside the box"	_____
Organizational Skills	
Know the business	_____
Use technical/functional expertise	_____
Use financial/quantitative data	_____
Strategic (Broad Business Perspective) Skills	
Recognize "big picture" impact	_____
Promote corporate citizenship	_____
Focus on customer needs	_____
Commit to quality	_____
Manage profitability	_____

Interpretation: We do not provide a scoring key for this questionnaire. Its purpose is simply to raise your awareness of the types of skills that are required to be a successful team member in business.

Virtual Teams

Some teams conduct most of their work by sending electronic messages to each other rather than conducting face-to-face meetings. A **virtual team** is a small group of people who conduct almost all of their collaborative work by electronic communication rather than by face-to-face meetings. Email, including IM (instant messaging), is the usual medium for sharing information and conducting meetings. *Groupware* and other screen-sharing software is another widely used approach to conducting an electronic meeting. Using groupware, several people can edit a document at the same time or in sequence. Desktop videoconferencing, such as using a webcam or Skype, is another technological advance that facilitates the virtual team.

virtual team
A small group of people that conducts almost all of its collaborative work by electronic communication rather than face-to-face meetings.

DEVELOPING TEAMWORK SKILLS

Many organizations make some use of virtual teams and electronic meetings. Strategic alliances in which geographically dispersed companies work with each other are ideally suited for virtual teams. It is less expensive for the field technician in Iceland to hold an electronic meeting with her counterparts in the United States, Africa, Mexico, and California than it is to bring them all together in one physical location. Virtual teams are sometimes the answer to the challenge of hiring workers with essential skills who do not want to relocate. Because the members of a virtual team might be working in different countries, they are often considered to be multicultural teams.

With team members geographically dispersed, precise communications are all the more important for virtual teams. The virtual team members usually need a formal document outlining the objectives, job responsibilities, and team goals. Another communication problem takes place when the virtual team is composed of both in-house workers and those in remote locations. The office-bound members become jealous of the seemingly cushy setup enjoyed by the telecommuters. One solution to this problem is for every member of the team to be given a chance to prove that he or she can work off-site.[5] Another consideration is that the work should be distributed fairly among office-bound workers and virtual team members. Last-minute assignments are often handed to the first in-house worker the manager sees.[6]

Establishing trust is a major challenge in a virtual team because the team members have to rely on people they never see to carry out their fair share of the workload, and to exchange reliable information. Trust is also needed in terms of what information should be shared outside of the team. For example, if the team is behind schedule on a project, can each member be trusted not to inform outsiders about the problem? One virtual team had an external communication norm that prohibited team members from conveying negative information to anyone outside the team.[7]

Despite the efficiency of virtual teams, there are times when face-to-face (or at least telephone) interaction is necessary to deal with complex and emotional issues. Negotiating a new contract between management and a labour union, for example, is not well suited to an electronic meeting.

ADVANTAGES AND DISADVANTAGES OF TEAMS AND TEAMWORK

LEARNING OBJECTIVE 2

Groups have always been the building blocks of organizations. Yet groups and teams have recently grown in importance as the basic unit for organizing work. In an attempt to cope with numerous changes in the outside world, many organizations have granted teams increased independence and flexibility. The increased acceptance of teams suggests that group work offers many advantages. Nevertheless, it is useful to specify several of these advantages and also examine the potential problems of groups. Being aware of these potential pitfalls can often help a person avoid them. These same advantages and disadvantages also apply to group decision-making, described in Chapter 7.

Ambrophoto/Fotolia

Advantages of Group Work and Teamwork

Group work and group decision making offer several advantages over individual effort. Because so much of what is accomplished in organizations is done by groups, it may appear that groups and teams have many advantages. However, the importance of this topic warrants mentioning a few of the advantages of groups, teams, and group decision making.

Synergy. If several knowledgeable people are brought into the decision-making process, a number of worthwhile possibilities may be uncovered. It is also possible to gain synergy, whereby the group's total output exceeds the sum of each individual's contribution. For example, it would be rare for

112 CHAPTER 6

person working alone to build a complete racing car. Groups and teams are the building block of the larger organization.

Work Accomplishment and High Productivity. Without groups, including teams, an organization could not get its work accomplished. Clarence Otis, Jr., the CEO of Darden Restaurants (which includes Olive Garden, Red Lobster, and Bahama Breeze), says that the thrust of his leadership is to build the team because the team accomplishes so much of the work.[8]

A major justification for relying on teams in the workplace is that under the right circumstances, they can enhance productivity and profitability. The right circumstances include an atmosphere that promotes teamwork. A classic example is the Canadian company Bombardier, which grew in spite of recessions. CEO Pierre Beaudoin attributes this financial success to its organizational culture, including its focus on values, goal setting, and strong teamwork. Beaudoin believes in teams and team goal setting to attain higher organizational goals and has moved the company from one of fragmentation to one of team productivity.[9]

A broad perspective about the advantages of groups is that because of groups and teams, large organizations can be built that provide useful goods and services to the world. For example, a company such as Apple, Inc., or Johnson & Johnson, is only possible because of group effort. Furthermore, the existence of large organizations, including business firms, colleges, universities, and hospitals, helps advance civilization.

Acceptance and Commitment. Group decision making is also helpful in gaining acceptance and commitment. The argument is that people who contribute to making a decision will feel some ownership about implementing the decision. Under these conditions, it becomes more difficult to object to a decision because your contribution was included in the decision. At times, managers will deliberately ask for input into a decision they have already made as a manipulative way of gaining acceptance for and commitment to the decision.

Avoidance of Major Errors. Team members often evaluate each other's thinking, so the team is likely to avoid major errors. An advertising specialist was developing an advertising campaign to attract seniors to live in a retirement community. The proposed ads had photographs of senior citizens engaged in playing shuffleboard, visiting the pharmacy, and sleeping in a hammock. Another team member on the project pointed out that many seniors perceive themselves to be energetic and youthful. Ads emphasizing advanced age might therefore backfire. A successful advertising campaign was then developed that featured seniors in more youthful activities, such as jogging and dancing.

Increased Job Satisfaction. Working in teams and groups also enhances the job satisfaction of members. Being a member of a work group makes it possible to satisfy more needs than working alone. Among these needs are affiliation, security, self-esteem, and self-fulfillment. (Chapter 11 provides more details about psychological needs.)

A major reason that groups and teams contribute to worker satisfaction is that many people find working in groups to be a natural way of life. In school, sports, and the community, they have been accustomed to working collaboratively and therefore feel more comfortable in group than in individual effort.

Disadvantages of Group Work and Teamwork

Group activity has some potential disadvantages for both individuals and the organization, as described in the following paragraphs. Some of these disadvantages serve as alerts for preventing problems.

Time Wasting. Teams and other groups often waste time because they talk too much and act too little. Teams that have been together for a length of time, for example, may spend part of their meeting time in personal conversation rather than work tasks. At times, committees appear to also suffer from inaction. Abigail Johnson, president of Fidelity Employer Services Division, says that committees are not effective decision makers. "They have tended to be slow and overly risk averse. Even worse, I believe, they can drain an organization of talent, because the group can only be as good as the average."[10]

Pressures toward Conformity.
A major problem is that members face pressures to conform to group standards of performance and conduct, as just implied. Some teams might shun a person who is much more productive than his or her co-workers. Also, to be liked by co-workers, as well as to avoid conflict, a group member will sometimes agree with the opinion of other group or team members even when the member does not agree with the thoughts or ideas of the team.

Conformity in dress and appearance is also apparent in many work groups. You might want to examine a photo of Google, Microsoft, or Apple employees and observe how much conformity in dress you find. Conformity in dress, however, is not much of a disadvantage except when a group member is dissatisfied because of the pressure to dress in the same manner as co-workers.

Self-Assessment Quiz 6-3 gives you an opportunity to think about your tendencies toward conformity.

Shirking of Individual Responsibility (Social Loafing).
Shirking of individual responsibility is another problem frequently noted in groups. Unless work is assigned carefully to each team member, an undermotivated person can often squeeze by without contributing his or her fair share to a group effort. **Social loafing** is the psychological term for shirking individual responsibility in a group setting. The social loafer risks being ostracized (shunned) by the group but may be willing to pay the price rather than work hard. Loafing of this type is sometimes found in groups such as committees and project teams. Have you ever encountered a social loafer on a group project at school?

social loafing
Shirking individual responsibility in a group setting.

Fostering of Conflict.
At their worst, teams and other groups foster conflict on the job. People within the work group often bicker about such matters as doing a fair share of the undesirable tasks within the department. Cohesive work groups can also become xenophobic (fearful of outsiders). As a consequence, they may grow to dislike other groups and enter into conflict with them. A customer service group might put considerable effort into showing up a sales group because the latter makes promises to customers that the customer service group cannot keep. For example, a sales representative might promise that a customer can get a loaner if his or her equipment needs repair, although customer service has no such policy.

Groupthink.
A well-publicized disadvantage of group decision making is **groupthink**, a deterioration of mental efficiency, reality testing, and moral judgment in the interests of group solidarity. Simply put, groupthink is an extreme form of consensus. The group atmosphere values getting along more than getting things done. The group thinks as a unit, believes it is impervious to outside criticism, and begins to have illusions about its own invincibility. As a consequence, the group loses its powers of critical analysis.[11] Groupthink appears to have contributed to several of the major financial scandals of the previous decade. Members of top management got together to vote themselves huge bonuses just before filing bankruptcy for their company. Several of the executives, including a few from Enron Corporation, were later sent to prison for their outrageous decisions.

groupthink
A deterioration of mental efficiency, reality testing, and moral judgment in the interests of group solidarity.

Two conditions are important for overcoming the potential disadvantages of teams and groups.[12] First, the members must strive to act like a team following some of the suggestions given in the upcoming pages. Second, the task given to the group should require collective effort instead of being a task that could better be performed by individuals. For example, an international business specialist would probably learn to conjugate verbs in a foreign language better by working alone than on a team. What is your opinion on this issue? Figure 6-1 presents more information about key factors associated with effective work teams and groups. The more of these factors that are present, the more likely it is that a given team or group will be productive.

SELF-ASSESSMENT QUIZ 6-3

The Conformity Quiz

Directions: Circle the extent to which each of the following statements describes your behaviour or attitude: Agree Strongly (AS); Agree (A); Neutral (N); Disagree (D); Disagree Strongly (DS). You may have to respond in terms of any team or group experience you have had if you are not currently a member of a work team, a class project team, or a sports team. Consider that having someone who is familiar with your behaviour and attitudes helps you respond accurately.

		AS	A	N	D	DS
1.	I rarely question the decision reached by the team.	5	4	③	2	1
2.	Whatever the group wants is fine with me.	⑤	4	3	2	①
3.	My clothing distinguishes me from the other members of the team.	①	2	3	4	5
4.	I consider myself to be one of the gang.	5	4	3	②	1
5.	I rarely express disagreement during a group discussion.	5	④	3	2	1
6.	I routinely have lunch with other members of the team.	⑤	4	③	2	1
7.	My teammates sometimes complain that I think too independently.	1	②	3	4	5
8.	My preference is to piggyback on the ideas of others rather than contributing the ideas of my own.	5	4	③	2	1
9.	When I notice that the other members of the team make the same error in speech, I will copy them rather than sound different.	5	4	3	②	1
10.	I am often the first person to get up at the scheduled ending of the meeting.	1	2	③	4	5
11.	I do almost all of my creative thinking for the team task when I'm with the team.	5	4	3	②	1
12.	I'm particularly careful not to criticize an idea submitted by the team leader.	5	4	3	②	1
13.	The number of hours I work per week corresponds closely to the number worked by my teammates.	5	④	3	②	1
14.	When I think it is necessary, I bring information to the group conflicting with the path we are following.	1	②	3	4	5
15.	I would rather keep my mouth closed than point out weaknesses in a teammate's ideas.	5	4	3	②	1
16.	I've been called a maverick on more than one occasion by teammates.	1	②	3	4	5
17.	I encourage team members to express doubts about proposed solutions to problems.	1	②	③	4	5
18.	I invite criticism of my ideas.	1	②	3	4	5
19.	When the team laughs at a comment, I laugh too even if I don't think the comment was funny.	5	4	3	2	①
20.	Most of my social life centres on activities with my teammates.	5	4	3	2	①

Interpretation: Calculate your score by adding the numbers you have circled, and use the following guide:

80–100 You are a high-conforming individual who readily goes along with the team without preserving your individuality. In an effort to be liked, you might be overcompromising your thinking.

40–79 You have probably achieved the right balance between following group norms (standards of conduct) and expressing your individuality. With actions and attitudes like this, you are on your way to becoming a good team player, yet also in a position to attain individual recognition.

20–29 You are highly individualistic, perhaps to the point of not working smoothly in a team setting. Be careful that you are not going out of your way to becoming a nonconformist, thereby interfering with your ability to be an effective team player.

Skill Development: Examine your responses to the 20 questions, because the response might give you a clue to needed development—often just by making a subtle change within your control. Here are two examples: If you answered Agree Strongly or Agree to question 8, you might work toward contributing ideas of your own. If you answered Disagree or Disagree Strongly to question 14, you might work toward helping the team think more critically about the path it is following.

DEVELOPING TEAMWORK SKILLS

FIGURE 6-1 Key Characteristics of Effective Teams and Work Groups

- The group has collective efficacy, or a belief that it can handle the assigned task.
- The team has clear-cut goals linked to organizational goals so that group members feel connected to the entire organization. However, the group does not have so many goals that confusion results. Goals include having a mission that helps explain what the group is attempting to accomplish.
- Group members are empowered so that they learn to think for themselves rather than expecting a supervisor to solve all the difficult problems. At the same time, the group believes it has the authority to solve a variety of problems without first obtaining approval from management.
- Group members are assigned work they perceive to be challenging, exciting, and rewarding. As a consequence, the work is self-rewarding.
- Members depend on one another to accomplish tasks, and work toward a common goal. At the same time, the group believes in itself and that it can accomplish an independent task.
- Diversity exists within the group, including differences in education, experience, and cultural background. Different backgrounds lead to more creative problem solving. Also, the differences prompt more discussion and analysis. (Your Golden Personality Type can be used to assign diverse members to a team.)
- Members receive extensive training in technical knowledge, problem-solving skills, and interpersonal skills.
- Members receive part of their pay related to team or group incentives rather than strictly based on individual performance.
- Group size is generally about 6 people, rather than 10 or more.
- Team members have good intelligence and personality factors, such as conscientiousness and pride, that contribute to good performance.
- There is honest and open communication among group members and with other groups in the organization.
- Members have the philosophy of working as a team—6 brains, not just 12 hands.
- Members are familiar with their jobs, co-workers, and the work environment. This experience adds to their expertise. The beneficial effects of experience may diminish after a while because the team needs fresh ideas and approaches.
- The team has emotional intelligence in the sense that it builds relationships both inside and outside the team. Included in emotional intelligence are norms that establish mutual trust among members, a feeling of group identity, and group efficacy.
- Stronger-performing group members assist weaker-performing group members to accomplish their task, particularly when the performance of the "weakest link" in the group is key for group performance.

Sources: Alexander D. Stajkovic, Dongseop Lee, and Anthony J. Nyberg, "Collective Efficacy, Group Potency, and Group Performance: Meta-analysis of Their Relationships, and Test of a Mediation Model," *Journal of Applied Psychology*, May 2009, p. 815; Stanley M. Gulley, Kara A. Incalcaterra, Aparna Joshi, and J. Matthew Beaublien, "A Meta-analysis of Team Efficacy, Potency, and Performance: Interdependence and Level of Analysis as Moderators of Observed Relationships," *Journal of Applied Psychology*, October 2002, pp. 819–832; Stephen R. Covey, "Secrets behind Great Teams," *USA Weekend*, July 11–13, 2008, p. 7; Katherine W. Phillips, Katie A. Liljenquist, and Margaret A. Neale, "Is the Pain Work the Gain? The Advantages and Liabilities of Agreeing with Socially Distinct Newcomers," *Personality and Social Psychology Bulletin*, March 2009, pp. 336–350; Shawn L. Berman, Vanessa Urch Druskat, and Steven B. Wolff, "Building the Emotional Intelligence of Groups," *Harvard Business Review*, March 2001, pp. 80–90; Claus W. Langred, "Too Much of a Good Thing? Negative Effects of High Trust and Individual Autonomy in Self-Managing Work Teams," *Academy of Management Journal*, June 2004, pp. 385–389; Bernhard Weber and Guido Hertel, "Motivation Gains of Inferior Group Members: A Meta-analytical Review," *Journal of Personality and Social Psychology*, No. 6, 2007, pp. 973–993.

TEAM MEMBER ROLES

A major challenge in learning to become an effective team member is to choose the right roles to occupy. A **role** is a tendency to behave, contribute, and relate to others in a particular way. If you successfully carry out positive roles, you will be perceived as a contributor to team effort. If you do not, you will be perceived as a poor contributor. Brian Waterman, a community recreation coordinator for Toronto Parks and Recreation, often leads team-building workshops to help his staff develop a strong team spirit. According to Waterman, "A good team player is an attentive listener, has creative abilities, shows initiative and is willing to help others." These are just a few of the effective roles that team members must learn to play in order to be effective.[13] In this section we describe a number of the most frequently observed positive roles played by team members. This is followed by an activity in which the roles can be practised.

Self-Assessment Quiz 6-4 will help you evaluate your present inclinations toward occupying effective roles as a team member. Also refer to your Golden Personality Type profile to examine your behaviours and preferences on a team.

According to the role theory developed by R. Meredith Belbin and his group of researchers, there are nine frequent roles occupied by team members. All of these roles are influenced to some extent by an individual's personality.[14]

LEARNING OBJECTIVE 3

role
A tendency to behave, contribute, and relate to others in a particular way.

1. **Creative problem solver.** The creative problem solver is imaginative and unorthodox. Such a person solves difficult problems. A potential weakness of this role is that the person tends to ignore fine details and becomes too immersed in the problem to communicate effectively.

2. **Resource investigator.** The resource investigator is extroverted, enthusiastic, and communicates freely with other team members. He or she will explore opportunities and develop valuable contacts. A potential weakness of this role is that the person can be overly optimistic and may lose interest after the initial enthusiasm wanes.

3. **Coordinator.** The coordinator is mature, confident, and a natural team leader. He or she clarifies goals, promotes decision making, and delegates effectively. A downside to occupying this role is that the person might be seen as manipulative and controlling. Some coordinators delegate too much by asking others to do some of the work they (the coordinators) should be doing.

4. **Shaper.** The shaper is challenging, dynamic, and thrives under pressure. He or she will use determination and courage to overcome obstacles. A potential weakness of the shaper is that he or she can be easily provoked and may ignore the feelings of others.

5. **Monitor-evaluator.** The monitor-evaluator is even-tempered, engages in strategic (big-picture and long-term) thinking, and makes accurate judgments. He or she sees all the options and judges accurately. A potential weakness of this role occupant is that he or she might lack drive and the ability to inspire others.

6. **Team worker.** The team worker is cooperative, focuses on relationships, and is sensitive and diplomatic. He or she is a good listener who builds relationships, dislikes confrontation, and averts friction. A potential weakness is that the team worker can be indecisive in a crunch situation or crisis.

7. **Implementer.** The implementer is disciplined, reliable, conservative, and efficient. He or she will act quickly on ideas, and convert them into practical actions. A potential weakness is that the implementer can be inflexible and slow to see new opportunities.

8. **Completer-finisher.** The completer-finisher is conscientious and eager to get the job done. He or she has a good eye for detail, and is effective at searching out errors. He or she can be counted on for finishing a project and delivering on time. A potential weakness is that the completer-finisher can be a worrier and reluctant to delegate.

9. **Specialist.** The specialist is a single-minded self-starter. He or she is dedicated and provides knowledge and skill in rare supply. A potential weakness of the specialist is that he or she can be stuck in a niche with little interest in other knowledge and may dwell on technicalities.

Practice
Team Player Roles

SELF-ASSESSMENT QUIZ 6-4

Team Player Roles

Directions: For each of the following statements about team activity, check "Mostly Agree" or "Mostly Disagree." If you have not experienced such a situation, imagine how you would act or think if placed in that situation. In responding to the statements, assume that you are filling out the questionnaire with the intent of learning something about yourself.

		Mostly Agree	Mostly Disagree
1.	It is rare that I ever miss a team meeting.	_____	_____
2.	I regularly compliment team members when they do something exceptional.	_____	_____
3.	Whenever I can, I avoid being the note-taker at a team meeting.	_____	_____
4.	From time to time, other team members come to me for advice on technical matters.	_____	_____
5.	I like to hide some information from other team members so I can be in control.	_____	_____
6.	I welcome new team members who come to me for advice and to learn the ropes.	_____	_____
7.	My priorities come first, leaving me with very little time to help other team members.	_____	_____
8.	During a team meeting, it is not unusual for several people at a time to look to me for my opinion.	_____	_____
9.	If I think the team is moving in an unethical direction, I will say so explicitly.	_____	_____
10.	Rarely will I criticize the progress of the team, even if I think such criticism is deserved.	_____	_____
11.	It is not unusual for me to summarize the progress of the team in a team meeting, even if not asked.	_____	_____
12.	To conserve time, I attempt to minimize contact with my teammates outside our meetings.	_____	_____
13.	I intensely dislike going along with a consensus decision if the decision runs contrary to my thoughts on the issue.	_____	_____
14.	I rarely remind teammates of our mission statement as we go about our work.	_____	_____
15.	Once I have made up my mind on an issue facing the team, I am unlikely to be persuaded in another direction.	_____	_____
16.	I am willing to accept negative feedback from team members.	_____	_____
17.	Just to get a new member of the team involved, I will ask his or her opinion.	_____	_____
18.	Even if the team has decided on a course of action, I am not hesitant to bring in new information that supports another position.	_____	_____
19.	Quite often I talk negatively about one team member to another.	_____	_____
20.	My teammates are almost a family to me because I am truly concerned about their welfare.	_____	_____
21.	When it seems appropriate, I joke and kid with teammates.	_____	_____
22.	My contribution to team tasks is as important to me as my individual work.	_____	_____
23.	From time to time I have pointed out to the team how we can all improve in reaching our goals.	_____	_____
24.	I will keep fighting to get my way even when the team does not support my viewpoint and wants to move toward consensus.	_____	_____
25.	I will confront the team if I believe that the members are thinking too much alike.	_____	_____

Total Score _____

Scoring and Interpretation: Give yourself one point (+1) for each time your responses agree with those given below.

Question Number	Positive Role Answer	Question Number	Positive Role Answer	Question Number	Positive Role Answer
1.	Mostly agree	10.	Mostly disagree	19.	Mostly disagree
2.	Mostly agree	11.	Mostly agree	20.	Mostly agree
3.	Mostly disagree	12.	Mostly disagree	21.	Mostly agree
4.	Mostly agree	13.	Mostly disagree	22.	Mostly agree
5.	Mostly disagree	14.	Mostly disagree	23.	Mostly agree
6.	Mostly agree	15.	Mostly disagree	24.	Mostly disagree
7.	Mostly disagree	16.	Mostly agree	25.	Mostly agree
8.	Mostly agree	17.	Mostly agree		
9.	Mostly agree	18.	Mostly agree		

20–25 You carry out a well-above-average number of positive team roles. Behaviour of this type contributes substantially to effective teamwork. Study the information in this chapter to build upon your already-laudable sensitivity in occupying various positive roles within the team.

10–19 You carry out an average number of positive team roles. Study carefully the roles described in this chapter to search for ways to carry out a greater number of positive roles.

0–9 You carry out a substantially below-average number of positive team roles. If becoming an effective team player is important to you, you will need to assiduously search for ways to play positive team roles. Study the information in this chapter carefully.

The weaknesses in the first nine roles point to problems the team leader or manager can expect to emerge, and therefore an allowance should be made. Belbin refers to these potential problems as *allowable weaknesses* because an allowance should be made for them. To illustrate, if a team worker has a tendency to be indecisive in a crisis, the team should not have high expectations of the team worker when faced with a crisis. Team workers will be the most satisfied if the crisis is predicted and decisions involving them are made before the pressure mounts.[15]

Another perspective on team roles is that team members will sometimes engage in *self-oriented roles*. Members will sometimes focus on their own needs rather than those of the group. The individual might be overly aggressive because of a personal need such as wanting a bigger budget for his or her project. The individual might hunger for recognition or power. Similarly, the person might attempt to dominate the meeting, block others from contributing, or serve as a distraction. One of the ploys used by distracters recently is to engage in cellphone conversations during a meeting, blaming it on "those people who keep calling me."

The many roles just presented overlap somewhat. For example, the implementer might engage in specialist activities. Do not be concerned about the overlap. Instead, pick and choose from the many roles as the situation dictates—whether or not overlap exists. Skill-Building Exercise 6-1 gives you an opportunity to observe these roles in action. The behaviour associated with the roles just described is more important than remembering the labels. For example, remembering to be creative and imaginative is more important than remembering the specific label *creative problem solver*.

GUIDELINES FOR THE INTERPERSONAL ASPECTS OF TEAM PLAY

The purpose of this and the following section is to help you increase your effectiveness as a team player by describing the necessary skills, actions, and attitudes. You can regard these *behaviours* (the collective term for skills, actions, and attitudes) as goals for personal

LEARNING OBJECTIVE 4

SKILL-BUILDING EXERCISE 6-1

Team Member Roles

A team of approximately six people is formed to conduct a 20-minute meeting on a significant topic of their choosing. The possible scenarios follow:

Scenario A: Management Team. A group of managers are pondering whether to lay off one-third of the workforce in order to increase profits. The company has had a tradition of caring for employees and regarding them as the company's most precious asset. However, the CEO has said privately that times have changed in our competitive world, and the company must do whatever possible to enhance profits. The group wants to think through the advisability of laying off one-third of the workforce, as well as explore other alternatives.

Scenario B: Group of Sports Fans. A group of fans have volunteered to find a new team name to replace "Redskins" for the local baseball team. One person among the group of volunteers believes that the name "Redskins" should be retained because it is a compliment, rather than an insult, to Native Canadians. The other members of the group believe that a name change is in order, but they lack any good ideas for replacing a team name that has endured for over 40 years.

Scenario C: Community Group. A community group is attempting to launch an initiative to help battered adults and children. Opinions differ strongly as to what initiative would be truly helpful to battered adults and children. Among the alternatives are establishing a shelter for battered people, giving workshops on preventing violence, and providing self-defence training. Each group member with an idea strongly believes that he or she has come up with a workable possibility for helping with the problem of battered people.

While the team members are conducting their heated discussion, other class members make notes on which team members carry out which roles. Students should watch for the different roles as developed by Belbin and his associates, as well as the self-oriented roles. For example, students in the first row might look for examples of the plant. Use the role worksheet that follows to help make your observations. Summarize the comment that is indicative of the role. An example would be noting in the shaper category: "Linda said naming the team the 'Canadian Rainbows' seems like too much of an attempt to be politically correct."

Creative Problem Solver: _____
_____
_____

Resource Investigator: _____
_____

Coordinator: _____
_____

Shaper: _____
_____

Monitor-Evaluator: _____
_____

Team Worker: _____
_____

Implementer: _____
_____

Completer-Finisher: _____
_____

Specialist: _____
_____

Self-Oriented Roles: _____
_____
_____

Understanding team member roles will contribute to working effectively as a member of a team. However, two key contributors to effective team play are recognizing individual differences and having good communication skills. The same two factors are fundamental for effectiveness in any setting involving interaction between and among people. Here is an example of how recognizing individual differences and having effective communication skills can help in a team setting: Max and Beth are teammates, and Max notices that Beth is shy and somewhat sullen. (He observes individual differences.) Max gives Beth a playful fist in the air, and says, "Come on Beth, we need your contribution in the 10 o'clock meeting. You have one of the sharpest minds on the team, and you're hiding it from us." With such warm encouragement, Beth then has the courage to contribute more to the morning meeting.

---

improvement. Identify the actions and attitudes for which you need the most improvement, and proceed accordingly with self-development. Apply the model for skill development presented in Chapter 1.

One convenient method of classifying team activities in pursuit of goals is to categorize them as people-related or task-related. Remember, however, that the categorization of people- versus task-related activities is not entirely accurate. For example, if you are challenging your teammates with a difficult goal, are you focusing more on the people (offering them a motivational challenge) or the task (achieving the goal)? We begin with people-related actions and attitudes (see also Figure 6-2), followed in the next section by task-related actions and attitudes.

FIGURE 6-2 Interpersonal Aspects of Team Play

> 1. Trust team members.
> 2. Display a high level of cooperation and collaboration.
> 3. Recognize the interests and achievements of others.
> 4. Give and receive helpful criticism.
> 5. Share the glory.
> 6. Take care not to rain on another person's parade.

BACK TO THE OPENING CASE

A key aspect of Ann Livermore being a good team player was to not care about experiencing a decrease in her power and authority because her company acquired a large outsourcing firm. She said that her main concern was the prosperity of her employer, HP. In crediting Livermore for her team spirit, recognize that Livermore already has had an outstanding career and was once a candidate to become CEO. She still has enough responsibility left to satisfy her needs for power and influence. A person still pursuing loftier positions might not have such a strong team spirit.

Trust Team Members

The cornerstone attitude of an outstanding team player is to trust team members, including the leader. Working on a team is akin to a small-business partnership. If you do not believe that the other team members have your best interests at heart, it will be difficult for you to share opinions and ideas. You will fear that others will make negative statements behind your back.

Trusting team members also includes believing that their ideas are technically sound and rational until proven otherwise. Another manifestation of trust is taking risks with other team members—for example, trying out one of their unproven ideas. You can also take a risk by submitting an unproven idea and not worrying about being ridiculed.

Display a High Level of Cooperation and Collaboration

Cooperation and collaboration are synonymous with teamwork. If you display a willingness to help others by working cooperatively with them, you will be regarded as a team player. If you do not cooperate with other team members, the team structure breaks down. Collaboration at the team level refers to working jointly with others to solve mutual problems. Although working with another person on a given problem may take longer than working through a problem yourself, the long-term payoff is important. You have established a climate favourable to working on joint problems where collective action is necessary.

Achieving a cooperative team spirit is often a question of making the first move. Instead of grumbling about poor teamwork, take the initiative and launch a cooperative spirit in your group. Target the most individualistic, least cooperative member of the group. Ask the person for his or her input on an idea you are formulating. Thank the person, then state that you would be privileged to return the favour.

Another way of attaining good cooperation is to minimize confrontations. If you disagree with the opinion of another team member, patiently explain the reasons for your differences and look for a workable way to integrate both your ideas. A teammate might suggest, for example, that the team stay until midnight to get a project completed today. You have plans for the evening and are angered by the suggestion. Instead of lashing out at your teammate, you might say, "I agree we need to put in

> ## SKILL-BUILDING EXERCISE 6-2
>
> ### The Scavenger Hunt
>
> The purpose of this teamwork exercise is to demonstrate the importance of cooperation and collaboration in accomplishing a task under pressure. The class is divided into teams of about five students. How much time you can devote to the task depends upon your particular class schedule. The instructor will supply each team with a list of items to find within a prescribed period of time—usually about 35 minutes. Given the time constraints, the group will usually have to conduct the hunt on campus. Following is a representative list of items to find in an on-campus scavenger hunt:
>
> - A piece of chalk
> - A cap from a beer bottle
> - A tie
> - A pop can
> - A brick
> - A flash drive
>
> When the groups return within 30 minutes, you hold a public discussion about what you learned about teamwork, and what insights you acquired.

extra time and effort to get the job done. But why can't we spread out this extra effort over a few days? In this way those of us who cannot work until midnight this evening can still contribute."

A side advantage of cooperation within the group is that the part of the brain associated with pleasure is activated when people cooperate. According to team building specialist Anna Maravelas, "It is intrinsically rewarding for human beings to pull together."[16]

Skill-Building Exercise 6-2 is a widely used technique for demonstrating the importance of cooperation and collaboration.

Recognize the Interests and Achievements of Others

A fundamental tactic for establishing yourself as a solid team player is to actively recognize the interests and achievements of others. Let others know you care about their interests. After you make a suggestion during a team meeting, ask, "Would my suggestion create any problems for anybody else?" or "How do my ideas fit into what you have planned?"

Recognizing the achievements of others is more straightforward than recognizing interests. Be prepared to compliment any tangible achievement, in a realistic way that is commensurate with the achievement; to do otherwise is to compromise your sincerity. For example, do not call someone a genius just because he or she showed you how to compute an exchange rate from one currency to another. Instead, you might say, "Thank you. I'm very impressed by your knowledge of exchange rates."

A technique has been developed to enable the entire team to recognize the interests and achievements of others. Playing the *anonymous praise* game, each team member lists what he or she admires about a specific co-worker. The team leader collects the responses and sends each team member the comments made about him or her. Using this technique, team members see a compilation of praise based on how co-workers perceive them. The anonymous praise game helps overcome the hesitancy some people have to praise another person face to face.[17]

Give and Receive Helpful Criticism

The outstanding team player offers constructive criticism when needed but does so diplomatically. To do otherwise is to let the team down. A high-performance team demands sincere and tactful criticism among members. No matter how diplomatic you are, keep your ratio of criticism to praise small. Keep two time-tested principles in mind. First, attempt to criticize the person's work, not the person. It is better to say, "The conclusion is missing from your analysis" than "You left out the conclusion." (The latter statement hurts because it sounds like your teammate did something wrong.)

Another key guideline for criticism is to ask a question rather than make a declarative statement. By answering a question, the person being criticized is involved in improving his or her work. In the above example, it would be effective to ask, "Do you think your report would have a greater impact if it contained a conclusion?" In this way, the person being criticized contributes a judgment about the conclusion. The person has a chance to say, "Yes, I will prepare a conclusion."

Criticism works both ways, so the effective team player is willing to accept helpful criticism, such as "You are speaking too fast for several of our team members for whom English is their second language." Such feedback assists the team member to be more sensitive and responsive to another team member.

Share the Glory

An effective team player shares praise and other rewards for accomplishment even if he or she is the most deserving. Shared praise is usually merited to some extent because teammates have probably made at least some contribution to the achievement that received praise. For example, if a team member comes up with a powerful suggestion for cutting costs, it is likely that somebody else in the group sparked his or her thinking. Effective examples of sharing glory are easy to find. Think back to watching athletes and other entertainers who win a title or an award. Many of them are gracious enough to share the glory. Shortly after he retired, hockey legend Wayne Gretzky told a television reporter, "I never would have accomplished what I did if I hadn't played with such a great group of people."

Take Care Not to Rain on Another Person's Parade

As teamwork specialist Pamela Lovel observes, we all have achievements and accomplishments that are sources of pride. Belittling the achievements of others for no legitimate reason provokes tension and anger. Suppress your feelings of petty jealousy.[18] An example would be saying to someone who is proudly describing an accomplishment, "Don't take too much credit. It looks to me like you were at the right place at the right time." If you support teammates by acknowledging their accomplishments, you are more likely to receive their support when you need it.

GUIDELINES FOR THE TASK ASPECTS OF TEAM PLAY

The task aspects of team play are also key to becoming an effective team player. Below we describe seven major task-related tactics (see Figure 6-3). As mentioned earlier, a task aspect usually has interpersonal consequences.

LEARNING OBJECTIVE 5

FIGURE 6-3 Task Aspects of Team Play

1. Provide technical expertise (or knowledge of the task).
2. Assume responsibility for problems.
3. See the big picture.
4. Believe in consensus.
5. Focus on deadlines.
6. Help team members do their jobs better.
7. Be a good organizational citizen.

DEVELOPING TEAMWORK SKILLS

Provide Technical Expertise (or Knowledge of the Task)

Most people are selected for a work team primarily because of their technical expertise. *Technical* refers to the intimate details of any task, not just tasks in engineering, physical science, and information technology. The sales promotion specialist on a product development team has technical expertise about sales promotion, whether or not sales promotion requires knowledge of engineering or computers.

As team consultant Glenn Parker observes, to use your technical expertise to outstanding advantage you must be willing to share it.[19] Some experts perceive their esoteric knowledge as a source of power. As a consequence, they hesitate to let others share their knowledge for fear of relinquishing power. Technical experts must communicate effectively with team members in other disciplines who lack the same technical background. Those who cannot explain the potential value of their contributions may not receive much attention.

Assume Responsibility for Problems

The outstanding team player assumes responsibility for problems. If the task of solving a problem has not been assigned, he or she says, "I'll do it." For instance, one team member might note that true progress on the team's effort is blocked until the team benchmarks (compares itself) with other successful teams. The effective team player might say, "You are right, we need to benchmark. If it's okay with everybody else, I'll get started on the benchmarking project tomorrow. It will be my responsibility." Taking responsibility must be combined with dependability. The person who takes responsibility for a task must produce, time after time.

Stephen Coburn/Fotolia

See the Big Picture

Effective team players need to think conceptually, or see the big picture. Discussion can get bogged down in small details in team effort, and the team might lose sight of what it is trying to accomplish. The team player (possibly the team leader) who can help the group focus on its broader purpose plays a vital role. The following case history illustrates what it means to see the big picture.

> *A group of retail sales associates and customer service representatives were sent to a one-day seminar about customer service training. The group was sent to training because customer service ratings at their store were below the level store executives thought was acceptable. During the lunch breaks, the conversation quickly turned to the fact that the coffee was not as hot as desired, the snacks were mediocre, the restrooms were too far from the meeting room, and the presenter had a phony smile and told goofy jokes. Next came a few complaints about a couple of the PowerPoint slides having too much detail.*
>
> *Alyssa, an experienced sales associate, stepped in with a comment. She noted, "I think all of you have valid complaints, but your points are minor. We are here to learn how to improve customer service. If we want our store to survive, and earn bigger bonuses, we have to learn what we can to help us do our jobs better. Whether or not you like our trainer's smile or jokes, he is trying to be helpful." The group returned after lunch with a more determined effort to focus on the purpose of the seminar—picking up ideas to improve customer service.*

Believe in Consensus

A major task-related attitude for outstanding team play is to believe that consensus has merit. Consensus is general acceptance of a decision by the group. Some members may not be thrilled about the decision, yet all of them are willing to support it. Believing that consensus is valuable enables you to participate fully in team decisions without thinking that you have sacrificed your beliefs or the right to think independently. To believe in consensus is to believe that the democratic process has relevance for organizations and that ideal solutions are not always possible.

Focus on Deadlines

A notable source of individual differences among work group members is how much importance they attach to deadlines. Some work group members may regard deadlines as moral contracts, to be broken only in emergencies. Others may view deadlines as arbitrary dates imposed by someone external to the group. Still others may perceive deadlines as moderately important. Differences in perception about the importance of deadlines influence the group's ability to meet deadlines.[20]

Keeping the group focused on deadlines is valuable task behaviour because meeting them is vital to team success. But on many teams, the existence of divergent attitudes toward deadlines makes discussing their importance all the more helpful.

Help Team Members Do Their Jobs Better

Your stature as a team player will increase if you take the initiative to help co-workers make needed work improvements. Helping other team members with their work assignments is a high-level form of cooperation. Make suggestions in a constructive spirit rather than displaying an air of superiority. Identify a problem that a co-worker is having, and then suggest alternatives he or she might be interested in exploring. Avoid saying to team members that they "should" do something, because many people become defensive when told what they should do. The term *should* is usually perceived as a moral judgment of one person by another, such as being told that you should save money, should learn a second language, or should improve your math skills.

Be a Good Organizational Citizen

A comprehensive way of carrying out the task aspects of team play (as well as relationship aspects) is to help out beyond the requirements of your job description. As discussed in Chapter 2, such extra-role activity is referred to as organizational citizenship behaviour—working for the good of the organization even without the promise of a specific reward. As a result of many workers being good organizational citizens, the organization functions more effectively in such ways as improved product quantity and quality.[21] Good citizenship on the job encompasses many specific behaviours, including helping a co-worker with a job task and refraining from complaints or petty grievances. A good organizational citizen would carry out such specific acts as picking up litter in the company parking lot. He or she would also bring a reference to the office that could help a co-worker solve a job problem. Most of the other team player tactics described here are related to organizational citizenship behaviour.

A recent synthesis of studies about the type of team processes described in this chapter supports the relevance of such actions by team members. (A team process is essentially an action taken by one or more team members.) A group of researchers examined the results of a variety of team member processes in 147 different samples of workers. The major conclusion reached was that teamwork processes are positively associated with both team member performance and satisfaction.[22] You can therefore have some assurance that if you engage in the activities described in this chapter, your efforts will help increase performance and satisfaction.

Skill-Building Exercise 6-3 will help you integrate the many suggestions presented here for developing teamwork skills.

SKILL-BUILDING EXERCISE 6-3

Habitat for the Homeless

Organize the class into teams of about six people. Each team takes on the assignment of formulating plans for building temporary shelters for the homeless. The task will take about one hour and can be done inside or outside the classroom. The dwellings you plan to build, for example, might be two-room cottages with electricity and indoor plumbing.

During the time allotted for the task, formulate plans for going ahead with Habitat for the Homeless. Consider dividing up work by assigning certain roles to each team member. Sketch out tentative answers to the following questions:

1. How will you obtain funding for your venture?
2. Which homeless people will you help?
3. Where will your shelters be located?
4. Who will do the actual construction?

After your plan is completed, evaluate the quality of the teamwork that took place within the group. Specify which teamwork skills were evident and which ones did not surface. Search the chapter for techniques you might use to improve teamwork. The skills used to accomplish the habitat task could relate to the team skills presented in Self-Assessment Quiz 6-2, the interpersonal aspects of team play, the task aspects of team play, or some team skill not mentioned in this chapter. Here is a sampling of the many different skills that might be relevant in this exercise:

- Speaks effectively
- Displays a high level of cooperation and collaboration
- Listens to others
- Provides knowledge of the task
- Innovates solutions to problems
- Sees the big picture
- Thinks outside the box
- Focuses on deadlines

DEVELOPING TEAM LEADERSHIP SKILLS

LEARNING OBJECTIVE 6

leadership
The ability to inspire support and confidence among the people who are needed to achieve common goals.

participative leadership
Sharing authority with the group.

As organizations continue to increase their use of teams, some of the best opportunities for practising leadership occur as a team leader. **Leadership** is the ability to inspire support and confidence among the people who are needed to achieve organizational goals. A team leader thus does this within a team and typically reports to a higher-level manager. The team leader is not a boss in the old-fashioned sense but a facilitator or coach who shares decision making with team members. (A facilitator is a person who helps make things happen without taking control.) A team leader practises **participative leadership,** or sharing authority with the group. Many of the interpersonal and task aspects of team play that have just been reviewed are applicable here; the major difference is the team leader uses these strategies as the team leader to facilitate excellent team work and achievement of organizational goals. Self-Assessment Quiz 6-5 gives you an opportunity to gauge your attitudes toward being a participative leader.

✓ Practice
What Style of Leader Are You or Would You Be?

SELF-ASSESSMENT QUIZ 6-5

What Style of Leader Are You or Would You Be?

Directions: Decide whether each of the following statements is "Mostly True" or "Mostly False."

		Mostly True	Mostly False
1.	I am more likely to take care of a high-impact assignment myself than turn it over to a group member.	_____	_____
2.	I would prefer the analytical aspects of a manager's job rather than working directly with group members.	_____	_____
3.	An important part of my approach to managing a group is to keep the members informed almost daily of any information that could affect their work.	_____	_____
4.	It's a good idea to give two people in the group the same problem and then choose what appears to be the best solution.	_____	_____

5. It makes good sense for the leader or manager to stay somewhat aloof from the group, so he or she can make a tough decision when necessary.

6. I look for opportunities to obtain group input before making a decision, even on straightforward issues.

7. I would reverse a decision if several of the group members presented evidence that I was wrong.

8. Differences of opinion in the work group are healthy.

9. I think that activities to build team spirit, like fixing up a poor family's house together on a Saturday, are an excellent investment of time.

10. If my group were hiring a new member, I would like the person to be interviewed by the entire group.

11. An effective team leader today uses email for about 98 percent of communication with team members.

12. Some of the best ideas are likely to come from the group members rather than the manager.

13. If our group were going to have a banquet, I would get input from each member on what type of food should be served.

14. I have never seen a statue of a committee in a museum or park, so why bother making decisions by a committee if you want to be recognized?

15. I dislike it intensely when a group member challenges my position on an issue.

16. I typically explain to group members what method they should use to accomplish an assigned task.

17. If I were out of the office for a week, most of the important work in the department would get accomplished anyway.

18. Delegation of important tasks is something that would be (or is) very difficult for me.

19. When a group member comes to me with a problem, I tend to jump right in with a proposed solution.

20. When a group member comes to me with a problem, I typically ask that person something like "What alternative solutions have you thought of so far?"

Scoring and Interpretation: The answers in the participative/team-style leader direction are as follows:

1. Mostly false
2. Mostly false
3. Mostly true
4. Mostly false
5. Mostly false
6. Mostly true
7. Mostly true
8. Mostly true
9. Mostly true
10. Mostly true
11. Mostly false
12. Mostly true
13. Mostly true
14. Mostly false
15. Mostly false
16. Mostly false
17. Mostly true
18. Mostly false
19. Mostly false
20. Mostly true

If your score is 15 or higher, you are most likely (or would be) a participative or team-style leader. If your score is 5 or lower, you are most likely (or would be) an authoritarian leader.

Skill Development: The quiz you just completed is also an opportunity for skill development. Review the 20 questions and look for implied suggestions for engaging in participative leadership. For example, question 20 suggests that you encourage group members to work through their own solutions to problems. If your goal is to become an authoritarian leader (one who makes decisions primarily on his or her own), the questions can also serve as useful guidelines. For example, question 19 suggests that an authoritarian leader looks first to solve problems for group members.

FIGURE 6-4 Developing Teamwork

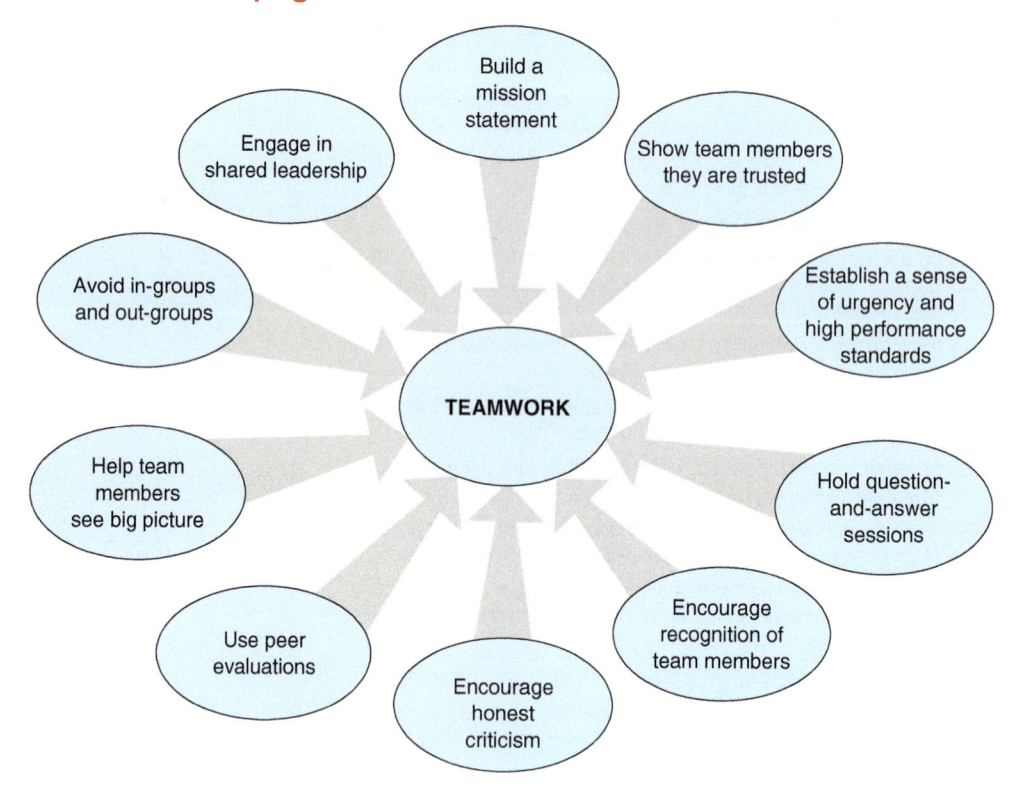

- Build a mission statement
- Show team members they are trusted
- Establish a sense of urgency and high performance standards
- Hold question-and-answer sessions
- Encourage recognition of team members
- Encourage honest criticism
- Use peer evaluations
- Help team members see big picture
- Avoid in-groups and out-groups
- Engage in shared leadership

→ TEAMWORK

On the pages that follow we describe the techniques that would contribute to your effectiveness as a team leader, as outlined in Figure 6-4. Note the similarities and overlap with the strategies to become an effective team player.

Engage in Shared Leadership

A major initiative for building teamwork is for the team leader to share, or distribute, leadership responsibilities among group members, depending on the task facing the group. So-called *collective leadership* is a reality of the modern workplace. Few leaders have enough skills to provide effective leadership in all situations.[23] The team leader might ask Ruby, who is skilled getting budget approvals, to take leadership of the budget project. Another time the team leader might ask Eric to take leadership on a project for recapturing lost customers because he is effective at damage control.

Research conducted by Craig L. Pearce and his associates at the Graduate School of Management at the University of California suggests that teams that perform poorly are often dominated by the team leader. In contrast, high-performing teams have a shared leadership structure. Part of the team's success can be attributed to the team spirit stemming from the shared leadership. If the organizational or national culture does not favour shared leadership, the good results might not be forthcoming.[24]

Build a Mission Statement

A starting point in developing teamwork is to specify the team's mission. The mission statement should contain a specific goal and purpose and should be optimistic and uplifting. Here is an example from a service team at a Volvo dealership:

> *To plan and implement a level of automobile service and repair of the highest quality, at a competitive price, that will delight customers and retain their loyalty.*

128   CHAPTER 6

SKILL-BUILDING EXERCISE 6-4

Developing a Team Mission Statement

The class organizes into teams of about six people and appoints a team leader. Each team plays the role of a specific team within a company, government agency, or hospital; an example would be the customer service team at a gas and electric company. The task is to develop a mission statement approximating the type described in the text. The team leader might also take notes for the group.

Remember that a mission statement contains a goal and a purpose and is uplifting and optimistic. It should also differentiate your team from other teams within the organization (class). Allow about 20 minutes for preparing the mission statements. The groups then compare mission statements. One representative from each group presents the mission statements to the rest of the class.

The leader can help develop the mission statement when the team is first formed or at any other time. Developing a mission statement for a long-standing team breathes new life into its activities. Being committed to a mission improves teamwork, as does the process of formulating a mission statement. A mission statement, however, needs to honestly represent the true goals and purpose of the team. An unrealistic mission statement that is not fully supported will do little for team morale or team development. Skill-Building Exercise 6-4 gives you practice in developing a mission statement for a team.

Show Your Team Members That They Are Trusted

An effective leader is perceived as honest and trustworthy, and he or she trusts team members (this is an interpersonal aspect of team play). The leader should recognize and reward ethical behaviour, particularly when there is a temptation to be dishonest—as when reporting a quality defect to a customer or preparing tax returns. Raise expectations of honesty by telling group members you are confident they will act in ways that bring credit to the organization.[25]

A practical way of demonstrating trust in group members is to avoid closely monitoring their work, and second-guessing their decisions about minor matters such as the best type of border for a report. A **micromanager** is one who closely monitors most aspects of group members' activities, sometimes to the point of being a "control freak." As a result, the group members do not feel that the leader or manager trusts them to make even the smallest decisions. One manager checked travel websites himself for the best deal after a team member booked plans for a business trip. As a result, team members felt that they were not trusted to care about the financial welfare of the company.

micromanager
One who closely monitors most aspects of group members' activities, sometimes to the point of being a "control freak."

Establish a Sense of Urgency and High Performance Standards

To build teamwork, members need to believe that the team has urgent, constructive purposes. A demanding performance challenge helps create and sustain the team. Team members also want to know exactly what is expected of them. The more urgent and relevant the rationale, the more likely it is that the team will perform well.[26] Based on this information, as a team leader you might project a sense of urgency and encourage setting high goals.

Hold Question-and-Answer Sessions with the Team

An effective way of demonstrating participative or team leadership is to hold question-and-answer sessions with team members. Both leader and members ask and answer questions, such as "How can we make an even bigger contribution to the company?" The Quality Department at Delta Dental Plan of California used question-and-answer sessions with success. The process not only boosted morale and made managers more accessible to employees, but also yielded more than 1000 employee suggestions in the first year. The department head said, "This program totally revolutionized the company.

Now employees from other divisions are eager to work in our department."[27] CEO Michael Stern of Michael Stern Associates, a Canadian executive search firm, states that listening is a critical skill for leaders. Not only encouraging the questions, but also listening carefully to the questions and answers, is an important skill for team leaders.[28]

Encourage Team Members to Recognize Each Other's Accomplishments

Members of a high-spirited team look for ways to encourage and praise each other, including the traditional "high five" signifying an important contribution to the team. Encouragement and praise from the team leader is important, but team members also play an important role in giving positive reinforcement to each other. Team spirit develops as members receive frequent positive feedback from each other.[29] Skill Building Exercise 6-5 lets team members practise how to recognize others' accomplishments. Which team behaviour earlier in the chapter does this reflect?

Encourage Honest Criticism

A superficial type of camaraderie develops when team members avoid honestly criticizing one another for the sake of group harmony. Avoiding criticism can result in groupthink. As a team leader, you should therefore explain that being a good team player includes offering honest feedback on mistakes and flawed ideas. The team benefits from mutual criticism, as we saw earlier in the chapter. A stronger team spirit will develop because team members realize they are helping one another through honest feedback. An example of honest criticism took place in the shipping department of a manufacturer of small kitchen appliances:

> One member of a customer service team had designed a satisfaction survey to mail to customers. The purpose of the survey was to investigate whether the packing materials were of satisfactory quality. Another member said, "Are you sure you want to do this? Would we just annoy our customers by asking about packing ingredients? Why waste more paper? We've never had a complaint about packing materials."

The person whose idea was challenged was miffed at first, but then expressed appreciation. She said, "I guess I went a little overboard on trying to measure customer satisfaction. Maybe we should save our survey dollars for a more important issue."

SKILL-BUILDING EXERCISE 6-5

Recognizing Team Accomplishments

The class organizes into teams of about six, ideally into teams or groups that have already worked with each other during the course. If you have not worked with each other, you will have to rely on any impressions you have made of the other members of the team during the course. Team members will be equipped with about six 3 × 5 index cards. (Any other small-size piece of paper will work.) Each member of the team thinks carefully about what other members of the team have accomplished during the course, including contribution to team problem solving, class participation, or perhaps some accomplishment outside of class.

Assume that you have six members on the team. Prepare a card for each member by jotting down whatever accomplishments you have observed of the other team members. Each person therefore prepares five cards that will be handed to the person name on the card, and then given to that person. Each team member will receive five "accomplishment cards," one from the other five members. Each member studies his or her accomplishment cards, consisting of statements of accomplishments, and perhaps a couple of words of praise. Here are two examples:

> I like the way you showed up on time for our study group, and were prepared for action. Nice job, Ben.
>
> A few times you came up with great ideas in our problem-solving groups. Shauna, you are a really nice team player.

After all cards have been read carefully, discuss your feelings about their cards and their potential contribution to teamwork. Cover observations, such as the following:

- How much closer to the group do you feel now?
- How much have your efforts in being a team player paid off?
- How useful would this technique of accomplishment recognition be for a workplace team?
- What potential disadvantages do you see to the technique?

Use Peer Evaluations

In the traditional performance-evaluation system, the manager evaluates group members at regular intervals. With peer-evaluation systems, the team members contribute to the evaluation by submitting evaluations of one another. The evaluations might consist of filling out rating forms about one another's performance. Sometimes brief essays are written about other team members and then synthesized by the team leader.

Peer evaluations contribute to teamwork because team members realize that helping one another becomes as important as helping the boss. Similarly, team members recognize that pleasing one another counts as much as pleasing the boss.

As a team leader, you might not have the authority to initiate a peer-evaluation system without first checking with your manager. Making a recommendation for peer input into evaluations might demonstrate that you are committed to participative leadership.

Help Team Members See the Big Picture

The team is likely to work together more smoothly when members have a clear understanding of how their work contributes to the company. Communicating the mission as described earlier is a good starting point. Showing the team its specific contribution to the overall organization is equally important. As the team leader you might create a flow chart that tracks an order from the time it is taken to when it is delivered. Show the team its role at each step. The team members may be aware of how they contribute to the team, but not how the team contributes to the success of the organization.[30] The team leader of a shipping department explains to his team regularly, "Let's keep this clearly in mind. A big factor in determining whether a customer stays with us is whether the goods arrive on time and in good shape." This is also an important task aspect of team play!

Minimize Formation of In-Groups and Out-Groups

An established leadership theory, the **leader-exchange model**, provides useful information for the aspiring team leader. According to this theory, leaders establish unique working relationships with group members. By so doing, they create in-groups and out-groups. The in-groups become part of a smoothly functioning team headed by the leader. Out-group members are less likely to experience good teamwork.[31] Figure 6-5 depicts the major concept of the leader-exchange model.

The in-group may develop because the leader prefers certain group members and therefore is motivated to form good working relationships with them. Conversely, the

leader-exchange model
A theory explaining that group leaders establish unique working relationships with group members, thereby creating in-groups and out-groups.

FIGURE 6-5 The Leader-Member Exchange Model

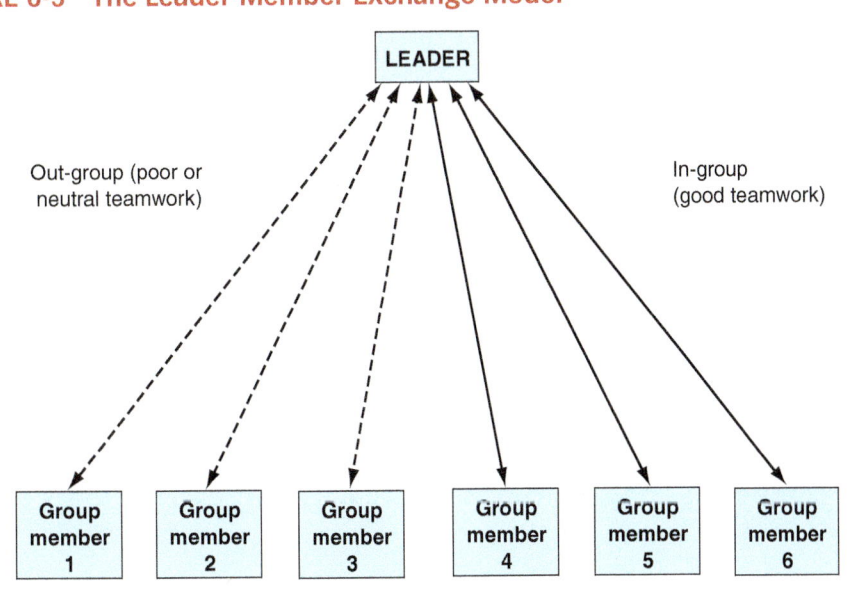

leader may neglect to form good relationships with people with whom he or she has limited rapport. First impressions count heavily when the leader decides on who is "in" and who is "out." A team leader should therefore guard against the formation of out-groups just because he or she is not fond of several team members or because a given team member gives a poor first impression.

The leader-exchange model does not mean that the team leader should avoid forming unique relationships with team members—what should be avoided is forming an out-group. One study investigated the relationships a group of female sales managers established with both male and female members of their sales groups. Treating members differently based on their needs contributed to leadership effectiveness, as evidenced in good team results.[32] An example of a unique relationship would be to give more recognition to a sales representative who craved recognition.

Access the eText in MySearchLab to learn more about this chapter's self-assessment quizzes.

To Watch ✻ Explore ✓ Practice ✓ Study and Review, visit MySearchLab

Developing Your Human Relations Skills and Reinforcing Concepts

Summary ✓ Practice Glossary Flashcards

- To be successful in the modern organization, it is necessary to be an effective team player in both traditional (face-to-face) and virtual teams.
- Advantages of groups and teams include synergy, avoiding major errors, increased acceptance of and commitment to decisions, and increased job satisfaction; disadvantages of group and team work include tendencies toward inactivity and conformity, tolerance of social loafing, conflict, and making bad decisions with group consensus.
- Effective team roles are creative problem solver, resource investigator, coordinator, shaper, monitor-evaluator, team worker, implementer, completer-finisher, and specialist.
- Guidelines for the interpersonal aspects of team play include trusting team members, being cooperative and collaborative, recognizing the interests and achievements of others, sharing the glory, and not raining on another's parade.
- Guidelines for the task aspects of team play include providing technical expertise, taking responsibility for problems, seeing the big picture, believing in consensus, focusing on deadlines, and helping others to do their jobs.
- An effective team leader employs a variety of the following interpersonal skills: engages in shared leadership, builds a mission statement, trusts team members, establishes a sense of urgency and high performance standards, holds question-and-answer sessions, encourages members to recognize others' accomplishments, encourages honest criticism, uses peer evaluations, helps members see the big picture, and minimizes the formation of in-groups and out-groups.

Interpersonal Relations Case 6-1

Leah Puts on Her Team-Player Face

Leah was happy to find a position as a scanning technician at a business process outsourcing company, Expert Resource, Inc. A major part of Expert's business was converting paperwork related to human resources management into digital form. Clients would mail their forms, such as medical claims, to Expert, and scanning technicians would insert the claim forms into large scanning machines to make the conversion to digital. Clients would then have digital instead of paper documents for health claims and other human resources records.

The scanning technicians had to interact with other employees in several ways. Many of the claims received contained illegible identifying information, so they had to be sent to a security department that attempted to obtain the proper identification for the forms. The scanning technicians were expected to help level the workload among the technicians. For example, if one of the technicians was overwhelmed, and another was caught up, the latter was supposed to help out the former. Also, the company frequently held small celebrations in the office. A typical celebration would be a brunch in honour of a new employee joining the company.

Leah believed that if she performed well in her position as a scanning technician, she would be eligible for promotion to the information technology department. Eventually being promoted to a supervisor position was also within the realm of possibility. Leah also recognized that having good skills and speed in scanning documents were not sufficient to be promoted to a supervisory position. Her size-up of the situation was that being a good team player would be required to be considered for promotion. Leah then set out to develop the reputation of being a good team player.

The next Monday morning, Leah arrived at the office with a box of doughnuts that she placed in the break room, with a note attached that said, "Enjoy your coffee or tea this morning with a treat from your co-worker Leah." Several of the other scanning technicians thanked Leah; however, one technician said to her, "Why did you bring us doughnuts? You're not our supervisor."

A week later, Leah implemented another tactic designed to boost her reputation as a team player. She sent an email to the other technicians informing them that they were free to send her an email or an IM anytime they were overloaded with documents to scan. Leah said that she would help the overloaded co-worker so long as she was caught up on her own work.

A week later Lean reflected, "I think I am developing a reputation as a good team player, but I can't give up yet. I think I know a way to really cement being regarded as a strong team player." Leah then wrote an email to the other scanning technicians, as well as her supervisor. The email read in part:

> We all know that it takes a village to raise a child. But did you also know that it takes a group of friendly and cooperative co-workers to get a scanning technician up to speed? I want to thank you all for your cooperation and friendliness. You have been very helpful to me.

Case Questions

1. How effective do you think Leah's initiatives are in helping her develop a reputation as a strong team player?
2. If you were Leah's supervisor, how would you react to the emails she sent to the group?
3. What advice might you offer Leah to help her advance her reputation as a team player?

Interpersonal Relations Case 6-2

Ruth Waves a Red Flag

Carlos is the team leader of a cost-reduction team at a well-established baked-goods company that produces bakery products under its own label, as well as private labels for grocery-store chains such as Metro and Price Chopper. Top-level management formed the team to arrive at suggestions for reducing costs throughout the organization. A transcript of one of the meetings is presented next.

Carlos: We've been gathering information for a month now. It's about time we heard some specific suggestions.

Jack: At the top of my list is cutting pension benefits. Our pension payments are higher than the minimum required by law. Our medical benefits are way above average. If we cut back on pension benefits, no current employees would be adversely affected.

Melissa: I like your analysis, Jack. No sense risking laying off employees just to keep retirees happy.

Jordan: We should make absolutely certain there are no legal complications here. Then we can sharpen our cost-cutting knives and dig right in.

Gunther: I'd support cutting pension benefits. It would probably reduce expenses more dramatically than the ways I have uncovered.

Carlos: There seems to be consensus so far that we should consider making recommendations about cutting pension benefits. Ruth, what do you think?

Ruth: I think it is much too early to reach consensus on such a sensitive issue. Cutting pension benefits would create panic among our retirees. Our older employees would be screaming as well. We'll have an avalanche of negative publicity in the media.

Jordan: Hold on, Ruth. I said the team should first check out this idea with the legal department.

Ruth: Just because cutting pension benefits could squeeze by legally doesn't mean that it's a good idea. We haven't examined the negative ramifications of cutting pension benefits. Let's study this issue further before word leaks out that we're taking away the golden egg.

Carlos: Maybe Ruth has a point. Let's investigate this issue further before making a recommendation.

Case Questions

1. What role, or roles, is Ruth occupying on the cost-reduction team?
2. How effective does she appear to be in her role?
3. What role, or roles, is Jack occupying on the cost-reduction team?
4. How effective does he appear to be in his role?
5. How effective is Carlos in his role as a team leader?

Questions for Discussion and Review

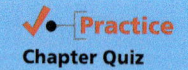

Practice Chapter Quiz

Multiple Choice

1. All of the following are advantages of group and team work except
   a. increased job satisfaction.
   b. synergy.
   c. conformity.
   d. error avoidance.

2. A good example of groupthink would be
   a. company executives taking a voluntary pay cut when profits diminish to help the company recover.

   b. a company team promoting the marketing and selling of a new sports product without a detailed analysis of its safety.
   c. changing hiring practices to adhere to new diversity legislation.
   d. company executives refusing to sell a new drug that has not had several trials to test for possible side effects.

3. All of the following are effective team member strategies except
   a. never criticizing other team members.
   b. trusting other team members.
   c. sharing the glory.
   d. collaborating with other members.

4. Participative leadership can be defined as:
   a. Everyone is equal on a team and leadership is shared equally.
   b. The team leader shares the leadership with the team as a facilitator or coach.
   c. There is no leader on the team.
   d. None of the above

5. Many skills that assist people in being effective team members also assist with being an effective team leader, including
   a. establishing high performance standards.
   b. recognizing team member accomplishments.
   c. minimizing the formation of in-groups and out-groups.
   d. using peer evaluations.

Short Answer

6. Part of being a good team player is helping other members. How can members of a workplace team help each other?
7. What should the other team members do when they uncover a social loafer?
8. What is the potential downside of heavily emphasizing the *specialist* role?
9. What team leader roles do you feel are the most important for motivating other team members to achieve goals? Explain your reasoning.
10. Open MySearchLab to the Web Exercises and choose exercise 3. Can you integrate competition and cooperation through teamwork on a sports team? Go to the link and read the article and summarize the main points of building a strong team that can also be competitive.

Answers to multiple choice questions: 1. c,   2. b,   3. a,   4. b,   5. b.

The Web Corner

www.timeanalyzer.com/lib/teamroles.htm
Belbin's team roles to improve team performance

www.quintcareers.com/team_player_quiz.html
Take the quiz "Are You a Team Player: A Quintessential Careers Quiz."

Internet Skill Builder: Becoming a Better Team Player
The purpose of this exercise duplicates the major purpose of the chapter—finding practical suggestions for improving your teamwork skills. Visit several websites that deal with enhancing teamwork skills from the standpoint of the individual, not the manager. An example of such a website is www.confidencecenter.com.

Write down at least three concrete suggestions you find, and compare these suggestions to those made in this chapter. If the opportunity arises, practise one of these skills in the next 10 days and observe the results.

MySearchLab

Visit **MySearchLab** to find self-grading review quizzes in the eText, discipline-specific media and readings, access to a variety of academic journals, and Associated Press news feeds, along with a wide range of writing, grammar, and research tools and to help hone writing and research skills.

CHAPTER 7
Group Problem Solving and Decision Making

You may not know the name Chip Wilson, but you likely know the name of his business, Lululemon, especially if you are a woman. Building on his experience in the skate and snowboard business, Chip Wilson founded the company (Lululemon Athletica Inc.) in 1998. It is worth over a billion dollars, and has also launched a successful sales website. Chip transformed Lululemon from a yoga-inspired grassroots female-clothing company in Vancouver to an international retail phenomenon.

How has he accomplished this transformation from sportswear store to household name? Two of Chip's main strategies are his marketing creativity and his realignment of sales teams.

Dotshock/Shutterstock

LEARNING Objectives

After reading and studying this chapter and doing the exercises, you should be able to

1. Discern the difference between rational and political decision making.
2. Use the general approach to group problem solving.
3. Make effective use of brainstorming.
4. Use of the nominal group technique effectively.
5. Increase the efficiency of group problem solving through email and groupware.
6. Pinpoint several suggestions for being an effective meeting participant.

Lululemon sends its employees to attend local workout classes and show off the latest collection. Lululemon stores sometimes host community events, and local yoga instructors teach free classes, in the stores. "They go beyond simply putting the right merchandise out in a store. They really connect with the customer in terms of being part of a community," says Maureen Atkinson, a senior partner at J. C. Williams Group in Toronto. "People want to look healthy and body-aware and like they do yoga, even if they don't."

The stores represent a community that offers healthy lifestyle changes to men and women (as well as teens and preteens) for better health and fitness. His salespeople are not "sales people" but instead are called "educators," and "shoppers" are called "clients." Sales teams are well versed in helping guests plan their fitness and lifestyle goals, a creative approach of having teams assist in solving the problems of their guests.[1]

The sales associates at Lululemon demonstrate how working as a team with customers achieves company as well as personal goals. Part of having high-level interpersonal skills is the ability to work closely with others in solving problems and making decisions. Applying the concepts presented in this chapter will improve your group problem-solving and decision-making skills. You will receive guidelines for applying several major group problem-solving methods. As a starting point in studying these techniques, first think through your present level of receptiveness toward group problem-solving by doing Self-Assessment Quiz 7-1.

RATIONAL VERSUS POLITICAL DECISION MAKING IN GROUPS

Group decision making is the process of reaching a judgment based on feedback from more than one individual. Most people involved in group problem solving may share the same purpose in agreeing on a solution and making a decision. Nevertheless, they may have different agendas and use different methods. Two such different approaches to group decision making are the rational model and the political model.

The **rational decision-making model** is the traditional, logical approach to decision making, based on the scientific method. It is grounded in establishing goals and alternatives, examining consequences, and hoping for optimum results. The search for optimum results is based on an economic view of decision making—the idea that people hope to maximize gain and minimize loss when making a decision. For example, a work team would choose the lowest-cost, highest-quality supplier even though the team leader was good friends with the sales representative of a competitor.

LEARNING OBJECTIVE 1

group decision making
The process of reaching a judgment based on feedback from more than one individual.

rational decision-making model
The traditional, logical approach to decision making, based on the scientific method.

GROUP PROBLEM SOLVING AND DECISION MAKING

> ### SELF-ASSESSMENT QUIZ 7-1
>
> #### My Problem-Solving Tendencies
>
> **Directions:** Describe how well you agree with the following statements. Use the following scale: Disagree Strongly (DS); Disagree (D); Neutral (N); Agree (A); Agree Strongly (AS).
>
> | | | DS | D | N | A | AS |
> |----|--|----|---|---|---|----|
> | 1. | Before reaching a final decision on a matter of significance, I like to discuss it with one or more people. | 1 | 2 | 3 | 4 | 5 |
> | 2. | If I'm facing a major decision, I like to get away from others to think it through. | 5 | 4 | 3 | 2 | 1 |
> | 3. | I get lonely working by myself. | 1 | 2 | 3 | 4 | 5 |
> | 4. | Two heads are better than one. | 1 | 2 | 3 | 4 | 5 |
> | 5. | A wide range of people should be consulted before an executive makes a major decision. | 1 | 2 | 3 | 4 | 5 |
> | 6. | To arrive at a creative solution to a problem, it is best to rely on a group. | 1 | 2 | 3 | 4 | 5 |
> | 7. | From what I've seen so far, group decision making is a waste of time. | 5 | 4 | 3 | 2 | 1 |
> | 8. | Most great ideas stem from the solitary effort of great thinkers. | 5 | 4 | 3 | 2 | 1 |
> | 9. | Important legal cases should be decided by a jury rather than a judge. | 1 | 2 | 3 | 4 | 5 |
> | 10.| Individuals are better suited than groups to solving technical problems. | 5 | 4 | 3 | 2 | 1 |
>
> Total Score _____
>
> **Scoring and Interpretation:** Add the numbers you circled to obtain your total score.
>
> **46–50** You have strong positive attitudes toward group problem solving and decision making. You will therefore adapt well to the decision-making techniques widely used in organizations. Be careful, however, not to neglect your individual problem-solving skills.
>
> **30–45** You have neutral attitudes toward group problem solving and decision making. You may need to remind yourself that group problem solving is well accepted in business.
>
> **10–29** You much prefer individual to group decision making. Retain your pride in your ability to think independently, but do not overlook the contribution of group problem solving and decision making. You may need to develop more patience for collaborative work.

The rational model also assumes that each alternative is evaluated in terms of how well it contributes to reaching the goals involved in making the decision. For example, if one of the goals in relocating a factory was to reduce energy costs and taxes, each alternative would be carefully examined in terms of its tax and energy consequences. A team member might say, "Setting up a factory in the Thunder Bay area sounds great. It's true that taxes are low, the labour market is wonderful, and we can access many federal grants. But did you know that the energy costs are very high because of the amount of heating required?"

The **political decision-making model** assumes that people bring preconceived notions and biases into the decision making situation. Because the decision makers are politically motivated (focused on satisfying their own interests), the individuals often do not make the most rational choice. The growing field of behavioural economics is based on the idea that many decisions are irrational or politically based. Revenge and cheating are among the irrational behaviours that underlie the behaviour of many employees and customers.[2] Most computer hackers make their decision to create a virus or destroy computer records based on revenge, cheating, or a sadistic delight in creating misfortune for others.

People who use the political model may operate on the basis of incomplete information. Facts and figures that conflict with personal biases and preferences might get blocked out of memory or rationalized away. A team member might say, "Those heating costs are exaggerated. I've heard that if you use geothermal heating units, heating costs go way down."

Another unintentional contributor to political decision making is **blind spots**—areas of unawareness about our attitudes, thinking, and behaviours that contribute to poor decisions. Shawn O. Utsey, a psychology professor at Virginia Commonwealth University, says that blind spots prevent us from making sound decisions by distorting vision, impairing judgment, and impairing personal and professional growth. An example of a

---

political decision-making model

An approach that assumes people bring preconceived notions and biases into the decision-making situation.

blind spots

Areas of unawareness about our attitudes, thinking, and behaviours that contribute to poor decisions.

frequent blind spot would be not stopping to think, particularly when under pressure.[3] For example, a person might purchase a luxury SUV on the spot that will wind up creating a monthly negative cash flow.

Greed and gluttony are major contributors to irrational (or political) decision making. During the early 2000s, an astounding number of financial managers decided to invest in subprime mortgage loans and then convert these loans into equity investments. Eventually, many holders of these high-risk mortgages were unable or unwilling to make their payments.[4] As the securities collapsed in value, an enormous stock market crisis took place. The securities were based on complex mathematic models, yet were believed in because the investment bankers were looking for ways to capture millions of dollars in bonuses for themselves.

In the relocation example at hand, two of the members might give the thumbs-up to Thunder Bay for reasons that satisfy their own needs. One team member might be attracted to the Canadian north as an avid camper and therefore want to move to Thunder Bay. Another member might have retired parents living in Thunder Bay and be interested in living near them.

In practice, it is sometimes difficult to determine whether a decision maker is being rational or political. Have you ever noticed that many hotels do not have a 13th floor? The reason is both rational and political. The hotel manager might say rationally, "Many people are superstitious about the number 13, so they will refuse to take a room on the 13th floor. If we want to maximize room use, the rational decision for us is to label the 13th floor as 14. In this way, we will avoid the irrational (political) thinking of guests."

Although the examples about political and irrational decision making have been related mostly to individuals, the same problems may surface in group decision making. This is true because a group decision is still based on what takes place in the brains of its members.

GUIDELINES FOR USING GENERAL PROBLEM-SOLVING GROUPS

Solving problems effectively in groups requires skill. The effort is often worthwhile because participation in group decision making frequently leads to better acceptance of the decision, and stronger commitment to the implications of the decision. For example, a group involved in making decisions about cost cutting might be more willing to carry through with the suggestions than if participants had not made the decision. Group decision making can also lead to higher-quality decisions and innovations because the group collectively has more information than might individuals.[5] Similarly, the group might come up with better suggestions for cost cutting because of group members sharing information.

LEARNING OBJECTIVE 2

Here we examine three aspects of group problem solving useful in making more effective decisions: working through the group problem-solving steps, managing disagreement about the decision, and aiming for inquiry rather than advocacy.

Working through the Group Problem-Solving Steps

When team members get together to solve a problem, they typically hold a discussion rather than rely on formal problem-solving techniques. Several team members might attempt to clarify the true nature of the problem, and a search then begins for an acceptable solution. Although this technique can be effective, the probability of solving the problem well (and therefore making the right decision) increases when the team follows a systematic procedure.

The Problem-Solving Steps. The following guidelines represent a time-tested way of solving problems and making decisions within a group.[6] You may recognize these steps as having much in common with the scientific method. The same steps are therefore ideal for following the rational decision-making model. Two other aspects of group decision making will be described here: managing disagreement and inquiry versus advocacy.

Assume that you are a team member of a small business that distributes food supplies to hospitals, nursing homes, and schools. Your business volume is adequate, but you have a cash-flow problem because some of your customers take more than 30 days to pay their bills. Here is how problem solving would proceed following the steps for effective group problem solving and decision making:

1. **Identify the problem.** Describe specifically what the problem is and how it manifests itself. The surface problem is that some customers are paying their bills late. Your company's ultimate problem is that it does not have enough cash on hand to pay expenses.

2. **Clarify the problem.** If group members do not see the problem the same way, they will offer divergent solutions to their individual perceptions of the problem. To some team members, late payments may simply mean the company has less cash in the bank. As a result, the company earns a few dollars less in interest. Someone else on the team might perceive the problem as mostly an annoyance and inconvenience. Another person may perceive late payers as being immoral and therefore want to penalize them. The various perceptions of these problem solvers contribute to their exercising a political model of decision making. It is important for the group to reach consensus that the ultimate problem is that there is not enough cash on hand to run the business, as explained in step 1.

3. **Analyze the cause.** To convert the existing situation into the desired one, the group must understand the cause or causes of specific problems and find ways to overcome them. Late payment of bills (over 30 days) can be caused by several factors. Customers may have cash-flow problems of their own; they may have slow-moving, bureaucratic procedures; or they may be understaffed. Another possibility is that the slow-paying customers are dissatisfied with the service and are holding back on payments in retaliation. Research, including interviewing customers, may be needed to analyze the cause or causes of the problem.

4. **Search for alternative solutions.** Remember that there are usually many alternative solutions to a problem. The ones you choose to focus on will depend on your analysis of the causes. Assume that you have found that customers are satisfied with your service but were slow in paying bills for a variety of other reasons. Your team then gets creative and develops a number of alternatives. Among them are offering bigger discounts for quick payment, dropping slow-paying customers, sending out your own bills more promptly, and using follow-up phone calls to bring in money. Another possibility would be to set up a line of credit that would enable your firm to take out short-term loans to cover expenses until your bills were paid.

5. **Select alternatives.** Identify the criteria that solutions should meet and then discuss the pros and cons of the proposed alternatives. No solution should be laughed at or scorned. Specifying the criteria that proposed solutions should meet requires you to think deeply about your goals. For example, your team might establish the following criteria for solutions: that they (a) improve cash flow; (b) do not lose customers; (c) do not cost much to implement; and (d) do not make the company look desperate. The pros and cons of each proposed alternative can be placed on a flip chart, whiteboard, or computer screen.

For many complex problems, it is best to select an alternative solution based on a variety of options. The blended options solutions will often be stronger because it contains several useful ideas.[7] At the same time, several group members will be satisfied that at least part of their suggestion was incorporated in the final solution. For example, if the problem under group discussion was choosing a theme for decorating a new office, several ideas might be selected. An advertising agency used group decision making to arrive at a dual theme for decorating the office: cool yet affluent.

> ### SKILL-BUILDING EXERCISE 7-1
>
> #### A General Problem-Solving Group
>
> The class is divided into groups of about six people. Each group takes the same complicated problem through the nine steps for effective group decision making. Several of the steps will be hypothetical, because this is a simulated experience. Pretend you are a task force composed of people from different departments in the company. Choose one of the following possibilities:
>
> **Scenario 1:** Your company wants your task force to decide whether to purchase a corporate jet for members of senior management or require them to continue to fly on commercial airlines.
>
> **Scenario 2:** You are employed by Hewlett-Packard Corp., an information technology giant that specializes in computers and printers. Data supplied by the marketing research department indicates that the consumption of HP inkjet cartridges by consumers worldwide is declining faster than anticipated. At the same time, private-label refill cartridges are selling much faster than anticipated. Your task force is asked to recommend a plan for increasing the consumption of inkjet cartridges.

6. **Plan for implementation.** Decide what action is necessary to carry out the chosen solution to the problem. Suppose your group decides that establishing a bank line of credit is the most feasible alternative. The company president or the chief financial officer might then meet with several local banks to apply for a line of credit at the most favourable rate. Your group also chooses to initiate a program of friendly follow-up telephone calls to encourage more rapid payment.

7. **Clarify the contract.** The contract is a restatement of what group members have agreed to do and deadlines for accomplishment. In your situation, several team members are involved in establishing a line of credit and initiating a system of follow-up phone calls.

8. **Develop an action plan.** Specify who does what and when to carry out the terms of the contract. Each person involved in implementing alternatives develops an action plan in detail that stems logically from the previous step.

9. **Provide for evaluation and accountability.** After the plan is implemented, reconvene to discuss progress and to hold people accountable for results that have not been achieved. In the current example, progress will be measured in at least two objective ways. You can use accounting measures to evaluate whether the cash-flow situation has improved and whether the average cycle time on accounts receivable has decreased.

When to Apply the Problem-Solving Steps. The above steps for effective group problem solving are best applied to complex problems. Straightforward problems of minor consequence (such as deciding on holiday decorations for the office) do not require all the steps. Nevertheless, remember that virtually every problem has more than one feasible alternative as a solution. For practice in using the steps just described, do Skill-Building Exercise 7-1.

The Importance of Collective Efficacy. How well a given group solves a problem depends on many of the characteristics of an effective work group outlined in Figure 6-1 (the previous chapter). Of particular relevance is the group's level of confidence that it can solve the problem at hand. **Collective efficacy** is a group's belief that it can handle certain tasks. Collective efficacy influences a group to initiate action, how much effort it will apply to the task, and how long the group's effort will be sustained.[8] If the group members say spontaneously, "We can do it, let's go," they will usually be successful in solving the problem, assuming they have the necessary knowledge and talent.

collective efficacy
A group's belief that it can handle certain tasks. If a group is high in collective efficacy, it will more likely be successful in solving problems.

> ### BACK TO THE OPENING CASE
>
> Lululemon sells a "lifestyle" of being more active and healthier. Their clothes are rarely discounted and their culture is attractive to large numbers of women. What do you think their store teams are like? Perhaps, their store teams are characterized by collective efficacy and the belief that they make a difference in the lives of their clients.

GROUP PROBLEM SOLVING AND DECISION MAKING

SKILL-BUILDING EXERCISE 7-2

Solving a Few Unusual Problems

Use group problem solving to find a solution to the three problems described next. Each problem is designed to capitalize on the group's ability to search for creative alternatives and think flexibly. Answers to the three problems are found at the end of the references for this chapter toward the end of the text.

Problem 1: Seven Tennis Balls in a Tube

Seven tennis balls are located at the bottom of a six-foot vertical pipe with a diameter of four inches, bolted securely to the floor. Your job is to remove the balls without destroying the pipe.

Problem 2: The Too-Low Bridge

A couple has rented a large truck to move their belongings to a new house in the country. As they are driving down a country road, they encounter an overhead bridge that appears to be somewhat low. Before barrelling through the bridge, the couple climbs up on the hood to discover that indeed the bridge is 1.5 inches too low and their truck will hit the bridge and not be able to go under. Ten minutes later, the couple drives right under the bridge. What solution did they find to the problem of their rented truck being too tall?

Problem 3: The Aging Members of HOG

A few years ago, managers at Harley-Davidson recognized that they were losing a lot of their members of HOG (Harley Owner's Group) because many Harley drivers had reached the age whereby they perceived driving a traditional motorcycle to be too dangerous. A problem-solving group was formed, and they arrived at a solution that prevented a lot of older HOG members from slipping away. Some of those HOG members are now as happy as a pig dipped in mud. What product do you think the Harley-Davidson problem-solving group developed?

Source: The seven-ball problem is from Dodge Fernald, *Psychology* (Upper Saddle River, NJ: Prentice Hall, 1997), p. 288.

Skill-Building Exercise 7-2 gives you an opportunity to solve a few more of the perplexing type of problems that companies and people may face.

Managing Disagreement about Group Decision Making

A major reason that group decision making does not proceed mechanically is that disagreement may surface. Such disagreement is not necessarily harmful to the final outcome of the decision because those who disagree may have valid points, and may help prevent groupthink. For committees and other groups to work well, they should be composed of people with different perspectives and experiences who are not hesitant to speak their minds.[9]

The idea is to manage disagreement so the decision-making process does not break down and the dissenters are not squelched. In one study, conflicts about decisions were examined among 43 cross-functional teams engaged in new product development. Disagreements about major issues led to positive outcomes for team performance (as measured by managers' ratings) under two conditions.[10]

First, the researchers concluded, dissenters have to feel they have the freedom to express doubt. To measure such freedom, participants in the study responded to such statements as "I sometimes get the feeling that others are not speaking up although they harbour serious doubts about the direction being taken." (Strongly disagreeing with this statement would suggest that group members had the freedom to express doubt.)

Second, doubts must be expressed collaboratively (trying to work together) rather than contentiously (in a quarrelsome way). An example of collaborative communication would be having used the following statement during decision making: "We will be working together for a while. It's important that we both [all] feel comfortable with a solution to this problem." An example of contentious communication would be high agreement with the statement "You're being difficult and rigid."

More recent research lends strength to the idea that teams are more likely to make optimal decisions when they take the time to debate the issues and thoughtfully discuss alternative solutions. A study about hiring pilots for long-distance flights found that when groups disagreed over who to hire, there was more information sharing. Also, the strong disagreement led to more intense discussions that prompted participants to repeat their reasoning in front of other group members. A debate over which candidate to hire encourages team members to focus on information that may be inconsistent with how they formed their original opinion.[11]

Conflict-resolution techniques, as described in Chapter 9, are another potentially useful approach to managing disagreement about decision making.

Aiming for Inquiry versus Advocacy in Group Decision Making

Another useful perspective on group decision making is to compare the difference between group members involved in *inquiry* (looking for the best alternative) versus *advocacy* (fighting for one position). Inquiry is an open process designed to generate multiple alternatives, encourage the exchange of ideas, and produce a well-reasoned solution. Decision makers who care more about the good of the firm than personal gain are the most likely to engage in inquiry. According to David A. Garvin and Michael A. Roberto, this open-minded approach doesn't come easily to most people.[12]

Instead, most groups charged with making a decision tend to slip into the opposite mode, called *advocacy*. The two approaches look similar, because under either mode the group members are busily immersed in work and appear to be searching for the best alternative. Yet the results from the two modes are quite different. Using an advocacy approach, participants approach decision making as a contest with the intent of selecting the winning alternative. One member of the group might be trying to gain the largest share of the budget and become so passionate about winning budget share that he loses objectivity. Advocates might even withhold important information from the group, such as not revealing that their budget is big enough considering their decreased activity.

With an advocacy approach, the disagreements that arise tend to separate the group into antagonistic camps. Personality conflicts come into play, and one person might accuse the other side of not being able to see the big picture. In contrast, an inquiry-focused group carefully considers a variety of alternatives and collaborates to discover the best solution.

Conflict-resolution methods can be useful in helping the decision makers overcome the advocacy approach. As part of resolving the conflict, the group leader must make sure everyone knows that his or her viewpoint is being carefully considered.

GUIDELINES FOR BRAINSTORMING

In many work situations, groups are expected to produce creative and imaginative solutions to problems. When the organization is seeking a large number of alternatives for solving problems, **brainstorming** is often the technique of choice. Brainstorming is a group problem-solving technique that promotes creativity by encouraging idea generation through non-critical discussion. Alex Osborn, who developed the practice of brainstorming, believed that one of the main blocks to organizational creativity was the premature evaluation of ideas.[13] The basic technique is to encourage unrestrained and spontaneous participation by group members. The term *brainstorm* has become so widely known that it is often used as a synonym for a clever idea.

Brainstorming is used both as a method of finding alternatives to real-life problems and as a creativity-training program. In the usual form of brainstorming, group members spontaneously call out alternative solutions to a problem facing them. Any member is free to improve or "hitchhike" upon the contribution of another person. At the end of the session, somebody sorts out the ideas and edits those that are less refined.

Brainstorming is widely used to develop new ideas for products, find names for products, develop advertising slogans, and solve customer problems. Brainstorming has also been used to develop a new organizational structure in a government agency and is now widely used in developing software. Adhering to a few simple rules or guidelines helps ensure that creative alternative solutions to problems will be forthcoming. The brainstorming process usually falls into place without frequent reminders about guidelines. Nevertheless, here are nine rules to improve the chances of having a good session. Unless many of these rules are followed,

LEARNING OBJECTIVE 3

brainstorming

A group problem-solving technique that promotes creativity by encouraging idea generation through non-critical discussion.

Explore

Mastering Business Communication: Brainstorming Sessions

brainstorming becomes a free-for-all, and is not brainstorming in its original intent.

1. **Group size should be about five to seven people.** If there are too few people, not enough suggestions are generated; if there are too many, the session becomes uncontrolled. However, brainstorming can be conducted with as few as three people.
2. **Everybody is given the chance to suggest alternative solutions.** Members spontaneously call out alternatives to the problem facing the group. (Another approach is for people to speak in sequence.)
3. **No criticism is allowed.** All suggestions should be welcome; it is particularly important not to use derisive laughter.
4. **Freewheeling is encouraged.** Outlandish ideas often prove quite useful. It is easier to tame a wild idea than to originate one.
5. **Quantity and variety are very important.** The greater the number of ideas put forth, the greater the likelihood of a breakthrough idea.
6. **Combinations and improvements are encouraged.** Building upon the ideas of others, including combining them, is very productive. "Hitchhiking" or "piggybacking" is an essential part of brainstorming.
7. **Notes must be taken during the session by a person who serves as the recording secretary.** The session can also be taped, but this requires substantial time to retrieve ideas.
8. **Invite outsiders to the brainstorming session.** Inviting an outsider to the brainstorming session can add a new perspective the "insiders" might not think of themselves.
9. **Do not become overly structured by following any of the above eight "rules" too rigidly.** Brainstorming is a spontaneous group process.

A widely accepted suggestion for brainstorming effectiveness is to have diverse group members. Diversity includes differences in age, sex, race, experience levels, and educational background, as well as functional background (e.g., marketing and information technology).[14] The diversity contributes to different perspectives that facilitate a variety of ideas surfacing during the brainstorming session.

According to one observer, the most productive brainstorming sessions take place in physically stimulating environments as opposed to a drab conference room. Natural light may stimulate thinking, so work in a room with windows or outside if weather permits. Changing from a seated position to walking around from time to time can be mentally stimulating. Food and drink also contribute to an enhanced environment for brainstorming.[15]

Another useful perspective on brainstorming is that the process really involves establishing and attaining a series of goals. The rules for brainstorming can be interpreted as goals, as with the following examples:

- Establish the goal of establishing as many ideas as possible.
- Establish the goal of avoiding criticism.
- Establish the goal of attempting to combine ideas and build on them.[16]

Brainstorming is an effective technique for finding a large number of alternatives to problems, particularly when the list of alternatives is subsequently refined and edited. Brainstorming in groups is also valuable because it contributes to job satisfaction for many people. Skill-Building Exercise 7-3 gives you an opportunity to practise a commercially useful application of brainstorming.

One curious feature of brainstorming is that individuals working alone typically produce more useful ideas than those placed in a group. Brainstorming by individuals working alone is referred to as **brainwriting**. When electronic brainstorming is described in the next

BlueSkyImages/Fotolia

brainwriting
Brainstorming by individuals working alone.

SKILL-BUILDING EXERCISE 7-3

Stretch Your Imagination

A global contest was organized by Stanford University through its Technology Ventures Program. Anyone in the world was permitted to enter. The assignment was to take ordinary rubber bands and "add value" to them. Entries were submitted by video, posting them on YouTube. Entrants included people from many different occupations, including computer scientist. The winner received the Genius Award.

Here is where you fit in. Through brainstorming, come up with at least six ways of adding value (making more useful) a rubber band, or a bunch of rubber bands. You must stretch your imagination to be successful. After the brainstorming sessions have been completed, perhaps taking 10 minutes of class time, a representative of each group might share results with the class. Students might then assign a Genius Award to the entry that seems the most useful. Or, the instructor might be the judge.

Source: The facts about the contest stem from Lee Gomes, "Our Columnist Judges a Brainstorming Bee, and Meets a Genius," *The Wall Street Journal*, March 5, 2008, p. B1.

SKILL-BUILDING EXERCISE 7-4

Brainstorming versus Brainwriting

One-half of the class is organized into brainstorming groups of about six people. The rest work by themselves. Groups and individuals then work on the same problems for 10 minutes. The brainstorming groups follow the aforementioned guidelines. Individuals jot down as many alternatives as come to mind without interacting with other people. After the problem-solving sessions are completed, compare the alternatives developed by the groups and individuals.

The class chooses one of the following problems so that solutions to the same problem can be compared:

1. How might we reduce the carbon dioxide emissions in our community?
2. How can we earn extra money, aside from holding a regular job?
3. How can we find new people to date?
4. How can we save money on food costs?
5. How can we use Twitter and Facebook to make money?

section, we will analyze why some people generate fewer ideas in a group setting. Skill-Building Exercise 7-4 gives you a chance to compare brainstorming and brainwriting.

GUIDELINES FOR THE NOMINAL GROUP TECHNIQUE

A team leader or other manager who must make a decision about an important issue sometimes needs to know what alternatives are available and how people will react to them. In such cases, group input may be helpful. Spoken brainstorming is not advisable, because the problem is still in the exploration phase and requires more than a list of alternative solutions.

A problem-solving technique called the **nominal group technique (NGT)** was developed to fit the situation. The NGT is a group problem-solving technique that brings people together in a structured meeting with limited interaction. The group is called "nominal" (in name only) because people first present their ideas without interacting with each other, as they would in a real group. However, group discussion does take place at a later stage in the process. Figure 7-1 outlines the nominal group technique.

A problem that is an appropriate candidate for NGT is a decision about which suppliers or vendors should be eliminated. Many companies are shrinking their number of suppliers because they believe that working with a smaller number of suppliers can lead to higher-quality components. It is easier to train a small number of suppliers, and it is also possible to build better working relationships when fewer people are involved. Also, with fewer suppliers there are fewer transactions to bother with.

A decision of this type can lead to hurt feelings and breaking up of old friendships. Suppose Pedro, the team leader, is empowered to make this decision about reducing the number of suppliers. The NGT involves a six-step decision process:

1. Work-team members are assembled because they will all participate in the decision to reduce the number of companies that serve as suppliers to the team. All team members are told in advance of the meeting and the agenda. The meeting is called, and an office assistant is invited to help take care of the administrative details of the meeting.

LEARNING OBJECTIVE 4

nominal group technique (NGT)

A group problem-solving technique that brings people together in a structured meeting with limited interaction.

FIGURE 7-1 The Nominal Group Technique

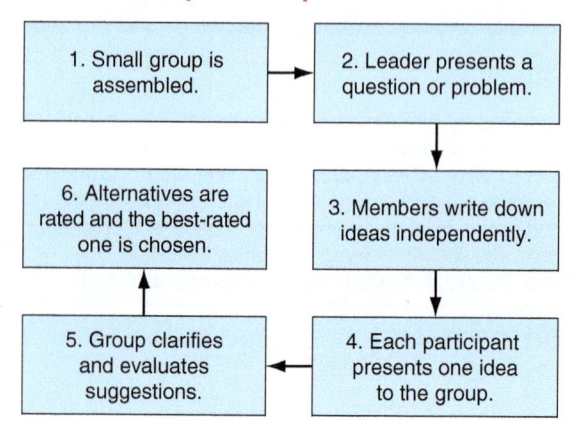

```
1. Small group is          →    2. Leader presents a
   assembled.                      question or problem.
                                           ↓
6. Alternatives are              3. Members write down
   rated and the best-rated         ideas independently.
   one is chosen.
        ↑                                  ↓
5. Group clarifies         ←    4. Each participant
   and evaluates                    presents one idea
   suggestions.                     to the group.
```

2. The team leader presents a specific question. Pierre tells the group, "Top management says we have to reduce our number of suppliers by two-thirds. It's too difficult to keep track of all these different suppliers and train them to meet our quality specs. I dislike terminating a supplier as much as anybody, but I can understand the logic of top management. Right now our team is doing business with 12 suppliers, and we should shrink that number to 4. Your assignment is to develop criteria for choosing which suppliers to eliminate. I also need to know how you feel about the decision you make on supplier reduction and how it might affect the operations of our team."

3. Individual team members write down their ideas independently, without speaking to other members. Using notepads, email, or word processors, the five team members write down their ideas about reducing the number of suppliers by two-thirds.

4. Each team member in turn presents one idea to the group. Sometimes these ideas are presented to the group by the team leader without identifying which person contributed the idea. In this way, ideas are submitted anonymously. The group does not discuss the ideas. The office assistant summarizes each idea by writing it on a flip chart. Here are the ideas submitted by each team member:

    Alternative A. We'll carefully study the prices offered by all 12 suppliers. The eight suppliers with the highest average prices for comparable goods are given the boot. I like this idea because our team will save the company a bundle of money.

    Alternative B. Let's keep the four suppliers who have the best quality record. We'll ask each supplier if it has won a quality award. If a supplier has won a quality award, the company is put on the retained list. We'll include awards from their customers or outside standards such as ISO 9000. If we find more than four suppliers have won awards, we'll retain those with the most impressive awards.

    Alternative C. I say we reward good service. We keep the 4 suppliers among the 12 who have been the most prompt with deliveries. We'll also take into account how good the suppliers have been about accepting returns of damaged or defective merchandise.

    Alternative D. Here's an opportunity to get in good with top management. Stop kidding each other. We know that the plant's general manager [Jake] has his favourite suppliers. Some of them are his fishing and golfing buddies. The suppliers who are friends with Jake get our vote. In this way, Jake will think our team shows really good judgment.

    Alternative E. Let's reward the suppliers who have served us best. We'll rate each supplier on a 1-to-10 scale on three dimensions: the quality of goods they have provided us, price, and service in terms of prompt delivery and returns policy. We could do the ratings in less than one hour.

5. After each team member has presented his or her idea, the group clarifies and evaluates the suggestions. The length of the discussion for each of the ideas varies

SKILL-BUILDING EXERCISE 7-5

The Nominal Group Technique

With a clear understanding of the mechanics of the NGT as described in the text, the technique can be demonstrated in about 30 minutes. The class is divided into groups of about seven. One person plays the role of the team leader, who can also assume the responsibility of the office assistant (recording information on flip charts or a computer).

You are the key member of a motion picture and television film production company. You have a contract to produce a series of four films. The problem you face is which North American (United States, Canadian, or Mexican) city to choose as the film site. The president has ruled out Hollywood because expenses are too high. Solve this problem using the NGT, and make a decision about which city to choose for your film site.

---

substantially. For example, the idea about rating suppliers on three criteria might precipitate a 30-minute discussion. The discussion about retaining the plant manager's political connections might last only five minutes.

6. The meeting ends with a silent, independent rating of the alternatives. The final group decision is the pooled outcome of the individual votes. The team members are instructed to rate each alternative on a 1-to-10 scale, with 10 being the most favourable rating. The ratings that follow are the pooled ratings (the sum of the individual ratings) received for each alternative. The maximum score is 50 (10 points, 5 raters).

Alternative A, price alone: 35

Alternative B, quality-award record: 30

Alternative C, good service: 39

Alternative D, plant manager's favourites: 14

Alternative E, combination of quality, price, and service: 44

Team leader Pierre agrees with the group's preference for choosing the four suppliers with the best combination of quality, price, and service. He schedules a meeting to decide which suppliers meet these standards. Pierre brings the team's recommendations to the plant manager, and they are accepted. Although the team is empowered to make the decision, it is still brought to management for final approval. To practise the nominal group technique, do Skill-Building Exercise 7-5.

USING STANDUP MEETINGS TO FACILITATE PROBLEM SOLVING

LEARNING OBJECTIVE 5

Problem solving and decision making can sometimes be improved by conducting meetings while standing up instead of sitting down. The general idea is that participants standing up in the problem-solving group are likely to be more alert and will come to a decision more quickly—that is, they literally "think well on their feet." Few people would be willing to stand for several hours, so they reach a decision quickly.

Many meeting leaders who use standup meetings are pleased with the results in terms of reaching high-quality decisions rapidly. At United Parcel Service (UPS), every morning and several times a day, managers assemble workers for a required standup meeting that lasts precisely three minutes. Among the topics covered are local information, traffic conditions, or customer complaints. Each meeting ends with a safety tip. The 180-second limit helps enforce punctuality throughout UPS.[17] Many problem-solving meetings at Google are held standing up. For example, details about a recent version of the Google results page were hammered out at a meeting of 10 people.[18]

A team of researchers investigated the effectiveness of standup meetings.[19] Study participants were 555 students in an introduction-to-management course who were offered extra credit for participating in the study. The students were randomly assigned to five-person groups, producing 111 groups. They were divided almost equally into standup and sit-down groups.

GROUP PROBLEM SOLVING AND DECISION MAKING

All groups were assigned the Lost on the Moon exercise, which presents a scenario involving a crash on the moon. Participants were asked to rank 15 pieces of equipment that survived the crash in terms of their importance for survival. Correct answers to the problem were the ranking of the equipment given by NASA astronauts and scientists. The major results of the experiment were as follows:

1. Sit-down meetings lasted about 34 percent longer than the standup meetings (788 seconds versus 589 seconds).
2. Sit-down and standup meetings made decisions of equal quality.
3. More suggestions about task accomplishment were used by groups in the sit-down meetings than in the standup meetings.
4. Participants in the sit-down meetings were more satisfied than participants in the standup meetings.

One implication for this study is that people make decisions more quickly when standing up, without sacrificing decision quality. However, people prefer to sit down. In general, if you think that a task can be performed in 30 minutes or less, a standup meeting is likely to be effective.

USING EMAIL AND GROUPWARE TO FACILITATE GROUP DECISION MAKING

The presence of so many teams in the workplace means that people must work collectively and that they must make decisions together. Collective effort usually translates into meetings. Without any meetings, people are working primarily alone and thus are not benefiting from working in teams. Yet with too many meetings, it is difficult to accomplish individual work, such as dealing with email, making telephone calls, analyzing information, and preparing reports.

Appropriate use of email and groupware can facilitate interaction among team members and group decision making, while at the same time minimizing the number of physical meetings. Such use of email and other electronic tools makes possible the virtual teams described in Chapter 6.

Using Email to Facilitate Meetings

By using email, team members can feed important information to all other members of the team without the ritual of entering a meeting and passing around handouts.[20] Using email, many small details can be taken care of in advance of the meeting. During the meeting, major items can be tackled. The typical use of email is to send brief memos to people on a distribution list. A more advanced use of email is to distribute word processing documents, spreadsheets, graphics, and photographs as attachments. If the subject of the meeting deals with uncomplicated issues, text messaging can be used instead of email.

Think back to the decision reached by the team using the nominal group technique. As a follow-up to the meeting, the team was to get together to rate all 12 suppliers on quality, price, and service. Using email, the group could cut down substantially on the amount of time they would have to spend in a group meeting. They might even be able to eliminate a group meeting. Pierre might instruct the team members to send their ratings and explanations to each other within 10 working days.

Each team member would then rate all 12 suppliers on quality, service, and price. The ratings would then be sent to all other team members by email. Pierre could tally the results and report the final tally to each team member by email. Since all team members could have performed the same calculation themselves, there would be no claims of a biased decision. A team meeting could be called to discuss the final results if Pierre or the other team members thought it was necessary.

Pushing the use of email too far can inhibit rather than enhance group decision making and teamwork. If people communicate with each other almost exclusively by email, the warmth of human interaction and facial expressions is lost, and piggybacking of ideas is possible by reading each other's ideas on a computer monitor. The wink of an eye, the shared laughter, and the encouraging smiles that take place in a traditional meeting make an important contribution to team effort, including group problem solving. Also, face-to-face interaction facilitates creativity as people exchange ideas.

Using Groupware to Facilitate Group Problem Solving

The application of email just described can be considered part of groupware because email was used to facilitate work in groups. Electronic brainstorming also relies on groupware because software is applied to facilitate group decision making. Using electronic brainstorming, as well as the other electronic approaches to group problem solving, participants are free to comment on, or suggest a modification of, the ideas of other contributors. Assume that Sara, a marketing assistant at a bicycle company, enters the following comment on her email: "I say, let's push for selling more adult tricycles in British Columbia because many seniors move there for the climate." Engineering technician Jason then adds to Sara's comment: "I love Sara's idea. But why limit the marketing push to British Columbia? There is a large senior crowd in Ontario and Quebec."

At its best, groupware offers certain advantages over single-user systems. Some of the most common reasons people use groupware are as follows:[21]

- To facilitate communication by making it faster, clearer, and more persuasive
- To communicate when it would not otherwise be possible
- To enable telecommuting (working from home)
- To reduce travel costs
- To bring together multiple perspectives and expertise
- To assemble groups with common interests where it would not be possible to gather a sufficient number of people face-to-face
- To facilitate group problem solving

Another example of groupware is a *shared whiteboard* that allows two or more people to view and draw on a common drawing surface even when they are at a distance. Several programs, such as Edistorm, offer a wide variety of shared spaces for problem solving, including polling, sharing, and brainstorming. The link to group decision making is that drawing sketches and diagrams might be an important part of the decision making. An example would be a sales team suggesting ways of dividing a geographic territory for selling. Yet another electronic approach to meetings is for all participants to post comments on a social networking site such as Facebook. In this way, all participants see the comments made by the other participants. Many companies have developed websites of their own modelled after Facebook. Lastly, online surveys can be used with such software as Survey Monkey. Prior to a meeting, group members can be surveyed on a variety of issues to assist in decision making and problem solving. For example, a conference-organizing team may want to examine possible venues for the conference. Using an online survey, the team can vote on possible venues and guest speakers to save time during the face-to-face meeting where more important issues can be addressed. Such surveys can be done anonymously or with voters' names also published with the results.

An advantage of virtual problem solving is that it avoids the problem of a couple of people dominating the meeting, and some people making no contribution because they are timid. A more human-relations-oriented perspective is that in-person meetings are useful for a final discussion or vote because of the exchange of ideas possible.[22] A problem with anonymity in problem solving is that many workers want to receive credit for their good ideas.

Despite all these potential applications and benefits of groupware, the system will break down unless almost all the parties involved use the software successfully. For example, all members of the virtual team must be willing to get online at the same time to have a productive meeting.

SUGGESTIONS FOR BEING AN EFFECTIVE MEETING PARTICIPANT

LEARNING OBJECTIVE 6

Except for virtual meetings such as those made possible by groupware, group problem solving takes place within the context of a face-to-face meeting. A major problem with most meetings is that they frustrate the participants, particularly those who are accomplishment-oriented. Steven G. Rogelberg and his associates conducted an online survey of 980 participants from the United States, Australia, and the United Kingdom. The more meetings the accomplishment-oriented workers attended, the worse they felt about their job and the lower their feelings of well-being. The meetings appeared to have been perceived as an interruption to the tasks these ambitious people set out to accomplish.[23] However, many workers do enjoy the social interaction involved in meetings, as well as a change of pace from individual work.

Meetings are not likely to be eliminated despite their unpopularity with accomplishment-oriented workers. A possible solution is for meeting participants to conduct themselves in a professional, task-oriented manner. In this way, meetings will most likely be shorter and more productive. A few key suggestions follow for being an effective meeting participant.[24]

- Arrive at the meeting prepared, such as having studied the support material and agenda, thought through your potential contribution, and taken care of some details by email beforehand.
- Arrive on time, and stay until the meeting is completed. The meeting leader will often wait for the last participant before getting down to business. Leaving early distracts other participants.
- Do not hog the meeting or sit silently. Meetings are much more effective when the participants make balanced contributions.
- Use constructive nonverbal communication rather than slouching, yawning, looking bored and frustrated, leaving the room frequently, chewing gum, checking your cell phone or laptop computer, or engaging in similar negative behaviours.
- Converse only with others in the meeting when someone else is not speaking. Some executives will oust from a meeting if they engage in *sidebar conversations*.
- Be prepared to offer compromise solutions when other meeting participants and the meeting leader are haggling about a conflict of opinion.
- When possible, have data ready to support your position, such as estimating from industry data how much money your suggestion will save the company.

Access the eText in MySearchLab to learn more about this chapter's self-assessment quizzes.

From studying these suggestions, you will observe that conducting yourself productively and professionally in a meeting is yet another job-oriented, interpersonal skill.

To Watch, Explore, Practice, Study and Review, visit MySearchLab

Developing Your Human Relations Skills and Reinforcing Concepts

Summary   ✓ Practice / Glossary Flashcards

- Group problem solvers and decision makers most often use either the rational or the political model. The rational model is the traditional, logical approach to decision making, based on the scientific method; the political model assumes that people bring preconceived notions and biases into the decision-making situation.
- Better decisions are reached when the group takes time to work through the general approach to problem-solving steps: (a) identify the problem; (b) clarify the problem; (c) analyze the cause; (d) search for alternative solutions; (e) select alternatives; (f) plan for implementation; (g) clarify the contract; (h) develop an action plan; and (i) provide for evaluation and accountability.
- Brainstorming is used to generate a large number of solutions to problems either as a group or electronically. Brainstorming allows participants to be creative with their ideas with noncritical discussion.
- The nominal group technique (NGT) is recommended for a situation in which a leader needs to know what alternatives are available and how people will react to them. NGT is a highly effective technique for coming up with good decisions and solutions by a team.
- Email and various types of groupware can be used to improve group decision making because members can feed information to one another without having to meet as a group.
- People who are effective at meetings engage in several positive behaviours, including arriving prepared and on time, participating effectively, using constructive nonverbal communication, offering solutions, and having data ready to support their positions in a discussion.

Interpersonal Relations Case 7-1

Pet Groomers on Wheels Get into a Huddle

Ted and Erin, a married couple, both loved pets and both craved becoming small-business owners. So several years ago while still holding down corporate positions, they launched a new business, Pet Groomers on Wheels. The basic model of the business is to make house calls to groom pets at the pet owner's home.

The key services for dogs are shampoos, haircuts, nail clips, teeth polishing, and ear cleaning. Except for the shampoos, the services are similar for cats. Ted and Erin travel in a van fully equipped with their supplies, and the pet grooming is conducted in the van rather than bringing all the equipment into the customer's home. Ted and Erin started the operation part-time by making their calls at night and on weekends. Soon it appeared the business was ready to become a full-time business, so the couple both quit their corporate positions.

Operating in the prosperous Greater Toronto area, Pet Groomers on Wheels has far exceeded the sales volume and profits projected by Ted and Erin. To successfully manage all the client demands, the couple hired two close relatives, Tanya and Nick, to make some of the calls. To help keep Tanya and Nick motivated—as well as not going into competition with Pet Care on Wheels—Ted and Erin made them part owners of the business.

After three years of operation, Pet Groomers on Wheels has generated $85,000 in profits beyond paying Ted, Erin, Tanya, and Nick salaries of an average of $65,000 each. In the process of preparing the income tax for Pet Groomers, Erin decided that the company was not managing its money effectively by leaving the profits in a chequing account. After chatting about the situation with Ted, they agreed that the company should manage its money more professionally. Ted said jokingly, "I guess we could run to Vegas and parlay the money into a fortune. Or we could take a comparable risk and invest in the stock market."

Erin replied, "I have a better idea. Let's get together with Tanya and Nick, and really thrash out what to do with Pet Groomers profits. We can all have dinner together, followed by a no-holds-barred problem-solving session."

Case Questions

1. Does the problem facing the owners of Pet Groomers on Wheels seem suited for going through the steps for group problem solving? If not, what other problem-solving technique would you recommend?

2. Take the problem of what to do with Pet Groomers's profits through the group problem-solving steps, even if you have to make assumptions about some of the data for the steps.

3. Compare the conclusion you reach in response to question 2 with the conclusion reached by other individuals or groups in the class.

Interpersonal Relations Case 7-2

The Torpedoed Submarine Rolls

Chad is the sales manager at Guarino's Bakery, a supplier of bread products, cakes, and pastries to local restaurants and stores. He enjoys the challenge of his job and welcomes the opportunity to practise the skills and techniques of a professional manager. Chad has acquired some of these techniques through experience and many others through reading business books and course work.

During the past three months, five accounts have stopped ordering from Guarino's the Italian bread they use for submarine sandwiches. The president and owner, Angelo Guarino, told Chad, "Our submarine bread sales are being torpedoed. Our reputation is getting so bad that we'll soon be out of business. Find out by next week what has gone wrong with our line of bread. Max [head baker] swears the bread hasn't changed."

"Angelo, I've been trying hard to find the answer," responded Chad. "So far, the only clue I have is that our submarine rolls just don't taste right. Something is wrong, but our customers don't know what it is. Several of them have complained that their customers say the bread is just not as good as in the past."

Angelo retorted, "Then go back and investigate some more. We've got to know what's wrong."

Chad said to himself, "Now is the time for action. But I'm not sure what action. Should I take a survey of dissatisfied customers? Should I increase the advertising budget?"

Case Questions

1. How might the problem facing Guarino's Bakery be resolved through group decision making?
2. Which technique should Chad use to solve the problem of customer resistance to the submarine rolls?
3. What is the underlying, or true, problem facing Guarino's Bakery?

Questions for Discussion and Review

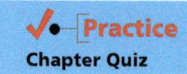

✓ **Practice Chapter Quiz**

Multiple Choice

1. A good example of political decision making would be to
   a. evaluate a new company location based on the cost of living for employees.
   b. vote for a certain supply company because your sister works for the company.
   c. base employee bonuses on productivity.
   d. hire a new employee based on qualifications.

2. All of the following are rules for brainstorming except:
   a. Invite outsiders to the brainstorming session.
   b. Take notes during the session.
   c. Carefully criticize ideas that do not fit the criterion.
   d. Add ideas to ones that have already been presented.

3. Standup meetings
   a. are, on average, longer than sit-down meetings.
   b. tend to be a drain on team production.
   c. usually result in the same quality of results as sit-down meetings.
   d. increase worker satisfaction more than sit-down meetings.

4. A shared whiteboard that allows two or more people to view and draw on a common surface electronically is an example of
   a. groupware.
   b. groupthink.
   c. group dynamics.
   d. group drawing.

5. All of the following are suggestions for more effective meetings except:
   a. Arrive at the meeting prepared.
   b. Be punctual.
   c. Engage in positive nonverbal behaviours.
   d. Make sure that you contribute more than the other group members.

Answers to multiple choice questions: 1. b, 2. c, 3. c, 4. a, 5. d.

Short Answer

6. What, if any, accommodations should be made in electronic brainstorming for group members who have poor keyboarding skills?
7. Identify two work-related problems for which the nominal group technique is particularly well suited.
8. Companies have known about standup meetings for many years, and the results have been favourable in terms of productivity. Why, then, are such meetings still not very popular?
9. Which group decision-making technique described in this chapter do you think members of top management are the most likely to use? Why?
10. Using your MySearchLab, log on to the videos and watch the video "Conflict" from Chapter 9. What rules was this team breaking in regard to brainstorming? What suggestions do you have to get this team back to developing better ideas with less conflict?

The Web Corner

www.mindtools.com
Techniques for group and individual problem solving, and creativity

http://www.businessballs.com/problemsolving.htm
From Businessballs, more information on problem-solving and decision-making

Internet Skill Builder: Where Did I Put That Great Idea I Had?

Many people involved in group brainstorming hit upon useful ideas when away from the brainstorming session, then forget the idea by the time they get to the session. So during the session, they fail to make an outstanding contribution. Search the Internet for some cool ideas for recording your ideas. An example would be sending yourself an email or voicemail message if you come upon a useful idea while hiking. You are encouraged to look widely for a couple of concrete suggestions for filing your creative ideas on the spot. Remember that fresh ideas are the building block for all types of groups, as well as individual problem solving.

MySearchLab

Visit **MySearchLab** to find self-grading review quizzes in the eText, discipline-specific media and readings, access to a variety of academic journals, and Associated Press news feeds, along with a wide range of writing, grammar, and research tools and to help hone writing and research skills.

CHAPTER 8
Cross-Cultural Relations and Diversity

Leanne was very excited when she was chosen to fly to China to discuss the details of a tender her company had succeeded in obtaining. The company she works for builds intricate measuring equipment used in mining and other geographic and geologic operations. As part of the marketing division, Leanne was to fly to China and meet with officials from the Chinese company for the final signing of all documentation and to familiarize herself with the company's operations.

Leanne had learned in similar dealings in Canada and the United States that the giving of a small gift when being treated to a meal is proper business etiquette. She had brought an elegant gift wrapped in beautiful white-and-black paper in the event such an occasion arose. As it happened, on her last evening in China—when all the business had been concluded—Leanne was invited out to dinner with Yen Lo, the owner, and his wife. Pleased with her gift of a carving done by a Canadian artist, Leanne was surprised by its stony reception. The rest of the evening was not very pleasant.

When Leanne returned home, she decided to approach an Asian friend of hers about the incident. When she told her about the gift, her friend suddenly interjected, "Oh my, you gave them a gift for mourning. We wrap gifts for those who have had a loved one die in black and white!"

Leanne made a mistake that is common when interacting with those from other cultures. She assumed that there were few differences between her North American cultural background and that of someone with an Asian upbringing. People often assume that, with technology, a global marketplace, and instant communication, differences between people are diminishing. While this may be true in some cultures, the assumption may hurt future business.

Cultures around the world still differ from each other in many ways and work to maintain their differences: their own set of beliefs, ideas, and ways of doing things, including how to do business. Being part of a global economy and

Echo/Cultura/Getty Images

LEARNING Objectives

After reading and studying this chapter and doing the exercises, you should be able to

1. Recognize who fits under the diversity umbrella.
2. Describe the major values accounting for cultural differences.
3. Overcome many cross-cultural communication barriers.
4. Improve your cross-cultural relations.

---

global marketplace means that employees need to be more aware of cultural differences and other diversity issues. A competent employee would have researched Chinese customs before departing. With some prior knowledge of Chinese culture, Leanne would not have made such an embarrassing—and perhaps costly—mistake.

While many employees may have the opportunity to visit other countries, an extensive knowledge of cultural differences and diversity is also required for work within our own country. Canada is a diverse nation, and the workplace reflects this diversity. Not only is the workforce becoming more diverse, but business has also become increasingly international. Small- and medium-sized firms, as well as corporate giants, are increasingly dependent on trade with other countries. Furthermore, most manufactured goods contain components from abroad.

All this workplace diversity has an important implication for the career-minded individual. To succeed in today's workplace, you must be able to relate effectively to people from different cultural groups from within and outside this country. Being able to relate to a culturally diverse customer base is also necessary for success, as is working with others from different cultural or ethnic backgrounds. To become more familiar with the cultural diversity in Canada, Figure 8-1 presents a statistical picture of Canadian diversity with a look toward the future.

This chapter presents concepts and techniques you can use to sharpen your ability to work effectively with people from diverse backgrounds. To get you started thinking about your readiness to work in a culturally diverse environment, take Self-Assessment Quiz 8-1.

THE DIVERSITY UMBRELLA

LEARNING OBJECTIVE 1

Improving cross-cultural relations includes understanding the true meaning of appreciating diversity. To appreciate diversity, a person must go beyond tolerating people from different racial and ethnic groups and treating them fairly. The true meaning of valuing diversity is to respect and enjoy a wide range of cultural and individual differences. Appreciating these differences is often referred to as *inclusion* to emphasize unity rather than diversity. To be diverse is to be different in some measurable way, even if what is measurable is not visible (such as religion or sexual orientation).

To be highly skilled in interpersonal relations, one must recognize and appreciate individual and demographic (group or category) differences, as well as cultural differences. People from the same demographic group often come from many different cultures. For example, the Asian demographic group is composed of many different cultures. Some people are more visibly diverse than others because of physical features or disabilities. Yet

FIGURE 8-1 A Statistical Picture of a Culturally Diverse Population Now and in the Future

Canada is an increasingly diverse country. Below are some interesting statistics about our national diversity now and into the future.

- In 2006, 17% of Canada's population consisted of young people under 15 years of age, 69% of persons aged 15 to 64 years, and 13% of persons aged 65 years and over. The most recent population projections show that toward the middle of the 2010 decade, the proportion of elderly might exceed the proportion of children, a historic first.
- Strong immigration to Canada in recent decades has led to a rise in the number of foreign-born persons and the portion of the population that they represent. Thus, from 1986 to 2006, the immigrant population went from 3.9 million to 6.2 million, accounting for respectively 15.6% and 19.8.% of the Canadian population. In 2017, this may lead to one in five Canadians being foreign-born.
- Visible minority numbers will also continue to increase. In 2017, approximately 20% of the Canadian population may belong to a visible minority group.
- The largest visible minority groups are the Chinese and South Asians. The visible minority groups that might increase the most rapidly between now and 2017 are West Asians, Koreans and Arabs, with their populations increasing by 150%, 120%, and 118%, respectively.
- Between 1996 and 2006, the population reporting Aboriginal identity grew by 45%, to reach close to 1.2 million persons, representing 3.8% of the Canadian population. The rest of the population grew more slowly (8%) during the same period.
- In 2006, the vast majority (98%) of Canadians knew enough of one of the two official languages (English and French) to conduct a conversation. Two-thirds (68%) of the population knew only English while 13% knew only French. The proportion of bilingual Canadians—those capable of conducting a conversation in either English or French—was 17% according to the 2006 Census. It was 12% in 1951.
- The highest speakers of non-official languages in 2006 were Chinese (3.9% of the population), Spanish (2.4%), Italian (2.1%), German (2.0%), Punjabi (1.5%), and Arabic (1.2%).

Source: Statistics Canada (2008), "Some Facts about the Demographic and Ethnocultural Composition of the Population," http://www.statcan.gc.ca/pub/91-003-x/2007001/4129904-eng.htm accessed 02/01/2013.

the diversity umbrella is supposed to include everybody in an organization. To value diversity is therefore to appreciate individual differences among people.

The diversity umbrella continues to include more people as the workforce encompasses a greater variety of people. The goal of a diverse organization is for persons of all cultural backgrounds to achieve their full potential, unrestrained by group identities such as sex, nationality, or race.[1] Another important goal is for these groups to work together harmoniously.

Figure 8-2 presents a broad sampling of the ways in which workplace associates can differ from one another. Studying this list can help you anticipate the types of differences to understand and appreciate in a diverse workplace. The differences include cultural as well as individual factors. Individual factors are also important because people can be discriminated against for personal characteristics as well as group factors. Many people, for example, believe they are held back from promotion because of their weight-to-height ratio.

A diverse workforce is noted to have many consequences to the organization, mostly positive, but some negative. A sampling of these consequences is as follows:

- Multicultural experiences are strongly associated with creative thinking, and creative outcomes such as ideas for new products.[2] If you work with people from different cultures on the job or associate with them in personal life, your creativity is likely to be enhanced.

SELF-ASSESSMENT QUIZ 8-1

Cross-Cultural Skills and Attitudes

Listed below are skills and attitudes that various employers and cross-cultural experts think are important for relating effectively to co-workers in a culturally diverse environment.

	Applies to Me Now	Not There Yet
1. I have spent some time in another country.	____	____
2. At least one of my friends is deaf, blind, or uses a wheelchair.	____	____
3. Currency from other countries is as real as the currency from my own country.	____	____
4. I can read in a language other than my own.	____	____
5. I can speak in a language other than my own.	____	____
6. I can write in a language other than my own.	____	____
7. I can understand people speaking in a language other than my own.	____	____
8. I use my second language regularly.	____	____
9. My friends include people of races different from my own.	____	____
10. My friends include people of different ages.	____	____
11. I feel (or would feel) comfortable having a friend with a sexual orientation different from mine.	____	____
12. My attitude is that although another culture may be very different from mine, that culture is equally good.	____	____
13. I would be willing to (or already do) hang art from different countries in my home.	____	____
14. I would accept (or have already accepted) a work assignment of more than several months in another country.	____	____
15. I have a valid passport.	____	____

Interpretation: If you answered "Applies to Me Now" to 10 or more of the preceding questions, you most likely function well in a multicultural work environment. If you answered "Not There Yet" to 10 or more of the questions, you need to develop more cross-cultural awareness and skills to work effectively in a multicultural work environment. You will notice that being bilingual gives you at least five points on this quiz.

Sources: Several ideas for statements on this quiz are derived from Ruthann Dirks and Janet Buzzard, "What CEOs Expect of Employees Hired for International Work," *Business Education Forum*, April 1997, pp. 3–7; and Gunnar Beeth, "Multicultural Managers Wanted," *Management Review*, May 1997, pp. 17–21.

✓ **Practice**
Cross-Cultural Skills and Attitudes

- A diverse workforce helps generate more profits through such means as having employees on board who look similar to and share the same customs as their customers.[3] Allstate and Walmart exemplify companies whose culturally diverse workforce helps them attract more customers.
- Cultural diversity within groups can sometimes lead to so much conflict and disagreement that productivity suffers. Diversity in educational background and age can also lead to conflict. However, a study in Germany found that in teams where the need for intellectual stimulation was relatively high, team performance increased in the presence of diversity in educational experience and age.[4]
- The setting of the diverse workgroup can sometimes influence whether or not cultural diversity leads to enhanced performance. A compilation of many studies found that relations-oriented diversity led to high performance in service industry settings. (Relations-oriented includes race, ethnicity, gender, and age.) In contrast, this type of diversity had slightly negative effects in manufacturing settings.[5]

FIGURE 8-2 The Diversity Umbrella

- Race
- Sex (or gender)
- Religion
- Age (young, middle-age, and old)
- Ethnicity (country of origin)
- Education
- Abilities
- Mental disabilities (including attention deficit disorder)
- Physical disabilities (including hearing status, visual status, able-bodied, wheelchair user)
- Values and motivation
- Sexual orientation (heterosexual, homosexual, bisexual, transsexual)
- Marital status (married, single, cohabitating, widow, widower)
- Family status (children, no children, two-parent family, single parent, grandparent)
- Personality traits
- Functional background (area of specialization)
- Technology interest (high-tech, low-tech, technophobe)
- Weight status (average, obese, underweight, anorexic)
- Hair status (full head of hair, bald, wild hair, tame hair, long hair, short hair)
- Tobacco status (smoker versus nonsmoker, chewer versus nonchewer)
- Styles of clothing and appearance (dress up, dress down, professional appearance, casual appearance)
- Socio-economic status, such as some groups having low income and formal education, whereas others have high income and high formal education

UNDERSTANDING CULTURAL DIFFERENCES

LEARNING OBJECTIVE 2

The groundwork for developing effective cross-cultural relations is to understand cultural differences. The information about different communication patterns between men and women presented in Chapter 4 is relevant here. We discuss six aspects of understanding cultural differences: (1) cultural sensitivity including political correctness; (2) cultural intelligence; (3) respect for all workers; (4) cultural fluency; (5) dimensions of differences in cultural values; and (6) avoidance of cultural bloopers. To work smoothly with people from other cultures, it is important to become competent in all six areas.

Cultural Sensitivity and Political Correctness

To relate well to someone from a foreign country, a person must be alert to possible cultural differences. When working in another country, you must be willing to acquire knowledge about local customs and learn how to at least passably speak the native language. When working with people from different cultures, even fellow Canadians, you must be patient, adaptable, flexible, and willing to listen and learn. The characteristics just mentioned are part of **cultural sensitivity**, an awareness of and willingness to investigate the reasons why people of another culture act as they do.[6] A person with cultural sensitivity will recognize certain nuances in customs that will help him or her build better relationships with people from different cultural backgrounds.

cultural sensitivity
An awareness of, and a willingness to investigate, the reasons why people of another culture act as they do.

158 CHAPTER 8

Another aspect of cultural sensitivity is **political correctness**—being careful not to offend or slight anyone, and being civil and respectful.[7] An effective use of political correctness would be to say, "We need a ladder in our department because we have workers of different heights who need access to the top shelves." It would be politically incorrect to say, "We need ladders because we have some short workers who cannot reach the top shelves." Carried too far, political correctness can push a person in the direction of being too bland and imprecise in language. The ultra-politically-correct person, for example, will almost never mention a person's race, sex, ethnicity, or health status when referring to another worker. For example, he or she would not make a statement like, "Sadie is German, so she was a natural to be our liaison with the manufacturing group." (The cultural stereotype here is that Germans are quite interested in manufacturing technology and think precisely.)

Empathy is a major trait and skill that facilitates cultural sensitivity and political correctness. You have to take the other person's perspective, and ask yourself questions like, "How would I like it if somebody snarled and said an ugly word when he or she looked at my favourite food?" Kim Oliver and Sylvester Baugh offer this insight into developing the type of empathy helpful in building cross-cultural relations in the workplace: "We want to try to develop an understanding for the majority about what it might be like to be the minority, and help the minority understand what it's like to be the majority."[8]

Cultural Intelligence

An advanced aspect of cultural sensitivity is to be able to fit in comfortably with people of another culture by observing the subtle cues they give about how a person should act in their presence. **Cultural intelligence (CQ)** is an outsider's ability to interpret someone's unfamiliar and ambiguous behaviour the same way that person's compatriots would.[9] With high cultural intelligence, a person would be able to figure out what behaviour would be true of all people and all groups, such as rapid shaking of a clenched fist to communicate anger. Also, the person with high cultural intelligence could figure out what is unique to this group, and those aspects of behaviour that are neither universal nor peculiar to the group. These ideas are so abstract that an example may clarify.

> *An English Canadian manager served on a design team that included two German engineers. As other team members floated their ideas, the engineers condemned them as incomplete or underdeveloped. The manager concluded that Germans in general are rude and aggressive.*
>
> *With average cultural intelligence the Canadian would have realized he was mistakenly equating the merit of an idea with the merit of the person presenting it. The Germans, however, were able to make a sharp distinction between the two. A manager with more advanced cultural intelligence might have tried to figure out how much of the two Germans' behaviour was typically German and how much was explained by the fact that they were engineers.*

Similar to emotional intelligence, cultural intelligence encompasses several different aspects of behaviour. The three sources of cultural intelligence relate to the cognitive, the emotional/motivational, and the physical, shown in Figure 8-3, and explained as follows:[10]

1. **Cognitive (the head).** The cognitive part of CQ refers to what a person knows and how he or she can acquire new knowledge. Here you acquire facts about people from another culture such as their passion for football (soccer in North America), their business practices, and their promptness in paying bills. Another aspect of this source of cultural intelligence is figuring out how you can learn more about the other culture.

2. **Emotional/motivational (the heart).** The emotional/motivational aspect of CQ refers to energizing one's actions and building personal confidence. You need both confidence and motivation to adapt to another culture. A man on a business trip to Africa might say to himself, "When I greet a work associate in a restaurant, can I really pull off kissing him on both cheeks? What if he thinks I'm

political correctness
Being careful not to offend or slight anyone, and being extra civil and respectful.

cultural intelligence (CQ)
An outsider's ability to interpret someone's unfamiliar and ambiguous behaviour the same way that person's compatriots would.

CROSS-CULTURAL RELATIONS AND DIVERSITY

FIGURE 8-3 The Components of Cultural Intelligence

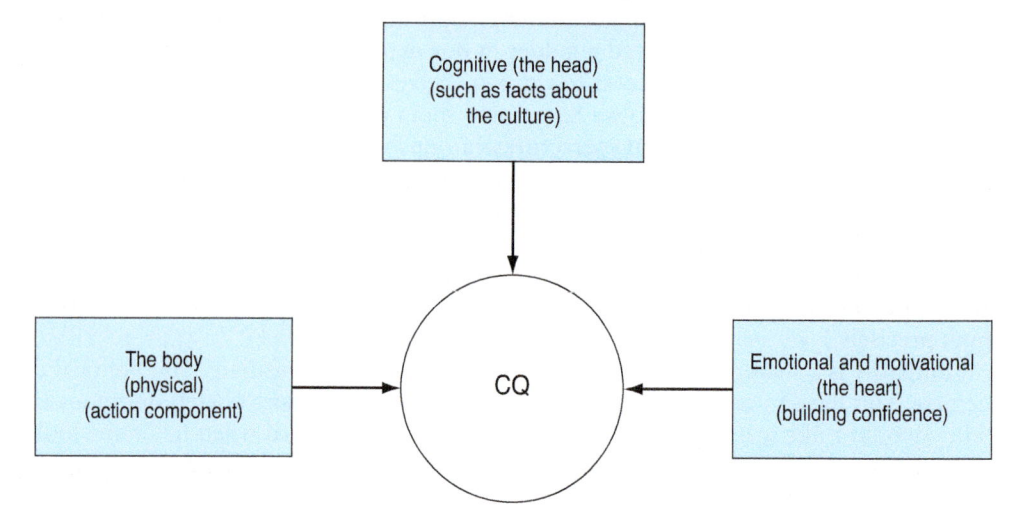

```
                    Cognitive (the head)
                    (such as facts about
                       the culture)
                              |
                              v
  The body                                    Emotional and motivational
  (physical)     ──────►   CQ   ◄──────           (the heart)
  (action component)                            (building confidence)
```

weird?" With strong motivation, the same person might say, "I'll give it a try. I kind of greet my grandfather the same way back in Quebec."

3. **The body (physical).** The body aspect of CQ is the action component. The body is the element for translating intentions into actions and desires. Kissing the same-sex African work associates on both cheeks is the *physical* aspect just mentioned. We often have an idea of what we should do, but implementation is not so easy. You might know, for example, that when entering an Asian person's home you should take off your shoes, yet you might not actually remove them—thereby offending your Asian work (or personal life) associate.

To practise high cultural intelligence, the mind, heart, and body have to work together. You need to figure out how to act with people from another culture; you need motivation and confidence to change; and you have to translate your knowledge and motivation into action. So when you are on a business trip to London, go ahead and hold your fork in your left hand!

Respect for All Workers and Cultures

An effective strategy for achieving cross-cultural understanding is to simply respect all others in the workplace, including their cultures. An important component of respect is to believe that although another person's culture is different from yours, it is equally good.

Respect comes from valuing differences. Respecting other people's customs can translate into specific attitudes, such as respecting one co-worker for wearing a yarmulke on Friday or another for wearing African clothing to celebrate Kwanzaa. Another way of being respectful would be to listen carefully to the opinion of a senior worker who says the company should never have converted to voice mail and a voice recognition system in place of assistants answering the phone (even though you disagree).

Company policies that encourage respect for the rights of others are likely to create a positive influence on tolerance throughout the firm. An example is that many employers have taken steps to recognize and affirm the existence of gay and lesbian workers. Among these steps are the publication of formal statements of nondiscrimination and the inclusion of issues about sexual orientation in diversity training programs. A major policy change has been to grant same-sex couples the same benefits granted to opposite-sex couples.

Another formal (official) way of demonstrating respect for all workers is to provide for the presence of **employee network (or affinity) groups**. Such a group is composed of employees throughout the company who affiliate on the basis of group characteristics, such as race, ethnicity, gender, sexual orientation, or physical-ability status. The network group provides members of the same demographic or cultural group an avenue for sharing ideas with management. Employee network groups at McDonald's, for example, include the African-American Council, the Hispanic Employee Network, the Asian Employee Network, and the Gays, Lesbians and Allies at McDonald's.[11]

A study of 537 gay and lesbian employees working for a variety of organizations demonstrated that the more prevalently a company's policies deal with respect, the more equitably sexual minorities are likely to be treated. More equitable treatment, in turn, was associated with gays and lesbians being more satisfied with their work and less likely to leave the firm.[12]

employee network (or affinity) groups

A group composed of employees throughout the company who affiliate on the basis of group characteristics, such as race, ethnicity, gender, sexual orientation, or physical-ability status.

Cultural Fluency

A high-level goal in understanding cultural differences is to achieve **cultural fluency**, the ability to conduct business in a diverse, international environment.[13] Achieving cultural fluency includes a variety of skills, such as relating well to people from different cultures and knowing a second language. Cultural fluency also includes knowledge of the international business environment, such as how the exchange rate can affect profits. Having high cultural intelligence would contribute to cultural fluency because such intelligence makes it easier to work well with people from other cultures. If you are culturally fluent, you will also find it easier to make friends (real and virtual) from other cultures.

cultural fluency

The ability to conduct business in a diverse, international environment.

BACK TO THE OPENING CASE

Leanne failed to develop her cultural fluency. With a bit of study about the culture of China, she would not have made such a cultural blooper and offended her hosts. Leanne will likely not make this mistake again, leading her to better cultural fluency and more able to make meaningful connections with others from diverse cultures.

Skill-Building Exercise 8-1 is a warm-up activity for achieving cultural sensitivity, and perhaps respect for all workers.

Dimensions of Differences in Cultural Values

One way to understand how national cultures differ is to examine their values or cultural dimensions. The formulation presented here is based on the worldwide research in 62 societal cultures and builds on previous analyses of cultural dimensions.[14] The cultural dimensions presented here are those most directly related to interpersonal skills. Keep in

SKILL-BUILDING EXERCISE 8-1

Developing Cultural Sensitivity

Carefully observe how products and services such as tennis shoes, notebooks, bicycles, and banking services are marketed and sold in Canada, and then attempt to find out how they are marketed and sold in other countries. For a convenient reference source, interview foreign students and foreigners outside class about these products and services. Your digging for information might uncover such nuggets as the following:

- In India, cricket champions are celebrities, comparable to Canadian hockey stars, and they endorse soft drinks such as Coca-Cola and Pepsi.
- In Hungary, peanut butter is considered a luxury food item.
- In some countries in warm climates, meat is freshly killed and hung on hooks for sale—without refrigeration or freezing.

After conducting these product and service interviews, arrive at some kind of interpretation or conclusion. Share your insights with other class members.

Source: "Teaching International Business," *Keying In* (The Newsletter of the National Business Education Association), January 1999, p. 1.

CROSS-CULTURAL RELATIONS AND DIVERSITY 161

mind that these cultural dimensions are stereotypes that apply to a representative person from a particular culture, and are not meant to insult anybody. These cultural dimensions are differences between national societies and may not be representative of a given individual. As with gender stereotypes in communication, individual differences are substantial. For example, many Americans are not assertive, and many French are willing to work 70 hours per week.

1. Performance orientation is the degree to which a society encourages, or should encourage, and rewards group members for performance improvement and excellence. Countries high on this dimension are the United States and Singapore, whereas those low on this dimension are Russia and Greece.
2. Assertiveness is the degree to which individuals are (and should be) assertive, confrontational, and aggressive in their relationships with one another. Countries scoring high on this dimension are the United States, Canada, and Austria, whereas those low on this dimension are Sweden and New Zealand. Assertive people enjoy competition in business, in contrast to less assertive cultural groups who prefer harmony, loyalty, and solidarity.
3. Time orientation is the importance nations and individuals attach to time. People with an urgent time orientation perceive time as a scarce resource and tend to be impatient. People with a casual time orientation view time as an unlimited and unending resource and tend to be patient. North Americans are noted for their urgent time orientation. They frequently impose deadlines and are eager to get started doing business. Asians, Mexicans, and Middle Easterners, in contrast, are patient negotiators.
4. Humane orientation is the degree to which a society encourages and rewards, and should encourage and reward, individuals for being fair, altruistic, caring, and kind toward others. Egypt and Malaysia rank high on this cultural dimension, and France and Germany rank lower.
5. In-group collectivism is the degree to which individuals express, and should express, pride, loyalty, and cohesiveness in their organizations and families. Asian societies emphasize collectivism, as do Egypt and Russia. One consequence of collectivism is taking pride in family members and the organizations that employ them.
6. Gender egalitarianism is the degree to which a culture minimizes, and should minimize, gender inequality. European countries emphasize gender egalitarianism, and so do the United States and Canada. South Korea is an example of a country that is low on gender egalitarianism, and is male-dominated.
7. Acceptance of power and authority is the degree to which members of a society expect, and should expect, power to be distributed unequally. Individuals who accept power and authority expect the boss to make the major decisions. These same individuals are more formal; however, being formal toward people in positions of authority has decreased substantially throughout the world in recent years. Examples of societies that score high on acceptance of power and authority are Thailand, Brazil, France, and Japan.
8. Work orientation is the number of hours per week and weeks per year people expect to invest in work versus leisure, or other non-work activities. Many North American corporate professionals typically work about 55 hours per week, take 45-minute lunch breaks, and take two weeks of vacation. North Americans tend to have a stronger work orientation than Europeans but a weaker one than Asians. For example, U.S. employees average 1804 hours of work per year, compared with 1407 for Norwegian workers and 1564 for the French. Workers in seven Asian countries including South Korea, Bangladesh, and China worked 2200 hours per year.[15]

9. Social-support-seeking is the degree to which people seek out others to help them with difficult problems through such means as listening, offering sympathy, and giving advice. Asians and Asian Americans are more reluctant to explicitly request support from close others than are European Americans. The hesitancy comes about because the Asians and Asian Americans are more concerned about negative relationship consequences, such as disrupting group harmony or receiving criticism from the other person. Another possible reason for the hesitancy is that Asians and Asian Americans expect social support without having to ask.[16]

How might someone use information about cultural differences to improve his or her interpersonal relations on the job? A starting point would be to recognize that a person's national values might influence his or her behaviour. Assume that you wanted to establish a good working relationship with a person from a high *humane orientation culture*. An effective starting point would be to emphasize care and concern when communicating with the individual.

Attitudes toward acceptance of power and authority can make a difference in establishing working relationships. A worker who values deference to age, gender, or title might shy away from offering suggestions to an elder or manager to avoid appearing disrespectful. This worker would need considerable encouragement to collaborate in decision making.[17] *Time orientation* may create a conflict if you are committed to making deadlines and a team member has a laid-back attitude toward time. You might explain that although you respect his attitudes toward time, the company insists on getting the project completed on time.

Self-Assessment Quiz 8-2 will help you think about how cultural dimensions might be influencing your interpersonal relations in the workplace.

SELF-ASSESSMENT QUIZ 8-2

Charting Your Cultural Dimension Profile

Directions: For each of the nine cultural dimensions, circle the number that most accurately fits your standing on the dimension. For example, if you perceive yourself to be "highly humane," circle 6 on the fourth dimension (item 4).

1. High performance orientation / Low performance orientation
   1 2 3 4 5 6 7
2. Low assertiveness / High assertiveness
   1 2 3 4 5 6 7
3. Urgent time orientation / Casual time orientation
   1 2 3 4 5 6 7
4. High humane orientation / Low humane orientation
   1 2 3 4 5 6 7
5. In-group collectivism / In-group individualism
   1 2 3 4 5 6 7
6. High gender egalitarianism / Low gender egalitarianism
   1 2 3 4 5 6 7
7. High acceptance of power and authority / Low acceptance of power and authority
   1 2 3 4 5 6 7
8. Work orientation / Leisure orientation
   1 2 3 4 5 6 7
9. Social-support-seeking / Social support avoidance
   1 2 3 4 5 6 7

Scoring and Interpretation: After circling one number for each dimension, use a pen or pencil to connect the circles, thereby giving yourself a profile of cultural values. Do not be concerned if your line cuts through the names of the dimensions. Compare your profile to others in the class. Should time allow, develop a class profile by computing the class average for each of the nine points and then connecting the points.

Cultural Bloopers

An effective way of being culturally sensitive is to minimize actions that are likely to offend people from another culture, based on their values. Cultural bloopers are most likely to take place when you are visiting another country. The same bloopers, however, can also be committed when dealing with people from a different culture within your own country. To avoid these bloopers, you must carefully observe persons from another culture. Studying another culture through reading is also helpful.

E-commerce and other forms of Internet communication have created new opportunities for creating cultural bloopers. Website developers and those responsible for adding content must have good cross-cultural literacy, including an awareness of how the information might be misinterpreted. Here are examples of three potential problems:

- Numerical date formats can be readily misinterpreted. To an American, 4/9/13 would be interpreted as April 9, 2013 (or 1913!). However, many Europeans would interpret the same numerical expression as September 4, 2013.
- Colours on websites must be chosen carefully. For example, in some cultures purple is the colour of royalty, whereas in Brazil purple is associated with death.
- Be careful of metaphors that may not make sense to a person for whom your language is a second language. Examples include "ethical meltdown," "Cat got your tongue?" and "over the hill."

English has become the language of business and science throughout the world, yet communicating in a customer's native tongue has its advantages. Being able to communicate your message directly in your customer's mother tongue provides a competitive advantage. Bilingualism also has career implications. Some telemarketing, banking, engineering, and financial service companies are searching for workers with bilingual skills. The two major contributing factors are the growing immigrant population and because companies are engaged more in international business.[18]

Furthermore, according to the research firm IDC, consumers are four times more likely to purchase a product online if the website is in their preferred language.[19] The translator, of course, must have good knowledge of the subtleties of the language to avoid committing a blooper. An English-to-French translator used the verb *baiser* instead of *baisser* to describe a program of lowering prices. *Baisser* is the French verb "to lower," but *baiser* means "kiss." Worse, in slang *baiser* is a verb that refers to intimate physical relations!

Keep two key facts in mind when attempting to avoid making cultural mistakes. One is that members of any cultural group show individual differences. What one member of the group might regard as an insensitive act, another might welcome. Recognize also that one or two cultural mistakes will not peg you permanently as a boor. Skill-Building Exercise 8-2 will help you minimize certain cultural bloopers.

OVERCOMING CROSS-CULTURAL BARRIERS

LEARNING OBJECTIVE 3

We have already discussed the importance of overcoming communication barriers in Chapter 4. Cultural differences create additional barriers. The following guidelines will help you overcome cross-cultural communication barriers.

1. **Be sensitive to the fact that cross-cultural communication barriers exist.** If you are aware of these potential barriers, you will be ready to deal with them. When you are dealing with a person in the workplace with a different cultural background than your own, solicit feedback to minimize cross-cultural barriers to communication. Being aware of these potential barriers will help you develop cultural sensitivity.
2. **Show respect for all workers.** The same behaviour that promotes good cross-cultural relations in general helps overcome communication barriers. A widely used comment that implies disrespect is to say to a person from another culture, "You have a funny accent." Should you be transposed to that person's culture, you, too, might have a "funny accent."
3. **Use straightforward language and speak slowly and clearly.** When working with people who do not speak your language fluently, speak in an easy-to-understand

SKILL-BUILDING EXERCISE 8-2

Cultural Mistakes to Avoid with Selected Cultural Groups

Europe

Great Britain
- Asking personal questions. The British protect their privacy.
- Thinking that a business person from England is unenthusiastic when he or she says "Not bad at all." English people understate positive emotion.
- Gossiping about royalty.

France
- Expecting to complete work during the French two-hour lunch.
- Attempting to conduct significant business during August—*les vacances* (vacation time).
- Greeting a French person for the first time and not using a title such as "sir" or "madam" (or "monsieur," "madame," or "mademoiselle").

Italy
- Eating too much pasta, as it is not the main course.
- Handing out business cards freely. Italians use them infrequently.

Spain
- Expecting punctuality. Your appointments will usually arrive 20 to 30 minutes late.
- Making the American sign for "okay" with your thumb and forefinger. In Spain (and many other countries) this is vulgar.

Scandinavia (Denmark, Sweden, Norway)
- Being overly conscious of rank. Scandinavians pay relatively little attention to a person's place in the hierarchy.

Asia

All Asian countries
- Pressuring an Asian job applicant or employee to brag about his or her accomplishments. Asians feel self-conscious when boasting about individual accomplishments; they prefer to let the record speak for itself. In addition, they prefer to talk about group rather than individual accomplishment.

Japan
- Shaking hands or hugging Japanese people (as well as other Asians) in public. The Japanese consider these practices offensive.
- Not interpreting "We'll consider it" as "No" when spoken by a Japanese business person. Japanese negotiators mean "No" when they say "We'll consider it."
- Not giving small gifts to Japanese people when conducting business. The Japanese are offended when they do not receive these gifts.
- Giving your business card to a Japanese business person more than once. The Japanese prefer to give and receive business cards only once.

China
- Using black borders on stationery and business cards. Black is associated with death.
- Giving small gifts to Chinese people when conducting business. The Chinese are offended by these gifts.
- Making cold calls on Chinese business executives. An appropriate introduction is required for a first-time meeting with a Chinese official.

Korea
- Saying no. Koreans feel it is important to have visitors leave with good feelings.

India
- Telling Indians you prefer not to eat with your hands. If the Indians are not using cutlery when eating, they expect you to do likewise.

Mexico and Latin America

Mexico
- Flying into a Mexican city in the morning and expecting to close a deal by lunch. Mexicans build business relationships slowly.

Brazil
- Attempting to impress Brazilians by speaking a few words of Spanish. Portuguese is the official language of Brazil.

Most Latin-American countries
- Wearing elegant and expensive jewellery during a business meeting. Most Latin Americans think people should appear more conservative in business settings.

Note: A cultural mistake for Canadians and Americans to avoid when conducting business in most other countries is to insist on getting down to business quickly. North Americans in small towns also like to build a relationship before getting down to business. The preceding suggestions will lead to cross-cultural skills development if practised in the right setting. During the next 30 days, look for an opportunity to relate to a person from another culture in the way described in these suggestions. Observe the reaction of the other person for feedback on your cross-cultural effectiveness.

---

manner. Minimize the use of idioms and analogies specific to your language. A computer analyst from Greece left confused after a discussion about a software problem with her manager. The manager said, "Let's talk about this another time because *I can't seem to get to first base with you.*" (The manager was referring to the fact that the conversation was headed nowhere because he couldn't come to an agreement with the analyst.) The computer analyst did not ask for clarification because she did not want to appear uninformed.

4. **Observe cultural differences in etiquette.** Violating rules of etiquette without explanation can erect immediate communication barriers. A major rule of etiquette in many countries is that people address each other by surname unless they have worked together for a long time. On the other hand, the superior might

encourage your being on a first-name basis with him or her. Be aware that although an increasing number of cultures are moving toward the informal approach, it is best to err on the side of formality.

5. **Be sensitive to differences in nonverbal communication.** Stay alert to the possibility that your nonverbal signal may be misinterpreted by a person from another culture. For example, an engineer for a Manitoba company was asked a question by a German co-worker. He signalled okay by making a circle with his thumb and forefinger. The German worker stormed away because in his country the same gesture is a vulgar personal insult. One area of nonverbal communication that often is misinterpreted is the use of interpersonal space. Cultures vary in what is considered appropriate distances between people when speaking. The results from a study done at the University of Montreal demonstrated cultural differences. Anglo Saxons used the largest zone of personal space, followed by Asians, and Mediterraneans and Latinos used the least amount of interpersonal distance.[20]

6. **Do not be diverted by style, accent, grammar, or personal appearance.** Although these superficial factors are all related to business success, they are difficult to interpret when judging a person from another culture. It is therefore better to judge the merits of the person's statement or behaviour.[21] A brilliant individual from another culture may still be learning your language and thus make basic mistakes in speaking it. Also, he or she might not yet have developed sensitivity to the dress style of your culture.

7. **Be attentive to individual differences in appearance.** A major cross-cultural insult is to confuse the identity of people because they are members of the same race or ethnic group. An older economics professor reared in China and teaching in Canada had difficulty communicating with students because he was unable to learn their names. The professor's defence was "So many of these Canadians look alike to me." Recent research suggests that people have difficulty seeing individual differences among people of another race because they code race first, such as thinking, "He has the nose of an African-American." However, people can learn to search for more distinguishing features, such as a dimple or eye colour.[22] In this way, individual differences are recognized.

8. **Be aware of and understand that prejudice and discrimination still exist and that members of different cultures have experienced and continue to experience much prejudice and discrimination.** While human rights codes, labour laws and practices, and company policies may all aspire to equality for all, this has not always been the case for many minorities. Prejudice and discrimination can be very subtle and continue for many minorities in Canada. Articles continue to point out that racism against black Canadians is still prevalent.[23] Also, current news articles continue to underscore the many inequalities faced by Canadian Aboriginals. Many programs and services have been implemented to assist Aboriginals in developing skills to succeed in the business world and run their own businesses, such as The Entrepreneurial Spirit: Introduction to Entrepreneurship, Business and Financial Management for Aboriginal Entrepreneurs, launched by the Canadian Bankers Association. Also, with continued growth of the First Nations Bank, there will continue to be more employment and business opportunities for Canadian Aboriginals.[24] The key point here is that while you may not be prejudiced or discriminatory, many people you encounter may have been the victims of such attitudes or treatment and you need to be sensitive to those experiences.

TECHNIQUES FOR IMPROVING CROSS-CULTURAL RELATIONS

LEARNING OBJECTIVE 4

Depending on where you choose to work, your contact with various cultures and groups will vary. If you work in larger urban centres, the cultural and ethnic diversity will be more pronounced than in more rural settings. If you choose to work in a large urban centre, you will likely encounter a wide range of cultural diversity. However, all settings will

SKILL-BUILDING EXERCISE 8-3

Cross-Cultural Relations Role-Play

One student plays the role of Ritu, a call centre representative in Bombay, India. Her specialty is helping customers with cellphone problems. Another student plays the role of Todd, an irate Canadian. His problem is that he cannot get his camera-equipped cell phone to transmit his photos by email. He is scheduled to attend a party in two hours, and wants to take loads of photos with his cell phone. Todd is impatient, and in the eyes of Ritu somewhat overbearing. Ritu is good-natured and pleasant, but feels she must help Todd solve his problem without being bullied by him. Because Ritu is instructed to spend the minimum time necessary to resolve the problem, she spends about five minutes on this problem.

The observers should make note of how well Ritu has made the necessary cross-cultural adaptations.

---

have a large diversity of groups. It is in your best personal and professional interest, then, to learn skills that will help you succeed in this culturally diverse nation.

Cultural Training

For many years, companies and government agencies have prepared their workers for overseas assignments. The method most frequently chosen is **cultural training**, a set of learning experiences designed to help employees understand the customs, traditions, and beliefs of another culture. In today's diverse business environment and international marketplace, learning about individuals raised in different cultural backgrounds has become more important. Many industries therefore train employees in cross-cultural relations.

Cultural training is also important for helping people of one culture understand their customers from another culture in particular, such as Chinese people learning to deal more effectively with their American customers. For example, in one training program Chinese businesspeople are taught how to sprinkle their email with English phrases like "How are you?" "It was great to hear from you," and "Can we work together?"[25] To practise improving your cross-cultural relations, do Skill-Building Exercise 8-3.

cultural training
A set of learning experiences designed to help employees understand the customs, traditions, and beliefs of another culture.

Cultural Intelligence Training

A newer development in assisting people to work more effectively with workers from other cultures is *cultural intelligence training*, a program based on the principles of cultural intelligence described earlier in this chapter. A key part of the training is to learn the three contributors to CQ—head, heart, and body. Instead of learning a few simple guidelines for working effectively with people from another culture, the trainee is taught strategies for sizing up the environment to determine which course of action is best. The culturally intelligent overseas worker would learn how to determine how much humour to interject into meetings, what kind of handshake is most appropriate, and so forth. The following excerpt will give you a feel for what is involved in cultural intelligence training:

> *A Canadian manager is attempting to interpret a "Thai smile." First, she needs to observe the various cues provided in addition to the smile gesture itself (e.g., other facial or bodily gestures, significance of others who may be in proximity, source of the original smile gesture) and to assemble them into a meaningful whole and make sense of what is really experienced by the Thai employee. Second, she must have the requisite motivation (directed effort and self-confidence) to persist in the face of confusion, challenge, or apparently mixed signals. Third, she must choose, generate, and execute the right actions to respond appropriately. So what does this smile mean and does it have the same meaning as it does to us?*
>
> *If any of these elements is deficient she is likely to be ineffective in dealing with the Thai employee. A high-CQ manager has the capability to deal with all three facets as they act in unison.*[26]

As the example illustrates, to be culturally intelligent you need to apply cognitive skills, have the right motivation, and then put your knowledge and confidence into action.

Armed with such skills you would know, for example, whether to greet a Mexican worker on a business trip to Texas with a handshake, a hug, or a kiss on both cheeks.

Language Training

Learning a foreign language is often part of cultural training, yet it can also be a separate activity. Knowledge of a second language is important because it builds better connections with people from other cultures than does relying on a translator. Building connections with people is still important even if English has become the international language of business. Many workers, aside from international business specialists, also choose to develop skills in a target language. Speaking another language can help build rapport with customers and employees who speak that language. As mentioned earlier, it is easier to sell to customers when using their native language.

Companies invest heavily in helping employees learn a target language because it facilitates conducting business in other countries. For this reason companies that offer language training and translation services are currently experiencing a boom. Medical specialists, police officers, and firefighters also find second language skills to be quite helpful because clients under stress, such as an injured person, are likely to revert to their native tongue. Learning a second language is particularly important when many of your customers and employees do not speak your country's official language.

As with any other skill training, investments in language training can pay off only if the trainee is willing to work hard at developing the new skill outside the training sessions. Allowing even 10 days to pass without practising your target language will result in a sharp decline in your ability to use that language.

Skill-Building Exercise 8-4 presents a low-cost, pleasant method of enhancing your foreign language and cross-cultural skills.

Diversity Training

diversity training

Training that attempts to bring about workplace harmony by teaching people how to get along better with diverse work associates.

The general purpose of cultural training is to help workers understand people from other cultures. Understanding can lead to dealing more effectively with them as work associates or customers. **Diversity training** has a slightly different purpose. It attempts to bring about workplace harmony by teaching people how to get along better with diverse work associates. Quite often the program is aimed at minimizing open expressions of racism and sexism. In recent years, diversity training has acquired the additional goal of accepting all dimensions of diversity based on the belief that enhanced business performance will result. For example, learning how to relate effectively to diverse customers can increase sales.[27]

Forms of Diversity Training. Diversity training takes a number of forms. Nevertheless, all centre on increasing awareness of and empathy for people who are different in some noticeable way from oneself. Training sessions in appreciating cultural diversity focus on the ways that men and women or people of different races reflect different values, attitudes, and cultural backgrounds. These sessions can vary from several hours to several

---

SKILL-BUILDING EXERCISE 8-4

Using the Internet to Help Develop Foreign-Language Skills

A useful way of developing skills in another language, and learning more about another culture, is to create a "bookmark" or "favourite" written in your target language and designate it as your home page. In this way, each time you go to the Internet on your own computer, your home page will contain fresh information in the language you want to develop.

To get started, use a search engine such as Yahoo! or Google that offers choices in several languages. Enter a search word such as "newspaper" or "current events" in the search probe. After you find a suitable choice, bookmark that newspaper as your home page. For example, imagine that French is your target language and culture. The Yahoo! France search engine might have brought you to www.france2.fr. This website, written in French, keeps you abreast of French and international news, sports, and cultural events. Now every time you access the Internet, you can spend five minutes practising your second language. You can save a lot of travel costs and time using the Internet to improve multicultural awareness.

days. Training sessions can also be held over a long period of time. Sometimes the program is confrontational, sometimes not.

An essential part of relating more effectively to diverse groups is to empathize with their points of view. To help training participants develop empathy, representatives of various groups explain their feelings related to workplace issues, including how they have felt different in a way that made them feel uncomfortable. A representative segment of a training program designed to enhance empathy took the following format. A minority group member was seated at the middle of a circle. First, the co-workers listened to an Indian woman explaining how she felt excluded from the in-group composed of whites and Asian Canadians in her department. "I feel like you just tolerate me. You do not make me feel that I am somebody important." The next person to sit in the middle of the circle was a Muslim. He complained about people wishing him Merry Christmas. "I would much prefer that my co-workers stop to think that I do not celebrate Christian holidays. I respect your religion, but it is not my religion."

Another form of diversity training is cross-generational diversity, or relating effectively to workers much older or younger than you. Cross-generational awareness training is one component in the corporate training program. The premise behind the program is that after acquiring cognitive knowledge, engaging in dialogue, and role-playing, employees will learn to accept people's differences, some of which are age-driven. For example, younger employees might feel less guilty than seniors when calling in sick just to have a day's vacation. Another part of cross-generational training would be to help older and younger generations appreciate their different preferences in communication. An example would be sending emails rather than text messages for disseminating brief bits of information.

Explore

Simulation: Cross-Cultural Relations and Diversity

Concerns about Diversity Training. Diversity training has frequently improved cross-cultural relationships in the workplace. Yet such programs can also create ill will and waste time. One problem is that participants are sometimes encouraged to be too confrontational and express too much hostility. Companies have found that when employees are too blunt during these sessions, it may be difficult to patch up interpersonal relations in the work group later on.

Another potential negative consequence of diversity training is that it sometimes results in perpetuating stereotypes about groups, such as people from Latin America not placing much value on promptness for meetings. A related problem is that diversity training might focus too much on differences instead of similarities.[28] For example, even if people are raised with different cultural values, they must all work harmoniously together to accomplish work. Although a worker believes that relationships are more important than profits, he or she must still produce enough to be a good investment for the company.

Skill-Building Exercise 8-5 provides you an opportunity to simulate an empathy-building experience in a diversity training program.

Cross-Cultural and Cross-Gender Mentoring Programs

An advanced method of improving cross-cultural relations is mentoring members of targeted minority groups. The mentoring demonstrates the company's interest in enhancing cross-cultural relations, and simultaneously enhances the minority group members'

SKILL-BUILDING EXERCISE 8-5

Developing Empathy for Differences

Class members come up to the front of the room one by one and give a brief presentation (perhaps even three minutes) of any way in which they have been perceived as different, and how they felt about this perception. Sometimes this exercise is referred to as "When I Felt Different." The difference refers to feeling different from the majority. The difference can be of any kind, relating to characteristics such as ethnicity, race, choice of major, physical appearance, height, weight, hair colour, or body piercing. After each member of the class (perhaps even the instructor) has presented, class members discuss what they learned from the exercise. It is also important to discuss how this exercise can improve relationships on the job.

Access the eText in MySearchLab to learn more about this chapter's self-assessment quizzes.

opportunities for advancement. To achieve cross-culture and cross-gender mentoring, companies often assign the member of the minority group a mentor who is typically an experienced manager. For example, a 24-year-old Canadian Aboriginal woman might be mentored by a 45-year-old Caucasian middle manager. Or a minority group member might be the mentor, such as a 45-year-old African-Canadian woman mentoring a 24-year-old Indian man.

As described in Chapter 12, mentors might help the person being mentored in such ways as making the right contacts and learning useful professional skills. A challenge noted with cross-cultural and cross-gender mentoring is a shortage of mentors with the right knowledge and interpersonal skills.

To Watch Explore Practice Study and Review, **visit MySearchLab**

Developing Your Human Relations Skills and Reinforcing Concepts

Summary

- The diversity umbrella includes all cultures and the development of cross-cultural relations. Six key aspects of understanding cultural differences are: (1) cultural sensitivity; (2) cultural intelligence; (3) respect for all workers and all cultures; (4) cultural fluency—the ability to conduct business in a diverse, international environment; (5) differences in cultural values; and (6) avoidance of cultural bloopers.
- Countries differ in their national values, leading to differences in how most people from a given country will react to situations. The dimensions studied here are (1) performance orientation, (2) assertiveness, (3) time orientation, (4) humane orientation, (5) in-group collectivism, (6) gender egalitarianism, (7) acceptance of power and authority, (8) work orientation, and (9) social-support-seeking.
- Communication barriers created by cultural differences can often be overcome by (1) being sensitive to the fact that these barriers exist; (2) showing respect for all workers; (3) using straightforward language and speaking slowly and clearly; (4) observing cultural differences in etiquette; (5) being sensitive to differences in nonverbal communication; (6) not being diverted by style, accent, grammar, or personal appearance; (7) being aware of the continued existence of prejudice and discrimination; and (8) being attentive to individual differences in appearance.
- Improve cross-cultural relations by increasing intercultural competence through (1) cultural training, (2) language training, (3) diversity training, and (4) mentoring programs.

Interpersonal Relations Case 8-1

What to Do with Shabana?

Shabana was raised in Pakistan and graduated from the University of Punjab with a major in commerce. She then moved to Toronto to live with her married aunt, as well as to begin a career in business in Canada. Shabana is fluent in her native Punjabi, but also has spoken and written English since the beginning of her primary education.

Having a sponsor in Canada made it possible for Shabana to enter the job market in Toronto. In addition to having a good formal education, Shabana makes a positive physical appearance that includes a warm smile and a comfortable, relaxed manner. After a two-month-long job search, Shabana found employment as a store associate in a cellphone store of one of the major mobile phone providers. She was content with this position because she thought it would be a stepping stone to store management in the field of consumer electronics.

Shabana enjoyed interacting with the other store associates, as well as the customers. An important part of her role was explaining some of the intricacies of cell phones, as well as the contracts, to customers. She willingly worked Saturday nights and Sunday afternoons, store hours unpopular with other associates.

From time to time, Shabana was perplexed about why some customers did not understand her. With a few of the older customers, Shabana attributed their lack of understanding to limited knowledge of technology, or hearing impairments. One customer looked straight at Shabana and said, "I do not understand a word you are saying."

One day Trevor, the store manager, took Shabana aside and told her, "You are a wonderful sales associate in many ways. The other associates enjoy working with you, and you get along well with many of our customers. Yet we are getting too many complaints by email and phone that many of our customers cannot understand you. It seems like some of these Toronto people just can't understand English with a Pakistani accent.

"Maybe some of our customers aren't the most sophisticated, but they are still customers. And we need every dollar we can take it to meet our sales goals. You need to become better understood by all our customers, or we can't keep you as a sales associate."

A little perplexed, Shabana replied, "I am so sorry to know that I have disappointed you and some of our valued customers. Please give me several weeks to correct this situation of my not being so well understood by all our customers."

Trevor replied, "Okay, but I am going to keep close watch on your progress."

Case Questions

1. What should Shabana do to improve her ability to be understood by more customers?
2. Is the problem of language comprehension in this case really a problem of customers not being too sharp mentally?
3. What actions do you recommend that Trevor take to help Shabana improve her ability to be understood by her customers? Or should he just fire her?
4. To what extent do you think Trevor is practising job discrimination by even hinting that he might fire Shabana if she is not better understood by a wider variety of customers?

Interpersonal Relations Case 8-2

Akiak Wants to Fit In

Akiak Nori was raised in Arviat, Nunavut, and then attended a career school in Thunder Bay, Ontario, majoring in electronic technology. Approaching graduation, he sorted through dozens of job offers he had obtained, several of which did not even require an in-person interview.

Akiak accepted a position with a construction company in Sudbury, Ontario, because of the job opportunities and the long brisk winters that would be natural and comfortable for him. He was assigned to a construction team for new buildings, and was also assigned maintenance work for existing electronic systems in office buildings, factories, and mills.

Akiak's goal from the first day on the job was to perform well and fit in with his co-workers. He recognized that fitting in with a non-Eskimo group would require some patience on his part. Akiak had been counselled by several teachers that patience was not one of his strong points.

During employee orientation, two other new employees asked Akiak if his name meant "kayak" in Eskimo language. With a smile, Akiak replied, "No, it means brave. I guess my parents thought I would have to be brave to grow up in Arviat, where you have to be tough to survive."

Later that morning, Akiak was asked if ice fishing and seal hunting were his two favourite sports. "Not at all," said Akiak, smiling. "We had a first-rate hockey rink in town, so I got to love hockey. And, I'm a big Sudbury Wolves [a Junior A Hockey team] fan. That's why I took a job in Sudbury."

During lunch, Mary, another new employee, asked Akiak, "Tell me Akiak, are you an Eskimo? Or are you an Inuit? I don't want to make a mistake."

Akiak responded, "It's no mistake to call me an Eskimo. It's no mistake to call me an Inuit. Some people think that the term 'Eskimo' is wrong, and that we should be called Inuit. It doesn't matter to me or to my friends and family. We like both terms.

"Yet, Mary, the mistake you are making is not thinking of me as just another Canadian. Nunavut is one of the Canadian territories. We vote. And we learn English in school and eat at McDonald's."

"I'm sorry," said Mary. "I was just trying to be friendly."

Ned, the supervisor of the orientation program, said to the group. "I think we have asked Akiak enough about his cultural heritage for now. Yet I have just one favour to ask Akiak. I wish he would show us how he positions his arm, head, and body to spear a big fish."

Akiak said with a sarcastic tone, "Time out. I'm taking a break from this orientation right now. I have to go back to my igloo and chew on some frozen fish."

Case Questions

1. What does this case tell us about cultural sensitivity?
2. How might have Akiak's co-workers related better to him during the orientation?
3. How might have Akiak done a better job of relating to his new co-workers so far?
4. Does Akiak "have an *attitude*" (a negative attitude problem)?

Questions for Discussion and Review

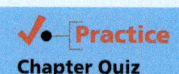

✓ Practice
Chapter Quiz

Multiple Choice

1. Cultural sensitivity can be defined as
   a. an awareness and willingness to investigate and understand cultural differences.
   b. paying more attention to cultural differences than similarities.
   c. ignoring other cultures.
   d. sympathizing with those who are different from us.

2. Cultural intelligence includes three sources:
   a. Physical, emotional, and auditory
   b. Cognitive, emotional, and physical
   c. Auditory, cognitive, and emotional
   d. None of the above
3. Sonia is from New Zealand and dislikes speaking up in business meetings about how to outsell the competition. Sonia is likely low in the cultural value of
   a. time orientation.
   b. assertiveness.
   c. humane orientation.
   d. work orientation.
4. All of the following are recommended strategies to overcome cross-cultural barriers except:
   a. Show respect for all workers.
   b. Speak as you would normally.
   c. Be sensitive to differences in nonverbal communication.
   d. Observe cultural differences in etiquette.
5. Diversity training attempts to
   a. increase employees' cultural intelligence.
   b. teach employees new languages.
   c. teach employees customs of other cultures.
   d. teach employees how to get along with fellow employees from other cultures.

Short Answer

6. How can a person demonstrate to others on the job that he or she is culturally fluent (gets along well with people from other cultures)?
7. Provide an example of cultural insensitivity of any kind that you have seen, read about, or can imagine.
8. If you were a supervisor, how would you deal with a group member who had a very low acceptance of power and authority?
9. How useful is the adage "When in Rome, do as the Romans do" for someone who wants to work in another country for a while?
10. Open your MySearchLab and click on "Simulation: Cross-Cultural Relations and Diversity." Work through the discussion questions at the end of the simulation. What is one strategy that you would recommend to make workplaces more inclusive of all cultures?

Answers to multiple choice questions: 1. a, 2. b, 3. b, 4. b, 5. d.

The Web Corner

www.diversityinc.com
Extensive information, including videos, about cultural diversity in organizations

www.berlitz.com
Information about language training and cultural training in countries throughout the world; investigate in your second language to enhance the cross-cultural experience

Internet Skill Builder: Avoiding Cultural Insensitivity

One of the most effective ways of hampering relationships with people of another culture is to be grossly insensitive. If you can avoid these errors, you will be on your way toward at least acceptable relationships with people from another domestic or foreign culture. Two examples of cultural insensitivity uncovered on the Internet are:

1. In Alberta, Canada, a sign in the window of a large chain restaurant read, "No drunken Indians allowed."
2. Walmart performed poorly in Germany because it did not recognize the cultural fact that Germans do not like to spend a lot of time shopping by walking through a giant store and waiting in line.

Search the Internet for other examples of cultural insensitivity. You might have to dig hard to find these nuggets, but the activity will help you become more culturally sensitive and aware.

MySearchLab

Visit **MySearchLab** to find self-grading review quizzes in the eText, discipline-specific media and readings, access to a variety of academic journals, and Associated Press news feeds, along with a wide range of writing, grammar, and research tools and to help hone writing and research skills.

CHAPTER 9
Resolving Conflicts with Others

Karen was one of a team of five workers who repaired and installed desktop and laptop computers for individuals and small businesses. Her company, Elite Computers, also installed new software and repaired virus damage. Karen enjoyed the technical challenges in her work, as well as the opportunity to work directly with a variety of clients and provide them valuable assistance.

A major challenge facing Karen and her teammates was that some of the on-site repair work had to be done on Saturdays and Sundays to accommodate clients who worked on weekends as well as weekdays. When their computers were down, some clients could not wait until Monday for an Elite technician to begin the repairs.

Blaj Gabriel /Shutterstock

LEARNING
Objectives

After reading and studying this chapter and doing the exercises, you should be able to

1. Specify why so much interpersonal conflict exists in organizations.
2. Recognize your typical method of resolving conflict.
3. Identify the five modes of handling conflict.
4. Develop effective techniques for resolving conflict and negotiating.
5. Combat sexual harassment in the workplace.

One of Karen's teammates, Charlie, often seemed to have an excuse for not making a weekend client visit when it was his turn. Several times Charlie sent Karen an urgent text message saying that he or a family member was sick, and that he needed Karen to take the service call for him. Each time, Charlie ended his message with "Please help. I'll return the favour later."

One Saturday at 8 a.m. Karen received a voice message from Charlie that read, "One of our biggest clients, Silver Motor Sales, has a system breakdown, and needs help this morning. It could be a virus attack. I have to take my brother to the emergency room. Please go to Silver Motors for me, ASAP."

Karen thought, "This dependency of Charlie on me has gotten out of hand. I don't know if he is lying. But if our team screws up with Silver Motors, we will all look bad. Maybe I should call Fred [the team leader]. I think Charlie is taking advantage of me. I've got to work on my problem with him."

The situation of computer repair technicians Karen and Charlie illustrates how so often it becomes imperative to resolve conflicts with a co-worker to fix an intolerable problem. This chapter will help you improve your ability to resolve conflicts with people at work. The same techniques are also useful in personal life. To improve your understanding of how to resolve conflict, this chapter will present specific techniques and also explain why so much conflict exists. To get you started relating the topic of conflict to you, take Self-Assessment Quiz 9-1.

SOURCES OF INTERPERSONAL CONFLICT IN ORGANIZATIONS

A **conflict** is a situation in which two or more goals, values, or events are incompatible or mutually exclusive. A conflict is also a strife, quarrel, or battle, such as would be the case if computer repair technician Karen told Charlie he was a lazy jerk, and he replied that she was callous and unfeeling about his problems.

Conflict between and among people has many sources or causes. In this section, we describe six of the leading sources. A seventh category, workplace violence, is both a cause and a consequence of conflict. If you understand the cause of a conflict, it can help you resolve the conflict and help prevent a similar recurrence. For example, if you learn that much conflict on the job is caused by people being uncivil toward each other, you might remind yourself to behave civilly. You can also learn how to deal with uncivil co-workers so that they treat you less rudely. Although specific sources of conflict can be identified, keep in mind an important fact—all conflict includes the underlying theme of incompatibility between your goals, values, or events and those of another person.

LEARNING OBJECTIVE 1

conflict
A situation in which two or more goals, values, or events are incompatible or mutually exclusive.

RESOLVING CONFLICTS WITH OTHERS

LEARNING OBJECTIVE 2

SELF-ASSESSMENT QUIZ 9-1

Collaborative versus Competitive Styles of Conflict Management

Answer on a 1-to-5 scale how well you agree with each of the following statements: Disagree Strongly; Disagree; Neutral; Agree; Agree Strongly.

		Disagree Strongly	Disagree	Neutral	Agree	Agree Strongly
1.	I like to see the other side squirm when I resolve a dispute.	5	4	3	2	1
2.	Winning is everything when it comes to settling conflict.	5	4	3	2	1
3.	After I have successfully negotiated a price, I like to see the seller smile.	1	2	3	4	5
4.	I have a "smash-mouth" attitude toward resolving conflict.	5	4	3	2	1
5.	In most conflict situations, one side is clearly right, and the other side is clearly wrong.	1	2	3	4	5
6.	I think there are effective alternatives to strikes for settling union versus management disputes.	1	2	3	4	5
7.	The winner should take all.	5	4	3	2	1
8.	Conflict on the job is like a prize fight: The idea is to knock out the opponent.	5	4	3	2	1
9.	I like the idea of tournaments in which first-round losers receive another opportunity to play.	1	2	3	4	5
10.	Nice guys and gals usually finish first.	1	2	3	4	5

Scoring and Interpretation: Add the point value of your scores to obtain your total. Scores of 40 and higher suggest that you prefer a *collaborative*, or *win–win*, approach to resolving conflict. You tend to be concerned about finding long-term solutions to conflict that will provide benefits to both sides. Scores of 39 and lower suggest that you prefer a *competitive* approach to resolving conflict. You want to maximize gain for yourself, with little concern about the welfare of the other side.

Competition for Limited Resources

An underlying source of job conflict is that few people can get all the resources they want. These resources include money, material, and human resources (or personnel). Conflict arises when two or more people squabble over who should get the resources. Even in a prosperous organization, resources have to be distributed in such a manner that not everybody gets what he or she wants.

Assume that you believe you need to have a document scanner immediately accessible the full workday. The company, however, has decided that 10 people must share one scanner. As a result, you are likely to enter into conflict with the others sharing the scanner. The conflict will be intense if several of your co-workers also think they need full-time access to the scanner.

Role Conflict

A major source of conflict (and stress) on the job relates to being put in a predicament. You are experiencing **role conflict** when you have to choose between competing demands or expectations. If you comply with one aspect of a role, compliance with the other is difficult or impossible. An important example would be receiving contradictory orders from two people above you in your company. If you comply with the wishes of one person, you will antagonize the other.

Role conflict can take various forms. You might be asked to accomplish two objectives that are in apparent conflict. If your boss asked you to hurry up and finish your work but also make fewer mistakes, you would experience this type of conflict (plus perhaps a headache!). Another type of problem occurs when two or more people give you

role conflict
The situation that occurs when a person has to choose between two competing demands or expectations.

CHAPTER 9

incompatible directions. Your immediate supervisor may want you to complete a crash project on time, but company policy temporarily prohibits authorizing overtime payments to clerical help or hiring office temporaries.

Role conflict also results when two different roles that you play are in conflict. Your company may expect you to travel 50 percent of the time, whereas your spouse threatens a divorce if you travel over 25 percent of the time. Finally, a form of role conflict takes place when the role(s) your organization expects you to occupy are in conflict with your basic values. Your company may ask you to fire substandard performers, but this could be in conflict with your humanistic values.

Competing Work and Family Demands

Balancing the demands of career and family life has become a major role conflict facing today's workforce. Caring about work and family responsibilities is more likely to intensify work–family conflict. The challenge is particularly intense for employees who are part of a two-wage-earner family. **Work–family conflict** occurs when an individual's roles of worker and active participant in social and family life compete with one another. This type of conflict is frequent because the multiple roles are often incompatible. Imagine having planned to attend your child's solo recital and then being ordered at the last minute to be present at an after-hours meeting. Work–family conflict can lead to interpersonal conflict because your boss or co-workers might think that you are asking them to cover for you while you attend to personal matters.

work–family conflict
A state that occurs when an individual's role as a worker clashes with his or her role as an active participant in social and family life.

Work-to-Family and Family-to-Work Conflict.
Work–family conflict can be viewed from two perspectives, with both leading to conflict and stress. A person's work can interfere with family responsibilities, or family responsibilities can interfere with work. In the above example, the person might say, "This is terrible. The meeting called for at the last minute will block me from attending my child's solo recital." Or, the same person might say, "This is terrible. My child's solo recital is going to block me from attending an important last-minute meeting."

An analysis of many scientific studies on the subject found that work demands can create some stress and low satisfaction at home, and that personal demands can create some stress and low satisfaction on the job.[1] Have you ever noticed that problems at work or school can negatively influence personal life? Have you also noticed that problems in personal life can negatively influence work or school? An international survey found that Canadians feel the most stressed at work, with 41 percent stating that they "often" or "almost always" experience stress at work, with work-family conflict being one of the sources of the stress.[2]

Another study investigated the effect of work–family conflict on the emotions of guilt and hostility among employed adults. The study also explored how work–family conflict, guilt, and hostility affected job satisfaction and marital satisfaction. It was found that work-to-family conflict and family-to-work conflict led to guilt and hostility at work and at home, respectively. A sidelight finding of interest to the study of human relations is that hostile people suffer even more conflict at home and on the job.[3]

The Issue of Work–Life Choices.
A continuing debate exists over whether a person can give equal balance between work and family life, and still advance far in his or her career. If getting far in your field requires 60 hours per week of hard work, you might not be able to meet that demand and still be a full contributor to family life. Jack Welch, former GE chief executive and now business writer and educator, told participants at a human resources conference, "There are work–life choices, and you make them, and they have consequences."[4]

Another issue related to work–life choices is that when managers perceive subordinates to be experiencing family–work conflict, there is a tendency for the bosses to think that the subordinate is not a good candidate for promotion. A study with supervisors in a large transportation company found that managers tended to categorize women as experiencing greater family–work conflict even when the women did not perceive themselves to have much family–work conflict. As a result, the managers downgraded their perception

RESOLVING CONFLICTS WITH OTHERS   177

of the women supervisors fit for the job, as well as their promotability.[5] Even if the managers' perceptions were biased, the supervisors still had to deal with these misperceptions.

Making a work–life (or work–family) choice can sometimes reduce conflict. It is helpful to develop a general guideline about how much time a person wants to invest in both work and family life, and then be satisfied with the compromise. Certain types of careers have to be excluded in order to spend most evenings and weekend in family and other personal activities. For example, to be a successful small business owner or a Toronto Stock Exchange financial analyst typically requires working between 60 and 70 hours per week. From the opposite standpoint, certain types of social activities have to be controlled to attain career success. An adult who wants to play video games and visit social networking sites for a combined nine hours per day will not succeed in most careers. After choices are made about type of work and type of personal life activities, work–family conflict will be minimized.

Company Initiatives to Reduce Work–Family Conflict. Companies can often avoid or minimize serious work–family conflict among employees by implementing equitable time-off policies. The underlying company attitude is that all employees need a work–life balance. Encouraging such an atmosphere of goodwill among co-workers can help prevent conflicts and resentments when one employee leaves early to take care of family responsibility.[6]

Many companies offer flexible working hours to a majority of their employees. In this way, a worker might be able to meet family demands that take place during typical working hours. An example would be taking off the morning to care for an ill parent, and working later that same evening to make up the time. People who are exceptionally good at organizing their time and efforts will often experience less work–family conflict, by such behaviours as staying on top of work to minimize periods of time when they are completely work-centred.[7]

Personality Clashes

personality clash
An antagonistic relationship between two people based on differences in personal attributes, preferences, interests, values, and styles.

Many workplace disagreements arise because people simply dislike each other. A **personality clash** is an antagonistic relationship between two people based on differences in personal attributes, preferences, interests, values, and styles. A personality clash reflects negative chemistry between two people, while personal differences are based more specifically on a clash of values.

People involved in a personality clash often have difficulty specifying why they dislike each other. The end result, however, is that they cannot maintain an amiable work relationship. One peculiarity about personality clashes is that people who get along well may begin to clash after working together for a number of years. A contributing factor is that as both people change and the situation changes, the two people may no longer be compatible.

Bullies in the Workplace

aggressive personalities
Persons who often verbally, and sometimes physically, attack others.

bullies
Persons who verbally, and sometimes physically, attack others.

Co-workers naturally disagree about topics, issues, and ideas. Yet some people convert disagreement into an attack that puts down other people and damages their self-esteem. As a result, conflict surfaces. **Aggressive personalities**, more commonly known as **bullies**, are people who often verbally, and sometimes physically, attack others. Verbal aggression takes the form of insults, teasing, ridicule, and profanity. Aggression may also be expressed as attacks on the victim's character, competence, background, and physical appearance.[8]

Among the typical behaviours of bullies are interrupting others, making humiliating comments and gestures, ranting in a loud voice, and making threats. One bullying manager would frequently ask people, "Are you going to be stupid the rest of your life?" Psychological harassment or workplace bullying costs Canadian companies millions of dollars in productivity.[9] Bullied workers complain of a range of psychological and physical ailments, including anxiety, sleeplessness, headache, irritable bowel syndrome, skin problems, panic attacks, and low self-esteem.[10] A few Canadian provinces have passed legislation making workplace bullying illegal. Quebec, in 2004, implemented anti-bullying legislation for non-unionized workplaces and is the first jurisdiction in

Canada to pass such legislation. Of 2200 complaints that were filed in the first two years of the legislation, over 1000 were considered to have merit.[11] In 2007, Saskatchewan followed suit by passing legislation making workplace bullying illegal in that province. In 2010, Ontario passed legislation that provides employees protection from workplace violence and harassment. With the passage of Bill 168, an amendment to the *Ontario Occupational Health and Safety Act*, employers are required to take reasonable steps to ensure the safety of employees.[12]

There are few Canadian statistics on the prevalence of workplace bullying, but there is little doubt that this is a problem in Canada. The Workplace Mental Health Promotion (a collaboration of the Canadian Mental Health Association and the University of Toronto) uses the statistics of the Workplace Bullying Institute as a reference for bullying in Canada. Online interviews with 7740 adults conducted by the Workplace Bullying Institute found that 60 percent of bullies are male, and 40 percent are female. An estimated 37 percent of American workers have been bullied on the job. Male bullies appear to choose men and women as targets in equal number. In contrast, women choose their targets as women 71 percent of the time.[13] Gary Namie, research director at the Bullying Institute, says that one reason women often choose other women as targets "is probably some idea that they can find a less confrontational person or someone less likely to respond to aggression with aggression."[14] Female bullies sometimes sabotage their competition through intimidation or by limiting access to important meetings and committees; withholding information, assignments, and promotions; or blocking the way to mentors and higher management.

Incivility and Rudeness

A milder form of aggression in the workplace is being rude or uncivil toward work associates. **Incivility** (or employees' lack of regard for one another) has gained attention as a cause of workplace conflict. What constitutes being uncivil or rude depends upon a person's perceptions and values.

Imagine two people having a business lunch together. One of them answers his cell phone during lunch, and while still eating engages the caller in conversation. To some people this everyday incident would be interpreted as double rudeness—interrupting lunch with a cellphone call and eating while talking. Another person might perceive the cellphone incident to be standard behaviour in a multitasking world. Rudeness also includes swearing at co-workers, a cubicle-dweller shouting loudly on the phone while making a personal call, and performing other work at a meeting. Typical forms of "other work" are sorting through paper mail, texting on a cell phone, or surfing the Internet on a notebook computer.

A study conducted by Lisa Penney found that 69 percent of 300 workers she surveyed reported experiencing condescending behaviour and put-downs in the workplace. Also, those who reported incivility on the job were more likely to engage in counterproductive behaviours including bad-mouthing their company, missing deadlines, and being rude to customers or clients. "Even though incivility may not seem like a very serious thing," says Penney, "it is related to behaviours that have more serious consequences" that can affect profits.[15] An investigation using many forms of data collection with 2400 people found that being treated in an uncivil manner leads employees to decrease work effort, time on the job, and productivity. When incivility is not curtailed, job satisfaction and loyalty to the company also diminish.[16]

A survey of workplace incivility was conducted with three different workplace groups, including university employees, attorneys, and federal court employees. Overall, employees subjected to incivility tended to feel frustrated, annoyed, and a little bit offended. Also, when employees are subjected to co-workers or managers who yell and swear, make them the object of mean jokes, or intentionally exclude them from friendship-building activities, their morale and performance often suffers.[17] (Does this finding surprise you?)

To put rudeness and incivility in perspective, it may simply be part of modern life where self-expression counts for everything and manners nothing. Rudeness in the

incivility
In human relations, employees' lack of regard for each other.

Watch
Skills for Workplace Success: Conflict

workplace is therefore just a natural extension of rudeness occurring in everyday life.[18] Yet a person who has good manners and behaves civilly can capitalize on these behaviours in his or her career.

Cross-Generational Conflict

As explained in Chapter 2, differences in values across generations lead to differences in behaviour. And these value-based differences in behaviour can lead to conflict, such as disputes about Gen Y workers wanting members of Gen X and Baby Boomers to be continuously logged on to instant messaging (IM). The following list presents three examples of potential work-related conflict across generations. The illustrations presented are stereotypes that apply to a *typical* member of each generation.

- **Preferred approach to communication.** Gen X members prefer to send text messages, use cell phones, and IM. Gen Y members prefer email, IM, and cell phones. Some Gen Y members prefer abbreviated conversation rather than fully explaining what they mean. Baby Boomers prefer email, cell phones, and face-to-face communication.

- **Approach to problem solving.** Gen X members prefer to form a team to brainstorm a solution, as well as use the web and social networking for research. Gen Y members prefer to think up a list of solutions on their own, then call a meeting to discuss the alternative solutions. Baby Boomers like to think about what has worked in the past and how it can be replicated. Then they call a meeting to discuss possible alternatives. Traditionalists (born 1922–1945) tend to be thorough and detail-oriented. Gen Y (millennials) will often multitask while solving a problem. Often they want to move quickly to another problem because of a short attention span, whereas traditionalists and Baby Boomers may want to drag out a problem.

- **Requirement for being respected.** Gen X members want to have their ideas valued by co-workers. Gen Y members want to have their professionalism and growing knowledge valued. Baby Boomers want to have their decades of work experience and input still valued.[19]

Although cross-generational conflict is mild in nature, it can still lead to miscommunication and hard feelings that disrupt work.

Workplace Violence (A Cause and Effect of Conflict)

Aggression can also take the extreme form of the shooting or knifing of a former boss or colleague by a mentally unstable worker recently dismissed from the company. Much workplace violence is perpetuated by disgruntled workers or former employees harbouring unresolved conflicts. For example, on April 6, 1999, Pierre Lebrun shot and killed four of his colleagues at an Ottawa city bus garage. A 1994 survey by the Canadian Union of Public Employees showed that almost 70 percent of respondents believed that verbal aggression was the leading form of workplace violence, but physical violence in the workplace is more common in this country than you might think. A 1998 survey by the International Labour Organization found Canada to be among the top five nations in terms of workplace violence, including general and sexual assaults.[20] A 2004 Canadian study found that almost one in five violent incidents occurred in the victim's workplace. There were almost 356,000 violent incidents in Canadian workplaces that year.[21]

Workplace violence is often predictable, with the worker who may erupt into violence showing early signals, according to Lynne McClure, a specialist in managing high-risk employees.[22] Predictors of workplace violence include the following employee behaviours and verbal expressions: talk about weaponry, paranoid (highly suspicious) or antisocial behaviour, reference to not being heard by management, expression of extreme desperation, history of violence, and being a loner who does not fit into the group. Multiple behaviours such as those just described might be reported to the manager or human resource professional. Yet you need to be careful about referring a co-worker who displays just one predictor of violent behaviour.

CONFLICT MANAGEMENT STYLES

The information presented thus far is designed to help you understand the nature of conflict. Such background information is useful for resolving conflict because it helps you understand what is happening in a conflict situation. The next two sections offer more specific information about managing and resolving conflict. Before describing specific methods of resolving conflict, it is useful to present more detail about five general styles, or modes, of handling conflict. You received preliminary information on four of these five styles when you completed Self-Assessment Quiz 9-1.

As shown in Figure 9-1, Kenneth Thomas has identified five major styles of conflict management. Each style is based on a combination of satisfying one's own concerns (assertiveness) and satisfying the concerns of others (cooperativeness).[23]

Competitive Style

The competitive style is marked by a desire to advance one's own concerns at the expense of the other party, or to dominate. A person with a competitive orientation is likely to engage in power struggles in which one side wins and the other loses (an approach referred to as *win–lose*). "My way or the highway" is a win–lose strategy. The competitive style works best when quick, decisive action is essential, such as in an emergency.

Accommodative Style

The accommodative style favours appeasement, or satisfying the other's concerns without taking care of one's own. People with this orientation may be generous or self-sacrificing just to maintain a relationship. Irate customers can be accommodated with full refunds, just to calm them down. The intent of such accommodation might also be to retain the customer's loyalty.

Accommodation sounds harmless, but according to Sidney Simon, when it runs unchecked at the expense of what somebody really wants it can lead to debilitating resentment, sickness, or even violence.[24] The problem is that the suppressed feelings create inner conflict and stress. Accommodation works best when you are wrong, or when the issues are more important to the other side. For example, an automobile sales associate might say yes to a last-minute demand for another $50 concession, rather than continuing to haggle.

FIGURE 9-1 Conflict-Handling Styles According to Degree of Cooperation and Assertiveness

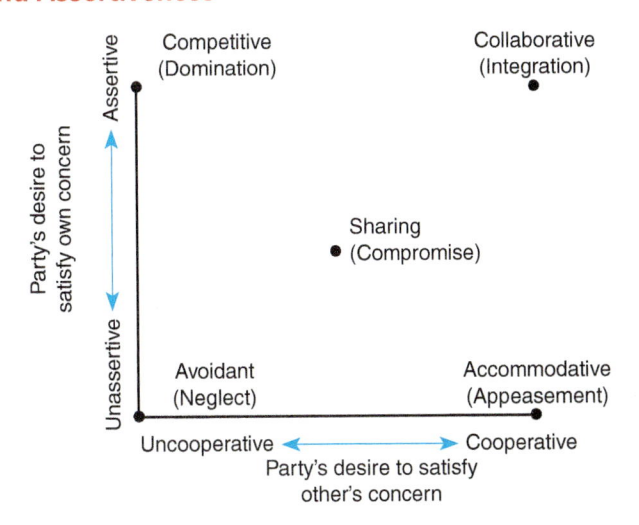

Source: Kenneth W. Thomas, "Organizational Conflict," in Steven Kerr, ed., *Organization Behaviour* (Columbus, Ohio: Grid Publishing, 1979), p. 156. Reprinted with permission of John Wiley & Sons.

Sharing Style

The sharing style lies halfway between domination and appeasement. Sharers prefer moderate but incomplete satisfaction for both parties, which results in a compromise. The term *splitting the difference* reflects this orientation, and is commonly used in such activities as purchasing a house or car. The sharing (or compromising) style is well suited to a situation in which both sides have equal power, yet are committed to mutually exclusive goals such as the buyer and seller of the house wanting to maximize financial gain.

Collaborative Style

In contrast to the other styles, the collaborative style reflects a desire to fully satisfy the desires of both parties. It is based on an underlying philosophy of **win–win**, the belief that after conflict has been resolved, both sides should gain something of value. The use of a win–win approach is genuinely aimed at arriving at a settlement that meets the needs of both parties, or at least does not badly damage the welfare of the other side. The option chosen results in a *mutual gain*. When collaborative approaches to resolving conflict are used, the relationships among the parties are built on and improved. The following example uses a win–win approach to resolve conflict.

> *Karma is an office assistant in a company that supplies food to restaurants, hospitals, and nursing homes. According to her budget analysis, Karma needed a 5 percent salary increase to meet her monthly expenses. The company owner explained that there was no money in the budget for a salary increase. A cordial discussion about the issue led to an option for mutual gain. Karma would receive the 5 percent salary increase as long as she increased her productivity enough to cover the increase. Her target was to increase her productivity to the point that the company could decrease the hours worked by an office temporary. The amount of the decrease covered the 5 percent salary increase.*

Mobile phone companies in search of antenna sites have led to win–win conflict resolution between companies and communities. Many of these companies have integrated antennas into church steeples, highrise buildings, forest-fire towers, and other tall structures without defacing them. The company wins by having an antenna to provide cell-phone service, and community groups do not object to the sight of a freestanding antenna. At the same time, the church wins by having a new steeple.

Collaborating is particularly important when both sides must be committed to the solution, such as the situation with the hidden cell antennas. Divorcing parents also need collaboration in their division of assets because they need to work together long-term for the good of the children.

Finding win–win solutions to problems (or options for mutual gain) is one of the most important conflict-resolution skills. To practise this skill, do Skill-Building Exercise 9-1.

Avoidant Style

The avoider is a combination of uncooperative and unassertive. He or she is indifferent to the concerns of either party. The person may actually be withdrawing from the conflict to rely upon fate. Avoiding works well when an issue is trivial, or there are more pressing issues to worry about. For example, a supervisor might not bother reprimanding workers who are a few minutes late because the supervisor is flooded with other work.

In the following description of specific techniques for resolving conflict, attempt to relate most of them to these five key styles. For example, you will observe that the confrontation and problem-solving technique reflects the collaborative style.

---

win–win

The belief that after conflict has been resolved, both sides should gain something of value.

SKILL-BUILDING EXERCISE 9-1

Win–Win Conflict Resolution

The class organizes into small problem-solving groups. Each group spends about 10 minutes finding a win–win solution to one of the following conflict situations.

1. Two co-workers want you to work with them after hours in establishing an online marketing firm. You do not want to take time away from your primary career to get involved in a side business. However, you want to maintain cordial relations with these two co-workers.
2. William, an accountant, wants workmates to call him "William." Yet several people in the office persist in calling him "Bill" or "Will."
3. You are offered a transfer within your company to an exciting job that you want strongly. Your manager says he cannot let you go because you are too valuable.
4. A group of workers at a small business would like a giant-screen, high-definition television set placed in the employee lounge to enhance their enjoyment of breaks. The business owner wants to keep employees satisfied but concludes that investing about $4000 in a television set for the lounge is too big an investment.

After the groups have found their solutions for mutual gains, specify carefully what gain each side attained. Share your solutions with other class members to obtain their feedback about the effectiveness of the mutual gains.

GUIDELINES AND TECHNIQUES FOR RESOLVING CONFLICTS

LEARNING OBJECTIVE 4

Explore

Mastering Business Communication: Resolving Conflict

Interpersonal conflict in organizations is inevitable. A career-minded person must therefore learn effective ways of resolving conflict. This section describes methods of conflict resolution that you can use on your own. All are based somewhat on the underlying model of win–win, or integrating the interests of both parties. Integrating both interests focuses on resolving the underlying concerns of the parties in conflict. By dealing with these concerns, it is more worthwhile for both sides to resolve the conflict than it is to have no agreement.

> Suppose a woman named Molly Coors wanted to open a beer brewery and name her beer Coors. The company lawyers from Coors-Molson, which owns the rights to the brand name Coors, would attempt to block her from using the same brand name—even if her family name is Coors. Molly Coors would hire her own lawyer to fight back. Two key concerns must be addressed. Molly Coors's underlying concern is that she feels her rights have been violated because she cannot name a business after herself. And Molly must deal with Coors-Molson's concern about a smaller company capitalizing on its well-known name (brand equity).

After reading the various strategies in this chapter, what advice might you give Molly in her efforts to name her company Coors?

Confrontation and Problem Solving

The ideal approach to resolving any conflict is to confront the real issue and then solve the problem. **Confrontation** means taking a problem-solving approach to differences and identifying the underlying facts, logic, or emotions that account for them. When conflicts are resolved through confronting and understanding their causes, people feel responsible for finding the soundest answer.[25]

confrontation
Taking a direct problem-solving approach in a conflict to resolve differences to maintain a good working relationship.

Confrontation can proceed gently, in a way that preserves a good working relationship, as shown by the following example. Assume that Mary, the person working at the desk next to you, loudly cracks chewing gum while she works. You find this behaviour both distracting and nauseating. If you do not bring the problem to Mary's attention, your annoyance will probably intensify with time. Yet you are hesitant to enter into an argument about something that a person might regard as a human right (the right to chew gum in public places).

A psychologically sound alternative is for you to approach her directly in this manner:

You: Mary, there is something bothering me that I would like to discuss with you.

She: Go ahead, I don't mind listening to other people's problems.

You: My problem concerns something you are doing that makes it difficult for me to concentrate on my work. When you chew gum you make loud cracking noises that grate on my nerves. It may be my problem, but the noise does bother me.

She: I guess I could stop chewing gum when you're working next to me. It's probably just a nervous habit.

When resolving conflict through confrontation and problem solving, as well as other methods of conflict resolution, it is helpful to bring closure by shaking hands, repeating your individual commitments, and then saying "Thank you." Following through on your commitments is also essential for effective conflict resolution.[26]

BACK TO THE OPENING CASE

Karen needs to resolve her conflict with Charlie in a way that will still preserve their working relationship. Perhaps informing their boss of the problem is not the most effective approach from the standpoint of preserving the relationship. Instead, it would be constructive for Karen to meet with Charlie to use the technique of confrontation and problem solving. Karen should let Charlie know clearly how difficult it is to cover for him so frequently. A slightly more aggressive approach would be for Karen to bring along a co-worker who also has been inconvenienced by Charlie. The two-on-one approach can be powerful, so long as Charlie does feel "ganged-up on." Karen acting alone, or accompanied by co-workers, should take a gentle, constructive approach.

Constructive Handling of Criticism

Learning to profit from criticism is an effective way of benefiting from conflict. People who benefit from criticism are able to stand outside themselves while being criticized. It is as if they are watching the criticism from a distance and looking for its possible merits. People who take criticism personally anguish when receiving negative feedback. Following are several specific suggestions for dealing with criticism, including two methods that will often get the other party on your side.[27]

1. **See yourself at a distance.** Place an imaginary Plexiglas shield between you and the person giving the criticism. Attempt to be a detached observer looking for useful information.

2. **Ask for clarification and specifics.** Ask politely for more details about the negative behaviour in question so you can change if change is warranted. If your boss is criticizing you for being rude to customers, you might respond: "I certainly do not want to be rude. Can you give me a couple of examples of how I was rude? I need your help in working on this problem." After asking questions, you can better determine whether the criticism is valid.

3. **Decide on a response.** An important part of learning from criticism is to respond appropriately to the critic. Let the criticizer know what aspects of the criticism you agree with. Apologize for the undesirable behaviour, such as saying, "I apologize for being rude to customers. I know what I can do differently now. I'll be more patient so as not to appear rude."

4. **Look for a pattern in terms of other criticism.** Is the criticism you are receiving something you have heard several times before from different people? The more times you have heard the same criticism, the more likely it is to be valid. If three different supervisors have told you that you do not follow through with your promises to get work done, the criticism is most likely valid.

5. **Disarm the opposition.** As an extension of the point just made, you will often decide to agree with the criticizer because the person has a legitimate complaint about you. If you deny the reality of that person's complaint, he or she will continue to harp on the point and the issue will remain unresolved. By agreeing with the criticism of you, you may set the stage for a true resolution of the problem.

Agreeing with criticism made by a person with formal authority over you is effective because by doing so you are then in a position to ask for his or her help in improving the situation. Rational managers realize that it is their responsibility to help subordinates overcome problems, not merely to criticize them. Imagine that you have been chronically late with reports during the past six months. It is time for a performance review, and you know that you will be reprimanded for your tardiness. You also hope that your manager will not downgrade all other aspects of your performance because of your tardy reports. Here is how disarming the opposition would work in this situation:

Your manager: Have a seat. It's time for your performance review, and we have a lot to talk about. I'm concerned about some things.

You: So am I. It appears that I'm having a difficult time getting my reports in on time. I wonder if I'm being a perfectionist. Do you have any suggestions?

Your manager: Well, I like your attitude. Maybe you are trying to make your reports too perfect before you turn them in. I think you can improve in getting your reports in on time. Try not to figure everything out to five decimal places. We need thoroughness around here, but we can't overdo it.

Disarming is effective because it takes the wind out of the other person's sails and has a calming effect. The other person is often waiting to clobber you if you deny guilt. If you admit guilt, you are more difficult to clobber. Skill-Building Exercise 9-2 gives you an opportunity to practise disarming the opposition.

Reframing

Another useful approach to resolving conflict is to re-examine or *reframe* the conflict situation by looking at in a different light. Following are two practical approaches to reframing, one by searching for the positives in the situation, and the other by asking questions.

Reframing through Cognitive Restructuring. An indirect way of resolving interpersonal conflict is to lessen the conflicting elements in a situation by viewing them more positively. According to the technique of **cognitive restructuring**, you mentally convert negative aspects into positive ones by looking for the positive elements in a situation.[28] How you frame or choose your thoughts can determine the outcome of a conflict situation. Your thoughts influence your actions. If you search for the beneficial elements in the situation, there will be less area for dispute. Although this technique might sound like a *mind game* to you, it can work effectively.

Imagine that a co-worker of yours, Don, has been asking you repeated questions about how to carry out a work procedure. You are about ready to tell Don, "Go bother somebody else; I'm not paid to be a trainer." Instead, you look for the positive elements in the situation. You say to yourself, "Don has been asking me a lot of questions. This does

cognitive restructuring
Mentally converting negative aspects into positive ones by looking for the positive elements in a situation.

SKILL-BUILDING EXERCISE 9-2

Disarming the Opposition

In each of these two scenarios, one person plays the role of the person with more power in the situation. The other person plays the role of the individual attempting to disarm the criticizer.

1. A representative from a credit organization telephones you at work to inform you that you are 60 days behind schedule on your car payment. The agent wants a settlement as soon as possible. Unfortunately, the credit agent is correct. Run this scenario for about five minutes.
2. Your manager calls you into the office to discuss the 10-page report you just submitted. The boss says in a harsh tone,

"Your report is a piece of trash. I counted 25 word-use mistakes such as writing *whether* for *weather* and *seen* for *scene*. (Your spell checker couldn't catch these errors.) Besides that, I can't follow many of your sentences, and you left out the table of statistics. I'm wondering if you are qualified for this job."

Observers of the role-play will judge how effective the person being criticized was in reducing some of the anger directed against him or her. Look also for any changes in attitude on the part of the criticizer.

> ### SKILL-BUILDING EXERCISE 9-3
>
> #### Reframing through Cognitive Restructuring
>
> The following are examples of negative statements about co-workers. Cognitively restructure (reframe) each comment in a positive way.
>
> **Negative:** Nancy is getting on my nerves. It takes her two weeks longer than anyone else on the team to complete her input.
>
> **Positive:**
>
> **Negative:** My boss is driving me crazy. He is forever telling me what I did wrong and making suggestions for improvement. He makes me feel like I'm in elementary school.
>
> **Positive:**

take time, but answering these questions is valuable experience. If I want to become a manager, I will have to help group members with problems."

After having completed this cognitive restructuring, you can then deal with the conflict situation more positively. You might say to Don, "I welcome the opportunity to help you, but we need to find a mutually convenient time. In that way, I can concentrate better on my own work." To get started with cognitive restructuring, do Skill-Building Exercise 9-3.

Reframing by Asking Questions. Another way to use reframing is to ask step back, take a deep breath, and then ask the following questions about the conflict situation that arises within the work group:

- Do I fully understand the situation?
- Am I sure what my co-worker is really saying?
- Is the person really angry with me or just worried and anxious?
- Have I missed something important?

Negotiating and Bargaining

negotiating
Conferring with another person to resolve a problem.

Conflicts can be considered situations calling for **negotiating**, or conferring with another person to resolve a problem. When you are negotiating a fair salary for yourself, you are trying to resolve a conflict. At first, the demands of the two parties may seem incompatible, but through negotiation a salary figure may emerge that satisfies both.

Another perspective on negotiation is that people are not just negotiating for the economic value of the negotiation. They are also negotiating for intangibles, such as feeling good about the negotiation process, the other party, and themselves.[29] For example, after the negotiation is complete, the individual might want to be perceived as an honest, sincere professional, rather than as a dishonest person out to maximize gain.

Managers and staff specialists must negotiate both internally (e.g., with subordinates, managers, and team leaders) and externally (e.g., with suppliers and government agencies). Considerable negotiation also takes place among co-workers. Team members, for example, sometimes negotiate among themselves about work assignments. One might say to the other, "I'm willing to be note-taker this year if there is some way I can cut back on the number of plant visits I make this year." Six leading negotiating tactics are presented on the following pages. Before studying them, do Self-Assessment Quiz 9-2.

Understand the Other Party's Perspective. As in being a good listener, empathy can be an important part of negotiation. Deepak Malhotra and Max H. Bazerman observe that negotiators often channel too much effort into pushing their own position and too little into understanding the other side's perspective.[30] To obtain a good deal, or sometimes any deal at all, negotiators have to dig for information about *why* the other side wants what it demands. Inaccurate assumptions about the other side's motives can lead negotiators to propose solutions to the wrong problems, waste money, or kill a deal. How about a personal life example for dog lovers?

> *You have wanted a Great Dane puppy for a long time. You enter into negotiations with the owner of the puppy and his mother. The owner is asking $900, and is*

SELF-ASSESSMENT QUIZ 9-2

The Negotiator Quiz

Directions: The following quiz is designed to give you insight into your tendencies toward being an effective negotiator. Answer each statement "Mostly True" or "Mostly False" as it applies to you.

	Mostly True	Mostly False
1. Settling differences of opinion is a lot of fun.	_____	_____
2. I try to avoid conflict and confrontation with others as much as possible.	_____	_____
3. I am self-conscious asking people for favours they have not spontaneously offered me.	_____	_____
4. I am generally unwilling to compromise.	_____	_____
5. How the other side feels about the results of our negotiation is of little consequence to me.	_____	_____
6. I think very well under pressure.	_____	_____
7. People say that I am tactful and diplomatic.	_____	_____
8. I'm known for my ability to express my viewpoint clearly.	_____	_____
9. Very few things in life are not negotiable.	_____	_____
10. I always (or would always) accept whatever salary increase is offered to me.	_____	_____
11. A person's facial expression often reveals as much as what the person actually says.	_____	_____
12. I wouldn't mind taking a few short-range losses to win a long-range battle.	_____	_____
13. I'm willing to work long and hard to win a small advantage.	_____	_____
14. I'm usually too busy talking to do much listening.	_____	_____
15. It's fun to haggle over price when buying a car.	_____	_____
16. I almost always prepare in advance for a negotiating session.	_____	_____
17. When there is something I need from another person I usually get it.	_____	_____
18. It would make me feel cheap if I offered somebody only two-thirds of his or her asking price.	_____	_____
19. People are usually paid what they are worth, so there's no use haggling over starting salaries.	_____	_____
20. I rarely take what people say at face value.	_____	_____
21. It's easy for me to smile when involved in a serious discussion.	_____	_____
22. For one side to win in negotiation, the other side has to lose.	_____	_____
23. Once you start making concessions, the other side is bound to get more than you.	_____	_____
24. A good negotiating session brings out my competitive urges.	_____	_____
25. When negotiations are completed, both sides should walk away with something valuable.	_____	_____
Total Score	_____	_____

Scoring and Interpretation: Score yourself +1 for each of your answers that agrees with the scoring key. The higher your score, the more likely it is that you currently have good negotiating skills, *providing your self-assessment is accurate*. It might prove useful to also have somebody who has observed you negotiate on several occasions answer the Negotiator Quiz for you. Scores of 7 or lower and 20 or higher are probably the most indicative of weak or strong negotiating potential. Here is the scoring key:

1. Mostly true	8. Mostly true	15. Mostly true	22. Mostly false
2. Mostly false	9. Mostly true	16. Mostly true	23. Mostly false
3. Mostly false	10. Mostly false	17. Mostly true	24. Mostly true
4. Mostly false	11. Mostly true	18. Mostly false	25. Mostly true
5. Mostly false	12. Mostly true	19. Mostly false	
6. Mostly true	13. Mostly true	20. Mostly true	
7. Mostly true	14. Mostly false	21. Mostly true	

✓ Practice
The Negotiator Quiz

adamant about her demands. If you are low on empathy, you will raise such negotiating points as how much the little Great Dane is costing the owner in food; that you will pay cash; and that the little fellow is ugly and therefore is only worth $500. (You might get invited off the premises in a hurry.) In contrast, with high empathy and a detective-like mind, you recognize that the owner wants the puppy to go to a wonderful home. So, if she asks for a lot of money, the potential owner is likely to be really interested in finding someone who truly wants the dog, and would therefore probably take good care of the puppy.

With this negotiating point in mind, you point out what great care you will give the Great Dane, what a spacious yard you have, how you would take him jogging every day, and how he would be your dream dog. The owner is happy because one of her key motives is for the pup to have a wonderful home. She is touched and agrees to your offer of $600.

Another key part of understanding the other party's perspective is that you look for common ground. Your talk of care and concern about the dog's health indicates that both you and the owner have a humanitarian attitude toward dogs.

To understand the other party's perspective, you often have to prepare in advance. Obtain as much information as you can about the other party's side before the negotiation session. A basic example is that many prospective car buyers first research the fair value of a vehicle before making an offer. Knowing how long the vehicle has been sitting on the lot or in the showroom is also useful advance information because dealers often borrow money to build inventory.

Focus on Interests, Not Positions.
Rather than clinging to specific negotiating points, keep your overall interests in mind and try to satisfy them. Remember that the true object of negotiation is to satisfy the underlying interests on both sides, as in the case of Bill Molson. Part of focusing on interests is to carefully study the other side's comments for clues to the type of agreement that will satisfy both of you.

Here is how this strategy works: You are considering accepting a job offer that will enable you to work on the type of problems you prefer and also to develop your professional skills. You have a starting salary in mind that would make you very happy—15 percent higher than you are currently making. Your negotiating position is thus your present salary plus 15 percent. However, your true interests are probably to have more discretionary income than at present. (You want to make more purchases and invest more.) You will therefore be better off negotiating for a work situation that spreads your money further. You can now accept the offer by negotiating other points in addition to a 15-percent-higher salary, including (1) work location in an area with a lower cost of living, (2) a better opportunity for earning a bonus, or (3) a generous expense account. During the negotiations you may discover that the other party is looking for a talented employee at a salary and benefits the company can afford.

Compromise.
The most widely used negotiating tactic is **compromise**, settlement of differences by mutual concessions. One party agrees to do something if the other party agrees to do something else. Compromise is a realistic approach to resolving conflict. Most labour–management disputes are settled by compromise. For instance, labour may agree to accept a smaller salary increase if management will subcontract less work to other countries.

compromise
Settlement of differences by mutual concessions.

Some people argue that compromise is not a win–win tactic. The problem is that the two parties may wind up with a solution that pacifies both but does not solve the problem. One example would be purchasing for two department heads half the new equipment each one needs. As a result, neither department really shows a productivity gain. Nevertheless, compromise is both inevitable and useful.

Begin with a Plausible Demand or Offer, Yet Allow Room for Negotiation.
The common-sense approach to negotiation suggests that you begin with an extreme, almost fanciful demand or offer. The final compromise will therefore be closer to your true

demand or offer than if you opened the negotiations more realistically. However, a plausible demand is useful because it shows you are bargaining in good faith. Also, if a third party has to resolve a conflict, a plausible demand or offer will receive more sympathy than an implausible one will. An example would be an arbitrator giving only a minimum settlement to an investor who wanted $10 million in damages for having received bad advice from an investment broker. (The arbitrator thinks that a $10 million settlement would be ridiculous.)

Although it is advisable to begin with a plausible demand, one must still allow room for negotiation. A basic strategy of negotiation is to begin with a demand that allows room for compromise and concession. If you think you need $5000 in new software for your department, you might begin negotiations by asking for a $7000 package. Your boss offers you $4000 as a starting point. After negotiation, you may wind up with the $5000 you need.

Make Small Concessions Gradually. Making steady concessions leads to more mutually satisfactory agreements in most situations. Gradually, you concede little things to the other side. The hard-line approach to bargaining is to make your concession early in the negotiation and then grant no further concession. The tactic of making small concessions is well suited to purchasing a new car. To reach a price you consider acceptable, you might grant concessions such as agreeing to finance the car through the dealer or purchasing a service contract.

Know Your Best Alternative to a Negotiated Agreement (BATNA). The reason you would probably negotiate would be to produce something better than the result obtainable without negotiating. The goal of negotiating is thus not just to agree, but to obtain more valuable results than would otherwise have occurred. When you are aware of your best alternative to a negotiated agreement (BATNA), it sets a floor to the agreement you are willing to accept. Your BATNA becomes the standard that can protect both parties from accepting terms that are too unfavourable. It also keeps you from walking away from terms that would be beneficial for you to accept.

What might a BATNA look like in practice? Suppose you are negotiating a starting salary for a full-time, professional position. The figure you have in mind is $45,000 per year. Your BATNA is $38,500, because this is the salary your future in-laws will pay you to enter the family business. You will therefore walk away from any offer of less than $38,500—just taking salary into account.

Knowing the other side's BATNA is also important, because it helps define the other participant's bargaining zone. Understanding one another's bargaining zones makes it possible to arrive at mutually profitable trade-offs. In the preceding salary negotiations, the company's BATNA might be to hire a less well-educated job candidate at $30,000 and then upgrade his or her knowledge on the job.

An underlying advantage of knowing your BATNA is that it capitalizes on the power of a positive "no." Famous negotiator William Ury reasons that being able to say no to a demand places you in a strong position.[31] During negotiations, a statement such as "I am not willing to make that big a concession" can bring you respect because you are standing up for your principles. For best effect, "no" should be expressed in a friendly and firm manner.

Use Anger to Your Advantage. Master negotiators make selective use of anger as a negotiating and bargaining tool. When a person becomes genuinely angry, the anger can energize him or her to be more resourceful and creative while bargaining. If you are angry with an issue or a negotiating point, the other side may be willing to submit to your demand rather than receive more of your anger. The director of a company wellness program might say with an angry look toward top management, "Why is there money in the budget for all kinds of frills like corporate jets, when a program that is preventing millions of dollars in lost productivity has to grovel for a decent budget?"

The downside of anger is that it can degenerate into incivility and personal insults. A touch of anger can be effective, but overdone it becomes self-defeating. You have to size up how far you can push people before damaging a work relationship—or being fired. To make effective use of anger during negotiation, it has to be used at the right time, with the right tone, and in the right amount.[32] A person who is always angry will often not be taken seriously.

Effective negotiation, as with any other form of conflict resolution, requires extensive practice and knowledge of basic principles and techniques. As a starting point you might take one of the negotiating tactics just described and practise it where the stakes are not so high. You might attempt to negotiate the price of a consumer electronics device, or negotiate for getting a particular Friday afternoon off from work.

Allow for Face-Saving. We have saved one of the most important negotiating and conflict resolution strategies for last. Negotiating does not mean that you should try to squash the other side. You should try to create circumstances that will enable you to continue working with that person if it is necessary. People prefer to avoid looking weak, foolish, or incompetent during negotiation or when the process is completed. If you do not give your opponent an opportunity to save face, you will probably create a long-term enemy.

Face-saving could work in this way. A small-business owner winds up paying a higher starting salary for director of manufacturing than she wanted. The employment agency who placed the director of manufacturing says to the business owner, "I know that Michel costs more than you have budgeted. But don't worry about it, you have made a great investment. Michel will increase your manufacturing productivity so much that his salary and benefits will be a bargain for you."

A major theme running through the various approaches to conflict resolution, including negotiating and bargaining, is that cooperating with the other side is usually preferable to competing. A study with 61 self-managing teams with 489 employees supports this idea of the superiority of cooperation over competition in successful conflict resolution. The style of conflict resolution was measured through questionnaires. For example, a statement geared toward cooperative behaviour was "We seek a solution that will be good for the whole team." Conflict efficacy was measured by a questionnaire indicating that the extent to which team members believed that they could successfully manage different conflict situations. Group effectiveness was measured by the ratings of supervisor and team leaders on productivity, quality, and cost savings—central reasons why self-directed teams are formed.

The study found that the cooperative approach to conflict was positively related to conflict efficacy. In contrast, the competitive approach to conflict was negatively related to conflict efficacy. Equally important, conflict efficacy was strongly associated with supervisory and team leader ratings of team effectiveness.[33]

Skill-Building Exercise 9-4 provides you the opportunity to practice negotiating in a scenario that most people encounter at least once in their career.

COMBATTING SEXUAL HARASSMENT: A SPECIAL TYPE OF CONFLICT

LEARNING OBJECTIVE 5

Watch
Skills for the Workplace: Language in the Office

Watch
Skills for the Workplace: Sexual Harassment

sexual harassment
Unwanted sexually oriented behaviour in the workplace that results in discomfort and/or interference with the job.

Many employees face conflict because a supervisor, co-worker, or customer is sexually harassing them. The *Canada Labour Code*, the *Canadian Human Rights Act*, the *Employment Equity Act*, and provincial and territorial *human rights codes* prohibit all types of harassment, including sexual harassment. The Human Rights Code covers the federal public service and federally regulated industries such as banks, communications, and interprovincial transportation. Provincial human rights codes, such as that of Ontario, prohibit all types of harassment and make employers responsible for preventing and discouraging harassment. If an employer fails to do so, the employee may file a complaint with the Ontario Human Rights Commission. Thus, business and industries not covered by the various provincial and federal codes still must provide harassment-free workplaces for all employees. According to Ministry of Labour, 41 percent of workers covered by major collective agreements have some form of negotiated protection against harassment, including **sexual harassment**.[34]

> ### SKILL-BUILDING EXERCISE 9-4
>
> **Negotiating a Starting Salary**
>
> A scenario for negotiation for many people is asking for a starting salary. In large organizations with many written rules and regulations, there is less opportunity for negotiating compensation (except for high-level executive positions) than in smaller firms.
>
> In the negotiating scenarios listed below, assume that you are applying for work with a small- or medium-sized firm. Assume also that you (a) have about three years of experience in the position in question, (b) have a good reputation including high job performance and a clean record, and (c) strongly want the position. Five positions are listed below along with a plausible starting salary that you are seeking. The sixth position allows for your unique situation.
>
> 1. Accountant, $49,500
> 2. Computer support specialist, $40,500
> 3. Telemarketer, $22,000
> 4. Fitness trainer, $30,500
> 5. Personal financial advisor, $57,500
> 6. Your field, your salary demands
>
> The other person involved in the role-play is the hiring manager, who has a general idea of what he or she would like to pay as a starting salary. The hiring manager is impressed with you, yet still wants to economize on the starting salary.
>
> Do not simply start debating a starting salary. Both sides should use at least two of the negotiation tactics described in this chapter.
>
> Several duos might try this negotiating activity in front of the class for approximately eight minutes. Observers should attempt to identify (a) how well the negotiation went, and (b) which specific negotiating tactics were used.

The focus here will be on sexual harassment, but keep in mind that all types of harassment or discrimination are illegal and that many of the suggestions in this section can also be used to battle other harassment or discrimination-based workplace incidents. For example, if Sophie is a woman of colour and feels that she is being denied a promotion because of this, a grievance can be launched in the same manner as a sexual harassment grievance. Most workplace codes have a similar procedure for all types of harassment and other complaints.

Division XV.1 of Part III of the Canada Labour Code establishes that all employees have the right to be free of sexual harassment in the workplace and requires employers to take positive action to prevent it. The Canada Labour Code defines sexual harassment as "any conduct, comment, gesture, or contact of a sexual nature that is likely to cause offence or humiliation to any employee or that might, on reasonable grounds, be perceived by that employee as placing a condition of a sexual nature on employment or on any opportunity for training or promotion."[35] The Supreme Court of Canada defines sexual harassment as unwelcome behaviour of a sexual nature in the workplace that negatively affects the work environment or leads to adverse job-related consequences for the employee.

Sexual harassment can include something as violent as rape or as subtle as making a sexually oriented comment about another person's body or appearance. Decorating the work area with pictures of nude people or displaying pornographic pictures on a computer are examples of more subtle sexual harassment. A Canadian Human Rights Tribunal identified three characteristics of sexual harassment. The first is that the encounters must be unsolicited and unwelcome to the complainant. An example of this type of behaviour is unwelcome sexual remarks. The second characteristic is that the conduct continues despite the complainant's protests, or, if it does stop, that there are negative employment consequences to the complainant. For instance, the comments do not stop, or the comments stop and the complainant is denied a promised promotion. Third, any perceived cooperation by the complainant must be due to employment-related threats or promises.[36] However, there is still much "grey area" when interpreting what behaviour is to be considered sexual harassment.

Despite codes, acts, and employer policies, sexual harassment continues to be a serious problem in the workplace. In the past decade, sexual harassment has received increasing attention due to the growing ranks of women in nontraditional work environments and recent high-profile cases, such as alleged coverups of harassment in the Canadian Armed Forces. Increasing numbers of men and women are also reporting sexual harassment. Recent surveys indicate that about one-half of working women experience some form of sexual harassment in the workplace. The largest Canadian survey to date, the Survey on Sexual Harassment in Public Places and at Work (SSHPPW), reported that

56 percent of Canadian working women had experienced sexual harassment in the year prior to the survey.[37] The most common incidents were staring, jokes, or comments about women, and jokes about the respondents themselves. While most research is devoted to men harassing women, this does not mean that women do not harass men, or that harassment does not take place between individuals of the same sex. A poll conducted in British Columbia indicated that 14 percent of 400 men polled said they had experienced sexual harassment at work.[38]

The Adverse Effects of Sexual Harassment

Aside from being unethical, immoral, and illegal, sexual harassment has adverse consequences for both the individual and the organization. According to the SSHPPW, almost one-third of the women surveyed reported that their job was affected by harassment; stress was the most common effect. Other effects included being hindered in or unable to do their job, preoccupation, stress at home, and a diminished trust in men.[39] A related study of the long-term effects of sexual harassment indicated that the negative effects remained two years after the incident. For example, 24 months after an incident of sexual harassment, many women still experienced stress, a decrease in job satisfaction, and lowered productivity.[40] These overt and hidden costs have a ripple effect (and resultant cost) that not only has an impact on the complainant and harasser but also affects the productivity of co-workers and supervisors.[41] Imagine if you were a co-worker of another employee who reported sexual harassment against your mutual supervisor.

Guidelines for Preventing and Dealing with Sexual Harassment

A starting point in dealing with sexual harassment is to develop an awareness of the types of behaviours that are considered sexual harassment. Often the difference is subtle. Suppose, for example, you placed copies of two nudes painted by Renoir, the French painter, on a co-worker's desk. Your co-worker might call that harassment. Yet if you took that co-worker to a museum to see the originals of the same nude prints, your behaviour usually would not be classified as harassment. One researcher and her colleagues have worked on a typology of sexual harassment that includes gender harassment (behaviours that indicate demeaning attitudes about women), unwanted sexual attention (both verbal and nonverbal), and sexual coercion (the use of threats or rewards to solicit sexual favours).[42] Following is a sampling of behaviours that will often be interpreted as sexual harassment.[43] If people refrain from these behaviours, many instances of sexual harassment will be avoided.

- **Inappropriate remarks and sexual implications.** Co-workers, subordinates, customers, and suppliers should not be referred to as sexual beings, and their appearance should not be referred to in a sexual manner. Telling a co-worker that she has gorgeous feet, or that he has fabulous biceps, is out of place at work.
- **Terms of endearment.** Refrain from calling others in the workplace by names such as "cutie," "sweetie pie," "honey," "dear," or "hunk." One might argue that these terms are simply *sexist* (they assume different roles for men and women) and that using them is not sexual harassment. However, this argument is losing ground because from a legal perspective any behaviour that puts people down based on their gender can be interpreted as harassment. Keep in mind also that some people find terms of endearment to have a sexual connotation. If you felt no physical attraction toward another adult, would you call that person "cutie" or "hunk"?
- **Suggestive compliments.** It is acceptable to tell another person he or she looks nice, but avoid making sexually tinged comments such as mentioning that the person's clothing shows off his or her body to advantage.

- **Physical touching.** To avoid any appearance of sexual harassment, it is best to restrict physical touching to handshakes and an occasional sideways hug. Hugging a long-term work associate is much more acceptable than hugging a new hire. Minimize such behaviours as adjusting a co-worker's earring, touching hair, and tweaking a person's chin.
- **Work-related kissing.** It is best to avoid all kissing in a work context—except, perhaps, a light kiss at an office party. It is much more professional to greet a work associate with a warm, sincere handshake.

There is little doubt that implementing an effective organizational policy that prohibits all harassment, including sexual harassment, will have positive benefits for all employees. An effective harassment policy should state that the organization is committed to providing a harassment-free workplace, clearly define what constitutes harassment, outline the procedures for reporting and investigating harassment internally, and clearly stipulate the consequences of harassment, including discipline or termination.[44] Also, the policy should clearly outline all of the steps that a person can take if he or she is being harassed, including who the people are that the employee can turn to for help.

The policy should also be widely disseminated so that it is available to everyone within the organization; a policy does not do much good if employees are unaware of its existence. Copies of the policy should be distributed to all employees and given to all new employees upon hire. Many organizations with an internal website post the policy in a readable or downloadable format.

Brief company training programs covering the type of information presented in this chapter are also part of a serious program to prevent and deal with sexual harassment. However, a one-time presentation of a 15-minute videotape about sexual harassment is insufficient. Periodic discussion about the topic is recommended.

Once sexual harassment has taken place, the victim will usually want to resolve the conflict. Two key strategies are either to use a formal complaint procedure or to resolve the conflict on your own. If you choose the latter course, you will save yourself the time of going through a lengthy investigation procedure. Figure 9-2 presents details about the two key strategies for dealing with sexual harassment. Skill-Building Exercise 9-5 offers you an opportunity to simulate controlling sexual harassment.

FIGURE 9-2 How to Deal with Sexual Harassment

The potential or actual victim of sexual harassment is advised to use the following methods and tactics to deal with the problem.

Formal Complaint Procedure. Whenever an employee believes that he or she has encountered sexual harassment, or if an employee is suspected to be the perpetrator of sexual harassment, the complainant should report the incident to his or her immediate supervisor (if that person is not the harasser) or to the next higher level of management if the supervisor is the harasser. The supervisor contacted is responsible for contacting a designated company official immediately regarding each complaint. The officer will explain the investigative procedures to the complainant and any supervisor involved. All matters will be kept strictly confidential, including private conversations with all parties.

Dealing with the Problem on Your Own. The easiest way to deal with sexual harassment is to speak up before it becomes serious. The first time it happens, respond with a statement such as: "I won't tolerate this kind of talk," or "I dislike sexually oriented jokes," or "Keep your hands off me."

Write the harasser a stern letter shortly after the first incident. Being confronted in writing dramatizes your seriousness of purpose in not wanting to be sexually harassed. Tell the actual or potential harasser: "You're practising sexual harassment. If you don't stop, I'm going to exercise my right to report you to management." Or: "I don't think I heard you right. Would you like to accompany me to the boss's office and repeat what you said to me?"

SKILL-BUILDING EXERCISE 9-5

Combating Sexual Harassment

The two role-plays in this exercise provide practice in applying the recommended techniques for combating sexual harassment. The activities have an implied sexual content, and they are for educational purposes only. Any students offended by these role-plays should exclude themselves from participating.

Scenario 1: The Offensive Jester. One student plays the role of Max, a man who delights in telling sexually oriented jokes and anecdotes in the office. He often brings a tabloid newspaper to the office to read sexually oriented passages to co-workers, both male and female. Another student assumes the role of Maxine, a woman in the office who takes offence to Max's sense of humour. She wants to convince Max that he is committing sexual harassment with his sexually oriented humour. Max does not see himself as committing sexual harassment.

Scenario 2: The Flirtatious Office Manager. One student assumes the role of Bertha, an office manager who is single. Another student plays the role of Bert, a married man who recently joined the company as an office assistant. Bert reports to Bertha, and she finds him physically attractive. Bertha visits Bert at his desk and makes such comments as "It looks like you have great quadriceps. I wonder what you look like in running shorts?" Bert wants to be on good terms with Bertha, but he feels uncomfortable with her advances. He also wants to behave professionally in the office.

Run both role-plays in front of the class for about eight minutes. Other students in the class will observe the role-plays and then provide feedback about how well Maxine and Bert were able to prevent or stop sexual harassment.

A major recommendation for documenting acts of sexual harassment is to keep a running diary of incidents against you. A log of the incidents is impressive to company officials, lawyers, and judges (should a lawsuit ultimately be involved). Examples of log entries from a woman and a man are given below:

- **January 17, 2012:** Jim Quattrone, the manager of accounts payable, asked me to have dinner with him for the sixth time, and I turned him down again. I said "no," "no," "no."
- **March 13, 2011:** Meg Evans, my supervisor, said that I would receive a much better performance evaluation if I could come over to her house for dinner. She said her husband would be out of town, so I could stay overnight if I wanted to. I felt so uncomfortable and pressured. I made up an excuse about having an exclusive relationship.

Access the eText in MySearchLab to learn more about this chapter's self-assessment quizzes.

To Watch · Explore · Practice · Study and Review, visit MySearchLab

Developing Your Human Relations Skills and Reinforcing Concepts

Summary

- A conflict is a situation in which two or more goals, values, or events are incompatible or mutually exclusive. Causes of conflict include competition for limited resources, role conflict, competing work and family demands, personality clashes, bullies, incivility and rudeness, and cross-generational conflict
- Five major styles of conflict management have been identified: competitive, accommodative, sharing, collaborative (win–win), and avoidant.
- Methods of conflict resolution include confrontation and problem solving, constructive handling of criticism, reframing, and negotiating and bargaining.
- Sexual harassment is a form of interpersonal conflict that has legal implications. Many companies have policies to prevent sexual harassment. Employees who do experience sexual harassment can either confront the harasser on their own or lodge a formal complaint.

Interpersonal Relations Case 9-1

The Apprehensive Sales Trainee

Maria was ecstatic about the position she just landed as a sales representative for a company that provides payroll and human resources services for small companies throughout the country. She was to be assigned a sales territory in the Edmonton, Alberta, area, where she lived with her husband and three young children. Before working her territory, Maria had to attend 10 days of training and orientation at the company headquarters in Vancouver.

One of the key trainers in the program was the national sales manager, Todd, an energetic and successful-looking man in his early forties. During a beverage break at the first morning of the training program, Todd approached Maria and complimented her on her "great tan" and "fabulous appearance." Maria was not particularly comfortable with the comments, but she let them pass.

Before the dinner meeting at the second night of the program, Todd came over to Maria and engaged her in a brief conversation about how she was enjoying the sales training. He then handed her a business card and said, "I imagine you might get lonely being away from home for so long, so here is my business card. Please get in touch if you would just like to hang out a little with me." Maria thought that Todd was stepping over the line of good business judgment, but she just smiled politely and said, "Thanks anyway, but I am so overwhelmed with all this great information I am receiving, I have no spare time."

The following morning, Maria received a text message from Todd on her BlackBerry that said, "Your beauty is devastating. Get back."

Maria later phoned her best friend in Edmonton and said, "Todd carries a lot of weight being the national sales manager. But I think his behaviour toward me borders on sexual harassment. Yet five days into my job, I guess I shouldn't attempt to rat on a company executive."

Maria's friend replied, "You have got to do something. That sales manager is a predator."

Case Questions

1. To what extent is Todd engaging in sexual harassment toward Maria?
2. If Todd is guilty, what type of sexual harassment is he committing?
3. What steps should Maria take so that she can stop the harassment, yet still maintain a good working relationship with Todd?
4. What would be the positives and negatives of Maria filing a complaint about Todd with the company?

Interpersonal Relations Case 9-2

The Refrigerator Caper*

Two email messages were sent at a technology company in Nova Scotia, covering the same topic:

From: Nestor, Jenna
Sent: Tuesday, August 7, 12:50 p.m.
To: All employees on 3rd, 4th, and 8th floors
Subject: Re: Refrigerator Etiquette
Importance: High

To the person who ate my lunch:

I would like to thank you for completely taking it upon yourself to deny me sustenance this afternoon. It is completely inappropriate to take things that are not yours. Are we in Grade 1?

Please read Diana's email that I have copied below. I would be happy to read it out loud and explain it to you if it is too hard to understand.

Jenna

A Very Angry Victim

P.S. In case you were wondering what that extra flavour was, each and every day I take the time to spit in my lunch. I hope you enjoyed it.

*The company involved in this incident chose to remain anonymous.

From: Sanders, Diana
Sent: Monday, July 30, 4:32 p.m.
To: All employees on 3rd, 4th, and 8th floors
Subject: Refrigerator Etiquette

Over the past month, a number of employees have been disappointed when they went to grab their lunch out of the refrigerator. Unfortunately, they found that someone had either taken part of their lunch out of their lunch bag and or the entire lunch was missing.

Please be respectful of others and do not eat anything from the fridge that is not your personal property. If you bring your lunch, please label with your name and date. Thank you for your immediate cooperation and consideration of co-workers.

Diana Sanders

Director of Administration

Case Questions

1. What is the exact conflict in this situation? What is the source of the conflict?
2. What is your evaluation of Jenna Nestor's method of resolving the conflict over the stolen lunch?
3. How can professional adults really act in this manner?

Questions for Discussion and Review

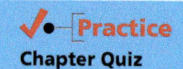

✓ Practice Chapter Quiz

Multiple Choice

1. Two managers are having a disagreement about allocation of monies to upgrade employees' computer workstations. One manager sees this as imperative. The other manager would prefer to allocate these funds to purchase new company vehicles and the computer upgrades could wait until the next budget process. This source of conflict is likely
   a. a personality clash.
   b. competition over limited resources.
   c. cross-generational conflict.
   d. None of the above

2. Nick often readily gives into his manager's demands without offering his views even when he thinks that the demands are unreasonable. He likely relies on the _____ style of conflict management.
   a. competitive
   b. sharing
   c. avoidant
   d. accommodative

3. You receive a poor performance review at your job. Initially you are furious, but after some careful thought you realize that there is some merit in the critique and that this review is also an opportunity for self-improvement. This is an example of
   a. cognitive restructuring.
   b. disarming the opposition.
   c. bargaining.
   d. confrontation.

4. A good negotiator knows to
   a. never use anger.
   b. make a large concession right at the beginning.
   c. make small concessions gradually.
   d. begin with a large demand.

5. A manager continually calls one of her subordinates "sweetie." He feels very uncomfortable with this endearment, but is too shy to confront her. What would be his best course of action?
   a. Just let it go. He is being too sensitive and she likely means nothing by calling him "sweetie."

Answers to multiple choice questions: 1. b,   2. d,   3. a,   4. c,   5. b.

b. Report to her manager that this is making him very uncomfortable and let the manager deal with this issue as sexual harassment.
c. Take another position within the organization that does not report to her.
d. Call her "sweetie" as well in hopes that she also feels uncomfortable with this label and thus may cause her to stop calling him "sweetie."

Short Answer

6. Why might it be useful for you to know a work associate's conflict style?
7. Have you ever attempted to disarm the opposition? How effective was the tactic?
8. How might a student use cognitive restructuring to get over feeling angry after receiving a low grade in a course? How might a student increase a poor grade by using negotiation?
9. Studies have shown that women working in male-dominated positions, such as a female construction supervisor or bulldozer operator, are more likely to experience sexual harassment than women in other fields. What explanation can you offer for this finding?
10. Open your MySearchLab and click on professional videos. Watch the one that deals with conflict during the brainstorming session. Answer the questions at the end of the video. If you were this unit's manager, how would you have handled the conflict?

The Web Corner

www.ehow.com
Resolving workplace conflict

www.canada.justice.gc.ca
The site for Justice Canada

http://wmhp.cmhaontario.ca/workplace-mental-health-core-concepts-issues/issues-in-the-workplace-that-affect-employee-mental-health/harassment-violence-bullying-and-mobbing#_ftn1
A Canadian resource site about bullying and harassment

Internet Skill Builder: Finding Suggestions for Resolving Conflict on YouTube

YouTube.com often has a generous sampling of brief videos about resolving conflict that apply mostly to personal life, but some are about the workplace. Visit the site, watch a handful of videos about conflict resolution, and look for a few serious messages. Look for any similarities between the information presented in YouTube videos and in this chapter. Also, does it appear that any of the videos you find present a humorous aspect to conflict resolution?

MySearchLab

Visit **MySearchLab** to find self-grading review quizzes in the eText, discipline-specific media and readings, access to a variety of academic journals, and Associated Press news feeds, along with a wide range of writing, grammar, and research tools and to help hone writing and research skills.

CHAPTER 10

Becoming an Effective Leader

Mary DiSalvo is the director of operations at a printing company that specializes in printing shrink-wrapped labels for food and consumer products, including bottled water, orange juice, and packaged meat. Company CEO Bruce Denton observed that over a six-year period, DiSalvo's group had the highest productivity and lowest employee turnover at the company. Denton had a hunch that DiSalvo's passion for people and her love of printing had something to do with her outstanding record. However, he wanted more insight into what made for the superb leadership at his company. So with Mary's permission, an outside human relations specialist interviewed several people about their experiences working in the company, and what they thought of Mary's leadership.

Edhar/Shutterstock

LEARNING Objectives

After reading and studying this chapter and doing the exercises, you should be able to

1. Identify key leadership traits for personal development.
2. Develop several attitudes and behaviours that will help you appear charismatic.
3. Develop your skills for coaching and training.
4. Develop your leadership potential.

Cheryl, a shipping supervisor, described DiSalvo's leadership in these terms: "Mary is so gung-ho about labels and production efficiency that her excitement rubs off on you. She makes us feel that we are on a crusade to produce the best labels in the business. At the same time, she really cares about everybody who works at the company. I remember when she personally went to help out a production worker whose house was severely damaged by a tree falling on it."

Jeff, a quality technician, expressed these ideas to the human relations interviewer: "I don't have too much direct contact with Mary because she is two levels up the ladder from me. But I feel her impact almost every day. Mary is committed to quality, and her emails to the company about quality make me feel that my work is very important. Mary is the hardest worker in the plant, so she sets a good example for us. She also has a great, warm smile and a cheerful attitude that makes you want to do your best."[1]

As in the story just presented, effective leaders have a combination of admirable qualities, including expertise, a passion to succeed, high energy, and the ability to inspire others. In working toward improving your leadership ability, the following definition is a goal to strive for. **Leadership** is the ability to inspire support and confidence among the people who are needed to achieve company goals. A company president might have to inspire thousands of people, while a team leader is concerned with inspiring about six people. Both of these leaders nonetheless play an important role.

Leadership has also been defined in many other ways. An analysis of 221 definitions of leadership concluded that they basically all say the same thing—leadership is about one person getting one or more other people to do something.[2] The something usually refers to attaining a worthwhile company goal. In other words, the leader makes a difference.

Becoming a leader does not necessarily mean that the company has to put you in charge of others (or assign you a formal leadership position). You can also rise to leadership when people come to respect your opinion and personal characteristics and are thus influenced by you. Leadership is thought by many to exist at all levels, with people anywhere in the organization being able to influence others if they have the right skills or know the right work procedures.[3] Your greatest opportunity for exerting leadership will come about from a combination of holding a formal position and exerting personal influence. An individual with appealing personal characteristics and expertise who is placed in a position of authority will find it relatively easy to exert leadership.

The purpose of this chapter is twofold: (1) to make you aware of the basic concepts you will need to become a leader; and (2) to point you toward developing skills necessary for leadership effectiveness. As well, we will cover two other areas where you can practise your leadership skills in a more informal way: coaching and training others.

leadership
The ability to inspire support and confidence among the people who are needed to achieve common goals.

BECOMING AN EFFECTIVE LEADER

KEY LEADERSHIP TRAITS TO DEVELOP

LEARNING OBJECTIVE 1

Explore
Simulation: Leadership

An important part of being an effective leader is to have the "right stuff." In this section and the following one about charisma, we describe personal attributes that help a person lead others in many situations. While this list does not include all the necessary traits for effective leadership, the items included have been well documented in research.

Also, recognize that radically different situations require a different set of leadership characteristics. For example, a leader may need to be more assertive with group members performing distasteful work than with those whose work is enjoyable. Even if traits are but one facet of understanding leadership, they play an important role. Traits help explain individual differences in leadership.[4] For example, an assertive and self-confident leader will be able to take decisive actions.

Each of the 10 leadership traits described next, and shown in Figure 10-1, can be developed. For such development to take place, you need to be aware of the importance of the personal characteristic, and then monitor your own behaviour to make progress. To assist you with such development, the description of each trait is accompanied by a suggestion for improvement.

Self-Confidence and Leadership Efficacy

In virtually every leadership setting, it is important for the leader to be realistically self-confident. A leader who is self-assured without being bombastic or overbearing instills confidence in group members. Self-confidence was among the first leadership traits researchers identified. A series of research studies have shown that increased self-confidence can bring about improvement in performance, including helping a group attain its goals.[5] In addition to being self-confident, the leader must project that self-confidence to the group.[6] Self-confidence is not only a personality trait. It also refers to the behaviour a person exhibits in a number of situations. It is similar to being cool under pressure. We can conclude that a person is a self-confident leader when he or she retains composure during a crisis, such as when the company suffers flood damage during a busy season.

FIGURE 10-1 10 Key Leadership Traits

People who possess the traits listed below are usually well suited to being an effective leader. However, many other traits and behaviours are also important contributors to effective leadership.

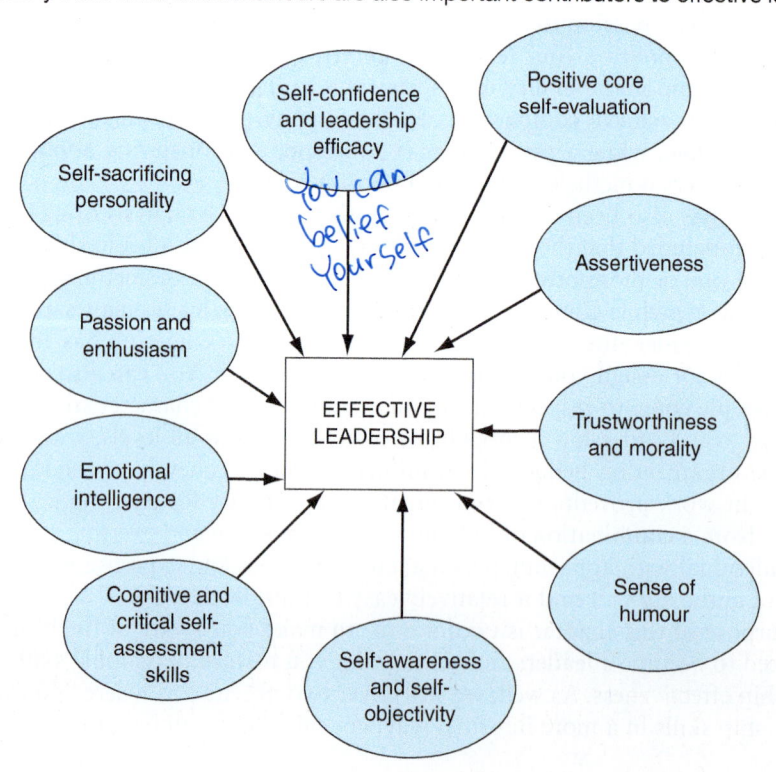

- Self-confidence and leadership efficacy
- Positive core self-evaluation
- Self-sacrificing personality
- Assertiveness
- Passion and enthusiasm
- Trustworthiness and morality
- Emotional intelligence
- Sense of humour
- Cognitive and critical self-assessment skills
- Self-awareness and self-objectivity

→ EFFECTIVE LEADERSHIP

The inclusion of a feeling of efficacy in combination with self-confidence helps better pinpoint how confidence works. *Leadership efficacy* is a form of efficacy associated with confidence in the knowledge, skills, and abilities valuable for with leading others. In essence, the leader is confident that he or she has the tools necessary to lead a group. Another insight into leadership efficacy is that it helps the leader step up to meet his or her challenges.[7] The confidence therefore extends beyond attitudes about the self. A leader who had been a successful racquet sports director at one athletic club might have the leadership efficacy to carry out the many aspects of that role at another club.

You can appear more self-confident to the group by using definitive wording, maintaining good posture, and making appropriate gestures such as counting off significant points of a speech with fingers for emphasis. Developing self-confidence is a lifelong process of performing well in a variety of situations. You need a series of easy victories to establish self-confidence. Further development of this trait requires performing well in challenging circumstances. Taking risks, such as volunteering to work on an unfamiliar project, contributes to self-confidence when the risk proves to be worthwhile. As your self-confidence builds in several situations, you will also develop a strong sense of leadership efficacy.

Positive Core Self-Evaluation

The core self-evaluation was described in Chapter 2 as closely related to self-esteem (Chapter 3 details self-esteem and its components). In more detail, the core self-evaluation captures a person's self-assessment. Its four components are self-esteem, locus of control, self-efficacy, and emotional stability (low neuroticism).[8] Except for locus of control, these traits have already been defined in Chapters 2 and 3. In addition, we described how self-esteem in the form of self-confidence can be developed.

Locus of control deals with the way people look at causation in their lives. If you believe that you are controlled mostly by outside events beyond your control, you would have an external locus of control. A marketing specialist with an external control might say, "Our computer system is down today, so there is nothing constructive I can do. I'll just wait until the system is running again." With an internal locus of control, the marketing specialist might say, "The computer is down, which will slow me down. However, I'll work on whatever I can do that does not require the company computer. I can do some research on markets in Africa with my smart phone."

An internal locus of control is better for leadership than an external locus of control. Leaders who believe that they can control events are more likely to inspire others and provide direction. High emotional stability is better for leadership than low emotional stability. Anyone who has ever worked for an unstable supervisor will attest to the importance of emotional stability as a leadership trait. Emotional stability is important for a leader because group members expect and need consistency in the way they are treated.

A useful tactic for developing an internal locus of control is to examine challenging situations, and search for what aspect of those situations might be in your control. The department leader might be informed that because of low profits, salaries will be frozen for the next year. The leader might say, "Okay, external events have created conditions for discontent in my department. However, I can still use recognition and interesting work assignments to boost morale." Emotional stability is difficult to develop, but people can learn to control many of their emotional outbursts.

locus of control
The way people look at causation in their lives.

Assertiveness

A widely recognized leadership trait is **assertiveness**, being forthright in expressing demands, opinions, feelings, and attitudes. If you are self-confident, it is easier to be assertive with people. An assertive team leader from the Ottawa area might say, "I know that the ice storm put us out of business for four days, but we can make up the time by working smart and pulling together. Within 30 days, we will have met or surpassed our goals for the quarter." This statement reflects self-confidence in the

assertiveness
Forthrightness in expressing demands, opinions, feelings, and attitudes.

team leader's leadership capabilities and assertiveness in expressing exactly what this leader thinks.

Assertiveness helps leaders perform many tasks and achieve goals. Among them are confronting group members about their mistakes, demanding higher performance, and setting high expectations. An assertive leader will also make legitimate demands on higher management, such as asking for equipment needed by the group. A recent experiment with students suggested that being assertive in the form of talking loudly and frequently is often perceived to be a leadership quality. The study indicated that individuals who have the tendency to behave in assertive and self-assured ways attain influence because such behaviour makes them appear confident. However, being dominant is not sufficient for being perceived as a leader over time. You need to back up loud talk with constructive actions.[9]

Being assertive differs significantly from being aggressive or passive (or nonassertive). Aggressive people express their demands in an overly pushy, obnoxious, and abrasive manner. Passive people suppress their own ideas, attitudes, feelings, and thoughts as if they were likely to be perceived as controversial. Nonassertive people are also too accommodating.

Developing assertiveness is much like attempting to become less shy. You must force yourself to take the opportunity to express your feelings and demands. For example, if something a teammate does annoys you, make the statement, "I enjoy working with you in general, but what you are doing now annoys me." You can also practise expressing positive emotion, such as telling a co-worker, "I'm happy that you and I are working on this project together, because I like your approach to work."

Expressing demands is easier for most people to practise than expressing feelings. People who do start expressing their demands are often surprised at the result. For example, if you are contemplating the purchase of an item that is beyond your budget, try this statement: "I like this product very much. Yet all I have to spend is $100 below your asking price. Can we do business?"

For a reading on your own level of assertiveness, do Self-Assessment Quiz 10-1.

Trustworthiness and Morality

Group members consistently believe that leaders must display honesty, integrity, and credibility—and therefore trustworthiness. Leaders themselves believe that honesty makes a difference in their effectiveness. Being honest with team members helps to build trust, which in turn leads to good cooperation and team spirit. Right Management Consultants conducted a survey of 570 employees in which they found that the white-collar workers valued honesty and integrity in a manager more than any other trait. When asked, "What is the most important trait or attribute that the leader of your company should possess?" 24 percent of the survey participants cited honesty, and 16 percent named integrity/morals and ethics.[10] Leaders themselves believe that honesty makes a difference in their effectiveness.

It is almost an axiom in leadership studies that integrity is important for effective leadership. (Leaders who are trustworthy typically have high integrity.) Like most concepts in human relations, *integrity* has several connotations. Yet, the two key meanings of **integrity** are (a) consistency of words and deeds, and (b) being true to oneself.[11] Being true to oneself refers to sticking with one's principles, such as a sales manager who preaches high ethics not giving kickbacks to customers for the purpose of closing a sale.

In recent years, trust in business leaders has been damaged by financial scandals in well-known companies. Executives enriched themselves by selling company stock just before the time they correctly forecast that the stock price would tumble. On the Canadian political scene, incidents such as the outrageous hotel expenditures by federal and provincial members of Parliament (remember the $16 bottle of orange juice?) have left many Canadians distrustful of political leaders.

In trusting group members, the leader has to be willing to give up some control over them, such as letting group members make more decisions and not challenging their

integrity
(a) Consistency of words and deeds, and (b) being true to oneself.

SELF-ASSESSMENT QUIZ 10-1

The Assertiveness Scale

Directions: Indicate whether each of the following statements is "Mostly True" or "Mostly False" as it applies to you. If in doubt about your reaction to a particular statement, think of how you would generally respond.

		Mostly True	Mostly False
1.	It is extremely difficult for me to turn down a sales representative when that individual is a nice person.	✓	
2.	I express criticism freely.	✓	
3.	If another person is being very unfair, I bring it to his or her attention.		✓
4.	Work is no place to let your feelings show.	✓	
5.	No use asking for favours; people get what they deserve.	✓	
6.	Business is not the place for tact; say what you think.		✓
7.	In a supermarket line, if a person looks as if he or she is in a hurry, I let that person in front of me.	✓	
8.	A weakness of mine is that I'm too nice a person.		✓
9.	I usually give other people what they want rather than do what I think is best, just to avoid an argument.	✓	
10.	If the mood strikes me, I will laugh out loud in public.		✓
11.	People consider me too outspoken.		✓
12.	I am quite willing to return merchandise that I find has a minor blemish.		✓
13.	I dread having to express anger toward a co-worker.		✓
14.	People often say that I'm too reserved and emotionally controlled.		✓
15.	Nice guys and gals finish last in business.		✓
16.	I fight for my rights down to the last detail.		✓
17.	I have no misgivings about returning an overcoat to the store if it doesn't fit me right.	✓	
18.	After I have an argument with a person, I try to avoid him or her.	✓	
19.	I insist on my spouse (or roommate or partner) doing his or her fair share of undesirable chores.	✓	
20.	It is difficult for me to look directly at another person when the two of us are in disagreement.		✓
21.	I have cried in front of friends more than once.	✓	
22.	If someone near me at a movie keeps up a conversation with another person, I ask him or her to stop.		✓
23.	I am able to turn down social engagements with people I do not particularly care for.		✓
24.	It is in poor taste to express what you really feel about another individual.		✓
25.	I sometimes show my anger by swearing at or belittling another person.	✓	
26.	I am reluctant to speak up at meetings.	✓	
27.	I find it relatively easy to ask friends for small favours such as giving me a ride to work while my car is being repaired.	✓	
28.	If another person is talking very loudly in a restaurant and it bothers me, I tell that person.		✓
29.	I often finish other people's sentences for them.	✓	
30.	It is relatively easy for me to express love and affection toward another person.	✓	

(Continued)

> **Scoring Key**
>
> | | | | |
> |---|---|---|---|
> | 1. Mostly false | 9. Mostly false | 17. Mostly true | 25. Mostly true |
> | 2. Mostly true | 10. Mostly true | 18. Mostly false | 26. Mostly false |
> | 3. Mostly true | 11. Mostly true | 19. Mostly true | 27. Mostly true |
> | 4. Mostly false | 12. Mostly true | 20. Mostly false | 28. Mostly true |
> | 5. Mostly false | 13. Mostly false | 21. Mostly true | 29. Mostly true |
> | 6. Mostly true | 14. Mostly false | 22. Mostly true | 30. Mostly true |
> | 7. Mostly false | 15. Mostly true | 23. Mostly true | |
> | 8. Mostly false | 16. Mostly true | 24. Mostly false | |
>
> **Interpretation:** Score yourself one point (+1) for each of your answers that agrees with the scoring key. If your score is 15 or less, it is probable that you are currently nonassertive. A score of 16 through 24 suggests that you are assertive. A score of 25 or higher suggests that you are aggressive. Retake this quiz about 30 days from now to give yourself some indication of the stability of your answers. You might also discuss your answers with a close friend to determine whether that person has a similar perception of your assertiveness.

expense accounts. The following anecdote told by Fred Smith, the founder of FedEx, illustrates what trust can mean in an organization:

> *A blizzard shut down a radio relay located on top of a mountain, cutting phone service to several FedEx offices. The phone company said it would take five days to repair the problem. On his own, a FedEx telecommunications expert named Hal chartered a helicopter to get to the site. The pilot was unable to land, but he got close enough to the ground for Hal to jump safely. Hal slogged through the deep snow and fixed the problem.*

According to Smith, Hal went to such great lengths to keep the organization going because there was mutual trust between employer and employee. Hal knew he would not be reprimanded for going to such expense to fix the telephone problem.[12]

Being moral is closely linked to trustworthiness because a moral leader is more likely to be trusted. A leader with high morality would perceive that he or she had an ethical responsibility to group members, as well as to outsiders.[13] The moral leader would therefore not give preferential treatment to workers with whom he had an outside-of-work friendship. At the same time the moral leader would not try to fool customers or make up false excuses for not paying bills on time to suppliers.

Chapter 14, about ethical behaviour, provides details concerning honesty on the job. Being honest is an effective way of getting others to trust you. A starting point in developing a strong sense of honesty is to follow a variation on the Golden Rule: Be as honest with others as you want them to be with you.

Sense of Humour

A sense of humour is borderline between being a trait and a behaviour. However you classify it, the effective use of humour is considered an important part of a leader's role. Humour serves such functions in the workplace as relieving tension and boredom and defusing hostility. Because humour helps the leader deal with tension and conflict in the workplace, it helps him or her exert power over the group. A study conducted in a large Canadian financial institution indicated that leaders who made frequent use of humour had higher-performing units. (Another interpretation is that it's easier to laugh when the group is performing well!) Among the forms of humour used by the managers were "[using] humour to take the edge off during stressful periods" and "[making] us laugh at ourselves when we are too serious."[14]

Self-effacing humour is the choice of comedians and organizational leaders alike. When you are self-effacing, nobody else is insulted or slighted; yet a point can be made. Creativity is required for humour. Just as creativity can be enhanced with practice, so can a sense of humour. To gather some experience in making humorous comments in the workplace, do Skill-Building Exercise 10-1.

SKILL-BUILDING EXERCISE 10-1

The Witty Leader

Groups of about five students gather in problem-solving groups to invent humorous comments a leader might make in the following scenarios. After the problem-solving groups have formulated their witty comments, the comments can be shared and compared. Groups also have the option of deciding that a particular scenario is too grim for humour.

Scenario 1: A store manager wants to communicate to employees that inventory slippage (merchandise stolen from the store by customers or store associates) has increased to an unacceptable level—twice the industry average.

Scenario 2: A leader has to communicate to the group that salaries have been frozen for another year due to limited business. The leader knows that group members have been eagerly awaiting news about the salary increase.

Scenario 3: Due to an unprecedented surge in orders, all salaried personnel will be required to work about 65 hours per week for the next 10 weeks. Further, the office and factory must be staffed on Saturdays and Sundays.

Scenario 4: A consulting firm that specializes in helping companies downsize their workforce has seen the demand for their services decline substantially in recent months. The company must therefore downsize itself. The company founder has to announce the layoff decision to the company.

Observers might rate the attempts at humour on a 1 (low) to 10 (high) scale. Observe also if any of the role players made you laugh.

Self-Awareness and Self-Objectivity

Effective leaders are aware of their strengths and limitations. This awareness enables them to capitalize on their strengths and overcome their weaknesses. A leader, for example, might realize that he or she is naturally distrustful of others. Awareness of this problem cautions the leader to not distrust people without good evidence. Another leader might realize that he or she is adept at counselling team members. This leader might then emphasize that activity in an effort to improve performance. Self-objectivity refers to being detached or non-subjective about your perceived strengths and limitations.

Another way in which self-awareness and self-objectivity contribute to leadership effectiveness is that these traits help a person become an authentic leader. Such a leader demonstrates passion for his or her purpose, practises values consistently, and leads with the heart as well as the head. Instead of being a phony, or acting out of character, the person is a genuine. Authenticity helps the leader be perceived as trustworthy.[15] "Being yourself" thus contributes to leadership effectiveness, assuming that you have personal qualities, such as those presented in this chapter, that facilitate leadership. Mary, the leader described in the chapter opener, appears to be an authentic leader.

You can enhance your self-awareness and self-objectivity by regularly asking for feedback from others. You then compare the feedback to your self-perception of your standing on the same factor. You might, for example, think that you communicate in colourful, interesting terms. In speaking to others about your communication style, you might discover that others agree. You can then conclude that your self-awareness about your communication skills is accurate.

Another technique for improving self-awareness and self-objectivity is to do a number of the type of self-examination exercises found in this text. Even if they do not describe you exactly, they stimulate you to reflect on your characteristics and behaviours.

Cognitive Skills Including Critical Assessments

Mental ability, as well as personality, is important for leadership success. To inspire people, bring about constructive changes, and solve problems creatively, leaders need to be mentally sharp. Problem-solving and intellectual skills are referred to collectively as **cognitive** factors. The term *cognition* refers to the mental process or faculty by which knowledge is gathered.

cognitive factors
The collective term for problem-solving and intellectual skills.

Stephen Coburn/Shutterstock

BECOMING AN EFFECTIVE LEADER

Knowledge of the Business. A major reason that cognitive skills have increased in importance for leadership is that they enable the leader to acquire knowledge. The processing of knowledge is now considered to be the *core competence* (key ability) of organizations. The leader's role is to both originate useful ideas and collect them from smart people throughout the organization.[16] Two cognitive skills were discussed in Chapter 2: cognitive ability and the personal factor of openness to experience. Another cognitive skill of major importance is *knowledge of the business,* or technical skill. An effective leader has to be technically or professionally competent in some discipline, particularly when leading a group of specialists. It is difficult for the leader to establish rapport with group members when he or she does not know what they are doing. A related damper on leadership effectiveness is when the group does not respect the leader's technical skill.

One of a large number of examples of how knowledge of the business is helpful for occupying a leadership position these days took place at the Cadillac division of General Motors Co. Vehicle designer Bryan Nesbitt was appointed to head the Cadillac brand. Typically, marketing and sales executives were chosen to head brands. Nesbitt had built a positive reputation when he designed the Chrysler PT Cruiser.[17] Such close knowledge of the business was thought necessary for the prosperity (or perhaps survival) of the Cadillac.

Critical Assessments. Another major reason cognitive skills are so important for leadership is that they facilitate making critical assessments, or thinking critically, about challenges facing the group or entire organization. You will recall that critical thinking refers to making a judgment after analytically evaluating a problem. Almost any course you have ever taken is supposed to improve your critical thinking ability. Making a critical assessment often boils down to sizing up a situation, and analyzing how the group can profit from this situation. Muhtar Kent, the CEO of Coca-Cola, is effective at making critical assessments, as illustrated in his analysis of how the future is bright for Coca-Cola:

> Kent insists that the beverage industry is better positioned than many other businesses to weather economic difficulties. He says rapid urbanization and blossoming of the middle class in big emerging nations are juicing demand for on-the-go beverages. So many people are moving to urban centres that it's like "adding a city the size of New York to the world every three months."[18]

(We might add to Kent's analysis that there are many more outlets for Coca-Cola brands in cities than rural areas.)

Independent Decision Making. High intelligence is particularly important for leaders, when they have the opportunity to make decisions by themselves and provide direction (such as giving technical instructions) to group members.[19] Problem-solving ability is less important when the leader delegates most of his or her responsibilities to others (or empowers them). High intelligence is important for three major aspects of the leader's job. One aspect is dealing with tasks, such as developing ideas for cost cutting. A second aspect is working with and through other people, or the human relations focus. The third is judging oneself and adapting one's behaviour accordingly, as in self-awareness and self-objectivity.[20]

Increasing one's mental ability, or raw intelligence, may not be easy to accomplish. Yet people can develop their cognitive skills by continuous study and by working on challenging problems. The mere act of keeping up with developments in your field can keep you mentally sharp. The comments about enhancing cognitive skills in Chapter 2 are also relevant here.

Emotional Intelligence

Emotional intelligence, as described in Chapter 2, refers to the ability to recognize your emotions and those of people around you. Emotional intelligence also refers to being able to work effectively with the emotions of others to resolve problems, through listening and empathizing. Research conducted by Daniel Goleman in many different firms suggests that superb leaders all have one trait in common: superb emotional intelligence.[21] A specific example is that an effective manager or leader can often recognize the motives behind an employee's actions. In this regard, consider the following scenario:

> Visualize yourself as a team leader. Vanessa, one of the team members, says to you, "I'm worried about Rick. I think he needs help. He looks like he has a drinking problem."
>
> If you have good emotional intelligence, you might think to yourself, "I wonder why Vanessa is telling me this. Is she simply being helpful? Or is she out to stab Rick in the back?" So you would seek some tangible evidence about Rick's alleged problem before acting. You would also seek to spend more time with Vanessa so you can better understand her motives.
>
> With much less emotional intelligence, you would immediately get in touch with Rick, accuse him of having a drinking problem, and tell him to get help or get fired.

Emotional intelligence is also reflected in a leader who incorporates the human touch into business activities, such as building personal relationships with employees and customers. Several years ago Robert A. Eckert was recruited from Kraft Foods to become chairman and CEO of toy maker Mattel. At the time Mattel was in deep financial trouble, and key Mattel managers were leaving the company. Eckert moved quickly to bring the famous toy manufacturer back to health. The first steps he took were to share meals with employees in the company cafeteria at every opportunity. During these lunches he engaged in candid dialogue with employees chosen at random. He reassured employees that their personal growth and development was a major part of his plans for rebuilding Mattel. Eckert notes, "In this case the emotional intelligence I'd developed over the years was even more important to my success than my traditional, analytical management skills were."[22]

Emotional intelligence can be developed through working on some of its components, as described in Chapter 2. It is also important to develop the habit of seeking to understand the feelings and emotions of people around you. Also, ask yourself, "How do I feel about what's going on here?" When you have a hunch about people's motives, look for feedback in the future to see if you were right. For example, in the scenario given above, investigation might indicate that Vanessa and Rick are indeed rivals and have a personality clash.

Passion and Enthusiasm

A prominent characteristic of effective leaders is the passion and enthusiasm they have for their work, much like the same quality in creative people. The passion reflects itself in such ways as an intense liking for the business, the customers, and employees. Passion is also reflected in a relentless drive to get work accomplished and an obsession for achieving company goals. Passion for their work is especially evident in entrepreneurial leaders and small-business owners who are preoccupied with expanding their businesses. Many leaders use the term "love" to describe their passion for their work, business, and employees.

Passion and enthusiasm are particularly evident among entrepreneurial leaders. When business founders talk about their products or service, you can hear the excitement in their voices. A representative comment by an entrepreneur is "I love what I do, so it isn't work at all."[23] To display passion and enthusiasm for your work, you must first find work that creates an inner spark. The work that you choose should be at least as exciting as your favourite pastime. If not everything about your job excites you, search for its most satisfying or *intrinsically motivating* elements. For example, the Mattel executive described above is so excited about the interpersonal aspects of his work that his passion inspires employees.

BECOMING AN EFFECTIVE LEADER   207

Self-Sacrificing Personality

A final trait to be discussed here that contributes to leadership effectiveness is a **self-sacrificing personality**—a tendency to be more concerned about the welfare and interests of others than those of oneself. The self-sacrificing personality translates into a behaviour while occupying a leadership role, because the leader acts in the best interest of group members. The self-sacrificing leader is sometimes referred to as a servant leader because his or her primary focus is to serve the group.

Leaders with a self-sacrificing personality are ethical and often forgo personal interests in order to focus on the mission and purpose of the group. Such a leader would be more concerned about the group having high morale and being productive than getting a large financial bonus. Self-sacrificing leaders often engage in personally risky behaviours to benefit the group. An example would be taking the risk of going over budget to purchase appropriate furnishings for the employee lounge, thereby maintaining morale. A leader with a self-sacrificing personality is typically a good role model for the group in terms of focusing more on the needs of others than being self-centered.[24]

Dave & Les Jacobs/Blend Images/Corbis

self-sacrificing personality
A tendency to be more concerned about the welfare and interests of others than those of oneself.

LEARNING OBJECTIVE 2

charisma
A special quality of people whose purposes, powers, and extraordinary determination differentiate them from others.

Explore
Simulation: Team Management

SUGGESTIONS FOR DEVELOPING CHARISMA

The study of leadership in recent years has emphasized the importance of inspirational leaders who guide others toward great heights of achievement. Such leaders are said to possess **charisma**, a special quality of leaders whose purposes, powers, and extraordinary determination differentiate them from others.[25] Being charismatic can make a leader's job easier, because leaders have to energize group members.[26]

An important fact about charisma is that it reflects a subjective perception on the part of the person being influenced. Past Prime Minister Pierre Elliott Trudeau, for instance, was described as having "indubitable leadership qualities" by one of his opponents, Quebec premier Lucien Bouchard. Yet he was also disliked by others such as Raymond Villeneuve, a former Front de Libération du Québec (FLQ) terrorist who described Trudeau as a "very good traitor."[27]

The term *charisma* is most frequently used in association with nationally and internationally known leaders. Yet first-level supervisors, team leaders, and minor sports coaches can also be charismatic. A naturally dynamic personality is a major component of charisma, but a person can engage in many tangible actions that also contribute to charisma. Following are a number of suggestions for behaving charismatically, all based on characteristics and behaviours often found in charismatic leaders. If you are not currently a leader, remember that being perceived as charismatic will help you become one.

1. **Communicate a vision.** A charismatic leader offers an exciting image of where the organization is headed and how to get there. A vision is more than a forecast because it describes an ideal version of the future of an entire organization or an organizational unit such as a department. Richard Branson, the colourful British entrepreneur, has inspired hundreds of employees with his vision of the Virgin brand's potential in dozens of fields with hundreds of his companies. Among his accomplishments in realizing this vision have been the Virgin Atlantic airline, Virgin Megastores, and Virgin Cinema. A visionary leader should also have the courage to communicate the vision to others, and to help implement the vision.[28] For the paralegal supervisor, part of implementing the vision might be teaching new technology skills to the paralegals. Michael Stern, president and CEO of Michael Stern Associates, an executive search firm in Toronto, Ontario, lists vision and being able to communicate such a vision as an essential leadership trait.[29]

> ### SKILL-BUILDING EXERCISE 10-2
>
> **Creating a Vision**
>
> The class breaks into small problem-solving groups. Each group constructs a vision for a unit of an organization or for a total organization of its choosing. Students can choose an organization with which they are familiar or a well-known business firm or government agency. The vision should be approximately 25 words long and depict a glorious future. A vision is not simply a straightforward goal, such as "In 2013 our firm will gross $10 million in sales." Remember, the vision statement you draw up should inspire people throughout the organization.
>
> If class time permits, volunteers can share their visions with other class members who will provide feedback on the clarity and inspirational qualities of the visions presented.

An important part of communicating a vision for good effect is to be clear about what needs to be done to build a better future, even if the future is next week. Based on his study of some of the world's most successful business leaders, Marcus Buckingham concludes that the leader should define the future in vivid terms so that people can see where they are headed.[30]

Skill-Building Exercise 10-2 will give you a chance to develop visioning skills (a buzzword in business).

> ### BACK TO THE OPENING CASE
>
> Several of Mary DiSalvo's leadership qualities were mentioned in the opening case. She also is a leader with vision. She says, "As food product safety becomes more of an issue in our world, the importance of secure labelling and packaging will multiply, and our company will be at the forefront."

2. **Make frequent use of metaphors and analogies.** To inspire people, the charismatic leader uses colourful language and exciting metaphors and analogies. Develop metaphors to inspire people around you. A commonly used one after a group has suffered a setback is: "Like the phoenix, we will rise from the ashes of defeat." To pick up the spirits of her maintenance group, a maintenance supervisor said, "We're a lot like the heating and cooling system in a house. A lot of people don't give us much thought, but without us their lives would be very uncomfortable."

3. **Inspire trust and confidence.** Make your deeds consistent with your promises. As mentioned earlier in this chapter, being trustworthy is a key leadership trait. Get people to believe in your competence by making your accomplishments known in a polite, tactful way. The *socialized charismatic* is likely to inspire trust and confidence because such a leader is ethical and wants to accomplish activities that help others rather than pursuing personal ends such as glory and power.[31]

4. **Be highly energetic and goal-oriented.** Impress others with your energy and resourcefulness. To increase your energy supply, exercise frequently, eat well, and get ample rest. Closely related to being goal-oriented is being optimistic about what you and the group can accomplish. People also associate optimism with energy. Being grumpy is often associated with being low on energy. You can also add to an image of energy by raising and lowering your voice frequently and avoiding a slow pace.

5. **Be emotionally expressive and warm.** A key characteristic of charismatic leaders is the ability to express feelings openly. Assertiveness is therefore an important component of charisma. In dealing with team members, refer to your feelings at the time, such as "I'm excited because I know we are going to hit our year-end target by mid-October." A study with firefighters showed that leaders who were perceived to be charismatic contributed to the happiness of the group particularly when the leader expressed positive emotion and had a positive outlook.[32]

Nonverbal emotional expressiveness, such as warm gestures and frequent touching (nonsexual) of group members, also exhibits one's charisma. Remember, however, that many people resent being touched when at work. Frequent smiling is another way of being emotionally expressive. Also, a warm smile seems to indicate a confident, caring person, which contributes to a perception of charisma.

6. **Make ample use of true stories.** An excellent way of building rapport is to tell stories that deliver a message. People like to hear stories about how a department or company went through hard times when it started, such as how Dell Computer began in a dormitory room at the University of Texas. Telling positive stories has become a widely accepted technique for building relationships with employees. Storytelling adds a touch of warmth to the teller and helps build connections among people who become familiar with the same story.

7. **Be candid and direct.** Practise saying what you want directly, rather than being indirect and evasive. If you want someone to help you, don't ask, "Are you busy?" Instead, ask, "Can you help me with a problem I'm having right now?"

8. **Make everybody you meet feel that he or she is important.** For example, at a company social gathering, greet and, if appropriate, shake the hand of every person you meet. Also, thank people frequently, both orally and by written notes.

9. **Increase the effectiveness of your handshake.** Shake firmly without creating pain, and make enough eye contact to notice the colour of the other person's eyes. When you take that much trouble, you project care and concern.[33]

10. **Stand up straight and use other nonverbal signals of self-confidence.** Practise having good posture. Minimize fidgeting, scratching, foot-tapping, and speaking in a monotone. Walk at a rapid pace, without appearing to be panicked. Dress fashionably, without going to the extreme that people notice your clothes more than they notice you.

11. **Be willing to take personal risks.** Charismatic leaders are typically risk takers, and risk taking adds to their charisma. Risks you might take would include extending additional credit to a start-up business, suggesting a bright but costly idea, and recommending that a former felon be given a chance in your firm.

12. **Be self-promotional.** Charismatic leaders are not shy. Instead, they toot their own horns and allow others to know how important they are. Without appearing self-absorbed, you, too, might let others know of your tangible accomplishments. Explain to others the key role that you played on your team or how you achieved a few tough goals.

Despite the importance of developing charisma, being excessively and flamboyantly charismatic can backfire, because others may perceive you as self-serving. Therefore, the idea is to sprinkle your charisma with humility, such as admitting when you make a mistake. Also, in recent years top-level management at some companies have replaced high-charisma, rock-star leaders with ones who concentrate more on running the business instead of garnering publicity for themselves.

COACHING AND TRAINING OTHERS

LEARNING OBJECTIVE 3

Coaching and training are two direct approaches to helping others in the workplace that provide opportunities to practise several leadership skills. In the traditional organization, managers have most of the responsibility for coaching and training, with some assistance from the human resources department. In the new workplace, team members share responsibility for coaching and training. High-tech companies, such as Google and Microsoft, heavily emphasize workers sharing knowledge with each other. Open workspaces, including the presence of whiteboards, are used to facilitate workers exchanging ideas and passing along information. Although coaching and training are described separately in the following subsections, recognize that the two processes are closely related.

Coaching Skills and Techniques

Most readers probably have some experience in coaching, whether or not the activity was given a formal label. If you have helped somebody else improve his or her performance on the job, on the athletic field, in a musical band, or on the dance floor, you have some coaching experience. In the workplace, **coaching** is a method of helping workers grow and improve their job competence by providing suggestions and encouragement. According to Donald Brooks of KPMG Canada, coaching is providing a person with "alternative ways of acting or performing [a] task to produce better results."[34] The suggestions for coaching presented next are generally easier to implement if you have formal authority over the person being coached. Nevertheless, with a positive, helpful attitude on your part, co-workers are likely to accept your coaching.

Konstantin Chagin/Shutterstock

coaching
A method of helping workers grow and develop and improve their job competence by providing suggestions and encouragement.

peer coaching
A type of helping relationship based on qualities, such as high acceptance of the other person, authenticity, mutual trust, and mutual learning.

Ideal Characteristics of Peer Coaching. Considerable workplace coaching is performed by professional coaches who specialize in helping managers improve their interpersonal skills.[35] Our focus here is coaching by workers themselves rather than by paid professionals. **Peer coaching** is a type of helping relationship based on qualities, such as high acceptance of the other person, authenticity, mutual trust, and mutual learning. According to researchers Polly Parker, Douglas T. Hall, and Kathy E. Kram, peer coaching has five critical qualities, to be described next. These qualities, however, tend toward being an ideal state and we cannot realistically expect all peer coaching to attain this high status.

1. **Equal status of peers.** The equal status of peers eliminates the power relationships found in many other relationships, such as superior–subordinate relationship. Peers are able to plan and initiate their learning opportunities and work toward a shared goal of mutual learning.

2. **Personal and professional development of both peers.** Peers strive to obtain an in-depth understanding of the subjective experiences, including the worldview of the other peer. Each person attempts to make sense of the other person's worldview. Each participant chooses issues of personal interest to express and explore.

3. **Integration of reflection and practice.** Effective peer coaching requires personal reflection on one's own actions and behaviours. Through reflection, the peer coach builds awareness of cognitive, emotional, and spiritual dimensions of himself or herself.

4. **Importance of attention to process.** Peer coaching provides a medium for peers to learn a process for how to do a better job of attending to other people. The focus is on understanding the self and other people rather than acquiring content or facts.

5. **Accelerating career learning.** Peer counselling helps people learn rapidly and continually, which helps them succeed in the modern world.[36]

We emphasize again that these characteristics of a peer coach are ideals to strive for. You can still be an effective peer coach by learning the coaching skills and techniques described next without attaining all the five characteristics described above.

Suggestions for Coaching. Coaching other employees requires skill. One way of acquiring this skill is to study basic principles and then practise them on the job. Another way is to coach under simulated conditions, such as role-playing and modelling an effective coach. Here are 11 suggestions for effective coaching, as outlined in Figure 10-2. For the best results, combine them with the suggestions for effective listening presented in Chapter 4.

1. **Build relationships.** A starting point in being an effective coach is to build relationships with co-workers before coaching them. Having established rapport with co-workers or subordinates facilitates entering into coaching relationships with them. The suggestions below about giving encouragement and support are

BECOMING AN EFFECTIVE LEADER   211

FIGURE 10-2 Coaching Skills and Techniques

> 1. Build relationships.
> 2. Provide specific feedback.
> 3. Make criticism pain-free and positive.
> 4. Encourage the person you are coaching to talk.
> 5. Ask powerful questions.
> 6. Give emotional support.
> 7. Give some constructive advice.
> 8. Coach with "could," not "should."
> 9. Interpret what is happening.
> 10. Allow for modelling of the desired performance and behaviours.
> 11. Applaud good results.

part of relationship building. Another vital aspect of relationship building is to be trusted by the people you coach.[37] For example, the person being coached has to believe that the coach is trying to help rather than undermine him or her.

2. **Provide specific feedback.** Instead of stating generalities about an area of improvement for another person, pinpoint areas of concern. A generality might be "You just don't seem as if you're into this job." A specific on the same problem might be "You neglect to call in on days that you are off sick. When you do that, you're letting down the team." Sometimes it can be effective to make a generalization (such as not being "into the job") after you first produce several concrete examples. Closely related to minimizing generalizations is to avoid exaggerating—for example, saying such things as, "You are always letting down the team." Specific feedback is sometimes referred to as *behavioural feedback*, because it pinpoints behaviour rather than personal characteristics or attitudes. "Neglecting to call in" pinpoints behaviour, whereas "not into the job" focuses more on an attitude.

3. **Make criticism pain-free and positive.** To be an effective coach, you will inevitably have to point out something negative the person you coach has done, or is planning to do. It is helpful to come right to the point about your criticism, such as "In our department meeting this morning, you acted so angry and hostile that you alienated the rest of the group. I know that you are generally a positive person, so I was surprised. My recommendation is that you keep your bad days to yourself when in a meeting." The positive aspect is important because you want to maintain good communications with the person you coach, whether you are the person's supervisor or co-worker.[38]

4. **Encourage the person you are coaching to talk.** Part of being a good listener is encouraging the person being coached to talk. Ask the person you are coaching open-ended questions. Closed questions do not provide the same opportunity for self-expression, and they often elicit short, uninformative answers. Assume you are coaching a co-worker on how to use the company's instant messaging system properly. An effective, open-ended question might be "Where are you having the biggest problems using the system?" A closed question covering the same topic might be "Do you understand how to use instant messaging?" The latter question would not provide good clues to specific problem areas faced by your co-worker.

5. **Ask powerful questions.** A major role for the coach is to ask powerful or tough questions that help the protégé think through the strengths and weaknesses of what he or she is doing or thinking. The powerful question is confrontational in a helpful way. The person being coached might be thinking of using an

application of digital storytelling to sell a product. Your powerful question might be "How will you purchase the required software in order to design your project?"

6. **Provide emotional support.** By being helpful and constructive, you provide much-needed emotional support to the person who needs help in improving job performance. A coaching session should not be an interrogation. An effective way of providing emotional support is to use positive rather than negative motivators. For example, as a team leader you might say to a team member, "If you learn how to analyze manufacturing costs, you will be eligible for an outstanding performance review." A negative motivator on the same topic might be "If you don't learn how to analyze manufacturing costs, you're going to get zapped on your performance appraisal."

    Workers who are performing well can also profit from praise and encouragement, often so they can perform even better. Also, even the best performers have flaws that might be preventing them from elevating their performance.[39] As a team leader or co-worker, you can therefore make a contribution by giving emotional support to a star performer.

7. **Give some constructive advice.** Giving too much advice interferes with two-way communication, yet some advice can lead to improved performance. Assist the person being coached to answer the question "What can I do about this problem?" Advice in the form of a question or suppositional statement is often effective. One example is: "Could the root of your problem be that you haven't studied the user manual?"

8. **Coach with "could," not "should."** When helping somebody to improve, tell the person that he or she *could* do something, rather than that he or she *should* do it. *Should* implies the person is doing something morally wrong, as illustrated by the following statement: "You should recycle the used-up laser cartridges." *Could* leaves the person with a choice to make: to accept or reject your input and weigh the consequences.[40]

9. **Interpret what is happening.** An interpretation given by the person doing the coaching is an explanation of why the person being coached is acting in a particular manner. The interpretation is designed to give the person being coached insight into the nature of the problem. For instance, a food service manager might be listening to the problems of a cafeteria manager with regard to cafeteria cleanliness. After listening awhile, the food service manager might say, "You're angry and upset with your employees because they don't keep a careful eye on cleanliness. So you avoid dealing with them, and it only makes problems worse." If the manager's diagnosis is correct, interpretation can be extremely helpful.

10. **Allow for modelling of desired performance and behaviour.** An effective coaching technique is to show the person being coached an example of what constitutes the desired behaviour. A customer service manager was harsh with customers when facing heavy pressure. One way the supervisor coached the service manager was by taking over the manager's desk during a busy period. The service manager then watched the supervisor deal tactfully with demanding customers.

11. **Applaud good results.** Effective coaches on the playing field and in the workplace are cheerleaders. They give positive reinforcement by applauding desired results. Some effective coaches shout in joy when the person coached achieves outstanding results; others give high-fives or clap their hands in applause.[41]

Many people are concerned that if they offer too much coaching and feedback to others, they will be perceived as interfering with their work, or being a *micromanager*. In reality, the majority of workers believe that they do not receive enough coaching and guidance on the job. RainmakerThinking Inc. has conducted long-term research suggesting that the undermanaged worker struggles because his or her supervisor is not sufficiently engaged to provide the needed direction and support.[42]

SELF-ASSESSMENT QUIZ 10-2

Characteristics of an Effective Coach

Directions: Following is a list of traits, attitudes, and behaviours of effective coaches. Indicate next to each of these whether you need to improve (e.g., "need to become more patient"). Prepare an action plan for improving each one you need to develop.

Trait, Attitude, or Behaviour	Action Plan for Improvement
Empathy	*Sample:* Will listen until I understand other person's point of view.
	Your own:
Listening skill	*Sample:* Will concentrate extra hard to listen.
	Your own:
Ability to size up people	*Sample:* Will jot down observations about people upon first meeting, then verify in the future.
	Your own:
Diplomacy and tact	*Sample:* Will study book of etiquette.
	Your own:
Patience toward people	*Sample:* Will practise staying calm when someone makes a mistake.
	Your own:
Concern for welfare of others	*Sample:* When interacting with another person will ask self, "How can this person's interests best be served?"
	Your own:
Self-confidence	*Sample:* Will attempt to have at least one personal success each week.
	Your own:
Non-competitiveness with team members	*Sample:* Will keep reminding myself that all boats rise with the same tide.
	Your own:
Enthusiasm for people	*Sample:* Will search for the good in each person.
	Your own:
Work on my personal development thereby by example	*Sample:* Overcome projecting the attitude that people who disagree leading with me are really stupid.
	Your own:
Develops trust and respect[43]	*Sample:* Consistently tells the truth to people.
	Your own:

One implication of the coaching suggestions just presented is that some people are more adept at coaching than others. Self-Assessment Quiz 10-2 provides insight into the "right stuff" required for being an effective coach. After doing the exercise and reading the suggestions, you will be prepared for Skill-Building Exercise 10-3 about coaching.

Training Others

training
The process of helping others acquire a job-related skill.

One direct way of helping others in the workplace is to train them. **Training** is the process of helping others acquire a job-related skill. The emphasis on continuous learning by employees to keep up with changes in technology and work methods has helped elevate the importance of on-the-job training.[44] Another training opportunity for some workers is to assist in the remedial learning of lesser-skilled employees. According to a Conference Board report, nearly half of 217 employers surveyed indicated that they provide remedial training to strengthen employees' writing, math, and problem-solving deficiencies.[45] Even if employees lacking basic skills do receive classroom instruction, they may still need the assistance from workers at a higher skill level.

Supervisors and trainers are responsible for much of the training in organizations. Yet, as mentioned at the outset of the chapter, to save money more responsibility for

> ## SKILL-BUILDING EXERCISE 10-3
>
> ### Coaching a Mediocre Performer Role-Play
>
> Visualize a busy sports medicine clinic, and you are the chief administrator. You recognize that many of your patients urgently need the medical help your clinic offers because they have been injured substantially while participating in sports. Yet a good proportion of your patients are visiting the clinic for rehabilitation exercises that they can do on their own or learn from downloaded videos. As a consequence, being pleasant and hospitable is a requirement for all staff members, physicians, physical therapists, and support personnel alike. You want to keep your practice thriving through the rehabilitation patients.
>
> One of your intake specialists, Tanya, goes about her work in a bland, mechanical manner. She makes relatively few errors in processing patient information, but she expresses very little warmth and appreciation toward patients. You have frequently observed patients appearing perplexed and displeased when Tanya deals with them. You have decided to get started coaching Tanya this afternoon toward becoming a warmer, more cheerful intake specialist.
>
> One student plays the role of the chief administrator, and one student plays the role of Tanya, who doesn't have a clue as to why you want to coach her. To your knowledge, you are a thoroughly professional sports medicine intake specialist.
>
> For both scenarios, observers rate the role players on two dimensions, using a 1-to-5 scale from Very Poor to Very Good. One dimension is "effective use of coaching techniques" (for the chief administrator). The second dimension is "acting ability." A few observers might voluntarily provide feedback to the role players in terms of sharing their ratings and observations. The course instructor might also provide feedback.

training has shifted to workers themselves. Also, as organizations operate with fewer managers, co-workers have more responsibility to train each other. Vancouver City Savings Credit Union is one organization that successfully uses peer training to train new employees, with very good results.[46]

While training others, keep in mind the following time-tested principles that aid learning—and therefore training. Applying these principles consistently will increase the chances that the people you are training will acquire new skills. A considerable amount of training has shifted to e-learning (also referred to as *distance learning* and *online learning*), especially for acquiring cognitive knowledge and skills.[47] Traditional training principles apply to e-learning, and you will still have opportunities to help the trainee. Many e-learners still need to ask questions, such as "I've been studying the new payroll system that we have started to use but I am still having some problems with some of the pay deductions. I'm doing something wrong. Can you help?" The training principles are as follows:

1. **Encourage concentration.** Not much learning takes place unless the trainee concentrates carefully on what is being learned. Concentration improves the ability to do both mental and physical tasks. In short, encourage the person you are training to concentrate.

2. **Motivate interest.** People learn best when they are interested in the problem facing them. Explain to the trainee how the skill being taught will increase his or her value as an employee, or relate the skill to the person's professional goals. Trainees can be encouraged to look for some relationship between the information at hand and their personal welfare. With this relationship in mind, the person will have a stronger intention to learn. This is an effective example of the WIIFM principle discussed in the next chapter. For example, when training new professors to use more online learning activities, explaining how such activities save time (a valuable commodity) is often a motivator to learn new online techniques.

3. **Remind learners to intend to remember.** We often fail to remember something because we do not intend to commit it to memory. Many executives are particularly effective at remembering the names of employees and customers. When one executive was asked how she could commit so many names to memory, she replied, "I look at the person, listen to the name, and try hard to remember." An example of reminding a protégé to remember would be to advise him or her to memorize the company mission statement.

4. **Ensure the material is meaningful.** The material to be learned should be organized in a meaningful manner. Each successive experience should build on the ones

before. In training another person how to process a customer order, you might teach the skill in terms of the flow of activities from customer inquiry to product delivery.

5. **Provide feedback on progress.** As a person's training progresses, motivation may be maintained and increased by providing feedback on progress. To measure progress, it may be necessary to ask the trainee questions or request a job sample. For example, you might ask the person being trained on invoices to prepare a sample invoice.

6. **Ask the trainee to reflect on what he or she has learned.** Research indicates that if you think carefully about what you have learned, your retention of the information increases. The idea is to step back from the experience to carefully and persistently ponder its meaning to you.[48] After participating in a team development exercise involving whitewater rafting, a person might reflect, "What did I really learn about being a better team player? How was I perceived by my teammates in the rubber raft? Did they even notice my contribution? Or did they think I was an important part of the team success?"

7. **Deal with trainee defensiveness.** Training is sometimes impeded because the person being trained is defensive about information or skills that clash with his or her beliefs and practices. The person might have so much emotional energy invested in the status quo that he or she resists the training. For example, a sales representative might resist learning how to use e-commerce because she believes that her warm smile and interpersonal skills have made her an excellent communicator. She is concerned that if she communicates with customers exclusively through email, her human touch will be lost. Sensing this defensiveness, the trainer is advised to talk about e-commerce as being a supplement to, but not a substitute for, in-person communication. (However, the sales rep might also be worried that her position will be eliminated.)

8. **Take into account learning style.** Another key factor that influences training is **learning style**, the way in which a person best learns new information. An example of a learning style is passive learning. People who learn best through passive learning quickly acquire information by studying texts, manuals, magazine articles, and websites. They can juggle images in their mind as they read about abstract concepts such as supply and demand, cultural diversity, or customer service. Others learn best by doing rather than studying—for example, learning about customer service by dealing with customers in many situations.

learning style
The way in which a person best learns new information.

Another key dimension of learning styles is whether a person learns best by working alone or cooperatively in a study group. Learning by oneself may allow for more intense concentration, and one can proceed at one's own pace. Learning in groups through classroom discussion allows people to exchange viewpoints and perspectives.

Because of differences in learning styles, you may decide to design training to fit these differences. For example, if your trainees prefer cooperative learning you could combine learning from reading books, articles, and online information with discussions in a conference room.

To start applying these principles of learning to training, do Skill-Building Exercise 10-4.

SKILL-BUILDING EXERCISE 10-4

Designing a Training Program

The class organizes into training-design teams of approximately six people. Each team sketches the design of a training program to teach an interpersonal skill to employees, such as being polite to customers or interviewing job candidates. The teams are not responsible for selecting the exact content of the training program they choose. Instead, they are responsible for designing a training program based on the principles of learning.

The activity should take about 15 minutes and can therefore be done inside or outside class. After the teams have designed their programs, they can compare the various versions.

DEVELOPING YOUR LEADERSHIP POTENTIAL

LEARNING OBJECTIVE 4

Much of this text deals directly and indirectly with information that could improve your leadership effectiveness. Chapter 4, on communications, is a case in point. Improving your communications effectiveness would be one way to better your ability to lead people. Formal education and leadership development programs also contribute to increased leadership potential. (Many such programs include some of the activities found in this chapter.)

Our approach to developing leadership potential is based on the assumption that leaders are both born and made.[49] You need some basic cognitive and personality characteristics to have the potential to be a leader, yet you need to develop these characteristics through experience and practice. A person who has good problem-solving ability, and is charismatic, still needs to assume leadership responsibility and engage in certain actions to become an effective leader. Among these dozens of activities would be recognizing the accomplishments of others.

First-level supervisory jobs are an invaluable starting point for developing your leadership potential. It takes considerable skill to manage a rapid-service (fast-food) restaurant or direct a public playground during the summer. First-level supervisors frequently face situations in which group members are poorly trained, poorly paid, and not well motivated to achieve company objectives. Motivating and inspiring entry-level workers is one of the major challenges facing organizations.

Below we describe six additional strategies for developing your leadership potential. Also, see Skill-Building Exercise 10-5 about maintaining a personal leadership journal.

1. **Acquire broad experience.** Because leadership varies somewhat with the situation, a sound approach to improving leadership effectiveness is to attempt to gain supervisory experience in different settings. A person who wants to become an executive would be well advised to gain supervisory experience in at least two different organizational functions, such as marketing and operations.

    Procter & Gamble, long noted for its development of leaders and managers, emphasizes broad experience. If a promising young brand assistant wants to become an executive, the company tries to give him or her as broad an experience as possible. The person might be appointed as assistant manager of Cascade detergent. Later, he or she will run laundry products in Canada, before eventually overseeing all of Northeast Asia.[50]

2. **Model effective leaders.** Another strategy for leadership development is to observe capable leaders in action and then model some of their approaches. You may not want to copy a particular leader entirely, but you can incorporate a few of the behaviour patterns into your own leadership style. For instance, most inexperienced leaders have difficulty confronting others. Observe how a skilled confronter

SKILL-BUILDING EXERCISE 10-5

My Personal Leadership Journal

An important aid in your development as a leader might be to maintain a journal or diary of your leadership experiences. Make a journal entry within 24 hours after you have carried out a leadership action of any kind, or failed to do so when the opportunity arose. You will therefore have entries dealing with leadership opportunities both capitalized upon and missed. An example: "A few of my neighbours were complaining about trash flying around the neighbourhood on trash pickup days, particularly when the wind was strong. I took the initiative and sent emails and flyers to neighbourhood residents discussing what could be done about the problem. I suggested that people pack their recycling boxes more tightly. I also suggested ever-so-politely that people should pick up their own flying trash. Soon the problem just about disappeared."

Also include in your journal such entries as feedback you receive on your leadership ability, leadership traits that you appear to be developing, and leadership ideas you learn about. Also, keep a list of leadership articles and books you intend to read. You might also want to record observations about significant acts of leadership or leadership blunders that you have observed in others, either first-hand or through the media.

Review your journal monthly, and make note of any progress you think you have made in developing your leadership skills. Also, consider preparing a graph of your progress in developing leadership skills. The vertical axis can represent skill level on a 1-to-100 scale, and the horizontal axis might be divided into time intervals, such as calendar quarters.

handles the situation, and try that person's approach the next time you have unfavourable news to communicate to another person.

3. **Self-develop leadership traits and behaviours.** Study the leadership traits and behaviours described earlier in this chapter. As a starting point, identify several attributes you think you could strengthen within yourself, given some determination and perhaps combined with the right training program. For example, you might decide that with some effort you could improve your sense of humour. You might also believe that you could remember to encourage honest criticism within the team. It is also helpful to obtain feedback from valid sources (such as a trusted manager) about which traits and behaviours you particularly need to develop.

4. **Become an integrated human being.** A philosophical approach to leadership suggests that the model leader is first and foremost a fully functioning person. According to William D. Hitt, mastering the art of leadership comes with self-mastery. Leadership development is the process of self-development. As a result, the process of becoming a leader is similar to the process of becoming an integrated human being. For example, you need to develop values that guide your behaviour before you can adequately guide the behaviour of others.

   The model (or ideal) leader, according to Hitt, must possess six character traits: identity (know thyself), independence, authenticity, responsibility, courage, and integrity.[51] All of these traits have everyday meanings, but they can also have personal meanings. Part of becoming an integrated person is to answer such questions as "What do I mean when I say I have integrity?"

   Another approach to becoming an integrated human being, and therefore a more effective leader, is to figure out how you perceive the world. For example, if you perceive yourself as inferior to most people, you will forever be in competition with others to impress them. You will even compete rather than work collaboratively with team members.[52]

5. **Practise a little leadership.** An effective way of developing your leadership skills is to look for opportunities to exert a small amount of helpful leadership, in contrast to waiting for opportunities to accomplish extraordinary deeds. The "little leadership" might involve such behaviours as mentoring a struggling team member, coaching somebody about how to use a new high-tech device, or making a suggestion about improving a product. In the words of Michael E. McGill and John W. Slocum, Jr., "For those who want to stand atop the dugout, dance with the elephants, fly with the buffaloes, soar with eagles, or perform other mystical and heroic acts of large leadership, our little leadership may seem all too managerial, too modest, and too mundane."[53]

6. **Help your leader lead.** According to Michael Useem, leaders need your assistance so they can do a good job. "If people are afraid to help their leaders lead, their leaders will fail."[54] A group member is often closer to the market and closer to how the product is used. Therefore, he or she can provide useful information to the person in the formal leadership position. When you help the people above you avoid a mistake or capitalize upon an opportunity, you help the entire company. At the same time you are developing your ability to take the initiative and lead.

Access the eText in MySearchLab to learn more about this chapter's self-assessment quizzes.

To **Watch** **Explore** **Practice** **Study** and **Review**, visit MySearchLab

Developing Your Human Relations Skills and Reinforcing Concepts

Summary   ✓ Practice Glossary Flashcards

- Traits that contribute to leadership effectiveness include self-confidence and leadership efficacy, positive core self-evaluation, assertiveness, trustworthiness and morality, a sense of humour, self-awareness and self-objectivity, cognitive skills including critical assessment, emotional intelligence, passion and enthusiasm, and a self-sacrificing personality.
- Suggestions for behaving charismatically include the following: communicate a vision; inspire trust and confidence; be highly energetic and goal-oriented; be emotionally expressive and warm; make ample use of true stories; be candid and direct; make everyone you meet feel important; increase the effectiveness of your handshake; stand up straight and nonverbally communicate self-confidence; be willing to take personal risks; and be self-promotional.
- Suggestions for effective coaching are build relationships provide specific feedback, make criticism pain-free and positive, encourage the person you are coaching to ask powerful questions, give emotional support, give some constructive advice, coach with "could" not "should," interpret what is happening, allow for modelling of the desired performance and behaviours, and applaud good results.
- Training involves helping people acquire job skills. To facilitate training, apply principles of learning such as the following: (1) encourage concentration; (2) use motivated interest; (3) remind learners to intend to remember; (4) ensure the meaningfulness of material; (5) give feedback on progress; (6) ask the trainee to reflect on what he or she has learned; (7) deal with trainee defensiveness; and (8) take into account learning style.
- Leadership potential can be developed through the following five strategies: (1) acquire broad experience; (2) model effective leaders; (3) self-develop leadership traits and behaviours; (4) become an integrated human being (a fully functioning person); (5) practise small leadership acts; and (6) help your leader lead.

Interpersonal Relations Case 10-1

So Is This How You Learn Leadership?

Len Olsen, age 23, was proud to be selected as part of the leadership program at a national chain of family restaurants. Workers selected for the leadership program are considered to be in line for running individual restaurants, and also as potential candidates in the long run for leadership positions in corporate headquarters. Before entering the key phase of the leadership program, all candidates must first work a minimum of one year as a server or bartender at one of the company stores (restaurants).

Len worked one year as a server in a downtown Montreal restaurant, and then was assigned to another Montreal restaurant to begin his formal leadership training as an assistant manager. His assignments as an assistant manager included scheduling the wait staff, conducting preliminary screen interviews of job applicants, and resolving problems with customers. After three months on the job, Len was asked by a member of the corporate human resources staff how his leadership training program was going; he replied, "I'm a little bit skeptical. I don't think I'm learning much about leadership."

When asked why he didn't think he was learning much about leadership, Len listed what he considered three recent examples of the type of responsibilities he faced regularly:

- At 11:00 yesterday morning, I received a phone call from Annie, one of the servers. She told me she wouldn't be able to work that afternoon because her Labrador retriever had become quite ill and she had to take the Lab to the vet. I told Annie that we desperately needed her that afternoon because of a large luncheon party. Annie told me her dog was more important to her than the job.

- Two weeks ago, Gus, one of our salad chefs, showed up to work absolutely drunk. I told him that working while drunk was absolutely against the company rules. He got a little belligerent, but I did get him to take a taxi home at the company's expense.
- Two days ago, a customer in the restaurant spilled a cup of hot coffee on herself while answering a call on her cell phone. She told me that the coffee was too hot and that she was going to sue the restaurant. I explained to her tactfully that unless she was truly burned, she had no claim. I offered to have the restaurant pay for her dry cleaning, and then she calmed down.

Olsen then said to the human resources manager, "What has stuff like this got to do with leadership? I mean, I'm not creating great visions or inspiring hordes of people. In what way am I becoming a leader?"

Case Questions

1. What is your opinion of the contribution of Olsen's representative experiences to his development as a leader?
2. What else can the restaurant chain do to help Olsen and others in the leadership program develop as leaders?

Interpersonal Relations Case 10-2

The Reality Coach

Kara was excited about her new position as Internet sales manager at a food supplement company. The company's dozens of products included pills and liquids for improving skin health, lowering blood pressure, improving digestion, and improving vision. Many of the company's sales were in bulk to supermarkets, pharmacies, and health food stores. In addition, many orders came in over the Internet and by toll-free numbers. Kara's responsibilities included revitalizing the company website periodically, and finding ways to direct more traffic to it.

During Kara's first week on the job, she was assigned a coach and mentor, Malcolm, the manager of order fulfillment. Malcolm was to act in the dual role of coaching and mentoring Kara, in addition to assisting in her *onboarding* (getting oriented into the company). During their first meeting, Malcolm was friendly and constructive, saying that his role was to help Kara in any feasible way.

The second meeting between Kara and Malcolm was quite brief, with Malcolm asking Kara if she was having any problems he could provide assistance with. Kara replied that all was going well so far.

One week later, Malcolm dropped by Kara's cubicle, and said to her, "I've noticed that Internet sales have been flat since you came on board. What is it that you are doing that is adding value to the company?" Kara replied that enhancing Internet sales takes considerable time.

Ten days later, Malcolm sent Kara an email asking that she meet with him in his cubicle at 4:00 p.m. Malcolm asked Kara how she was doing, and then said he had some advice for her as her coach and mentor. "Quite frankly, I think you could make a more professional appearance. Your hair is too long, and you wear too much dangling jewellery. I think that you need to tone down your appearance a little to be successful as an Internet sales manager."

Kara replied, "Nobody else has complained. Besides, most of my important interactions are over the Internet, and not with customers face to face. So long hair and dangling jewellery should not be a problem."

Kara was beginning to wonder if Malcolm was really a help or just an irritant. She then devoted most of her energies the next couple of weeks in revamping and modernizing the company website. Her boss, as well as several co-workers, made approving comments about the new site. Malcolm, however, had his own opinion. He said to Kara in person, "I have heard that a few people like the changes you made to the website. But Kara, I am disappointed. You just tweaked the site instead of making radical changes that would increase sales substantially. I know that you can do better."

Kara replied, "Malcolm, isn't there anything I can do to please you? Are you my coach and mentor, or just my heckler?"

Malcolm retorted, "Do you think you might be too thin-skinned to succeed in business? As your coach and mentor I have to be frank. Otherwise I can't help you."

Case Questions

1. How effective do you think Malcolm is in his role as Kara's coach and mentor?
2. What suggestions can you offer Malcolm to be more effective in his role?
3. What suggestions might you offer Kara so that she can benefit more from the coaching and mentoring the company is providing her?

Questions for Discussion and Review

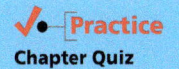

Practice Chapter Quiz

Multiple Choice

1. An effective leader would
   a. never criticize a team member's work.
   b. aggressively confront a team member who is obviously wrong.
   c. be the first to speak about a company issue loudly rather than letting others speak first.
   d. be forthright in expressing his or her feelings.

2. All of the following are key leadership traits, according to your text, except
   a. self-confidence.
   b. passivity.
   c. sense of humour.
   d. passion.

3. Charismatic people
   a. use true stories to build rapport.
   b. never tell true stories, as this is far too personal.
   c. let others develop a vision for the organization.
   d. never take risks.

4. A good trainer
   a. only shares simple assignments so as not overwhelm the person being mentored.
   b. ignores learning styles.
   c. provides feedback on progress.
   d. solves problems for his or her trainee.

5. An effective coaching statement to the person being coached would be
   a. "You should have done that differently."
   b. "How could you have done that differently to get a better result?"
   c. "Let me show you the right was so you don't make the same stupid mistake."
   d. None of the above

Short Answer

6. Informal observation suggests that people who were voted "most likely to succeed" in high school are frequently found in leadership positions later in life. What explanation can you offer for the frequent accuracy of these predictions of success?

7. What can you do this week to increase your charisma?

8. How might one employee coach or train another employee by use of Twitter and text messaging?

9. Many human resources professionals believe that training employees is the best method of enhancing organizational productivity. Why do you think this might be true?

10. Open your MySearchLab, click on the simulation cases library, and click on this chapter and the leadership case study. This is a simulation case for you to work through. Do you have other suggestions that you would use to help employees manage a transition effectively?

Answers to multiple choice questions: 1. d, 2. b, 3. a, 4. c, 5. b.

The Web Corner

www.ccl.org
Center for Creative Leadership

www.core-edge.com
Attaining power and charisma; includes a video

www.jobshadow.org
Job shadowing as a form of mentoring

http://www.ucl.ac.uk/hr/osd/resources/documents/coaching_toolkit.pdf
A coaching toolkit

Internet Skill Builder: Mentoring Online

As mentioned in the chapter, many mentors stay in touch with the people they mentor primarily through email and websites, including company and social networking sites. Such virtual networking has advantages and disadvantages. Search the Internet for three useful ideas about how to mentor effectively online. Try the search terms "virtual mentoring" and "online mentoring," and other terms you think might work. Think through which of these ideas you would use as an online mentor.

MySearchLab

Visit **MySearchLab** to find self-grading review quizzes in the eText, discipline-specific media and readings, access to a variety of academic journals, and Associated Press news feeds, along with a wide range of writing, grammar, and research tools and to help hone writing and research skills.

CHAPTER 11
Skills for Motivating and Helping Others

Motivation consultant Bob Nelson says on his website (www.nelson-motivation.com) that giving merchandise awards creates some problems. He notes that often the trinkets that employees are given to motivate them are perceived as a joke to many employees. "In other instances," he notes, "trinkets have become an outright insult. Sure, the first coffee mug you get for finishing a project is nice, but how many coffee mugs does one person need? Same with pen sets, T-shirts, and even certificates of appreciation. Just yesterday, I was reviewing the employee focus group comments on the topic of recognition from a large client. I noted employees were clear about what they did not want:

- 'No pens, pen sets, or watches'
- 'No clocks, paperweights, or T-shirts'
- 'Too many mugs'

pressmaster/Fotolia

LEARNING Objectives

After reading and studying this chapter and doing the exercises, you should be able to

1. Motivate many people by responding to their self-interests.
2. Apply positive reinforcement to motivate people in many situations.
3. Make effective use of recognition to motivate others.
4. Apply expectancy theory as a comprehensive way of motivating others.
5. Demonstrate how being a nurturing, positive person can influence the development of co-workers.
6. Deal more effectively with difficult people on the job.

"Trophies, plaques, nominal gifts, and mementos fall into the same category from the employees' perspective. And printing your organization's logo on the merchandise doesn't magically transform it into something of value, especially if the object is something employees could have purchased themselves."[1] Nelson is well known internationally for his expertise about employee motivation. For example, his website, books, and articles are used by many businesses and organizations, including the Government of Nova Scotia.

The comments of Bob Nelson (the "guru of thank you") hint at the complexity of motivating people. Handing out trinkets alone may not be an effective motivational device. **Motivation** has two meanings: (1) an internal state that leads to effort expended toward objectives and (2) an activity performed by one person to get another to accomplish work.

We often think of a manager or leader attempting to motivate group members. Yet many people in the workplace have a need to motivate others. To accomplish their work, people must motivate individuals who report to them, co-workers, supervisors, or customers. Developing motivational skills will therefore help you accomplish more work than you would if you relied strictly on the good nature and team spirit of others. An integral part of motivating others in the workplace is the development of positive relationships to accomplish work and achieve goals.

This chapter describes how to develop motivational skills based on four related explanations of motivation. We progress from the simplest to the most complex explanation as well as some techniques for motivating yourself. Developing positive relationships through nurturing others is a also a key strategy to helping others become motivated in the workplace. However, despite our best attempts, dealing with uncooperative people may hamper our best efforts, and strategies to deal with difficult people conclude this chapter. To start thinking through how to motivate others, do Self-Assessment Quiz 11-1.

motivation
An internal state that leads to effort expended toward objectives; an activity performed by one person to get another to accomplish work.

MOTIVATION SKILL BASED ON THE PRINCIPLE OF "WHAT'S IN IT FOR ME?"

LEARNING OBJECTIVE 1

The most fundamental principle of human motivation is that people are motivated by self-interest. This principle is referred to as "What's in it for me?" or WIIFM (pronounced *wiff'em*). Reflect on your own experience. Before working hard to accomplish a task, you probably want to know how you will benefit. If your manager asks you to work extra hours to take care of an emergency, you will most likely oblige. Yet underneath you might be thinking "If I work these extra hours, my boss will think highly of me. As a result, I will probably receive a good performance evaluation and maybe a better-than-average salary increase."

SELF-ASSESSMENT QUIZ 11-1

My Approach to Motivating Others

Instructions: Describe how often you act or think in the way indicated by the following statements when you are attempting to motivate another person. Circle the appropriate number for each statement. Scale: Very Infrequently (VI); Infrequently (I); Sometimes (S); Frequently (F); Very Frequently (VF).

	VI	I	S	F	VF
1. I ask the other person what he or she is hoping to achieve in the situation.	1	2	(3)	4	5
2. I attempt to figure out whether the person has the ability to do what I need done.	1	2	(3)	4	5
3. When another person is heel-dragging, it usually means he or she is lazy.	5	4	3	(2)	1
4. I explain exactly what I want to the person I'm trying to motivate.	1	2	(3)	4	5
5. I like to give the other person a reward up front so that he or she will be motivated.	5	4	3	(2)	1
6. I give lots of feedback when another person is performing a task for me.	1	(2)	3	4	5
7. I like to belittle another person enough so that he or she will be intimidated into doing what I need done.	5	4	3	(2)	1
8. I make sure that the other person feels treated fairly.	1	2	3	(4)	5
9. I figure that if I smile nicely I can get the other person to work as hard as I need.	5	4	3	(2)	1
10. I attempt to get what I need done by instilling fear in the other person.	5	(4)	3	2	1
11. I specify exactly what needs to be accomplished.	1	2	(3)	4	5
12. I generously praise people who help me get my work accomplished.	1	2	3	(4)	5
13. A job well done is its own reward. I therefore keep praise to a minimum.	5	(4)	3	2	1
14. I make sure that I let people know how well they have done in meeting my expectations on a task.	1	2	3	(4)	5
15. To be fair, I attempt to reward people similarly no matter how well they have performed.	(5)	4	3	2	1
16. When somebody doing work for me performs well, I recognize his or her accomplishments promptly.	1	2	3	(4)	5
17. Before giving somebody a reward, I attempt to find out what would appeal to that person.	1	2	3	(4)	5
18. I make it a policy not to thank somebody for doing a job he or she is paid to do.	5	4	(3)	2	1
19. If people do not know how to perform a task, motivation will suffer.	1	2	3	(4)	5
20. If properly laid out, many jobs can be self-rewarding.	1	2	3	(4)	5

Total Score __68__

Scoring and Interpretation: Add the circled numbers to obtain your total score.

90–100 You have advanced knowledge and skill with respect to motivating others in a work environment. Continue to build on the solid base you have established.

50–89 You have average knowledge and skill with respect to motivating others. With additional study and experience, you will probably develop advanced motivational skills.

20–49 To effectively motivate others in a work environment, you will need to greatly expand your knowledge of motivation theory and techniques.

Source: The idea for this quiz and a few items are from David A. Whetton and Kim S. Cameron, *Developing Management Skills*, 5th ed. (Upper Saddle River, NJ: Prentice Hall, 2002), pp. 302–303.

Margin notes:

attempt: try to do

specify: identify clearly and definitely

accomplish: achieve or complete successfully

generously: in a way that shows a willingness to give money, help, kindness. especially more than usual

If your instructor asks you to prepare a lengthy research paper, you might be motivated to work to the best of your ability. But before getting down to the task, it is likely that questions will have raced through your mind, such as "Will this paper elevate my grade?" or "Will I pick up information that will help me in my career?"

Why Help Others? A perplexing issue is how the WIIFM principle explains why people are motivated to help others. Why would a company president donate gift baskets of food to the homeless? Why hire a virtually unemployable person for a nonproductive job in the mailroom? People who perform acts of social good receive the reward of feeling better about themselves. In psychological terms, they satisfy their needs to nurture (take care of) others. More cynically, helping the unfortunate leads to recognition for being a humanitarian.

The widespread willingness of people to contribute to websites that provide useful information to others gives additional insights into what satisfaction many people obtain from working for free. According to Prabhakar Raghavan, chief of Yahoo!, approximately 4 to 6 percent of Yahoo's users contribute their energies for free in such matters as reviewing films or handling questions at Yahoo! Answers. The motivation is often pride. At other times, Net volunteers combine their motivation to help others with the motivation to build their online presence, or *personal brand*. ThisNext is a social network where participants exchange shopping leads, and many volunteers help run the site. Gordon Gould, the operator of ThisNext, says that volunteer workers prosper because "They can build their brands."[2] The takeaway here is that even when people do not get paid for working, they are usually obtaining an important personal benefit.

Applying the WIIFM Principle. A person can be highly motivated, mildly motivated, or only slightly motivated, depending on the intensity of his or her WIIFM principle. A company might offer outstanding performers the opportunity to work at home one day per week. Employees who are intensely motivated to work at home will work virtually up to capacity to achieve a rating of outstanding performer. A Canadian study by Hewitt Associates found that of 232 companies surveyed, 60 percent currently offer the option of working at home and 70 percent of the companies planned to have this option in place by 2009.[3] According to Human Resources Development Canada, working at home is becoming more widespread (spurred on by technology) and has been gaining in popularity.[4]

To use the WIIFM principle in motivating others, you must find out what needs, desires, or motives a person is attempting to satisfy. In general language, responding to the needs of people is referred to as *touching their hot buttons*. You find out what these needs are by asking people what they want or by observing what interests them. For instance, the way a manager might motivate a recognition-hungry group member is to tell that person, "If you perform 10 percent above quota for six consecutive months, we will have a luncheon to congratulate you."

The Importance of Needs. One of the reasons needs are so important in understanding motivation is that needs lead to behaviour, or what people actually do. A person might be extraverted because of a need to affiliate with others, so that person might be motivated by the opportunity to work closely with others. Another person might be conscientious partly because of a need for achievement. This individual might be motivated by the opportunity to accomplish useful work.[5]

Employee needs have been classified in many ways, yet most of these lists overlap. According to a representative classification, 99 percent of employees are motivated by one or more of the following seven needs:

1. **The need for achievement.** Employees with strong achievement needs seek the satisfaction of completing projects successfully. They want to apply their talents to attain success, and they find joy in accomplishment for its own sake.
2. **The need for power.** Employees with a strong power need derive satisfaction from influencing and controlling others, and they aspire to becoming executives. These employees like to lead and persuade and be in charge of resources such as budgets.

SKILL-BUILDING EXERCISE 11-1

Background Work for the WIIFM

The class divides into pairs of students. In each pair, one student plays the role of a team leader who is developing a plan to highly motivate the team member being interviewed. The other student plays the role of the team member being interviewed. The twist to this role-play, however, is that the team member reflects on his or her actual motivators.

The team leader might ask several or all of the following questions while conducting an interview for approximately 15 minutes. In addition, when the team member reveals an important piece of information, the team leader will dig for more details. The team leader should use effective listening skills, as described in Chapter 4. Suggested interview questions are as follows:

1. Why are you working on this team?
2. What can the company do to make you really happy?
3. What would be a fair reward for performing up to your capacity? On a 1-to-10 scale, how badly do you want this reward?
4. What would you consider an outstanding reward for performing up to your capacity? On a 1-to-10 scale, how badly do you want this reward?
5. What would you consider a fantasy reward for performing up to your capacity? On a 1-to-10 scale, how badly do you want this reward?
6. What do you hope to get out of this job?

A brief class discussion might follow the completion of the interviews. A key issue to address in the discussion is the extent to which the interview would be helpful in motivating the team member.

---

3. **The need for affiliation.** Employees with a strong need for affiliation derive satisfaction from interacting with others, being part of a work group, and forming friendships. The same employees are motivated to avoid working alone for long periods of time.

4. **The need for autonomy.** Employees with a strong need for autonomy seek freedom and independence, such as having almost complete responsibility for a project. The same employees are motivated to avoid working in a team effort for long periods of time. Many industrial sales representatives (those who sell to companies) have a strong need for autonomy.

5. **The need for esteem.** Employees with a strong need for esteem want to feel good about themselves, and they judge their worth to a large extent based on how much recognition and praise they receive.

6. **The need for safety and security.** Employees with strong needs for safety and security seek job security, steady income, ample medical and dental insurance, and a hazard-free work environment.

7. **The need for equity.** Employees with a strong need for equity seek fair treatment. They often compare working hours, job responsibilities, salary, and privileges with those of co-workers, and they will become discouraged if co-workers are receiving better treatment.[6]

Recognizing such needs, as well as other needs and interests, helps you apply the WIIFM principle. Skill-Building Exercise 11-1 gives you the opportunity to do the preliminary work needed for applying this principle.

USING POSITIVE REINFORCEMENT TO MOTIVATE OTHERS

The most widely used formal method of motivating people in the workplace is **behaviour modification**, an attempt to change behaviour by manipulating rewards and punishments. Behaviour modification is based on a fundamental principle of human behaviour: the **law of effect**. According to the law of effect, behaviour that leads to a positive consequence for the individual tends to be repeated, whereas behaviour that leads to a negative consequence tends not to be repeated.

The focus of behaviour modification on the job is to reward employees for behaving in ways that support what the organization is attempting to accomplish, such as improved productivity. Our approach to skill development in behaviour modification is to emphasize positive reinforcement, because this is the modification strategy most widely used in the workplace. **Positive reinforcement** means increasing the probability that behaviour will be

---

LEARNING OBJECTIVE 2

behaviour modification
An attempt to change behaviour by manipulating rewards and punishments.

law of effect
Behaviour that leads to a positive consequence for the individual tends to be repeated, whereas behaviour that leads to a negative consequence tends not to be repeated.

positive reinforcement
An attempt to increase the probability that behaviour will be repeated by rewarding people for making the desired response.

repeated by rewarding people for making the desired response. The phrase *increasing the probability* means that positive reinforcement improves learning and motivation, but is not 100 percent effective. The phrase *making the desired response* is also noteworthy. To use positive reinforcement properly, a reward must be contingent upon doing something right. Simply paying somebody a compliment or giving the person something of value is not positive reinforcement. Behaviour modification involves linking consequences to what the person has or has not accomplished.

Positive reinforcement is easy to visualize with well-structured jobs such as data entry or producing parts. Yet positive reinforcement is also used to encourage desired behaviour in highly paid, complex jobs. An accountant who developed a new method for the company to get paid faster might be rewarded with two extra days of vacation. A survey of how companies are using rewards indicated that a growing number of firms are giving specific rewards to workers who reach targeted business results.[7] As an example, a web specialist might be rewarded for developing a new corporate website that attracted more visitors who stayed longer and led to achieving or exceeding a specified sales volume.

Negative reinforcement (or *avoidance motivation*) means rewarding people by taking away an uncomfortable consequence of their behaviour. It is the withdrawal or avoidance of a disliked consequence. You are subject to negative reinforcement when you are told your insurance rate will go down if you receive no traffic violations for 12 months. The uncomfortable consequence removed is a high insurance premium. Removing the undesirable consequence is contingent upon your making the right response—driving within the law.

Be careful not to make the common mistake of confusing negative reinforcement with punishment. Negative reinforcement is the opposite of punishment. It involves rewarding someone by removing a punishment or uncomfortable situation.

To use behaviour modification effectively, certain rules and procedures must be followed. Although using rewards and punishments to motivate people seems straightforward, behaviour modification requires a systematic approach. The rules are specified from the standpoint of the person trying to motivate another individual, such as a group member, co-worker, supervisor, or customer.

Rule 1: State Clearly What Behaviour Will Lead to a Reward. The nature of good performance, or the goals, must be agreed upon by the manager and group member. Clarification might take this form: "We need to decrease by 40 percent the number of new credit card customers who have delinquent accounts of 60 days or more." Workers also need to know specifically which types of behaviour will lead to punishment, such as being late for work three or more times in one month.

Rule 2: Choose an Appropriate Reward. An appropriate reward or punishment is both effective in motivating a given person and feasible from the standpoint of the individual or the company. If one reward does not motivate the person, try another. The importance of choosing the right reward underscores the fact that not all rewards are reinforcers. A reward is something perceived as valuable by the person giving the reward. However, if the reward does not lead to strengthening a desired response (such as wearing safety goggles), it is not a true reinforcer.[8]

Figure 11-1 provides a list of factors by employees as to what would satisfy them on the job. At the same time, these factors can be translated into potential rewards for employees. For example, if employees value bonuses, a high-performing employee might be given some assurance of receiving a bonus for above-average employment. Because all of these factors are ranked as *important* job factors by employees, all of them are potentially appropriate rewards.

negative reinforcement
Rewarding people by taking away an uncomfortable consequence of their behaviour.

BACK TO THE OPENING CASE

Bob Nelson found that trinkets such as logoed mugs, T-shirts, pen sets, or other small items were not perceived as rewards for good work. This brings home the idea that rewards are only perceived as rewards if the employee perceives the recognition gift as something valuable. The theory of behaviour modification and positive reinforcement give credibility to Nelson's findings.

FIGURE 11-1 What Workers Want from Their Jobs and Their Employers

1. Competitive salary
2. 100 percent of health-care coverage paid by employers
3. Company-matched retirement investments
4. Bonus programs
5. Flexible schedules
6. Compressed workweek
7. Good relationship with the boss
8. Being treated with respect
9. Making a contribution to the company and perhaps society.

Note: Although only factors 1, 2, and 3 are in rank order, factors 4 through 9 are also considered important for job satisfaction.

Source: Table prepared from survey of 1051 workers presented in "Listen Up Employers; Employees Know What They Want This Labor Day," www.kronos.com, August 2, 2006, p. 1. The survey was conducted by Harris Interactive and sponsored by Kronos Incorporated. Factor 9 is from Timothy R. Clark, "Engaging the Disengaged," *HR Magazine*, April 2008, p. 112.

Rule 3: Supply Ample Feedback. Behaviour modification cannot work without frequent feedback to individuals. Feedback can take the form of simply telling people they have done something right or wrong. Brief email messages or handwritten notes are other forms of feedback. Many effective motivators make extensive use of handwritten thank-you notes. Negative feedback by email should be written tactfully to avoid resentment.

Rule 4: Schedule Rewards Intermittently. Rewards should not be given on every occasion of good performance. **Intermittent rewards** sustain desired behaviours longer and also slow down the process of behaviours fading away when they are not rewarded. If each correct performance results in a reward, the behaviour will stop shortly after a performance in which the reward is not received. Another problem is that a reward given continuously may lose its impact. A practical value of intermittent reinforcement is that it saves time. Few managers or team leaders have enough time to dispense rewards for every correct action by group members.

Rule 5: Make Sure the Rewards Follow the Observed Behaviour Closely in Time. For maximum effectiveness, people should be rewarded soon after doing something right. A built-in, or intrinsic, feedback system, such as a computer program's working or not working, capitalizes on this principle. If you are administering rewards and punishments, strive to administer them the same day they are earned. Suppose a coworker feeds you exactly the information you need to make a PowerPoint presentation for the group. Send your co-worker an email or text message of appreciation the same day. Or be old-fashioned and thank him or her in person.

Rule 6: Make the Reward Fit the Behaviour. People inexperienced in applying positive reinforcement often overdo the intensity of spoken rewards. When an employee does something of an ordinary nature correctly, a simple word of praise such as "Good job" is preferable to something like "Fantastic performance." A related idea is that the magnitude of the reward should vary with the magnitude of the accomplishment.

Rule 7: Make the Reward Visible. Another important characteristic of an effective reward is the extent to which it is visible, or noticeable, to other employees. When other workers notice the reward, its impact multiplies because other people observe what kind of behaviour is rewarded.[9] Assume that you are informed about a coworker's having received an exciting assignment because of high performance. You might strive to accomplish the same level of performance. Rewards should also be visible, or noticeable, to the employee. A reward of 10 dollars per week added to a

intermittent rewards

Rewards given for good performance occasionally, but not always.

> **SKILL-BUILDING EXERCISE 11-2**
>
> **Positive Reinforcement**
>
> In both of the following scenarios, one student plays the role of the person attempting to modify the behaviour of (motivate) the other individual. Another student plays the role of the person who is the recipient of these motivation attempts.
>
> **Scenario 1: Rewarding a Customer Service Representative.** The customer service manager carefully reviews customer service reports to discover that one service rep has resolved the most complaints for four weeks in a row. Since this rep has been on the job only six months, the manager wants to make sure the rep feels amply rewarded and appreciated. The manager calls the rep into his or her office to discuss this outstanding performance and give an appropriate reward.
>
> **Scenario 2: Rewarding Your Boss.** The group member has just received a wonderful assignment from the boss, offering the opportunity to spend a few days with key customers who are located out of town. This is the group member's first really exciting extra assignment. As a consequence, the worker wants to encourage the boss to keep him or her in mind for future assignments of this nature. The boss was not expecting to be rewarded for making an assignment that fit the company's needs.
>
> Others in the class observe the two scenarios so they can provide feedback on how well behaviour modification principles were applied to provide reinforcement.

person's paycheque might hardly be noticeable, after payroll deductions. However, a bonus cheque for $200 might be very noticeable.

Rule 8: Change the Reward Periodically. Rewards do not retain their effectiveness indefinitely. Employees and customers lose interest in striving for a reward they have received many times in the past. This is particularly true of a repetitive statement such as "Nice job" or "Congratulations." It is helpful for the person giving out the rewards to study the list of potential rewards and try different ones from time to time.

A general approach applying to the previous rules is to look for creative ways to apply behaviour modification. The creativity might be in the selection of the reward, or how the reward is administered. Here are a few ideas:

- **Applause.** Choose an especially effective employee, and at the end of the week or month have co-workers gather and clap for the person.
- **Giraffe award.** Give a certificate saying, "Thanks for sticking your neck out." The name of the reward and the certificate reward risk-taking.
- **Safety jackpot.** Managers give "lotto" cards to employees who follow safety practices. Workers scratch off the cards to learn how many points they have won. Points are then redeemed via a gift catalogue or website.[10]

Now do Skill-Building Exercise 11-2 to practise several of these rules for using positive reinforcement.

USING RECOGNITION TO MOTIVATE OTHERS

Motivating others by giving them recognition and praise can be considered a direct application of positive reinforcement. Nevertheless, recognition is such a potentially powerful motivator that it merits separate attention. Also, recognition programs to reward and motivate employees are a standard practice in business and nonprofit firms. One Sears Canada store gives "employees of the month" preferred parking spaces to reward top performance in various departments. Outstanding sales representatives ("beauty consultants") receive recognition and, at Mary Kay, rewards in the form of pink cell phones, pink Buicks, and pink Cadillacs—in Canada and the United States, as well as in China and other countries.[11] The pink, however, is just a tinge of pink to give it a modern look. In keeping with the theme of this text, our emphasis is on individual, rather than organizational, use of recognition to motivate.

LEARNING OBJECTIVE 3

Why Recognition Is a Strong Motivator

Recognition is a strong motivator because the craving for recognition is a normal human need. At the same time, recognition is effective because most workers feel they do not receive enough of it. Several studies conducted over a 50-year time span have indicated that employees welcome praise for a job well done as much as a regular paycheque. This finding should not be interpreted to mean that praise is an adequate substitute for salary. Employees tend to regard compensation as an entitlement, whereas recognition is perceived as a gift.[12] Workers, including your co-workers, want to know that their output is useful to somebody.

Recognition is also important as a motivator because it is often tied in with other motivators. Receiving a pay increase based on performance is a form of positive reinforcement. At the same time, the pay raise provides recognition for having performed well. An extensive study of call centres in North American financial and retail industries over a seven-year period provides evidence of how recognition is tied in with promotions. Call centre employees were more interested in promotion than in pay increases exclusively. Promotion, as they perceived it, brought them formal recognition as well as changes in status and responsibilities.[13]

Approaches to Giving Recognition

To appeal to the recognition needs of others, identify a meritorious behaviour and then recognize that behaviour with an oral, written, or material reward. Email, instant messaging, and text messaging are useful vehicles for providing quick recognition when in-person appreciation is not feasible. Also, sometimes people like to print a copy of the recognition they receive. The rules for the use of positive reinforcement are directly applicable. An additional suggestion relates closely to making rewards visible: Time your praise for when it will do the most good. Praise delivered during a staff meeting, for example, can be a potent form of recognition.[14] The recognition award should help the employee feel appreciated for having made a contribution. The economic value of the award, such as engraved metal bowl, is much less important.

Some specific examples of using recognition to sustain desired behaviour (a key aspect of motivation) follow:

- A co-worker shows you how to use Twitter more effectively for advertising. Three days later, you send her an email message with a copy to the boss: "Hi Jessica, your suggestion about using Twitter to gain some visibility for our new product was dynamite. We've significantly increased the number of company followers." (You are reinforcing Jessica's helpful and cooperative behaviour.)

- As the team leader, you receive a glowing letter from a customer about how Lin, one of your team members, solved the customer's problem. You have the letter laminated and present it as a gift to Lin. (The behaviour you are reinforcing is good customer service.)

- One member of your department, Ahmed, is a mechanical engineer. While at a department lunch taking place during National Engineers Week, you stand up and say, "I want to toast Ahmed in celebration of National Engineers Week. I certainly wouldn't want to be sitting in this office building today if a mechanical engineer hadn't assisted in its construction." (Here the only behaviour you are reinforcing is Ahmed's goodwill, so your motivational approach is general rather than specific.)

A high-powered approach to recognizing the achievements of others is for the manager, supervisor, or team leader to hold personal celebrations of outstanding accomplishment. The celebration takes place in person in contrast to disseminating an electronic message, thereby making the celebration more personal. Such types of public recognition might be part of an employee recognition and celebration program. Personal celebrations include having a meal in a restaurant or in the workplace in honour of an outstanding accomplishment such as a major cost-saving suggestion, a major sale, or receiving a patent. Intense group recognition of this type will often boost the self-esteem of the employee who is celebrated.

Fine Points about Using Recognition to Motivate Others

An outstanding advantage of recognition, including praise, as a motivator is that it is no cost or low cost, yet powerful. Recognition thus provides an enormous return on investment in comparison to a cash bonus. Nevertheless, a challenge in using recognition effectively is that not everyone responds well to the same form of recognition. A good example is that highly technical people tend not to like general praise such as "Great job" or "Awesome." Instead, they prefer a laid-back, factual statement of how their output made a contribution. Furthermore, women are slightly more responsive to praise than are men, as revealed in a study of working adults.[15]

Giving recognition to others as a motivational tactic is more likely to be effective if a culture of recognition exists within the company. This is true because the person giving the recognition will feel that what he or she is doing fits what top management thinks is appropriate behaviour. At the same time, the recipient of the recognition is likely to take it seriously.

The rules for positive reinforcement described above also apply to giving recognition. For example, a recognition reward given too frequently either becomes stale or regarded as an entitlement. In one business firm, the CEO traditionally bought lunch for all employees every Friday to recognize their contributions. Soon, employees were asking him to be reimbursed for lunch if they ate outside of the company on a Friday.[16]

USING EXPECTANCY THEORY TO MOTIVATE OTHERS

So far we have described motivating others through applying the principle of "What's in it for me?" (WIIFM) and behaviour modification, including recognition. We now shift to expectancy theory, a more comprehensive explanation of motivation that includes elements of the two other approaches. Expectancy theory is given special attention here for three reasons. First, the theory is comprehensive because it incorporates many different aspects of motivating others. Second, expectancy theory can help you diagnose motivational problems. Third, it gives the person attempting to motivate others many guidelines for triggering and sustaining constructive effort from group members.

LEARNING OBJECTIVE 4

Capsule Overview of Expectancy Theory

The **expectancy theory** of motivation is based on the premise that how much effort people expend depends on the reward they expect to receive in return. (Notice the similarity to WIIFM?) Expectancy theory assumes that people are rational and logical. In any given situation, they want to maximize gain and minimize loss. The theory assumes that people choose among alternatives by selecting the one they think they have the best chance of attaining. Further, they choose the alternative that appears to have the biggest personal payoff. How intensely they want that alternative is also an important consideration. Given a choice, people select an assignment they think they can handle, and that will benefit them the most.

An example will help clarify the central thesis of expectancy theory. Hector, a 27-year-old credit analyst at a machine tool company, recognizes that he needs to increase his income by about $500 per month to cover his expenses. After carefully reviewing his options, Hector narrows his alternatives to the following three choices:

1. Work as a dining-room server one night a week and on most weekends, with a variable income of somewhere between $600 and $850 per month.
2. Work for an income tax preparation service about four months per year for 20 hours per week, yielding an annual income of about $7000.
3. Work extra hard at his regular job, including taking a course in corporate finance, to improve his chances of receiving a promotion and a salary increase of $700 per month.

Hector rejects the first choice. Although he knows he can do the work, he anticipates several negative outcomes. He would much prefer to engage in extra work related to his field of expertise. The unpredictable income associated with being a dining-room server is also a concern. Hector sees merit in the second alternative, because income tax preparation work relates to his accounting background. Further, the outcome (amount of pay) is relatively certain. But Hector also has some concerns that working so many extra hours for four months a year could hurt his performance on his day job.

Hector decides to take a chance with the third alternative of going all out to position himself for promotion. He is confident he can elevate his performance, but he is much less certain that hard work will lead to promotion. Yet Hector attaches such high value to being promoted and upgrading his professional credentials that he is willing to gamble.

Basic Components of Expectancy Theory

All versions of expectancy theory have the following three major components: effort-to-performance expectancy, performance-to-outcome expectancy, and valence.[17] Figure 11-2 presents a glimpse of expectancy theory.

Effort-to-performance expectancy is the probability assigned by the individual that effort will lead to performing the task correctly. An important question rational people ask themselves before putting forth effort to accomplish a task is this: "If I put in all this work, will I really get the job done properly?" Each behaviour is associated in the individual's mind with a certain expectancy, or subjective hunch of the probability of success.

Expectancies range from 0 to 1.0. The expectancy would be 0 if the person thought that there was no chance of performing the task correctly. An expectancy of 1.0 would signify absolute faith in being able to perform the task properly. Expectancies thus influence whether you will even strive to earn a reward. Self-confident people have higher expectancies than do those with low self-confidence. Being well-trained will also increase your subjective hunch that you can perform the task.

The importance of having high expectancies for motivation meshes well with a thrust in work motivation that emphasizes the contribution of **self-efficacy**, your confidence in your ability to carry out a specific task. If you have high self-efficacy about the task, your motivation will be high. Low self-efficacy leads to low motivation. Some people are poorly motivated to skydive because they doubt they will be able to pull the rip cord while free-falling at 200 kilometres per hour. A more technical definition and explanation will help you appreciate self-efficacy's contribution to motivation.[18]

Self-efficacy refers to an individual's convictions (or confidence) about his or her abilities to mobilize the motivation, cognitive resources, and course of action needed to successfully execute a specific task within a given context.

In short, if you are confident about your task-related skills, you will get your act together to do the task. This is one reason motivators need to give people the skills and confidence they need for them to exert effort.

Performance-to-outcome expectancy is the probability assigned by the individual that performance will lead to certain outcomes or rewards. When people engage in a particular behaviour, they do so with the intention of achieving a desired outcome or reward. Performance-to-outcome expectancies also range from 0 to 1.0. If you believe there is no chance of receiving the desired reward, the assigned probability is 0. If you believe the reward is certain to follow from performing correctly, the assigned probability is 1.0. For

---

effort-to-performance expectancy
The probability assigned by the individual that effort will lead to performing the task correctly.

self-efficacy
Confidence in one's ability to carry out a specific task.

performance-to-outcome expectancy
The probability assigned by the individual that performance will lead to outcomes or rewards.

FIGURE 11-2 A Basic Version of Expectancy Theory

Person will be motivated under these conditions:
- A. Effort-to-performance expectancy is high: Person believes he or she can perform the task.
- B. Performance-to-outcome expectancy is high: Person believes that performance will lead to certain outcomes.
- C. Valence is high: Person highly values the outcomes.

example: "I know for sure that if I show up for work every day this month, I will receive my paycheque."

A **valence** is the value, worth, or attractiveness of an outcome. It signifies how intensely you want something (as described in WIIFM). In each work situation there are multiple outcomes, each with a valence of its own. Remember Hector, the credit analyst? The potential outcomes of working part-time as an income tax preparer would include extra income, new experience, and interference with his day job.

In the version of expectancy theory presented here, valences range from −100 to +100. A valence of +100 means that you desire an outcome strongly. A valence of −100 means that you are strongly motivated to avoid an outcome, such as being fired. A valence of 0 means that you are indifferent toward an outcome, and it is therefore of no use as a motivator. An outcome with a probable valence of 0 would be as follows: To gain the cooperation of co-workers, you promise them gold stars as a reward (or outcome).

Skill-Building Exercise 11-3 will help sensitize you to the importance of estimating valences when attempting to motivate others. A major problem faced by managers and others who attempt to motivate others is that they have limited knowledge about the valences of their motivators (or rewards).

valence
The value, worth, or attractiveness of an outcome.

How Moods Influence Expectancy Theory

Expectancy theory emphasizes the rational side of people, yet emotions still play a key role in determining the impact of expectancies, instrumentalities, and valences. Moods are

Explore
Simulation: Motivating Others

SKILL-BUILDING EXERCISE 11-3

Estimating Valences for Applying Expectancy Theory

Directions: Listed here are rewards and punishments (outcomes) stemming from job scenarios. Also included is a space for rating the reward or punishment on a scale of −100 to +100. Work with about six teammates, with each person rating all the rewards and punishments. Compute the mean (average) rating for each reward and punishment.

Potential Outcome — Rating (−100 to +100)

1. A 20 percent salary increase
2. Profit-sharing plan in successful company
3. Stock ownership in company
4. Fully paid three-day leave
5. $7000 performance bonus
6. $300 gift certificate
7. Outstanding performance review
8. Above-average performance review
9. One-step promotion
10. Two-step promotion
11. Flexible working hours
12. Chance to work at home one day per week
13. Chance to do more of preferred task
14. Take over for supervisor when supervisor is away
15. Fancy job title without change in pay
16. Bigger work area
17. Private office
18. Company-paid cell phone
19. Wall plaque indicating accomplishment
20. Employee-of-the-month designation
21. Warm smile and word of appreciation
22. Compliment in front of others
23. Threat of being suspended for one month
24. One-month suspension without pay
25. Demotion to undesirable job
26. Being fired
27. Being fired combined with promise of negative references
28. Being put on probation
29. Being ridiculed in front of others
30. A 30 percent pay reduction

After completing the ratings, discuss the following topics:

1. Which outcomes received the most variable ratings?
2. Which outcomes received the most similar ratings?
3. Which are the three most desirable rewards?
4. Which are the three most undesirable punishments?

Another analytical approach would be to compute the class mean for all 30 outcomes. Each student could then compare his or her rating with the class average.

To apply this technique to the job, modify the preceding outcomes to fit the outcomes available in your work situation. Explain to team members that you are attempting to do a better job of rewarding and disciplining and that you need their input. The ratings made by team members will give strong clues to which rewards and punishments would be the most effective in motivating them.

SKILLS FOR MOTIVATING AND HELPING OTHERS

relatively long-lasting emotional states that do not appear to be tied to a clear source of the emotion. For example, a person might be in a good mood despite experiencing a negative situation such as an automobile breaking down. Also, people may feel glum despite good news such as having won a prize.

Several studies have shown that moods shape people's perceptions of expectancies and valence in expectancy theory. A positive mood increases the perceived connection between effort and performance (E→P expectancy), between performance and desired outcome (P→O expectancy), and in the valence attached to those outcomes. When we are in a good mood, we are more likely to believe that we can accomplish a task, so we have more of a "can do" attitude. We are also more optimistic about the outcomes (rewards) of our effort, and the outcomes look even better to us.[19] The opposite might also be true—when we are in a bad mood we feel less capable of task accomplishment; we are more pessimistic about getting the reward; and the reward appears less enticing.

Lisa F. Young/Fotolia

Diagnosing Motivation with Expectancy Theory

An important potential contribution of expectancy theory to interpersonal relations is that it helps a person diagnose whether motivation is present, and the intensity of the motivation. In performing your diagnosis, seek answers to the following questions:

1. Does the person I am attempting to motivate have the skills and self-efficacy to do the job? If the person feels ill equipped to perform, he or she will be discouraged and show very little motivation.
2. What assurance does the person have that if he or she performs the work the promised reward will be forthcoming? Does the company have a decent reputation for following through on promises? What about me? Have I established my credibility as a person who follows through on promises? (If you and/or the company are not trusted, motivation could be reduced to zero.)
3. How badly does the person want the reward being offered in the situation? Am I offering a reward that will make it worthwhile for the person to do what I need done? If the sum of the valences of the outcomes in the situation is close to 0 (some positive, some negative), motivation will be absent.
4. Are there any 0s in response to the first three questions? If there are, motivation will be absent, because the expectancy theory equation is Motivation = (Effort-to-performance expectancies) × (Performance-to-outcome expectancies) × (The sum of the valences for all the outcomes). Remember what happens when you multiply by 0 in an equation.
5. Is the person in a reasonably good mood? Perhaps the person is poorly motivated today because of being in a bad mood.

Guidelines for Applying Expectancy Theory

The information about expectancy theory presented so far provides ideas for motivating others. Here we present several additional specific guidelines to improve your skill in motivating others.

1. **Train and encourage people.** If you are a manager, you should give employees the necessary training and encouragement to be confident that they can perform the required task. Some employees who appear to be poorly motivated might simply lack the right skills and self-efficacy.
2. **Make the link between rewards and performance explicit.** Employees should be reassured that if they perform the job up to standard, they will receive the promised reward. It is sometimes helpful for employees to ask co-workers whether they received promised rewards.

SKILL-BUILDING EXERCISE 11-4

Applying Expectancy Theory

One student plays the role of the manager of telemarketing (selling over the telephone). Another student plays the role of Terry, a telemarketing specialist who has been with the company for three months. Terry is 40 percent below target in selling magazine renewals. The manager calls Terry into the office for a discussion of the problem.

Terry goes on at length to explain how confusing the job has become. Terry makes comments such as "I don't even know if I have the right kind of voice for this job. People I reach on the phone think I'm just a kid." Terry also wonders what kind of money he can make in this job and whether it is a dead-end job. (The student who plays the role of Terry can improvise about more of these kinds of problems.)

The manager will apply expectancy theory to motivate Terry to achieve satisfactory performance. Other class members should jot down statements the manager makes that indicate the use of expectancy theory. Also, observe whether it appears that Terry is being helped.

---

3. **Make sure the rewards are substantial enough.** Some rewards fail to motivate people because, although they are the right kind, they are not in the right amount. The promise of a large salary increase might be motivational, but a 1 percent increase will probably have little motivational thrust for most workers.

4. **Understand individual differences in valences.** To motivate others in the workplace effectively, you must discover individual differences in preferences for rewards. An attempt should be made to offer a worker rewards to which he or she attaches a high valence. For instance, one employee might value a high-adventure assignment; another might attach a high valence to a routine, tranquil assignment. Also keep individual differences in mind when attempting to motivate customers. One customer might attach a high valence to a volume discount, while another might favour follow-up service.

5. **Use the Pygmalion effect to increase effort-to-performance expectancies.** The **Pygmalion effect** is the phenomenon that people will rise (or fall) to the expectations another person has of them. Even if these expectations are not communicated explicitly, the other person will catch on to the nonverbal language. As the levels of expectation increase, so will performance. High expectations thus become a self-fulfilling prophecy.

Pygmalion effect
The phenomenon that people will rise (or fall) to the expectations that another person has of them.

It is difficult to keep all the points made about expectancy theory in your head at the same time. Nevertheless, with practice and by referring to this text and your notes, you can apply many of the ideas. Skill-Building Exercise 11-4 will help you get started in applying expectancy theory.

MOTIVATING OTHERS BY NURTURING AND MENTORING

Our personality influences how well we can motivate and help others in the workplace. For example, it does not matter how well you can apply expectancy theory or reinforce others if you fail to come across as caring and helpful. In fact, if you do not come across as caring, your co-worker may be wondering if you have ulterior motives or a hidden agenda when offering your assistance. Among the key helping roles are nurturing others, mentoring, coaching and training, and helping difficult people become more cooperative. Here we will examine nurturing others, as coaching and training were discussed in the previous chapter as part the development of leadership skills. We will finish this chapter with examining difficult people in the workplace and how we can deal with them effectively.

LEARNING OBJECTIVE 5

Do Self-Assessment Quiz 11-2 to gain preliminary insight into your attitudes toward helping others in the workplace.

Being a Nurturing, Positive Person

A major strategy for helping others grow and develop is to be a nourishing, positive person. A **nurturing person** promotes the growth of others. Nurturing people are positive and supportive and typically look for the good qualities in others. A **toxic person** stands in

nurturing person
One who promotes the growth of others.

toxic person
One who dwells exclusively on the failings of others and whose pessimistic behaviours undermine the group.

SELF-ASSESSMENT QUIZ 11-2

Attitudes Toward Helping Others

Directions: Describe how well you agree with the following statements by circling the appropriate letter after each statement: Disagree (D); Neutral (N); Agree (A).

1.	If I see a co-worker make a mistake, I do not inform him or her of the mistake.	D	N	A
2.	It should be part of everybody's job to share skills and ideas with co-workers.	D	N	A
3.	The manager should have exclusive responsibility for coaching people within the work unit.	D	N	A
4.	I can think of many instances in my life when somebody thanked me for showing him or her how to do something.	D	N	A
5.	I have very little patience with co-workers who do not give me their full cooperation.	D	N	A
6.	To save time, I will do a task for another person rather than invest the time needed to show him or her how to do it.	D	N	A
7.	I would take the initiative to take an inexperienced worker under my wing.	D	N	A
8.	As a child, I often took the time to show younger children how to do things.	D	N	A
9.	Rather than ask a co-worker for help, I will wait until the manager is available to help me.	D	N	A
10.	It is best not to share key information with a co-worker because that person could then perform as well as or better than me.	D	N	A

Total Score: _____

Scoring and Interpretation: Use the following score key to obtain your score for each answer, and then calculate your total score.

1. D = 3, N = 2, A = 1
2. D = 1, N = 2, A = 3
3. D = 3, N = 2, A = 1
4. D = 1, N = 2, A = 3
5. D = 3, N = 2, A = 1
6. D = 3, N = 2, A = 1
7. D = 1, N = 2, A = 3
8. D = 1, N = 2, A = 3
9. D = 3, N = 2, A = 1
10. D = 3, N = 2, A = 1

25–30 Very positive attitudes toward helping, developing, and training others in the workplace. Such attitudes reflect strong teamwork and a compassion for the growth needs of others.

16–24 Mixed positive and negative attitudes toward helping, developing, and training others in the workplace. You may need to develop more sensitivity to the growth needs of others to be considered a strong team player.

10–15 Negative attitudes toward helping, developing, and training others in the workplace. Guard against being so self-centred that it will be held against you.

---

contrast to a nourishing person because he or she dwells on the negative.[20] Visualize the following scenario to appreciate the differences between nurturing and toxic people:

> *Randy, a purchasing specialist, enters the office, where two co-workers are talking. One is a nurturing person, the other toxic. With a look of panic, Randy says, "I'm sorry to barge in like this, but can anybody help me? I've been working for three hours preparing a file on the computer, and it seems to have vanished. Maybe one of you can help me retrieve it."*
>
> *Margot, the nourishing person, says, "I'm no computer expert, but since I'm not the one who lost the file, I can be calm enough to help. Let's go right now." Ralph, the toxic person, whispers to Margot: "Tell Randy to use his computer manual. If you help him now, you'll only find him on your doorstep every time he needs help."*

If you listen to toxic people long enough, you are likely to feel listless, depressed, and drained. Toxic people have been described as *energy vampires* because they suck all the positive energy out of you.[21] Nurturing people, in contrast, are positive, enthusiastic, and supportive.

The guideline for skill development here is to engage in thoughts and actions every day that will be interpreted by others as nourishing. Following are three actions and attitudes that support being a nourishing person:

1. **Recognize that most people have growth needs.** Almost everybody has a need for self-fulfillment, although people vary widely in the extent of this need. If you recognize this need in others, it may propel you toward helping people satisfy their need. You might engage in interactions with co-workers such as sharing new skills with them, forwarding relevant news articles from the Internet, or telling them about an important new website you have discovered. You might also tell them about an exciting course you have taken that has increased your self-confidence.

2. **Team up with a co-worker in your department or another one so the two of you can form a buddy system.** Children in swimming programs and even soldiers in combat use the buddy system. The same system can be used by you and a friend to keep each other informed of decisions and events that could affect your careers. You might nurture your buddy by telling about growth opportunities in the company he or she might not have heard about. Your buddy would reciprocate. One person told her buddy about expanding opportunities for company employees who were fluent in both English and French. The two buddies, who already knew some French, worked together to become fluent.

3. **Be a role model for others.** An indirect way of being a nurturing, positive person is to conduct yourself in such a way that others will model your behaviour. By serving as a role model, you help another person develop. How to become a role model for co-workers is as comprehensive a topic as learning to be successful. Among the many factors that make you role-model material are a strong work ethic, job expertise, personal warmth, good speaking ability, a professional appearance, and great ethics. Do you qualify yet, or do you need some more work?

Being a nurturing, positive person is a lifelong process rather than a tactic that can be used at will. Nevertheless, making a conscious attempt to be nurturing and positive can help you develop the right mindset. Skill-Building Exercise 11-5 provides an opportunity to practise being a positive person.

Being a Mentor to Co-Workers

In Homer's tale *The Odyssey*, Mentor was a wise and trusted friend as well as a counsellor and advisor. The term *mentor* has become a buzzword in the workplace. A **mentor** is generally defined as an individual with advanced experience and knowledge who is committed to giving support and career advice to a less experienced person. The less experienced person is the **protégé** (from the French word for *protected*). Here we look at various characteristics of mentoring, followed by behaviours that will be useful to you in mentoring others.

mentor
An individual with advanced experience and knowledge who is committed to giving support and career advice to a less experienced person.

protégé
The less experienced person in a mentoring relationship who is helped by the mentor.

SKILL-BUILDING EXERCISE 11-5

The Nurturing, Positive Person

One student plays the role of Pat, a worker who is experiencing difficulty on the job and in her personal life. Pat approaches Leslie, a co-worker, during lunch in the company cafeteria and says, "What a day! I just received a rotten performance appraisal. If my work doesn't improve within a month, the company may let me go. To add to my woes, my fiancé has threatened to break off the engagement if I don't get a big raise or a promotion. I feel like my whole world is collapsing." The other person plays the role of Leslie, who attempts to be nurturing and positive in order to help get Pat out of the doldrums. Run the role-play for about 10 minutes.

The rest of the class provides feedback on Leslie's skill in being nurturing and helpful. Jot down specific behaviours you think are most effective.

Characteristics and Types of Mentoring

The term *mentoring* is used so widely and in so many contexts that it can refer to almost any type of helping relationship. From a more technically precise perspective, mentoring is characterized as:

- A unique relationship between two people
- A learning partnership that involves emotional and task-related career support
- A reciprocal helping relationship
- A frequently changing relationship between the mentor and the mentored[22]

A mentor is usually older or more experienced than the protégé and may be in a higher job category (although this is not always the case). For present purposes, however, be aware that one co-worker can be a mentor to another. The Vancouver-based company 1-800-GOTJUNK? purposely hires employees over the age of 40. The people director of the company feels that the younger people can learn from their more-seasoned colleagues.[23] However, mentoring is not always just about age. As long as you are more experienced and wiser than a co-worker in some important aspect of the job, you can be a mentor. A person who is not a manager can also be a mentor in another important way. He or she can select an entry-level person in the firm and serve as the inexperienced person's coach and advisor. Even when a person has a high-ranking person as a mentor, you can also be his or her mentor. The reason is that having more than one mentor improves a person's chances for developing job and career skills.[24]

Mentoring is more important than ever, because it supports the modern, team-based organization. Also, after years of downsizing, many organizations have fewer managers available to mentor employees. Co-workers often have to fill this void. More people work together as equals, and they are expected to train and develop one another. Mentoring facilitates such learning and also supports the current emphasis on continuous learning.[25]

Mentoring often takes the form of the mentor and protégé communicating by email, referred to as *virtual or online mentoring*. As the time of corporate professionals and managers has become more scarce, virtual mentoring is more practical. Also, virtual mentoring gives the protégé an opportunity to be mentored by someone who is geographically distant, even overseas. The person being mentored might send a quick email to the mentor explaining that he just received an outstanding performance review. The mentor might reply back with an email of encouragement. When asked about a problem facing the protégé, the mentor might reply with advice quickly. Answers by the mentor within 48 hours are recommended to communicate an attitude of concern.[26] Skype is also used in virtual mentoring, giving an opportunity for mentor and protégé to see each other, which is more typical of traditional mentoring.

Mentoring co-workers can take place in one of two ways. With informal mentoring, the mentor and protégé come together naturally, in the same way that friendships develop. The formal approach is for the company to assign you somebody to mentor. Several studies have shown that mentoring is likely to be more effective when both the mentor and protégé have some input into the matching.[27] Measures of mentoring effectiveness include rate of promotions, salary increases, and job satisfaction. Being mentored is also a career-advancement tactic, and will be discussed in Chapter 16.

Serving as a mentor is an excellent way of helping others on the job. Mentoring is also gaining acceptance off the job. Many communities have developed programs whereby working adults volunteer to serve as mentors to youths. Mentoring in many of these programs is designed to help adolescents and teenagers succeed at school, avoid a life of crime and substance abuse, and gain early experiences in the workplace.

Specific Mentoring Behaviours

To be a mentor, a person engages in a wide range of helping behaviors, all related to being a trusted friend, coach, and teacher. To prepare you for mentoring a less experienced person, a list of specific mentoring behaviours follows:[28]

- **Sponsoring.** A mentor actively nominates somebody else for promotions and desirable positions. In some situations, one person is asked to nominate a co-worker for a promotion to supervisor or team leader or for a special assignment.
- **Coaching.** A mentor gives on-the-spot advice to the protégé to help her or him improve skills. Coaching is such an important part of helping others that it receives separate mention in this chapter.
- **Protecting.** A mentor might shield a junior person from potentially harmful situations or from the boss. For example, the mentor might tell her protégé, "In your meeting today with the boss, make sure you are well prepared and have all your facts at hand. He's in an ugly mood and will attack any weakness."
- **Sharing challenging assignments.** One member of the team does not ordinarily give assignments to another, yet in some situations you can request that your protégé help you with a difficult task. You would then offer feedback on your protégé's performance. The purpose of these high demands is to help the protégé develop more quickly than if he or she were not offered new challenges.
- **Acting as a referral agent.** The mentor sometimes refers the protégé to resources inside and outside the company to help with a particular problem. For example, the protégé might want to know how one goes about getting the employee benefits package modified.
- **Role-modelling.** An important part of being a mentor is demonstrating to the protégé a pattern of values and behaviours to emulate. Several of the specific behaviours associated with being a role model were described earlier in connection with being a positive, nurturing person.
- **Giving support and encouragement.** A mentor can be helpful just by giving support and encouragement. In turn, the protégé is supposed to support the mentor by offering compliments and defending the mentor's ideas. In a team meeting, for example, the protégé might make a statement such as "I think John's ideas will work wonders. We should give them a try."
- **Counselling.** A mentor listens to the protégé's work problems and offers advice. Given that counselling plays such a central role in helping others, it too receives separate mention in this chapter.
- **Providing friendship.** A mentor is, above all, a trusted friend, and the friendship extends two ways. *Trusted* means that the mentor will not pass on confidential information or stab you in the back.
- **Encouraging problem solving.** Mentors help their protégés solve problems by themselves and make their own discoveries. A comment frequently made to mentors is "I'm glad you made me think through the problem myself. You jogged my mind."
- **Explaining the ropes.** A general-purpose function of the mentor is to help the protégé learn the ropes, which translates into explaining the values and "dos and don'ts" of the organization.
- **Teaching the right skills.** The original role of the mentor in teaching skills (such as a master teaching an apprentice) is highly relevant today. Among the many skills a mentor can help the protégé develop are those dealing with information technology, customer service, corporate finance, and producing high-quality work.
- **Encouraging continuous learning.** A major role for the modern mentor is to encourage the protégé to keep learning. Part of encouraging lifelong learning is to emphasize that formal education and an occasional workshop are not sufficient for maintaining expertise in today's fast-changing workplace. The individual has to stay abreast of new developments through courses and self-study. A specific way in which the mentor can encourage continuous learning is to ask the protégé questions about new developments in the field.

As implied by the preceding list, mentoring is a complex activity that involves a variety of helping behaviours. To develop mentoring skills, you need to offer help to several people for at least six months. In preparation for becoming a mentor, it is helpful to think

> **SKILL-BUILDING EXERCISE 11-6**
>
> ### Selecting a Protégé
>
> To be a successful mentor, it is necessary to select protégés who will respond well to your advice and coaching. Since the mentor–protégé relationship is personal, much like any friendship, one must choose protégés carefully. In about 50 words (in the space provided), describe the type of person you would like for a protégé. Include cognitive, personality, and demographic factors in your description (refer to Chapter 2 for ideas). Indicate why you think the characteristics you chose are important.
>
> **My Ideal Protégé**
>
> As many class members as time allows can present their descriptions to the rest of the class. Look for agreement on characteristics of an ideal protégé.

of the type of person you would prefer to have as a protégé. Skill-Building Exercise 11-6 is designed to help you think through this issue. Be prepared for a potential protégé seeking you out because many people serious about advancing their careers search for potential mentors with whom they have rapport. Similarly, if you are looking for a mentor, take the initiative to establish contact with someone you like and who you think could help you. A study conducted at York University recommends that companies using a mentoring system for training match mentor and protégé carefully and ensure that mentors are trained in mentoring skills.[29]

Mentoring is designed to help another individual grow and develop; yet mentoring can also help your employer at the same time. Workers who receive mentoring are likely to feel more satisfied about their jobs and stay with the organization longer. A study with over 1300 Army officers showed that officers who were mentored felt more emotionally committed to the Army than did their non-mentored counterparts. Furthermore, mentored officers felt more likely to stay in the Army, and were less likely to leave the military voluntarily.[30]

Mentoring has also been successful in promoting a more diverse workforce representation in a business or organization. The Bank of Montreal is notable for several of its mentoring initiatives and programs to increase the bank's employee diversity.[31]

Helping Difficult People

LEARNING OBJECTIVE 6

A challenge we all face from time to time is dealing constructively with workers who seem intent on creating problems. For a variety of reasons, these difficult or counterproductive people perform poorly themselves or interfere with the job performance of others. A **difficult person** is an individual who creates problems for others yet has the skill and mental ability to be more productive. Below we briefly describe various types of difficult people and then emphasize methods for helping them behave more productively. To pretest your skill in dealing with and helping difficult people, do Self-Assessment Quiz 11-3.

difficult person

An individual who creates problems for others, even though he or she has the skill and mental ability to do otherwise.

Types of Difficult People

Dozens of types of difficult people have been identified, with considerable overlap among the types. For example, one method of classifying difficult people might identify the *dictator*, while another method might identify the same individual as the *bully*. Our purposes will be served by listing a sampling of the many types of difficult people found in the workplace and as customers. As you read the following list, look for familiar types:[32]

- **Know-it-alls** believe they are experts on everything. They have opinions on every issue, yet when they are wrong they pass the buck or become defensive.
- **Blamers** are workers who never solve their own problems. When faced with a challenge or hitch, they think the problem belongs to the supervisor or a group member.
- **Gossips** spread negative rumours about others and attempt to set people against each other.
- **Bullies** cajole and intimidate others. They are blunt to the point of being insulting, and will sometimes use harsh, vulgar language to attain their goals. Bullies constantly make demands on workmates.

SELF-ASSESSMENT QUIZ 11-3

Helping Difficult People

Directions: For each of the following scenarios, choose the method of handling the situation you think would be the most effective. Make a choice, even though more than one method of handling the situation seems plausible.

1. A co-worker in the cubicle next to you is talking loudly on the telephone about the fabulous weekend she and a few friends enjoyed. You are attempting to handle a challenging work problem. To deal with this situation, you
    a. get up from your chair, stand close to her, and say loudly, "Shut up, you jerk. I'm trying to do my work."
    b. slip her a handwritten note that says, "I'm happy that you had a great weekend, but I have problems concentrating on my work when you are talking so loudly. Thanks for your help."
    c. get the boss on the phone and ask that she please do something about the problem.
    d. wait until lunch and then say to her, "I'm happy that you had a great weekend, but I have problems concentrating on my work when you are talking so loudly. Thanks for your help."

2. One of your co-workers, Olaf, rarely carries his fair load of the work. He forever has a good reason for not having the time to do an assignment. This morning he has approached you to load some new software onto his personal computer. You deal with this situation by
    a. carefully explaining that you will help him, providing he will take over a certain specified task for you.
    b. telling him that you absolutely refuse to help a person as lazy as he is.
    c. counselling him about fair play and reciprocity.
    d. reviewing with him a list of five times he has asked other people to help him out. You then ask if he thinks this is a good way to treat co-workers.

3. In your role as supervisor, you have noticed that Diane, one of the group members, spends far too much work time laughing and joking. You schedule a meeting with her. As the meeting opens, you
    a. joke and laugh with her to establish rapport.
    b. explain to Diane that you have called this meeting to discuss her too-frequent laughing and joking.
    c. talk for a few moments about the good things Diane has done for the department, then confront the real issue.
    d. explain to Diane that she is on the verge of losing her job if she doesn't act more maturely.

4. As a team member, you have become increasingly annoyed with Jerry's ethnic, racist, and sexist jokes. One day during a team meeting, he tells a joke you believe is particularly offensive. To deal with the situation, you
    a. meet privately with the team leader to discuss Jerry's offensive behaviour.
    b. catch up with Jerry later when he is alone, and tell him how uncomfortable his joke made you feel.
    c. confront Jerry on the spot and say, "Hold on, Jerry. I find your joke offensive."
    d. tell the group an even more offensive joke to illustrate how Jerry's behaviour can get out of hand.

5. You have been put on a task force to look for ways to save the company money, including making recommendations for eliminating jobs. You interview a supervisor about the efficiency of her department. She suddenly becomes rude and defensive. In response, you
    a. politely point out how her behaviour is coming across to you.
    b. get your revenge by recommending that three jobs be eliminated from her department.
    c. explain that you have used up enough of her time for today and ask for another meeting later in the week.
    d. tell her that unless she becomes more cooperative, the interview cannot continue.

Scoring and Interpretation: Use the following key to obtain your score:

1.	2.	3.	4.	5.
a. 1	a. 4	a. 1	a. 2	a. 4
b. 4	b. 1	b. 4	b. 4	b. 1
c. 2	c. 3	c. 3	c. 3	c. 2
d. 3	d. 2	d. 2	d. 1	d. 3

18–20 You have good intuition about helping difficult people.
10–17 You have average intuition about helping difficult people.
5–9 You need to improve your sensitivity about helping difficult people.

SKILLS FOR MOTIVATING AND HELPING OTHERS

- **Repulsives** are people whose poor personal hygiene, eating habits, appearance, or foul language disrupts the tranquility of others.
- **Yes-people** agree to any commitment and promise any deadline, yet rarely deliver. Although sorry about being late, they cannot be trusted to deliver as promised.
- **No-people** are negative and pessimistic and quick to point out why something will not work. They are also inflexible, resist change, and complain frequently.
- **Jekyll-and-Hydes** have a split personality. When dealing with supervisors, customers, or clients, they are pleasant, engaging people; yet when carrying out the role of supervisors they become tyrannical.
- **Whiners** gripe about people, processes, and company regulations. They complain about being overworked and underpaid, or not receiving assignments up to their true capabilities.
- **Backstabbers** pretend to befriend you and encourage you to talk freely about problems or personality clashes you face. Later, the backstabber reports the information—often in exaggerated form—to the person you mentioned in a negative light. Or the backstabber simply says negative things about you behind your back to discredit you to others.
- **High-maintenance types** require considerable attention from others in such forms as demanding much of the supervisor's time, making unusual requests to the human resources department, and taking the maximum number of sick days and personal days allowable. High-maintenance types are often a combination of several of the previous types described above.
- **Clods** are master procrastinators who can find plenty of excuses as to why a project has not been started. When the clod finally gets started on a project, the work proceeds so slowly that other people who need the clod's input fall behind schedule and become stressed.
- **Minimalists** are apathetic and low-performing, and do just enough work to avoid being fired. They do the bare minimum, are thrive on being mediocre.
- **Office cheats** take claim for the ideas of other people, and benefit from these ideas, leaving the originator of the idea without receiving deserved credit, and feeling frustrated because of the stolen ideas.

Tactics for Dealing with Difficult People

How one deals most effectively with a difficult person depends to some extent on the person's type. For example, you may need different tactics to deal with a co-worker who gets nothing done than you would need with a co-worker who makes too many mistakes but insists she knows it all. Bullies are another type of difficult person to deal with in the workplace. Figure 11-3 presents specific ideas for dealing with a bully. (You will recall that bullying was described in Chapter 9 as a source of workplace conflict.)

The following techniques are broadly applicable to helping difficult people change to a more constructive behaviour pattern. This general approach should prove more helpful than being concerned with specific tactics for each type of difficult person you encounter. A principle to keep in mind in dealing with difficult people is that they vary in their amount of personality disturbance.

Stay Calm. A good starting point in dealing with many types of difficult people is to stay calm so that you can confront the other person in a professional manner. Staying calm also helps you think of a useful approach on the spot. Imagine that an exploder is upset because the new chair she was assigned has a broken height adjustment. You might calmly say to her, "I can imagine that having a chair that does not adjust is inconvenient, but what would you like me to do?" When you are calm, the difficult person's anger will often simmer down, and the problem that triggered the person can be solved.

Provide Ample Feedback. The primary technique for dealing with counterproductive behaviour is to feed back to the difficult person how his or her behaviour affects you. Focus on the person's behaviour rather than on his or her characteristics or values. If a

FIGURE 11-3 How to Be a Bully Buster

> Christine Pearson, a management professor at the University of North Carolina at Chapel Hill, says that employees can take steps to keep uncivil behaviour out of the workplace.
>
> - The first step is to admit to yourself that you are being bullied and that the bullying is unfair and unjustified.
> - If the bully is affecting you physically, see your doctor.
> - Stand up for yourself and be confident.
> - Check out your body language. If you stoop, hang your head, or hunch over, you may be giving off victim signals.
> - Try not to show that the bully has upset you; the bully may get bored and leave you alone.
> - Don't suffer in silence; tell someone you trust.
> - Find out about your rights, consider using any complaints procedure available in your company, and if necessary consult a lawyer.

Source: Survey cited in Mark Schoeff, Jr., "A U.S. Training Upgrade," *Workforce Management*, September 14, 2009, p. 32.

repulsive type is annoying you by constantly eating when you are working together, say something to this effect: "I have a hard time concentrating on the work when you're eating." Such a statement will engender less resentment than saying, "I find you repulsive, and it annoys me." As in coaching, it is better to avoid *should* statements because they often create defensiveness instead of triggering positive behaviour. Instead of saying, "You shouldn't be eating when you are working," you might try, "Could you find another place to eat when we are working together?"

Feedback will sometimes take the form of confrontation, and it is important not to lose emotional control during the confrontation. If the difficult person has criticized you unjustly in your eyes, attempt not to be defensive. Ask the difficult person exactly what he or she is upset about rather than argue. In this way, the burden of responsibility is now back on the antagonist. For example, if a bully was swearing at you during a meeting, later ask for the reason behind the outburst. Following the technique of disarming the opposition described in Chapter 9, you might agree with at least one of the bully's points. This will tend to establish rapport.[33] An example here would be, "Yes, I should have consulted you before making the final report. I apologize for the oversight."

Criticize Constructively. Feedback sets the stage for criticism. It is best to criticize in private and to begin with mild criticism. Base your criticism on objective facts rather than subjective impressions. Point out, for example, that the yes-person's lack of follow-through resulted in $10,000 in lost sales. Express your criticism in terms of a common goal. For example, "*We* can get the report done quickly if *you'll* firm up the statistical data while I edit the text." When you criticize a co-worker, avoid acting as if you have formal authority over the person.

Help the Difficult Person Feel More Confident. Many counterproductive employees are simply low in self-confidence and self-efficacy. They use stalling and evasive tactics because they are afraid to fail. Working with your manager or team leader, you might be able to arrange a project or task in which you know the difficult person will succeed. With a small dose of self-confidence and self-efficacy, the person may begin to complain less. With additional successes, the person may soon become less difficult.[34] Self-confidence building takes time. However, self-efficacy can build more quickly as the person learns a new skill.

Use Tact and Diplomacy. Tactful actions on your part can sometimes take care of co-workers' annoying behaviour without confrontation. Close your door, for example, if noisy co-workers are gathered outside. When the subtle approach fails, it may be necessary to proceed to a more confronting type of feedback.

Tact and diplomacy can still be incorporated into confrontation. In addition to confronting the person, you might also point out a strength of the individual. In dealing with a know-it-all you might say, "I realize you are creative and filled with good ideas. However, I wish you would give me an opportunity to express my opinion."

Use Non-hostile Humour. Non-hostile humour can often be used to help a difficult person understand how his or her behaviour is blocking others. Also, the humour will help you defuse the conflict between you and that person. The humour should point to the person's unacceptable behaviour yet not belittle him or her. Assume that you and a co-worker are working jointly on a report. For each idea that you submit, your co-worker gets into the know-it-all mode and informs you of important facts you have neglected. Following is an example of non-hostile humour that might jolt the co-worker into realizing that his or her approach is annoying:

> *If there is ever a contest to choose the human being with a brain that can compete against a Zip drive, I will nominate you. But even though my brain is limited to human capacity, I still think I can supply a few facts for our report.*

Your humour may help the other person recognize that he or she is attempting to overwhelm you with facts at his or her disposal. You are being self-effacing and thereby drawing criticism away from your co-worker. Self-effacement is an effective humour tactic in such situations.

Work Out a Deal. A direct approach to dealing with problems created by a difficult person is to work out a deal or negotiated solution. Workers who do not carry their load are successful in getting others to do their work. The next time such a worker wants you to carry out a task, agree to it if he or she will reciprocate by performing a task that will benefit you. For working out a deal to be effective, you must be specific about the terms of the deal. The worker may at first complain about your demands for reciprocity, so it is important to be firm.

Reinforce Civil Behaviour and Good Moods. In the spirit of positive reinforcement, when a generally difficult person is behaving acceptably, recognize the behaviour in some way. Reinforcing statements would include, "It's fun working with you today" and "I appreciate your professional attitude."

Ask the Difficult Person to THINK Before Speaking. Human relations specialist John Maxwell suggests that you ask the difficult person to THINK before he or she speaks, with "THINK" referring to this acronym:[35]

- T   Is it true?
- H   Is it helpful?
- I   Is it inspiring?
- N   Is it necessary?
- K   Is it kind?

Although Maxwell's suggestion is aimed at difficult people, is would be a helpful rule of thumb for building relationships with people in many situations.

Report Behaviour That Continues to Be Unacceptable or Inappropriate. If the behaviour is truly problematic, such as bullying or harassment, do not hesitate to report the behaviour to your manager (or his or her boss if the problem person is your manager). If you have exhausted all of your ideas and nothing has worked, to continue to have to deal with this person can become very disheartening and stressful. Most organizations do have policies and procedures in place (and in some cases it is law) to assist you when you are the victim of repeated hostility, bullying, or harassment of any kind.

SKILL-BUILDING EXERCISE 11-7

Dealing with Difficult People

In both of the following scenarios, one person plays the role of a group member whose work and morale suffer because of a difficult person. The other person plays the role of the difficult person, who may lack insight into what he or she is doing wrong. It is important for the suffering person to put emotion into the role.

Scenario 1: The Bully. A bully is present at a meeting called to plan a company morale-boosting event. Several students play the roles of the group members. One student plays the role of a group member who suggests that the event centre on doing a social good such as refurbishing a poor family's house or conducting a neighbourhood cleanup. Another student plays the role of a bully who thinks the idea is "a bummer"—pointlessly unpleasant. The group member being intimidated decides to deal effectively with the bully.

Scenario 2: A No-Person. One student plays the role of a worker with a lot of creative energy whose manager is a no-person. The energetic worker has what he or she thinks is a wonderful way for the company to generate additional revenue: conducting a garage sale of surplus equipment and furnishings. The worker presents this idea to the no-person manager, played by another student. When the manager acts true to form, the worker will attempt to overcome his or her objections.

The tactics for dealing with difficult people just described require practice to be effective. When you next encounter a difficult person, try one of the tactics that seems to fit the occasion. Role-plays, such as those presented in Skill-Building Exercise 11-7, are a good starting point for employing the appropriate tactic in dealing with difficult people.

Access the eText in MySearchLab to learn more about this chapter's self-assessment quizzes.

To Watch Explore Practice Study and Review, visit **MySearchLab**

SKILLS FOR MOTIVATING AND HELPING OTHERS   245

Developing Your Human Relations Skills and Reinforcing Concepts

Summary ✓ Practice Glossary Flashcards

- Motivation is an internal state that leads to effort being expended toward achieving objectives and to an activity performed by one person to get another person to work.
- Theories of how to motivate others include
  - the "What's in it for me?" (WIIFM) principle: People can be motivated through their self-interest.
  - behaviour modification, a theory and technique that changes behaviour by using positive reinforcement and punishments: Recognition is a powerful motivator.
  - expectancy theory of motivation: People are decision makers who choose among alternatives by selecting the one that appears to have the biggest personal payoff at the time.
- Mentors nurture and help others by sponsoring, coaching, protecting, sharing challenging assignments, and acting as a referral agent.
- Dealing with difficult people is a major challenge in helping others. Tactics for dealing with them include staying calm, giving ample feedback, criticizing constructively, helping the difficult person feel more confident, using tact and diplomacy, using humour, working out a deal, reinforcing civil behaviour and good moods, and asking the person to "THINK" before speaking.

Interpersonal Relations Case 11-1

On Time at Prime Time

Prime Time Furniture is a manufacturer and distributor of inexpensive, ready-to-assemble furniture for the home and small business, including home-based businesses. Among its products are bookcases, television stands, computer workstations, and kitchen tables. Some of the higher-end products are manufactured at the Wisconsin factory and distribution centre. The vast majority of products, however, are imported from Malaysia and then placed in the distribution centre until sold.

Demand for ready-to-assemble furniture has increased steadily as more people are looking for ways to reduce household expenses. To meet the increased demand, more companies have entered the field, making the business more competitive and therefore reducing prices.

Eton Westin, the distribution centre manager, searches continuously for ways to make the centre more efficient. During a two-hour productivity meeting with supervisors, Westin learned that employee lateness is costing Prime Time a lot of money. Ashley Novak explained the problem in these terms:

"We are short-handed as it is. When an employee is late it makes it more difficult to ship on time. We have learned the hard way that when we do not ship on time, we lose some business. A big part of our business now comes from online sales through Amazon and other resellers. These outfits promise rapid delivery, and when we don't ship on time, we get heat from both the resellers and the end customers." (The resellers inform the end customer that Prime Time Furniture is the source of the furniture.)

Jimmy Gerber, the director of administration and human resources, said he had an idea for improving punctuality that has worked in other companies. The program is set up by a company specializing in performance improvement. Gerber then outlined the basics of the program.

"We run a punctuality race with each department being represented by a horse, assigned a name by the department. The consulting company sets up the race with their own software, and we visit our race website any time we want. The setup looks like a video game. You can see graphically the relative positions of the horses as they run the 'punctuality race.'"

"Every time a worker arrives on time, that fact is entered into the database, and the department's horse gets two points. Every time a worker is late the department's horse is penalized two points. Coming back from breaks on time earns one point, and coming back late is a one-point penalty. Leaving work, or leaving early, also follows the same one-point value."

"At the end of each month, the points are totalled. The team with the winning horse can then convert the points into gifts from a catalogue or gift certificates to a few selected restaurants."

Westin asked the group for their opinion on the horse race to improve punctuality. "I'm a little concerned," he said. "Isn't this too childlike? I mean, running a horse race for coming to work on time. Let's get real."

"With due respect, Eton," said Liz Lopez, the shipping supervisor, "adults are motivated by games and small prizes. We are all children at heart, even Prime Time employees."

Case Questions

1. What do you predict will be the outcome of the horse-race motivation program if implemented?
2. Which approach, or approaches, to motivating people does this horse-race program represent?
3. What other program for improving punctuality might you recommend?

Interpersonal Relations Case 11-2

The Nightmare in the Logistics Department

Larry Smits was happy to join the distribution department of his company as a logistics specialist. His position centred on keeping track of shipments to customers and from vendors. A distribution specialist works extensively with computers to track shipments, but part of the job description involves telephone and face-to-face contact with company insiders and outsiders.

Larry enthusiastically explained his new job to his girlfriend: "Here's a great opportunity for me. I'll be using a sophisticated software system, and I'll have lots of contact with a variety of people. I'll be talking to marketing executives, purchasing agents, truckers, package-delivery people, and office assistants. Equally good, I'll be learning about a very important part of the business. If the company doesn't ship goods to customers, we can't collect money. And if we don't receive shipments of supplies that we need, we can't produce anything ourselves."

During the first four months on the job, Larry's enthusiasm continued. The job proved to be as exciting as he had anticipated. Larry got along well with all his co-workers and developed his closest friendship with Rudy Bianchi, a senior distribution specialist. Rudy said that since he had several more years of experience than Larry, he would be willing to help him with any job problem he encountered. One day Larry took Rudy up on his offer. Larry was having a little difficulty understanding how to verify the accuracy of tariffs paid to several European countries. Part of Larry's job was to make sure the company was paying its fair share of tariffs, but no more than necessary. Larry sent Rudy an email message asking for clarification on three tariff questions. Rudy answered promptly and provided Larry with useful information.

When Larry next saw Rudy in person during lunch, he thanked him again for the technical assistance. "No problem," said Rudy. "I told you that I'm always willing to help a buddy. By sharing knowledge, we multiply our effectiveness." Larry detected a trace of insincerity in Rudy's message but later thought he might be overreacting to Rudy's colourful way of expressing himself.

Several days later Larry was reviewing a work assignment with his supervisor, Ellie Wentworth. She said to him, "How are you coming along with the problems you were having understanding how to verify tariffs? That's a key part of your job, you know."

Larry explained to Ellie that he wasn't having any real problems, but that he had asked for clarification on a couple of complicated rates. He also pointed out that he quickly obtained the clarification he needed. Larry thought to himself, "Oh, I guess Ellie must have misinterpreted a comment by Rudy about my clarifying a few tariff rates with him. I doubt Rudy would have told our boss that I was having trouble. Why should I be paranoid?"

One week later Rudy stopped by Larry's cubicle. At the moment, Larry had the classified ad section of the *Globe and Mail* on his desk. "Are you job hunting, Larry? You're a rising star in our department. Why look elsewhere?"

"I'm not job hunting," said Larry. "I was just curious to see what kind of demand exists for logistics specialists. It's just part of my interest in the field. It's reassuring to know we're part of a growing profession."

"That's a great answer," said Rudy. "I was just pulling your chain a little anyway."

A week later Ellie was reviewing some work assignments with Larry. As the discussion about the work assignment was completed, Ellie said, "I think highly of how you're progressing in your job, Larry, but I want to make sure of one thing. Before we give you another major assignment, I want to know if you're happy in your job. If for any reason you are planning to leave the company, please let us know now."

"What are you talking about?" said Larry with a puzzled expression. "I intend to be with the company for a long, long time. I can't imagine what gave you the impression that I am not happy here."

As Larry left the office, he was furious. He began to wonder if someone might be spreading malicious rumours about him. He muttered silently, "It couldn't be Rudy. He's supposed to be my friend, my mentor. But I have to get to the root of this problem. I feel like I'm being sabotaged."

Case Questions

1. What devious technique might Rudy, or another co-worker, be using against Larry?
2. What motivation might a co-worker have for raising questions about Larry's job knowledge and loyalty to the company?
3. How should Larry deal with his suspicions?
4. How effectively has Ellie dealt with her two concerns about Larry?

Questions for Discussion and Review

Practice Chapter Quiz

Multiple Choice

1. A good example of positive reinforcement in the workplace would be
   a. giving an employee a mug for a new idea that saves the company money.
   b. giving an employee an extra day off for an idea that saves the company money.
   c. giving an employee a plaque for an idea to increase sales.
   d. none of the above, as reinforcers vary among people and not all rewards are reinforcers.
2. In expectancy theory, valence refers to
   a. the worth or attractiveness of a given outcome.
   b. the effort required to obtain a given outcome.
   c. the outcome itself which is called a valence.
   d. the task.
3. A nurturing person
   a. babies co-workers as would a parent.
   b. promotes the growth of others in the workplace.
   c. dwells on the negative.
   d. none of the above
4. All of the following are characteristics of an effective mentor except:
   a. Provides friendship
   b. Gives support and encouragement
   c. Is a superior to the person being mentored
   d. Encourages continuous learning
5. A recommended strategy to deal with a difficult person in the workplace is to
   a. help the person feel more confident.
   b. ignore the person when he or she is behaving badly.
   c. report the person to your superior immediately.
   d. insult the person right back when the person hurls an insult at you.

Short Answer

6. For what purpose would someone need to motivate his or her supervisor?
7. If people really live by the WIIFM principle, how can a leader still achieve teamwork?
8. How do individual differences show themselves in attempting to motivate others?
9. What is your opinion on whether workers have a responsibility to help each other grow and develop?
10. Open your MySearchLab and click on the case simulation "Motivating Others." Work through the scenario about a business person and his manager answering the case questions at the end. When you have completed these questions, what was your most significant learning after completing this case?

Answers to multiple choice questions: 1. d,   2. a,   3. b,   4. c,   5. a.

The Web Corner

www.zeromillion.com
Search for "Positive Reinforcement in the Workplace."

http://lmiworks.ca/CareerGuide/resources/JobShadowingAndMentoring.pdf
Job shadowing as a form of mentoring

www.bluesuitmom.com/career/management/difficultpeople.html
Strategies for dealing with difficult people

www.bbll.com/ch26.html
A chapter from the web "book" *Lessons in Lifemanship* about motivating others

Internet Skill Builder: Motivating Other People

Visit www.nelson-motivation.com to watch a five-minute video clip of one of Bob Nelson's talks. After watching, answer the following questions: (1) What have I learned that I could translate into a skill motivating other people as well as employees? (2) Which theory, or approach, to motivation does Nelson emphasize in his presentation?

MySearchLab

Visit **MySearchLab** to find self-grading review quizzes in the eText, discipline-specific media and readings, access to a variety of academic journals, and Associated Press news feeds, along with a wide range of writing, grammar, and research tools and to help hone writing and research skills.

CHAPTER 12
Positive Political Skills

Todd Averett is director of global supply chain design and sourcing at Payless ShoeSource, the largest family footwear dealer in the Western Hemisphere. The official name of the company is now Collective Brands, Inc. Averett wrote the following about the importance of organizational citizenship behaviour at his company:

> Most organizational leaders, when asked, would say they prefer to staff their organizations with individuals who are good "organizational citizens"—individuals who go above and beyond the call of duty. In recent years Payless ShoeSource has strived

Robert Kneschke/Fotolia

LEARNING Objectives

After reading and studying this chapter and doing the exercises, you should be able to

1. Explain the importance of political skill and social intelligence for becoming skilled at using positive political tactics.
2. Manage effectively the impression you give, including developing an awareness of the rules of business etiquette.
3. Implement political techniques for building relationships with managers and other key people.
4. Implement political techniques for building relationships with co-workers and other worker associates.
5. Avoid committing political blunders.

to develop a culture that focuses on principles and values related to organizational citizenship. At Payless, this focus began with the realization at the executive level that to reach our full potential as an organization, the hearts and minds of our Associates had to be fully engaged in achieving common goals. For Payless, a retailer in a competitive market, this meant moving from a culture of "results at all costs" to a culture driven by "Guiding Values." These Guiding Values are: personal accountability, risk taking and innovation, teamwork, change, and open communication. To change the culture, Payless had to convince employees to let go of longstanding norms and accept, on faith, that living the Guiding Values would bring greater success for both the company and themselves.

Similar to Payless's Guiding Values, the essence of organizational citizenship is employee behaviour that goes above and beyond the call of duty. Perhaps more importantly, these behaviours represent, or are the manifestations of, beliefs that individuals have about their roles at work.[1]

The comments by the learning and development director at Payless Shoes emphasize one of the themes of this chapter: Organizational citizenship behaviour helps the company, and is also good organizational politics because such behaviour helps you develop a solid relationship with your manager and co-workers. The proper use of positive political tactics helps build good interpersonal relationships. In turn, these good relationships can facilitate achieving career goals. Recognize, however, that being competent in your job is still the most effective method of achieving career success. After skill come hard work and luck as important success factors.

A fourth ingredient is also important for success—positive political skills. Few people can achieve success for themselves or their group without having some awareness of the political forces around them and how to use them to advantage. It may be necessary for the career-minded person to take the offensive in using positive and ethical political tactics. As used here, **organizational politics** refers to gaining power through any means other than merit or luck. (Luck, of course, is what happens when preparation meets opportunity.) Politics are played to achieve power, either directly or indirectly. **Power** refers to the ability or potential to control anything of value and to influence decisions. The results of such power may take diverse forms like being promoted, being transferred, receiving a salary increase, or avoiding an uncomfortable assignment.

Organizational politics can also be regarded from the standpoint of interpersonal relationships and sizing up the environment. As described by author and speaker Donna Cardillo, office politics refers to understanding the unwritten rules of the workplace that involve getting along with others, getting recognized for one's efforts, and following the protocol of how things get accomplished.[2]

organizational politics
Interpersonal relations in the workplace by which power is gained or held through any means other than merit or luck.

power
The ability or potential to control anything of value and to influence decisions.

FIGURE 12-1 Relationship among politics, power, and influence

Political tactics, such as developing contacts with key people, lead to power, which enables one to control and influence others.

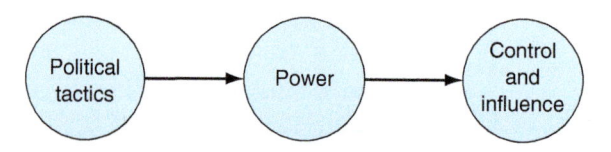

Political tactics → Power → Control and influence

As you study this chapter, it will become evident that communication skills and team player skills are necessary for being skilled at politics. Figure 12-1 depicts the relationship among politics, power, and control and influence. Political tactics, such as developing contacts with key people, lead to power, which enables one to control and influence others.

In this chapter, we approach skill development in organizational (or office) politics from several standpoints. Information is presented about such topics as managing the impression you make, using political tactics to improve interpersonal relationships, and avoiding hazardous political mistakes. To measure your current tendencies toward playing politics, do Self-Assessment Quiz 12-1.

Explore
Organizational Politics Questionnaire

SELF-ASSESSMENT QUIZ 12-1

Organizational Politics Questionnaire

Directions: Answer each question "Mostly Agree" or "Mostly Disagree," even if it is difficult for you to decide which alternative best describes your opinion.

		Mostly Agree	Mostly Disagree
1.	The boss or team leader is always right.	_____	_____
2.	It is wise to flatter important people.	_____	_____
3.	If you do somebody a favour, remember to cash in on it.	_____	_____
4.	Given the opportunity, I would cultivate friendships with powerful people.	_____	_____
5.	I would be willing to say nice things about a rival to get that person transferred from my department.	_____	_____
6.	If it would help me get ahead, I would take credit for someone else's work.	_____	_____
7.	Given the chance, I would offer to help my boss build some shelves for his or her den.	_____	_____
8.	I laugh heartily at my boss's humour, even if I do not think it is funny.	_____	_____
9.	Dressing for success is silly. At work, wear clothing that you find to be the most comfortable.	_____	_____
10.	Never waste lunchtime by eating with somebody who can't help you solve a problem or gain advantage.	_____	_____
11.	I think using email to zap somebody for his or her mistakes, and sending copies to key people, is a good idea.	_____	_____
12.	If somebody higher up in the organization offends you, look for ways to get even with him or her.	_____	_____
13.	Honesty is the best policy, even if it means insulting somebody.	_____	_____
14.	Power for its own sake is one of life's most precious commodities.	_____	_____
15.	If I had a legitimate gripe against my employer, I would air my views publicly (for instance, distributing my comments over the Internet).	_____	_____

16. I would invite my boss or team leader to a party at my home even if I didn't like him or her. _____ _____
17. An effective way to impress people is to tell them what they want to hear. _____ _____
18. Having a high school or skyscraper named after me would be an incredible thrill. _____ _____
19. Hard work and good performance are usually sufficient for career success. _____ _____
20. Even if I made only a minor contribution to a project, I would get my name listed as being associated with it. _____ _____
21. I would never publicly correct mistakes made by my boss or team leader. _____ _____
22. I would never use my personal contacts to gain a promotion. _____ _____
23. If you happen to dislike a person who receives a big promotion in your firm, don't bother sending that person a congratulatory note. _____ _____
24. I would never openly criticize a powerful executive in my organization. _____ _____
25. I would stay late in the office just to impress my boss or team leader. _____ _____

Scoring and Interpretation: Give yourself a +1 for each answer you gave in agreement with the keyed answer. Note that we did not use the term *correct* answer. Whether an answer is correct is a question of personal values and ethics. Each question that receives a score of +1 shows a tendency toward playing organizational politics. The scoring key is as follows:

1. Mostly agree
2. Mostly agree
3. Mostly agree
4. Mostly agree
5. Mostly agree
6. Mostly agree
7. Mostly agree
8. Mostly agree
9. Mostly disagree
10. Mostly agree
11. Mostly agree
12. Mostly disagree
13. Mostly disagree
14. Mostly agree
15. Mostly disagree
16. Mostly agree
17. Mostly agree
18. Mostly agree
19. Mostly disagree
20. Mostly agree
21. Mostly agree
22. Mostly disagree
23. Mostly disagree
24. Mostly agree
25. Mostly agree

In an earlier version of this test, based on a sample of 750 men and women managers, professionals, administrators, sales representatives, and business owners, the mean score was 10. Scores of 1 through 7 suggest a below-average tendency to play politics. Scores between 8 and 12 suggest an average tendency to play office politics. Scores of 13 and above suggest an above-average tendency to play office politics and a strong need for power.

Sources: Andrew J. DuBrin, "Career Maturity, Organizational Rank, and Political Behavior Tendencies: A Correlational Analysis of Organizational Politics and Career Experience," *Psychological Reports*, 63 (1988), pp. 531–37; DuBrin, "Sex Differences in Endorsement of Influence Tactics and Political Behavior Tendencies," *Journal of Business and Psychology*, Fall 1989, pp. 3–14.

POLITICAL SKILL AND OTHER HUMAN RELATIONS SKILLS

Political skill does not stand alone, separated from other human relations skills. Here we look at how political skill relates to awareness of one's surroundings, emotional intelligence and social intelligence, relationship building with the leader, and coping with an unjust environment.

LEARNING OBJECTIVE 1

Sensitivity to Your Surroundings

For starters, being sensitive to your surroundings and to other people helps make you politically aware. Cultural sensitivity, as described in Chapter 8 about cross-cultural relations and diversity, is a specific type of sensitivity to one's surroundings that deals with sizing up the cultural environment.

Imagine that you are applying for a position at Research In Motion (RIM) doing exactly the kind of work you want. You have seen photos of RIM employees, and you visited its headquarters before your interview just to see what the company looks like. No RIM worker including the founders is ever seen in a business suit, yet this fact escapes you. You show up for your interview wearing a business suit and leather shoes as if you were applying for a position as an investment banker trainee at a Wall Street firm. Zap, you're done. The RIM employees wearing jeans, casual shirts and blouses, and running shoes think you would be a poor cultural fit despite your intelligence and talent. You were not sensitive enough to the environment to choose the appropriate attire for you interview.

Monkey Business/Fotolia

Emotional Intelligence and Social Intelligence

Political skill relates to emotional intelligence because you need to be able to read the emotions of others to establish rapport with them. For example, a person with good emotional intelligence would ask for a raise when the boss appeared to be in a good mood. Also, the person would avoid asking for a raise when the boss was upset, preoccupied, and in an ugly mood.

Political skill is also directly related to **social intelligence**, an understanding of how relationships with bosses and colleagues, family, and friends shape our brains and affect our bodies. Social intelligence is a book-length subject, yet we can take away a couple of basic lessons that are linked to positive political skill.[3] Social intelligence tells us that good relationships act like vitamins, energizing us to perform well. In contrast, bad relationships are like poison that undermines our cognitive efficiency and creativity. The person with good social intelligence would work at having positive relationships with others on the job, so as to being able to concentrate on the task and perform well.

social intelligence
An understanding of how relationships with bosses and colleagues, family, and friends shape our brains and affect our bodies.

Another aspect of having social intelligence would be to recognize that being arrogant or derisive toward others can cause emotional distress that impairs the brain's ability to learn and think clearly. So a good team player or a manager would relate more positively toward others in order to help attain a productive workplace.

CEO Steve Bennett of Intuit exemplifies a manager who deliberately practises social intelligence. For instance, he gives constructive criticism but avoid angry attacks. During one meeting, he criticized a senior manager who was dominating a meeting even though the subject was not his field of expertise. Bennett attempted to criticize him in a joking way rather than being hostile.[4]

Relationship Building with the Leader

A major purpose of organizational politics including political skill is to develop good relationships with your superior, as described later in this chapter. More specifically, strong political skills can help you develop a higher-quality leader–member exchange (LMX). A new study suggests that having good political skills can help a person develop a positive LMX even when the two parties are demographically different. Previous research had shown that LMXs tend to be more positive when the leader and group member are demographically similar, such as being the same sex or race, or similar in age.

The study in question involved 189 participants in a retail service organization. Seventy-six percent of the sample were white (Caucasian), and 56 percent were women. The average age of participants was 30. Participants took a self-administered political skill inventory that measured their interpersonal skills such as ease of communication, sincerity, and relationship-building skills. Political skill was shown to improve relationships with racially dissimilar leaders and group members (better LMX scores). It was also found that the quality of the LMX was not due to gender or age.

The researchers concluded that political skill enables subordinates who are racially dissimilar to their co-workers to get around the potential relationship problems based on these differences.[5]

Overcoming the Effects of Injustice

To illustrate further the positive impact of political skill, some evidence suggests that having political skill can help overcome the effects of unfairness in the organization. The study in question was a government agency, and two types of justices were measured by questionnaires—procedural and distributive. Procedural justice is the perceived fairness of the policies and procedures used to make decisions. Distributive justice is how fairly outcomes or rewards are distributed based on these procedures, such as receiving a deserved salary increase. Political skill was measured by the political skill inventory mentioned above, and job performance was measured by supervisory ratings of performance.

The study found that under conditions of injustice, political skill was associated with high performance. Highly politically skilled workers were rated similarly regardless of the level of distributive justice. In other words, having good political skill helped overcome the effects of low justice. Another finding was that under conditions of injustice, low political skill is harmful to performance ratings.[6] You need political skills to help combat an unfair system.

IMPRESSION MANAGEMENT AND ETIQUETTE

Being an effective, responsible contributor is not always sufficient to gain you the attention you deserve. It may also be necessary to make others aware of your capabilities. **Impression management** is a set of behaviours directed at improving one's image by drawing attention to oneself. Often the attention is directed toward superficial aspects of the self, such as clothing and appearance. Impression management also includes telling people about your accomplishments and appearing self-confident. Our presentation of impression management includes a listing of specific tactics and a discussion of business etiquette.

LEARNING OBJECTIVE 2

impression management

A set of behaviours directed at improving one's image by drawing attention to oneself.

Tactics of Impression Management

Managing the impression you create encompasses dozens of specific tactics, limited only by what you imagine will impress others. Part of your power in the organization stems from your formal position, as well as how you are perceived by others. Creating the right image is the practice of impression management.[7]

Although impression management can be used in a variety of relationships, it is most commonly found in the attempt of a worker to please the manager. For example, impression management is frequently used during performance evaluation in order to impress the manager with the worker's accomplishments. Six positive tactics of impression management are described next.

Display Organizational Citizenship Behaviour. We mention organizational citizenship behaviour in several places in our study of human relations because of its contribution to effective interpersonal relationships. A highly effective and meritorious way of creating a good impression is to step outside your job description to help co-workers and the company. You become admired for going beyond the call of duty.[8] Organizational citizenship behaviour is generally aimed at helping others, yet it is possible that the motive underlying citizenship behaviour is to foster a good impression. A prime example is that volunteering for special assignments helping others may provide workers with an opportunity to show off their talents and knowledge, leading to an enhanced image.

Impression management theorists argue that a primary human motive is to be viewed positively by others, and to avoid being viewed negatively. Engaging in organizational citizenship behaviour is an effective means of being viewed positively in the sense of having positive motives for engaging in constructive behaviours, such as collecting relief funds for a co-worker whose apartment burned down.

Whether or not organizational citizenship behaviour has an element of trying to look good, the balance of evidence is that citizenship behaviour helps both individuals and the organization. Based on 168 studies involving more than 50,000 workers, it was found that organizational citizenship behaviour helped individuals receive better performance ratings and salary increases. Organizations benefited in such ways higher productivity, lowered costs, and better customer service.[9]

BACK TO THE OPENING CASE

Todd Averett and other managers at Payless ShoeSource have continued to emphasize the importance of organizational citizenship behaviour as a corporate value. One of many positive consequences is that the employees build good relationships with managers, and are satisfied with their good working conditions. Employee turnover is low by industry standards, and profits are high.

Build Trust and Confidence. A key strategy for creating a positive impression with your immediate superior and higher ranking managers is to build trust and confidence. Project the authentic impression of a person who can be trusted to carry out responsibilities faithfully and ethically. Rather than take action without permission (e.g., spending beyond budget), know the bounds of your authority and work within those bounds. Be aware that your boss has other responsibilities, so do not take more than your fair share of his or her time. You will generate an impression of confidence if you suggest alternative solutions to the problems you bring to your manager.[10]

Be Visible and Create a Strong Presence. An essential part of impression management is to be perceived as a valuable contributor on the job. Visibility is attained in many ways, such as regular attendance at meetings and company social events, being assigned to important projects, and doing volunteer work in the community. Helping in the launch of a new product or redesigning work methods are other ways of attaining visibility and creating a strong presence. Face-to-face visibility is perhaps the best, but electronic visibility can also be effective. This includes making intelligent contributions to company intranets and blogs, and sending email messages of substance to the right people. Saying nice things about your company on social networking sites is valuable also. Terry Bragg observes that many employees are shocked to learn that they lost their jobs during a downsizing because upper management did not know that they were valuable contributors.[11]

Admit Mistakes. Many people believe that to create a good impression, it is best to deny or cover up mistakes. In this way, you will not appear vulnerable. A higher level of political skill is to admit mistakes, thereby appearing more forthright and trustworthy. The simple statement "I goofed" will often gain you sympathy and support, whereas an attempted cover up will decrease your social capital. For purposes of impression management, the bottom line of being wrong is to (a) admit the error, (b) request guidance, (c) step up repair, and (d) learn from it.[12] Requesting guidance is important because it conveys the impression that you have humility and that you trust the advice and counsel of others. Here is an example of this tactic in action:

> *Cindy, a call centre operator, is listening on the phone to a woman rant and rave about a $5.87 charge on her credit card that seems unwarranted. Thinking that she has the telephone receiver covered, Cindy says in a sigh of exasperation to a co-worker, "I'm about to scream. I'm talking to the biggest jerk of year right now." Unfortunately "the biggest jerk of the year" heard the comment and reported it to Cindy's supervisor.*
>
> *During a review of the incident with her supervisor, Cindy said, "Yes indeed, I made the comment," and then asked how to deal with the pressures of such an overreacting customer. Cindy offered to send a written apology to the customer. So far, Cindy has learned from her error and not repeated the incident.*

Minimize Being a Yes-Person. A conventional view of organizational politics suggests that being a yes-person is an excellent way of developing a good relationship with higher-ups, and generating the impression of a loyal and supportive subordinate. The yes-person operates on the principle "The boss is always right." Often the boss cultivates yes-person behaviour among subordinates by being intimidating, and unapproachable.[13] When working for an emotionally secure and competent manager, you are likely to create a better impression by not agreeing with all the boss's ideas and plans. Instead, express constructive disagreement by explaining how the boss's plan might be enhanced, or an error might be avoided.

> *Assume that you work in the marketing department of Jitterbug, a simplified cell phone that focuses on the senior market. Your boss suggests an advertising theme suggesting that even people with arthritis and who are technically challenged can easily operate a Jitterbug. Your intuition tells you this theme would be a humiliating insult to seniors. So you respond to your boss, "I know that Jitterbug targets seniors, but I suggest that we tone down the terms "arthritis" and "technically challenged." Why not be positive and state that the keys are easy to manipulate, and that the Jitterbug is as easy to operate as a landline phone?"*

Create a Healthy Image. A superficial yet important part of impression management is to project a healthy, physically fit appearance. Appearing physically fit in the workplace has gained in importance as many business firms offer workers rewards for being physically fit and avoiding smoking and obesity. Among the rewards offered by employers are electronic gadgets, discounted health insurance, and cash bonuses. At IBM Corp., employees get as much as $300 annually for exercising regularly, quitting smoking, or logging on to the company's preventive-care website.[14] The fitness centre at IBM Canada's new software lab in Markham is one of the most popular amenities with its 2500 employees and a key selling point for recruiting new talent, says Deborah Earley, Human Resources Manager. The doors of the Active Blue fitness centre officially swung open for business in early October 2001, and they haven't stopped swinging since.[15] Canada Life Assurance is an example of a company that has embraced health and fitness and its benefits for employees. After 23 years Canada Life's award-winning "Life in Action" program continues to thrive with over 30 percent of its 1800 employees actively participating. The 560-square-metre facility provides a hub for their comprehensive fitness and wellness programs.[16]

Projecting an image of emotional fitness also contributes to a healthy image. *Emotional fitness* would include such behaviours as appearing relaxed, appropriate laughing and smiling, and a minimum of nervous mannerisms and gestures. Being physically fit helps project emotional fitness. When managing the impression you create, be mindful of the advice offered by William L. Gardner III: Be yourself. When selecting an image, do not attempt to be somebody you are not, because people will see through this. Gardner concludes, "Make every effort to put your best foot forward—but never at the cost of your identity or integrity!"[17] Impression management is geared toward looking good, but not creating a false impression.

You need good political skills to be effective at impression management. A study of 204 employees working on environmental issues indicated that when employees with good political skill use impression management tactics, they are likely to receive higher job performance ratings from their supervisor. In contrast, individuals low in political skill who engage in impression management tend to be seen less positively by their supervisors.[18] In other words, you need a little finesse and sensitivity to people to be good at office politics.

Another essential part of impression management is to avoid creating a negative impression through such behaviours as being absent or late frequently, speaking poorly, or talking in a meeting while the presenter is speaking. The discussion of etiquette helps guide a person away from behaviours that would bring him or her negative attention.

Skill-Building Exercise 12-1 gives you an opportunity to try out a highly practical application of impression management.

SKILL-BUILDING EXERCISE 12-1

The Elevator 30-Second Speech

A long-standing suggestion in career development and impressing higher-ups is to make a 30-second impromptu presentation when you have a chance encounter with a key person in your organization. If you work in an office tower, the chance encounter is likely to take place in an elevator—and it is generally frowned upon to have long conversations in an elevator. So the term *elevator speech* developed to describe a brief opportunity to impress a key person. Imagine that you have a chance encounter with a high-ranking executive in your area on the elevator, escalator, parking lot, or during a company picnic, or some other location. You then give that person a 30-second pitch geared to make a positive impression. Because you must boil your pitch down to 30 seconds, you will need to prepare for a long time.

About six different pairs (impresser and person to be impressed) will carry out this role-play in front of the class. The evaluators will put themselves in the role of the key person who was the target of the 30-second evaluation. Consider using the following scale, and answering the two questions:

_____ Wow, I was impressed. (5 points)
_____ I was kind of impressed with the person I ran into. (4 points)
_____ He or she left me with at least an average impression. (3 points)
_____ I found the person to be somewhat annoying. (2 points)
_____ That person I met left with a terrible impression. (1 point)

1. What did I like about person's 30-second pitch?
2. What did I see as possible areas for improvement?

Find a mechanism to feed back some of your observations to the role-players. Volunteer to present the findings in class, give the person your comments on notepaper, or send him or her an email or text message.

Business Etiquette

business etiquette
A special code of behaviour required in work situations.

▶ Watch
Business Lunch Etiquette

A major component of managing your impression is practising good etiquette. **Business etiquette** is a special code of behaviour required in work situations. The term *manners* has an equivalent meaning. Both manners and etiquette generally refer to behaving in a refined and acceptable manner. Jim Rucker and Anna Sellers explain that business etiquette is much more than knowing how to use the correct utensil or how to dress in a given situation. Business people today must know how to be at ease with strangers and with groups, be able to offer congratulations smoothly, know how to make introductions, and know how to conduct themselves at company social functions. Studying etiquette is important because knowing and using proper business etiquette contributes to individual and business success.[19]

People who are considerate of the feelings of others, and companies that are courteous toward customers, are more likely to succeed than their rude counterparts. Another perspective on etiquette is that it is a way of presenting yourself with the kind of polish that shows you can be taken seriously. So many people are rude and uncivil today that practising good etiquette will often give you a competitive advantage.[20]

Business etiquette includes many aspects of interpersonal relations in organizations, as described in the following discussion.[21] We have already discussed in Chapter 5 several aspects of etiquette in relation to the digital workplace. What is considered proper etiquette and manners in the workplace changes over time and may vary with the situation. At one time, addressing one's superior by his or her first name was considered brash. Today it is commonplace behaviour. A sampling of etiquette guidelines is nevertheless helpful. A general principle of being considerate of the feelings of work associates is more important than any one act of etiquette or courtesy. Keep in mind, also, that you will find a few contradictory statements in writings about etiquette.

Etiquette for Work Behaviour, Including Clothing. General work etiquette includes all aspects of performing in the work environment, such as completing work on time, punctuality, being a good team player, listening to others, and following through. For instance, having the courtesy to complete a project when it is due demonstrates good manners and respect for the work of others.

Clothing might be considered part of general work behaviour. The casual standards in the information technology field, along with dress-down days, have created confusion about proper office attire. A general rule is that *casual* should not be interpreted as sloppy, such as torn jeans or a stained sweatshirt. Many companies have moved back toward emphasizing traditional business attire, such as suits for men and women. In many work situations, dressing more formally may constitute proper etiquette.

Introductions. The basic rule for introductions is to present the lower-ranking person to the higher-ranking person regardless of age or sex. "Ms. Barker [the CEO], I would like you to meet my new co-worker, Pierre Lacome." (Observe that the higher-ranking person's name is mentioned first.) If the two people being introduced are of equal rank, mention the older one first. Providing a little information about the person being introduced is considered good manners. When introducing one person to the group, present the group to the individual. "Sid Foster, this is our information systems team." When being introduced to a person, concentrate on the name and repeat it soon, thus enhancing learning. A fundamental display of good manners is to remember people's names and to pronounce them correctly. When dealing with people senior to you or of higher rank, call them by their last name and title until told otherwise. (Maybe Ms. Barker, above, will tell you "Please call me Kathy.")

It is good manners and good etiquette to remember the names of work associates to whom you are introduced, even if you see them only occasionally. If you forget the name of a person, it is better to admit this than to guess and come up with the wrong name. Just say, "I apologize, but I've forgotten your name. Tell me once more, and I won't forget."

A major change in introducing people is that men and women are now both expected to extend their right hand when being introduced. Give a firm but not overpowering handshake, and establish eye contact with the person you are greeting. However, some people are concerned about handshakes being unhygienic, so be willing to use the modern fist-to-fist light touch often used in social life. If the other person extends the fist, you do the same.

Relationships between Men and Women and between People of Different Ages. Social etiquette is based on chivalry and the gender of the person, whereas business etiquette is based on generally equal treatment for all. Women should no longer be treated differently when approaching a door, riding in an elevator, or walking in the street. According to the new rules, the person in the lead (no matter the sex or age) should proceed first and hold the door for the others following. However, a man should still follow a woman when using an escalator. When using stairs, a man usually follows a woman going up and precedes her going down. Men no longer have to walk next to the street when walking with one or two women. Correct etiquette now states that men should always walk on either side, but not in the middle of two women. Elders should still be respected, but not in such ways as holding doors open for them, helping them off with their overcoats, or getting coffee for them.

Unless you are good friends who typically hug when meeting, it is best to avoid touching others of the same or opposite sex except for a handshake. Some people believe that nonsexual touching is part of being charming and warm, yet many workers are offended when touched by another worker. The subject is controversial because public figures often drape their arms around others, and physical touching is part of the ritual of offering congratulations in sports. Of note, many athletic coaches have switched to fist-to-fist touching to say hello or offer congratulations to teenagers and young children to avoid being charged with sexually suggestive contact.

Dining. Etiquette surrounding meals involves planning for the meeting, making seating arrangements, paying the bill, tipping, using proper table manners, and appropriate drinking of alcoholic beverages. We all know not to slurp spaghetti one strand at a time, pour ketchup over sauce, or leave a 50-cent tip. Less obvious are the following guidelines:

- Arrange seating for meal meetings in advance.
- Establish with the server who will be paying the cheque.
- Place your napkin on your lap immediately after being seated.
- Bread should not be used to push food onto a fork or spoon.
- Attempt to pace your eating speed to that of others at the table.
- The wait staff, not the diners, should be responsible for moving plates around the table.
- Circulate rolls and bread to the right, not the left.
- Order an alcoholic beverage only when invited to do so by the person sponsoring the meal, and then only if he or she does. Avoid drunkenness or getting tipsy.

Working in a Cubicle. Workplace cubicles were invented by fine arts professor Bob Probst in the 1960s, and they have been praised and condemned ever since. The praise generally relates to saving the company money on office space and having more open communication. The condemnation usually relates to lack of privacy, and therefore ties in directly with workplace etiquette.

Cubicles represent a major etiquette challenge because a variety of co-workers and superiors can observe your everyday work behaviour.[22] Among the many etiquette challenges for the cubicle dweller are (a) speaking low enough into a wired phone so as not to annoy others or reveal confidential information, (b) not allowing a personal cell phone ring during the workday, (c) not displaying material on the computer that others might find offensive, unless it is business-related, (d) not wearing a sports cap indoors unless an acceptable part of the company culture, and (e) not attending to personal hygiene such as dental flossing, hair spraying, or nail clipping.

Cubicle sizes have been shrunk recently to save on company real estate. As a result, people work even closer to each other physically. The etiquette challenges just mentioned have thereby intensified, particularly with respect to invading the privacy of others.[23]

Cross-Cultural Relations. What constitutes proper etiquette may differ from culture to culture. Be alert to differences in etiquette in areas such as gift giving, dining, drinking alcoholic beverages, and when and where to discuss business. Many of these differences in customs were described in Chapter 8.

Violating these customs is poor etiquette. For example, using the index finger to point is considered rude in most Asian and Middle Eastern countries. Also, people in Middle Eastern countries tend to stand as close as two or three inches from the person with whom they are talking. To back away is interpreted as an insult. An American visitor to China nearly lost a major sale because after receiving a business card from the Chinese company representative, he stuffed it in his pocket without first carefully reading the card. Proper etiquette in China is to carefully read the giver's business card, and perhaps holding it with both hands out of respect. We emphasize again that stereotypes such as those just mentioned refer to typical behaviour and are accurate perhaps only about 70 percent of the time.

Suppose you are in doubt about the proper etiquette for any situation, and you do not have a handbook of etiquette readily available. As a substitute, observe how your host or a successful person in the group behaves.

Interacting with People with Disabilities. Many able-bodied people are puzzled by what is proper etiquette in working with people with disabilities. Be as natural and open as you can. In addition, consider these guidelines for displaying good manners when dealing with a physical disability:

- Speak directly to a person with a disability, not to the person's companion.
- Don't assume that a person with a disability needs help. If someone is struggling, ask for permission to assist.
- When talking to a person in a wheelchair, place yourself at that person's eye level.
- When speaking to a person with impaired vision; identify yourself and anyone who may be with you. Do not shout when speaking to a blind person.
- Treat a person with a disability as you would anyone else except for the differences noted in this list.[24]
- To get the attention of a deaf person, tap the person's shoulder or wave your hand. According to the Canadian Hearing Society, if the person has an interpreter, you should speak directly to the deaf person and not to the interpreter.[25]

As shown in Figure 12-2, impression management combined with managing relationships and avoiding political blunders contribute to being a more polished and successful professional worker.

Skill-Building Exercise 12-2 gives you an opportunity to practise appropriate etiquette in several situations.

FIGURE 12-2 Relationship between Positive Political Behaviours and Individual Success

Impression management, building relationships with influential people, and avoiding political blunders all contribute to being a more polished and successful professional worker

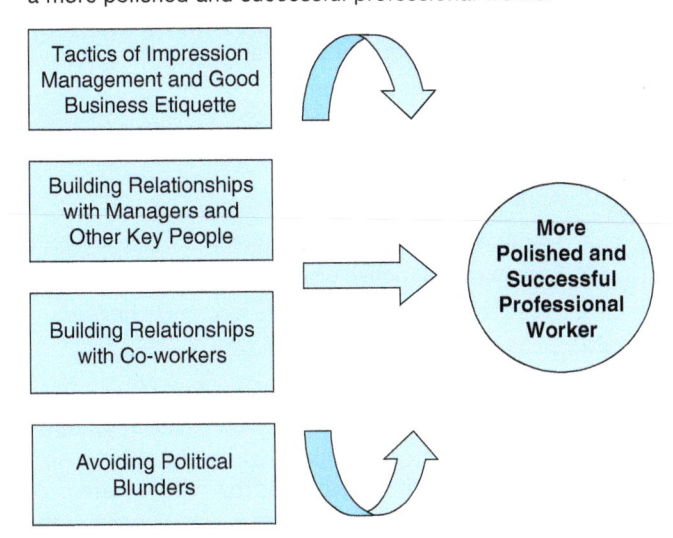

- Tactics of Impression Management and Good Business Etiquette
- Building Relationships with Managers and Other Key People
- Building Relationships with Co-workers
- Avoiding Political Blunders

→ More Polished and Successful Professional Worker

SKILL-BUILDING EXERCISE 12-2

Business Etiquette

An effective way of improving business etiquette is to be disciplined enough to use one's best manners and courtesy in real-life situations. Role-playing etiquette scenarios can also contribute to helping you develop the right mindset for using good etiquette.

Scenario 1: Dining Etiquette. A small group of students plan to conduct a high-etiquette meal at a local fast-food restaurant during non-peak hours. Pretend the plastic eating utensils are fine silver and that the Styrofoam cups are crystal. Assume that your Big Mac is Beef Wellington or that your submarine sandwich is a delicately prepared capon. Each class member uses his or her best etiquette. At the same time, each group member carefully observes the etiquette displayed by the other members.

At the conclusion of the meal, critique each other's etiquette. If you were courteous enough to invite your instructor to your high-etiquette meal, get his or her feedback.

Scenario 2: Etiquette for Communicating with a Person in a Wheelchair. One person (as a potential buyer) sits in a chair as if it were a wheelchair. The other person is to introduce themselves and conduct a five-minute conversation about the product they are selling. Other students will observe the behaviour of the salesperson as to whether the correct etiquette was used in talking to the customer. Also observe if the introduction was done well and the person has good manners.

BUILDING RELATIONSHIPS WITH MANAGERS AND OTHER KEY PEOPLE

The political purpose of building good relationships with managers is to acquire power through such means as gaining a recommendation for promotion or a key assignment. A good relationship with the boss is also important for the basic purpose of receiving a good performance evaluation. Building these good relationships with managers is also important because it helps create a positive, supportive work environment. Good relationships can also be established with managers for the nonpolitical purpose of trying to get the job accomplished. The strategies and tactics described next are outlined in Figure 12-3 and should be used on a regular basis.

LEARNING OBJECTIVE 3

Network with Influential People

A basic success strategy is developing contacts, or networking, with influential people. In addition to making contacts, networking involves gaining the trust and confidence of the

networking
Developing contacts with influential people, including gaining their trust and confidence.

POSITIVE POLITICAL SKILLS

FIGURE 12-3 Strategies and Tactics for Building Relationships with Managers and Other Key People

1. Network with influential people.
2. Help your manager succeed.
3. Understand unwritten boundaries.
4. Volunteer for assignments.
5. Flatter influential people sensibly.
6. Use information power.
7. Appear cool under pressure.
8. Laugh at your manager's humour.
9. Express constructive disagreement.
10. Present a clear picture of your accomplishments.

influential people. (Networking for job finding is described in Chapter 17.) Before you can network with influential people, you must identify the power players.[26] You might make observations of your own, such as listening for whose names are mentioned frequently by people in the company. Asking the opinions of others about which people influence decision making can be illuminating. Sometimes a person without a fancy job title might be a highly influential person. An example is that an administrative assistant might exert heavily influence the decisions of his or her boss.

Networking also takes place with people both inside and outside the organization who are not your managers. Developing contacts with influential people is likely to pay big career dividends.

A standard procedure is to create a card or computer file of the people in your network and update it frequently. To keep your network effective, it is necessary to contact people on your list periodically. Developing a network of influential people requires alertness and planning. You need to identify influential people and then think of a sensible reason to contact them. Below are several possibilities.

- Send an email message to a high-ranking manager, offering a money-saving or revenue-producing suggestion. A related tactic is to inform the person of something of significance you have done in the past that might lie directly in his or her area of interest. Social networking sites such as Facebook, LinkedIn, and Twitter can be used for networking with influential people. An influential person who joins such a site is usually open to making new contacts. (You may find, however, that many influential people are not willing to become your "friend." However, you will often be able to at least send them a message.)
- Do a standout job as a member of a task force or committee that includes a high-ranking official.
- Discuss your career plans with a neighbour who has an outstanding position.
- Take the initiative to develop a friendship with an influential person who is a member of your athletic club, other club, or place of worship.

Networking is so often used—and abused—that suggestions and guidelines for networking etiquette have emerged. A starting point is to be clear, concise, and specific when making requests of networking contacts.[27] Explain, for example, that you want to become an industry specialist and would like to acquire specific information. Be frank about the amount of time you would want from the network member, such as 15 minutes per month of email and telephone contact.

After making contact with a potential network member, explain the benefit this person is likely to derive from his or her association with you. Provide a *benefit statement* for interacting with you and helping you with your career.[28] Indicate specifically how this person might benefit from you being in his or her network. (If a person is in your network, you are also in that person's network.) If the potential network member is more powerful than you, it is still possible to think of what benefit you might be able to provide. Two examples follow:

- I would like to contact you a few times a year about career concerns. In return, I would be happy to help you identify some groups on Twitter that might be worthwhile for our company to contact.
- In return for my receiving career advice from you from time to time, I would be happy to collect information for you about how people in my area perceive one of your products. I have lots of useful contacts in my community.

Avoid being a pest. Many influential people are bombarded with requests to be part of someone's network, so ask for a modest amount of time and assistance. Good networking etiquette is to request a collaborative relationship in which you give as much as you get. The benefit statement just mentioned will place you in a collaborative relationship with the influential person.

Help Your Manager Succeed

The primary reason you are hired is to help your manager achieve the results necessary to succeed. Avoid an adversarial relationship with your manager. Determine both obvious and subtle ways of ensuring the manager's success. One subtle way of increasing your manager's chances for success is to help that person out when he or she is under attack from another department. One example of this would be to supply information to support your manager's position on a controversial issue or to publicly back your manager's position on the issue. Also keep in mind the cornerstone tactic of performing your job superbly. Your manager will then share in your success.

A specific relationship-building advantage of helping your manager succeed is that he or she is likely to develop loyalty toward you in such matters as recommending you for a bigger salary increase and giving you a better performance evaluation. And during a downsizing, you are less likely to be tapped for job loss.

Understand Unwritten Boundaries

A person skilled at positive organizational politics is able to read unwritten rules about who has the authority to do what. According to psychologist Judith Sills, there exist *unwritten boundaries*, or dividing lines of behaviour appropriate to different roles. Many workers struggle with office problems that are boundary issues in disguise. Sills observes that boundaries for office interactions are like the rope lanes in a swimming pool. The purpose of the ropes is to enhance safety, but they can be budged or even removed depending on need, skill, and circumstance.

Unwritten boundaries deal with such issues as when it is appropriate to correct your boss, how much anger to display, which influential people you can invite to a social engagement, and whose speech or appearance you can criticize. A person with an exaggerated sense of his or her worth may have trouble that a boundary exists at all, such as one woman who felt free to protest angrily when her boss changed something in her report.[29] Two other examples of unacceptable boundary crossing are (a) a man who told a vice-president that his hairpiece looked phony and (b) a woman who told her boss that she needed to upgrade her information technology skills to be a credible leader.

An example of successful boundary crossing took place when an accounts receivable specialist sent an unsolicited email to the director of marketing. The young worker said that he grew up in Mexico and would be happy to provide input for the company's plans to penetrate the Mexican market. Although the accounts receivable worker was from outside of the marketing department, he was invited to participate in a focus group about expanding into the Mexican market.

Look for indicators about whether boundaries can be crossed in your company. First, count the layers in your company's organization structure. The more layers (or more hierarchical) the company, the less welcome boundary-crossing is likely to be. Look for established border crossings. Observe where people of different rank in the company mix.

Among the possibilities are the fitness centre, the cafeteria, and after-hours drinks. Make your first attempts at border-crossing at those places.[30]

Volunteer for Assignments

An easily implemented method of winning the approval of superiors is to become a "hand-raiser." By volunteering to take on assignments that do not fit neatly into your job description, you display the kind of initiative valued by employers. Among the many possible activities to volunteer for are fundraising campaigns assigned to your company, project membership, and working overtime when most people prefer not to (e.g., on a Saturday in July). As noted under the discussion of networking, task-force assignments are also useful for being noticed by key people in the organization. As a team member, volunteer to assume any leadership responsibility you think you can handle. If your team offers rotating leadership assignments, express interest in taking your turn.

Flatter Influential People Sensibly

One of the most effective relationship builders is to flatter people sensibly and credibly. Despite the risk of being called obsequious or a cheap office politician, the flatterer wins. A study on how to advance in big business pointed out that a company's top employees tend to be equal in performance. So advancing was based on image (30 percent) and contact time with the manager (50 percent). Flattery can play a big role in both.[31] Another study indicated that even at the highest positions in business, flattery helps a person get ahead. Specifically, ingratiating oneself with the CEO, including flattery, was a major factor in receiving an appointment as a director on the board of major companies.[32] Not monitoring or negatively scrutinizing the CEO's activities also worked in a person's favour for obtaining a board appointment.[33] One might interpret not finding fault with a CEO to be a subtle form of flattery.

Flattery is likely to be effective because most people want to receive accolades, even if not completely warranted. People who pay us compliments are likely to be treated kindly in turn.[34] Remember, however, the discussion about recognition in Chapter 11, suggesting that less technically oriented people are often the most receptive to praise and flattery. Flattery geared toward the more technically oriented person might have to be more concrete and tied to specific accomplishments. Recent evidence supports the idea that constructive compliments are not overblown. Descriptions of what went right are more effective than evaluative phrases such as "magnificent" or "extraordinary." An effective, general-purpose piece of flattery is to tell another person that you are impressed by something he or she accomplished. Rather than telling an influential person that he or she is a genius, you might say to a manager after a meeting,[35] "Everyone in the meeting was listening so attentively when you gave your report. And the industry statistics you found really drove home the point."

Another way of flattering somebody is to listen attentively. If you actively listen to the other person, he or she will feel flattered. The person might think, "What I have to say is valuable. This person really cares about what I have to offer." Flattery can also take the form of quoting another person, or referring to something he or she said to you earlier.

During the next two weeks, try out the flattery tactic with an influential person. In the interim, do Skill-Building Exercise 12-3.

Use Information Power

Power accrues to those who control vital information. At the same time, being a source of useful information will help you build constructive working relationships with managers. You will be relied on as an important contributor. Controlling vital information includes knowing how to gain access to useful information that others do not know how to retrieve. Many workers are aware of the mechanics of using the Internet, but fewer have the skills to use it to retrieve commercially useful information. During a tight labour market, for example, human resources specialists can

> **SKILL-BUILDING EXERCISE 12-3**
>
> **Flattering an Influential Person**
>
> As a perceptive, intelligent reader, you have probably already guessed the nature of this role-play. One student plays the role of a newcomer to the organization who is seeking to advance, or at least to secure, his or her position in the organization. Another person plays the role of a vice-president visiting the newcomer's department. The company holds this vice-president in high esteem because he or she recently spearheaded the introduction of a highly successful product, a *smart mattress* that adjusts to the temperature and firmness requirements of its user. In some models the two sides of the mattress can have different settings to adapt to the heat and firmness preferences of two users sharing the mattress.
>
> The newcomer is asked to escort the vice-president to another part of the building. The walk should take about five minutes, giving the newcomer an opportunity to work in some flattery. Fortunately, the newcomer has read the sales literature about the smart mattress, and has even tried one out in the factory showroom. Although the vice-president is not naïve, he or she is proud of his or her accomplishments. The two role-players conduct the five-minute walk, perhaps circling the classroom.

acquire power if they know how to use the Internet to find talented people who might want to join the company.

Information power is closely related to *expert power*, which refers to having valuable expertise. If your expertise or skill is in high demand at the moment, power will flow in your direction. Currently, an important type of expert power is being able to use social networking sites to gain publicity for products (including creating a buzz for the product), and to recruit employees.

Appear Cool under Pressure

Showing signs of panic generally hurts your reputation with influential people. In contrast, appearing to be in control emotionally when things around you are falling apart helps convey the impression that you are worthy of additional responsibility. Being cool under pressure is part of emotional stability, and it is a key leadership characteristic. If you can remain calm when others are not, this will enhance your reputation. For example, a deadline was moved up for an important business presentation. The office assistant calmly assured his manager that he would have the handouts prepared for the new and tight deadline. The manager could then work on her presentation without worrying about handouts. When offered a promotion to another department, his manager cited this as an example of his ability to stay calm in a stressful situation.

Laugh at Your Manager's Humour

When you indicate by your laughter that you appreciate your manager's sense of humour, it helps establish rapport between the two of you. An indicator of good two-way communication between people is that the two parties comprehend each other's subtle points. Most humour in the workplace deals with subtle meanings about work-related topics. To implement the tactic of laughing at your manager's jokes, do not worry excessively about having heard the joke before.

Express Constructive Disagreement

At one time the office politician thought an effective way of pleasing the boss was to be a "yes-person." Whatever the supervisor thought was right, the yes-person agreed with. A more intelligent tactic in the modern business world is to be ready to disagree in a constructive manner when you sincerely believe the boss is wrong. In the long run you will probably earn more respect than if you agree with the boss just to please that person. Constructive disagreement is based on a careful analysis of the situation and is also tactful.

The right way to disagree means not putting your manager in a corner or embarrassing your manager by confronting him or her loudly or in public. If you disagree with your boss, use carefully worded, inoffensive statements. In this way you minimize the chances of a confrontation or hostile reaction. Remember the smart mattress mentioned in Skill-Building Exercise 12-3? Suppose the marketing vice-president claims that the mattress is geared exclusively toward the senior citizen market, and you disagree. You might say, "I think that marketing our smart mattress to seniors is a breakthrough. Yet I also see some other possibilities. There are loads of cold-sensitive young people who wanted a heated mattress. Also, a lot of young people with athletic injuries or orthopaedic problems would welcome an adjustable mattress. Does my thinking make any sense?"

The reason constructive disagreement helps you build a good relationship with most managers is that the boss comes to respect your job knowledge and your integrity. However, if you are working with a very insecure boss, he or she may be taken aback by disagreement. In that case, you have to be extra tactful in expressing disagreement.

Present a Clear Picture of Your Accomplishments

"What have you done for me lately?" is a question on the minds of many managers. To the extent that you can clearly document what you have accomplished recently, as well as in the past, you are therefore likely to enhance your relationship with your manager. You can help your manager better understand your contributions by explaining exactly what work you are doing, problems you are solving, and the successes you are attaining. Document legitimately what you have accomplished, and communicate it in a factual, matter-of-fact manner. The occasional FYI email provides useful documentation, provided you do not seem to be bragging.[36] A collection agent might report to her boss, "In March, I collected an average of $310 from my block of delinquent accounts. So far, I have collected at least something from 25 out of the 31 accounts I am currently assigned. We should be getting something from three more of these delinquent accounts."

BUILDING RELATIONSHIPS WITH CO-WORKERS AND OTHER WORK ASSOCIATES

LEARNING OBJECTIVE 4

Another strategy for increasing your power is to form alliances with co-workers and other work associates. You need the support of these people to get your work accomplished. Also, when you are being considered for promotion, co-workers and other work associates may be asked their opinion of you. Under a peer-evaluation system, the opinion of co-workers about your performance counts heavily. Long-term research conducted by Tom Rath of the Gallup Organization with many thousands of employees emphasizes the contribution of friendships and alliances in the workplace. Rath concludes that employees who have a best friend in the office are more productive and more likely to have positive interactions with customers, share ideas, and stay longer on the job. Also, many workers succeed or fail based on the support and involvement of best friends.[37] (The term *best* appears to imply that the contact is not simply an acquaintance or someone on your contact list on a social networking website.)

Another perspective on the importance of cooperation in the workplace is that cooperation enhances happiness and satisfaction. Long-term research by the University of Haifa psychology professor Richard Schuster says that it is natural for humans, as well as other animals, to want to cooperate. Schuster posits that evolution has prodded us toward enjoying the company of other people, and toward cooperation. He adds that social behaviour is its own reward.[38]

Figure 12-4 lists eight strategies and techniques for developing good interpersonal relationships at or below your level. The information about developing teamwork skills presented in Chapter 6 is also relevant here.

Maintain Honest and Open Relationships

Although being honest may appear to contradict organizational politics, it is representative of the nature of positive politics. Giving co-workers frank but tactful answers

FIGURE 12-4 **Strategies and Tactics for Developing Relationships with Co-workers and Other Work Associates**

1. Maintain honest and open relationships.
2. Make others feel important.
3. Be diplomatic.
4. Exchange favours.
5. Ask advice.
6. Share constructive gossip.
7. Minimize microinequities.
8. Follow group norms.

to their requests for your opinion is one useful way of developing open relationships. Assume that a co-worker asks your opinion of an email he intends to send to his supervisor. As you read it, you find it somewhat incoherent and filled with spelling and grammatical errors. An honest response to this message might be: "I think your idea is a good one. But I think your email needs more work before that idea comes across clearly."

Accurately expressing your feelings, whether positive or negative, also leads to constructive relationships. If you have been singled out for good performance, let other team members know that you are happy and proud. If you arrive at work upset over a personal problem and appearing obviously fatigued, you can expect some reaction. A co-worker might say, "What seems to be the problem? Is everything all right?" A dishonest reply would be, "Everything is fine." In addition to making an obviously untrue statement, you would also be perceived as rejecting the person who asked the question. If you prefer not to discuss your problem, an honest response would be, "Thanks for your interest. I am facing some problems today. But I think things will work out."

Another advantage of honest and open relationships is that they foster collaboration, which improves teamwork and organizational performance. When John Thain was the chairman and chief of Merrill Lynch & Co., he said, "Fostering teamwork, collaboration, and cross-selling enable us to generate innovations and ideas to give us the best competitive advantage."[39]

One of the swiftest ways of breaking down honest and open relationships with co-workers is to **backstab**—an attempt to discredit by underhanded means, such as innuendo, accusation, or the like. The backstabber will pretend to be your friend, but will say something negative behind your back in an attempt to discredit you. For example, your rival might say to the manager, "I'm worried about the health of _____. She seems so preoccupied that it's difficult to get her attention to talk about any work problems." During times of decreased job security, including downsizings due to mergers, workers are more likely to say negative things about co-workers to gain advantage. Also, when a promotion is at stake, co-workers are more likely to say negative things about each other to a common boss.[40]

backstab
An attempt to discredit by underhanded means, such as innuendo, accusation, or the like.

Make Others Feel Important

A fundamental principle of fostering good relationships with co-workers and others is to make them feel important. Visualize that everyone in the workplace is wearing a small sign around the neck that says, "Please make me feel important."[41] Although the leader has the primary responsibility for satisfying this recognition need, co-workers also play a key role. One approach to making a co-worker feel important would be to bring a notable accomplishment of his or hers to the attention of the group. Investing a small amount of time in recognizing a co-worker can pay large

POSITIVE POLITICAL SKILLS

dividends in terms of cultivating an ally. Expressing an interest in the work of others helps them feel important. A basic way to accomplish this is to ask other employees questions such as the following:

- How is your work going?
- How does the company use output from your department?
- How did you establish all the contacts you did to be so successful in sales?
- How did you develop the skills to do your job?

Expressing an interest in the work of others is also an effective tactic because so many people are self-centred. They are eager to talk about their own work, but rarely pause to express a genuine interest in others. Expressing an interest in the work of others is also effective because it is a form of recognition.

Self-Assessment Quiz 12-2 gives you an opportunity to think about your tendencies toward making others feel important.

Be Diplomatic

Despite all that has been said about the importance of openness and honesty in building relationships, most people fail to be convinced. Their egos are too tender to accept the raw truth when faced with disapproval of their thoughts or actions. Diplomacy is still an essential part of office politics. Translated into action, diplomacy often means finding the right phrase to convey disapproval, disagreement, or discontent. Below is an example of a delicate situation and a diplomatic response to it.

SELF-ASSESSMENT QUIZ 12-2

How Important Do I Make People Feel?

Directions: Indicate on a 1-to-5 scale how frequently you act (or would act if the situation presented itself) in the ways indicated below: Very Infrequently (VI); Infrequently (I); Sometimes (S); Frequently (F); Very Frequently (VF). Circle the number underneath the column that best fits your answer.

		VI	I	S	F	VF
1.	I do my best to correctly pronounce a co-worker's name.	1	2	3	4	5
2.	I avoid letting other people's egos get too big.	5	4	3	2	1
3.	I brag to others about the accomplishments of my co-workers.	1	2	3	4	5
4.	I recognize the birthdays of friends in a tangible way.	1	2	3	4	5
5.	It makes me anxious to listen to others brag about their accomplishments.	5	4	3	2	1
6.	After hearing that a friend has done something outstanding, I shake his or her hand.	1	2	3	4	5
7.	If a friend or co-worker recently received a degree or certificate, I would offer my congratulations.	1	2	3	4	5
8.	If a friend or co-worker finished second in a contest, I would inquire why he or she did not finish first.	5	4	3	2	1
9.	If a co-worker showed me how to do something, I would compliment that person's skill.	1	2	3	4	5
10.	When a co-worker starts bragging about a family member's accomplishments, I do not respond.	5	4	3	2	1

Total Score _____

Scoring and Interpretation: Total the numbers corresponding to your answers. Scoring 40 to 50 points suggests that you typically make people feel important; 16 to 39 points suggests that you have a moderate tendency toward making others feel important; 10 to 15 points suggests that you need to develop skill in making others feel important. Study this chapter carefully.

During a staff meeting, a co-worker suggests that the entire group schedule a weekend retreat to formulate a five-year plan for the department. The boss looks around the room to gauge the reactions of others to the proposal. You want to say, "What a stupid idea! Who needs to ruin an entire weekend to do something we could easily accomplish on a workday afternoon?" The diplomatic response is: "I've heard that retreats sometimes work. But would spending that much time on the five-year plan be cost-effective? Maybe we could work on the plan during one long meeting. If we don't get the planning accomplished in that time frame, we could then consider the retreat."

Exchange Favours

An important part of human interaction on and off the job is to reciprocate with others. Exchanging favours with others can make it easier for people to accomplish their work because they are able to call on assistance when needed. The adept political player performs a favour for another employee without asking a favour in return. The favour is then cashed in when a favour is needed. Here are three typical exchanges:

- A paralegal agrees to help another overburdened paralegal in the same law office, knowing that the other paralegal will reciprocate if needed in the future.
- A credit manager agrees to expedite a credit application for a sales representative. In reciprocation, the sales rep agrees to not commit the company to a delivery date on the next sale until the customer's credit has been evaluated.
- An assistant restaurant manager agrees to substitute for another assistant manager on New Year's Eve. One month later the first person asks the second to take over her shift, so she can get away for the weekend.

Ask Advice

Asking advice on technical and professional topics is a good way of building relationships with other employees. Asking for advice from another person—someone whose job does not require giving it—will usually be perceived as a compliment. Asking advice transmits the message, "I trust your judgment enough to ask your opinion on something important to me." You are also saying, "I trust you enough to think that the advice you give me will be in my best interest."

To avoid hard feelings, inform the person whose advice you are seeking that his or her opinion will not necessarily be binding. A request for advice might be prefaced with a comment such as, "I would like your opinion on a problem facing me. But I can't guarantee that I'll be in a position to act on it." As with any other political tactic, asking for advice must be done in moderation. Too much advice asking can make you appear to indecisive or a pest.

Share Constructive Gossip

An effective way of building workplace relationships is to share constructive gossip with others. Gossip serves as a socializing force because it is a mode of forging intimate relationships for many employees; workers get close to one another through the vehicle of gossip. It also serves as the lifeblood of personal relationships on the job. If you are the person supplying the gossip, people will develop positive attitudes toward you. **Positive gossip** is unofficial information that does not attack others, is based on truth, and does not leak confidential information. Given these restrictions, here is an example of positive gossip:

positive gossip
Unofficial information that does not attack others, is based on truth, and does not leak confidential information.

- "I heard that business is really picking up. If this week is any example, the company's profits for the quarter will far exceed expectations."
- "I heard yesterday that the director of public relations just finished her doctorate in business administration. I bet she will have some good ideas for improving some of our public relations strategies."

Kzenon/Fotolia

microinequity
A small, semiconscious message we send with a powerful impact on the receiver.

group norms
The unwritten set of expectations for group members.

Minimize Microinequities

A potent way of alienating co-workers is to snub them, or put them down, in a small way without being aware of your behaviour. A **microinequity** is a small, semiconscious message we send with a powerful impact on the receiver, or a subtle slight. It might take the form of ignoring another person, a snub, or a sarcastic comment. Understanding microinequities can lead to changes in one-on-one relationships that may profoundly irritate others.[42]

Imagine that you are in line in the company cafeteria with three co-workers. You turn around and notice an old friend from school who is visiting the company. Next, you introduce your old friend to two of the co-workers with you, but not the third. That co-worker is likely to feel crushed and irritated, and it will take you a while to patch your relationship. Looking at a microinequity from the standpoint of the receiver, a work associate might say to you, "Some computer illiterate sent me an email this morning without the attachment he said was there." You respond, "Excuse me, but that *computer illiterate* was me."

To overcome giving microinequities, it is important to think through the consequences of what you are doing and saying before taking action. In the cafeteria situation above, you might say to yourself, "Here comes time for an introduction, and this is not easy for me. I will remember to introduce everybody to my old friend."

Follow Group Norms

A summary principle to follow in getting along with other employees is to heed **group norms**, the unwritten set of expectations for group members. If you do not deviate too far from these norms, the group will accept much of your behaviour. Group norms also take the form of social cues about how to act, and therefore contribute to the organizational culture. Representative group norms include the following: (1) help co-workers with problems if you have the right expertise; (2) do not wear formal business attire on casual dress days; (3) have lunch with your co-workers at least once a week; (4) do not complain to the boss about a co-worker unless his or her negative behaviour is outrageously bad; (5) do not take a sick day unless you are really sick; (6) take your turn in bringing snacks to a meeting at least once a month; and (7) side with your co-workers rather than management when there is a dispute between the two groups.

If you do not deviate too far from these norms, the group will accept much of your behaviour. If you do deviate too far, you will be subject to much rejection and therefore lose some of your power base. Yet if you conform too closely to group norms, higher-level management may perceive you as unable to identify with management. Employees are sometimes blocked from moving up the ladder because they are regarded as "one of the gang."

Some of the relationship building described in the above eight strategies and tactics is now being done on company social networking sites. These sites are being used to connect employees who have limited opportunity to meet face to face, or who simply prefer the Internet for most of their social interactions. Often the company social networking sites are supplemented with websites such as Facebook and Twitter because so many employees from the same firm might be members. For many workers, social networks provide a desirable way of communicating because they include photos, videos, and personal information like hobbies and music preferences, all of which are good for relationship building.

Skill-Building Exercise 12-4 provides an opportunity to practise several of the techniques for building interpersonal relationships with co-workers and other work associates.

SKILL-BUILDING EXERCISE 12-4

Getting Along with Co-workers Role-Play

An inventory auditor in a department store chain decides to take action aimed at getting along better with co-workers. In each of the following two scenarios, one person plays the role of the inventory auditor. Another person plays the role of an employee whom the auditor is attempting to cultivate.

Scenario 1: Exchanging Favours. The auditor decides to strike a bargain with a store associate. (The role player decides what this exchange of favours should be.) Unknown to the auditor, the store associate is concerned about an inventory audit because he is worried about being accused of stealing merchandise.

Scenario 2: Express an Interest in the Co-worker's Work. The auditor decides to express an interest in a tech fixer because he can be a valuable ally when conducting an inventory audit. The inventory audit is computerized, and the appropriate software is confusing and crashes frequently. The tech fixer has a heavy workload and is not much prone to small talk, but he does get excited talking about information technology.

For both scenarios, observers rate the role players on two dimensions, using a 1-to-5 scale from very poor to very good. One dimension is "effective use of human relations techniques"; the second is "acting ability." A few observers might voluntarily provide feedback to the role players in terms of sharing their ratings and observations. The course instructor might also provide feedback.

After these scenarios have been completed, the class might discuss favours they have exchanged on the job that helped build relationships. Strive for at least five students to present examples of exchanges that enhanced their working relationships.

AVOIDING POLITICAL BLUNDERS

LEARNING OBJECTIVE 5

A strategy for not losing whatever power you have accumulated is to refrain from making power-eroding blunders. Committing these politically insensitive acts can also prevent you from attaining power. Self-Assessment Quiz 12-3 will get you started thinking about blunders. Several leading blunders are described in the following list.

1. **Criticizing your manager in a public forum.** The oldest saw in human relations is "Praise in public and criticize in private." Yet in the passion of the moment, you may still surrender to the irresistible impulse to criticize your manager publicly. As a result, the manager will harbour resentment toward you and perhaps block your chances for advancement.

2. **Bypassing the manager.** Many people believe that because most organizations are more democratic today, it is not important to respect the layers of authority (the chain of command). In reality, following etiquette is highly valued in most firms. Going around the manager to resolve a problem is therefore hazardous. You might be able to accomplish the bypass, but your career could be damaged and your recourses limited. It is much better to work out differences with your manager using standard methods of resolving conflict.

3. **Displaying disloyalty.** Being disloyal to your organization is a basic political blunder. Making it known that you are looking for a position elsewhere is the best-known form of disloyalty. Criticizing your company in public settings, praising the high quality of competitors' products, and writing angry internal email messages about your company are others. You may not get fired, but overt signs of disloyalty may land you in permanent disfavour.

4. **Being a pest.** Common wisdom suggests that diligently pressing for one's demands is the path to success. This may be true up to a point, but when assertiveness is used too often it becomes annoying to many people. The unduly persistent person comes to be perceived as being a pest, which has serious political consequences. An example of being a pest would be asking your manager every month when you are going to receive the raise you deserve.

5. **Being (or being perceived as) a poor team player.** An employee is expected to be a good team player in almost all organizations because cooperation makes collective effort possible. If you are a poor team player, or are perceived as such, your chances for promotion will diminish because you will be recognized as having poor interpersonal skills. Among the ways to be perceived as a poor team player

Practice
The Blunder Quiz

SELF-ASSESSMENT QUIZ 12-3

The Blunder Quiz

Indicate whether you agree or disagree with the following statements.

		Agree	Disagree
1.	It's fine to criticize your manager in a meeting so long as the criticism is valid.	_____	_____
2.	If I objected to a decision made by top management I would send a companywide email explaining my objection.	_____	_____
3.	I am willing to insult any co-worker if the insult is deserved.	_____	_____
4.	I see no problem in using competitors' products or services and letting my superiors know about it.	_____	_____
5.	If I thought the CEO of my company were way overpaid, I would send him or her an email making my opinion known.	_____	_____
6.	Never bother with company-sponsored social events, such as holiday parties, unless you are really interested.	_____	_____
7.	I would not attend a company social function if I had the chance to attend another social activity of more interest to me.	_____	_____
8.	I'm very open about passing along confidential information.	_____	_____
9.	I openly criticize most new ventures my company or department is contemplating.	_____	_____
10.	I avoid any deliberate attempt to please or impress co-workers.	_____	_____

Scoring and Interpretation: The greater the number of statements you agree with, the more prone you are to political blunders that can damage your interpersonal relationships and your career. You need to raise your awareness level of blunders on the job.

are to engage in social loafing, miss numerous department meetings, take too much credit for group accomplishments, and minimize your interactions with co-workers. In short, if you ignore all the advice about team-play presented in Chapter 6, you will be committing a political blunder.

6. **Burning your bridges.** A potent political blunder is to create ill will among former employers or people who have helped you in the past. The most common form of bridge-burning occurs when a person departs from an organization. A person who leaves involuntarily is especially apt to express anger toward those responsible for the dismissal. Venting your anger may give a temporary boost to your mental health, but it can be detrimental in the long run.

7. **Indiscreet behaviour in private life.** Employees are representatives of the company, so their behaviour off the job is considered to contribute to their performance—particularly for managers, supervisors, and professionals with visible jobs. Embarrassing the company will often lead to dismissal, combined with a negative reputation that will be difficult to shake for purposes of future employment. Indiscreet behaviour in private life that can lead to dismissal includes being caught shoplifting, a citation for drunk driving, being arrested for a drug offense, charges of sexual harassment or rape, and assault and battery.

8. **Making derogatory comments about your employer on the Internet.** Large numbers of employees in recent years have been reprimanded or fired because they wrote nasty comments about their company on a blog or social networking site. (One such comment on Twitter: "Our CEO should hire a bodyguard. He rakes in millions yet fires thousands.") As we all know, a rant about your company or boss on a social networking site becomes a permanent record, and will almost inevitably be referred to a company executive. Even if you are not fired or severely reprimanded for your public display of hostility, you will have lost considerable political capital—even if your rant is merited.

If you want to overcome having committed a blunder, avoid defensiveness. Demonstrate that you are more interested in recovering from the blunder than in trying to share the blame for what happened. Focus on solutions to the problem rather than on fault-finding. Suppose you have been too critical of your team leader in a recent team meeting. Explain that your attempts to be constructively critical backfired and that you will choose your words more carefully in the future.

Another way to patch up a blunder is to stay poised. Admit that you made the mistake and apologize, but don't act or feel inferior. Mistakes are inevitable in a competitive work environment. Avoid looking sad and distraught. Instead, maintain eye contact with people when you describe your blunder.

Access the eText in MySearchLab to learn more about this chapter's self-assessment quizzes.

To Watch Explore Practice Study and Review, **visit MySearchLab**

Developing Your Human Relations Skills and Reinforcing Concepts

Summary
✓ **Practice**
Glossary Flashcards

- Positive political tactics help build good interpersonal relationships. Political skill is related to awareness of one's surroundings, emotional and social intelligence, relationship building with the leader, and coping with an unjust environment.
- Managing the impression you create encompasses a wide range of behaviours designed to create a positive influence on work associates.
- Part of impression management includes business etiquette. Areas of business etiquette include work behaviour and clothing, introductions, relationships between men and women and between people of different ages, working in a cubicle, cross-cultural relations, and interaction with people with disabilities.
- Political strategies and tactics for building relationships with managers include the following: networking with influential people; helping your manager succeed; understanding unwritten boundaries; volunteering for assignments; flattering influential people sensibly; using information power; admitting mistakes; appearing cool under pressure; laughing at your manager's humour; expressing constructive disagreement; and presenting a clear picture of your accomplishments.
- Political strategies and tactics for developing relationships with co-workers and other work associates include maintaining honest and open relationships, making others feel important, being diplomatic, exchanging favours, asking for advice, sharing constructive gossip, minimizing microinequities, and following group norms.
- A strategy for not losing whatever power you have accumulated is to refrain from making political blunders such as criticizing your manager publicly, bypassing your manager, displaying disloyalty, being a pest, being a poor team player and burning your bridges, indiscreet behaviour in private life, and making derogatory comments about your employer on the Internet.

Interpersonal Relations Case 12-1

What Do My Table Manners Have to Do with the Job?

Suzanne Limeau was mentally set for a wonderful day. She was returning to AutoPay Inc. for her third job interview for a position as a human resources representative. As an HR rep Suzanne would have a variety of responsibilities including answering employee questions about benefits, organizing company parties and picnics, and conducting exit interviews with employees who quit the firm.

Suzanne reasoned that the third interview should be mostly to confirm the opinion of AutoPay managers that she was an excellent candidate for the position. Suzanne admired how AutoPay had grown into one of the largest payroll processing companies in the region, managing payroll and other human resource functions for hundreds of small employers. She also admired the professional appearance and behaviour of almost all the AutoPay workers she met.

Two hours before leaving for the job interview, Suzanne received an email message from her prospective boss, Steve Adams. The message indicated that there would be a slight change of schedule. Instead of her arriving at 10:00 a.m., Adams wanted Suzanne to arrive at 11:30 a.m. Adams and a few other company representatives decided they wanted to take her to lunch. The setting for the lunch would be Silo's, an upscale restaurant that emphasized Italian specialties.

On company premises, Suzanne met briefly with three company representatives and exchanged a few pleasantries. At this point, Suzanne knew that any heavy questions would be asked over lunch. The inevitable question about

Suzanne's motives for entering human resources came up before the group even ordered: "Why do you want to work in human resources?" Suzanne knew to avoid the stereotypical answer, "Because I like people."

Instead, Suzanne explained that she enjoyed working with the complexity of people, and that she believed strongly that taking care of human resources translates directly into profits. Adams blurted out, "Great answer, Suzanne."

The server came to the table and asked for drink orders. Two people ordered a glass of club soda, one person ordered tonic water, and Suzanne asked for a Blue Light. "And, don't forget," she added, "I would like another one during the meal."

Suzanne ordered clams over linguini for an entrée. When the server asked if the diners wanted dessert, only Suzanne said yes. Her choice was Neapolitan ice cream.

Conversation flowed freely during the lunch, and Suzanne was feeling confident that she would receive a job offer. After lunch, Adams took her aside, thanked her for joining the group for lunch, and said that she would be hearing from them soon.

A week passed without hearing from Adams or another company representative. Suzanne sent an email thanking the company for the three interviews, and pointed out that she was still enthused about the prospects of working for AutoPay. Two days later a letter arrived in the mail explaining that the company had decided to offer the job to another candidate. A little bit shocked and disappointed, Suzanne telephoned Adams and asked if she could please be told exactly why she was turned down for a job, when she seemed so qualified, and the company seemed so interested.

"We all thought you were a strong candidate, Suzanne," answered Adams. "But my boss said we could not hire a person with such poor manners."

"Poor manners? What are you talking about?" inquired Suzanne.

"My boss and I noticed three faux pas. First, you were the only person to order an alcoholic beverage, and you ordered two. Second, you sucked in a strand of linguini more than once. Third, you were the only person to order dessert. I am very sorry."

Disappointed and angry, Suzanne asked, "What do my table manners have to do with the job? I didn't get drunk, and I wasn't a slob."

Case Questions

1. How justified were the company managers in turning down Suzanne based on their perception of her table manners?
2. Should Steve Adams have warned Suzanne Chavez that her table manners would be a factor in evaluating her job qualifications?
3. How might Suzanne benefit from the time she invested in her interviews with AutoPay?

Interpersonal Relations Case 12-2

Passed-Over Pete

Pete Gupta was enjoying his career as a real estate agent at Barclay Properties, a real estate development company. The business model adopted by the founders of Barclay is to purchase and then rehabilitate distressed office buildings. Many of the older buildings the company rehabilitated were then converted into mixed used, such as office space, retail space, and loft condominium apartments. Part of the plan was to restore majestic older buildings, thereby fitting into the environmental trend of preserving what exists rather than consuming enormous amounts of energy and material in the construction of new office towers.

As Barclay Properties continued to expand, seven agents were working full-time, all of whom reported to Katie Logan, the company co-founder. Gupta's major responsibility was to find tenants as well as condominium buyers for the rehabilitated buildings. His passion for the business, combined with his knowledge of the business and sales skills, enabled him to become the leading agent in terms of sales volume.

Katie Logan specialized in supervising rehabilitation of the older buildings. Her role required that she spend considerable time with architects, construction firms, and local zoning boards. Ralph Parsons, the other co-founder, concentrated his efforts more in finding properties and working with financial institutions to fund the projects. Logan and Parsons agreed that Barclay had expanded enough to warrant hiring a manager to provide leadership to the sales group. Katie Logan enjoyed working with the real estate agents, but she was too occupied with other activities to provide much assistance or direction to the agents.

Logan and Parson agreed jointly that it would be a plus for the firm to offer the promotion to sales director to one of the seven agents. The new director of sales would continue to contribute as a sales agent, but would also function as the manager of the group. After considerable discussion, the director of sales position was offered to Sara Morales, who readily accepted the offer. For the previous year, Morales was the third-highest producer in terms of dollar volume.

After learning of Morales's appointment, Pete Gupta demanded an explanation from Logan and Parsons. He said angrily, "I am the number one agent here, and you didn't even discuss the promotion with me. What's going on?"

Logan responded, "Ralph and I are well aware that you are a star performer, and we expect that you will make Barclay a long-term career. But we needed more of a team player for the sales director position. We see you as an individual star who doesn't get too involved with the rest of the sales group. The buzz we obtained from your colleagues is that you are great with clients, but that you are a lone wolf. You don't appear to have too much interest in working as a team member. You never share your expertise with the guys and gals in the group."

Gupta replied, "I thought the name of this game is bring in the big bucks. Spending time with colleagues seems less important."

Parsons said in response, "Sales volume is obviously very important. But we needed a little more of an internal person for this position."

Case Questions

1. In what way does this case study relate to lateral relations?
2. What do you think of the logic behind the decision of Logan and Parsons to pass over Pete Gupta?
3. What tactics should Gupta use if he wants to reverse his image as a lone wolf?
4. How ethical was it for the co-founders to listen to "buzz" about Gupta to help them reach their decision?
5. What should Logan and Parsons do to increase the chances that Gupta will not quit because he was passed over for promotion?

Questions for Discussion and Review

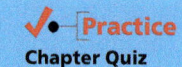

Practice Chapter Quiz

Multiple Choice

1. A good example of organizational leadership behaviour is
   a. staying within your job description at all times.
   b. helping a co-worker with a major project even though it is not within the scope of your job description.
   c. agreeing to all of your manager's suggestions.
   d. dressing well for work.

2. Flattery can be an excellent strategy to building relationships with influential people if the comments are
   a. realistic and deserved.
   b. effusive and delivered in an excited tone in front of others.
   c. only delivered in front of others.
   d. Do not use flattery as it is usually recognized for what it is and often backfires.

3. All of the following are suggested strategies for building relationships with co-workers except:
   a. Maintain open and honest relationships.
   b. Exchange favours.
   c. Gossip whenever the opportunity presents itself.
   d. Follow group norms.

4. Group norms are
   a. unwritten set of expectations about how to act in the workplace.
   b. written guidelines that employees are expected to follow in the workplace.
   c. identical in most organizations.
   d. semiconscious messages that have a powerful impact on the receiver.

5. Posting pictures on a public social network site of overtly doing illegal drugs
   a. should be of no concern to the workplace as this is private life.
   b. is acceptable in most workplaces.
   c. shows poor judgment but should not affect work.
   d. is considered a major political blunder that will affect work prospects.

Short Answer

6. To what extent are office-politics skills important for a person who is technically competent and hard-working?

7. Identify three job positions in which you think practising good business etiquette would be extremely important.

8. It has been said that although most businesspeople can see through flattery, the technique still works. How would you explain this observation?

9. Give an example of a microinequity that you have been subjected to, or that you have observed happen to another person. Explain why the incident is a microinequity.

10. Open your MySearchLab, click on the professional videos for this chapter, and watch the video on business etiquette in a shared workspace. Answer the questions at the end of the video about Brian's lack of etiquette. What other suggestions would you give to Brian to help him improve his business etiquette?

Answers to multiple choice questions: 1. b, 2. a, 3. c, 4. a, 5. d

The Web Corner

http://www.mayoclinic.com/health/stress/wl00049
Reduce stress at work by getting along with your boss

http://www.mindtools.com/pages/article/newCDV_85.htm
Managing office politics

www.executiveplanet.com
Guide to international business culture and etiquette in more than 35 countries

Internet Skill Builder: Sharpening Your Compliments

An important part of being a skilled office politician, as well as a government one, is to compliment people effectively. The information about flattery contained in the chapter gave you some ideas about how to use compliments effectively. Search the Internet for a few more useful suggestions for giving compliments to others. A good starting point for this assignment is www.kissmegoodnight.com, because it provides intelligent suggestions about giving compliments. Try out this week the best idea you find in this skill-building assignment. Observe the results of your compliment so that you can refine your technique.

MySearchLab

Visit **MySearchLab** to find self-grading review quizzes in the eText, discipline-specific media and readings, access to a variety of academic journals, and Associated Press news feeds, along with a wide range of writing, grammar, and research tools and to help hone writing and research skills.

CHAPTER 13

Customer Satisfaction Skills

As Tanya Polanski approached the receptionist counter at the hotel, she was tired, frustrated, and confused. "Everything has gone wrong for me the past two days," she explained to Kathy Chang, the receptionist. "My flight from Bejing arrived 10 hours late. I was delayed at customs for an hour. The man said they were doing a random inspection of passengers, even though I didn't look or act like a terrorist. When I tried to use my credit card at the airport, they told me the computer wasn't working so I had to come back a couple of hours later."

"You certainly have had a difficult couple of days, Ms. Polanski," said Chang. "After you are settled in your room, you will start to feel much better. Let me access your reservations." After checking her computer, Chang said, "There seems to be a little problem here. We do not have reservations for you."

Alliance/Fotolia

LEARNING Objectives

After reading and studying this chapter and doing the exercises, you should be able to

1. Explain the three components of customer experience (or service).
2. Enhance your ability to satisfy customers by using general principles of customer satisfaction.
3. Create bonds with present or future customers.
4. Have a plan for dealing effectively with customer dissatisfaction.

In tears, Polanski said, "Has everything gone crazy in Canada? I made these reservations three months ago for the Holiday Inn right on this avenue."

"I understand why you are upset. Let's work out this problem together. Could it be that you made reservations at our other Holiday Inn, a little closer to downtown? It's on the same street. I will check into our worldwide reservation system right now."

"You're in luck, Ms. Polanski," said Chang after a few minutes at the terminal. "Your reservations are at our other Holiday Inn, just five blocks away.

"I will have our van take you there right away, and I will phone ahead to make sure you get to the front of the line as soon as possible. Enjoy your stay in Canada, and we look forward to seeing you again."

"Thank you, thank you, you have saved my day," replied Polanski.

Maybe the hotel receptionist in question is naturally gifted in interpersonal skills, or maybe she combined the right personality traits with the right training to become a compassionate and helpful hotel receptionist. Either way she has a lesson for workers at all levels in many different types of jobs. Outstanding customer service enhances a company's reputation, and leads to repeat business. This chapter presents information and exercises that can enhance your ability to satisfy both external and internal customers at a high level.

External customers fit the traditional definition of customers, which includes clients, guests, and patients. External customers can be classified as retail or industrial. The latter would include a company that buys from another, such as purchasing steel or a gross of printer cartridges. In contrast, *internal customers* are the people you serve within the organization, those who use the output from your job, or anyone you depend on. Much of this text deals with better serving internal customers, because improved interpersonal relationships increase the satisfaction of work associates. However, the emphasis in this chapter is on satisfying external customers.

Customer satisfaction skills are required by all workers who are in contact with external customers, such as sales representatives, customer service representatives (those who back up sales and take care of customer problems), and store associates. Workers in a wide variety of jobs need good customer satisfaction skills. The founder of a technology consulting firm observes, "Ninety percent of the time when a client has an issue with a consultant, it's related to soft skills."[1] Another way of understanding the importance of customer satisfaction skills is to recognize that employees who can satisfy customers contribute heavily to profits. The chief executive of a firm that surveys approximately 20 million customers a year for retail and restaurant chains concludes: "A good employee or a good sales associate might be worth five or 10 times an average one. We've seen that. It's unreal."[2]

CUSTOMER SATISFACTION SKILLS

Practice
The Customer-Service Orientation Quiz

SELF-ASSESSMENT QUIZ 13-1

The Customer-Service Orientation Quiz

Directions: Answer each of the following statements about dealing with customers as "Mostly True" or "Mostly False." The statements relate to your attitudes, even if you lack direct experience in dealing with customers. Your experiences as a customer will also be helpful in responding to the statements.

		Mostly True	Mostly False
1.	All work in a company should be geared to pleasing customers.	_____	_____
2.	The real boss in any business is the customer.	_____	_____
3.	Smiling at customers improves the chances of making a sale.	_____	_____
4.	I would rather find a new customer than attempt to satisfy one who is difficult to please.	_____	_____
5.	Dealing with customers is as rewarding as (or more rewarding than) dealing with co-workers.	_____	_____
6.	I enjoy (or would enjoy) helping a customer solve a problem related to the use of my product or service.	_____	_____
7.	The best way to get repeat business is to offer steep discounts.	_____	_____
8.	In business, your customer is your partner.	_____	_____
9.	Dealing directly with customers is (or would be) the most boring part of most jobs.	_____	_____
10.	If you have the brand and model the customer wants, being nice to the customer is not so important.	_____	_____
11.	A good customer is like a good friend.	_____	_____
12.	If you are too friendly with a customer, he or she will take advantage of you.	_____	_____
13.	Now that individual consumers and companies can shop online, the personal touch in business is losing importance.	_____	_____
14.	Addressing a customer by his or her name helps build a relationship with that customer.	_____	_____
15.	Satisfying a customer is fun whether or not it leads to a commission.	_____	_____

Scoring and Interpretation: Give yourself a +1 for each of the following statements receiving a response of "Mostly True": 1, 2, 3, 5, 6, 8, 11, 14, and 15. Give yourself a +1 for each of the following statements receiving a response of "Mostly False": 4, 7, 9, 10, 12, and 13.

13–15 You have a strong orientation to providing excellent customer service.

8–12 You have an average customer service orientation.

1–7 You have a below-average orientation to providing excellent customer service.

Various aspects of developing customer satisfaction skills are divided into three parts in this chapter: general principles, bonding with customers, and dealing with customer dissatisfaction. To reflect on your attitudes toward satisfying customers, do Self-Assessment Quiz 13-1.

THE THREE COMPONENTS OF CUSTOMER EXPERIENCE (SERVICE)

LEARNING OBJECTIVE 1

A useful starting point in becoming skilled at satisfying customers is to understand how customers form impressions of their experience. The term *experience* is often used as to replace *service* because customer service is often perceived as getting help from a call centre or returning merchandise in a retail store. According to the research of marketing professors Leonard L. Berry, Eileen A. Wall, and Lewis P. Carbone, customers form three clues about the service experience based on their presence or absence. A clue is anything

FIGURE 13-1 Clue Influences on Customer Perceptions

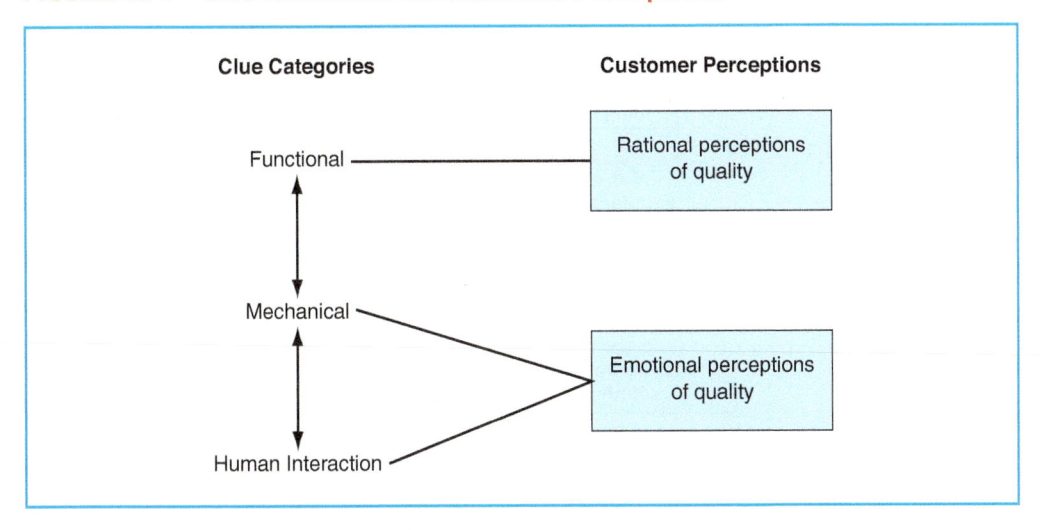

Clue Categories → **Customer Perceptions**

- Functional → Rational perceptions of quality
- Mechanical → Emotional perceptions of quality
- Human Interaction → Emotional perceptions of quality

Source: Adapted from Leonard L. Berry, Eileen A. Wall, and Lewis P. Carbone, "Service Clues and Customer Assessment of the Service Experience: Lessons from Marketing," *Academy of Management Perspectives,* May 2006, p. 46. Reprinted with permission of the Academy of Management Review.

the customer can see, hear, taste, or smell. It is often small clues that influence a customer's overall perception of an experience, such as a customer service rep yawning while taking care of the person's problem.[3]

The key point is that customers form perceptions based on three components of the experience. First are *functional clues* derived from the technical performance of the service, such as the technician from the call centre enabling you to get your new printer up and running. Second are *mechanical clues* stemming from the sensory presentation of the service, including sights, smells, sounds, tastes, and textures. At The Bay stores, the mechanical clues include the red-yellow-green colour scheme, the wide isles, and the checkout counters. Third are the *human interaction clues* detected from the behaviour and appearance of service providers. Such clues include the service provider's choice of words, tone of voice, enthusiasm, body language, and dress. Much of this chapter deals with the human-touch (interaction) component of the customer experience.

Human interaction in the service experience offers the biggest opportunity to deepen customers' emotional connection to the company and the service provider. For example, many customers return to a given restaurant because the server is so polite, friendly, and helpful—assuming the food and decor are also satisfactory.

Figure 13-1 presents an overview of the three components of, or clues about, customer experience. Notice that only the functional clues are based mostly on rational perceptions of quality of service. If the call-centre technician gets your printer working, you are not so concerned about his or her lack of warmth and enthusiasm. In contrast, the mechanical and human interaction clues are based mostly on emotional perceptions of the quality of service. For example, you might return to a hotel mostly because of the view of the bay and the soothing beige colours in the room. For the customer service to be truly outstanding, all three clues should be positive.

FOLLOWING THE GENERAL PRINCIPLES OF CUSTOMER SATISFACTION

Knowing how to satisfy customers is a subset of effective interpersonal relations in organizations. Nevertheless, there are certain general principles that will sharpen your ability to satisfy customers and thereby improve customer retention. This section presents eight key principles for satisfying customers. Remember, however, that satisfaction is considered a minimum expectation. If you do an outstanding job of satisfying customers, they will experience delight, as shown in Figure 13-2.

LEARNING OBJECTIVE 2

FIGURE 13-2 Levels of Customer Satisfaction

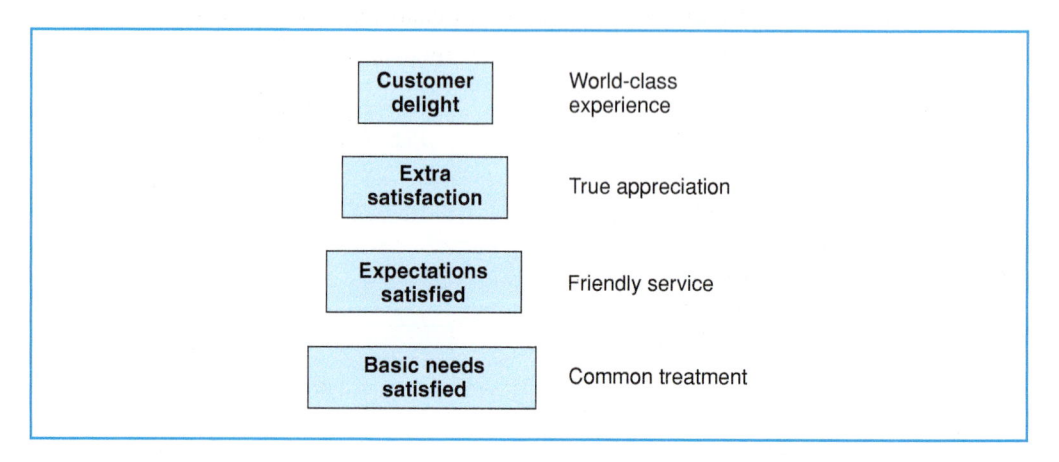

Customer delight	World-class experience
Extra satisfaction	True appreciation
Expectations satisfied	Friendly service
Basic needs satisfied	Common treatment

Customer satisfaction is important for several reasons. To begin with, without satisfying customers, a business would cease to exist. The slogan of WestJet Airlines, "Because owners care," illustrates a customer satisfaction focus as a priority provided by caring staff who are all part-owners of the company. Satisfied customers are likely to tell friends and acquaintances about their satisfactory experiences, helping a firm grow its business. In contrast, dissatisfied customers—especially those with an unresolved problem—are likely to tell many people about their dissatisfaction, thus dissuading a large number of people from becoming new customers. Studies indicate that an upset or angry customer tells an average of between 10 and 20 other people about an unhappy experience.[4] Customer satisfaction is also highly valued because it breeds customer loyalty, which in turn is very profitable. Repeat business is a success factor in both retail and industrial companies.

Another reason for satisfying customers is the humanitarian aspect. Satisfying people enhances their physical and mental health, whereas dissatisfaction creates negative stress. Have you ever been so angry at poor service that you experienced stress?

Be Satisfied So You Can Provide Better Customer Service

Employees who are happy with their jobs are the most likely to satisfy customers. Treating employees well puts them in a better frame of mind to treat their customers well. For example, an extensive case history analysis of Sears found a strong relationship between employee and customer satisfaction. Employees who were satisfied influenced customers to be satisfied, resulting in more purchases and profits.[5] According to consumer behaviour specialist James Hazen, good service comes down to creating a positive and memorable customer experience. For example, Starbucks can command a premium price for its coffee beverages not simply because of the quality of its beans and its stylish cardboard cups, but because of the overall experience. And the employees—particularly the baristas—are part of that experience.[6] Although Starbucks has reduced many prices in recent years, its customers still have the option of purchasing lower price coffee at fast-food chains and convenience stores.

Acting alone, you cannot improve company conditions that contribute to job satisfaction. What you can control to some extent, however, are your own related attitudes and beliefs. Following is a checklist of the ones over which you can exert some control:

- **Interest in the work itself.** Job satisfaction stems directly from being interested in what you are doing. People who love their work experience high job satisfaction and are therefore in the right frame of mind to satisfy customers.
- **A feeling of self-esteem.** If you have high self-esteem you are more likely to experience high job satisfaction. High-status occupations contribute more to self-esteem than do those of low status. Feelings of self-esteem also stem from doing work the

individual sees as worthwhile. This perception is less influenced by external standards than is the status associated with a particular job or occupation.

- **Optimism and flexibility.** An optimistic and flexible person is predisposed to be a satisfied employee. A pessimistic and rigid person will most likely be a dissatisfied employee. Every company has its share of people who will always find something to complain about. Evidence suggests that a tendency toward optimism versus pessimism is inherited.[7] If you have a predisposition toward pessimism, it does not mean that you cannot become more optimistic with self-discipline. You can, for example, look for the positive aspects of a generally unpleasant situation.

- **Positive self-image.** People possessing a positive self-image are generally more satisfied with their jobs than are those possessing a negative self-image. One explanation is that the people who view themselves negatively tend to view most things negatively. You have to like yourself before you can like your job.

- **Positive expectations about the job.** People with positive expectations about their jobs are frequently more satisfied than are those with low expectations. These expectations illustrate a self-fulfilling prophecy. If you expect to like your job, you will behave in such a way that those expectations will be met. Similarly, if you expect your job not to satisfy your needs, you will do things to make your expectations come true. Assume that a worker expects to earn low commissions in a sales job. The person's negativity may come through to customers and prospective customers, thereby ensuring low customer satisfaction and low commissions.

- **Effective handling of abuse from customers.** Customer service workers are often verbally abused by customers over such matters as products not working, merchandise returns not being acceptable, and the customer having been charged a late fee. Automated telephone-answering systems often force callers to hack through a thicket of prompts before reaching a human being. By the time a live person is reached, the customer is angry and ready to lash out at the customer service representative.[8] To prevent these oral tirades from damaging one's job satisfaction, it is essential to use effective techniques of dealing with criticism and resolving conflict as described in Chapter 9. The section on dealing with dissatisfied customers presented later in this chapter is also important.

High job satisfaction contributes to good customer service in another important way. Employees who are satisfied with their jobs are more likely to engage in service-oriented organizational citizenship behaviour. As you will recall, *organizational citizenship behaviour* relates to going beyond your ordinary job description to help other workers and the company. A customer service worker with high organizational citizenship behaviour will go beyond ordinary expectations to find ways to solve a customer problem.[9] A member of the tech support staff in a consumer electronics store volunteered to drop by a customer's house to help him install a programmable DVD, even though such home visits were not required. As a result of the technician's kindness, the man purchased a $6000 high-definition TV from the store.

Receive Emotional Support from Co-workers to Give Better Customer Service

Closely related to the idea that satisfied workers can better satisfy customers is the finding that the emotional support of co-workers often leads to providing better customer service. According to a research study, the support of co-workers is even more important than supervisory support. The participants in the study were 354 customer service workers employed in service-based facilities. Customer satisfaction surveys were collected from 269 customers. The major finding was that employees who perceived their co-workers to be supportive had a higher level of commitment to their customers.

The researchers concluded that it is important to have a supportive group of co-workers by your side to help you perform service-related duties. In this study, supervisory

Explore

Simulation: Customer Service

support was less important than co-worker support in terms of bringing about a strong customer orientation. (A *customer service orientation* includes a desire to help customers, and a willingness to act in ways that would satisfy a customer.) Another important conclusion drawn from the study was that customer satisfaction was positively associated with the strength of the service worker's customer orientation.[10]

BACK TO THE OPENING CASE

The hotel receptionist portrayed in the chapter opener exemplifies a service worker with a strong customer orientation. She recognized the psychological distress of the customer and lessened it by offering her a complimentary ride to the correct hotel. What may have been the effects if she had not been so gracious? Do you think that Ms. Polanski would have ever stayed at a Holiday Inn again?

Research also supports the idea that the type of leadership sales representatives receive influences the type of relationships the reps build with customers. The study in question involved 300 pairs of sales managers and 1400 salespeople reporting directly to them. Sales managers who were charismatic and good at setting visions strongly affected the use of customer-oriented selling behaviours, such as building good relationships. Other key factors related to building good relationships with customers were the level of support the sales workers received from the organization, and how much cohesiveness (closeness) they felt with co-workers.[11]

A similar study conducted in Taiwan with 450 hair stylists and 112 store managers found that charismatic and visionary leaders enhanced employee service. In turn, better service was associated with customers coming back to the salon.[12] You probably already knew that if your hairstylist gives good service, you will return—but now there is a quantitative study to support your belief.

The major point here is that the organization plays an important role in your ability or willingness to build relationships with customers. A thought to take away is that if you perceive your manager to be charismatic, you are more likely to provide better customer service.

Understand Customer Needs and Put Them First

Explore
Simulation: Interpersonal Communication

The most basic principle of selling is to identify and satisfy customer needs. One challenge is that many customers may not be able to express their needs clearly. To help identify customer needs, you may have to probe for information. For example, the associate in a camera and video store might ask, "What uses do you have in mind for a video camera?" Knowing such information will help the associate identify which camcorder will satisfy the customer's needs.

The concept of adding value for customers is widely accepted as a measure of satisfying customer needs. If you satisfy customer needs, you are adding value for them. A person might be willing to pay $20 more per ticket to watch an athletic event if the extra $20 brought a better view and a chair instead of a backless bench. (The better view and more comfortable back add value for the spectator.) After customer needs have been identified, the focus must be on satisfying those needs rather than the needs of oneself or the company. Assume that the customer says, "The only convenient time for me to receive delivery this week would be Thursday or Friday afternoon." The sales associate should not respond, "On Thursday and Friday our truckers prefer to make morning deliveries." Instead, the associate should respond, "I'll do whatever is possible to accommodate your request."

Explore
Mastering Business Communcations: Listening Skills

A major contributor to identifying customer needs is to listen actively to customers. Listening can take place during conversations with customers, and "listening" can also mean absorbing information sent by email and written letters. A policy at Southwest Airlines is that if a customer (or employee) has an idea, a manager must respond instantaneously.[13]

Focus on Solving Problems, Not Just Taking Orders

In effective selling, sales representatives solve problems as well as take orders. An example is the approach taken by sales representatives for Xerox Corp. Instead of focusing on the sale of photocopiers and related equipment, the sales reps look to help customers solve their information-flow problems. The solution could involve selling machines, but it might also involve selling consulting services.

Consultative selling is also referred to as customer-centric. A **customer-centric sales process** emphasizes a low-pressure environment in which the sales staff act as consultants, offering information and explaining how the product or service can help solve a customer's problem. The customer-centric approach is visible at an Apple Store. At an Apple Store, customers can obtain free assistance from the Genius Bar.[14] The same holds true for TELUS stores, where customers can come in with their cell phones and get immediate assistance for problems with their phones.

The focus on problem-solving enables sales representatives to become partners in the success of their customers' businesses. By helping the customer solve problems, the sales representative increases the value of the supplier-customer relationship to the customer. The customer is receiving consulting services in addition to the merchandise or service being offered. In some situations, a store associate can capitalize on the same principle. If the customer appears unsure about a purchase, ask him or her what problem is being faced that the product will solve. The following scenario in a computer store illustrates this point:

Customer: I think I would like to buy this computer. I'm pretty sure it's the one I want. But I don't know too much about computers other than how to use them for word processing, email, and basic research.

Store Associate: I am happy you would like to purchase a computer. But could you tell me what problems you are facing that you want a computer to help you solve?

Customer: Right now I feel I'm not capitalizing on the Internet revolution. I want to do more online, and get into digital photography so I can send cool photos to friends all over. I also want to purchase music online, so I can walk around with an iPod like my friends do.

Store Associate: To solve your problem, you will need a more powerful computer than the one you are looking at. I would like you to consider another model that is about the same price as the one you have chosen. The difference is that it has the memory you need to email photos and download music from a subscription service.

Respond Positively to Moments of Truth

An effective customer contact person performs well during situations in which a customer comes in contact with the company and forms an impression of its service. Such a situation is referred to as a **moment of truth**. If the customer experiences satisfaction or delight during a moment of truth, he or she is likely to return when the need for service arises again. A person who is frustrated or angered during a moment of truth will often not be a repeat customer. A moment of truth is an important part of customer service because what really matters in a service encounter is the customer's perception of what occurred.[15] Visualize a couple who have just dined at an expensive restaurant as part of celebrating their anniversary. The food, wine, and music might have been magnificent, but the couple perceives the service as poor because one of them slipped on ice in the restaurant parking lot.

You can probably visualize many moments of truth in your experiences with service personnel. Reflect on how you were treated by a store associate when you asked for assist-

customer-centric sales process

A sales process emphasizing a low-pressure environment in which the sales staff acts as consultants, offering information and explaining how the product or service can help solve a customer's problem.

moment of truth

Situation in which a customer comes in contact with a company and forms an impression of its service.

FIGURE 13-3 A Cycle-of-Service Chart for Obtaining a Car Loan at a Bank

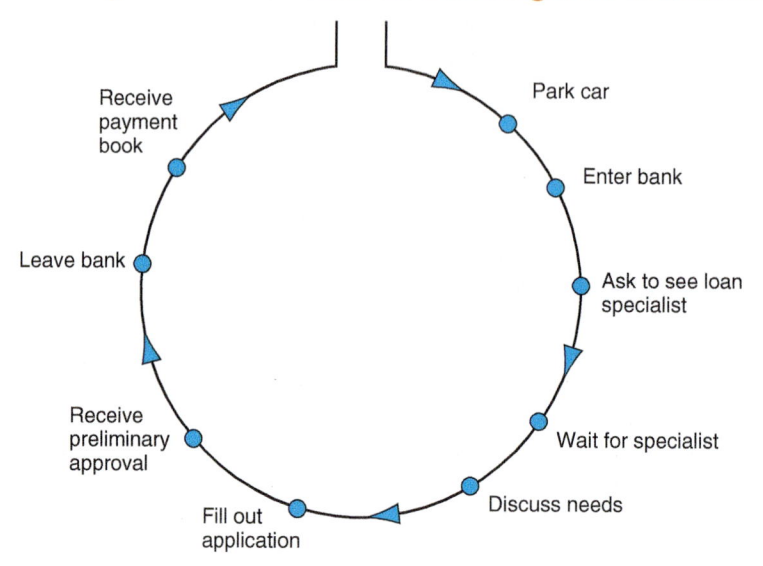

- Park car
- Enter bank
- Ask to see loan specialist
- Wait for specialist
- Discuss needs
- Fill out application
- Receive preliminary approval
- Leave bank
- Receive payment book

ance; the instructions you received when an airplane flight was cancelled; or how you were treated when you inquired about financial aid. Each business transaction has its own moment of truth. Yet they all follow the theme of a key interaction between a customer and a company employee.

One way you can track moments of truth is to prepare a cycle-of-service chart, as shown in Figure 13-3. The **cycle-of-service chart** summarizes the moments of truth encountered by a customer during the delivery of a service.[16] To gain insight into these charts, do Skill-Building Exercise 13-1.

cycle-of-service chart
A method of tracking the moments of truth with respect to customer service.

Be Ready to Accept Empowerment

A major strategy for improving customer service is to empower customer contact employees to resolve problems. **Empowerment** refers to managers transferring, or sharing, power with lower-ranking employees. In terms of customer relations, it means pushing decision making and complaint resolution downward to employees who are in direct contact with customers. The traditional method of dealing with all but the most routine customer problems is for the customer contact worker to refer them to the manager. Many manufacturing firms and service firms now authorize customer contact workers to take care of customer problems themselves, within limits. Employees at Ritz-Carlton hotels have the authority to spend up to $2000 to solve a customer problem. At less luxurious hotels, such as the Hampton Inn, any worker can offer a guest a free night of lodging to compensate for a service problem.

empowerment
The process of managers transferring, or sharing, power with lower-ranking employees.

Empowerment is not giving away the store, especially because limits are established to the customer contact worker's authority. Empowerment does involve taking a reasonable risk based on company principles to provide meaningful customer service. For empowerment to work, the company must grant decision-making latitude to employees.

SKILL-BUILDING EXERCISE 13-1

Moments of Truth

The class breaks into small groups to discuss what can go right versus what can go wrong during customer moments of truth. First refer to the cycle-of-service chart shown in Figure 13-3. Discuss what can go right or wrong at each moment of truth. Discuss what can go right or wrong at each moment of truth. Second, have the team develop its own cycle-of-service chart for another service, using its own experiences and imagination. After making the two analyses, discuss the usefulness of a cycle-of-service chart for improving customer satisfaction.

For additional practice in identifying the three components of customer of service, label each moment of truth into one of three perceptions: functional, mechanic, or human interaction. For example, you might have observed that the retail store had a nice scent (a perception of mechanics).

The employees, in turn, must be willing to accept empowerment (or decision-making authority).[17] Imagine yourself in a customer contact position. For empowerment to work effectively, you should be able to answer the following statements affirmatively:

- I am willing to arrive at a quick decision as to whether the company or the customer is right.
- I would be willing to admit to a customer that the company has made a mistake.
- I would be willing to take the risk that at times I will lose money for the company on a given transaction.
- I would be comfortable making an out-of-the-ordinary decision about a customer problem without consulting a manager.

Enhance Customer Service through Information Technology

Much has been said and written about how information technology has depersonalized customer service, such as having customers select from a long menu of choices on a touch-tone telephone. Information technology, however, also plays an important role in recording customer preferences and individualizing service. A major contribution of information technology to enhancing customer service is to develop individualized appeals to customers. With the right software in place, you can make a direct appeal to customer preferences based on past purchases, and the habits of customers with similar preferences. For example, the Fairmont and Delta hotel chains keep track of customer preferences such as what kinds of pillows you prefer and your preference of room location (near an elevator for example) when you join their free customer preference clubs. If you have purchased online at a major retailer like Amazon.ca, you may be familiar with this technology. Two examples follow:

1. Computerized information tells you immediately what the customer on the phone or online has bought in the past, so you may ask a question such as, "Two years ago you installed a centralized vacuum cleaning system. Do you need another set of bags by now?"
2. Speaking to the person, or sending an email message to the customer, you may say, "Last year you purchased a heated doghouse for your Yorkshire terrier. Our information suggests that people who own a heated doghouse are also interested in dog sweaters. Please take a moment to look at our new line of dog sweaters for canines that appreciate warmth."

Developing individualized appeals to customers is likely to be included in customer relationship management (CRM) software. The complex software is used to implement a strategy of interacting with your customers to bring them more value, and more profits to your firm. One of its basic purposes is to make the company easier for customers to do business with, including facilitating placing orders over the Internet.[18] As such, the individual customer service worker would not have the authority to install such a system. Yet the individual worker can always look for ways to apply the CRM system (such as that provided by Salesforce.com, or SAP) in a way that best serves the customer.

A major challenge in providing good customer service when using information technology is preserving the human touch. Here are some hints for adding a personal touch into your electronic communications to help build customer loyalty.

Using Voice Mail

1. Vary your voice tone and inflection when leaving messages and in your greeting to avoid sounding bored or uninterested in your job and the company.
2. Smile while leaving your message—somehow a smile gets transmitted over the telephone wires or optic fibres!
3. Use voice mail to minimize "telephone tag" rather than to increase it. If your greeting specifies when you will return, callers can choose to call again or to leave a message. When you leave a message, suggest a good time to return your call. Another way to minimize telephone tag is to assure the person you are calling that you will keep trying.

4. Place an informative and friendly greeting (outgoing message) on your voice mail or answering machine. Used effectively, a voicemail greeting will minimize the number of people irritated by not talking to a person.

5. When you are leaving a voicemail message, include specific, relevant information. As mentioned above, be specific about why you are calling and what you want from the person called. The probability of receiving a return call increases when you leave honest and useful information. If you are selling something or asking for a favour, be honest about your intent.

6. When leaving your message, avoid the most common voicemail error by stating your name and telephone number clearly enough to be understood. Most recipients of a message dislike intensely listening to it several times to pick up identifying information.

7. The company using computerized calls (or "robocalls") should determine if these calls are perceived as helpful or so annoying that they harm business.[19] One of the many uses of an automated calling service is to remind patients of upcoming medical and dental appointments. Some patients appreciate the reminder, whereas others slam down the phone in disgust because they expect more a more personal touch from a dental or medical office.

Using Email[20]

1. Use the customer's name. Begin with a personal greeting, for example, "Hello, Lisa King." Many companies now greet customers by their first name only, but some customers consider this practice very rude. However, few people are likely to be offended when you use both their first and last names.

2. Choose a human email address. "MarySmith@hotmail.com" feels more personal than an odd sequence of numbers, letters, and dashes.

3. Be conversational. Mention events you have shared, such as "I enjoyed seeing you at the company meeting."

4. Sign your name. Don't neglect your signature. "Best regards, Jim Woods."

Avoid Rudeness and Hostility toward Customers

We have reserved the most frequently violated principle of good customer service for last: Avoid being rude to customers. Although rudeness to customers is obviously a poor business practice, the problem is widespread. Rudeness of customer contact personnel is a major problem from the employer's standpoint. A widely practised form of rudeness is for two store associates to converse with each other about non-work matters while a customer waits for attention. And how about a store associate making a personal phone call or texting while waiting on you?

Rude treatment creates more lost business than does poor product quality or high prices. Several years ago McDonald's franchises were facing a downturn in sales. Surveys indicated that one of the problems facing McDonald's Corporation was the indifferent and rude behaviour by many frontline workers. McDonald's then increased the training of store employees and upgraded the menu, to achieve a substantial rebound in sales.

Rudeness is sometimes a form of hostility, because rudeness, such as grimacing at a customer, stems from anger. Being outright hostile toward customers can be a bigger problem than rudeness, which is more subtle. The impact of service provider hostility on customer satisfaction was explored by studying 142 naturally occurring service interactions at a telephone service centre of a bank. A typical interaction would be a customer phoning the bank to inquire about an account balance. (Today, such calls would only be in reference to what appeared to be inaccuracies in the online statement, or the one retrieved through the automated phone service.) Service interactions usually lasted about two minutes. Customers were later contacted to complete a quality survey about their transaction. Hostility was measured through raters' judgment of the tone of the service providers' voices.

A major finding of the study was that when the technical performance (e.g., providing the information needed) was low, hostility by the service provider lowered customer satisfaction considerably. When the technical performance of the service provider was good,

SELF-ASSESSMENT QUIZ 13-2

Am I Being Rude?

Directions: Following is a list of behaviours of customer contact workers that many would interpret as rude. Indicate whether you have engaged in such behaviour in your dealings with customers, or whether you would be likely to do so if your job did involve customer contact.

	Yes	No
1. I talk to a co-worker while serving a customer.	___	___
2. I conduct a telephone conversation with someone else while serving a customer.	___	___
3. I address customers by their first names without having their permission.	___	___
4. I address customers as "You guys."	___	___
5. I chew gum or eat while dealing with a customer.	___	___
6. I laugh when customers describe an agonizing problem they are having with one of our company's products or services.	___	___
7. I minimize eye contact with customers.	___	___
8. I say the same thing to every customer, such as "Have a nice day," in a monotone.	___	___
9. I accuse customers of attempting to cheat the company before carefully investigating the situation.	___	___
10. I hurry customers when my break time approaches.	___	___
11. I comment on a customer's appearance in a flirtatious, sexually oriented way.	___	___
12. I sometimes complain about or make fun of one customer when I am serving another.	___	___
13. I sometimes look and act impatient if a customer fumbles around trying to locate his or her credit card, debit card, or cash.	___	___

Interpretation: The more of these behaviours you have engaged in, the ruder you are and the more likely that you are losing potential business for your company. If you have not engaged in any of these behaviours, even when faced with a rude customer, you are an asset to your employer. You are also tolerant.

✓ Practice
Am I Being Rude?

---

hostility had a less negative impact on service quality.[21] When you get the information you need from a service provider, you are willing to put up with a few angry tones! The overall message supports a human relations perspective: Being hostile toward customers lowers their perception of the quality of service.

To elevate your awareness level about rudeness among customer-contact personnel, do Self-Assessment Quiz 13-2.

CREATING A BOND WITH YOUR CUSTOMER

Another key perspective on achieving customer satisfaction and delight is to create a bond—or emotional relationship—with customers. The rationale is that if you form warm, constructive relationships with your customers, they will keep buying from your company. Staying focused on the importance of customers will help provide the motivation for forming such a bond. The willingness to form a bond with the customer is part of having a **strong customer orientation**, defined as "a set of basic individual predispositions and an inclination to provide service, to be courteous and helpful in dealing with customers and associates."[22] You may recall Self-Assessment Quiz 13-1 about customer orientation at the outset of the chapter. Service-oriented organizational citizenship behaviour relates to the same idea of focusing on customer needs.

Creating a bond is aimed at increasing sales, but it also enhances service. If the customer relies on and trusts the sales representative, the customer will perceive the service to be of high quality. Similarly, people perceive medical and legal services to be of high quality if they

LEARNING OBJECTIVE 3

strong customer orientation
A set of individual predispositions and an inclination to provide service, to be courteous and helpful in dealing with customers and associates.

trust the physician or lawyer. Virtually all of the principles and techniques presented in this chapter will help form a bond with customers. However, six key principles are as follows:

1. Create a welcoming attitude, including a smile.
2. Provide exceptional service.
3. Show care and concern.
4. Make the buyer feel good.
5. Build a personal relationship.
6. Invite the customer back.

Create a Welcoming Attitude, Including a Smile

An effective starting point in creating a customer bond is to use enthusiastic expressions, including a smile, when greeting customers. Attempt to show a sincere, positive attitude that conveys to customers and prospects "I'm here to make you happy."[23] In addition to being an effective greeting, smiling is also a natural relationship builder and can help you bond with your customer. Smile several times at each customer meeting, even if your customer is angry with your product or service. A cell phone that has a recording function is a useful device for getting feedback on the quality of your smile. Practising your smile in front of a mirror might feel a little less natural, but it is still helpful. Smiling at customers has a potential disadvantage, despite its general effectiveness. If your smile is too friendly and inviting, the customer might think that you want to get to know him or her outside the business relationship.

Smiling is such a key part of bonding with customers that the smiles of customer service workers have been the subject of scientific study. Twenty pairs of first-year college students who were trained as coders for the experiment observed 220 employee-consumer encounters in food/coffee services. Customers were later asked to report their mood, appraisal of service quality, and encounter satisfaction. Several of the findings were as follows: Even in brief encounters, substantial smiling by employees made customers smile in return. Smiling employees were perceived as providing quality service, and the customers felt overall satisfaction with their encounters. Smiling somehow did not affect customer mood after the encounter. One interpretation of the study is that service employees should keep smiling, but not to the point that they lack authenticity.[24] Phony smiles backfire in work and personal life.

Provide Exceptional Service

The best-accepted axiom about keeping customers is to provide exceptional service. Many successful companies contend that good service is their competitive advantage. An excellent example is State Farm Insurance. When the ice storm hit eastern Ontario and Quebec in the winter of 1997, State Farm Insurance handled thousands of damage claims resulting from the storm. Thousands of households were without electricity and other services for up to three weeks. The company provided emergency relief services and had claims adjusters on-site within hours of many claimants' calls. State Farm capitalized on this service with subsequent advertisements outlining its outstanding services during and after the storm.

Exceptional service includes dozens of customer transactions, including prompt delivery, a fair returns policy, accurate billing, and prompt attention to a customer's presence. Exceptional service also includes giving customers good advice about using the product or service. As shown in Figure 13-2, providing exceptional service leads to customer delight.

Show Care and Concern

During contacts with the customer, the sales representative should show concern for the customer's welfare. The representative should ask questions such as "How have you enjoyed the optical scanner you bought a while back?" and "How are you feeling today?" After asking the question, the sales representative should project a genuine interest in the answer.

Delta hotels follow up every stay with a customer survey. One of the key questions asks whether the client was greeted by their first name and asked about their stay. Repeat customers are to be greeted promptly with their name accompanied by a welcoming attitude and smile.

Make the Buyer (Customer) Feel Good

A fundamental way of keeping a relationship going is to make the buyer feel good about himself or herself. Also, the customer should be made to feel good because of having bought from the representative. Offer compliments about the customer's appearance or about a report he or she prepared that specified vendor requirements clearly. An effective feel-good line is "I enjoy doing business with you."

Sometimes giving the customer or potential customer a small treat will make that person feel good enough to take decisive action. Microsoft enterprise sales manager LaShonda Anderson-Williams reports: "I once had a purchase order that needed to be signed by the end of our fiscal year. We called the CFO's assistant, and she said it was sitting on his desk. So I sent her a basket of cookies. The next day she got him to sign. To get my $1.2 million deal done, I spent $40."[25] We caution that you need good sensitivity to the situation to avoid giving a small treat that could backfire. An example might be sending Bill Gates (ranked as one of the richest people in the world) a $25 gift certificate to Macy's in order to sell to his company.

Build a Personal Relationship

Interacting with customers in a personal way often enhances the customer experience, leading to repeat business. Interaction with pleasant staff members gives customers a temporary feeling of friendship that many of them value.

Executives at Staybridge Suites recognize how human interaction contributes to profitability, and use this principle as a guide for making investments in customer service. Staybridge, similarly to other extended-stay hotels, provides limited services and is sparsely staffed to reduce costs. Rooms are fully cleaned only once a week, and the front desk is usually staffed by only one or two people. Instead of providing loads of amenities, Staybridge concentrates its customer service on staff members interacting with guests.

"A lot of our guests really want that personal interaction—the thing they get from home that they'd like to get from a hotel," says Rob Radomski, the vice-president for brand management for Staybridge Suites. "There are conversations between guests and staff about projects they're working on, and their family back home, and the kid, the dog." Staybridge also offers "Sundowner receptions" on Tuesday, Wednesday, and Thursday evenings in the lobby. General managers are required to attend the receptions in which guests are given a free meal and an opportunity to socialize. Radomski believes the meals are cost-effective in terms of developing customer loyalty.[26]

Another way of building relationships with large numbers of customers is to interact with them through company blogs or the social media. The company representative is authorized to chat with hundreds of customers and potential customers by placing informal comments on the authorized company blog. The worker lets out tidbits of information to customers without betraying company confidences or making defamatory statements about the company. However, the blog entries are not usually as positive as advertisements, which help form bonds with the customers. Many customers post replies and swap ideas with the company rep.

Company-approved blogs are widely used as customers demand information presented in a more unvarnished way. A major advantage of blogs is that they humanize large organizations, such as the company representative mentioning a favourite recipe as well as chatting about a new product.

Kadmy/Fotolia

SKILL-BUILDING EXERCISE 13-2

Bonding with Customers

Role players in this exercise will demonstrate two related techniques for bonding with customers: showing care and concern and making the buyer feel good.

Scenario 1: Show Care and Concern. A sales representative meets with two company representatives to talk about installing a new information system for employee benefits. One of the company representatives is from the human resources department and the other from the telecommunications department. The sales representative will attempt to show care and concern for both company representatives during the same meeting.

Scenario 2: Make the Buyer Feel Good. A couple, played by two role players, enters a new-car showroom to examine a model they have seen advertised on television. Although they are not in urgent need of a new car, they are strongly interested. The sales representative is behind quota for the month and would like to close a sale today. The rep decides to use the tactic "make the buyer feel good" to help form a bond.

For both scenarios, observers rate the role players on two dimensions, using a 1-to-5 scale from very poor to very good. One dimension is "effective use of human relations techniques." The second dimension is "acting ability." A few observers might voluntarily provide feedback to the role players in terms of sharing their ratings and observations. The course instructor might also provide feedback.

Invite the Customer Back

The Southern U.S. expression "Y'all come back, now!" is well suited to bonding with customers. Specific invitations to return may help increase repeat business. The more focused and individualized the invitation, the more likely its impact on customer behaviour. ("Y'all come back, now!" is sometimes used too indiscriminately to be effective.) Pointing out why you enjoyed doing business with the customer, and what future problems you could help with, is an effective technique. An industrial cleaning company supervisor might say, "Our crew enjoyed cleaning such a fancy office. Keep us in mind when you would like your windows to sparkle."

Despite the importance of forming a bond with your customer, getting too personal can backfire. Most customers want a business relationship with the company, and are not looking for a personal relationship with a company representative. As Daniel Askt observes, "Most customers want value and service without contending with a salesman who insists that he wants to be like family to you. Chances are you've already got a family, and for most of us, one is enough."[27]

Skill-Building Exercise 13-2 gives you an opportunity to practise techniques for bonding with customers.

DEALING WITH CUSTOMER DISSATISFACTION

LEARNING OBJECTIVE 4

Most companies put honest effort into preventing customer dissatisfaction. In addition to employing many of the principles and techniques already cited, many companies routinely survey customers to detect problem areas that could lead to dissatisfaction. A representative survey is shown in Figure 13-4. Despite all these efforts to achieve total customer satisfaction, some customer dissatisfaction is inevitable. One reason is that mistakes in serving customers are almost inevitable; for example, a piece of equipment may have a faulty component unknown to the seller. A second reason is that some customers have a predisposition to complain. They will find something to complain about with respect to any product or service. Visualize the billions of transactions that take place every year between Walmart service personnel and customers. Inevitably, some customer somewhere is going to rant and rave about poor service no matter how hard Walmart managers and store associates try to please.

An important point to remember in dealing with dissatisfied customers is that the negative personality traits of customers can bring down your level of customer service. For example, a study conducted in two major fast-food chains in Singapore found that customers who scored high on the trait of agreeableness tended to bring out positive emotion by the service personnel. In contrast, customers who scored high on negative affectivity (being disagreeable) brought out negative emotion among customer service

FIGURE 13-4   A Chain Restaurant Customer Satisfaction Survey

We would like to hear about your visit and how we can improve. Thank you!

Date: _____ Time: _____ AM/PM   Which location did you visit? _____

Name: _____

Address: _____

Email: _____

Phone: _____

Cheque Number: _____

Please rate us:	Poor	Fair	Good	Very Good	Excellent
Host/Hostess Hospitality	1	2	3	4	5
Server's Hospitality	1	2	3	4	5
Server's Attentiveness	1	2	3	4	5
Bartender's Hospitality	1	2	3	4	5
Bartender's Attentiveness	1	2	3	4	5
Quality of Food	1	2	3	4	5
Value of Meal	1	2	3	4	5
Cleanliness	1	2	3	4	5
Likely to Return	1	2	3	4	5
Manager Visit Table?	Yes	No			

Host/Hostess's Name: _____   Hair colour: _____

Server's Name: _____   Hair colour: _____

Bartender's Name: _____   Hair colour: _____

What did you order today or tonight? _____

Was this your first visit?   Would you like to be a Secret Shopper?
☐ Yes   ☐ No   ☐ Yes   ☐ No

Comments on your visit: _____
_____
_____

The information provided will be used to help us better serve you and will not be shared.

personnel.[28] A service worker cannot change the personality traits of customers, yet a little self-management of emotion is in order. The service worker might reflect, "I won't let this nasty customer get me down. I will do my best to do my job without overreacting." Be careful not to fake your emotion too frequently because it can create stress. Instead be assertive with a comment like "I want to help you, but might you tell me what you want in a more positive way?"

The next subsections describe four approaches to handling customer dissatisfaction: dealing with complaints and anger, involving the customer in working out a problem, handling an unreasonable request, and maintaining a realistic customer retention attitude.

Deal Constructively with Customer Complaints and Anger

In an era when customer satisfaction is so highly valued, both retail and industrial customers are likely to be vocal in their demands. When faced with an angry customer, use one or more of the following techniques recommended by customer satisfaction specialists.[29]

1. **Acknowledge the customer's point of view.** Make statements such as "I understand," "I agree," and "I'm sorry." Assume, for example, a customer says, "The accounts payable department made a $1000 overcharge on my account last month. I want this fixed right away." You might respond, "I understand how annoying this must be for you. I'll work on the problem right away."

2. **Avoid placing blame.** Suggesting that the customer is responsible for the problem intensifies the conflict. With the customer who claims to have been overcharged, refrain from saying, "Customers who keep careful accounts of their orders never have this problem."

3. **Use six magic words to defuse anger.** The magic words are *I understand* (that this is a problem), *I agree* (that it needs to be solved), and *I'm sorry* (that this happened to you). The six magic words help communicate your empathy, which is considered vital to dealing with customer problems.

4. **Apologize for the problems created by you or your company.** To recover from a breakdown in customer service, it is best to acknowledge an error immediately. Apologies are most effective when stated in the first person (such as "I created the problem"). The corporate "we're sorry" sounds less sincere than when one specific person accepts responsibility for what went wrong.

5. **Take responsibility, act fast, and be thorough.** This technique is essentially a simplified framework for managing customer dissatisfaction. Mark Delp, the manager of a fleet maintenance service, illustrates: "Suppose a customer calls about an oil leak after Fleet Response services a car. I have the car immediately picked up from the office and clean any oil spots that may have been left on the driveway. I make sure there are no further leaks. Furthermore, I apologize and accept full responsibility, even if the problem is not our fault, such as when a part fails."[30]

6. **Tell the difficult customers how much you value them.** Quite often customers with problems feel unappreciated. Just before resolving the problem of a difficult customer, explain how important he or she is to your firm. You might say, "We value your business, so I want to correct this for you quickly."[31] (Of course, you would value the customer even more after he or she becomes less difficult.)

7. **Follow up on the resolution of the problem.** Following up to see whether the resolution to the problem is satisfactory brings closure to the incident. The follow-up also helps the service deliverer know that he or she can rebound from an episode of customer dissatisfaction. One useful form of follow-up is to telephone the customer whose problem was solved. For example, a representative from the service department of an automobile dealership might telephone a customer whose new car required substantial warranty repairs. "Hello, this is Jill Gordon from Oak Automotive. We replaced your original transmission last month. How is the new transmission working?"

8. **Do your best to make sure the problem does not happen again.** The preceding steps are all valuable in resolving the complaints of angry customers. In addition, the customer needs some assurance that the problem will not happen again. Without such assurance, repeat business is at risk. The *recovery paradox* refers to the fact that customers will sometimes be more delighted by a skillful resolution of a problem than they are by service that was failure-free to begin with. For example, a customer might be delighted that a false roaming charge of $145 was removed from a phone bill—when the customer had never visited the country in which the charge occurred.

A less personal, and usually less effective, form of follow-up is to send a customer satisfaction questionnaire to the person with the problem. The questionnaire will often be interpreted as a company procedure that does not reflect specific concern about the individual's problem.

Involve the Customer in Working Out the Problem

Mistakes and problems in serving customers are inevitable, however hard the customer contact worker strives for perfection. To minimize the perception of poor service, the customer should be involved in deciding what should be done about the problem. By being involved in the solution, the customer is more likely to accept a deviation from the service originally promised. The ideal situation is for the customer service representative and dissatisfied customer to work as partners in resolving the problem. The following case history illustrates the technique of customer involvement and partnering.

Seth Bradbury is a sales promotion specialist at an advertising agency. A furniture store hired the agency to prepare and mail 3000 postcards advertising a new line of furniture. One side of the postcard contained a photograph of the furniture, and the other side contained product details and space for addressing and stamping the card. After the cards were mailed, Seth received an urgent call from the client. "The photograph of the furniture is printed vertically. It looks horrible. We agreed on a horizontal shot. This means 3000 cards have been mailed with a mistake."

After allowing the client to finish his complaint, Seth responded, "You're right, it is a vertical shot. Perhaps we misinterpreted your directions. However, I think your furniture still looks beautiful. The extra white space the vertical shot provides creates an interesting effect. It's unfortunate that the cards have already been mailed. What would you like us to do? It's important that you are satisfied."

The client responded, "I guess there's nothing we can do to change the photograph. Would you be willing to give us a discount off the price we agreed on?"

A survey conducted with more than 75,000 customers supports the importance of dealing directly with customer dissatisfaction. The customers in the study were people dealing directly with contact-centre representatives or using self-service channels. It was found that generous approaches to satisfying customers such as giving them a refund, a free product, or a free service such as expedited shipping did not have much impact on customer loyalty. What customers really want is a simple, rapid resolution to their problem.[32] For example, if a customer is not receiving the satellite television channels he or she subscribed to, all the customer wants is to receive the channels. A discount coupon will most likely not recapture his or her loyalty.

Anticipate How to Handle an Unreasonable Request

No matter how hard the customer contact worker attempts to provide outstanding customer service, at some point a customer comes along with an unreasonable request. Or the customer may raise an unfair objection. Speak to any experienced store associate to obtain a case history of "the customer from hell." For example, a small-business owner demanded that a store associate grant him exchange credit for six printer ribbons. The ribbons were purchased four years previously and were now obsolete.

Recognize that the customer who makes an unreasonable demand is usually aware it is unreasonable. The customer may not expect to be fully granted the request. Instead, the customer is bargaining by beginning with an unreasonable demand. The small-business owner who brought in the printer ribbons was probably looking to salvage whatever he could.

Sales representatives and other customer contact workers who stand their ground with dignity and courtesy generally will not lose customers with unreasonable requests. The suggestions presented next will help you deal with unreasonable demands while retaining the customer's business.[33]

- Let your customers retain their dignity by stating your position politely and reasonably.
- Avoid arguing with an upset customer. As the adage says, "You never win an argument with a customer."
- Appeal to your customer's sense of fair play and integrity. Explain that your intention is to do what is right and fair.
- Be firm by repeating the facts of the situation, but keep your temper under control.

SKILL-BUILDING EXERCISE 13-3

Dealing with Difficult Customers

The following scenarios require one person to play the role of the customer contact worker and another person to play the difficult customer. As usual, the role players project their feelings into the role-play by imagining how they would behave in the situation.

Scenario 1: One person is a store associate in a high-fashion women's clothing store. A woman who bought a $1000 gown the previous week brings the gown back today. She claims that she is returning the gown because it doesn't fit comfortably. The store associate strongly suspects the woman bought the gown to wear to a special occasion the past weekend and is now returning it as she no longer needs it.

Scenario 2: One person plays the role of a customer service representative in a consumer-electronics store. Another person plays the role of a customer who purchased a $3500 giant-screen television receiver three months ago. He comes up to the service rep's counter ranting about the store's ineptitude. The customer claims that the TV has broken down three times.

After the first repair, the TV worked for two weeks and then broke down again. The second repair lasted two weeks, only for the TV to break down during a Super Bowl party at his house. The customer is red in the face and shouting loudly. The service rep wants to resolve the customer's problem and prevent him from badmouthing the store.

- Accept responsibility for your decision rather than blaming company policy or your manager. Making somebody else the villain may intensify the problem.
- Be willing to say no to a customer when it is justifiable. Saying yes to an outrageous demand opens the door for a series of outrageous demands.

Maintain a Realistic Customer Retention Attitude

Some customers are too unreasonable, and therefore may not be worth keeping.[34] A realistic goal is to retain as many profitable customers as possible. At times it may be possible to retain a customer by modifying the service. For example, customers who do not pay their bills on time or at all might be changed to a prepaid service, as is done by phone companies and some Internet service providers.[35] In this way, the customers who have difficulty paying bills can still receive service.

An extreme example of a customer not worth keeping is the airline passenger who engages in *air rage*. Symptoms of air rage include (1) insisting on being served more alcoholic beverages than permissible by airline regulations, (2) sexually harassing or physically attacking flight attendants or other passengers, (3) refusing to fasten seat belts, (4) using electronic gear such as cell phones and laptops when not allowed by regulations, (5) smoking in the lavatory, and (6) using the aisles for a lavatory.

It is best to set limits for unruly customers and see if their behaviour changes. If the customer insists on creating disturbances, it is best to suggest the customer never return. Another problem is that some customers require so much service, or demand such high discounts, that they are unprofitable to retain. Good service to these customers means there is less time available to respond to the needs of profitable customers.

Customers can be unreasonable and unruly also because they are late paying their bills or do not pay them. Such customers divert resources away from more loyal and profitable customers and clients. Kishau Rogers, the owner of Websmith Group LLC, is a case in point. She finally had to drop or avoid clients who are high-maintenance or habitually late paying their bills. Her clients are mostly retail stores or entrepreneurs. They often asked for discounts because of their tight budgets or an expanded level of service beyond the agreed-upon contract. Rogers said that terminating 5 percent of her clientele "was the best decision I've made, because it really reduced the level of frustration I was experiencing. It freed me up to the clients that are loyal and pay on time."[36] In this way, the service she offered to other clients improved.

Access the eText in MySearchLab to learn more about this chapter's self-assessment quizzes.

Dealing diplomatically and effectively with difficult customers requires an awareness of tactics described in the previous several pages. Practice on the firing line is indispensable. The type of experience provided by Skill-Building Exercise 13-3 is also helpful.

To [Watch] [Explore] [Practice] [Study] and Review, visit MySearchLab

Developing Your Human Relations Skills and Reinforcing Concepts

Summary — Practice, Glossary Flashcards

- The three components of customer service experience are functional clues, mechanical clues, and human interaction clues.
- Eight key principles to increase customer satisfaction include keeping employees satisfied, receiving emotional support from co-workers, understanding customer needs and putting them first, focus on solving problems, responding positively to moments of truth, being ready to accept empowerment, improving customer service, and avoiding rudeness.
- Another key element in achieving customer satisfaction and delight is to create a bond—or emotional relationship—with customers. Six principles include showing a welcoming attitude, including a smile; providing exceptional service; expressing care and concern; making the buyer feel good; building a personal relationship; and inviting the customer back.
- Despite the best efforts on the company's part, some customer dissatisfaction is inevitable. Deal with customer dissatisfaction by acknowledging the customer's point of view, avoiding blaming the customer, using the six magic words to defuse anger, apologizing for the problem, taking responsibility, telling the customer how you value them, following up with the resolution, and doing your best to ensure the problem does not happen again.

Interpersonal Relations Case 13-1

The Rumpled Claims Forms

Rob is the supervisor of scanning operations at Insurance Resource, a firm that specializes in digitizing handwritten insurance claims. The client companies mail in their insurance claims in batches to Insurance Resource for processing into a digital format. In addition to scanning the handwritten documents, Insurance Resource also creates computer files for clients, and forwards the claims to the appropriate insurance company for reimbursement.

With profit margins being small in insurance claims processing, the document-scanning technicians must work rapidly as well as process a large volume of claims. One day when Rob asked Wendy to improve her speed, he received a response that he had heard many times in the past.

"How can I work fast when so many of these claims are rumpled, crumpled, and incomplete? We get some forms with missing names and addresses. The other scanning technicians say the same thing. We even have to stop to remove staples from the forms. If we are not careful, the staples get caught in scanners, and then we have to call tech support to de jam the machine."

"My speed problem is that some of our clients are just stupid. The speed problem is theirs, not ours. I know that we can send the documents with missing information to our research department. But that takes time from my scanning."

Rob replied, "Wendy, you have a point. Some of our clients make work difficult for us, but they are still valued customers. If we put too much pressure on them to give us claims forms that are easier to scan, they might look for another outsourcing firm.

"I'm going to get with Kim [vice-president of operations], and see if we can get a task force set up to work on this problem of difficult-to-scan documents right away."

Case Questions

1. In what way does this case deal with a customer service problem?
2. What steps do you recommend that Insurance Resource take to get clients to send the company documents that are easier to manage?
3. What suggestions can you offer Wendy and the other scanning technicians to process their work more effectively for now?

Source: Case researched by Stefanie Donaldson, Rochester, New York, January 2010.

Interpersonal Relations Case 13.2

The Troublesome Big Screen

The Chavez nuclear family consists of Maria, an office manager at a hospital; Tony, an ambulance medic; and their daughter Jennifer, a grade eight student. A happy family, they share many activities. Among their joint activities is watching MuchMusic (music television). The family regularly scrunch down to watch their favourite music shows on a 20-year-old, 30-inch colour television.

One Thursday evening, Jennifer said, "Mom and Dad, I have a great idea. Let's do something exciting with some of your money. Let's buy a big-screen TV so we can have more fun watching the rock channel."

Maria and Tony thought that Jennifer's idea had merit. However, they both agreed that a big-screen TV was a luxury item they could ill afford right now. Just before they fell asleep, the issue surfaced again. Maria said to Tony, "Deep down, we both agree with Jennifer. For less than $1000 we could bring much joy into our home."

Friday night the Chavez family visited Appliance City to look at television sets. Maria spotted a 48-inch TV that seemed ideal. A store associate, however, convinced them that the model they were inspecting was of mediocre quality. Instead, he recommended a domestic brand with a 60-inch screen that he claimed was the highest-quality model in its class. Spearheaded by Jennifer's exuberance, the Chavez family was convinced. The cost, including a three-year complete service warranty, was $1257.

The television set was delivered Monday evening as scheduled. For several days, the Chavez family enjoyed watching MuchMusic and other favourite programs on their new big-screen set. Friday evening, however, Maria, Tony, and Jennifer were mystified by an image that appeared on their screen. Shortly after Jennifer punched the menu button, an advertisement appeared on the screen touting the features of the set. Among the messages was one indicating that if the owner of this set were in a noisy room, he or she could mute the audio and watch the video.

Tony laughed as he explained that the demonstration mode was somehow triggered, and that the solution would be to just punch a few buttons. Next, Maria and he punched every button on the receiver and the TV remote control. The demonstration mode remained. Tony then pulled the plug and reinserted it, only for the demonstration mode to reappear.

Maria, Tony, and Jennifer then searched the owner's manual but found no information about the problem. Maria telephoned the dealer and got through to the service department after being placed on hold for six minutes. The service department said they knew nothing about the problem, but that she should speak to the sales department. After Maria explained her problem to a sales associate, she was told to speak to the service department.

Maria called back the service department and explained the problem again. A customer service specialist said that the store relied on an outside TV appliance repair firm to handle such problems. She said she would call the repair firm on Monday and that the firm would contact the Chavez family. By Tuesday morning the Chavez family still had not heard from the repair firm.

In desperation, Tony scanned a customer information booklet that came with the TV receiver. He found a list of 10 authorized service centres throughout North America that repaired his brand of television. Tony telephoned a service centre in Halifax. A cheerful woman answered the phone and listened to Tony's problem. With a sympathetic laugh, she said, "We get lots of calls like this. No problem. Just push the volume-up and volume-down buttons at the same time. The demo mode will disappear. The mode was activated when somebody pressed the menu up and down buttons at the same time." Tony raced into the living room and triumphantly restored the TV set to normal functioning.

The Friday after, a representative from the local television repair shop called. She said, "This is Modern TV and Appliance. Do you still need service on your set?" With anger in her voice, Maria explained how the problem was finally resolved.

Later that night, as the family gathered to watch MuchMusic, Maria said, "I guess we all love our new big-screen TV, but I wouldn't go back to Appliance City to buy even an electric can opener."

Case Questions

1. What mistakes in customer satisfaction principles did Appliance City personnel make?
2. What mistakes in customer satisfaction principles did Modern TV and Appliance make?
3. What would you do if you experienced a similar problem with an expensive TV receiver?

Questions for Discussion and Review

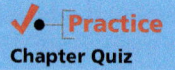

✓ Practice Chapter Quiz

Multiple Choice

1. Body language would be an example of a _____ clue, one of the components of customer service.

   a. technical
   b. human interaction
   c. mechanical
   d. sociological

2. The highest level of customer satisfaction is referred to as
   a. expectations satisfied.
   b. true appreciation.
   c. basic needs satisfied.
   d. customer delight.

3. According to your text, moments of truth are
   a. situations in which a customer realizes poor service.
   b. situations in which an employee realizes they are providing poor service.
   c. situations in which a customer comes in contact with a company and forms an impression of its service.
   d. situations in which a customer experiences exemplary service.

4. According to your text, which of the following results in the most lost business for a company?
   a. treating customers rudely
   b. long wait times for service
   c. pricing
   d. product quality

5. Which of the following is *not* a recommended strategy for dealing with customer complaints?
   a. Ignore the complaint; customers eventually stop calling to complain.
   b. Avoid placing blame on the customer.
   c. Apologize.
   d. Acknowledge the customer's point of view.

Short Answer

6. For what reason is a satisfied employee more likely to provide better customer service?
7. Describe a situation in your life in which you experienced customer delight. What made the experience delightful?
8. A couple walks into an automobile showroom and say they want a big, safe vehicle for them and their three children, yet they are unsure about what vehicle they should purchase. Describe how you might identify customer needs in this situation.
9. Visualize yourself as an executive at Hudson's Bay Company. Develop a policy to empower customer service desk associates to resolve customer problems, including the limits to their empowerment.
10. Log on to your MySearchLab to the chapter on customer service and click on the Simulations Cases Library. After working through the simulation of a doctor's office, do you have other suggestions that you think would improve the service in the doctor's office?

Answers to multiple choice questions: 1. b, 2. d, 3. c, 4. a, 5. a.

The Web Corner

www.sears.ca
Sears Canada (check out customer service)

www.customersatisfaction.com
Improving customer satisfaction and retention

www.customer-service.com
Improving your customer service

Internet Skill Builder: Building Customer Relationships

An axiom of business is that customer relationships are essential. Direct your Internet search for this assignment toward finding customer-relationship-building suggestions that can be converted into specific interpersonal skills, such as making a phone call to see how things are going. An example of a website that offers concrete suggestions for building customer relationships related to interpersonal skills is www.sideroad.com. Walk away from this exercise with a couple of ideas you might put into practice in dealing with customers.

MySearchLab

Visit **MySearchLab** to find self-grading review quizzes in the eText, discipline-specific media and readings, access to a variety of academic journals, and Associated Press news feeds, along with a wide range of writing, grammar, and research tools and to help hone writing and research skills.

CHAPTER 14

Enhancing Ethical Behaviour

Hudson's Bay Company (HBC) is a large Canadian business that has prided itself on its ethical practices including its ethical sourcing code. HBC includes The Bay, Zellers (which has been sold to Target), Home Outfitters, Fields, and Lord & Taylor (in the United States). HBC established the foundation for its ethical sourcing program in 1998, when it established a Code of Vendor Conduct (CVC). This program has evolved and now includes the Social Compliance Program (SCP), which was formalized in 2001, containing the CVC and a monitoring and remediation process. The overall goals of this comprehensive program are to improve factory conditions, educate buyers, and share industry knowledge. What this really means is that all of the products sold in HBC retail establishments must abide by the company's Social Compliance Program. Suppliers, especially those who produce their top brands for HBC, are carefully monitored to ensure that they

nyul/Fotolia

LEARNING Objectives

After reading and studying this chapter and doing the exercises, you should be able to

1. Recognize the importance of ethical behaviour for establishing good interpersonal relationships in organizations.
2. Recognize common ethical problems that occur in the workplace.
3. Follow guidelines and strategies for making ethical decisions and behaving ethically.

comply with all labour laws, satisfy employment standards (e.g., no child labour), adhere to environmental guidelines, and follow proper customs procedures for shipping.[1]

The company prepares a yearly Corporate Social Responsibility Report on all of its practices including its sourcing. It covers environmental sustainability, community investment, ethical sourcing, and associate (employee) development and wellness. The results are transparent and publicly available on the HBC website.[2]

The scenario above illustrates one company that conducts its business ethically. Ethics are an important part of workplaces today as there is more public scrutiny into business practices. Therefore, it is important to understand your own ethical values and ideas. We study ethics here because a person's ethical code has a significant impact on his or her interpersonal relationships. Our approach will emphasize the importance of ethics, common ethical problems, and guidelines for behaving ethically. Self-Assessment Quiz 14-1 gives you the opportunity to examine your ethical beliefs and attitudes.

WHY BE CONCERNED ABOUT BUSINESS ETHICS?

LEARNING OBJECTIVE 1

When asked why ethics is important, most people would respond with a statement resembling this one: "Ethics is important because it's the right thing to do. You behave decently in the workplace because your family and religious values have taught you what is right and wrong." All true so far, but the justification for behaving ethically is more complex, as described below. A major justification for behaving ethically on the job is to recognize that people are motivated by both self-interest and moral commitments. Most people want to maximize gain for themselves (remember the expectancy theory of motivation?). At the same time, most people are motivated to do something morally right. As one of many examples, vast numbers of people donate money to charity, although keeping that amount of money for themselves would provide more personal gain.

Many business executives want employees to behave ethically because a good reputation can help business. A favourable corporate reputation may enable firms to charge premium prices and attract better job applicants. A favourable reputation also helps attract investors, such as mutual fund managers who purchase stock in companies. Certain mutual funds, for example, invest only in companies that are environmentally friendly. Managers want employees to behave ethically because unethical behaviour is costly—for example, if it consists in employee theft, lost production time, or lawsuits.

Behaving ethically is also important because many unethical acts are also illegal, which can lead to financial loss and imprisonment. According to one estimate, North American industry loses about $400 billion annually to unethical or criminal behaviour.[3] A company that knowingly allows workers to engage in unsafe practices might be fined and the executives held personally liable. Further, unsafe practices can kill people. In

SELF-ASSESSMENT QUIZ 14-1

The Ethical Reasoning Inventory

Directions: Describe how well you agree with each of the following statements. Use the following scale: Disagree Strongly (DS); Disagree (D); Neutral (N); Agree (A); Agree Strongly (AS).

		DS	D	N	A	AS
1.	When applying for a job, I would cover up the fact that I had been fired from my most recent job.	5	4	3	2	1
2.	Cheating just a few dollars in one's favour on an expense account is okay if a person needs the money.	5	4	3	2	1
3.	Employees should inform on one another for wrongdoing.	1	2	3	4	5
4.	It is acceptable to give approximate figures for expense account items when one does not have all the receipts.	5	4	3	2	1
5.	I see no problem with conducting a little personal business on company time.	5	4	3	2	1
6.	Just to make a sale, I would stretch the truth about a delivery date.	5	4	3	2	1
7.	I would set up a customer with a date just to close a sale.	5	4	3	2	1
8.	I would flirt with my boss just to get a bigger salary increase.	5	4	3	2	1
9.	If I received $200 for doing some odd jobs, I would report it on my income tax return.	1	2	3	4	5
10.	I see no harm in taking home a few office supplies.	5	4	3	2	1
11.	It is acceptable to read the email messages and faxes of other workers, even when not invited to do so.	5	4	3	2	1
12.	It is unacceptable to call in sick just to take a day off, even if one only does it once or twice a year.	1	2	3	4	5
13.	I would accept a permanent, full-time job even if I knew I wanted the job for only six months.	5	4	3	2	1
14.	I would first check company policy before accepting an expensive gift from a supplier.	1	2	3	4	5
15.	To be successful in business, a person usually has to ignore ethics.	5	4	3	2	1
16.	If I felt physically attracted toward a job candidate, I would hire that person over a more qualified candidate.	5	4	3	2	1
17.	On the job, I tell the truth all the time.	1	2	3	4	5
18.	If a student were very pressed for time, it would be acceptable to either have a friend write a paper or purchase one.	5	4	3	2	1
19.	I would authorize accepting an office machine on a 30-day trial period, even if I knew we had no intention of buying it.	5	4	3	2	1
20.	I would never accept credit for a co-worker's ideas.	1	2	3	4	5

Scoring and Interpretation: Add the numbers you have circled to obtain your total score.

90–100 You are a strongly ethical person who may take a little ribbing from co-workers for being too straitlaced.

60–89 You show an average degree of ethical awareness, and therefore should become more sensitive to ethical issues.

41–59 Your ethics are underdeveloped, but you at least have some awareness of ethical issues. You need to raise your level of awareness of ethical issues.

20–40 Your ethical values are far below contemporary standards in business. Begin a serious study of business ethics.

recent history, two employees burned to death in a chicken processing plant in a fire they could not escape. Management had blocked the back doors to prevent employees from sneaking chicken parts out of the plant. Low ethics have also resulted in financial hardship for employees as company executives raid pension funds of other companies they purchase, sharply reducing or eliminating the retirement funds of many workers.

A subtle reason for behaving ethically is that a high standard of ethics increases the quality of one's working life. Ethics provides a set of guidelines that specify what makes for acceptable behaviour. Being ethical will point you toward actions that make life more satisfying for work associates. A company code of ethics specifies what constitutes ethical versus unethical behaviour. When employees follow this code, the overall quality of working life improves. Here are several sample clauses from ethical codes:

- Demonstrate courtesy, respect, honesty, and fairness.
- Do not use abusive language.
- Do not bring knives or other weapons to work.
- Do not offer bribes.
- Maintain confidentiality of records.
- Do not harass (sexually, racially, ethnically, or physically) subordinates, superiors, co-workers, customers, or suppliers.

To the extent that all members of the organization abide by this ethical code, the quality of working life will improve. At the same time, interpersonal relations in organizations will be strengthened.

COMMON ETHICAL PROBLEMS

To become more skilled at behaving ethically, it is important to familiarize yourself with common ethical problems in organizations. Whether or not a given situation presents an ethical problem for a person depends to some extent on its **moral intensity**, or how deeply others might be affected.[4] A worker might face a strong ethical conflict about dumping mercury into a water supply but would be less concerned about dumping cleaning fluid. Yet both acts would be considered unethical and illegal. Here we first look at why being ethical is not as easy as it sounds. We then look at some data about the frequency of ethical problems and an analysis of predictable ethical temptations, and also examine the subtle ethical dilemma of choosing between rights.

Why Being Ethical Isn't Easy

As analyzed by Linda Klebe Treviño and Michael E. Brown, behaving ethically in business is more complex than it seems on the surface for a variety of reasons.[5] To begin with, ethical decisions are complex. For example, someone might argue that hiring children for factory jobs in overseas countries is unethical. Yet if these children lose their jobs, many would starve or turn to crime to survive. Second, people do not always recognize the moral issues involved in a decision. The home-maintenance worker who found a butcher knife under the bed might not think that he has a role to play in perhaps preventing murder. Sometimes language hides the moral issue involved, such as when the term "file sharing" replaces "stealing" in regard to music.

Another complexity in making ethical decisions is that people have different levels of moral development. At one end of the scale some people behave morally just to escape punishment. At the other end of the scale, some people are morally developed to the point that they are guided by principles of justice and want to help as many people as possible. The environment in which we work also influences whether we behave ethically. Suppose a restaurant owner encourages such practices as serving customers food that was accidentally dropped on the kitchen floor. An individual server is more likely to engage in such behaviour to obey the demands of the owner.

LEARNING OBJECTIVE 2

moral intensity
In ethical decision making, how deeply others might be affected by the decision.

Dave Einsel/Getty Images

utilitarian predisposition

A belief that the value of an act's outcomes should determine whether it is moral.

A fundamental reason that being ethical is not always easy is that some people have a predisposition to be unethical. The predisposition works almost like a personality trait, compelling certain people to be devious. A person with a **utilitarian predisposition** believes that the value of an act's outcomes should determine whether it is moral.[6] A server with this predisposition might be willing to serve food that dropped on the floor so long as no customer became sick or sued the restaurant. A small-business owner with a utilitarian predisposition might be willing to sell fake luxury goods on the Internet so long as nobody complained and he or she was not caught. When asked about why he sold imitation watches, one vendor said, "What's the difference? My watches look like the real thing, and they tell time."

Another major contributor to ethical problems is the same factor that motivates people to do many things—acting out of self-interest. John Bogle, the founder and former chief executive of the Vanguard Groups of Mutual Funds, believes that self-interest contributed to the financial scandals of recent years. "But self-interest got out of hand. It created a bottom-line society in which success is measured in monetary terms. Dollars became the coin of the new realm. Unchecked market forces overwhelmed traditional standards of professional conduct, developed over centuries."[7] Another take on self-interest is that employee fraud intensifies during difficult financial times where workers are experiencing financial pressures in their personal lives. Among these frauds are cheque-forgery schemes, petty-cash thefts, and taking money from fabricated customer returns.[8] All of these schemes are illegal as well as unethical.

A Survey of the Extent of Ethical Problems

A substantial number of managers and employees engage in unethical behaviour, often because they feel pressured into making a quick profit. There has been substantial publicity in recent years of these misdeeds as well as those of Canadian government officials engaging in such behaviours as claiming exorbitant expenses while overseas. Feeling under pressure, in general, or not taking the time to think through the ethics of an issue, can lead to unethical behaviour in the name of saving time.

However, ethical violations are not limited to executives, but also occur among rank-and-file employees. Figure 14-1 presents data about unethical behaviour noticed by employees. As found in other surveys, lying is another widespread ethical problem in the workplace. Lying to either employees or outsiders was observed by 31 percent of employees. These findings might suggest that workers are observant of ethical problems, and willing to note them on a survey.

FIGURE 14-1 Questionable Workplace Behaviour as Reported by Employees

Despite a heightened emphasis on business ethics following scandals earlier this decade, a significant number of employees say they still witness questionable workplace behaviour. Here is the percentage of employees who say they observed certain behaviours in the previous year, according to a survey of 2852 workers by the Ethics Resource Center.

Lying to employees	19%
Engaging in conflicts of interest	16%
Lying to outside stakeholders	12%
Engaging in health and safety violations	11%
Producing poor product quality	9%
Stealing	9%
Sexual harassment	7%

Source: National Business Ethics Survey, Ethics Resource Center, Arlington, VA, 2009 survey. (www.ethics.org). Reprinted with permission.

FIGURE 14-2 Frequent Ethical Dilemmas

Many ethical temptations face the individual on the job, forcing him or her to think through ethical issues practically every workday.

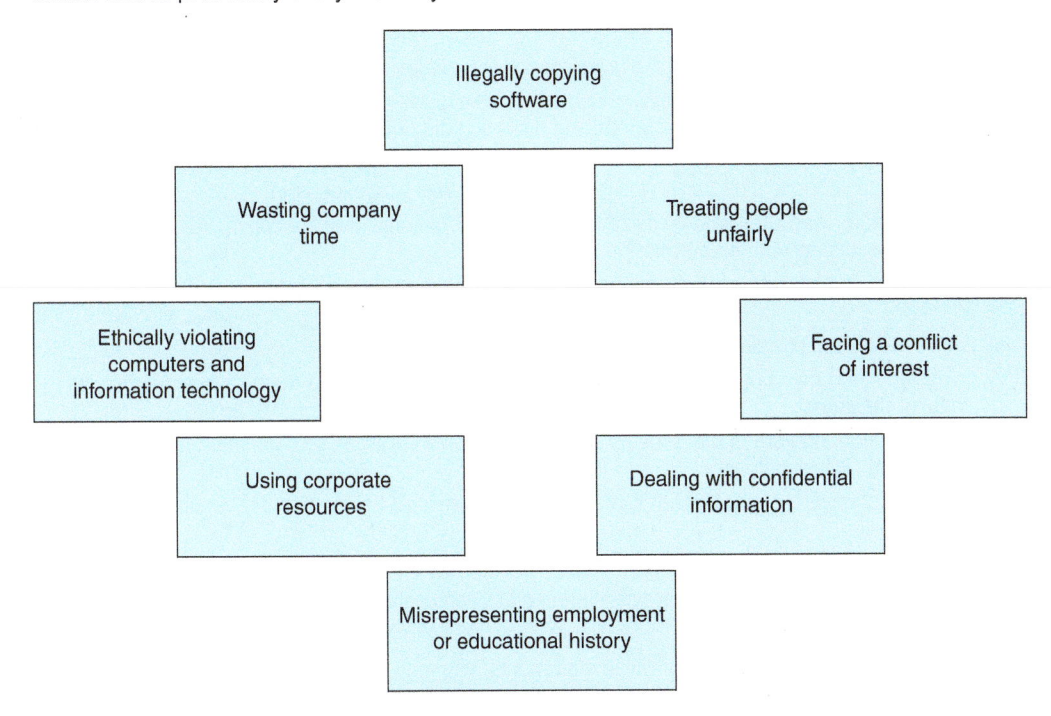

- Illegally copying software
- Wasting company time
- Treating people unfairly
- Ethically violating computers and information technology
- Facing a conflict of interest
- Using corporate resources
- Dealing with confidential information
- Misrepresenting employment or educational history

Frequent Ethical Dilemmas

Certain ethical mistakes, including illegal actions, recur frequently in the workplace. Familiarizing oneself with them can be helpful in monitoring one's own behaviour. Here we describe a number of common ethical problems faced by business executives as well as workers at lower job levels. Figure 14-2 outlines these problems.

The Temptation to Illegally Copy Software. A rampant ethical problem is whether to illegally copy software. According to the Business Software Alliance, approximately 35 percent of applications used in business are illegal.[9] There are a myriad of excuses that individuals and businesses use to justify their behaviour with excuses such as it is for educational purposes, no one is getting hurt, and the movie industry makes enough money already. No matter the excuse, such downloading is illegal. Self-Assessment quiz 14-2 examines your tendency to copy software (or at least your temptation to do so).

Treating People Unfairly. Being fair to people means practising equity, reciprocity, and impartiality. Fairness revolves around the issue of giving people equal rewards for accomplishing equal amounts of work. The goal of human resources legislation is to encourage making decisions about people based on their qualifications and performance—not on the basis of demographic factors such as sex, race, or age. A fair working environment is where performance is the only factor that counts (*equity*). Employer–employee expectations must be understood and met (*reciprocity*). Prejudice and bias must be eliminated (*impartiality*).

To treat people fairly—and therefore ethically—an overemphasis on political factors would be unethical. Yet this ethical doctrine is not always easy to implement. It is human nature to want to give bigger rewards (such as fatter raises or bigger orders) to people we like.

A major contributor to treating people unfairly is cronyism, or giving jobs to people who have done personal favours for you. Often the unqualified friend is given a position when competent, and qualified candidates are available. Cronyism is often practised in

▶ Watch
Making Ethical Decisions

> ### SELF ASSESSMENT QUIZ 14-2
>
> Examine the following statements and answer yes or no if you have ever done any of the following or have thought about doing so.
>
> 1. I have watched a movie on a CD that was not the actual movie CD produced by the movie rights holder. Yes ___ No ___
> 2. I have had friends copy me their purchased disks so I did not have to pay for it myself. Yes ___ No ___
> 3. I have copied a friend's disk as it was for school and it was very expensive. Yes ___ No ___
> 4. I often look for web sites where I can download movies or songs that are copyrighted and do not allow downloading without permission. Yes ___ No ___
> 5. I have done presentations with downloaded video clips without looking at copyright. Yes ___ No ___
> 6. I have purchased pirated movies or video games. Yes ___ No ___
> 7. I regularly lend my copyrighted disks to friends so that they can use them rather than buying them at the store. Yes ___ No ___
> 8. I really do not understand the issue as these companies are making so much money that my bit of "stealing" is insignificant. Yes ___ No ___
> 9. Software changes so quickly that it really does not matter if I copy an older version. Yes ___ No ___
> 10. I am using it only for educational purposes. Yes ___ No ___
> 11. Once I am finished, I delete the program immediately so I only use it for a few weeks. Yes ___ No ___
>
> If you have responded "yes" to any of these statements, you may have illegally copied or thought of copying software. Such assessment as this, gives you an opportunity to think about or rethink your beliefs and how you plan to respond to such temptations in the future.

government, where heads of government agencies are sometimes appointed mostly because they are a supporter and friend of the person in power. Cronyism is also sometimes found in business, with buddies, relatives, and lovers often being chosen over more qualified workers for a variety of positions.

Sexual Harassment. In Chapter 9, we looked at sexual harassment as a source of conflict and an illegal act. Sexual harassment is also an ethical issue, because it is morally wrong and unfair. All acts of sexual harassment fail an ethics test. Before sexually harassing another person, the potential harasser should ask, "Would I want a loved one to be treated this way?"

Conflict of Interest. Part of being ethical is making business judgments only on the basis of the merits or facts in a situation. Imagine that you are a supervisor who is romantically involved with a worker within the group. When it comes time to assign raises, it will be difficult for you to be objective. A **conflict of interest** occurs when your judgment or objectivity is compromised. Conflicts of interest often take place in the sales end of business. If a company representative accepts a large gift from a sales representative, it may be difficult to make objective judgments about buying from the representative. Yet being taken to dinner by a vendor would not ordinarily cloud one's judgment. Another common example of a conflict of interest is making a hiring decision about a friend who badly needs a job but is not well qualified for the position.

Blogging has created a new type of conflict of interest because many bloggers are paid for those kind, supposedly objective, comments they insert on the Internet about products and services. In the United States, the Federal Trade Commission now requires bloggers to clearly disclose any payments or freebies they receive from companies for publishing reviews about their products or services. Penalties include a maximum fine of up to $11,000 per violation.[10]

---

conflict of interest

A situation that occurs when a person's judgment or objectivity is compromised.

Websites that allow people to review hotels, resorts, and cruises have also been victims of unethical postings. On TripAdvisor (one hotel and restaurant review site), hotel companies have been accused of having their employees post negative reviews of competitors' hotels.[11] Proven or not, these allegations affect the confidence that hotel searchers can have in these reviews.

Dealing with Confidential Information. An ethical person can be trusted by others not to divulge confidential information unless the welfare of others is at stake. Suppose a co-worker tells you in confidence that she is upset with the company and is therefore looking for another job. Behaving ethically, you do not pass this information along to your supervisor even though it would help your supervisor plan for a replacement. Now suppose the scenario changes slightly. Your co-worker tells you she is looking for another job because she is upset. She tells you she is so upset that she plans to destroy company computer files on her last day. If your friend does find another job, you might warn the company about her contemplated activities.

The challenge of dealing with confidential information arises in many areas of business, many of which affect interpersonal relations. If you learned that a co-worker was indicted for a crime, charged with sexual harassment, or facing bankruptcy, there would be a temptation to gossip about the person. A highly ethical person would not pass along information about the personal difficulties of another person.

Misrepresenting Employment or Education History. Many people are tempted to distort in a positive direction information about their employment or education history on their job résumé, job application form, and during the interview. Distortion, or lying, of this type is considered to be unethical and can lead to immediate dismissal if discovered. Misrepresentation of credentials takes place at all job levels. Inflated credentials in the executive suite have been an embarrassment to many companies. A survey of 358 senior executives at 53 publicly traded companies has uncovered seven instances of inaccurate claims that an individual had received an academic degree. In recent years, misrepresentation of academic credentials has cost top corporate officials their positions at companies, including RadioShack Corp., vitamin maker Herbalife Ltd., and Usana Health Sciences, Inc.[12]

Use of Corporate Resources. A corporate resource is anything the company owns, including its name and reputation. If Jake Petro worked for Ford Motor Company, for example, it would be unethical for him to establish a body shop and put on his letterhead and website "Jake Petro, Manufacturing Technician, Ford Motor Company." Other uses of corporate resources fall more into the grey area. It might be quite ethical to borrow a laptop for the weekend from your employer to do work at home. But it would be less ethical to borrow the laptop to prepare personal income taxes. In the latter case you might be accused of using corporate resources for personal purposes. Loading personal software onto company computers so you can access your bank account and so forth also can be considered an ethical violation.

Ethical Violations with Computers and Information Technology. As computers dominate the workplace, many ethical issues have arisen in addition to pirating software. One ethical dilemma that surfaces frequently is the fairness of tracking the websites a person visits and those from which he or she makes purchases. Should it be allowable for this information to be sold? Another issue is the fairness of having an employee work at a keyboard for 60 hours in one week when such behaviour frequently leads to repetitive strain injury. Figure 14-3 lists some major ethical issues involved in computer use.

Wasting Company Time. Many workers waste company time in the pursuit of personal interests. Among these time wasters are making personal phone calls, shopping by phone or the Internet, visiting sports and pornography sites, talking about personal matters with co-workers, daydreaming, and spending long periods of time smoking outside the building. The problem has become so severe with cellphone calls and text

FIGURE 14-3　The 11 Commandments of Computer Ethics

> 1. Do not use a computer to harm other people. Avoid all obscene, defamatory, threatening, or otherwise harassing messages. Take precautions against others developing repetitive motion disorders.
> 2. Do not interfere with other people's computer work. (This includes intentionally spreading computer viruses.)
> 3. Do not snoop around in other people's files.
> 4. Do not use a computer to steal.
> 5. Do not use a computer to bear false witness.
> 6. Do not use or copy software for which you have not paid (see Figure 14-1).
> 7. Do not use other people's resources without authorization.
> 8. Do not appropriate other people's intellectual output.
> 9. Do not use the employer's computer for the personal promotion of commercial goods or services, unless granted permission by the employer.
> 10. Do think about the social consequences of the program you write.
> 11. Do use a computer in ways that show consideration and respect.

Source: Adapted and updated from Arlene H. Rinaldi and Florida Atlantic University, rinaldi@acc.fau.edu; "Code of Conduct for Computer and Network Use," http://www.rit.edu/computerconduct.

messaging that many employers forbid the use of cell phones while working. The section in Chapter 15 about personal productivity presents data about time wasting on the job.

You may have observed that these common ethical directions are not always clear-cut. Aside from obvious matters such as prohibitions against stealing, lying, cheating, and intimidating, subjectivity enters into ethical decision making. Skill-Building Exercise 14-1 provides an opportunity to try out your ethical reasoning.

Choosing between Two Rights: Dealing with Defining Moments

Ethical decision making usually involves choosing between two options: one we perceive to be right and one we perceive to be wrong. A challenging twist to ethical decision making is to sort through your values when you have to choose between two *rights*, or two morally sound choices. Joseph L. Badaracco, Jr., uses the term **defining moment** to describe choosing between two or more ideals in which we deeply believe.[13] If you can learn to work through defining moments, your ethical skills will be improved. Let's first take a non-work example to illustrate a defining moment.

Imagine yourself as a basketball referee in a league for boys 10 years old and younger. Luis, the smallest boy on the team, has a self-confidence problem in general, and he has not scored a goal yet this season. This is the final game of the season. The other team is ahead by 10 points, with one minute to go. Luis lets fly with a shot that goes into the basket, but his right heel is on the line. If the goal is allowed, Luis will experience one of the happiest moments in his life, and his self-confidence might increase.

You strongly believe in helping people grow and develop. Yet you also strongly believe in following the rules of sports. What should you do?

You may have recognized that a defining moment is a role conflict in which you have to choose between competing values. A CEO might deeply believe that she has an obligation to the stockholders to make a profit, and also believe in being generous and fair toward employees. However, to make a profit this year she will be forced to lay off

defining moment
A time when one must choose between two or more ideals in which one deeply believes.

SKILL-BUILDING EXERCISE 14-1

The Ethics Game

Citicorp (now part of Citigroup) has developed an ethics game called The Work Ethic. It teaches ethics by asking small teams of employees to confront difficult scenarios, such as those that follow. Discuss these ethical problems in teams. As you discuss the scenarios, identify the ethical issues involved.

Scenario 1: One of your assignments is to find a contractor to conduct building maintenance for your company headquarters. You invite bids for the job. High-Performance Cleaners, a firm staffed largely by teenagers from troubled families who have criminal records, bids on the job. Many of these teenagers also have severe learning disabilities and cannot readily find employment. High-Performance Cleaners proves to be the second-highest bidder. You

a. advise High-Performance Cleaners that its bid is too high for consideration and that your company is not a social agency.
b. award the bid to High-Performance Cleaners and justify your actions with a letter to top management by talking about social responsibility.
c. falsify the other bids in your report to management, making High-Performance Cleaners the low bidder—and thus the contract winner.
d. explain to High-Performance Cleaners that it lost the bid, but you will award the company a piece of the contract because of its sterling work with needy teenagers.

Scenario 2: You live in Toronto and your company sends you on a three-day trip to New York City. Your business dealings in the Big Apple will keep you there Wednesday, Thursday, and Friday morning. You have several friends and relatives in New York, so you decide to stay there until Sunday afternoon. Besides, you want to engage in tourist activities, such as taking a boat tour around Manhattan and visiting Radio City Music Hall. When preparing your expense report for your trip, you request payment for all your business-related costs up through Friday afternoon, plus

a. your return trip on Sunday.
b. the return trip and the room cost for Friday and Saturday nights.
c. the return trip and one-half of your weekend food expenses as well as two extra nights in the hotel.
d. the return trip and your food costs for the weekend (which you justify because you ate at fast-food restaurants on Wednesday, Thursday, and Friday).

Scenario 3: You are the leader of a self-managing work team in a financial services company. The work of your team has expanded to the point where you are authorized to hire another team member. The team busily interviews a number of candidates from inside and outside the company. The other team members agree that one of the candidates, Pat, has truly outstanding credentials. You agree that Pat is a strong candidate. Yet you don't want Pat on the team because you and Pat were emotionally involved with one another in the past for about a year. You think that working with Pat would disrupt your concentration and bring back hurtful memories. You decide to

a. tell the group that you have some negative information about Pat's past that would disqualify Pat for the job.
b. telephone Pat and beg that Pat find employment elsewhere.
c. tell the group that you agree Pat is qualified, but explain your concerns about the disruption in concentration and emotional hurt working with Pat would cause you.
d. tell the group that you agree Pat is right for the position and mention nothing about the past relationship.

Scoring and Observation: Scenario 1, about High-Performance Cleaners, raises dozens of ethical questions, including whether humanitarian considerations can outweigh profit concerns. Teams that chose "a" receive 0 points; "b," 20 points; "c," 10 points; "d," 10 points. (Answer "d" is best here, because it would not be fair to give the bid to the second-highest bidder. However, you are still finding a way to reward the High-Performance Cleaners for its meritorious work in the community. Answer "c" is the worst, because you would be outright lying.)

Scenario 2 raises ethical issues about using company resources. Teams that chose "a" receive 20 points; "b," 10 points; "c," 15 points; "d," 0 points. (Answer "a" is fairest, because the company would expect to reimburse you for your round trip plus the expenses up through Friday afternoon. Answer "c" is the worst, because it would be unjustified for you to be reimbursed for your vacation in New York.)

Scenario 3 raises issues about fairness in making selection decisions. Teams that chose "a" receive 20 points; "b," 10 points; "c," 15 points; "d," 0 points. (Answer "c" is the most ethical, because you are being honest with the group about the reason you do not wish to hire Pat. Answer "a" is the most unethical, because you are telling lies about Pat. Furthermore, you might be committing the illegal act of libel.)

Source: The concept of the game is from Karen Ireland, "The Ethics Game," *Personnel Journal*, March 1991, p. 74. The scenarios are original.

---

several good employees with long seniority. The CEO now faces a moment of truth. Badaracco suggests that the individual can work through a defining moment by discovering "Who am I?" You discover who you are by arriving at soul-searching answers to three questions:

1. What feelings and intuitions are coming into conflict in this situation?
2. Which of the values that are in conflict are the most deeply rooted in my life?
3. What combinations of expediency and shrewdness, coupled with imagination and boldness, will help me implement my personal understanding of what is right?

SKILL-BUILDING EXERCISE 14-2

Dealing with Defining Moments

The toughest ethical choices for many people occur when they need to choose between two *rights*. The result is a defining moment, because we are challenged to think in a deeper way by choosing between two or more ideals. Working individually or in teams, deal with the two following defining moments. Explain why these scenarios could require choosing between two rights, and explain the reasoning behind your decisions.

Scenario 1: You are the manager of a department in a business firm that assigns each department a fixed amount of money for salary increases each year. An average-performing member of the department asks you in advance for an above-average increase. He explains that his mother has developed multiple sclerosis and requires the services of a paid helper from time to time. You are concerned that if you give this man an above-average increase, somebody else in the department will need to receive a below-average increase.

Scenario 2: You are the team leader of an e-tailing (retail selling over the Internet) group. In recent months, each team member has been working about 60 hours per week, with little prospect of the workload decreasing in the future. Since the project is still losing money, higher management insists that one person be dropped from the team. One member of the team, Mildred, is willing to work only about 45 hours per week because she spends considerable time volunteering to work with autistic children. Mildred's work is satisfactory, but her output is the lowest in the group because of her shorter number of working hours. You must make a decision about whether to recommend that Mildred be dismissed.

Skill-Building Exercise 14-2 gives you an opportunity to deal with defining moments. The three questions just asked could help you find answers, but do not be constrained by these questions.

GUIDELINES FOR BEHAVING ETHICALLY

LEARNING OBJECTIVE 3

✳ Explore
Simulation: Ethics in the Workplace

Following guidelines for ethical behaviour is the heart of being ethical. Although many people behave ethically without studying ethical guidelines, they are usually following guidelines programmed into their minds early in life. The Golden Rule exemplifies a guideline taught by parents, grandparents, and kindergarten teachers. In this section, we approach ethical guidelines from five perspectives: (1) developing virtuousness; (2) following a guide to ethical decision making; (3) developing strong relationships with work associates; (4) using corporate ethics programs; and (5) following an applicable professional code of conduct.

Developing Virtuousness

A deep-rooted approach to behaving ethically is to have strong moral and ethical principles, or to be virtuous. A person of high virtue has good character, and genuine motivation and intentions. A major problem in becoming virtuous is to agree on what values constitute virtuousness. Management professor Edwin A. Locke has prepared a modern analysis of what values constitute virtue in a business environment.[14] Here we highlight his findings because they are representative of what constitutes virtuousness. Other observers might have a different list of virtuous values.

1. **Rationality** is a principle that leads to being virtuousness. Being rational includes taking reality (facts) seriously, thinking hard, thinking long-range, and thinking of the consequences of one's actions. A rational parachute technician would not ship a defective parachute just because it was close to quitting time, and he did not want to work late. And we hope that the manager is rational (and therefore ethical) when writing performance evaluations.

2. **Honesty,** the refusal to fake reality, is a value that contributes directly to ethical behaviour. Being dishonest can also be illegal, such as when a company lies to the Canadian Revenue Service about expenses it incurred or hides revenue when preparing a tax report. Dishonesty in terms of making false statements about the financial health of an enterprise has been one of the most frequent business frauds. Being caught lying can lead to dismissal by many employers.

An example of such a lie would be blaming someone else for a mistake of your own. *Integrity* means loyalty to one's rational convictions, or sticking with one's principles. If you believe that favouritism is immoral, then you would not recommend that the company hire a friend of yours who you know to be unqualified.

3. **Independence** refers to the responsibility of using your own rational judgment rather than relying too heavily on the thinking of others. In personal life, being independent means not relying too heavily on others for permanent support. A worker with a strong value of independence would not readily go along with the thinking of the group if he or she had a better idea.

4. **Productivity** means creating, or obtaining through trade, the material values your life requires. You are therefore virtuous if you are productive on the job and contribute enough to be worthy of your compensation. *Justice* refers to looking at the facts of the character and achievements of others and judging them objectively. To be just is to be fair, such as willing to pay somebody what they are worth, or paying a fair price for merchandise. When a big company executive "squeezes" a supplier to the point that the supplier can barely make a profit, the executive is not practising justice.

5. **Forgiveness** is a virtue providing the breach of morality was not too severe, such as forging an employee who ate a sandwich without paying when eating food without paying was not authorized. *Pride* in the context of virtues refers to working to perfect one's moral character. You would thus be proud because you are virtuous.

The above values that contribute to being virtuousness are useful in the study of human relations because they all translate into interpersonal skills, such as knowing how to be productive and treat people justly.

Following a Guide to Ethical Decision-Making

A powerful strategy for behaving ethically is to follow a guide for ethical decision making. Such a guide for making contemplated decisions includes testing the ethics of the decision. **Ethical screening** refers to running a contemplated decision or action through an ethics test. Such screening makes the most sense when the contemplated action or decision is not clearly ethical or unethical. If a sales representative were to take a favourite customer to McDonald's for lunch, an ethical screen would not be necessary. Nobody would interpret a Big Mac as a serious bribe. Assume, instead, that the sales rep offered to give the customer an under-the-table gift of $700 for placing a large offer with the rep's firm. The sales rep's behaviour would be so blatantly unethical that conducting an ethical screen would be unnecessary.

Several useful ethical screens, or guides to ethical decision making, have been developed. A guide developed by Treviño and Nelson is presented here, because it incorporates the basic ideas in other ethical tests.[15] After studying this guide, you will be asked to ethically screen two different scenarios. The eight steps to sound ethical decision making identified in the guide are as follows:

1. **Gather the facts.** When making an important decision in business, it is necessary to gather relevant facts. Ask yourself the following questions: "Are there any legal issues involved here?" "Is there a precedent in our firm with respect to this type of decision?" "Do I have the authority to make this decision?" "Are there company rules and regulations governing such decisions?"

   The manager of a child-care centre needed to hire an additional child-care specialist. One of the applicants was a 55-year-old male with experience as a father and grandfather. The manager judged him to be qualified, yet she knew that many parents would not want their preschool children to be cared for by a middle-aged male. Many people perceive that a younger woman is better qualified for child care than an older man. The manager therefore had to gather

ethical screening

Running a contemplated decision or action through an ethics test.

considerable facts about the situation, including facts about job discrimination and precedents in hiring males as child-care specialists.

2. **Define the ethical issues.** The ethical issues in a given decision are often more complicated than a first glance suggests. When faced with a complex decision, it may be helpful to talk over the ethical issues with another person. The ethical issues might involve character traits such as being kind and caring and treating others with respect. Or the ethical issues might relate to some of the common ethical problems described earlier in the chapter. Among them are conflict of interest, dealing with confidential information, and use of corporate resources.

    The manager of the child-care centre is facing such ethical issues as fairness, job discrimination, and meeting the demands of customers at the expense of job applicants. The manager is also facing a diversity issue: Should the workforce in a child-care centre be culturally diverse, or should only young women be hired?

3. **Identify the affected parties.** When faced with a complex ethical decision, it is important to identify all the affected parties. Major corporate decisions can affect thousands of people. If a company decides to shut down a plant and move its manufacturing to a low-wage country, thousands of individuals and many different parties are affected. Workers lose their jobs, suppliers lose their customers, local governments lose out on tax revenues, and local merchants lose many of their customers. You may need to brainstorm with a few others to think of all the parties affected by a given decision.

    The parties affected by the decision about hiring or not hiring the 55-year-old male include the applicant himself, the children, the parents, and the board of directors of the child-care centre. The government might also be involved if the man were rejected and filed charges of age and sex discrimination.

4. **Identify the consequences.** After you have identified the parties affected by a decision, the next step is to predict the consequences for each party. It may not be necessary to identify every consequence, yet it is important to identify the consequences with the highest probability of occurring and those with the most negative outcomes. The problem is that many people can be harmed by an unethical decision, such as a decision to avoid describing the full possible side effects of a diet program.

    Both short-term and long-term consequences should be specified. The company's closing a plant might create considerable short-term turmoil, but in the long term the company might be healthier. People participating in a diet program might achieve their short-term objective of losing weight. Yet in the long term, their health might be adversely affected because the diet is not nutritionally balanced.

    The *symbolic* consequences of an action are important. Every action and decision sends a message (the decision is a symbol of something). If a company moves manufacturing out of a community to save on labour costs, it means that the short-term welfare of domestic employees is less important than profit or perhaps the company surviving.

    Let us return to the child-care manager and the job applicant. If the applicant does not get the job, his welfare will be adversely affected. He has been laid off by a large employer and cannot find work in his regular field. His family will also suffer because he will not be able to make a financial contribution. Yet if the man is hired, the child-care centre may suffer. Many parents will say, "Absolutely not. I do not want my child cared for by a middle-aged man. He could be a child molester." (It may be unethical for people to have vicious stereotypes, yet they still exist.) If the child-care centre does hire the man, the act will symbolize the fact that the owners of the centre value diversity.

5. **Identify the obligations.** Identify the obligations and the reasons for each obligation when making a complex decision. The manufacturer of automotive brakes has an obligation to produce and sell only brakes that meet high safety standards. The obligation is to the auto manufacturer who purchases the brakes and, more important, to the ultimate consumer whose safety depends on effective brakes. The reason for the obligation to make safe brakes is that lives are at stake.

   The child-care manager has an obligation to provide for the safety and health of the children at the centre. She must also provide for the peace of mind of the parents and be a good citizen of the community in which the centre is located. The decision about hiring the candidate in question must be balanced against all these obligations.

6. **Consider your character and integrity.** A core consideration when faced with an ethical dilemma is to consider how relevant people would judge your character and integrity in the light of the decision you make. What would your family, friends, significant others, teachers, and co-workers think of your actions? To refine this thinking further, how would you feel if your actions were publicly disclosed in the local newspaper or by email? Would you want the world to know that you gave an under-the-table kickback or that you sexually harassed a frightened teenager working for you? If you would be proud for others to know what decision you made when faced with an ethical dilemma, you are probably making the right decision.

   The child-care manager might ponder how she would feel if the following information were released in the local newspaper:

   The manager of Good Times Child Care recently rejected the application of a 55-year-old man for a child-care-specialist position. She said that although Mr. _____ was well qualified from an experience and personality standpoint, she couldn't hire him. She said that Good Times would lose too much business because many parents would fear that Mr. _____ was a child molester or pedophile.

7. **Think creatively about potential actions.** When faced with an ethical dilemma, put yourself into a creative-thinking mode. Stretch your imagination to invent several options rather than thinking you have only two choices—to do or not do something. Creative thinking may point toward a third, and even a fourth, alternative. Imagine this ethical dilemma: A purchasing agent is told that if her firm awards a contract to the sales representative's firm, she will find a leather jacket of her choice delivered to her door. The purchasing agent says to herself, "I think we should award the contract to the firm, but I cannot accept the gift. Yet if I turn down the gift, I will be forfeiting a valuable possession that the company simply regards as a cost of doing business."

   The purchasing agent can search for another alternative. She can say to the sales rep, "We will give the contract to your firm because your product fits our requirements. I thank you for the offer of the leather jacket. But I would like you to give that jacket to the Salvation Army instead of to me."

   A creative alternative for the child-care manager might be to offer the applicant the next position that opens for an office manager or maintenance person in the centre. In this way, she would be offering a qualified applicant a job but placing him in a position more acceptable to parents. Or do you feel that this is a cop-out?

8. **Check your intuition.** So far, we have emphasized the rational side of ethical decision making. Another effective way of conducting an ethical screen is to rely on your intuition. How does the contemplated decision feel? Would you be proud of yourself or would you hate yourself if you made the decision? Imagine how you would feel if you took money from the handbag of a woman sleeping in the park. Would you feel the same way if you went ahead and took a kickback, sold

SKILL-BUILDING EXERCISE 14-3

Ethical Decision Making

Working in small groups, take one or more of the following ethical dilemmas through the eight steps for screening contemplated decisions. If more than one group chooses the same scenario, compare your answers for the various steps.

Scenario 1: To Recycle or Not. Your group is the top management team at a large insurance company. Despite the movement toward computerization, your firm still generates tonnes of paper each month. Customer payments alone account for truckloads of envelopes each year. The paper recyclers in your area claim they can hardly find a market any longer for used paper, so they will be charging you just to accept your paper for recycling. Your group is wondering whether to recycle.

Scenario 2: The Job Applicant with a Past. Emily has been working for the family business as an office manager for five years. Because the family business is being sold, Emily has started a job hunt. She also welcomes the opportunity to work in a larger company so she can learn more about how a big company operates. As she begins preparing her résumé, she ponders how to classify the year of unemployment prior to working at the family business. During that year she worked a total of 10 weeks in entry-level jobs at three fast-food restaurants. Otherwise she filled her time with such activities as walking in the park, watching daytime television shows, surfing the Internet, playing video games, and pursuing her hobby of visiting graveyards. Emily finally decides to tack that year onto the five years in the family business. She indicates on her résumé that she has been working *six* years at the family business. As Emily says, "It's a tight job market for office managers, and I don't want to raise any red flags." Evaluate the ethics of Emily's decision to fill in the year off from work, and perhaps offer her some advice.

Scenario 3: The High-Profit Toy. You are a toy company executive starting to plan your holiday season line. You anticipate that the season's hottest item will be Robo-Woman, a battery-operated crime fighter and superhero. Robo-Woman should wholesale for $18.50 and retail for $38. Your company figures to earn $10 per unit. You receive a sales call from a manufacturing broker who says he can produce any toy you want for one-third of your present manufacturing cost. He admits that the manufacturer he represents uses prison labour in China but insists that his business arrangement violates no law. You estimate you can earn $14 per unit if you do business with the manufacturing broker. Your decision is whether to do business with him.

---

somebody a defective product, or sold an 80-year-old man an insurance policy he did not need? How will the manager of the child-care centre feel if she turns down the man for the child-care specialist position?

You are encouraged to use the guide for ethical decision making when you next face an ethical dilemma of consequence. Skill-Building Exercise 14-3 gives you an opportunity to practise using these eight steps.

Developing Closer Relationships with Work Associates

A provocative explanation of the causes of unethical behaviour emphasizes the strength of relationships among people.[16] Assume that two people have close ties to one another, such as having worked together for a long time or knowing one another both on and off the job. As a consequence, they are likely to behave ethically toward one another on the job. In contrast, if a weak relationship exists between two people; either party is more likely to engage in unethical behaviour toward the other. The owner of an auto-service centre is more likely to behave unethically toward a stranger passing through town than toward a long-time customer. The opportunity for unethical behaviour between strangers is often minimized because individuals typically do not trust strangers with sensitive information or valuables.

The ethical skill-building consequence of information about personal relationships is that building stronger relationships with people is likely to enhance ethical behaviour. If you build strong relationships with work associates, you are likely to behave more ethically toward them. Similarly, your work associates—that is, all your contacts, both internal and external customers—are likely to behave more ethically toward you.

Self-Assessment Quiz 14-3 provides an opportunity to think of the ethical aspects of your relationships with co-workers.

Using Corporate Ethics Programs

Many organizations have various programs and procedures for promoting ethical behaviour. Among them are mission statements and guidelines that promote and encourage

SELF-ASSESSMENT QUIZ 14-3

The Ethical Workplace Relationships Inventory

Directions: Describe how well you agree with each of the following statements, using the following scale: Disagree Strongly (DS); Disagree (D); Neutral (N); Agree (A), Agree Strongly (AS). Circle the number in the appropriate column.

	DS	D	N	A	AS
1. I would give a sexually suggestive hug to a team member who I thought was physically attractive.	5	4	3	2	1
2. If I were asked to purchase pizza and soft drinks for the group, I would be willing to ask for more in reimbursement than I actually paid.	5	4	3	2	1
3. If I were the manager of my group, I would be willing to put pressure on group members to purchase direct sales items from me, such as beauty and health products.	5	4	3	2	1
4. I would be willing to recommend for promotion to a supervisor position a worker from a different racial group than my own.	1	2	3	4	5
5. If I didn't get along with my manager or team leader, I would be willing to start a rumour that he or she was undergoing bankruptcy.	5	4	3	2	1
6. To damage the reputation of a co-worker I didn't like, I would be willing to write a negative blog about the company and sign his or her name.	5	4	3	2	1
7. I like the idea of encouraging a co-worker to complain about a mutual boss, and then report those negative comments back to the boss.	5	4	3	2	1
8. If I were the team member who made a serious error on a project, I would quickly inform our team leader before the blame was placed on another team member.	1	2	3	4	5
9. If I heard that a company executive was arrested in a domestic violence incident, I would immediately inform other employees.	5	4	3	2	1
10. Stealing an idea from a co-worker, and then taking credit for that idea is totally unacceptable under any circumstance.	1	2	3	4	5

Total Score _____

Scoring and Interpretation: Add the numbers you have circled to obtain your total score.

45–50 You are strongly ethical in your relationships with co-workers.

30–44 You show an average degree of ethical behaviour in your workplace relationships and should therefore become more sensitive to ethical issues.

10–29 Your ethical values could lead you to develop a negative relationship with work associates, assuming that your unethical behaviour is caught. Begin a serious study of business ethics.

---

ethical behaviour, committees that monitor ethical behaviour, training programs in ethics, and vehicles for reporting ethical violations. The presence of these programs is designed to create an atmosphere in which unethical behaviour is discouraged and reporting of unethical behaviour is encouraged. In Canada, 90 percent of companies with over $1 billion in revenues have a published code of ethics.[17]

Ethics hotlines are one of the best-established programs to help individuals avoid unethical behaviour. Should a person be faced with an ethical dilemma, the person calls a toll-free line to speak to a counsellor about the dilemma. Sometimes employees ask for help interpreting a policy, for example: "Is it okay to ask my boss for a date?" or "Are we supposed to give senior citizen discounts to customers who qualify but do not ask for one?" At other times, a more pressing ethical issue might be addressed, such as: "Is it ethical to lay off a worker just five months short of his qualifying for a full pension?"

Sears has an ethics hotline the company refers to as an "Assist Line" because very few of the 15,000 calls it receives per year represent crises. Often the six full-time ethics specialists who handle the calls just listen; at other times they intervene to help resolve the problem. The Assist Line is designed to help with these kinds of calls: guidance about company policy; company code of conduct issues; workplace harassment and discrimination; selling practices; theft; and human resources issues. Employees and managers are able to access information and guidance without feeling they are facing a crisis. So the Assist Line is kind of a cross between "911" and "411" calls. At times an ethical problem of such high moral intensity is presented that employee confidentiality cannot be maintained. However, the Ethics Office handles the inquiries in as confidential a manner as practical and assigns them case identification numbers for follow-up.[18]

The link between the programs such as hot lines and individual ethical skills is that these programs assist a worker's skill development. For example, if you become comfortable asking about ethical issues, or turning in ethical violators, you have become more ethically skilled.

BACK TO THE OPENING CASE

This is HBC's Corporate Social Responsibility statement on its website: "Every day, we make choices. Some of those choices have an impact on our families and communities; some may reach around the world. At HBC, our goal is to foster and enhance sustainable business practices throughout our organization, particularly in the areas of the environment, associate wellness, community investment and ethical sourcing."[19] HBC is an example of a company that does more than talk about corporate social responsibility and this statement is realized through its programs that incorporate and track ethical behaviour within the organization.

Being Environmentally Conscious

Another ethical skill is to be *green* or to do your job in helping sustain the physical environment. (*Green* derives from the idea that green vegetations such as trees and forests are a plus for the environment.) The reasoning behind this statement is that it is morally responsible to protect the environment. Do not be concerned with taking sides on the issue of global warming. Whether or not humans and the carbon dioxide emissions they create have contributed to global warming, the physical environment needs your help.

The skill of being environmentally conscious has two major components. First is to take as many steps as you can individually to help preserve the environment, even in such small steps as carrying a reusable cloth bag to the grocery store, and using a refillable water bottle instead of buying bottled water. Second is to be an advocate for the environment by mentioning its importance at work. You might, for example, present data to management about how solar heating can save the company money in the long run, and how benches and walkways made from recycled tires and plastics are attractive and economical. Figure 14-4 gives you a starting point for contributing to a sustainable environment. You might want to add to this list with suggestions of your own, or those you find in the media and scientific articles.

You may need to use your persuasive communication skills to make an impact on the environment. And you will also need to use your positive political skills so that you will not be perceived as an environmental, tree-hugging pest.

You are invited to do Skill-Building Exercise 14-4 to get started right away in improving the physical environment.

FIGURE 14-4 Representative Suggestions for Helping a Company Contribute to a Sustainable Environment

1. Conserve energy by adjusting thermostats to keep working areas cooler during cold months, and warmer during warm months.
2. Do what you can to encourage your company and co-workers to send to recycling centres no-longer-in-use electronic devices, such as desktop computers, laptops, cell phones, and personal digital assistants.
3. Spread the word about the environmental good that be accomplished from making new products from recycled goods, such as paving stones and park benches made from recycled bottles and tires. The entire re-manufacturing industry relies on the reuse of manufactured materials.
4. Do what you can to create a buzz about the possibilities of photovoltaic technology that is used to convert sunlight into clean energy. Alert influential people to energy-saving and money-saving solar heating systems, such as solar buildings that provide solar hot water and solar heating.
5. Place a lawn on the roof that can reduce roof surface temperature and internal building temperatures.
6. Carpool to work with at least three co-workers, and provide preferred parking spaces for carpoolers and hybrid or electric cars.
7. Campaign for a four-day, 40-hour workweek, which can save enormous amounts of energy by less commuting along with less heating and cooling of the workplace. (However, if the employees drive considerably on their day off and use more heating and cooling at home, much of the energy savings will be lost.)
8. Encourage employee use of mass transportation, and provide company shuttle buses from locations convenient to where employees live.
9. Offer employees at least $2000 toward the purchase of a hybrid vehicle or electric car.
10. Turn off electronic machines when not in use unless starting and stopping them frequently uses more energy than leaving the machines turned on during working hours. Encourage the replacement of incandescent bulbs with fluorescent ones (providing the replacement bulb provides enough light for the purpose).
11. Recycle as many packages as possible and purchase products, such as office furniture and driveways, made from recycled products, including vehicle tires. When possible, use old newspapers for packing material instead of new paper and plastic.
12. Use mugs instead of Styrofoam and set up bins to recycle aluminum cans and plastic bottles.
13. When constructing a new building, seek environmental ratings. (There are several programs, including Leadership in Energy and Environmental Design [LEED] certification, Sustainability Tracking, Assessment, and Rating System [STAR, currently used at several Canadian Colleges], and Green Star in Australia).
14. Provide bicycle racks that enable employees to bike to work. Biking to work will save considerable energy as well as decrease carbon dioxide emissions.
15. Construct a system that captures rainwater to be reused for irrigation.
16. Grow as much vegetation on company premises as feasible, including celebrating special events by planting another tree. Use plants that are native to the region because native vegetation does not require as much maintenance, fertilizer, chemical sprays, or water.
17. Drink as much tap water as possible to minimize the use of bottled water, or filter tap water to one's specifications.
18. Combat litter and clutter in your work area and on company premises to help attain a pleasant, environmentally friendly atmosphere. Take such actions as alerting the

(Continued)

FIGURE 14-4 (Continued)

> company to exposed, rusted pipes, broken concrete in the parking lot, peeling paint, and broken fences.
>
> 19. Encourage people in your network not to drive at high speeds or sit in an idling vehicle while making phone calls or sending text messages. Encourage safe driving in general because vehicular accidents consume enormous amounts of energy, including tow trucks, salvage operations, and hospital stays. Also encourage people to walk on errands instead of driving, whenever feasible.
> 20. A general guideline is to use less stuff and less energy.
> 21. My suggestions: _____

Sources: Several of the ideas are from Ben Elgin and Brian Grow, "The Dirty Secret of Recycling Electronics," *Business Week*, October 27, 2008, pp. 40–44; Letita M. Aaron, "The Big Payback," *Black Enterprise*, May 2009, pp. 64–66; Michael Barbaro, "At Wal-Mart, Lessons in Self-Help," *The New York Times*, April 5, 2007, www.nytimes.com; Bryan Walsh, "Thank God It's Thursday," *Time*, September 7, 2009, p. 58; Melanie Warner, "Plastic Potion No. 9," *Fast Company*, September 2008, p. 88; Charles Lockwood, "Building the Green Way," *Harvard Business Review*, June 2006, pp. 129–137; David Roberts, "Another Inconvenient Truth," *Fast Company*, March 2008, p. 70; Tom Szaky, *Revolution in a Bottle* (New York: Portfolio, 2009).

Following an Applicable Professional Code of Conduct

Professional codes of conduct are prescribed for many occupational groups, including physicians, nurses, lawyers, paralegals, purchasing managers and agents, and real estate salespeople. A useful ethical guide for members of these groups is to follow the code of conduct for their profession. If the profession or trade is licensed by the province, a worker can be punished for deviating from the code of conduct specified. The code of conduct developed by the profession or trade is separate from the legal code, but usually supports the same principles and practices. Some of these codes of conduct developed by professional associations are 50 and 60 pages long, yet all are guided by the kind of ethical principles implied in the ethical-decision-making guide described earlier. Figure 14-5 presents a sampling of provisions from these codes. The Bank of Montreal has seven principles, two which are noted in Figure 14-5, that make up its Code of Business Conduct and Ethics. One of the websites at the end of this chapter lists hundreds of Canadian companies and a variety of codes of conduct, ethical practices, and regulations.

SKILL-BUILDING EXERCISE 14-4

Conducting an Environmental Audit

To create an environmentally friendly workplace, somebody has to take the initiative to spot opportunities for change. Organize the class into groups of about five, with one person being appointed the team leader. You might have to do the work outside of class because your assignment is to do an environmental audit of a workplace, including a nonprofit setting such as a place of worship, a school, or an athletic facility. If the audit is done during class time, evaluate a portion of the school, such as a classroom, an athletic facility, or the cafeteria. Your task is to conduct an environmental audit with respect to the energy efficiency and healthfulness of the workplace. Make judgments perhaps on a 1-to-10 scale plus comments about the following factors:

1. How energy-efficient is the workplace in terms of such factors as building insulation, use of fluorescent lighting, heating and cooling, and use of solar panels?
2. How safe is the environment in terms of pollutants, and steps to prevent physical accidents?
3. How aesthetic is the environment in terms of protecting against sight and sound pollution?

Summarize your findings and suggestions in a bulleted list of less than one page. Present them to classmates, and perhaps to a manager of the workplace. Classmates might comment on whether your findings will really improve the planet from an ecology standpoint.

FIGURE 14-5 Excerpts from Professional Codes of Conduct

Professional Organization	Samples of Ethical Guidelines, Conduct and Regulations
Sears Canada	1. Associates are required to conduct themselves with respect, cooperation, and dignity towards all those with whom they have dealings on behalf of Sears. 2. It is vital that we be truthful in all our business dealings with each other and with third parties. At no time should misleading information be provided to anyone, either verbally or in writing. We must always act in good faith.
Canadian Pacific Railway	1. Employees must avoid all actual or perceived conflicts of interest between their personal interests and their duties to CPR. 2. CPR and its employees shall comply with all legal requirements, both domestic and foreign, applicable to CPR's business.
Bank of Montreal	1. Everything we do and every decision we make will be guided by principles of honesty, integrity, fair dealing, respect and high ethical standards. 2. We must be alert to and immediately report concerns that may point to a breach of any laws, regulations or this Code to the appropriate persons or departments within BMO. Retaliation against a BMO employee for raising legitimate concerns under this Code is prohibited.

Sources: Sears Canada, http://www.sears.ca; Canadian Pacific Railway, http://www8.cpr.ca/cms/English/Investors/Governance/Policies/Code+of+Business+Ethics.htm; Bank of Montreal, http://www2.bmo.com/content/0,1089,divId-7_langId-1_navCode-4138,00.html.

Be Ready to Exert Upward Ethical Leadership

A politically delicate situation can arise when a worker wants to behave ethically, yet he or she works for an unethical manager. He or she might worry that being ethical will lead to being reprimanded or job loss. The ethical person working for an unethical boss might feel that his or her values are being compromised, such as a virtuous credit card specialist being told to approve credit cards for people who will probably wind up paying many late fees. **Upward ethical leadership** is leadership displayed by individuals who take action to maintain ethical standards, although higher-ups engage in questionable moral behaviours.[20]

At the extreme, an employee might blow the whistle on the boss, and report the unethical behaviour to top management or a government agency. An example would be telling Health Canada (which has a special department for reporting dangerous consumer products) that your company was selling cribs that could trap a baby's head after your boss refused to accept your complaint.

The upward leadership approach would be to attempt to resolve the problem before going to the extreme of whistleblowing. The employee who spots the immoral or unethical behaviour would use problem-solving and communication skills, along with conflict resolution skills. For example, the employee who spotted the potential head-trap problem might say to the boss, "I have a problem and I would like to discuss it with you." The employee would therefore be engaging the boss in helping solve the problem. Recognizing that you have less power than your boss, you would have to be diplomatic and nonaccusatory. It would be important to point to the problem (the pos-

upward ethical leadership
The leadership displayed by individuals who take action to maintain ethical standards, although higher-ups engage in questionable moral behaviours.

SKILL-BUILDING EXERCISE 14-5

Confronting the Unethical Boss

One student plays the role of Pierre, a manager who makes frequent business trips by airplanes. Pierre also likes to fly frequently on vacation, and appreciates accumulating frequent-flyer miles. Company policy allows employees to keep the frequent-flyer miles they accumulate for work. So Pierre will often take indirect trips to a destination to accumulate more air miles. For example, to fly to Halifax, he will fly from Toronto to Montreal, and then to Halifax to accumulate more miles even though he could have flown directly from Toronto to Halifax. This is more expensive than if he flew directly.

Another person plays the role of Kelly, the office administrative assistant who sometimes helps Pierre prepare his travel vouchers. Kelly, who has good knowledge of geography, notices this strange pattern of Fred taking indirect flights. She is also aware of company policy that permits employees to accumulate frequent-flyer miles on business trips. Kelley is disturbed about what she perceives to be an inappropriate use of company resources—and therefore an ethical violation.

Kelly decides to discuss with Pierre this ethical violation. The role-play takes place in Pierre's cubicle, and you can imagine how defensive Pierre is going to be.

Run the role-play for about five minutes. For both scenarios, observers rate the role players on two dimensions, using a 1-to-5 scale from very poor to very good. One dimension is "effective use of human relations techniques." Observers look to see if Kelly can preserve her sense of ethics while not doing too much damage to her relationship with her boss, Pierre. The second dimension is "acting ability." A few observers might voluntarily provide feedback to the role players in terms of sharing their ratings and observations. The course instructor might also provide feedback.

Access the eText in MySearchLab to learn more about this chapter's self-assessment quizzes.

sibility of an infant getting his or her head stuck) rather than accusing the boss of being unethical or immoral.

Skill-Building Exercise 14-5 gives you an opportunity to practise upward leadership skills for correcting unethical behaviour.

To Watch Explore Practice Study and Review, visit MySearchLab

Developing Your Human Relations Skills and Reinforcing Concepts

Summary

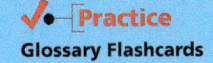

Practice Glossary Flashcards

- Behaving ethically is important for establishing good interpersonal relationships in the workplace. Understanding ethics is important for a variety of reasons. First, people are motivated by self-interest and a desire to be morally right. Second, practising good ethics can be good for business and help avoid illegalities. Third, a high standard of ethics improves the quality of working life.

- Commonly faced ethical dilemmas include illegally copying software, treating people unfairly including cronyism, sexually harassing co-workers, facing a conflict of interest, dealing with confidential information, misrepresenting employment and educational history, using corporate resources, ethically violating computers and information technology, and wasting company time.

- There are several guidelines and strategies to improve upon ethical behaviour. These include developing virtuousness, following a guide for ethical decision making, developing strong relationships with co-workers, using a corporate ethics program, being environmentally conscious, following a code of ethics, and exerting upward ethical leadership.

Interpersonal Relations Case 14-1

The Highly Rated, but Expendable Marsha

Department manager Nicholas had thought for a long time that Marsha, one of his financial analysts, created too many problems. Although Marsha performed her job in a satisfactory manner, she required a lot of supervisory time and attention. She frequently asked for time off when her presence was needed the most because of a heavy workload in the department. Marsha sent Nicholas many long and complicated email messages that required substantial time to read and respond to. When Nicholas responded to Marsha's email message, she would typically send another email back asking for clarification.

Marsha's behaviour during department meetings irritated Nicholas. She would demand more time than any other participant to explain her point of view on a variety of issues. At a recent meeting she took 10 minutes explaining how the company should be doing more to help the homeless and invest in the development of inner cities.

Nicholas coached Marsha frequently about the problems she was creating, but Marsha strongly disagreed with his criticism and concerns. At one time, Nicholas told Marsha that she was a high-maintenance employee. Yet Marsha perceived herself as a major contributor to the department. She commented once, "Could it be, Nick, that you have a problem with an assertive woman working in your department?"

Nicholas developed a tactic to get Marsha out of the department. He would give her outstanding performance evaluations, emphasizing her creativity and persistence. Marsha would then be entered into the company database as an outstanding employee, thereby making her a strong candidate for transfer or promotion. Within six months, a manager in a new division of the company took the bait. She requested that Marsha be recruited into her department as a senior financial analyst. Nicholas said to the recruiting manager, "I hate to lose a valuable contributor like Marsha, but I do not want to block her career progress."

Two months later, Marsha's new manager telephoned Nicholas, and asked, "What's the problem with Marsha? She's kind of a pill to have working with us. I thought she was an outstanding employee."

Nicholas responded, "Give Marsha some time. She may be having a few problems adjusting to a new environment. Just give her a little constructive feedback. You'll find out what a dynamo she can be."

Case Questions

1. How ethical was Nicholas in giving Marsha a high performance evaluation for purposes of making her attractive to other departments?
2. What should the manager do who was hooked by Nicholas's bait of the high performance evaluation?
3. What might the company do to prevent more incidents of inflated performance evaluations for the purpose of transferring an unwanted employee?

Interpersonal Relations Case 14-2

Am I Paid to Be My Manager's TV Repair Technician?

Karen worked for a division of a pharmaceutical company as a member of the technical support team. Among her many responsibilities were keeping the division's desktop computers, laptops, printers, and smart phones in working order. Gus, her manager, who had been with the company for about 10 years, had a general understanding of what the tech support staff was doing, but he was more of an administrator than a specialist in communication technology.

Several times in recent weeks, Gus complained to Karen and a few other team members about a problem he was having with a digital television set connected to an internal (rabbit-ears) antenna. During a lunch break, he explained to Karen, "I'm going a little crazy. I have four television sets at home. The two big ones are satellite-connected and they work just fine. I have a small set in the family room in the basement connected to rabbit ears, and the reception is reasonably good. I am picking up the digital signals with a few halts here and there, but I am getting the reception I need.

"The problem I have is with a relatively new set connected in our upstairs bedroom. I did the channel scan about one year ago, and I was getting the network channels I needed. A few weeks ago I stopped receiving the channels I needed. All that was left was HSN (Home Shopping Network). I must have done a channel scan 20 times to try to fix the problem. Plus, I rotated the antenna a few times. I called tech support at the manufacturer of my set, and the rep couldn't help. He told me to telephone the CRTC (Canadian Radio-television and Telecommunications Commission). I did that, followed the rep's instructions, and still no signal."

Karen agreed that Gus was facing a frustrating problem, but that many people using antennas on their TV sets have lost reception since the conversion from analogue to digital in 2009.

A week later, Gus spoke to Karen again about his TV reception woes. He then asked Karen, "How about you coming over after work some night to help straighten out my TV problem? My wife and I would really appreciate your help. You're a great tech fixer."

Karen pondered for a moment, thinking that Gus was making an unreasonable demand. She replied, "Gus, let me think about your request. I really don't know a lot about TV reception. Also, I am pretty much tied up after work for a couple of weeks."

With a frown on his face, Gus said, "Karen, I know you can help. Please don't let me down."

Case Questions

1. What do you see as any potential ethical issues in Gus's request that Karen attempt to fix his TV set reception problem?
2. What advice might you offer Karen for dealing with this problem?
3. How do Gus's demands fit into the category of expecting Karen to exhibit strong organizational citizenship behaviour?

Questions for Discussion and Review

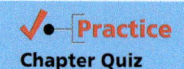

✓ Practice Chapter Quiz

Multiple Choice

1. Which of the following would *not* be considered an ethical violation?
   a. copying word processing software owned by your company with permission
   b. using corporate resources such as bringing company paper home for your personal printer
   c. surfing the Internet for your next vacation while at work
   d. telling your best friend about a recent company fine although it is currently confidential

2. Having to choose between two options, both that are morally right is known as a/an
   a. moment of truth.
   b. ethical dilemma.
   c. defining moment.
   d. "aha" experience.

3. According to your text, values that contribute to virtuousness include all of the following except
   a. rationality.
   b. forgiveness.
   c. honesty.
   d. skepticism.

4. According to the text, if a decision does not feel right, you should
   a. ignore those feelings and move ahead with the decision.
   b. re-examine the decision, as intuition is often important when it comes to being ethical.
   c. back out of the dilemma and not make any decision.

d. have someone else make the decision to avoid responsibility.
5. A new ethical area in decision making is
   a. human rights.
   b. environmental sustainability.
   c. prejudice and discrimination.
   d. computer software issues.

Short Answer

6. How can behaving ethically improve a person's interpersonal relationships on the job?
7. What would most likely be some of the specific behaviours of a manager who scored 20 points on the ethical reasoning inventory?
8. Virtually all accountants have studied ethics as part of their education, yet many business scandals involve accountants. What's their problem?
9. Check out the websites of a couple of major business corporations. What conclusion do you reach about whether an environmentally conscious (or green) person would fit in those companies?
10. Open your MySearchLab. Click on "professional videos" and watch the video "Making Ethical Choices." Answer the questions at the end of the video. Please note that the ethics test referred to at the end of the video is the Ethical Reasoning Inventory that is in Self-Assessment Quiz 14-1. How widespread do you think these behaviours are in organizations today? Is there any way to justify these behaviours?

Answers to multiple choice questions: 1. a, 2. c, 3. d, 4. b, 5. b.

The Web Corner

www.ethics.org
Ethics Resource Centre

www.cbsr.ca
Canadian Business for Social Responsibility; for businesses to promote transparent and ethical ways of doing business

http://globalethicsuniversity.com
An examination of many phases of business ethics

Internet Skill-Builder: Learning from Ethical Role Models

One of the many ways of learning ethical skills is to get good ideas from ethical role models. For example, you might observe a professor who takes the initiative to change a grade upward because she later discovered a calculation error. This Internet skill-builder is more abstract than some others, so you might find it a little frustrating. Search for a few specific ways in which you can learn from an ethical role model. To illustrate, you might learn from a business executive, sports figure, or public servant you admire.

MySearchLab

Visit **MySearchLab** to find self-grading review quizzes in the eText, discipline-specific media and readings, access to a variety of academic journals, and Associated Press news feeds, along with a wide range of writing, grammar, and research tools and to help hone writing and research skills.

CHAPTER 15
Personal Productivity and Stress Management

Canadian workers are feeling the pinch. How about you? Are you balancing work, school, a family, elderly relatives? No matter what you call it, many Canadians are feeling stressed in life and at work. Data from the national study on work–life balance in 2012 indicates that many Canadian workers are under stress. This study surveyed over 25,000 Canadian full-time workers across the country from a wide variety of organizations. Respondents ranged from Generation Y to Baby Boomers.

What were some of the findings in this survey? It underscores many of the stressors discussed in this chapter: Many people are balancing work and caring for young children at home while also providing care for elders (these people are referred to as the "sandwich generation").

Andrey_Arkusha/Fotolia

LEARNING Objectives

After reading and studying this chapter and doing the exercises, you should be able to

1. Reduce any tendencies you might have toward procrastination.
2. Identify attitudes and values that will increase your productivity.
3. Identify skills and techniques that will increase your productivity.
4. Pinpoint potential time wasters that drain your productivity.
5. Explain many of the symptoms and consequences of stress, including burnout.
6. Describe personality factors and job factors that contribute to stress.
7. Be prepared to manage your own stress effectively.

Many people are single parents, many work more than 40 hours per week, and many bring work home with them in the evenings. Work extension technology (WET) such as email has increased their stress levels. Balancing multiple roles (parent, caregiver, employee) has led to increased stress due to work–life (role) conflict and trying to find time to do everything that needs to be done. One in three respondents let work interfere with home life, and this type of conflict has a negative impact on work performance.

Overall, high levels of stress are a problem in Canadian organizations: 57 percent of respondents reported high levels of stress and a substantive proportion (40 percent) reported moderate levels of stress.[1]

These statistics illustrate two major workplace themes: Workers need to be productive, but at the same time they must find realistic ways of managing stress and avoiding burnout. Although this text is primarily about interpersonal skills, information about increasing personal productivity and managing stress is relevant. Being more productive and keeping stress under control enable you to focus better on interpersonal relationships.

The first half of this chapter describes various approaches to increasing personal productivity; the second half deals with the nature of stress and how it can be managed. The two topics are as closely related as nutrition and health. When your work is under control, you avoid the heavy stress of feeling overwhelmed. And when you effectively manage stress, you can be more productive.

INCREASING PERSONAL PRODUCTIVITY

Increasing personal productivity is more in vogue than ever. Companies strive to operate with smaller staffs than in the past by pushing workers to achieve higher productivity. At the same time, there is a movement toward simplifying personal life by reducing clutter and cutting back on tasks that do not add much to the quality of working life. **Personal productivity** refers to the amount of resources, including time, you consume to achieve a certain level of output.

We approach productivity improvement from four perspectives: (1) dealing with procrastination; (2) attitudes and values that increase personal productivity; (3) work habits and skills that increase personal productivity; and (4) overcoming time wasters.

Dealing with Procrastination

The person who indulges in **procrastination** delays action for no good reason. Procrastination lowers productivity because it wastes time and many important tasks never get done. Procrastination results in a gap between intention and action. A major reason why

LEARNING OBJECTIVE 1

personal productivity
A measure of a worker's output in relation to the resources, including time, that he or she consumes to achieve it.

procrastination
Delaying action for no good reason.

Practice
Procrastination Tendencies

SELF-ASSESSMENT QUIZ 15-1

Procrastination Tendencies

Directions: Circle Yes or No for each item:

1.	I usually do my best work under the pressure of deadlines.	Yes	No
2.	Before starting a project, I go through such rituals as sharpening every pencil, straightening up my desk more than once, and discarding bent paper clips.	Yes	No
3.	I crave the excitement of the "last-minute rush."	Yes	No
4.	I often think that if I delay something, it will go away, or the person who asked for it will forget about it.	Yes	No
5.	I extensively research something before taking action, such as obtaining three different estimates before getting the brakes repaired on my car.	Yes	No
6.	I have a great deal of difficulty getting started on most projects, even those I enjoy.	Yes	No
7.	I keep waiting for the right time to do something, such as getting started on an important report.	Yes	No
8.	I often underestimate the time needed to do a project and say to myself, "I can do this quickly, so I'll wait until next week."	Yes	No
9.	It is difficult for me to finish most projects or activities.	Yes	No
10.	I have several favourite diversions or distractions that I use to keep me from doing something unpleasant.	Yes	No

Total Yes Responses _____

Scoring and Interpretation: The greater the number of Yes responses, the more likely you have a serious procrastination problem. A score of 8, 9, or 10 strongly suggests that procrastination is lowering your productivity.

Watch
Workplace Etiquette

people procrastinate is that they want to feel good at the moment rather than reap future rewards. As such, procrastination is a form of impulsivity.[2] Why bother getting in touch with my boss to discuss my prospects for promotion when I can send a tweet to 500 people right now? Procrastination lowers productivity because it wastes time and many important tasks never get done. Another serious problem is that undone tasks rumble around in the back of your consciousness, decreasing your concentration. Chronic procrastination can even lead to debt, divorce, and job loss.

True, procrastinators can sometimes be productive people; but if they did not procrastinate, they would be even more so.

Many people regard procrastination as a laughable weakness, particularly because procrastinators themselves joke about it. Yet procrastination has been evaluated as a profound, debilitating problem, with between 20 and 25 percent of working adults identifying themselves as chronic procrastinators.[3] Approximately 90 percent of college students report problems with overdue papers and delayed studying. About 25 percent are chronic procrastinators, and many of them drop out of school.[4] The enormity of the problem makes it worthwhile to examine methods for bringing it under control. Do Self-Assessment Quiz 15-1 to think through your own tendencies toward procrastination—and don't wait until tomorrow.

Choose from among the following suggestions for controlling procrastination, based on those that appear to best fit your type of procrastination. A combination of techniques is likely to be the most effective.

1. **Commit to what you want in life.** If you are not committed to something you want in life, you are more likely to be a chronic procrastinator. The reason is that it is difficult to prioritize and take action. (See the later discussion about a personal mission and work habits.)[5] Your commitment to what you want in life will

often translate into forgoing short-term pleasure, such as stopping by a café, in order to finish a project due today.

2. **Calculate the cost of procrastination.** You can reduce procrastination by calculating its cost. You might lose out on obtaining a high-paying job you really want by not having your résumé and cover letter ready on time. Your cost of procrastination would include the difference in compensation between the job you do find and the one you really wanted. Another cost would be the loss of potential job satisfaction.

3. **Follow the "WIFO" principle, which stands for "worst in, first out."**[6] If you tackle the worst task on your list first, doing the other tasks may function as a small reward. You get to do what you dislike the least by doing first what you dislike the most. Following the WIFO principle is particularly effective when one is faced with several tasks simultaneously.

4. **Break up the task into manageable chunks.** To reduce procrastination, cut down a task that seems overwhelming into smaller projects that seem less formidable. If your job calls for preparing an enormous database, begin by assembling some readily available information. Then take the next step by assembling another small segment of the database—perhaps all customers whose last names begin with Z. Think of your task as pulling together a series of small databases that will fit into a master database.

5. **Make a commitment to other people.** Try to make it imperative that you get something done on time by making it a commitment to one or more other people. You might announce to co-workers that you are going to get something accomplished by a certain date. If you fail to meet this date, you are likely to feel embarrassed.

6. **Remove some clutter from your mind.** Procrastination escalates when people have many unfinished projects in the back of their minds, draining their concentration. Having too much to do can freeze us into inaction. Just eliminating a few trivial items from your to-do list can give you enough mental energy to overcome procrastination on a few major tasks. Note carefully that this approach to overcoming procrastination requires that you be self-disciplined enough to take the first step.

7. **Satisfy your stimulation quota in constructive ways.** If you procrastinate because you enjoy the rush of scrambling to meet deadlines, find a more constructive way of using busyness to keep you humming. If you need a high level of stimulation, enrich your life with extra projects and learning new skills. The fullness of your schedule will give you the stimulation you had been deriving from squeezing yourself to meet deadlines and get to appointments on time.[7]

8. **Eliminate tangible rewards you are giving yourself for procrastinating.** If you are procrastinating through socializing with co-workers, taking a walk to obtain a beverage, surfing the Internet, or any other pleasant experience—stop rewarding yourself. Just sit alone in your work area doing nothing while procrastinating. If you remove the pleasant activities from your stalling routine, you may be able to reduce procrastination.[8]

Attitudes and Values That Increase Personal Productivity

LEARNING OBJECTIVE 2

Developing good work habits and time-management practices is often a matter of developing the right attitudes toward your work and toward time. If, for example, you think that your schoolwork or job is important and that time is a precious resource, you will be on your way toward developing good work habits. In this section, we describe a group of attitudes, values, and beliefs that can help a person become more productive through better use of time and improved work habits.

Begin with a Mission and Goals. A mission, or general purpose, propels you toward being productive. Assume that a person says, "My mission is to be an outstanding professional in my field and a loving, constructive spouse and parent." The mission serves

SKILL-BUILDING EXERCISE 15-1

Using a Mission Statement and Goals to Power Work Habits

People with a well-defined mission statement and supporting goals tend to have better work habits and time-management skills than those who do not. The following exercise is designed to help you establish a mission statement and goals that will energize you to be more productive.

A. **Mission Statement:** To help develop your mission statement, or general purpose in life, ask yourself, "What are my five biggest wishes in life?" These wishes give you a hint of your purpose because they point toward an ideal purpose in life. Feel free to think big, because mission statements tend toward idealism.

B. **Long-Range Goals to Support Mission Statement:** Now write down what long-range goals would support your mission statement. Suppose your mission statement related to "creating a better life for disadvantaged people." Your long-range goals might include establishing a foundation that would fund your efforts. You would also need to be successful enough in your career to get the foundation started.

C. **Intermediate-Range Goals to Support Long-Range Goals:** Write down the intermediate-range goals needed to support the long-range goals. You will probably need to complete your education, obtain broad experience, and identify a lucrative form of self-employment.

D. **Weekly Goals to Support Intermediate-Range Goals:** Write down what you have to do this week to help you complete your education, such as researching and writing a paper for a particular course, registering for courses for next term, and inquiring about career opportunities in your field.

E. **Today's Goals to Support Weekly Goals (My To-Do List):** Here's where your lofty purpose in life gets translated into reality. What do you have to do today to get that paper written? Do you need to get your car battery replaced so you can get to the library to write your paper, so you can graduate, so you can become rich, so you can ultimately help all those disadvantaged people? Get going!

---

as a compass to direct your activities, such as being well organized in order to accomplish more work and be highly valued by your employer. Goals are more specific than mission statements; they support the mission statement, but the effect is the same. Being committed to a goal also propels you toward good use of time. If you know that you can obtain the position in international business that you really want by mastering a second language, you are likely to work diligently on learning that language. Skill-Building Exercise 15-1 gives you the opportunity to develop a mission statement and supporting goals.

Work Smarter, Not Harder. People caught up in trying to accomplish a job often wind up working hard, but not in an imaginative way that leads to good results. Much time and energy are therefore wasted. A working-smart approach also requires that you spend a few minutes carefully planning how to implement your task. An example of working smarter, not harder, is to invest a few minutes of critical thinking before conducting a telemarketing campaign for home replacement windows. Develop a list of homeowners of houses that are at least 15 years old. People with relatively new homes are poor prospects for replacing their windows.

A new perspective on working smarter, not harder, is to keep perfecting your skills through **deliberate practice**—applying a strong effort to improve target performance over time. Practice alone does not lead to nearly as much improvement as thinking through what you have done to look for areas for improvement.[9] Feedback from others is also helpful. Assume that a loan officer at a bank signs off on loans to small-business owners. She engages in deliberate practice by following the history of these loans to evaluate which business owners proved to be good risks, and those that proved to be poor risks. She frequently asks herself, "What did I miss here? What did I do right here?" In this way, the loan officer is working smarter by honing her risk-evaluation skills.

deliberate practice
Strong effort to improve target performance over time.

Value Orderliness and Cleanliness. An orderly desk, work area, briefcase, or hard drive does not inevitably indicate an orderly mind. Yet it does help most people become more productive because they can better focus their minds. Being surrounded by a collection of small, unfinished tasks interferes with your ability to focus on major tasks. Also, less time is wasted and less energy is expended if you do not have to hunt for information that you thought you had on hand. The central message of the best-seller *Getting Things*

Done by David Allen is that to achieve maximum efficiency and relaxation is to clear clutter both outside and inside your mind.[10] One way of clearing clutter from your mind is to write down your tasks on to-do lists. If you are orderly, you clear clutter.

Knowing where information is stored and what information you have available is a way of being in control of your job. When your job gets out of control, you are probably working at less than peak efficiency. Valuing cleanliness improves productivity in several ways. According to the Japanese system, cleanliness is the bedrock of quality. Also, after you have thoroughly cleaned your work area, you will usually attain a fresh outlook.

As with any suggestions about human behaviour, individual differences exist with respect to the impact of clutter on productivity. Internet guru Esther Dyson has a work area so cluttered that she gives the impression of being an exaggerated case of a person needing help from a personal productivity consultant. It has also been argued that focusing too much on tidiness might detract from creative thinking, and that many messy people, such as Albert Einstein, believe that a messy work area facilitates their creative thinking. To quote the great man, "If a cluttered desk is a sign of a cluttered mind, of what then, is an empty desk?"[11]

Value Good Attendance and Punctuality. Good attendance and punctuality are expected of both experienced and inexperienced employees. You cannot be productive if you are not physically present in your work area. The same principle applies whether you work on company premises or at home. One exception is that some people can work through solutions to job problems while engaged in recreation. Keep in mind, too, that being late for or absent from meetings, whether face to face or virtual, sends the silent message that you do not regard the meeting as being important. Whether the person is late or absent for work, or just for a meeting, the behaviour is interpreted by many as demonstrating irresponsibility.

Attain a Balance in Life and Avoid Being a Workaholic. A productive attitude to maintain is that overwork can lead to negative stress and burnout. Proper physical rest and relaxation can contribute to mental alertness and improved ability to cope with frustration. A strategy for preventing overwork is to strive for a balance in which you derive satisfaction from various spheres of life. Major spheres in addition to work include family life, romance, sports, the arts and music, faith, and intellectual growth.

A strongly recommended technique for attaining balance between work and other spheres of life is to learn how to say no diplomatically to your boss and family members.[12] For example, your boss might ask you to take on a project when you are already overloaded. It would be necessary to *occasionally* explain that you are so overloaded that you could not do a good job with the new assignment. And, you might have to *occasionally* turn down your family's or friend's request to take a weekend vacation when you face heavy work demands.

Neglecting the normal need for rest and relaxation can lead to **workaholism,** an addiction to work in which not working is an uncomfortable experience. Some types of workaholics are perfectionists who are never satisfied with their work and therefore find it difficult to leave it behind. In addition, the perfectionist-type workaholic may become heavily focused on control, leading to rigid behaviour and strained interpersonal relationships. Many workaholics take laptops to bed, and leave their cell phones on during the night to catch any potential calls from distant time zones. However, some people who work long and hard are classified as achievement-oriented workaholics who thrive on hard work and are usually highly productive.[13] For example, a person with strong family values might nevertheless work 65 hours per week for one year while establishing a new business.

workaholism
An addiction to work in which not working is an uncomfortable experience.

DragonImages/Fotolia

PERSONAL PRODUCTIVITY AND STRESS MANAGEMENT

Work Habits and Skills That Increase Personal Productivity

LEARNING OBJECTIVE 3

Overcoming procrastination and developing the right attitudes contribute to personal productivity, but effective work habits and skills are also essential. Six key work habits and skills are described next. They represent a mixture of traditional productivity boosters and those geared to information technology.

▶ Watch
Time Management and Organization Tips

Prepare a To-Do List and Set Priorities. At the heart of every time-management system is list-making, whether the list is put on an index card, in a daily planner, or on your smart phone. As already mentioned, the to-do list is the basic tool for achieving your daily goals, which in turn help you achieve bigger goals and your mission. Almost every successful person in any field composes a list of important and less important tasks that need to be done. Before you compose a useful list, you need to set aside a few minutes of quiet time every day to sort out the tasks at hand. This is the most basic aspect of planning.

The "Getting Things Done" system of time management guru David Allen is based on a to-do list. First, you transfer all the tasks floating around in your head onto paper or into software, and sort them into a system of prioritized lists. Second, you take the items on the to-do lists (such as "sanitize the bakery") into "next actions," or necessary steps to accomplish the goal.[14] For the task in question, you might send an email to a commercial cleaning company in your area.

As is well known, it is helpful to set priorities for items on the to-do list. A typical system is to use A to signify critical or essential items, B to signify important items, and C for the least important ones. Although an item might be regarded as a C (e.g., emptying the wood shavings from the electric pencil sharpener), it still makes a contribution to your management of time and sense of well-being. Accomplishing anything reduces some stress. Also, many people obtain satisfaction from crossing off an item on their list, however trivial. If you are at all conscientious, small, unaccomplished items will come back to interfere with your concentration.

To-do lists contribute enormously to productivity, yet a to-do list may have to be revamped to meet the changing demands of the day. Marissa Mayer, vice-president of Search Products and User Experience at Google, explains that she keeps a task list in a text file. She uses the list as high-priority things to focus on. "But at Google things can change pretty fast. This morning I had my list of what I thought I was going to do today, but now I'm doing entirely different things," says Mayer.[15] As a result, she quickly prepares a new to-do list.

Preparing to-do lists should not become an end in itself, with so much time devoted to list making that accomplishing some of the tasks are neglected. The compulsive list-maker sometimes neglects the big picture. Another danger is filling the to-do list with items you would have to accomplish anyway, such as "check email" or "handle customer inquiry." The to-do list can become so long that it becomes an overwhelming task.

Streamline Your Work and Emphasize Important Tasks. As companies continue to operate with fewer workers than in the past, despite prosperity, more unproductive work must be eliminated. Getting rid of unproductive work is part of *business process improvement*, in which work processes are radically redesigned and simplified. Every employee is expected to get rid of work that does not contribute to productivity or help customers.

In general, to streamline or reengineer your work, look for duplication of effort and waste. An example of duplication of effort would be to routinely send people email and voice mail covering the same topic. An example of waste would be to call a meeting for disseminating information that could easily be communicated by email.

Emphasizing important tasks means that you make sure to take care of A items on your to-do list. It also implies that you seek to accomplish a few work activities that, if done well, would make a big difference in your job performance. Although important tasks may take less time to accomplish than many routine tasks, they can represent the difference between success and failure. Five minutes of telephone conversation with a major customer might do more good for your company than three hours of arranging obsolete inventory in the warehouse.

Concentrate on One Important Task at a Time Instead of Multitasking. While working on important tasks, concentrate on what you are doing. Effective executives and professionals have a well-developed capacity to concentrate on the problem or person facing them, however surrounded they might be with other obligations. Intense concentration leads to crisper judgment and analysis and also minimizes major errors. Another useful by-product of concentration is that it helps reduce absent-mindedness. If you really concentrate on what you are doing, the chances diminish that you will forget what you intended to do.

While concentrating on an important task, such as performing analytical work or writing a report, avoid multitasking, or performing more than one activity simultaneously. Common forms of multitasking include surfing the Internet or reading email while engaged in a phone conversation with a co-worker or customer. Both experimental evidence and opinion has accumulated that multitasking while performing important tasks leads to problems in concentration, along with significant errors—for most people. Multitasking on routine tasks has less negative consequences, and can sometimes be a legitimate time saver. For example, waiting in line at the airport during business travel provides a good opportunity to review company documents or catch up on work-related news.

David E. Meyer, the director of the Brain, Cognition and Action Laboratory at the University of Michigan, notes that when people attempt to perform two or more related tasks at the same time or alternating rapidly—instead of doing them sequentially—two negative consequences occur. Errors increase substantially, and the amount of time to perform the task may double. Also, according to recent research about the brain, few people can concentrate on more than four tasks at once.[16]

Multitasking has enormous potential negative consequences when the lives of others are at stake, such as when driving a car, truck, or flying an airplane. How many motor vehicle accidents occur because people mistakenly believe that they can text while driving? According to the Canadian Council of Motor Transport Administrators (CCMTA)'s Distracted Driving Subcommittee: "Distracted driving is the diversion of attention from driving, as a result of the driver focusing on a non-driving object, activity, event or person. This diversion reduces awareness, decision-making or performance leading to increased risk of driver error, near-crashes or crashes. The diversion of attention is not attributable to a medical condition, alcohol/drug use and/or fatigue."[17] Using these devices while driving reduces the driver's awareness of their environment and consequently also significantly affects their attention to events around them. The use of such equipment has been shown to increase the chances of a collision from 38 to 400 percent depending on the type of study methodology used.[18]

Stay in Control of Paperwork and Electronic Work. Although it is fashionable to complain about paperwork in responsible jobs, the effective career person does not neglect it. (Paperwork includes electronic work, such as email and voice mail.) Paperwork involves taking care of administrative details, such as correspondence, invoices, human resources reports, and inventory forms. A considerable amount of electronic work results in paperwork because many email messages and attachments wind up being printed. Unless paperwork and electronic work are attended to, a job may get out of control. A small amount of time should be invested in paperwork every day. Non-prime time (when you are at less than your peak of efficiency but not over-fatigued) is the best time to take care of paperwork.

An effective technique is to respond quickly to high-priority email messages, and permanently delete those you will most likely not need to refer to again. Print and file only those email messages of high importance to avoid being overwhelmed with piles of old messages. For many types of work, it is important to be able to access old emails. However, some workers complain (brag?) of having 6000 emails in their inbox. In addition to clogging the servers, this large accumulation is distracting, thereby lowering productivity. Old emails should be archived, and others moved to appropriate folders.[19]

Communicating by email or telephone with co-workers in distant time zones creates special challenges in terms of staying in control of electronic work. Assume that Sumi, working in Toronto, has clients in London, England, who want to have telephone conferences at 9 a.m. their time. Sumi has to be on the phone at 3 a.m. her time, so it is best to make all her 3 a.m. calls one morning per week rather than having a life out of control because she has to be on the phone many mornings at 3 a.m.

PERSONAL PRODUCTIVITY AND STRESS MANAGEMENT

virtual office

A place of work without a fixed physical location, where the output is communicated electronically.

Work Productively from Your Home Office or Virtual Office.

A growing segment of the workforce works full- or part-time from home or from a **virtual office**. Such an office is a place of work without a fixed physical location from which the worker communicates his or her output electronically. A virtual office might be in a car or train, in a hotel room, on a park bench, or wherever the worker happens to be at the time. Many people adapt well to working at home and from virtual offices because they are self-starters and disciplined. Many other workers lack the self-discipline and effective work habits necessary to be productive outside a traditional office. Following is a list of representative suggestions for being productive while working independently:[20]

- Act as if you work in a traditional office. Set specific working hours, get dressed, go outside the house for a few minutes, then return and get to work. Also, close your home or virtual office at some regular time. Otherwise, you are open for business all the time. If you work at home, establish a clear workspace and let your family and friends know when you cannot be disturbed.
- Stay in touch with teammates to improve your team-player skills and avoid missing out on important information that could lower your effectiveness (such as missing an appointment at the traditional office).
- Minimize conducting your personal life at the same time as working (e.g., watching television, talking to neighbours, or shopping over the Internet during working hours).
- Schedule regular times for meals and snacks; otherwise you will lose many minutes and likely gain weight taking food and beverage breaks.

The practice of working at home or from virtual offices is increasingly popular, so these suggestions merit careful consideration. Several of these productivity ideas are also suited to the conventional office.

Improve Your Internet Search Skills.

An important job skill is searching the Internet for a variety of information. It follows that if you develop your Internet search skills you will become more productive by spending less time obtaining the results you need. First, it is important to rely on several search engines to seek needed information. Some search engines claim to be so comprehensive that no other is required. Such claims are exaggerated, because the same search word entered into different comprehensive engines will reveal a different list of sources.

Second, give careful thought to the search word or phrase you use. The more specific you are, the better. Assume that you want to find software to increase your productivity and that you enter the word "software" into a search engine. You will probably receive a message indicating that 3,500,000 entries have been located in response to your inquiry. You are better advised to use the search phrase "software for increasing personal productivity" (without the quotation marks).

Third, for many searches, framing the query as a phrase by enclosing it in quotation marks refines the number of hits (or sites) returned.[21] Simply put quotation marks before and after the search phrase, such as "software for improving work habits."

Fourth, if you do not find what you want in your initial search, reframe your question or change the search terms. How about "software for time management" or "computer programs for increasing personal efficiency"? Skill-Building Exercise 15-2 will help you make better use of the Internet to increase your personal productivity.

SKILL-BUILDING EXERCISE 15-2

Boosting Productivity through Work Habits on the Internet

This chapter has already given you ideas about using work habits to increase productivity. Here is a chance to make some personal applications of your own. Gather into small teams or work individually to identify 10 ways in which good work habits, as well as using the Internet, can increase personal productivity either on the job or at home. To supplement your own thinking, you might search the Internet for ideas on how the Internet is supposed to boost productivity.

Overcoming Time Wasters

Another basic thrust in improving personal productivity is to minimize wasting time. According to one survey, the average worker wastes 28 percent of the day with interruptions, such as checking email, responding to an instant message, clicking on YouTube, or posting a personal message on Twitter or Facebook. The wasted time includes doing the task and recovery time, with the combination resulting in an estimated productivity drain of $650 billion per year.[22] Recognize, however, that answer the phone or responding to an email with a legitimate work purpose is not an interruption—it is part of your job.

Many of the techniques already described in this chapter help save time, such as eliminating nonessential work. Whether an activity is a time waster depends on the purpose of the activity. Suppose you play computer solitaire for 10 minutes to reduce stress and then return to work refreshed. In contrast, another worker who spends 10 minutes playing solitaire just for fun is wasting time.

Figure 15-1 presents a list of common time wasters and ideas to overcome them. Being aware of time wasters will help sensitize you to the importance of minimizing

LEARNING OBJECTIVE 4

FIGURE 15-1 Ways to Prevent and Overcome Time Wasting

1. Get your desk, as well as your work space (usually a cubicle or office), in order for good because sorting through disorder wastes so much time. Also, keep track of important names, places, and things to avoid wasting time searching for them.
2. Use a time log for two weeks to track time wasters. (See Skill-Building Exercise 15-3.)
3. Avoid the computer as a diversion from work, such as sending jokes back and forth to work members, playing video games, and checking out recreational websites during working hours.
4. Cluster together tasks such as returning phone calls or responding to email messages. For example, in most jobs it is possible to be polite and productive by reserving two or three 15-minute periods per day for taking care of email correspondence.
5. Socialize on the job just enough to build your network. Chatting with co-workers is a major productivity drain.
6. Be prepared for meetings by, for example, having a clear agenda and sorting through the documents you will be referring to. Make sure electronic equipment is in working order before attempting to use it during the meeting.
7. Set a time limit for tasks after you have done them once or twice.
8. Prepare a computer template for letters and computer documents that you send frequently. (The template is essentially a form letter, especially with respect to the salutation and return address.)
9. When you arrive at work, be ready to get started working immediately. Greet people quickly, avoid checking your personal email, and shut off your cell phone.
10. Take care of as much email correspondence as you can after you have finished your other work, unless a key part of your job is dealing with email. It consumes substantial time.
11. Avoid perfectionism, which leads you to keep redoing a project. Let go and move on to another project.
12. Make use of bits of time—for instance, five minutes between appointments. Invest those five minutes in sending a work-related email message or revising your to-do list.
13. Minimize procrastination, the number one time-waster for most people.
14. Avoid spreading yourself too thin by doing too many things at once, such as having one project too many to handle. When you are overloaded, time can be wasted because of too many errors.
15. Manage interruptions by letting co-workers know when you are available for consultation, and when you need to work independently—except for emergencies. Respond to instant messages only if your job requires responding immediately. Batch your instant messages just as you would other emails.

Sources: Suggestion 1 is from Toddi Gutner, "Beat the Clock," *Business Week*, February/March 2008, p. 58; suggestions 6 and 7 are based on Stephen R. Covey with Hyrum Smith, "What If You Could Chop an Hour from Your Day for Things That Matter Most?" *USA Weekend*, January 22–24, 1999, pp. 4–5; suggestion 10 is from Anita Bruzzese, "Tips to Avoid Wasting Time," *Gannet News Service*, August 9, 2004. Support for suggestion 13 is found in Vince Thompson, "Make the Most of Your White Space," jobs@UpLadder.com, October 3, 2007. Data about the productivity drain of interruptions are analyzed in Quintus R. Jett and Jennifer M. George, "Work Interrupted: A Closer Look at the Role of Interruptions in Organizational Life," *Academy of Management Review*, July 2003, pp. 494–507.

SKILL-BUILDING EXERCISE 15-3

Maintaining a Time Log

An effective starting point to avoid wasting time is to identify how you spend the 168 hours you have each week (24 hours × 7 days). For two weeks, catalogue all the time you spend, down to as much detail as you can tolerate. Besides the large, obvious items, include the small, easy-to-forget ones. Keep track of any activity that requires at least five minutes. Major items would include working, attending class, studying, reading, watching television, sleeping, eating, going places, spending time with loved ones and friends (hanging out). Small items would include visiting the coffee shop or vending machine, purchasing gum, and clipping your nails. If you multitask, such as walking and listening to music, do not double-count the time.

When your time logs have been completed, search for complete wastes of time, or activities that could be shortened. You might find, for example, that you spend about 45 minutes per day in the pursuit and consumption of coffee. If you reduced that time to 30 minutes you would have an additional 15 minutes per day that you could invest in your career. However, if coffee time includes forming alliances with people or maintaining relationships, maybe the 45-minute-per-day investment is worthwhile.

---

them. Even if you save just 10 minutes per workday, the productivity gain over a year could be enormous.

To analyze whether you might be wasting time, do Skill-Building Exercise 15-3. Self-Assessment Quiz 15-2 gives you an opportunity to think through your tendencies toward a subtle type of time wasting.

SELF-ASSESSMENT QUIZ 15-2

Tendencies toward Perfectionism

Directions: Many perfectionists have some behaviours and attitudes described below. To help understand your tendencies toward perfectionism, rate how strongly you agree with each of the statements below on a scale of 0 to 4 by circling the appropriate number. 0 means disagree, 4 means agree.

1.	Many people have told me that I am a perfectionist.	0	1	2	3	4
2.	I often correct the speech of others.	0	1	2	3	4
3.	It takes me a long time to write an email because I keep checking and rechecking my writing.	0	1	2	3	4
4.	I often criticize the colour combinations my friends are wearing.	0	1	2	3	4
5.	When I purchase food at a supermarket, I usually look at the expiration date so I can purchase the freshest.	0	1	2	3	4
6.	I can't stand it when people use the term "remote" instead of "remote control."	0	1	2	3	4
7.	If a company representative asked me, "What is your *social*?" I would reply something like "Do you mean my *social insurance number*?"	0	1	2	3	4
8.	I hate to see dust on furniture.	0	1	2	3	4
9.	I like the Martha Stewart idea of having every decoration in the home just right.	0	1	2	3	4
10.	I never put a map back in the glove compartment until it is folded just right.	0	1	2	3	4
11.	Once an eraser on a pencil of mine becomes hard and useless, I throw away the pencil.	0	1	2	3	4
12.	I adjust all my watches and clocks so they show exactly the same time.	0	1	2	3	4
13.	It bothers me that clocks on personal computers are often wrong by a few minutes.	0	1	2	3	4
14.	I clean the keyboard on my computer at least once a week.	0	1	2	3	4
15.	I organize my email messages and computer documents into many different, clearly labelled files.	0	1	2	3	4
16.	You won't find old coffee cups or soft-drink containers on my desk.	0	1	2	3	4
17.	I rarely start a new project or assignment until I have completed my present project or assignment.	0	1	2	3	4

18.	It is very difficult for me to concentrate when my work area is disorganized.	0	1	2	3	4
19.	Cobwebs in chandeliers and other lighting fixtures bother me.	0	1	2	3	4
20.	It takes me a long time to make a purchase such as a digital camera because I keep studying the features on various models.	0	1	2	3	4
21.	When I balance my chequebook, it usually comes out right within a few dollars.	0	1	2	3	4
22.	I carry enough small coins and dollar bills with me so when I shop I can pay the exact amount without requiring change.	0	1	2	3	4
23.	I throw out any underwear or T-shirts that have even the smallest holes or tears.	0	1	2	3	4
24.	I become upset with myself if I make a mistake.	0	1	2	3	4
25.	When a fingernail of mine is broken or chipped, I fix it as soon as possible.	0	1	2	3	4
26.	I am carefully groomed whenever I leave my home.	0	1	2	3	4
27.	When I notice packaged goods or cans on the floor in a supermarket, I will often place them back on the shelf.	0	1	2	3	4
28.	I think that carrying around antibacterial cleaner for the hands is an excellent idea.	0	1	2	3	4
29.	If I am with a friend, and he or she has a loose hair on the shoulder, I will remove it without asking.	0	1	2	3	4
30.	I am a perfectionist.	0	1	2	3	4

Total Score _____

Scoring and Interpretation: Add the numbers you circled to obtain your total score.

91 or over You have strong perfectionist tendencies to the point that it could interfere with your taking quick action when necessary. Also, you may annoy many people with your perfectionism.

61–90 You have a moderate degree of perfectionism that could lead you to produce high-quality work and be a dependable person.

31–60 You have a mild degree of perfectionism. You might be a perfectionist in some situations quite important to you, but not in others.

0–30 You are not a perfectionist. You might be too casual about getting things done right, meeting deadlines, and being aware of details.

UNDERSTANDING AND MANAGING STRESS

A major challenge facing any worker who wants to stay healthy and have good interpersonal relationships is to manage stress effectively. There is little doubt that many people at the present time are feeling the effects of stress. Although *stress* is an everyday term, a scientific definition helps clarify its meaning. **Stress** is an adaptive response that is the consequence of any action, situation, or event that puts special demands on a person. Note that stress refers to a reaction to the situation, not the situation or force itself. A **stressor** is the external or internal force that brings on stress.

Individual differences play a key role in determining what events are stressful. Giving a presentation to management, for example, is stressful for some people but not for others. Some people perceive a presentation as a threatening and uncomfortable experience, while others might perceive the same event to be an invigorating challenge. The term *special* demands is also critical, because minor hassles, such as a pencil point that breaks, are usually not perceived as stressful. Yet a piling on of minor hassles, such as having 10 small things go wrong in one day, is stressful. This is true because stress is cumulative; a series of small doses of stress can create a major stress problem.

Our approach to understanding stress centres on its symptoms and consequences, personality and job factors that contribute to stress, and methods and techniques for stress management. Managing stress receives more emphasis because the same techniques can be used to combat a variety of stressors.

stress

An adaptive response that is the consequence of any action, situation, or event that places special demands on a person.

stressor

The external or internal force that brings about stress.

Symptoms and Consequences of Stress

LEARNING OBJECTIVE 5

The physiological changes that take place within the body in response to stress are responsible for most stress symptoms. These physiological changes are almost identical for both positive and negative stressors. Snowboarding, romantic attraction, and being downsized can make you feel about the same physically. The experience of stress helps activate hormones that prepare the body to fight or run when faced with a challenge. This battle against the stressor is referred to as the **fight-or-flight response**. It helps you deal with emergencies.

The brain is the organ that decides whether a situation is stressful and produces the behavioural and physiological responses. Yet the brain's response is based on personal experience and culture. Driving on a busy four-lane highway would rarely be stressful for someone who lives in Toronto, yet might be for someone from a small village in Northern Ontario. The brain senses stress as damage to well-being and therefore sends out a signal to the body to cope. The brain is thus a self-regulating system that helps us cope with stressors.

fight-or-flight response
The body's physiological and chemical battle against a stressor, in which the person either tries to cope with the adversity head-on or tries to flee from the scene.

Physiological Reactions
The activation of hormones when the body has to cope with a stressor produces a short-term physiological reaction. Among the most familiar symptoms are increases in heart rate, blood pressure, blood glucose, and blood clotting. The stress hormone cortisol and other chemical responses to a stress can increase the cardiovascular function and the immune system in the short term. To help yourself recognize these symptoms, try to recall your internal bodily sensations the last time you were almost in an automobile accident or heard some wonderful news. Less familiar changes are a redirection of the blood flow toward the brain and large muscle groups and a release of stored fluids from places throughout the body into the bloodstream.

If stress is continuous and accompanied by these short-term physiological changes, annoying and life-threatening conditions can occur. Damage occurs when stress levels rarely subside. Eventually the immune system is suppressed, and memory is impaired. When the immune system is impaired, the severity of many diseases and disorders increases. For example, people whose stress level is high recover more slowly from colds and injuries, and they are more susceptible to sexually transmitted diseases.

A stressful life event usually leads to a high cholesterol level (of the unhealthy type) and high blood pressure. Other conditions associated with stress are cardiac disease, migraine headaches, ulcers, allergies, skin disorders, irritable bowel syndrome, and cancer. People under continuous negative stress, such as having severe family problems or having a life out of control, also age more quickly partially because of cell damage.[23] (Have you ever observed that stressed-out friends of yours look older than their chronological age?) A study of 812 Swedish workers conducted over a 25-year period found that work stress doubles the risk of dying from a heart attack. Seventy-three of the workers died from cardiac disease during the study. The major type of stress studied was having high work demands with little control over the work, combined with being underpaid.[24]

A general behavioural symptom of intense stress is for people's weakest tendencies to be exaggerated. For instance, a person with a strong temper who usually keeps cool under pressure may throw a tantrum under extreme stress. Common stress symptoms are listed in Figure 15-2.

Job Performance Consequences.
Stress has both negative and positive consequences. **Hindrance stressors** are those stressful events and thoughts that have a negative effect on motivation and performance. Many of these have already been mentioned. In contrast, **challenge stressors** have a positive direct effect on motivation and performance.[25] A study with 215 employees across 61 offices of a state agency showed that when faced with challenge stressors, employees performed better on their regular tasks, citizenship behaviour, and customer service. In contrast, performance on the three dimensions decreased when employees experienced hindrance stressors. An example of a challenge stressor was having high responsibility; having to deal with a lot of red tape to get the job done was an example of a hindrance stressor.[26]

hindrance stressors
Those stressful events that have a negative effect on motivation and performance.

challenge stressors
Stressful events that have a positive direct effect on motivation and performance.

FIGURE 15-2 A Variety of Stress Symptoms

Mostly Physical and Physiological

Shaking or trembling	Mouth dryness
Dizziness	Upper and lower back pain
Heart palpitations	Frequent headaches
Difficulty breathing	Low energy and stamina
Chronic fatigue	Stomach problems
Unexplained chest pains	Constant craving for sweets
Frequent teeth-grinding	Increased alcohol or cigarette consumption
Frequent nausea	Frequent need to eliminate

Mostly Emotional and Behavioural

Difficulty concentrating	Anxiety or depression
Nervousness	Forgetfulness
Crying	Restlessness
Anorexia	Frequent arguments with others
Declining interest in sex	Feeling high-strung much of the time
Frequent nail-biting or hair-tugging	

Note: Anxiety is a general sense of dread, fear, or worry not linked to a specific event, such as being anxious about your future.

The right amount of stress prepares us for difficult challenges and spurs us on to peak intellectual and physical performance. An optimum level of stress exists for most people and most tasks.

In general, performance tends to be best under moderate amounts of stress. If the stress is too great, people become temporarily ineffective; they may freeze or "choke." Experiencing too little stress, people may become lethargic and inattentive. Figure 15-3 depicts the relationship between stress and performance. An exception to this relationship is that certain negative forms of stress are likely to lower performance even if the stress is moderate. For example, the stress created by an intimidating supervisor or worrying about radiation poisoning—even in moderate amounts—will not improve performance.

FIGURE 15-3 Relationship between Stress and Job Performance

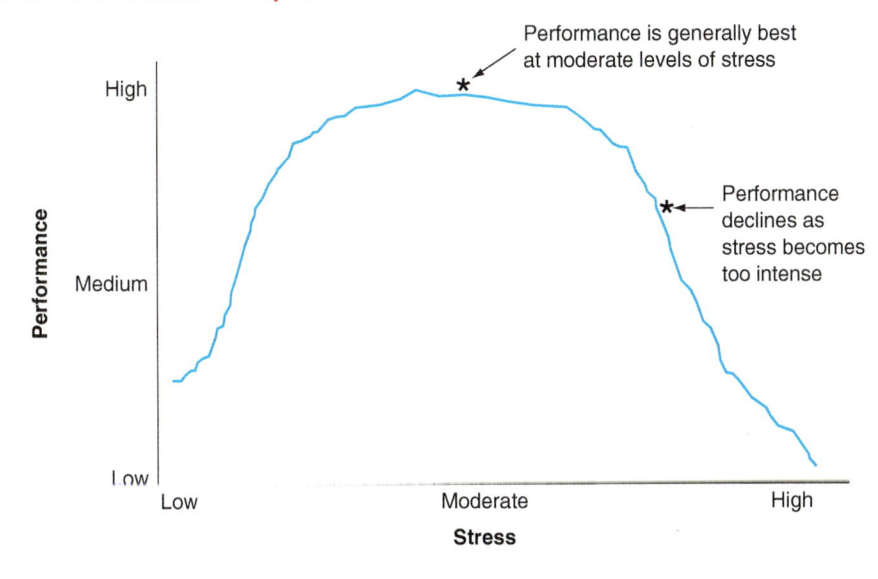

Performance is generally best at moderate levels of stress

Performance declines as stress becomes too intense

PERSONAL PRODUCTIVITY AND STRESS MANAGEMENT

Job stress can also lower job performance indirectly because distressed workers are more likely to be absent from the job, thereby not accomplishing as much work. A study of 323 health service workers in the United Kingdom found that job-related psychological distress, particularly depression, was associated with more days absent, and a greater number of times absent.[27]

The optimum amount of stress is a positive force that is the equivalent of finding excitement and challenge. Your ability to solve problems and deal with challenge is enhanced when the right amount of adrenalin flows in your blood to guide you toward peak performance. In fact, highly productive people are sometimes said to be hooked on adrenalin.

BACK TO THE OPENING CASE

According the latest national study on work–life balance in 2012, many workers are finding themselves in the wrong area of Figure 15-3 and are experiencing too much stress as they try to balance work and home. What can employers do to assist employees experiencing such high levels of stress? The study found that workplaces are doing little to alleviate this issue. Many organizational cultures still maintain "a work takes priority over family" stance, which does little for those experiencing this type of conflict. What would you recommend an employer do to assist workers to find better balance and less stress?

Burnout and Stress. One of the major problems of prolonged stress is that it may lead to burnout, a condition of emotional, mental, and physical exhaustion in response to long-term stressors. Burnout is also referred to as *work exhaustion* because fatigue is usually involved. Burned-out people are often cynical. Two other examples of burnout symptoms are irritability and impatience. According to Linda Duxbury, professor at Carleton University, members of the "sandwich generation" (see the opening discussion of this chapter) are often burned out. "People say they're short of sleep, grumpy, and they take it out on customers and colleagues at work."[28]

Burnout is a complex phenomenon with causes centring on five factors. First is a feeling of limited autonomy or control in the workplace. Not being able to decide how to accomplish a task is significant, as well as having little say in choosing what tasks to do. Second is receiving insufficient recognition for accomplishments. Third is not having advancement opportunities and feeling stifled on the job. Fourth is having poor relationships with co-workers, including not getting much respect. Fifth is working in an organizational culture incompatible with your belief system, such as a vegetarian working for a poultry producer.[29] A recent study with Dutch workers suggests that having a charismatic leader can help reduce some of the problems that lead to burnout.[30] For example, a charismatic leader is likely to give ample recognition.

The key feature of burnout is the distancing that occurs in response to work overload. Burnout sufferers shift into a mode of doing the minimum as a way of protecting themselves. They start leaving work early and dehumanizing their clients, patients, or customers. People experiencing burnout may do their job, but their heart is no longer in it.[31]

A synthesis of dozens of studies shows that burnout often damages the physical health of workers. Partly because burnout is a consequence of stress, burnout increases the risk for cardiovascular disease as much as well-known risk factors such as smoking, an elevated body mass index, and too much bad cholesterol. Other potential links between burnout and health problems include poor health behaviors and sleep disorder.[32]

Personality and Job Factors Contributing to Stress

LEARNING OBJECTIVE 6

Workers experience stress for many different reasons, including personal predispositions, factors stemming from the job, or the combined influence of both. If a person with an extreme negative predisposition has to deal with irate customers, he or she is most likely to experience substantial stress. Here we describe a sampling of important individual and organizational factors that contribute to job stress. Keep in mind, however, that a large number of potential stressors exist and that many of them overlap. For example, financial problems are a major source of stress, and they might contribute to relationship and health problems. Fighting about money harms relationships, and worrying about money can create health problems. Below we describe a sampling of important individual and organizational factors that contribute to job stress.

Personality Factors Predisposing People toward Stress. Individuals vary considerably in their susceptibility to job stress, based on their personality traits and characteristics. Four such factors are described next.

- **Low perceived control.** A key factor in determining whether workers experience stress is how much they believe they can control a given adverse circumstance. **Perceived control** is the belief that an individual has at his or her disposal a response that can control the negative aspects of an event. A survey of over 100 studies indicated that people with a high level of perceived control had low levels of physical and psychological symptoms of stress. Conversely, people with low perceived control are more likely to experience work stress.[33]

- **Low self-efficacy.** Self-efficacy, like perceived control, is another personal factor that influences susceptibility to stress. (Note that because self-efficacy is tied to a specific situation, it is not strictly a personality trait.) When workers have both low perceived control and low self-efficacy the stress consequences may be much worse. However, having high self-efficacy (being confident in one's abilities) softens the stress consequences of demanding jobs.[34] If you believe that you can successfully resolve a difficult problem, such as troubleshooting the reason for packages being sent to incorrect addresses, you will be less stressed.

- **Type A behaviour.** A person with **Type A behaviour** is demanding, impatient, and over-striving and is therefore prone to negative stress. Type A behaviour has two main components. One is the tendency to try to accomplish too many things in too little time. This causes the Type A individual to be impatient and demanding. The other component is free-floating hostility. Because of this sense of urgency and hostility, trivial things irritate these people. People with Type A behaviour are aggressive and hard-working.

    Type A personalities frequently develop cardiac disease, including heart attacks and strokes, at an early age. However, only certain features of the Type A personality pattern may be related to coronary heart disease. The heart attack triggers are hostility, anger, cynicism, and suspiciousness—and not other Type A characteristics such as impatience, ambition, and being work-driven.[35] In fact, hostility is more strongly associated with coronary heart disease in men than smoking, drinking, overeating, or high levels of bad (LDL) cholesterol.[36] Note that the heart attack triggers also make for strained interpersonal relationships.

- **Negative affectivity.** A major contributor to being stress prone is **negative affectivity**, a tendency to experience aversive emotional states. Negative affectivity is a pervasive disposition to experience emotional stress, including feelings of nervousness, tension, and worry. The same disposition also includes such emotional states as anger, scorn, revulsion, guilt, self-dissatisfaction, and sadness.[37] Such negative personalities seem to search for important discrepancies between what they would like and what exists. Poor interpersonal relationships often result from the frequent complaining of people with negative affectivity.

Job Sources of Stress. Almost any job situation can act as a stressor for some employees but not others. As just described, certain personality factors make it more likely that a person with them will experience job stress. Further, other personal life stressors may spill over into the workplace, such as being a member of the sandwich generation mentioned earlier, making it more likely that a person will experience job stress. Below we describe six frequently encountered job stressors, outlined in Figure 15-4.

Role Overload. Having too much work to do, or **role overload**, can create negative stress in two ways. First, the person may become fatigued and thus be less able to tolerate annoyances and irritations. Second, a person subject to unreasonable work demands may feel perpetually behind schedule, a situation that is itself a powerful stressor. Downsizing

---

perceived control
The belief that an individual has at his or her disposal a response that can control the negative aspects of an event.

Type A behaviour
A behaviour pattern in which the individual is demanding, impatient, and over-striving, and therefore prone to negative stress.

negative affectivity
A tendency to experience aversive emotional states.

role overload
Having too much work to do.

FIGURE 15-4 Six Significant Sources of Job Stress

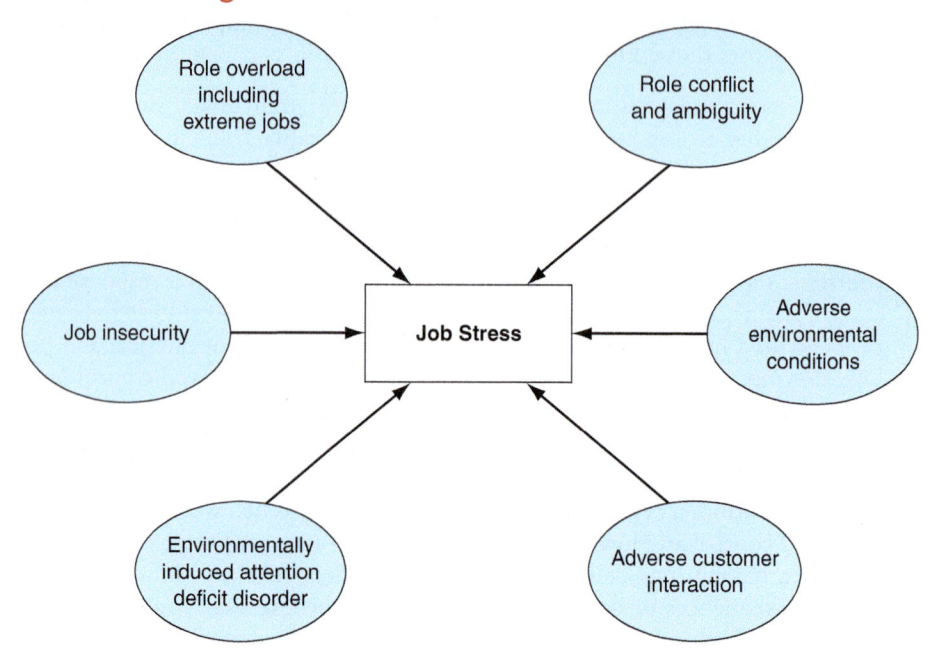

```
        Role overload              Role conflict
        including                  and ambiguity
        extreme jobs
              ↓                          ↓
Job insecurity  →      Job Stress      ←  Adverse
                                           environmental
                                           conditions
              ↑                          ↑
        Environmentally           Adverse customer
        induced attention          interaction
        deficit disorder
```

often creates overload because fewer people are left to handle the same workload as previously. (If work is carefully streamlined, role overload is minimized.) In a Canadian study, role overload was associated with both physical and emotional health problems. Of the sample, almost 60 percent of employees reported high levels of role overload. Employees who have high role overload are often less committed to their organization, report higher levels of job stress, and are less satisfied with their jobs. Also, employees with high role overload were more likely to have high rates of absenteeism and were more likely to report they intend to leave their jobs.[38]

According to a study from Health Canada, work culture is the most powerful predictor of role overload. For both men and women, the single most important aspect of work culture with respect to the prediction of role overload was the extent to which the employee believed the organization promoted a culture that was supportive of work–life balance. Work cultures that emphasize over-commitment to work, such as expecting extra hours at the office or taking work home in the evenings, contribute to overload.[39]

Work overload often takes the form of an **extreme job** in which the incumbent works at least 60 hours per week in a position that usually requires tight deadlines and heavy travel. Many of these jobs with long hours are found in information technology and financial services fields; yet many business owners work comparable hours. The availability of work associates across the globe in different time zones facilitates extreme jobs. One financial analyst who immigrated to the United States from India reportedly works 120 hours per week, leaving only 48 hours for non-work activities including sleep. Although many extreme job holders experience considerable job stress, many are exalted by the excitement and the high income.[40]

In extreme form, role overload can kill. For example, death from too much work is so common in Japan that the word *karoshi* has been coined to label the situation. In a celebrated case, a Toyota chief engineer worked up to 114 hours of overtime a month in the six months before he died of heart failure. For decades, the Japanese government has been attempting without much success to set limits on hours of work. The consequences of role overload show up in claims for death and disability from overwork, and also in suicides attributed to work fatigue. Among 2207 work-related suicides in Japanese companies in one year, the most frequent reason (672 suicides) was overwork.[41]

Role Conflict and Role Ambiguity. Role conflict is a major workplace stressor. People experience stress when they have to choose between two sets of expectations. Suppose an accountant is asked by her manager to state company earnings in a way that conflicts with the professional norms of accountants. If she complies with her manager, she will feel that

---

extreme job
A job in which the incumbent works at least 60 hours per week in a position that usually requires tight deadlines and heavy travel.

she is betraying her profession. If she insists on maintaining her professional norms, she will enter into dispute with the manager. The woman is likely to experience job stress.

Role ambiguity is a condition in which the job holder is faced with confusing or poorly defined expectations. Workers in many organizations are placed in situations in which they are unsure of their true responsibilities. Some workers who are placed on a self-managing work-team experience role ambiguity because they are asked to solve many problems by themselves. It is less ambiguous to have the manager tell you what to do. Many people experience stress symptoms when faced with role ambiguity.

role ambiguity
A condition in which a job holder is faced with confusing or poorly defined expectations.

Adverse Environmental Conditions.
A variety of adverse organizational conditions are stressors, as identified by national and provincial occupational safety and health agencies and boards. Among these adverse organizational conditions are unpleasant or dangerous physical conditions, such as crowding, noise, air pollution, or ergonomic problems. Enough polluted air within an office building can create a "sick building," in which a diverse range of airborne particles, vapours, moulds, and gases pollute the indoor environment. The result can be headaches, nausea, and respiratory infections, as well as the stress created by physical illness.[42]

Ergonomic problems refer to a poor fit between the physical and human requirements of a job. Working at a computer monitor for prolonged periods of time can lead to adverse physical and psychological reactions. The symptoms include headaches and fatigue, along with eye problems. Common visual problems are dry eyes and blurred or double vision. An estimated one out of five visits to vision-care professionals is for computer-related problems. Another vision-related problem is that people lean forward to scan the monitor, leading to physical problems such as back strain.

The repetitive-strain injury most frequently associated with keyboarding and the use of optical scanners is **carpal tunnel syndrome**. The syndrome occurs when repetitive flexing and extension of the wrist causes the tendons to swell, trapping and pinching the median nerve. Carpal tunnel syndrome creates stress because of the associated pain and misery. According to the Canadian Centre for Occupational Health and Safety, this disorder is fairly common. For example, 614 out of 982 supermarket checkers surveyed reported symptoms of carpal tunnel syndrome.[43] A less publicized problem is a sore thumb (overuse syndrome) related to continuous use of the space bar and mouse. The "BlackBerry thumb" stems from using the thumb to type on the very small keyboard.

carpal tunnel syndrome
A condition that occurs when repetitive flexing and extending of the wrist cause the tendons to swell, thus trapping and pinching the median nerve.

Thoughts of having to permanently leave a job requiring keyboarding constitute another potential stressor. If ergonomic principles, such as erect posture, are incorporated into computer usage, these stress symptoms diminish. Office chairs and desks developed in recent years allow for more flexibility of movement as workers shift rapidly between tasks such as moving toward the computer screen, placing feet on the desk, changing desk height, and turning for a face-to-face conversation.[44]

Commuting to and from work is a major stressor for many people that could be classified as an adverse environmental condition. We emphasize *for many people*, because individual differences again come into play. Some people enjoy driving, or being on a train or bus, for such reasons as the opportunity to listen to the radio or read. One study with commuters found that train rides of over one hour are particularly stressful for commuters. Longer commutes were associated with elevated cortisol (a stress hormone) poorer performance on a proofreading task given the study participants, and high levels of perceived commuting stress. The researcher also observed that for many workers commuting is the most stressful aspect of work.[45]

To avoid the stress of commuting in rush hour traffic, some workers leave home several hours before work, and then use the early arrival time to have breakfast, read the newspaper, or visit an athletic club near the work site.[46] Furthermore, a major reason many people work from home is to avoid the stresses associated with commuting.

Adverse Interaction with Customers and Clients and Emotional Labour.
Interactions with customers can be a major stressor. Part of the problem is that the sales associate often feels helpless when placed in conflict with a customer. The sales associate is told "The customer's always right." Furthermore, the store manager usually sides with the customer in a dispute. Unreasonable demands by clients and customers can also be stressful, such as customers who offer to buy a product or service below cost. Being subjected to sexual

harassment by clients and customers is another stressor widely experienced by store sales associates, especially young women.

Related to adverse customer interaction is the stressor of having to control the expression of emotion to please or to avoid displeasing a customer. Imagine having to smile at a customer who belittles you or your employer. Alicia A. Grandey, associate professor of psychology at Penn State University, defines **emotional labour** as the process of regulating both feelings and expressions to meet organizational goals.[47] The process involves both surface acting and deep acting. Surface acting means faking expressions, such as smiling, whereas deep acting involves controlling feelings, such as suppressing anger toward a customer you perceive to be annoying or unreasonable.

Sales workers and customer service representatives often experience emotional labour because so often they have to fake facial expressions and feelings so as to please customers. Nevertheless, according to one study, the top five occupations in terms of emotional labour demands are (1) police and sheriff's patrol officers, (2) social workers, (3) psychiatrists, (4) supervisors of police and detectives, and (5) registered nurses. Bill and account collectors ranked 15![48]

Engaging in emotional labour for prolonged periods of time can lead to job dissatisfaction, stress, and burnout. Surface acting creates more dissatisfaction. A contributing cause is that faking expressions and emotions takes a physiological toll, such as the intestines churning. Workers who engage in emotional labour may also develop cardiovascular problems and weakened immune systems. The good news is that being extraverted helps reduce some of the stress associated with both surface acting and deep acting.[49] (Perhaps if you like people, you can better tolerate their unruly behaviour.)

Environmentally Induced Attention Deficit Disorder. According to psychiatrist Edward Hallowell, many people suffer from an attention deficit disorder brought on by technology and activity overload. (The condition is similar to communication or information overload.) This problem appears to be a combination of the environment and the individual who chooses to overuse information technology devices. The symptoms of environmentally induced attention deficit disorder include frequently feeling rushed and impatient, being easily distracted, forgetfulness, and having little time for creative thought. In short, the person feels frazzled. A major cause of this type of attention deficit disorder is attempting to do more in less time.[50] Many of the suggestions about work habits and time management described later are useful in coping with environmentally induced attention deficit disorder.

Job Insecurity and Job Loss. Worrying about losing your job is a major stressor. Even when jobs are plentiful, having to search for another job and facing the prospect of geographic relocation are stressors for many people. Downsizing and corporate mergers (which usually result in downsizing) have contributed to job insecurity. The anticipation of layoffs among employees can increase negative stress and lower job performance. In addition, the survivors of a downsizing often experience pressure from fear of future cuts, loss of friends, and worry about a sudden increase in workload.[51]

Job loss is usually a more intense stressor than worrying about losing one's job. Losing a job often leads to the stressors of financial problems and relationship conflict. Some people who lose their job become so stressed and depressed that they commit suicide. An unfortunate example is that between 2006 and 2008, France Télécom laid off approximately 22,000 workers. Twenty-four laid off workers committed suicide, with the labour union blaming the layoffs for most of the suicides.[52] We hypothesize here that workers with

emotional labour
The process of regulating both feelings and expressions to meet organizational goals.

good resources, such as supportive friends and family, good professional contacts, and effective job search skills are the least likely to commit suicide after job loss.

So which of the job stressors described have the most adverse effect on job performance? An analysis of 69 groups, comprising 35,265 employees, indicated that role ambiguity and situational constraints are the most negatively related to job performance. A *situational constraint* refers to a situation in which conditions in an employee's job setting inhibit or constrain performance, such as improper machinery or inadequate supplies.[53] The job stressor, adverse environmental conditions, includes a few situational constraints.

Methods and Techniques for Managing Stress

LEARNING OBJECTIVE 7

Unless stress is managed properly, it may lead to harmful long-term consequences, including disabling physical illness and career impediment. Managing stress refers to controlling stress by making it a constructive force in your life. Managing stress thus involves both preventing and reducing stress. However, the distinction between methods of preventing and reducing stress is not clear-cut. For example, physical exercise not only reduces stress, it contributes to a relaxed lifestyle that helps you prevent stress.

A key principle about managing stress is that you are less likely to experience distress from stressors if you have the right resources. Having the right personality characteristics such as high perceived control, high self-efficacy, and not being hostile helps to ward off stress. External resources to help ward off negative stress include having a network of friends who provide support, an encouraging manager, and programs for helping distressed employees.[54] Assume, for example, that a worker is heavily stressed by a long rush-hour commute. If the company provides flexible working hours that help decrease commuting during rush hour, the worker experiences less of a hindrance stressor.

Coping with, or managing, stress can be undertaken through hundreds of activities, with substantial personal differences in which technique is effective. Running is a case in point. For many people, running or jogging is an excellent method of stress reduction. Others find running creates new stressors, such as aching knees, shin splints, dizziness from breathing in vehicle exhaust, and worry about being hit by vehicles. In general, coping efforts involve cognitions and behaviours aimed at managing the stressor and its associated emotions. For example, you may need to decrease the troublesome elements in your job (such as role overload) and also deal with the tension generated by overwork. Below we describe seven representative methods for managing stress and include a list of everyday stress-busters.

Eliminate or Modify the Stressor. The most potent method of managing stress is to eliminate or modify the stressor giving you trouble. One value of relaxation techniques is that they calm down a person enough so that he or she can deal constructively with the stressor. One helpful way to attack the cause of stress is to follow the steps in problem solving and decision making. You clarify the problem, identify the alternatives, weigh them, and select one. A difficulty, however, is that your evaluation of the real problem may be inaccurate. There is always a limit to self-analysis. For example, a person might think that work overload is the stressor when the true stressor is low self-efficacy.

A major strategy for modifying a stressor is to rethink your belief about a challenging situation. According to the **cognitive-behavioural approach to stress management**, people learn to recognize how pessimistic and distorted thoughts of gloom and doom create stress. After recognition of the problem, the person learns to replace the overly pessimistic thinking with more realistic or optimistic thinking. Assume that Mandy is stressed about the prospects of losing her job. Using a cognitive-behavioural approach to stress management, she begins to think, "Would losing this job really be that bad? If this job folds, I could move to Vancouver, where I've always wanted to live, and restart my career." Mandy is right on target because a synthesis of many studies found that cognitive-behavioural approaches are the most effective method of combating workplace stress.[55]

cognitive-behavioural approach to stress management
A method by which people learn to recognize how pessimistic and distorted thoughts of gloom and doom create stress.

Get Appropriate Physical Exercise. A moderate amount of physical exercise is a cornerstone of managing stress and achieving wellness. To manage stress it is important to select an exercise program that is physically challenging but does not lead to overexertion and

PERSONAL PRODUCTIVITY AND STRESS MANAGEMENT   343

muscle or bone injury. Competitive sports, if taken too seriously, can actually increase stress. Aerobic exercises are most beneficial because they make you breathe faster and raise your heart rate. Walking is highly recommended as a stress reducer because it is inherently relaxing, and offers many of the benefits of other forms of exercise with a minimum risk of physical danger. Doing housework, yard work, and washing and waxing a vehicle are examples of everyday forms of gentle exercise that offer the side benefits of getting tasks accomplished. A major mental and emotional benefit of physical exercise stems from endorphins produced in the thalamus portion of the brain when one exercises. The endorphins are associated with a state of euphoria referred to as a "runner's high." Endorphins also work like painkillers, adding to their stress-reduction value.

Physical exercise directly reduces stress, and also reduces the risk of disorders that are both debilitating themselves, and as a result become intense stressors. According to the Public Health Agency of Canada physical activity and exercise have many health benefits, including healthy growth and development, prevention of many chronic diseases, increased energy, decreased stress, and prolonged independence as we age.[56]

Many people seek to reduce and prevent stress through yoga, which is both physical exercise and a way of developing mental attitudes that calm the body and mind. One of yoga's many worthwhile goals is to solder a union between the mind and body, thereby achieving harmony and tranquility. Another benefit of yoga is that it helps people place aside negative thoughts that act as stressors.[57]

Get Sufficient Rest. Rest offers benefits similar to those of exercise, such as stress reduction, improved concentration, improved energy, and better tolerance for frustration. Achieving proper rest is closely linked to getting proper exercise. The current interest in adult napping reflects the awareness that proper rest makes a person less stress prone and increases productivity. A study was conducted of 23,681 healthy Greek adults over a six-year period, many of whom napped for about 30 minutes three times a week. Study participants who napped had 37 percent lower risk of dying from a heart attack than the people who did not. A criticism offered of this study is that the people who napped may also take better care of their bodies and mind in general.[58] The connection of this study to stress management is that many heart attacks are stress induced.

A growing number of firms have napping facilities for workers, and many workers nap at their desks or in their parked vehicles during lunch breaks. Workday power naps of about 15 minutes' duration serve as both energizers and stress-reducers.[59] Napping can help a worker become more productive and less stressed. A rested brain is a more effective brain. To keep the effectiveness of "power napping" in perspective, workers who get enough rest during normal sleeping hours have less need for a nap during working hours.

Maintain a Healthy Diet. Another practical method of stress reduction and prevention is to maintain a well-balanced, and therefore healthy, diet. Nutritious food is valuable for physical and mental health, making it easier to cope with frustrations that are potential stressors. Some non-nutritious foods, such as those laden with caffeine or sugar, tend to enhance a person's level of stress. According to Canada's Food Guide, from Health Canada, a healthy diet is one that

- emphasizes fruits, vegetables, whole grains, and fat-free or low-fat milk and milk products.
- includes lean meats, poultry, fish, beans, eggs, and nuts.
- is low in saturated fats, trans fats, cholesterol, salt (sodium), and added sugars.

These recommendations are for the general public over two years of age. There is also additional information for specific age groups, pregnant women, and First Nations peoples. A national food guide has also been created that reflects the values, traditions and food choices of First Nations, Inuit, and Métis, which is offered on Health Canada's website. Consult the complete guide shown in Figure 15-5 and visit Health Canada's website for more detailed information at www.hc-sc.gc.ca/fn-an/food-guide-aliment/index_e.html. The website for this guide provides more information about nutrition and healthy eating, including how to plan menus for healthy eating.

FIGURE 15-5 Canada's Food Guide

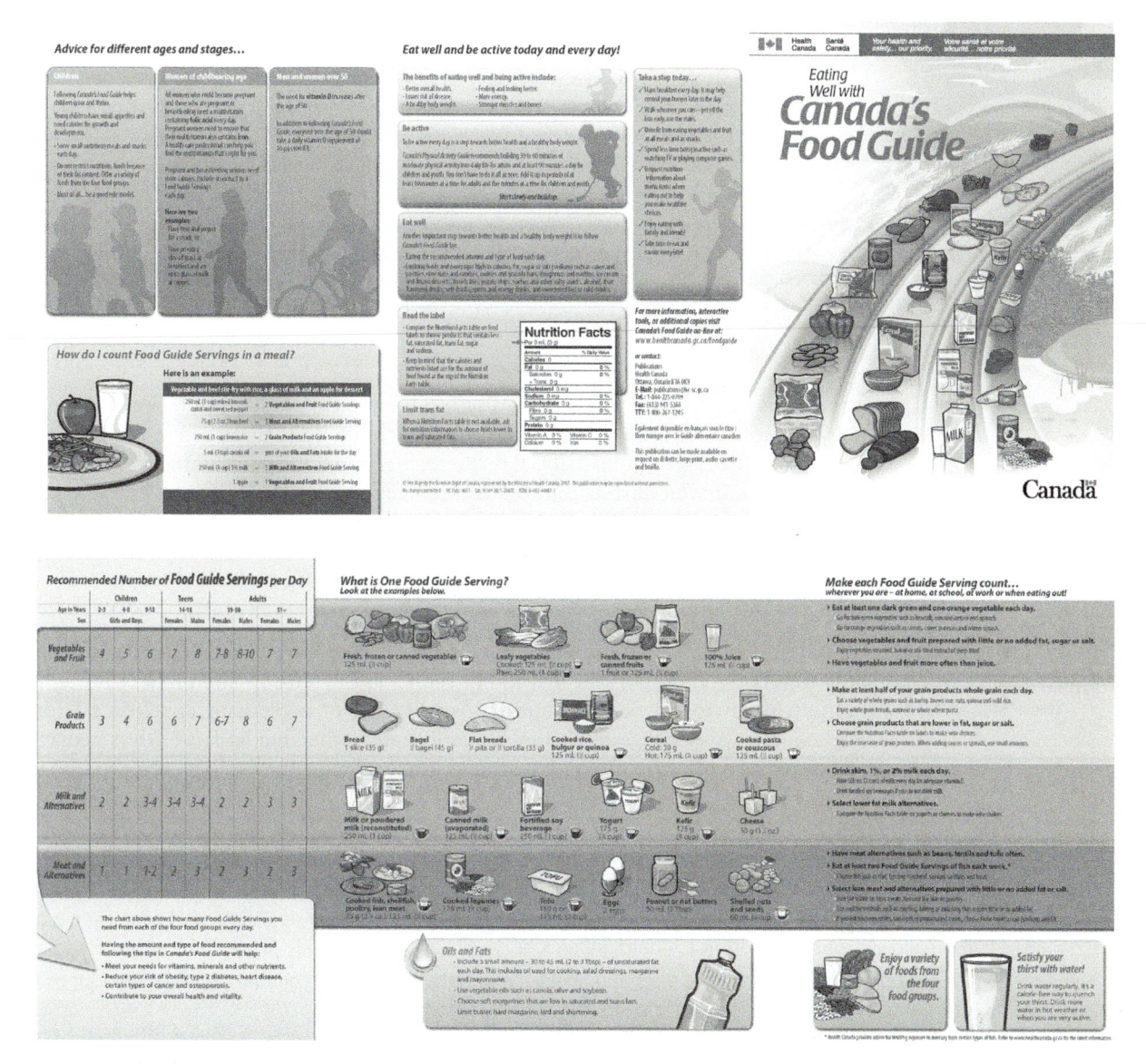

Source: "Eating Well with Canada's Food Guide." Health Canada, 2011. Reproduced with permission from the Minister of Health, 2013.

Build a Support Network. A **support network** is a group of people who can listen to your problems and provide emotional support. These people, or even one person, can help you through your difficult episodes. Members of your network can provide you with a sense of closeness, warmth, and acceptance that will reduce your stress. Also, the simple expedient of putting your feelings into words can be a healing experience. The way to develop this support network is to become a good listener yourself so that the other person will reciprocate. A support network is therefore a method of stress management based squarely on effective interpersonal skills.

support network
A group of people who can listen to your problems and provide emotional support.

Practise Visualization and Meditation. Perhaps the most effortless and enjoyable relaxation technique for managing stress is to visualize a pleasant experience, as explained in Skill-Building Exercise 15-4. Like so many stress-reduction techniques, including meditation, visualization requires concentration. Concentrating helps slow down basic physiological processes, such as the heart rate, and dissipates stress. Forcing yourself to concentrate is also valuable, given that a key symptom of stress is difficulty in concentration.

Meditation is a relaxation technique used to quiet the mind, as well as to relieve stress, and is more complicated than simple visualization. (The well-known *relaxation*

PERSONAL PRODUCTIVITY AND STRESS MANAGEMENT   345

> ### SKILL-BUILDING EXERCISE 15-4
>
> **Visualization for Stress Reduction**
>
> A standard, easy-to-use method for reducing stress symptoms is to visualize a pleasant and calm experience. If you are experiencing stress right now, try the technique. Otherwise, wait until the next time you perceive your body to be experiencing stress. In this context, visualization means picturing yourself doing something that you would like to do. Whatever fantasy suits your fancy will work, according to the advocates of this relaxation technique. Visualizations that work for some people include smiling at a loved one, floating on a cloud, caressing a baby, petting a kitten or puppy, and walking in the woods. Notice that all of these scenes are relaxing rather than exciting. What visualization would work for you?
>
> To implement the technique, close your eyes and bring the pleasant image into focus in your mind. Think of nothing else at the moment. Imagine that a videotape of the pleasant experience is playing on the television screen in your brain. Breathe softly and savour the experience. Slowly return to reality, refreshed, relaxed, and ready to tackle the challenges of the day.

response is essentially a form of meditation.) A typical meditation technique proceeds as follows: Hold your back straight, and relax the body. Take three gentle breaths, breathing in and out through the nostrils. Let the respiration follow its natural flow. Your body breathes as if it were fast asleep, yet you remain vigilant. If you get distracted, simply let go of the interrupting thought, and return to the breathing. It is helpful to count each inhale up to 21; every time your mind wanders, go back to 1. Practise meditating about 20 minutes a day, and meditate on the spot after a stressful event or thought.[60] The breathing part of meditation is so important that it is itself an everyday method of stress reduction.

Explore
Simulation: Productivity and Stress Management

Practise Everyday Methods of Stress Reduction. The simple expedient of learning how to relax is an important method of reducing the tension and anxiety brought about by both positive and negative stress. Visualization of a pleasant experience is one such method. Everyday suggestions for relaxation and other methods of stress reduction are presented in Figure 15-6. If you can accomplish these, you are less likely to need tranquilizing

FIGURE 15-6 Stress-Busters

- Take a deep breath and exhale slowly. Inhale and your heart beats faster. Exhale and your heart beats more slowly, and slows down the cardiac muscle.
- Place your thumbs behind your ears and spread your fingers on the top of your head. Move your scalp back and forth gently by rotating your fingers for 15–20 seconds.
- Give in to your emotions. If you are angry, disgusted, or confused, admit your feelings. Suppressing your emotions adds to stress.
- Take a brief break from the stressful situation and do something small and constructive, such as washing your car, emptying a wastebasket, or getting a haircut.
- Get a massage, because it can loosen tight muscles, improve your blood circulation, and calm you down.
- Get help with your stressful task from a co-worker, supervisor, or friend.
- Concentrate intensely on reading, surfing the Internet, a sport, or a hobby. Contrary to common sense, concentration is at the heart of stress reduction.
- Have a quiet place at home and have a brief idle period there every day.
- Take a leisurely day off from your routine.
- Finish something you have started, however small. Accomplishing almost anything reduces some stress.
- Stop to smell the flowers, make friends with a young child or elderly person, or play with a kitten or puppy.
- Strive to do a good job, but not a perfect job.
- Work with your hands, doing a pleasant task.
- Find somebody or something that makes you laugh, and have a good laugh.
- Minimize drinking caffeinated or alcoholic beverages, and drink fruit juice or water instead. Grab a piece of fruit rather than a can of beer.
- Help somebody less fortunate than you. The flood of good feelings will act like endorphins.

SKILL-BUILDING EXERCISE 15-5

Personal Stress Management Action Plan

Most people face a few powerful stressors in their work and personal life, but few people take the time to clearly identify these stressors or develop an action plan for remedial action. The purpose of this exercise is to make you an exception. Here is an opportunity to develop an inventory of your stressors, think through the problems they may be causing you, and develop action plans you might take to remedy the situation. Use the form below or create one with a word processing table or a spreadsheet.

Work or School Stressor	Symptoms This Stressor Is Creating for Me	My Action Plan to Manage This Stressor
1.		
2.		
3.		

Personal Life Stressor	Symptoms This Stressor Is Creating for Me	My Action Plan to Manage This Stressor
1.		
2.		
3.		

medication to keep you calm and in control. Your stress symptoms will ordinarily return, however, if you do not eliminate and modify the stressor. If the stress is from an emotional conflict you do not understand, assistance from a mental health professional is recommended.

Now that you have studied various method of managing stress, reinforce your thinking by doing Skill-Building Exercise 15-5.

Access the eText in MySearchLab to learn more about this chapter's self-assessment quizzes.

To Watch ✻ Explore ✓• Practice ✓• Study and Review, visit **MySearchLab**

Developing Your Human Relations Skills and Reinforcing Concepts

Summary ✓ Practice — Glossary Flashcards

- Procrastination, an enormous problem for many people, can be approached as follows: calculate the cost of procrastination; use the "worst in, first out" (WIFO) principle; break the task into manageable chunks; make a commitment to other people; remove some clutter from your mind; satisfy your stimulation quota in constructive ways; and eliminate rewards for procrastinating.
- Develop better attitudes and values at work by applying the following: (1) begin with a mission statement and goals; (2) play the inner game of work; (3) work smarter, not harder; (4) value orderliness and cleanliness; (5) value good attendance and punctuality; (6) attain a balance in life and avoid being a workaholic; and (7) increase energy.
- Skills that improve productivity include (1) Prepare a to-do list and set priorities, (2) streamline your work and emphasize important tasks, (3) concentrate on one important task at a time, (4) stay in control of paperwork and electronic work, (5) work productively from your home office or virtual office, and (6) improve your Internet search skills.
- Minimize time wasters at work such as daydreaming, surfing the Internet, and being unprepared for meetings.
- A major challenge facing any worker who wants to stay healthy and have good interpersonal relationships is to manage stress effectively. Individual differences play a big role in determining whether an event will lead to stress. The physiological changes that take place within the body in response to stress are responsible for most of the stress symptoms. The fight-or-flight response prepares us for battle against the stressor. The activation of hormones when the body has to cope with a stressor produces short-term physiological reactions, including an increase in heart rate and blood pressure. When stress levels rarely subside, these physiological changes create damage. Burnout, a condition of emotional, mental, and physical exhaustion is a response to long-term stressors.
- Four personality factors predisposing people toward stress are low perceived control, low self-efficacy, Type A behaviour, and negative affectivity. Frequently encountered job stressors are role overload, role conflict and ambiguity, adverse environmental conditions, environmentally induced attention deficit disorder, and job insecurity and job loss.
- You can cope with, or manage, stress through hundreds of activities, with substantial personal differences in which technique is effective. Seven representative stress-management methods are to eliminate or modify the stressor, get appropriate physical exercise, rest sufficiently, maintain a healthy diet, build a support network, practise visualization, and use everyday methods of stress reduction.

Interpersonal Relations Case 15-1

Rachel Runs the Treadmill

Six-thirty Tuesday morning, 38-year-old Rachel Proust hops out of her bed while her husband, Alex Proust, is still sleeping. Rachel's first stop is to wake up her nine-year-old daughter, and encourage her to start getting ready to meet the school bus on time. By 8 a.m. Rachel is in her car and on her way to her job as a business development specialist for a human resource outsourcing company. Her primary responsibility is to entice small- and medium-size companies to turn over most of their human resource functions to her firm.

Just as Rachel begins to manage her email and plan her agenda for the day, she places her right hand about three inches to the right of her heart. Rachel can feel the tightness next to her heart, and in her left arm. She thinks to herself, "This feels like I'm going to have a heart attack. It doesn't make sense for a woman my age to be a heart attack victim. But I'm happy that I have an appointment at the cardiology centre on Thursday."

At the North Side Cardiology Centre, Rachel is first interviewed by Nurse Practitioner Janet Trudeau before her interview with Dr. Harry Ching, the cardiologist. Trudeau first took a brief medical history, followed by an interview. Parts of the interview with Trudeau went as follows:

Trudeau: So tell me in more detail why you came to visit our cardiology centre.

Proust: I have these annoying chest pains next to my heart and in my left arm. The pains usually start when I am extremely aggravated and frustrated. I have the pains about once a day.

Trudeau: Do you ever faint or become light-headed during the pains?

Proust: No, my problem is just the pains. I keep doing whatever I'm doing when the pain hits.

Trudeau: Tell me about the situations you find so aggravating and frustrating.

Proust: I'm really stressing out. I have a ton of aggravations and worries. To begin with, my nine-year-old daughter, Samantha, has seizures. She is under treatment but the problem remains, and it's worrisome. I worry every day that Samantha will have a seizure and strike her head or get involved in an accident.

My work is also quite worrisome. I work mostly on commission selling human resource services. Our business has grown rapidly in the past few years, but we have kind of dried up the territory. I have to travel more to find new clients. My earnings are taking a turn downward despite the extra travel.

Trudeau: Are you the sole breadwinner in the family?

Proust: No, my husband, Alex, is an assistant manager at a Ruby Tuesday restaurant, and he makes a modest living. But talking about aggravation, my husband is a decent guy but he gives me chest pains. I think he cares much more about professional sports, especially the CFL and the NHL, than he does about Samantha and me. If he's watching a game, I can forget about talking about something serious.

And then, of course, Alex works the hours of a restaurant manager, which means that he is often working when I am not working, like on Saturdays and Sundays.

Trudeau: Any other major aggravations in your life?

Proust: Yes, commuting on busy highways. I can feel my chest pains starting when I think of sitting still for 15 minutes during rush-hour traffic.

Trudeau: Thank you, Rachel. I will be studying this information before your interview with Dr. Ching. Have a seat in the waiting room. He will be with you in about 10 minutes.

Later that day Proust had an extensive cardiology exam, including an electrocardiogram. Dr. Ching informed her that despite the muscle tension she was experiencing, her heart was in excellent condition.

Case Questions

1. What sources of stress does Rachel Proust appear to be facing?
2. What do you recommend Proust do about the stressors she is facing?
3. Given that Proust does not have a heart problem, should she be concerned about the stressors in her life? Explain your answer.
4. How might Proust organize her work and her life better to feel that her life is less out of control?

Interpersonal Relations Case 15-2

Stress-Busting at the Agriculture and Markets Group

The Agriculture and Markets group, part of a provincial health ministry, was having a demanding year. The mission of the group is to inspect grocery stores for possible health violations, such as unsanitary conditions and the sale of tainted food and meats. The group had a record number of complaints to investigate partly because so many stores were purchasing packaged goods, products, and meats from bottom-price suppliers in order to trim costs. At the same time, the Agriculture and Markets group was on a mandated cutback in spending. As a result, a few of the inspectors who had quit could not be replaced. The remaining inspectors were therefore carrying a much heavier workload.

The reality of a heavier workload with fewer staff available to make on-site visits created a high-pressure work environment. Michelle and Trevor, two of the more junior inspectors, decided together that the group needed to find a good way of blowing off steam. Their plan was to organize a few "prankster nights." On the first such night, six inspectors from the office got together to have a few drinks after work. During the drinking session at a bar close to the office, Michelle and Trevor announced their plan to relieve stress in a big way by pulling off a major prank.

The prank was the "popcorning" often executed by professional basketball players. The group would purchase a massive amount of popcorn and stuff it into the vehicle of their supervisor, Alicia Gordon, who typically parked her car in a remote spot in the garage to the government building. The three group members will pull off the prank on her sports car the next Monday during lunch hour.

Tuesday morning, every employee at the Department of Agriculture and Markets received an email explaining that a misdemeanor had been committed in the parking lot in the form of damaging Alicia's vehicle. The email also stated that the cruel act had violated the rights of Alicia Gordon to a harassment-free work environment. Anyone who knew who could have committed the hostile act of damaging Gordon's vehicle was urged to reply immediately to the email.

Michelle and Trevor quickly sent text messages to each other. Michelle wrote, "Can't Alicia take a joke? What's her problem?"

Trevor wrote back, "Maybe we did lower our stress. But I'm afraid our stress is going to bump up now."

Case Questions

1. What is your evaluation of the effectiveness of the stress-reduction techniques created by Michelle and Trevor?
2. What might have been a more effective method of the group from Markets and Agriculture to have used to decrease their stress?
3. What do you recommend Michelle, Trevor, and the rest of the group do with respect to taking responsibility for their prank?

Questions for Discussion and Review ✓ Practice Chapter Quiz

Multiple Choice

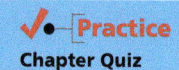

1. To manage procrastination, the WIFO principle refers to
    a. waiting for the right time to do the task you have been avoiding.
    b. tackling the easiest item on your to-do list.
    c. tackling the worst task on your to-do list first.
    d. working slowly but methodically on each task.
2. According to the text, the number one time waster at work for most people is
    a. perfectionism.
    b. procrastination.
    c. surfing the Internet.
    d. socializing with co-workers.
3. Performance is generally best at _____ levels of stress.
    a. moderate
    b. high
    c. low
    d. none of the above
4. Marty has been asked to promote a product to his customers that he knows is defective and performs poorly. He believes in being ethical and honest with customers, which is also part of the company's mission statement. This source of stress is referred to as
    a. role overload.
    b. role ambiguity.
    c. role conflict.
    d. burnout.
5. All of the following are recommended strategies for managing stress except
    a. practice meditation.
    b. get enough rest.
    c. build a support network.
    d. ignore the stressful situation.

Short Answer

6. Describe any way in which you have used information technology to make you more productive.
7. With millions of workers making regular use of personal digital assistants and smart phones throughout the world, why hasn't productivity in organizations taken a dramatic leap forward?
8. Why might having your stress under control improve your interpersonal relationships?
9. Interview a person in a high-pressure job in any field. Find out whether the person experiences significant stress and what methods he or she uses to cope with it.
10. Open your MySearchLab and click on the left-hand side "professional videos" and watch the video "Time Management and Organizational Tips." Answer the questions at the end of the video. As you consider these various ideas from the video, which ones do you feel you may try yourself? Are some ideas better than others? Why or why not?

Answers to multiple choice questions: 1. c,   2. b,   3. a,   4. c,   5. d.

The Web Corner

www.cmha.ca
Canadian Mental Health Association; a wide variety of information on mental health

www.hc-sc.gc.ca/index-eng.php
Health Canada; a wide variety of strategies to maintain good physical and mental health

http://www.student-affairs.buffalo.edu/shs/ccenter/stressprocrast.php
Overcoming procrastination for students

Internet Skill Builder

Go to www.getmoredone.com/tabulator.html to find the Pace Productivity Tabulator. This interactive module enables you to enter the time you spend on 11 major activities (such as employment, eating, sleeping, and television watching) and compare your profile to others'. You are also able to enter your ideal profile to see where you would like to be. You just follow the straightforward instructions. After arriving at your personal pie chart, ask yourself: "What have I learned that will enhance my personal productivity?"

MySearchLab

Visit **MySearchLab** to find self-grading review quizzes in the eText, discipline-specific media and readings, access to a variety of academic journals, and Associated Press news feeds, along with a wide range of writing, grammar, and research tools and to help hone writing and research skills.

GLOSSARY

action plan A series of steps designed to achieve a goal.
active listener A person who listens intently, with the goal of empathizing with the speaker.
aggressive personality A person who verbally, and sometimes physically, frequently attacks others.
alternative dispute resolution A formalized type of mediation, usually involving a hired professional who mediates a conflict between two or more parties.
assertiveness Forthrightness in expressing demands, opinions, feelings, and attitudes.
backstab An attempt to discredit by underhanded means, such as innuendo, accusation, or the like.
behaviour modification An attempt to change behaviour by manipulating rewards and punishments.
behavioural feedback Information given to another person that pinpoints behaviour rather than personal characteristics or attitudes.
behavioural interview An interview with questions that ask about a candidate's behaviour in relation to important job activities.
bias A prejudgment about something, not usually based on fact.
blind spots Areas of unawareness about our attitudes, thinking, and behaviours that contribute to poor decisions.
brainstorming A group problem-solving technique that promotes creativity by encouraging idea generation through non-critical discussion.
brainwriting Brainstorming by individuals working alone.
bullying Verbal and sometimes physical attacks on another without provocation.
burnout A condition of emotional, mental, and physical exhaustion in response to long-term stressors.
business etiquette A special code of behaviour required in work situations.
career path A sequence of positions necessary to achieve a goal.
carpal tunnel syndrome A condition that occurs when repetitive flexing and extending of the wrist cause the tendons to swell, thus trapping and pinching the median nerve.
casual time orientation A cultural characteristic in which people view time as an unlimited and unending resource and therefore tend to be patient.
challenge stressors Stressful events that have a positive direct effect on motivation and performance.
character trait An enduring, consistently exhibited characteristic of a person that is related to moral and ethical behaviour.
charisma A special quality of leaders whose purposes, powers, and extraordinary determination differentiate them from others. (However, people other than leaders can be charismatic.)
coaching A method of helping workers grow and develop and improve their job competence by providing suggestions and encouragement.
cognition The mental process or faculty by which knowledge is gathered.
cognitive behavioural approach to stress management A method by which people learn to recognize how pessimistic and distorted thoughts of gloom and doom create stress.

cognitive factors The collective term for problem-solving and intellectual skills.
cognitive fitness A state of optimized ability to remember, learn, plan, and adapt to changing circumstances.
cognitive restructuring Mentally converting negative aspects into positive ones by looking for the positive elements in a situation.
cognitive styles Mental processes used to perceive and make judgments from situations.
collective efficacy A group's belief that it can handle certain tasks. If a group is high in collective efficacy, it will more likely be successful in solving problems.
collectivism A belief that the group and society should receive top priority, rather than the individual.
communication The sending, receiving, and understanding of messages.
compromise Settlement of differences by mutual concessions.
concern for others An emphasis on personal relationships and a concern for the welfare of others.
conflict A situation in which two or more goals, values, or events are incompatible or mutually exclusive.
conflict of interest A situation that occurs when a person's judgment or objectivity is compromised.
confrontation Taking a direct problem-solving approach in a conflict to resolve differences to maintain a good working relationship.
consensus General acceptance by the group of a decision.
cultural fluency The ability to conduct business in a diverse, international environment.
cultural intelligence (CQ) An outsider's ability to interpret someone's unfamiliar and ambiguous behaviour the same way that person's compatriots would.
cultural sensitivity An awareness of, and a willingness to investigate, the reasons why people of another culture act as they do.
cultural training A set of learning experiences designed to help employees understand the customs, traditions, and beliefs of another culture.
customer relationship management (CRM) Software packages that enhance customer relations for a business.
customer-centric sales process A sales process emphasizing a low-pressure environment in which the sales staff acts as consultants, offering information and explaining how the product or service can help solve a customer's problem.
cyberbullying The use of information and communication technologies to bully, embarrass, threaten or harass another person. It also includes the use of information and communications technology (ICT) to engage in conduct or behaviour that is derogatory, defamatory, degrading, illegal, and/or abusive.
cycle-of-service chart A method of tracking the moments of truth with respect to customer service.
defensive communication The tendency to receive messages in such a way that self-esteem is protected.
defining moment A time when one must choose between two or more ideals in which one deeply believes.

deliberate practice Strong effort to improve target performance over time.

denial The suppression of information a person finds uncomfortable.

developmental need A specific area in which a person needs to change or improve.

difficult person An individual who creates problems for others, even though he or she has the skill and mental ability to do otherwise.

disability A physical or mental condition that substantially limits an individual's major life activities.

diversity training Training that attempts to bring about workplace harmony by teaching people how to get along better with diverse work associates.

effort-to-performance expectancy The probability assigned by the individual that effort will lead to performing the task correctly.

electronic brainstorming Method of generating ideas with the aid of a computer. Group members simultaneously and anonymously enter their suggestions into a computer, and the ideas are distributed to the monitors of other group members.

emotional intelligence Qualities such as understanding one's own feelings, empathy for others, and the regulation of emotion to one's own benefit.

emotional labour The process of regulating both feelings and expressions to meet organizational goals.

empathy In communication, imagining oneself in the receiver's role, and assuming the viewpoints and emotions of that individual.

employee network (or affinity) groups A group composed of employees throughout the company who affiliate on the basis of group characteristics, such as race, ethnicity, gender, sexual orientation, or physical ability status.

empowerment The process of managers transferring, or sharing, power with lower-ranking employees.

EQ Abbreviation for emotional intelligence, or emotional intelligence quotient, assessed by a variety of tests.

ethical screening Running a contemplated decision or action through an ethics test.

ethics The moral choices a person makes.

expectancy theory A motivation theory based on the premise that the effort people expend depends on the reward they expect to receive in return.

extinction Decreasing the frequency of undesirable behaviour by removing the desirable consequence of such behaviour.

extreme job A job in which the incumbent works at least 60 hours per week in a position that usually requires tight deadlines and heavy travel.

extreme job hunting An offbeat way of attracting an employer's attention, with a small probability of success.

feedback In communication, messages sent back from the receiver to the sender.

fight-or-flight response The body's physiological and chemical battle against a stressor, in which the person either tries to cope with the adversity head-on or tries to flee from the scene.

formality A cultural characteristic of attaching considerable importance to tradition, ceremony, social rules, and rank.

frame of reference A person's individual vantage point that causes him or her to perceive words and concepts differently.

g (general) factor A factor in intelligence that contributes to the ability to perform well in many tasks.

Galatea effect A type of self-fulfilling prophecy in which high expectations lead to high performance.

group decision making The process of reaching a judgment based on feedback from more than one individual.

group norms The unwritten set of expectations for group members.

groupthink A deterioration of mental efficiency, reality testing, and moral judgment in the interest of group solidarity.

groupware Technology designed to facilitate the work of groups.

high-context culture A culture that makes extensive use of body language.

hindrance stressors Those stressful events that have a negative effect on motivation and performance.

impression management A set of behaviours directed at improving one's image by drawing attention to oneself.

incivility In human relations, employees' lack of regard for each other.

individual differences Variations in how people respond to the same situation based on personal characteristics.

individualism A mental set in which people see themselves first as individuals and believe that their own interests take priority.

informal learning The acquisition of knowledge and skills that takes place naturally outside a structured learning environment.

informality A cultural characteristic of a casual attitude toward tradition, ceremony, social rules, and rank.

information overload A phenomenon that occurs when people are so overloaded with information that they cannot respond effectively to messages.

integrity (a) Consistency of words and deeds, and (b) being true to oneself.

intelligence The capacity to acquire and apply knowledge, including solving problems.

intermittent reward A reward that is given for good performance occasionally but not always.

internal customers The people within an individual's own company for whom the person performs a service in the course of doing his or her job.

interpersonal relations The technical term for relationships with people.

interpersonal skills training The teaching of skills in dealing with others.

intuition An experience-based way of knowing or reasoning in which the weighing and balancing of evidence are done automatically.

law of effect Behaviour that leads to a positive consequence for the individual tends to be repeated, whereas behaviour that leads to a negative consequence tends not to be repeated.

leader-exchange model A theory explaining that group leaders establish unique working relationships with group members, thereby creating in-groups and out-groups.

leadership The ability to inspire support and confidence among the people who are needed to achieve common goals.

learning style The way in which a person best learns new information.

locus of control The way people look at causation in their lives.

materialism An emphasis on assertiveness and the acquisition of money and material objects.

mediation A type of conflict resolution whereby the two conflicting parties appeal to a third party to aid in arriving at a mutually satisfactory solution.

mediator A person who has usually received special training in helping two (or more) conflicting parties arrive at a resolution that satisfies the needs of both parties.

mentor An individual with advanced experience and knowledge who is committed to giving support and career advice to a less experienced person.

message A purpose or idea to be conveyed.

metacommunicate To communicate about your communication, to help overcome barriers or resolve a problem.

microinequity A small, semiconscious message we send with a powerful impact on the receiver.

micromanager One who closely monitors most aspects of group members' activities, sometimes to the point of being a control freak.

mirroring Subtly imitating someone.

moment of truth Situation in which a customer comes in contact with a company and forms an impression of its service.

moral intensity In ethical decision-making, how deeply others might be affected by the decision.

motivation An internal state that leads to effort expended toward objectives; an activity performed by one person to get another to accomplish work.

motivational state Any active needs and interests operating at a given time.

multiple intelligences A theory of intelligence contending that people know and understand the world in distinctly different ways and learn in different ways.

multitasking (a) Having two or more projects that you are working on, but you do not work on these projects at the same time. (b) Doing two or more tasks simultaneously.

negative affectivity A tendency to experience aversive emotional states.

negative reinforcement (avoidance motivation) Rewarding people by taking away an uncomfortable consequence of their behaviour.

negotiating Conferring with another person to resolve a problem.

networking Developing contacts with influential people, including gaining their trust and confidence.

noise Anything that disrupts communication, including the attitudes and emotions of the receiver.

nominal group technique (NGT) A group problem-solving technique that calls people together in a structured meeting with limited interaction.

nonverbal communication The transmission of messages through means other than words.

nurturing person One who promotes the growth of others.

organization culture A system of shared values and beliefs that influence worker behaviour.

organizational citizenship behaviour The willingness to go beyond one's job description.

organizational politics Interpersonal relations in the workplace by which power is gained or held through any means other than merit or luck.

paraphrase To repeat in your own words what the sender says, feels, and means.

participative leadership Sharing authority with the group.

peak performance Exceptional accomplishment in a given task that includes a feeling of total involvement with the task.

peer coaching A type of helping relationship based on qualities, such as high acceptance of the other person, authenticity, mutual trust, and mutual learning.

perceived control The belief that an individual has at his or her disposal a response that can control the negative aspects of an event.

performance-to-outcome expectancy The probability assigned by the individual that performance will lead to outcomes or rewards.

personal brand For career purposes, what makes you unique, thereby distinguishing you from the competition.

personal productivity A measure of a worker's output in relation to the resources, including time, that he or she consumes to achieve it.

personality clash An antagonistic relationship between two people based on differences in personal attributes, preferences, interests, values, and styles.

personality Persistent and enduring behaviour patterns that tend to be expressed in a wide variety of situations.

person–organization fit The compatibility of the individual and the organization.

person–role conflict The situation that occurs when the demands made by the organization clash with the basic values of the individual.

political correctness Being careful not to offend or slight anyone, and being extra civil and respectful.

political decision-making model People bring preconceived notions and biases into the decision-making situation.

positive gossip Unofficial information that does not attack others, is based on truth, and does not leak confidential information.

positive reinforcement An attempt to increase the probability that behaviour will be repeated by rewarding people for making the desired response.

positive self-talk Saying positive things about yourself.

positive visual imagery Picturing a positive outcome in your mind.

power The ability or potential to control anything of value and to influence decisions.

proactive personality A person who is relatively unconstrained by situational forces and who brings about environmental change.

procrastination Delaying action for no good reason.

protégé The less experienced person in a mentoring relationship who is helped by the mentor.

Pygmalion effect The phenomenon that people will rise (or fall) to the expectations that another person has of them.

rational decision-making model The traditional, logical approach to decision making, based on the scientific method.

role A tendency to behave, contribute, and relate to others in a particular way.

role ambiguity A condition in which a job holder is faced with confusing or poorly defined expectations.

role conflict The situation that occurs when a person has to choose between two competing demands or expectations.

role overload Having too much work to do.

s (special) factors Specific components of intelligence that contribute to problem-solving ability.

self-concept What we think about ourselves and who we are.

self-efficacy Confidence in one's ability to carry out a specific task.

self-esteem The positive or negative evaluation that individuals make of themselves.

self-managing work team A small group of employees responsible for managing and performing technical tasks to deliver a product or service to an external or internal customer.

self-sacrificing personality A tendency to be more concerned about the welfare and interests of others than those of oneself.

sexual harassment Unwanted sexually oriented behaviour in the workplace that results in discomfort and/or interference with the job.

social intelligence An understanding of how relationships with bosses and colleagues, family, and friends shape our brains and affect our bodies.

social loafing Shirking individual responsibility in a group setting.

stress An adaptive response that is the consequence of any action, situation, or event that places special demands on a person.

stressor The external or internal force that brings about stress.

strong customer orientation A set of individual predispositions and an inclination to provide service, to be courteous and helpful in dealing with customers and associates.

summarization The process of summarizing, pulling together, condensing, and thereby clarifying the main points communicated by another person.

support network A group of people who can listen to your problems and provide emotional support.

synergy A situation in which the group's total output exceeds the sum of each individual's contribution.

team A small number of people with complementary skills who are committed to a common purpose, set of performance goals, and approach for which they hold themselves mutually accountable.

toxic person One who dwells exclusively on the failings of others and whose pessimistic behaviours undermine the group.

training The process of helping others acquire a job-related skill.

triarchic theory of intelligence An explanation of mental ability, holding that intelligence is composed of three different subtypes: analytical, creative, and practical.

Type A behaviour A behaviour pattern in which the individual is demanding, impatient, and over-striving, and therefore prone to negative stress.

universal training need An area for improvement common to most people.

upward ethical leadership The leadership displayed by individuals who take action to maintain ethical standards, although higher-ups engage in questionable moral behaviours.

urgent time orientation A cultural trait of perceiving time as a scarce resource, characterized by impatience.

utilitarian predisposition A belief that the value of an act's outcomes should determine whether it is moral.

valence The value, worth, or attractiveness of an outcome.
value The importance a person attaches to something.
virtual office A place of work without a fixed physical location, where the output is communicated electronically.
virtual team A small group of people that conducts almost all of its collaborative work by electronic communication rather than face-to-face meetings.

win–win The belief that after conflict has been resolved, both sides should gain something of value.
workaholism An addiction to work in which not working is an uncomfortable experience.
work–family conflict A state that occurs when an individual's role as a worker clashes with his or her role as an active participant in social and family life.

NOTES

CHAPTER 1

1. *Dale Carnegie Training* brochure, Spring/Summer 2005, p. 12.
2. Joanne Lozar Glenn, "Lessons in Human Relations," *Business Education Forum*, October 2003, p. 10.
3. Research cited in Bob Wall, *Working Relationships: The Simple Truth about Getting Along with Friends and Foes at Work* (Palo Alto, CA: Davies-Black, 1999).
4. George B. Yancey, Chante P. Clarkson, Julie D. Baxa, and Rachel N. Clarkson, "Example of Good and Bad Interpersonal Skills at Work," http://www.psichi.org/pubs/articles/article_368.asp, p. 2, accessed February 2, 2004.
5. Conference Board of Canada, Employability Skills 2000+, http://www.conferenceboard.ca/topics/education/learning-tools/employability-skills.aspx.
6. Edward Muzio, Deborah J. Fisher, Err R. Thomas, and Valerie Peters, "Soft Skill Quantification (SSQ) for Project Manager Competencies," *Project Management Journal*, June 2007, pp. 30–31.
7. Marshall Goldsmith, "How Not to Lose the Top Job," *Harvard Business Review*, January 2009, p. 77.
8. The model presented here is an extension of the one presented in Thomas V. Bonoma and Gerald Zaltman, *Psychology for Management* (Boston: Kent, 1981), pp. 88–92.
9. Gary P. Latham, "The Motivational Benefits of Goal-Setting," *Academy of Management Executive*, November 2004, pp. 126–127.
10. Susan B. Wilson and Michael S. Dobson, *Goal Setting: How to Create an Action Plan and Achieve Your Goals*, 2nd ed. (New York: American Management Association, 2008).
11. Roger B. Hill, "On-line Instructional Resources—Lesson 3, Interpersonal Skills," http://www.coe.uga.edu/~rhill/workethic/less3.htm, p. 1, accessed March 17, 2005.
12. Nancy Day, "Informal Learning Gets Results," *Workforce*, June 1998, pp. 30–36; Marcia L. Conner, "Informal Learning," *Ageless Learner*, 1997–2005, http://agelesslearner.com/intros/informal.html, p. 2.
13. Andrew Paradise, "Informal Learning: Overlooked or Overhyped?" pp. 1–2, http://www.astd.org/lc/2008/0708_paradise.html, accessed January 3, 2010.
14. Morgan W. McCall, Jr., *High Flyers: Developing the Next Generation of Leaders* (Boston: Harvard Business School Press, 1998).

CHAPTER 2

1. Jean-François Cusson, based on an interview with Captain Robert Piché. Translation by Gaston St-Jean, Association de réhabilitation sociale du Québec, http://www.asrsq.ca/fr/salle/porte-ouverte/0403/salle_por_040304.php, accessed October 14, 2012.
2. Marvin Zuckerman, "Are You a Risk Taker?" *Psychology Today*, November/December 2000, p. 53.
3. Remus Ilies and Timothy A. Judge, "On the Heritability of Job Satisfaction: The Mediating Role of Personality," *Journal of Applied Psychology*, August 2003, pp. 750–759.
4. Robert R. McRae and Juri Allik, eds., *The Five-Factor Model of Personality Across Cultures* (New York: Kluwer, 2002).
5. Sarah E. Strang and Karl W. Kuhnert, "Personality and Leadership Development Levels as Predictors of Leader Performance," *The Leadership Quarterly*, June 2009, p. 423.
6. Daniel Nettle, "The Evolution of Personality Variation in Human and Other Animals," *American Psychologist*, September 2006, p. 622.
7. Lawrence R. James and Michelle D. Mazerolle, *Personality in Work Organizations* (Thousand Oaks, CA: Sage, 2002).
8. Nicole M. Dudley, Karin A. Orvis, Justin E. Lebiecki, and José M. Cortina, "A Meta-Analytic Investigation of Conscientiousness in the Prediction of Job Performance: Examining the Intercorrelations and the Incremental Validity of Narrow Traits," *Journal of Applied Psychology*, January 2006, p. 51.
9. Gregory M. Hurtz and John J. Donovan, "Personality and Job Performance: The Big Five Revisited," *Journal of Applied Psychology*, December 2000, pp. 869–879.
10. David V. Day, Deidra J. Scheleicher, Amy L. Unckless, and Nathan J. Hiller, "Self-Monitoring Personality at Work: A Meta-Analytic Investigation of Construct Validity," *Journal of Applied Psychology*, April 2002, pp. 390–401.
11. Gerald L. Blakely, Martha C. Andrews, and Jack Fuller, "Are Chameleons Good Citizens? A Longitudinal Study of the Relationship between Self-Monitoring and Organizational Citizenship Behavior," *Journal of Business and Psychology*, Winter 2003, pp. 131–144; Research synthesized in Ori Brafman and Rom Brafman, "To the Vulnerable Go the Spoils," *Bloomberg Business Week*, June 14–June 2, 2010, p. 72.
12. Nathan P. Podsakoff, Whiting, S.W., Podsakoff, P.M., and Blume, B.D, "Individual- and Organizational-Level Consequences of Organizational Behaviors: A Meta-Analysis, *Journal of Applied Psychology*, January 2009, pp. 122–141.
13. Jeff Joireman, Dishan Kamdar, Denise Daniels, and Blythe Duell, "Good Citizens to the End? It Depends: Empathy and Concern with Future Consequences Moderate the Impact of a Short-Term Time Horizon on Organizational Citizenship Behaviors," *Journal of Applied Psychology*, November 2006, p. 1315.
14. Ryan D. Zimmerman, "Understanding the Impact of Personality Traits on Individuals' Turnover Decisions: A Meta-Analytic Path Model," *Personnel Psychology*, Summer 2008, pp. 309–348.
15. Cited in David Stipp, "A Little Worry Is Good for Business," *Fortune*, November 24, 2003, p. 68.
16. L. A. Witt, Lisa A. Burke, Murray R. Barrick, and Michael K. Mount, "The Interactive Effects of Conscientiousness and Agreeableness on Job Performance," *Journal of Applied Psychology*, February 2002, pp. 164–169.
17. Carl J. Thoresen, Jill C. Bradley, Paul D. Bliese, and Joseph D. Thoresen, "The Big Five Personality Traits and Individual Job Performance Growth Trajectories in Maintenance and Transitional Job Stages," *Journal of Applied Psychology*, October 2004, pp. 835–853.
18. Isabel Briggs Myers, *Introduction to Type*, 6th ed. (Mountain View, CA: CPP, Inc., 1996), p. 10. (Revised by Linda K. Kirby and Katharine D. Myers.)

357

19. John Patrick Golden, *Golden Personality Type Profiler Technical Manual* (San Antonio, TX: Pearson TalentLens, 2005).
20. Golden, *Golden Personality Type Profiler*, p. 27.
21. Golden, *Golden Personality Type Profiler*, p. 24.
22. Brian S. Young, Winfred Arthur, Jr., and John Finch, "Predictors of Managerial Performance: More Than Cognitive Ability," *Journal of Business and Psychology*, Fall 2000, pp. 53–72.
23. Roderick Gilkey and Clint Kitts, "Cognitive Fitness," *Harvard Business Review*, November 2007, pp. 53–66.
24. Robert J. Sternberg, *Beyond IQ: A Triarchic Theory of Human Intelligence* (New York: Cambridge University Press, 1985); Bridget Murray, "Sparking Interest in Psychology Class," *APA Monitor*, October 1995, p. 51.
25. Howard Gardner, *Leading Minds: An Anatomy of Leadership* (New York: Basic Books, 1996); http://www.funderstanding.com/multipleint.htm.
26. Malcolm Gladwell, *Outliers: The Story of Success* (Boston: Little, Brown, 2008). See also Geoff Colvin, "Why Talent Is Over-Rated," *Fortune*, October 27, 2008, pp. 138–147.
27. Charles G. Morris and Albert A. Maisto, *Psychology: An Introduction*, 11th ed. (Upper Saddle River, NJ: Prentice Hall, 2002), p. 11.
28. Sharon Begley, "Critical Thinking: Part Skill, Part Mindset and Totally Up to You," *The Wall Street Journal*, October 20, 2006, p. B1.
29. Daniel Goleman, Richard Boyatzis, and Annie McKee, "Primal Leadership: The Hidden Driver of Great Performance," *Harvard Business Review*, December 2001, pp. 42–51.
30. David A. Morand, "The Emotional Intelligence of Managers: Assessing the Construct Validity of a Nonverbal Measure of 'People Skills,'" *Journal of Business and Psychology*, Fall 2001, pp. 21–33.
31. Research cited in Mayer, Salovey, and Caruso, "Emotional Intelligence," p. 512.
32. Day et al, Predicting Psychological Health: Assessing the Incremental Validity of Emotional Intelligence beyond Personality, Type A Behaviour, and Daily Hassles, *European Journal of Personality*, 19, pp. 519–536, Jan 2005.
33. Shalom H. Schwartz, "Universals in the Content and Structure of Values: Theoretical Advances and Empirical Tests in 20 Countries," in Mark P. Zanna, ed., *Advances in Experimental and Social Psychology* (New York: Academic Press, vol. 25, 1992), pp. 1–65.
34. 2008 Annual Report of the APA Policy and Planning Board, "How Technology Changes Everything (and Nothing) in Psychology, *American Psychologist*, July/August 2009, p. 454.
35. Jeff Payne, "Generation Jones, Still Striving," *HR Magazine*, December 2008, p. 15. (From Readers section.)
36. Kenyon Wallace, "How Canadians Can Help Victims of Japan Quake and Tsunami," *Toronto Star*, March 11, 2011, http://www.thestar.com/news/world/article/952611--how-canadians-can-help-victims-of-the-japan-quake-and-tsunami.
37. David C. McClelland, "How Motives, Skills, and Values Determine What People Do," *American Psychologist*, July 1985, p. 815.
38. Jeffrey R. Edwards and Daniel M. Cable, "The Value of Value Congruence," *Journal of Applied Psychology*, May 2009, pp. 654–677.
39. Jean M. Twenge, *Generation Me* (New York: The Free Press, 2006).
40. "Get Ready for 'Millennials' at Work," *Manager's Edge*, January 2006, p. 1.

CHAPTER 3

1. Ric Mazereeuw, "It's a Dirty Job, but Someone Has to Get Rich," *Canadian Business*, 75(20) (October 28, 2002), pp. 38–41; interview with Brian Scudamore, "Beyond Junk," *Canadian Business*, 85(8) (2012), p. 46–48.
2. Michelle K. Duffy, Jason D. Shaw, Kristin L. Scott, and Bennett J. Tepper, "The Moderating Roles of Self-Esteem and Neuroticism in the Relationships between Group and Individual Undermining Behavior," *Journal of Applied Psychology*, September 2006, p. 1067.
3. April O'Connell, Vincent O'Connell, and Lois-Ann Kuntz, *Choice and Change: The Psychology of Personal Growth and Interpersonal Relationships*, 7th ed. (Upper Saddle River, NJ: Pearson/Prentice Hall, 2005), p. 3.
4. "Better Self-Esteem," http://www.utexas.edu/student/cmhc/booklets/selfesteem/selfest.html, 1999, p. 2.
5. "Better Self-Esteem," p. 2.
6. Cited in Randall Edwards, "Is Self-Esteem Really All That Important?" *The APA Monitor*, May 1995, p. 43.
7. Research reported in Jeffrey Zaslow, "The Most-Praised Generation Goes to Work," *The Wall Street Journal*, April 20, 2007, p. W7.
8. David De Cremer et al., "Rewarding Leadership and Fair Procedures as Determinants of Self-Esteem," *Journal of Applied Psychology*, January 2005, pp. 3–12.
9. Eugene Raudsepp, "Strong Self-Esteem Can Help You Advance," *CareerJournal.com (The Wall Street Journal)*, August 10, 2004.
10. Timothy A. Judge, Charlice Hurst, and Lauren S. Simon, "Does It Pay to Be Smart, Attractive, or Confident (or All Three)? Relationships among General Mental Ability, Physical Attractiveness, Core Self-Evaluation, and Income," *Journal of Applied Psychology*, May 2009, pp. 742–755. The definition of core self-evaluation is from Christian J. Resick, et al., "The Bright-Side and the Dark-Side of CEO Personality: Examining Core Self-Evaluations, Narcissism, Transformational Leadership, and Strategic Influence," *Journal of Applied Psychology*, November 2009, p. 1367.
11. Research reported in Melissa Dittman, "Study Links Jealousy with Aggression, Low Self-Esteem," *Psychology Today*, February 2005, p. 13.
12. Jon L. Pierce, Donald G. Gardner, Larry L. Cummings, and Randall B. Dunman, "Organization-Based Self-Esteem: Construct Definition, Measurement, and Validation," *Academy of Management Journal*, September 1989, p. 623.
13. Nathaniel Branden, *Self-Esteem at Work: How Confident People Make Powerful Companies* (San Francisco: Jossey-Bass, 1998); Timothy A. Judge and Joyce E. Bono, "Relationship of Core Self-Evaluations Traits—Self-Esteem, Generalized Self-Efficacy, Locus of Control, and Emotional Stability—with Job Satisfaction and Job Performance: A Meta-Analysis," *Journal of Applied Psychology*, February 2001, pp. 80–92.
14. Duffy et al., "The Moderating Roles of Self-Esteem and Neuroticism," p. 1069.
15. Quoted in Carlin Flora, "The Measuring Game: Why You Think You'll Never Stack Up," *Psychology Today*, September/October 2005, p. 44.
16. "Building Self-Esteem: A Self-Help Guide," *Health*, athealth.com/Consumer/disorder/self-esteem.html, p. 1.
17. Research mentioned in book review by E. R. Snyder in *Contemporary Psychology*, July 1998, p. 482.
18. "Better Self-Esteem," pp. 3–4.
19. "Better Self-Esteem," pp. 4–5.
20. Cited in "Self-Esteem: You'll Need It to Succeed," *Executive Strategies*, September 1993, p. 12.
21. Raudsepp, "Strong Self-Esteem Can Help You Advance."
22. "Building Self-Esteem: A Self-Help Guide," http://mentalhealth.samhsa.gov, p. 2, accessed September 7, 2007.
23. Marilyn E. Gist and Terence R. Mitchell, "Self-Efficacy: A Theoretical Analysis of Its Determinants and Malleability," *Academy of Management Review*, April 1992, pp. 183–211.
24. George P. Hollenbeck and Douglas T. Hall, "Self-Confidence and Leader Performance," *Organizational Dynamics*, Issue 3, 2004, pp. 261–264.
25. Jay T. Knippen and Thad B. Green, "Building Self-Confidence," *Supervisory Management*, August 1989, pp. 22–27.
26. Quoted in "Entrepreneurs Need Attitude: Power of Being Positive Can Help You to Succeed In Spite of Setbacks," *Knight Ridder*, September 16, 2002.
27. John Derbyshire, *We Are Doomed* (New York: Crown Forum, 2009).

28. D. Brian McNatt and Timothy A. Judge, "Boundary Conditions of the Galatea Effect: A Field Experiment and Constructive Replication," *Academy of Management Journal*, August 2004, pp. 550–565.
29. Price Pritchett, *HardOptimism: Developing Deep Strengths for Managing Uncertainty, Opportunity, Adversity, and Change* (Dallas, TX: Pritchett, 2004), p. 16.
30. Frances Thornton, Gayle Privette, and Charles M. Bundrick, "Peak Performance of Business Leaders: An Experience Parallel to Self-Actualization Theory," *Journal of Business and Psychology*, Winter 1999, pp. 253–264.
31. Joshua D. Margolis and Paul G. Stoltz, "How to Bounce Back from Adversity," *Harvard Business Review*, January/February 2010. pp. 91–92.

CHAPTER 4

1. Jim Blasingame, "There Are No Handshakes 'In the Clouds,'" *The Wall Street Journal* (Special Advertising Feature), October 13, 2009, B5.
2. Ritch Sorenson, Grace DeBord, and Ida Ramirez, *Business and Management Communication: A Guide Book*, 4th ed. (Upper Saddle River, NJ: Prentice Hall, 2001), pp. 6–10.
3. Sue Morem, "Nonverbal Communication Help for Salespeople," *http://www.careerknowhow/com/ask_sue/nonverbal.htm*.
4. Jeffrey Jacobi, *The Vocal Advantage* (Upper Saddle River, NJ: Prentice Hall, 1996).
5. Roberta H. Krapels and Vanessa D. Arnold, "Speaker Credibility in Persuasive Work Situations," *Business Education Forum*, December 1997, p. 25.
6. Amie Parnes, "Formal Business Dress Coming Back: Dot-Com Casual Wears Off," *The New York Times*, June 17, 2001.
7. Eric Kress, "The Unintended Word," *HR Magazine*, August 2006, p. 51.
8. Research presented in "We Can Measure the Power of Charisma," *Harvard Business Review*, January/February 2010, p. 34.
9. Robert Lee Hotz, "How Your Brain Allows You to Walk in Another's Shoes," *The Wall Street Journal*, August 17, 2007, p. B1.
10. Jared Sandberg, "'It Says Press Any Key. Where's the Any Key?'" *The Wall Street Journal*, February 20, 2007, p. B1.
11. Paul Hemp, "Death by Information Overload," *Harvard Business Review*, September 2009, p. 83.
12. Mark Henricks, "Can We Talk? Speaking Up About the Value of Dialogue," *Entrepreneur*, January 1998, p. 82.
13. Sharon Lund O'Neil, "An Empowered Attitude Can Enhance Communication Skills," *Business Education Forum*, April, 1998, pp. 28–30.
14. Jimmy Calano and Jeff Salzman, "Persuasiveness: Make It Your Power Booster," *Working Woman*, October 1988, pp. 124–125; Krapels and Arnold, "Speaker Credibility," pp. 24–26; Gayle Theiss, "Say It Smart," *Aspire*, November/December 1998, pp. 3–4.
15. Jean Mausehund and R. Neil Dortch, "Communications—Presentation Skills in the Digital Age," *Business Education Forum*, April 1999, pp. 30–32.
16. "Avoid Words That Mar Your Image," *Administrative Professional Today*, January 2009, pp. 1–2.
17. For more details, see Brian Fugere, Chelsea Hardaway, and Jon Warshawsky, *Why Business People Speak Like Idiots* (New York: Free Press, 2005).
18. Joann Baney, *Guide to Interpersonal Communication* (Upper Saddle River, NJ: Pearson/Prentice Hall, 2004), p. 7.
19. Quoted in Jessica Shambora, "Stop Talking and Start Listening," *Fortune*, November 9, 2009, p. 24.
20. Daniel Araoz, "Right Brain Management (RBM): Part 2," *Human Resources Forum*, September 1989, p. 4.
21. Cited in Matthew S. Scott "Five Keys to Effective Listening," *Black Enterprise*, March 2005, p. 113.
22. Ideas from Marshall Goldsmith cited in "Eliminate Bad Words," *Manager's Edge*, special issue, 2008, p. 5.
23. The information in this section is from Holly Weeks, "Taking the Stress out of Stressful Conversations," *Harvard Business Review*, July/August 2001, pp. 112–119. The quote is from page 117.
24. Deborah S. Roberts, "Communication + Stress = Breakdown," *Dartnell's Communication at Work*, sample issue, undated.
25. Deborah Tannen, *Talking from 9 to 5* (New York: William Morrow, 1994); Tannen, *You Just Don't Understand* (New York: Ballantine, 1990); John Gray, *Men Are from Mars, Women Are from Venus* (New York: HarperCollins, 1992).

CHAPTER 5

1. Many of the ideas in this list are based on the following sources: Louise Lee, "Cell? Well . . . Use Your Phone for Good, Not Evil," *Business Week Small Biz*, February/March 2009, p. 22; Cathrine Hatcher, "11 Rules For Good Cell Phone Etiquette," *http://cbs1tv.com*, accessed December 30, 2007; Amy Novotney, "Dangerous Distractions," *Monitor on Psychology*, February 2009, pp. 32–36.
2. The sources in endnote 1 above also apply to this. In addition: Christine Rosen, "Our Cell Phones, Ourselves," *The New Atlantis*, Summer 2004, p. 31; Alex Williams, "Mind Your BlackBerry or Mind Your Manners," *The New York Times*, "Cell Phone Etiquette at the Office, *Articlesbase*, April 27, 2009; Lynette Spicer, "Civility in the Workplace," *Iowa State University Extension*, *www.extension.iastate/edu/mt/civility*, May 4, 2009.
3. Quoted in Rosen, "Our Cell Phones, Ourselves," *The New Atlantis*, p. 31.
4. Research cited in Novotney, "Dangerous Distractions," p. 32.
5. Several of the suggestions for what to do and what not to do during a webcam interview are from Kiviat, "Résumé? Check. Nice Suit? Check. Webcam?" *Time Magazine*, November 9, 2009, p. 50.
6. Abby Ellin, "Auditioning in a Video Résumé," *The New York Times*, April 21, 2007, p. 3.
7. Paul Hemp, "Death by Information Overload," *Harvard Business Review*, September 2009, p. 85.
8. Carmen Pickering, "The Jury Has Reached its Verdict, or Has It?" *The Alberta Teacher's Association Magazine*, 89(2) (2008–9), http://www.teachers.ab.ca/Publications/ATA%20Magazine/Volume%2089/Number2/Articles/Pages/CyberbullyingintheCanadianLegalArena.aspx.
9. "Cyberbullying," updated March 2005, accessed February 28, 2013, http://www.cbc.ca/news/background/bullying/cyber_bullying.html.
10. Qing Li, "Cyberbullying in Schools: A Research of Gender Differences," *School Psychology International*, 27 (May 2006), pp. 157–170, accessed February 26, 2013, http://spi.sagepub.com/content/27/2/157.short.
11. For a useful perspective on how social networking is changing society, see Steven Johnson, "How Twitter Will Change the Way We Live." *Time*, June 15, 2009, pp. 32–37.
12. Bridget Carey, "Bosses Should Set Social Networking Rules," *The Miami Herald*, August 11, 2009.
13. Alex Taylor III, "Fixing Up Ford," *Fortune*, May 25, 2009, p. 49.
14. Alex Williams, "Mind Your BlackBerry or Mind Your Manners," *The New York Times*, June 22, 2009.
15. Joann S. Lublin, "Some Dos and Don'ts to Help You Hone Videoconference Skills," *The Wall Street Journal*, February 7, 2006, p. B1.
16. "Work à la Modem," *Business Week*, October 4, 1999, p. 176.
17. "Bridge Gaps with Remote Workers," *Manager's Edge*, July 2008, p. 1.
18. Michelle Conlin, "Telecommuting: Out of Sight, Yes. Out of Mind, No," *Business Week*, February 18, 2008, p. 060.
19. CTV News, "Social Media Used to Find Good Samaritan, Hunt Rioters," June 16, 2011, http://www.ctvnews.ca/social-media-used-to-find-good-samaritan-hunt-rioters-1.658011#ixzz28u5Yy38f.

20. Wendy Stueck, "Can Rioters Lose Their Jobs?" *The Globe and Mail*, August 24, 2012, accessed October 13, 2012, http://m.theglobeandmail.com/news/british-columbia/can-rioters-lose-their-jobs/article583947/?service=mobile.
21. Anita Hamilton, "Outsmart Your Haters," *Time*, October 6, 2008, pp. 67–68.
22. Bridget Carey and Niala Boodhoo, "How to Deal with What Feels Like Online Identity Theft," *The Miami Herald*, April 14, 2009.

CHAPTER 6

1. Carol Hymowitz, "H-P's Ann Livermore Keeps Eye on 'Team,'" *The Wall Street Journal*, June 2, 2008, p. B.
2. Conference Board report cited in "CEO Leadership Skips Teamwork, Article Says," *Democrat and Chronicle* (Rochester, NY), February 17, 2002, p. 1E.
3. Jon R. Katzenbach and Douglas K. Smith, "The Discipline of Teams," *Harvard Business Review*, March/April 1993, p. 112.
4. Claus W. Langfred, "Too Much Trust a Good Thing? Negative Effects of High Trust and Individual Autonomy in Self-Managing Teams," *Academy of Management Journal*, June 2004, pp. 385–399.
5. "Shepherding Communications When the Flock Is Scattered," *Flexible Workplace Management*, sample issue, 2001.
6. "Bridge Gaps with Remote Workers," *Manager's Edge*, July 2008, p. 1.
7. Arvind Malhotra, Ann Majchrzak, and Benson Rosen, "Leading Virtual Teams," *Academy of Management Perspectives*, February 2007, p. 62.
8. Cited in Adam Bryant, "Ensemble Acting, in Business," *The New York Times*, June 7, 2009.
9. Jon Miller, "Insights from McKinsey Interview with Bombardier CEO Pierre Beaudoin," Gemba Panta Rei (Kaizen Institute Lean Manufacturing Blog), March 2011, accessed October 20, http://www.gembapantarei.com/2011/03/insights_from_mckinsey_interview_with_bombardier_c.html.
10. "When Committees Spell Trouble: Don't Let Individuals Hide within a Group," *WorkingSMART*, August 1998, p. 1; Ross Kerber, "For Abigail Johnson, a Leadership Test," *The Boston Globe*, August 21, 2007, p. 1.
11. Irving L. Janus, *Victims of Groupthink: A Psychological Study of Foreign Policy Decisions and Fiascos* (Boston: Houghton Mifflin, 1972); Glen Whyte, "Groupthink Reconsidered," *Academy of Management Review*, January 1989, pp. 40–56.
12. Martha A. Peak, "Treating Trauma in Teamland," *Management Review*, September 1997, p. 1.
13. Neilia Sherman, "Fostering Teamwork," *Canadian Living*, September 2012, http://www.canadianliving.com/life/work/fostering_teamwork.php.
14. "R. Meredith Belbin," in *Business: The Ultimate Resource* (Cambridge, MA: Perseus, 2002), pp. 966–967; R. Meredith Belbin, *Management Teams* (London: Elsevier Butterworth-Heinemann, 2003); "Belbin® Team-Roles," http://www.belbin.com/belbin-teamroles.htm.
15. From a review of R. Meredith Belbin, *Management Teams*, by Colin Thomson appearing in http://www.accountingweb.co.uk., accessed April 14, 2004.
16. Cited in "Gather Round, People!" *Entrepreneur*, September 2009, p. 21.
17. "Fly in Formation: Easy Ways to Build Team Spirit," *WorkingSMART*, March 2000, p. 6.
18. Pamela Lovell, "Healthy Teams Display Strong Vital Signs," *Teamwork*, sample issue, the Dartnell Corporation, 1997.
19. Glenn M. Parker, *Cross-Functional Teams: Working with Allies, Enemies, & Other Strangers* (San Francisco: Jossey-Bass, 1994), p. 170.
20. Mary J. Waller et al., "The Effect of Individual Perceptions of Deadlines on Team Performance," *Academy of Management Review*, October 2001, p. 597.
21. Mark G. Ehrhant and Stefanie E. Naumann, "Organizational Citizenship Behavior in Work Groups: A Group Norms Approach," *Journal of Applied Psychology*, December 2004, pp. 960–974.
22. Jeffrey A. LePine et al., "A Meta-Analysis of Teamwork Processes: Tests of a Multidimensional Model and Relationships with Team Effectiveness Criteria," *Personnel Psychology*, Summer 2008, pp. 273–307.
23. Tamara L. Friedrich et al., "A Framework for Understanding Collective Leadership: The Selective Utilization of Leader and Team Expertise within Networks," *Leadership Quarterly*, December 2009, pp. 933–958.
24. Craig L. Pearce, Charles C. Manz, and Henry P. Sims, Jr., "Where Do We Go from Here? Is Shared Leadership the Key to Success?" *Organizational Dynamics*, July–September 2009, pp. 234–238.
25. "Bring Out the Leader in Everyone," *Managing People at Work*, sample issue, 2000p. 4.
26. Jon R. Katzenbach and Douglas K. Smith, "The Discipline of Teams," *Harvard Business Review*, March/April 1993, p. 118.
27. "Pump Up Your Leadership Style," *Manager's Edge*, March 2007, p. 3. Adapted from Patricia Fripp, "Leadership Lesson 2: 'I'm Glad You Asked,'" http://www.fripp.com.
28. Michael Stern, "The Right Stuff," *Canadian Business*, April 26, 2004, pp. 95–99.
29. "Bring Out the Leader in Everyone," p. 4.
30. "What It Takes to Be an Effective Team Leader," *Manager's Edge*, March 2000, p. 6.
31. Terri A. Scandura and Chester A. Schrieisheim, "Leader–Member Exchange and Supervisor Career Mentoring as Complementary Constructs in Leadership Research," *Academy of Management Journal*, December 1994, pp. 1588–1602; George Graen and J. F. Cashman, "A Role Making Model of Leadership in Formal Organizations: A Developmental Approach," in J. G. Hunt and L. L. Larson (eds.), *Leadership Frontiers* (Kent, OH: Kent State University Press, 1975), pp. 143–165.
32. Francis J. Yammarino, Alan J. Dubinsky, Lucette B. Comer, and Marvin A. Jolson, "Women and Transformational and Contingent Reward Leadership: A Multiple-Levels-of-Analysis Perspective," *Academy of Management Journal*, February 1997, pp. 205–222.

CHAPTER 7

1. Jacqueline Nelson, "Loco for Lulu," *Canadian Business*, April 29, 2001, http://www.canadianbusiness.com/article/21711--loco-for-lulu, accessed October 22, 2012.
2. Dan Ariely, "The End of Rational Economics," *Harvard Business Review*, July/August 2009, pp. 78–84.
3. Cited in Marcia A. Reed-Woodard, "What Were You Thinking?" *Black Enterprise*, January 2009, p. 87.
4. Thomas H. Davenport, "Make Better Decisions," *Harvard Business Review*, November 2009, p. 117.
5. Felix C. Brodbeck et al., "Group Decision Making under Conditions of Distributed Knowledge: The Information Asymmetries Model," *Academy of Management Review*, April 2007, pp. 459–460.
6. Andrew E. Schwartz and Joy Levin, "Better Group Decision Making," *Supervisory Management*, June 1990, p. 4.
7. Debra Wheatman, "Problem Solving in the Workplace," *San Francisco Examiner*, June 28, 2009.
8. Alexander D. Stajkovic, Dongseop Lee, and Anthony J. Nyberg, "Collective Efficacy, Group Potency, and Group Performance: Meta-Analysis of their Relationships, and Test of a Mediation Model," *Journal of Applied Psychology*, May 2009, p. 815.
9. Cited in Jason Zweig, "How Group Decisions End Up Wrong-Footed," *The Wall Street Journal*, April 25–26, 2009, p. B1.
10. Kay Lovelace, Debra L. Shapiro, and Laurie R. Weingart, "Minimizing Cross-Functional New Product Teams' Innovativeness and Constraint Adherence: A Conflict Communications Perspective," *Academy of Management Journal*, August 2001, pp. 779–793.

11. Stuart D. Sidle, "Do Teams Who Agree to Disagree Make Better Decisions?" *Academy of Management Perspectives*, May 2007, pp. 74–75. The Sidle article is a review of S. Schultz-Hardt et al., "Group Decision Making in Hidden Profile Situations: Dissent as a Facilitator for Decision Quality," *Journal of Personality and Social Psychology*, 6 (2006), pp. 1080–1093.
12. David A. Garvin and Michael A. Roberto, "What You Don't Know about Making Decisions," *Harvard Business Review*, September 2001, pp. 110–111.
13. Leigh Thompson, "Improving the Creativity of Work Groups," *Academy of Management Executive*, February 2003, p. 99.
14. "Better Brainstorming," *Manager's Edge*, September 2009, p. 4.
15. "Future Edisons of America: Turn Your Employees into Inventors," *WorkingSMART*, June 2000, p. 2.
16. Robert C. Litchfield, "Brainstorming Reconsidered: A Goal-Based View," *Academy of Management Review*, July 2008, pp. 649–668.
17. Owen Thomas, "The Three-Minute Huddle," *Business 2.0*, April 2006, p. 94.
18. "How Google Got Its New Look," *Bloomberg Businessweek*, May 10–May 16, 2010, p. 60.
19. Allen C. Bluedorn, Daniel B. Turban, and Mary Sue Love, "The Effects of Stand-Up and Sit-Down Meeting Formats on Meeting Outcomes," *Journal of Applied Psychology*, April 1999, pp. 277–285.
20. Howard Baker, "Promoting Interaction and Teamwork with Electronic Mail," *Business Education Forum*, October 1994, pp. 30–31.
21. "Introduction to Groupware," *http://www.usabilityfirst.com/groupware/intro.html*, accessed October 1, 2007.
22. "Nail Down Decision Making," *Manager's Edge*, July 2009, p. 1.
23. Erika Packard, "Meetings Frustrate Task-Oriented Employees, Study Finds," *Monitor on Psychology*, June 2006, p. 10; Steven G. Rogelberg, Desmond J. Leach, Peter B. Warr, and Jennfer L. Burnfield, "'Not Another Meeting!' Are Meeting Time Demands Related to Employee Well-Being?" *Journal of Applied Psychology*, January 2006, pp. 83–96.
24. Several of the suggestions are based on Rachel Zupek, "Horrible, Terrible Meeting Mistakes," *www.CNN.com*, August 29, 2007, pp. 1–3.

Solutions to the Problems in Skill-Building Exercise 7-2 The solution to "seven tennis balls in a tube" problem is to simply fill the pipe with water and the balls will float to the top. For the too-high truck, carefully deflate the four tires about 2 inches, and then drive through the tunnel under the bridge. Harley management solved the problem of the "aging members of HOG" quite nicely by developing a motor tricycle that has become popular. Harley has also made modifications to their other models to make them easier for older people to control, such as being more comfortable and less powerful.

CHAPTER 8

1. Joan Crockett, "Winning Competitive Advantage through a Diverse Workforce," *HRfocus*, May 1999, p. 9.
2. Angela Ka-yee Leung, William W. Maddox, Adam D. Galinsky, and Chi-yue Chu, "Multicultural Experience Enhances Creativity," *American Psychologist*, April 2008, pp. 169–181.
3. Michael Bowker, "Corporate Diversity Driving Profits," *Hispanic Business*, September 2008, pp. 12, 14.
4. Eric Kearney, Diether Gebert, and Sven C. Voelpel, "When and How Diversity Benefits Teams: The Importance of Team Members' Need for Cognition," *Academy of Management Journal*, June 2009, pp. 581–598.
5. Apnara Joshi and Hyuyntak Roh, "The Role of Context in Work Team Diversity Research: A Meta-Analytic Review," *Academy of Management Journal*, June 2009, pp. 599–627.
6. Arvind V. Phatak, *International Dimensions of Management* (Boston: Kent, 1983), p. 167.
7. Robin J. Ely, Debra Meyerson, and Martin N. Davidson, "Rethinking Political Correctness," *Harvard Business Review*, September 2006, p. 80.
8. Quoted in "Leveraging Diversity at Work," *Hispanic Business*, November 2006, p. 70.
9. P. Christopher Earley and Elaine Mosakowski, "Cultural Intelligence," *Harvard Business Review*, October 2004, p. 140. The example is from the same source, same page.
10. Earley and Mosakowski, "Toward Culture Intelligence: Turning Cultural Differences into a Workplace Advantage," *Academy of Management Executive*, August 2004, pp. 154–155.
11. Ann Pomeroy, "She's Still Lovin' It," *HR Magazine* December 2006, p. 60.
12. Scott B. Button, "Organizational Efforts to Affirm Sexual Diversity: A Cross-Level Examination," *Journal of Applied Psychology*, February 2001, pp. 17–28.
13. Charlene Marmer Solomon, "Global Operations Demand That HR Rethink Diversity," *Personnel Journal*, July 1994, p. 50.
14. Mansour Javidan, Peter W. Dorfman, May Sully de Luque, and Robert J. House, "In the Eye of the Beholder: Cross Cultural Lessons in Leadership from Project GLOBE," *Academy of Management Perspectives*, February 2006, pp. 69–70. Similar dimensions were described in Geert Hofstede, *Culture's Consequences: International Differences in Work Related Values* (Beverly Hills, CA: Sage, 1980); updated and expanded in "A Conversation with Geert Hofstede," *Organizational Dynamics*, Spring 1993, pp. 53–61; Hofstede, "Who Is the Fairest of Them All? Galit Ailon's Mirror," *Academy of Management Review*, July 2009, pp. 570–571. Dimension 8 is not included in the above research. Paul J. Taylor, Wen-Dong Li, Kan Shi, and Walter C. Borman, "The Transportability of Job Information across Countries," *Personnel Psychology*, Spring 2008, pp. 72–76.
15. Study reported in Bradley S. Klapper, "Report: U.S. Workers Are the Most Productive," Associated Press, September 2, 2007.
16. Heejung S. Kim, David K. Sherman, and Shelley E. Taylor, "Culture and Social Support," *American Psychologist*, September 2008, pp. 518–526.
17. Lee Gardenswartz and Anita Rowe, "Cross-Cultural Awareness," *HR Magazine*, March 2001, p. 139.
18. Ellyn Ferguson, "Many Firms Seek Bilingual Workers," Gannett News Service, May 13, 2007.
19. Darren Fonda, "Selling in Tongues," *Time*, November 26, 2001, pp. B12–B13.
20. Catherine Beaulieu, "Intercultural Study of Personal Space," *Journal of Applied Social Psychology*, (34) 4, pp. 794–805.
21. Roger E. Axtell, *Gestures: The Do's and Taboos of Body Language around the World* (New York: Wiley, 1990).
22. Siri Carpenter, "Why Do 'They All Look Alike'?" *Monitor on Psychology*, December 2000, p. 44.
23. "Let Down by the System," *Canada and the World Backgrounder*, April 1996, pp. 18–22.
24. Christopher Guly, "Banking on Aboriginal Entrepreneurs," *Canadian Banker*, November/December 1998, pp. 17–23.
25. Mei Fong, "Chinese Charm School," *The Wall Street Journal*, January 13, 2004, p. B1.
26. P. Christopher Earley and Randall S. Peterson, "The Elusive Cultural Chameleon: Cultural Intelligence as a New Approach to Intercultural Training for the Global Manager," *Academy of Management Learning and Education*, March 2004, p. 106.
27. Rohini Anahand and Mary-Frances Winters, "A Retrospective View of Corporate Diversity Training from 1964 to the Present," *Academy of Management Learning & Education*, September 2008, p. 356.
28. Gillian Flynn, "The Harsh Reality of Diversity Programs," *Workforce*, December 1998, p. 29.

CHAPTER 9

1. Michael T. Ford, Beth A. Heinen, and Krista L. Langkamer, "Work and Family Satisfaction and Conflict: A Meta-Analysis of Cross Domain Relations," *Journal of Applied Psychology*, January 2007, pp. 57–80.

2. "Canadian Workers Most Stressed," *Worklife*, 14, pp. 8–10, 2002.
3. Timothy A. Judge, Remus Ilies, and Brent A. Scott, "Work–Family Conflict and Emotions: Effects at Work and at Home," *Personnel Psychology*, Winter 2006, pp. 779–814.
4. Quoted in Naomi Schaefer Riley, "Work and Life—and Blogging the Balance," *The Wall Street Journal*, July 17, 2009, p. W11.
5. Jenny M. Hoobler, Sandy J. Wayne, and Grace Lemmon, "Bosses' Perceptions of Family–Work Conflict and Women's Promotability: Glass Ceiling Effects," *Academy of Management Journal*, October 2009, pp. 939–957.
6. Joyce M. Rosenberg, "Equitable Time-Off Policies Avert Staff Conflicts," Associated Press, September 3, 2007.
7. Kathryn Tyler, "Beat the Clock," *HR Magazine*, November 2003, p. 103.
8. Dominic A. Infante, *Arguing Constructively* (Prospect Heights, Illinois: Waveland Press, 1992).
9. Ross Marowits, "Anti-bullying Legislation Shows Its Teeth," *The Gazette* (Montreal), June 12, 2006, p. A.8.
10. Survey reported in Jessica Guynn, "Bullying Behavior Affects Morale as Well as the Bottom Line," Knight Ridder syndicated story, November 2, 1998.
11. Judith Sills, "When Personalities Clash," *Psychology Today*, November/December 2006, p. 61.
12. Lisa M. Barrow, "Why Workplace Bullying Legislation Makes Good Business Sense," LMSB Consulting, June 2010.
13. Gary Namie, "(Still) Bullying with Impunity: Labor Day Survey," *Workplace Bullying Institute*, September 2009; Namie, "U.S. Workplace Bullying Survey," *Workplace Bullying Institute and Zogby International*, September 2007.
14. Quoted in Mickey Meece, "Backlash: Women Bullying Women at Work," *The New York Times*, May 9, 2009.
15. Deborah Smith, "I/O Conference Examines Army Special Forces, Workplace Incivility," *Monitor on Psychology*, June 2003, p. 11.
16. Christine M. Pearson and Christine L. Porath, "On the Nature, Consequences and Remedies of Workplace Incivility: No Time for 'Nice'? Think Again," *Academy of Management Executive*, February 2005, pp. 7–30. The definition of *incivility* is from the same source, p. 7.
17. Lilia M. Cortina and Vicki J. Magley, "Patterns and Profiles of Responses to Incivility in the Workplace," *Journal of Occupational Health Psychology*, July 2009, pp. 272–288.
18. Comment made by John Derbyshire in a review of Lynne Truss, *Talk to the Hand* (New York: Gotham, 2005), *The Wall Street Journal*, November 5–6, 2005, p. P8; Loretta Chao, "As Workloads Increase, So Does Office Rudeness," *WSJ.com College Journal*, January 23, 2006, p. 1.
19. Chris Pentila, "Talking about My Generation," *Entrepreneur*, March 2009, p. 55; "The Multigenerational Workforce: Opportunity for Competitive Success," *SHRM Research Quarterly*, First Quarter 2009, pp. 1–2.
20. Press release of the International Labour Organization, *Violence on the Job—A Global Problem* (Geneva: ILO, July 20,1998), http://www.us.ilo.org/news/prsrls/violence.html.
21. Canadian Wire, "Workplace a Hotbed for Violent Incidents," *Winnipeg Free Press*, February 17, 2007, p. A.3.
22. Cited in Susan M. Heathfield, "Workplace Violence: Violence Can Happen; Recognizing the Potential for Workplace Violence," *About.com Human Resources*, 2009, http://www.humanresources.about.com.
23. Kenneth Thomas, "Conflict and Conflict Management," in Marvin D. Dunnette (ed.), *Handbook of Industrial and Organizational Psychology* (Chicago: Rand McNally College Publishing, 1976), pp. 900–902.
24. Simon, cited in Mark Liu, "You Can Learn to Be Less Accommodating—If You Want To," *Democrat and Chronicle* (Rochester, NY), April 25, 1999, p. 1C.
25. Robert R. Blake and Jane S. Mouton, *The Managerial Grid III* (Houston: Gulf Publishing, 1985), p. 101.
26. "7 Steps to Conflict Resolution," *Executive Leadership*, June 2007, p. 7. Adapted from The Common Sense Guy Blog, by Bud Bilanich, http://www.commonsenseguy.com.
27. The first three suggestions are from Conninrae Andreas and Steve Andreas, *Heart of the Mind* (Moab, Utah: Real People Press, 1991).
28. Kenneth Kaye, *Workplace Wars and How to End Them: Turning Personal Conflicts into Productive Teamwork* (New York: AMACOM, 1994).
29. Jared Curhan, Hilary Anger Elfenbein, and Heng Xu "What Do People Value When They Negotiate? Mapping the Domain of Subjective Value in Negotiation," *Journal of Personality and Social Psychology*, 3 (2006), pp. 493–512.
30. Deepak Malhotra and Max H. Bazerman, "Investigative Negotiation," *Harvard Business Review*, September 2007, pp. 72–78.
31. William Ury, *The Power of a Positive No* (New York: Random House, 2007).
32. Mark Diener, "Mad Skills," *Entrepreneur*, April 2003, p. 79.
33. Steve Alper, Dean Tjosvold, and Kenneth S. Law, "Conflict Management, Efficacy, and Performance in Organizational Teams," *Personnel Psychology*, Autumn 2000, pp. 625–642.
34. "Sexual Harassment Clauses," *Worklife Report*, 8(3) (1991), pp. 4–6.
35. Human Resources Development Canada, "Information on Labour Standards, 12: Sexual Harassment," http://www.labour.gc.ca/eng/standards_equity/st/pubs_st/harassment.shtml.
36. H. F. Schwind, H. Das, W. Werther, and K. Davis, *Canadian Human Resource Management*, 4th ed. (Toronto: McGraw-Hill Ryerson Canada, 1995).
37. Diane Crocker and Valery Kalemba, "The Incidence and Impact of Women's Experiences of Sexual Harassment in Canadian Workplaces," *Canadian Review of Sociology & Anthropology*, November 1999, pp. 541–559.
38. M. Jinenez, "Sexual Harassment at Work Prevalent in B.C., Poll Shows," *Vancouver Sun*, May 4, 1998, pp. A1–A2.
39. Crocker and Kalemba, "The Incidence and Impact of Women's Experiences of Sexual Harassment in Canadian Workplaces."
40. Theresa M. Glomb, Liberty J. Munson, and Charles L. Hulin, "Structural Equation Models of Sexual Harassment: Longitudinal Explorations and Cross-Sectional Generalizations," *Journal of Applied Psychology*, February 1999, pp. 14–28.
41. Barbara Orser, "Sexual Harassment Is Still a Management Issue, Conference Board of Canada," Gender Diversity Took Kit: Resource No. 1, 2001.
42. Crocker and Kalemba, "The Incidence and Impact of Women's Experiences of Sexual Harassment in Canadian Workplaces."
43. Kathleen Neville, *Corporate Attractions: An Inside Account of Sexual Harassment with the New Sexual Roles for Men and Women on the Job* (Reston, VA: Acropolis Books, 1992); Joanne Cole, "Sexual Harassment: New Rules, New Behavior," *HRfocus*, March 1999, pp. 1, 14–15.
44. Lauren M. Bernardi, "Maintaining a Harassment-Free Workplace," *Canadian Manager*, Spring 1998, pp. 13–16.

CHAPTER 10

1. Case history collected in Rochester, New York, January 2008.
2. E. D. Kort, "What, after All, Is Leadership? 'Leadership' and Plural Action," *Leadership Quarterly*, August 2008, p. 409.
3. Joseph A. Raelin, *Creating Leaderful Organizations: How to Bring Out Leadership in Everyone* (San Francisco: Berrett-Koehler, 2003).
4. Timothy A. Judge, Ronald F. Piccolo, and Tomek Kosalka, "The Bright and Dark Sides of Leader Traits: A Review and Theoretical Extension of the Leader Trait Paradigm," *Leadership Quarterly*, December 2009, p. 871.
5. George P. Hollenbeck and Douglas T. Hall, "Self-Confidence and Leader Performance," *Organizational Dynamics*, 3 (2004), pp. 254–269.

6. Shelley A. Kirkpatrick and Edwin A. Locke, "Leadership: Do Traits Matter?" *Academy of Management Executive*, May 1991, pp. 26–27.
7. Sean T. Hannah, Bruce J. Avolio, Fred Luthans, and P. D. Harms, "Leadership Efficacy: Review and Future Directions," *Leadership Quarterly*, December 2008, pp. 669–692.
8. Judge, Piccolo, and Kosalka, "The Bright and Dark Sides of Leader Traits," p. 866.
9. Cameron Anderson and Gavin Kilduf, "Why Do Dominant Personalities Attain Influence in Face-to-Face Groups? The Competence-Signaling Effects of Trait Dominance," *Journal of Personality and Social Psychology*, February 2009, pp. 491–503.
10. Survey cited in "What Are the Most Important Traits for Bosses?" *Employee Recruitment & Retention*, Sample Issue, 2006.
11. Michael E. Palanski and Francis J. Yammarino, "Integrity and Leadership: A Multi-Level Conceptual Framework," *Leadership Quarterly*, June 2009, p. 406.
12. Reported in "Developing Trust Pays Off," *Manager's Edge*, April 1999, p. 9.
13. Douglas R. May, Adrian Y. L. Chan, Timothy D. Hodges, and Bruce J. Avolio, "Developing the Moral Component of Authentic Leadership," *Organizational Dynamics*, 3 (2003), pp. 247–260.
14. Bruce J. Avolio, Jane M. Howell, and John J. Sosik, "A Funny Thing Happened on the Way to the Bottom Line: Humor as a Moderator of Leadership Style Effects," *Academy of Management Journal*, April 1999, pp. 219–227.
15. Bill George, Peter Sims, Andrew N. McLean, and Diana Mayer, "Discovering Your Authentic Leadership," *Harvard Business Review*, February 2007, p. 129.
16. Dale E. Zand, *The Leadership Triad: Knowledge, Trust, and Power* (New York: Oxford, University Press, 1997), p. 8.
17. John D. Stoll, "Fix-It Experts Appointed at GM," *The Wall Street Journal*, July 24, 2009, p. B2.
18. Betsy McKay, "Can New CEO Put Fizz Back in Coke?" *The Wall Street Journal*, June 30, 2008, p. B1.
19. Studies on this topic are reviewed in Timothy A. Judge, Amy Colbert, and Remus Ilies, "Intelligence and Leadership: A Quantitative Review and Test of Theoretical Propositions," *Journal of Applied Psychology*, June 2004, p. 548.
20. John Menkes, *Executive Intelligence: What All Great Leaders Have* (New York: Collins, 2006).
21. Daniel Goleman, "What Makes a Leader?" *Harvard Business Review*, November/December 1998, p. 92.
22. Robert A. Eckert, "Where Leadership Starts," *Harvard Business Review*, November 2001, pp. 53–61. The quote is from page 54.
23. Nancy Dahlberg, "One Trait Links All Successful Entrepreneurs: Passion," *The Miami Herald*, November 9, 2009, pp. 1–2.
24. David De Cremer, David M. Mayer, Marius van Dijke, Barbara S. Schouten, and Mary Bardes, "When Does Self-Sacrificial Leadership Motivate Prosocial Behavior? It Depends on Followers' Prevention Focus," *Journal of Applied Psychology*, July 2009, pp. 887–899.
25. Jay A. Conger, *The Charismatic Leader: Behind the Mystique of Exceptional Leadership* (San Francisco: Jossey-Bass, 1989).
26. Jack and Suzy Welch, "It's Not about Empty Suits," *Business Week*, October 16, 2006, p. 132.
27. Nelson Wyatt, "Sovereigntist and Federalist Quebecers Acknowledge Trudeau's Legacy in His Home Province," *Canadian Press*, September 29, 2000, http://www.canoe.ca/CNEWS-TrudeauNews/000929_trudeauque-cp.html.
28. Luisa Beltran, "Standout Performer," *Hispanic Business*, April 2007, p. 26.
29. Michael Stern, "The Right Stuff," *Canadian Business*, April 26, 2004.
30. Bill Breen, "The Clear Leader," *Fast Company*, March 2005, pp. 65–67.
31. Michael E. Brown and Linda K. Treviño, "Socialized Charismatic Leadership, Values, Congruence, and Deviance in Work Groups," *Journal of Applied Psychology*, July 2006, p. 955.
32. Amir Erez, Vilmos F. Misangi, Diane E. Johnson, Marcie A. LePine, and Kent C. Halverson, "Stirring the Hearts of Followers: Charismatic Leadership as the Transferal of Affect," *Journal of Applied Psychology*, May 2008, pp. 602–616.
33. Suggestions 7, 9, and 10 are from Roger Dawson, *Secrets of Power Persuasion* (Upper Saddle River, NJ: Prentice Hall, 1992), pp. 181–183.
34. Donald Brooks, "Vertical Team Building Releases an Organization's Pent-Up Energy," *Northern Ontario Business*, October 1994.
35. Diane Coutu and Carol Kauffman, "What Can Coaches Do for You?" *Harvard Business School*, January 2009, pp. 91–97.
36. Polly Parker, Douglas T. Hall, and Kathy E. Kram, "Peer Coaching: A Relational Process for Accelerating Career Learning," *Academy of Management Learning & Education*, December 2008, p. 490.
37. "Coaching—One Solution to a Tight Training Budget," *HRfocus*, August 2002, p. 7; Sharon Ting and Peter Scisco, eds., *The CCL Handbook of Coaching: A Guide for the Leader Coach* (San Francisco: Jossey-Bass, 2006).
38. Editors of *Manager's Edge: The Successful Manager's Guide to Giving and Receiving Feedback* (Alexander, VA: Briefings Publishing Group, 2004), p. 14.
39. "Coach Your Employees to Success with This Plan," *Manager's Edge*, May 2000, p. 1.
40. "Coach with 'Could,' not 'Should,'" *Executive Strategies*, April 1998, p. 1.
41. Andrew J. DuBrin, *Leadership: Research Findings, Practice, and Skills*, 6th ed. (Boston: Houghton Mifflin, 2010), p. 305.
42. Bruce Tulgan, "The Under-management Epidemic," *HR Magazine*, October 2004, p. 119.
43. This one item is from John M. Ivancevich and Thomas N. Duening, *Management: Skills, Application, Practice, and Development* (Cincinnati, OH: Atomic Dog Publishing, 2006), p. 282.
44. Pamela Babcock, "Always More to Learn," *HR Magazine*, September 2009, pp. 51–54.
45. Survey cited in Mark Schoeff, Jr., "A U.S. Training Upgrade," *Workforce Management*, September 14, 2009, p. 32.
46. Cy Charney, "Self-Directed Peer Training in Teams," *Journal for Quality & Participation*, October/November 1996, pp. 34–37.
47. Bill Roberts, "Hard Facts about Soft-Skills E-Learning," *HR Magazine*, January 2008, pp. 76–78.
48. Ian Cunningham and Linda Honald, "Everyone Can Be a Coach," *HRMagazine*, June 1998, pp. 63–66.
49. This issue is treated at length in Bruce J. Avolio, *Leadership in Balance: Made/Born* (Mahwah, NJ: Earlbaum, 2005).
50. Mina Kimes, "P & G's Leadership Machine," *Fortune*, April 13, 2008, p. 22.
51. William D. Hitt, *The Model Leader: A Fully Functioning Person* (Columbus, OH: Battelle Press, 1993).
52. Cheryl Dahle, "Natural Leader," *Fast Company*, December 2000, p. 270.
53. Michael E. McGill and John W. Slocum, Jr., "A *Little* Leadership Please?" *Organizational Dynamics*, Winter 1998, p. 48.
54. Bill Breen, "Trickle-Up Leadership," *Fast Company*, November 2001, pp. 70–72.

CHAPTER 11

1. Bob Nelson, "Why Formal Recognition Programs Don't Work," http://www.nelson-motivation.com. Reprinted with permission.
2. Quoted in Stephen Baker, "Will Work for Praise," *Business Week*, February 16, 2009, pp. 46–49.
3. Hewitt News and Information, "Canadian Employers Struggle to Attract and Retain Employees," *Canadian Manager*, Fall 2006, pp. 12–13.
4. Dr. Linda Duxbury and Dr. Chris Higgins, "The 2001 National Work–Life Conflict Study: Report One," Health Canada, March 2002; Human Resources Development Canada, *Report of the*

Advisory Group on Working Time and the Distribution of Work (Ottawa: 1994).
5. Piers Steel and Cornelius J. König, "Integrating Theories of Motivation," *Academy of Management Review*, October 2006, pp. 895–896.
6. Research summarized in "One of These Seven Things Will Motivate Any Employee in the Company," *The Motivational Manager*, sample issue, 1998 (Lawrence Ragan Communications, Inc.).
7. Jennifer J. Laabs, "Targeted Rewards Jump-Start Motivation," *Workforce*, February 1998, p. 90.
8. Fred Luthans and Alexander D. Stajkovic, "Reinforce for Performance: The Need to Go beyond Pay and Even Rewards," *Academy of Management Executive*, May 1999, p. 52.
9. Steven Kerr, *Ultimate Rewards: What Really Motivates People to Achieve* (Boston: Harvard Business School Publishing, 1997).
10. "Simple Rewards Are Powerful Motivators," *HRfocus*, August 2001, p. 10; Jennifer Laabs, "Satisfy Them with More Than Money," *Workforce*, November 1998, p. 43.
11. Martin Booe, "Sales Force at Mary Kay China Embraces the American Way," *Workforce Management*, April 2005, pp. 24–25.
12. Jennifer Laabs, "Satisfy Them with More Than Money," *Workforce*, November 1998, p. 43.
13. Philip Moss, Harold Salzman, and Chris Tilly, "Under Construction: The Continuing Evolution of Job Structures in Call Centers, *Industrial Relations*, 47 (2008), pp. 173–208.
14. "Time Your Praise to Make It Last," *WorkingSMART*, June 2000, p. 2.
15. Andrew J. DuBrin, "Self-Perceived Technical Orientation and Attitudes toward Being Flattered," *Psychological Reports*, 96 (2005), pp. 852–854.
16. Susan M. Heathfield, "Five Tips for Effective Employee Recognition," *About.com Human Resources*, August 6, 2009, http://www.humanresources.about.com.
17. The original version of expectancy theory applied to work motivation is Victor Vroom, *Work and Motivation* (New York: Wiley, 1964).
18. Alexander D. Stajkovic and Fred Luthans, "Social Cognitive Theory and Self-Efficacy: Going beyond Traditional Motivational and Behavioral Approaches," *Organizational Dynamics*, Spring 1998, p. 66.
19. Steve McShane, "Getting Emotional about Employee Motivation," *Currents* (published by McGraw-Hill), September 2004, p. 1; Amir Erez and Alice M. Isen, "The Influence of Positive Affect on the Components of Expectancy Motivation," *Journal of Applied Psychology*, December 2002, pp. 1055–1067.
20. Jeffrey Keller, "Associate with Positive People," Supplement to the *Pryor Report*, 1994.
21. Keller, "Associate with Positive People."
22. Tammy Ellen and Lillian Eby, eds., *The Blackwell Handbook of Mentoring: A Multiple Perspectives Approach* (Malden, MA: Blackwell Publishing, 2007).
23. Erin Pooley, "Canada's Best Workplaces: Fairness First," *Canadian Business Magazine*, April 23, 2007.
24. Monica C. Higgins and Kathy E. Kram, "Reconceptualizing Mentoring at Work: A Developmental Network Perspective," *Academy of Management Review*, April 2001, pp. 264–288.
25. Erik J. Van Slyke and Bud Van Slyke, "Mentoring: A Results-Oriented Approach," *HRfocus*, February 1998, p. 14.
26. Anne Field, "No Time to Mentor? Do It Online," *BusinessWeek*, March 3, 2003, p. 126; Stephenie Overman, "Mentors without Borders," *HR Magazine*, March 2004, pp. 3–85.
27. Tammy D. Allen, Lillian T. Eby, and Elizabeth Lentz, "Mentoring Behaviors and Mentorship Quality Associated with Formal Mentoring Programs: Closing the Gap between Research and Practice," *Journal of Applied Psychology*, May 2006, pp. 567–578.
28. Based mostly on Kathy E. Kram, *Mentoring at Work: Developmental Relationships in Organizational Life* (Glenview, IL: Scott, Foresman, 1985), pp. 22–39; Van Slyke and Van Slyke, "Mentoring," 1998, p. 14.

29. J. Lorinc, "The Mentor Gap," *Canadian Business*, September 1990, pp. 93–95.
30. Stephanie C. Payne and Ann H. Huffman, "A Longitudinal Examination of the Influence of Mentoring on Organizational Commitment and Turnover," *Academy of Management Journal*, February 2005, pp. 158–168.
31. BMO Financial Group, "Business Leaders Should Spend More Time Mentoring Women," speech by Rose M. Patten, Executive Vice-President, Human Resources and Head of Management, BMO Financial Group, given on January 14, 2003, at the Women in Capital Markets Mentoring Reception, Toronto, Ontario, www2.bmo.com/bmo/files/news%20release/4/1/Jan1403_RosePattenWCM_EN.html; Gillian Flynn, "Bank of Montreal Invests in Its Workers," *Workforce*, December 1997, pp. 30–38.
32. *Career Track* seminar, "How to Deal with Difficult People," 1995; Kenneth Kaye, *Workplace Wars and How to End Them: Turning Personal Conflicts into Productive Teamwork* (New York: AMACOM, 1994); "Tame the Best within You: How to Cope with Mood Swings in Yourself and Others," *WorkingSMART*, April 1999, p. 1; Joann S. Lublin, "Feeling Unappreciated? You May Find Griping Makes Things Worse," *The Wall Street Journal*, June 5, 2003, p. B1; Jared Sandberg, "Staff 'Handfuls' and the Bosses Who Coddle Them," *The Wall Street Journal*, October 8, 2003, p. B1.
33. Nando Pelusi, "Dealing with Difficult People," *Psychology Today*, September 1, 2006, http://www.psychologytoday.com/articles/200609/dealing-difficult-people.
34. "How to Deal with 'Problem' Workers," *Positive Leadership*, sample issue, distributed 2001; Martien Eerhart, "Top 7 Ideas for Dealing with Difficult Employees," http://top7business.com/archives/personnel/050499.html.
35. John C. Maxwell, *Winning with People: Discover the People Principles That Work for You Every Time* (Nashville, TN: Nelson Books, 2004), pp. 1428–1429.

CHAPTER 12

1. Todd Averett, Executive Commentary in response to Mark C. Bolino and William H. Turnley, "Going the Extra Mile: Cultivating and Managing Employee Citizenship Behavior," *Academy of Management Executive*, August 2003, pp. 72–73. Updated January 2010 through personal communication with Everett.
2. Cited in Linda Noeth, "All Those Unwritten Rules of the Office Also Guide Policy," *Democrat and Chronicle*, February 8, 2009, p. 2E.
3. Daniel Goleman, *Social Intelligence: The New Science of Human Relationships* (New York: Bantam, 2006); Carol Hymowitz, "Business Is Personal, So Managers Need to Harness Emotions," *The Wall Street Journal*, November 13, 2006, p. B1.
4. Hymowitz, "Business Is Personal."
5. Robyn L. Brouer, Allison Duke, Darren C. Treadway, and Gerald R. Ferris, "The Moderating Effect of Political Skill on the Demographic Dissimilarity—Leader–Member Exchange Quality Relationship," *Leadership Quarterly*, April 2009, pp. 61–69.
6. Martha C. Andrews, K. Michele Kacmar, and Kenneth J. Harris, "Got Political Skill? The Impact of Justice on the Importance of Political Skill for Job Performance," *Journal of Applied Psychology*, November 2009, pp. 1427–1437.
7. Amos Drory and Nurit Zaidman, "The Politics of Impression Management in Organizations: Contextual Effects," in Eran Vigoda-Gadot and Amos Drory eds., *Handbook of Organizational Politics* (Northampton, MA: Edward Elgar, 2006), p. 75.
8. Andrew J. DuBrin, *Impression Management in the Workplace: Research, Theory, and Practice* (New York: Routledge, 2011), p. 73.
9. Nathan P. Podsakoff, Steven W. Whiting, Philip M. Podasakoff, and Brian D. Blume, "Individual- and Organizational-Level Consequences of Organizational Citizenship Behaviors: A Meta-Analysis," *Journal of Applied Psychology*, January 2009, pp. 122–141.

10. "Career Article 103: Getting Along with Your Boss," *www.SeekingSuccess.com*, 2002–2006, p. 2.
11. Terry Bragg, "Nine Strategies for Successfully Playing Office Politics," *www.tbragg.addr.com*, July 15, 2005, p. 1, available *http://ehstoday.com/columns/ehs_imp_36855*.
12. Tamara E. Holmes, "Admitting When You're Wrong," *Black Enterprise*, May 2007, p. 124.
13. "Get Rid of 'Yes Men,'" *Manager's Edge*, Special Bulletin, Spring 2006, p. 2.
14. Daniel Yi, "For Many Employees, Fitness Has Its Prize," *The Los Angeles Times*, March 12, 2007.
15. Sue Pridham, "Workplace Fitness Facilities . . . A Popular Amenity with a Healthy Payback," *Office Life*, February 2002.
16. Pridham, "Workplace Fitness Facilities."
17. William L. Gardner III, "Lessons in Organizational Dramaturgy: The Art of Impression Management," *Organizational Dynamics*, Summer 1992, p. 45.
18. Kenneth J. Harris, K. Michele Kacmar, Suzanne Zivnuska, and Jason D. Shaw, "The Impact of Political Skill on Impression Management Effectiveness," *Journal of Applied Psychology*, January 2007, pp. 278–285.
19. Jim Rucker and Jean Anna Sellers, "Changes in Business Etiquette," *Business Education Forum*, February 1998, p. 45.
20. Paula Gamonal, "Business Etiquette: More Than Just Eating with the Right Fork," *Ravenwerks Business Etiquette Blog*, *http://www.ravenwerks.com*, accessed October 24, 2007.
21. This section of the chapter is based on "Business Etiquette: Teaching Students the Unwritten Rules," *Keying In*, January 1996, pp. 1–8; Rucker and Sellers, "Changes in Business Etiquette," pp. 43–45; Letitia Baldrige, *The Executive Advantage* (Washington, DC: Georgetown Publishing House, 1999); "Culture Shock?" *Entrepreneur*, May 1998, p. 46; Ann Perry, "Finer Points of the Meet and Eat," *Toronto Star*, January 2, 2004; Blanca Torres, "Good Dining Manners Can Help Bet a Bigger Slice of the Job Pie," *Baltimore Sun*, April 5, 2005; Erin White, "The Jungle: Focus on Recruitment, Pay and Getting Ahead," *The Wall Street Journal*, November 2, 2004, p. B8. The quotes are from the same sources.
22. James F. Thompson, *The Cubicle Survival Guide* (New York: Villard, 2007).
23. Sarah E. Needleman, "Office Space Is Crowded Out," *The Wall Street Journal*, December 7, 2009, p. B7.
24. "Disability Etiquette," *Human Resources Forum* (a supplement to *Management Review*), June 1997, p. 3; "Helping Today's Blind Children Become the Winners of Tomorrow," *American Blind Children's Council* (flyer), 2002.
25. "How to Use Sign Language Interpreters Effectively" Toronto: The Canadian Hearing Society.
26. Jared Sandberg, "How Office Tyrants in Critical Positions Get Others to Grovel," *The Wall Street Journal*, August 21, 2007, p. B1.
27. Deb Koen, "Jittery about Networking? Know the Etiquette," *Democrat and Chronicle* (Rochester, NY), April 14, 2002, p. 4E.
28. Brian Hilliard and James Palmer, *Networking Like a Pro* (Atlanta, GA: Agito Consulting, 2003) p. 52.
29. Judith Sills, "How to Be a Rising Star," *Psychology Today*, March/April 2006, pp. 38–39.
30. Sills, "How to Be a Rising Star," p. 39.
31. Research reported in Laura Lippman, "The Age of Obsequiousness: Flattering Your Way up the Corporate Ladder," *The Sun* (Baltimore, MD), October 24, 1994.
32. Research reported in Jennifer Reingold, "Suck Up and Move Up," *Fast Company*, January 2005, p. 34.
33. James D. Westphal and Ithai Stern, "Flattery Will Get You Everywhere (Especially If You Are a Male Caucasian): How Ingratiation, Boardroom Behavior, and Demographic Minority Status Affect Additional Board Appointments at U.S. Companies," *Academy of Management Journal*, April 2007, pp. 267–288.
34. Marshall Goldsmith, "All of Us Are Stuck on Suck-ups," *Fast Company*, December 2003, p. 117.
35. Research reported in Jeffrey Zaslow, "The Most-Praised Generation Goes to Work," *The Wall Street Journal*, April 20, 2007, p. W7.
36. Judith Sills, "How to Improve Your Credit Rating," *Psychology Today*, March/April 2008, p. 67.
37. Tom Rather, *Vital Friends: The People You Can't Afford to Live Without* (New York: Gallup Press, 2006).
38. Cited in Lea Winerman, "You Rub My Fin, I'll Rub Yours," *Psychology Today*, January 2009, pp. 56–59.
39. Susanne Craig, "Merrill CEO Presents New Leadership Team," *The Wall Street Journal*, April 30, 2008, p. C3.
40. Andrew J. DuBrin, *Political Behavior in Organizations* (Thousand Oaks, CA: Sage, 2009), p. 234.
41. Shelia Murray Bethel, *Making a Difference* (New York: G. P. Putnam's Sons, 1989).
42. Gary M. Stern, "Small Slights Bring Big Problems," *Workforce*, August 2002, p. 17; Joann S. Lublin, "How to Stop the Snubs That Demoralize You and Your Colleagues," *The Wall Street Journal*, December 7, 2004, p. B1.

CHAPTER 13

1. Quoted in Mark Hendricks, "Paying in Kind: How Can You Ensure Employees Give Service with a Smile?" *Entrepreneur*, February 2006, p. 82.
2. Quoted in Ryan Chittum, "Price Points: Good Customer Service Costs Money. Some Expenses Are Worth It—and Some Aren't," *The Wall Street Journal*, October 30, 2006, p. R7.
3. Leonard L. Berry, Eileen A. Wall, and Lewis P. Carbone, "Service Clues and Customer Assessment of the Service Experience: Lessons from Marketing," *Academy of Management Perspectives*, May 2006, pp. 43–57.
4. Paul R. Timm, *Customer Service: Career Success through Customer Satisfaction*, 2nd ed. (Prentice Hall, 2001), p. 8.
5. Anthony J. Rucci, Steven P. Kirn, and Richard T. Quinn, "The Employee-Customer-Profit Chain at Sears," *Harvard Business Review*, January/February 1998, pp. 82–97.
6. Quoted in Lin Grensing-Pophal, "Building Service with a Smile," *HR Magazine*, November 2006, p. 86.
7. Barry M. Stow and Jerry Ross, "Stability in the Midst of Change: A Dispositional Approach to Job Attitudes," *Journal of Applied Psychology*, August 1985, p. 471.
8. Sue Shellenbarger, "Domino Effect: The Unintended Results of Telling Off Customer-Service Staff," *The Wall Street Journal*, February 5, 2004, p. D1.
9. Lance A. Bettencourt, Kevin P. Gwinner, and Matthew L. Meuter, "A Comparison of Attitude, Personality, and Knowledge Predictors of Service-Oriented Organizational Citizenship Behavior," *Journal of Applied Psychology*, February 2001, pp. 29–41.
10. Alex M. Susskind, K. Michele Kacmar, and Carl P. Borchgrevink, "Customer Service Providers' Attitudes Relating to Customer Service and Customer Satisfaction in the Customer–Server Exchange," *Journal of Applied Psychology*, February 2003, pp. 179–187.
11. Craig A. Martin and Alan J. Bush, "Psychological Climate, Empowerment, and Customer-Oriented Selling: An Analysis of the Sales Manager–Salesperson Dyad," *Journal of the Academy of Marketing Science*, 3 (2006), pp. 419–438.
12. Hui Lao and Aichia Chuang, "Transforming Service Employees and Climate: A Multilevel, Multisource Examination of Transformational Leadership in Building Long-Term Service Relationships," *Journal of Applied Psychology*, July 2007, pp. 1006–1019.
13. "The Chairman of the Board Looks Back," *Fortune*, May 28, 2001, p. 70.
14. Jeremy Quittner, "The Art of the Soft Sell," *Business Week Small Biz*, October/November 2009, p. 50.
15. Richard B. Chase and Sriram Dasu, "Want to Perfect Your Company's Service? Use Behavioral Science," *Harvard Business Review*, June 2001, pp. 78–84.

16. Karl Abrecht, *The Only Thing That Matters* (New York: HarperCollins, 1992).
17. Susan Okula, "Customer Service: New Tools for a Timeless Idea," *Business Education Forum*, December 1998, p. 7; Robert F. Gault, "Managing Customer Satisfaction for Profit," *Management Review*, April 1993, p. 23.
18. Amanda C. Kooser, "Crowd Control," *Entrepreneur*, August 2003, pp. 33–34.
19. Ken Belson, "For Half a Cent, a Call That Informs, and Annoys," *The New York Times*, July 16, 2008, pp. 1–3.
20. Adapted from "For Extraordinary Service," *The Customer Service Professional*, October 1997, p. 3.
21. Lorna Ducet, "Service Provider Hostility and Service Quality," *Academy of Management Journal*, October 2004, pp. 761–771.
22. D. J. Cran, "Towards the Validation of the Service Orientation Construct," *The Service Industries Journal*, 14 (1994), p. 36.
23. Dot Yandle, "Helping Your Employees Give Customers What They Want," *Success Workshop* (A supplement to *Manager's Edge*), November 1998, p. 1.
24. Patricia B. Barger and Alicia A. Grandey, "Service with a Smile and Encounter Satisfaction: Emotional Contagion and Appraisal Mechanisms," *Academy of Management Journal*, December 2006, pp. 1229–1238.
25. Quoted in Jia Lunn Yang, "How to Sell in a Lousy Economy," *Fortune*, September 29, 2008, p. 102.
26. Ryan Chittum, "Price Points: Good Customer Service Costs Money," p. R7.
27. Daniel Akst, book review of *Hug Your Customers* by Jack Mitchell (New York: Hyperion, 2003), appearing in *The Wall Street Journal*, November 14, 2003, p. W9.
28. Hwee Hoon Tan, Maw Der Foo, and Min Hui Kwek, "The Effects of Customer Personality Traits on the Display of Positive Emotions," *Academy of Management Journal*, April 2004, pp. 287–296.
29. Donna Deeprose, "Helping Employees Handle Difficult Customers," *Supervisory Management*, September 1991, p. 6; Chip R. Bell and Ron Zemke, "Service Breakdown—The Road to Recovery," in *Service Wisdom: Creating and Maintaining the Customer Service Edge* (Minneapolis, MN: Lakewood Books, 1992).
30. Jan Norman, "Caring about Clients Helps Companies Handle Crises," Knight Ridder, December 3, 2000, p. 1G.
31. Hal Hardy, "Five Steps to Pleasing Difficult, Demanding Customers," *First-Rate Customer Service*, 1 (2005), p. 1.
32. "Customer Problem Clinics," in *Making . . . Serving . . . Keeping Customers* (Chicago: Dartnell, 1992).
33. "Customer Problem Clinics."
34. Timm, *Customer Service*, p. 43.
35. Vikas Mittal, Matthew Sarkees, and Feisal Murshed, "The Right Way to Manage Unprofitable Customers," *Harvard Business Review*, April 2008, p. 102.
36. Raymond Flandez, "It Just Isn't Working? Some File for Customer Divorce," *The Wall Street Journal*, November 10, 2009, p. B7.

CHAPTER 14

1. Industry Canada, "Corporate Social Responsibility: Hudson's Bay Co. (HBC): A Case Study in Ethical Sourcing," *http://www.ic.gc.ca/eic/site/csr-rse.nsf/eng/rs00168.html*, accessed April 1, 2013.
2. Hudson's Bay Company, 2011 Corporate Social Responsibility Report, *http://216.157.72.150/wp-content/uploads/2013/02/2011-Corporate-Social-Responsibility-Report.pdf*, accessed April 1, 2013.
3. Linda K. Treviño and Katherine A. Nelson, *Managing Business Ethics: Straight Talk about How to Do It Right* (New York: Wiley, 1995), pp. 24–35; "Why Have a Code of Ethics?" *The Fact Finder*, January 1995, p. 3; Ralph Estes, *Tyranny of the Bottom Line: Why Corporations Make Good People Do Bad Things* (San Francisco: Berrett-Koehler, 1996).
4. John S. McClenahen, "Your Employees Know Better," *Industry Week*, 248 (5) (March 1, 1999), pp. 12–14; Thomas M. Jones, "Ethical Decision Making by Individuals in Organizations: An Issue Contingent Model," *Academy of Management Review*, April 1991, p. 391.
5. Linda Kelbe Treviño, "Managing to Be Ethical: Debunking Five Business Ethics Myths," *Academy of Management Executive*, May 2004, pp. 69–72.
6. Scott J. Reynolds, "Moral Awareness and Ethical Predispositions: Investigating the Role of Individual Differences in the Recognition of Moral Issues," *Journal of Applied Psychology*, January 2006, p. 234.
7. John C. Bogle, "A Crisis of Ethic Proportions," *The Wall Street Journal*, April 21, 2009, p. A19.
8. Simona Covel, "Small Businesses Face More Fraud in Downturn," *The Wall Street Journal*, February 19, 2009, p. B5.
9. Data reported in "McAfee Anti-Piracy Information," *http://www.networkassociates.com/us/antipiracy_policy.htm*, accessed May 25, 2005.
10. "FTC: Bloggers Must Disclose Payments for Reviews," Associated Press, October 5, 2009.
11. The Economist, "Trip Advisor's Fake Battle" (blog), August 22, 2011, *http://www.economist.com/blogs/gulliver/2011/08/hotel-reviews*, accessed April 1, 2013.
12. Keith J. Winstein, "Inflated Credentials Surface in Executive Suite," *The Wall Street Journal*, November 13, 2008, p. B1.
13. Joseph L. Badaracco, Jr., "The Discipline of Building Character," *Harvard Business Review*, March/April 1998, pp. 114–124.
14. Edwin A. Locke, "Business Ethics: A Way out of the Morass," *Academy of Management Learning & Education*, September 2006, pp. 328–330.
15. Treviño and Nelson, *Managing Business Ethics*, pp. 71–75.
16. Daniel J. Brass, Kenneth D. Butterfield, and Bruce C. Skaggs, "Relationships and Unethical Behavior: A Social Network Perspective," *Academy of Management Review*, January 1998, pp. 14–31.
17. KPMG, 1997 KPMG Business Ethics Survey Report, *http://www.itcilo.it/english/actrav/telearn/global/ilo/code/1997kpmg.htm*; QLT Inc., *http://www.qlt.com*; Compaq Canada, *http://www6.compaq.ca*.
18. "Extolling the Virtues of Hot Lines," *Workforce*, June 1998, pp. 125–126; Daryl Koehn, "An Interview with William Griffin," *http://www.stthom.edu/cbes/griffin.html*, accessed May 27, 2005.
19. HBC Corporate Responsibility, *http://www3.hbc.com/hbc/social-responsibility*, accessed April 4, 2013.
20. Mary Uhl-Bien and Melissa K. Carsten, "Being Ethical When the Boss Is Not," *Organizational Dynamics*, 2 (2007), p. 197.

CHAPTER 15

1. Linda Duxbury and Christopher Higgins, "Revisiting Work–Life Issues in Canada: The 2012 National Study on Balancing Work and Caregiving in Canada," *http://www.healthyworkplaces.info/wp-content/uploads/2012/11/2012-National-Work-Long-Summary.pdf*, accessed May 1, 2013.
2. Stephen Kotler, "Escape Artists," *Psychology Today*, September/October 2009, pp. 73–75.
3. Data reported in Kotler, "Escape Artists," p. 75.
4. Maia Szalavitz, "Stand & Deliver," *Psychology Today*, July/August 2003, p. 50.
5. Cited in Kotler, "Escape Artists," p. 76.
6. The term *WIFO* has been contributed by Shale Paul, as cited in "Tips to Keep Procrastination under Control," Gannett News Service, November 9, 1998.
7. Dru Scott, *How to Put More Time in Your Life* (New York: New American Library, 1980), p. 1.
8. "Don't Procrastinate," *Practical Supervision*, undated sample issue, p. 7.
9. Christopher Percy Collier, "The Expert on Experts," *Fast Company*, November 2006, p. 116.
10. David Allen, *Getting Things Done* (New York: Penguin, 2001, 2007).

11. Quoted in Adrian Wooldridge, "Why Clean Up Your Desk? Delight in Disorder Instead," *The Wall Street Journal*, January 2, 2007, p. D7, book review of Eric Abrahamson and David Freedman, *A Perfect Mess* (New York: Little, Brown & Co., 2007).
12. Anne Fisher, "The Rebalancing Act," *Fortune*, October 6, 2003, p. 110; Andrea Kay, "Avoid 'Traps' to Gain the Free Time You Need," Gannet News Service, January 10, 2005.
13. Mildred L. Culp, "Working Productively with Workaholics While Minimizing Legal Risks," Passage Media, 1997.
14. Jana McGregor, "Getting Serious about Getting Things Done," *Business Week*, September 1, 2008, p. 069.
15. "Secrets of Greatness: Marissa Mayer," *Fortune*, March 20, 2006, p. 68.
16. The scientific information about multitasking is reviewed in Claudia Wallis, "The Multitasking Generation," *Time*, March 27, 2006, pp. 48–55. See also Joshua S. Rubinstein, David E. Meyer, and Jeffrey E. Evans, "Executive Control of Cognitive Processes in Task Switching," *Journal of Experimental Psychology— Human Perception and Performance*, 26(4) (January 2000), pp. 763–769.
17. Transport Canada, *Road Safety in Canada*, Cat. T46-54/1-2011E, http://www.tc.gc.ca/eng/roadsafety/tp-tp15145-1201.htm#intro, accessed May 10, 2013.
18. Claire Laberge-Nadeau, "Wireless Telephones and the Risk of Road Crashes," *Accident Analysis & Prevention*, 35(5) (2003), pp. 649–660; D. Redelmeier and R. Tibshirani, "Association between Cellular-Telephone Calls and Motor Vehicle Collisions," *The New England Journal of Medicine*, 336(7) (1997): 453–458.
19. Ellen Joan Pollock, "How I Got a Grip on My Workweek," *Business Week*, April 6, 2009, p. 086.
20. Amy Dunkin, "Saying 'Adios' to the Office," *Business Week*, October 12, 1998, p. 153; Heather Page, "Remote Control," *Entrepreneur*, October 1998, p. 148; Jenny C. McCune, "Telecommuting Revisited," *Management Review*, February 1998, p. 14; E. Jeffrey Hill, Brent C. Miller, Sara P. Weiner, and Joe Colihan, "Influences of the Virtual Office on Aspects of Work/Life Balance," *Personnel Psychology*, Autumn 1998, pp. 667–683.
21. John J. Fried, "Be a Sharp Web Detective," Knight Ridder, June 27, 1999.
22. Survey cited in Maggie Jackson, "May We Have Your Attention Please?" *Business Week*, June 23, 2008, p. 055.
23. Research reported in Christine Gorman, "6 Lessons for Handling Stress," *Time*, January 29, 2007, p. 82.
24. *British Medical Journal* study reported in "Trop de Stress au Travail Double le Risque de Mourir d'une Crise de Coeur," *Journal de Montréal*, October 18, 2002, p. 7.
25. Jeffery A. Lapine, Nathan P. Podsakoff, and Marcie A. Lepine, "A Meta-Analytic Test of the Challenge-Stressor-Hindrance-Stressor Framework: An Explanation for Inconsistent Relationships among Stressors and Performance," *Academy of Management Journal*, October 2005, pp. 764–775.
26. J. Craig Wallace et al., "Work Stressors, Role-Based Performance, and the Moderating Influence of Organizational Support," *Journal of Applied Psychology*, January 2009, pp. 254–262.
27. Gillian E. Hardy, David Woods, and Toby D. Wall, "The Impact of Psychological Distress on Absence from Work," *Journal of Applied Psychology*, April 2003, pp. 306–314.
28. Tavia Grant, "Life on overload: 'Sandwich Generation' Struggles with Burnout," *The Globe and Mail*, March 27, 2013, http://www.theglobeandmail.com/report-on-business/economy/life-on-overload-sandwich-generation-struggles-with-burnout/article10422434, accessed May 2, 2013.
29. Christina Maslach and Michael Leiter, *The Truth about Burnout* (San Francisco: Jossey-Bass, 1997). Research updated in interview, Emily Waters, "Burnout on the Rise: Recognizing the Unconventional Telltale Signs," *NY Workplace Examiner*, June 18, 2009.
30. Annebel H. B. De Hoog and Deanne N. Den Hartog, "Neuroticism and Locus of Control as Moderators of the Relationships of Charismatic and Autocratic Leadership with Burnout," *Journal of Applied Psychology*, July 2009, pp. 1058–1067.
31. Christina Maslach, *The Truth about Burnout* (San Francisco: Jossey-Bass, 1997). See also Dirk van Dierendonck, Wilmar B. Schaufeli, and Bram P. Buunk, "The Evaluation of an Individual Burnout Intervention Program: The Role of Equity and Social Support," *Journal of Applied Psychology*, June 1998, pp. 393–407.
32. Research reported in Deborah Smith Bailey, "Burnout Harms Workers' Physical Health through Many Pathways," *Monitor on Psychology*, June 2006, p. 11.
33. M. Afalur Rahim, "Relationships of Stress, Locus of Control, and Social Support to Psychiatric Symptoms and Propensity to Leave a Job: A Field Study with Managers," *Journal of Business and Psychology*, Winter 1997, p. 159.
34. Steve M. Jex and Paul D. Bliese, "Efficacy Beliefs as a Moderator of the Impact of Work-Related Stressors: A Multilevel Study," *Journal of Applied Psychology*, June 1999, pp. 349–361; Steve M. Jex, Paul O. Bliese, Sheri Buzell, and Jessica Primeau, "The Impact of Self-Efficacy on Stressor–Strain Relations: Coping Style as an Explanatory Mechanism," *Journal of Applied Psychology*, June 2001, pp. 401–409.
35. Jeffrey R. Edwards and A. J. Baglioni, Jr., "Relationships between Type A Behavior Pattern and Mental and Physical Symptoms: A Comparison of Global and Component Measures," *Journal of Applied Psychology*, April 1991, p. 276.
36. Edwards and Baglioni, "Relationships between Type A Behavior Pattern and Mental and Physical Symptoms"; related research reported in Etienne Benson, "Hostility Is among Best Predictors of Heart Disease in Men," *Monitor on Psychology*, January 2003, p. 15.
37. Peter Y. Chen and Paul E. Spector, "Negative Affectivity as the Underlying Cause of Correlations Between Stressors and Strains," *Journal of Applied Psychology*, June 1991, p. 398.
38. Dr. Linda Druxbury and Dr. Chris Higgins, *Work–Life Conflict in Canada in the New Millennium: A Status Report* (Ottawa: Health Canada, Healthy Communities Division, October 2003).
39. Dr. Chris Higgins and Dr. Linda Duxbury, "Who Is at Risk? Predictors of Work–Life Conflict: Report Four" (Ottawa: Public Health Agency of Canada, 2005), http://www.phac-aspc.gc.ca/publicat/work-travail/report4/index.html.
40. Sylvia Ann Hewlett and Carolyn Buck Luce, "Extreme Jobs: The Dangerous Allure of the 70-Hour Work Week," *Harvard Business Review*, December 2006, pp. 49–59.
41. Blaine Harden, "Japan's Overtime Proves to Be Killer," *Washington Post*, July 16, 2008.
42. William Atkinson, "Causes of Workplace Stress," *HR Magazine*, December 2000, p. 107; Michele Conlin, "Is Your Office Killing You?" *Business Week*, June 5, 2000, pp. 114–128.
43. Canadian Centre for Occupational Health and Safety, "OSH Answers: Carpal Tunnel Syndrome," http://www.ccohs.ca/oshanswers/diseases/carpal.html?print, accessed May 6, 2004.
44. Christina Binkley, "Sitting Pretty When You're Hard at Work," *The Wall Street Journal*, June 11, 2009, pp. D1, D7.
45. Study reported in Deborah Smith Bailey, "Longer Train Commutes Are More Stressful, Study Finds," *Monitor on Psychology*, September 2006, p. 12.
46. Larry Copeland, "Drivers Rising Earlier to Beat the Traffic," *USA Today*, September 16, 2007.
47. Alicia A. Grandey, "Emotion Regulation in the Workplace: A New Way to Conceptualize Emotional Labor," *Journal of Occupational Health Psychology*, 5(1) (2000), pp. 95–110; A. A. Grandey, "When "The Show Must Go On:' Surface Acting and Deep Acting as Determinants of Emotional Exhaustion and Peer-Related Service Delivery," *Academy of Management Journal*, February 2003, pp. 86–96.

48. Theresa M. Glomb, John D. Kammeyer-Mueller, and Maria Rotundo, "Emotional Labor Demands and Compensating Wage Differentials," *Journal of Applied Psychology*, August 2004, p. 707.
49. Timothy A. Judge, Erin Fluegge Woolf, and Charlice Hurst, "Is Emotional Labor More Difficult for Some Than Others? A Multilevel, Experience-Sampling Study," *Personnel Psychology*, Spring 2009, pp. 57–88.
50. Edward Hallowell, *CrazyBusy: Overstretched, Overbooked, and About to Snap—Strategies for Coping in a World Gone ADD* (New York: Ballantine Books, 2006); "Zen and the Art of Thinking Straight," *Business Week*, April 3, 2006, p. 116; Maggie Jackson, "Quelling Distraction: Help Employees Overcome 'Information Overload,'" *HR Magazine*, August 8, 2008, pp. 42–46.
51. Richard S. DeFrank and John M. Ivancevich, "Stress on the Job: An Executive Update," *Academy of Management Executive*, August 1998, pp. 55–56.
52. "Executive Quits after Suicides at France Télécom," Associated Press, October 6, 2009.
53. Simona Gilboa, Arie Shirom, Yitzhak Fried, and Cary Cooper, "A Meta-Analysis of Work Demand Stressors and Job Performance: Examining Main and Moderating Effects," *Personnel Psychology*, Summer 2008, pp. 227–271.
54. Jan de Jonge and Christian Dormann, "Stressors, Resources, and Strain at Work: A Longitudinal Test of the Triple-Match Principle," *Journal of Applied Psychology*, November 2006, pp. 1359–1374.
55. Katherine M. Richardson and Hannah R. Rothstein, "Effects of Occupational Stress Management Intervention Programs: A Meta-Analysis," *Journal of Occupational Health Psychology*, January 2008, pp. 69–93.
56. Public Health Agency of Canada, "Physical Activity," *http://www.phac-aspc.gc.ca/hp-ps/hl-mvs/pa-ap/index-eng.php*, accessed May 2, 2013.
57. Richard Corliss, "The Power of Yoga," *Time*, April 23, 2001, pp. 54–62; Stacy Forster, "Companies Say Yoga Isn't a Stretch," *The Wall Street Journal*, October 14, 2003, p. D4.
58. Lisa Belkin, "Some Respect, Please, for the Afternoon Nap," *The New York Times*, February 25, 2007. p. 1.
59. Harriet Johnson Brackey, "Snoozing Studies Alarm Experts," Knight Ridder, July 6, 1998; Donald J. McNerney, "Napping at Work: You Snooze, You Win!" *HRfocus*, March 1995, p. 3.
60. Katherine Ellison, "Mastering Your Own Mind," *Psychology Today*, October 2006, p. 75.

INDEX

A

Aaron, Letita M., 318*n*
Aboriginal peoples. *See* Canadian Aboriginals
abuse from customers, 283
acceleration of career learning, 211
accent, 166
acceptance, 113
accommodative style, 181
accomplishments, 48, 266
accountability, 141
achievement, need for, 225
action plan, 7–8, 141
Active Blue, 257
active listener, 76
active listening, 75–78, 78*f*
actual experience, 52
adverse environmental conditions, 341
adverse interaction with customers, 341–342
adversity, 58
advice, asking for, 269
advocacy, 143
affiliation needs, 113, 226
age, and relationships, 259
aggressive personalities, 178
agreeableness, 20, 26
air rage, 296
Air Transat, 18
Allen, David, 329, 330
Allen, Herb, 75
allowable weaknesses, 119
Alsop, Ron, 34*n*
alternative solutions, 140
Amazon.com, 287
analogies, 165, 209
analysis of cause of problem, 140
analytical subtype, 28
Anderson-Williams, LaShonda, 291
anger, 189–190
angry customers, 294
anonymous praise game, 122
anti-bullying legislation, 178–179
anxiety, 337*n*
appearance, 69
applause, 229
Apple, Inc., 113, 114
Apple Store, 285
Army, 240
Ash, Mary Kay, 47
Asia, 260
Asian demographic group, 155–156
Askt, Daniel, 292
assertiveness, 162, 201–202
assessment of reality, 7

assumption of responsibility for problems, 124
Atkinson, Maureen, 137
attendance, 329
attention deficit disorder, 342
attention paid to other person, 69
attention to process, 211
attitudes, and personal productivity, 327–329
audience, 74
Austria, 162
authenticity, 205
authority, 162, 163
autonomy, need for, 226
Averett, Todd, 250–251
avoidance motivation, 227
avoidance of major errors, 113
avoidant style, 182

B

Baby Boomers, 34, 34*t*, 35, 180
backing up conclusions, 74
backstab, 267
backstabbers, 242
Bahama Breeze, 113
balance in life, 329
Bangladesh, 162
Bank of Montreal, 240, 318, 319*f*, 319*n*
Barbaro, Michael, 318*n*
bargaining, 186–190
BATNA (best alternative to a negotiated agreement), 189
Baugh, Sylvester, 159
Bazerman, Max H., 186
Beaublien, J. Matthew, 116*n*
Beaudoin, Pierre, 113
behaviour modification, 226–229
behaviours, 119
Belbin, R. Meredith, 117, 119
belittling others, 123
benefit statement, 262
Bennett, Steve, 254
Berman, Shawn L., 116*n*
Berry, Leonard L., 280, 281*n*
best alternative to a negotiated agreement (BATNA), 189
bias, 22
Big Five, 19–22
big picture, 124, 131
Bill 168, 179
black Canadians, 166
blamers, 240
Blasingame, Jim, 63
blind spots, 138–139
blogs, 98, 291, 306

bodily/kinesthetic intelligence, 29
body language, 80
 see also nonverbal communication
body (physical) source of cultural intelligence, 160
Bogle, John, 304
Bouchard, Lucien, 208
bounce back from setbacks and embarrassments, 58
Bragg, Terry, 256
brainstorming, 143–145
brainwriting, 144–145
Branden, Nathaniel, 47
Branson, Richard, 208
Brazil, 162
broad experience, 217
Brooks, Donald, 211
Brown, Michael E., 303
Buckingham, Marcus, 209
buddy system, 237
bullies, 178–179, 240, 243*f*, 244
burning your bridges, 272
burnout, 338
business ethics. *See* ethics
business etiquette, 258–261
business process improvement, 330
Business Software Alliance, 305
bypassing the manager, 271

C

call centres, 230
calm, 242
Cameron, Kim S., 224*n*
Canada
 assertiveness, 162
 diversity in, 156*f*
 gender egalitarianism, 162
Canada Labour Code, 190, 191
Canada Life Assurance, 257
Canada's Food Guide, 344, 345*f*
Canadian Aboriginals, 166, 170, 344
Canadian Armed Forces, 191
Canadian Bankers Association, 166
Canadian Centre for Occupational Health and Safety, 341
Canadian Council of Motor Transport Administrators (CCMTA), 331
Canadian Human Rights Act, 190
Canadian Human Rights Tribunal, 191
Canadian Mental Health Association, 179
Canadian Pacific Railway, 319*f*, 319*n*
Canadian Red Cross, 35
Canadian Union of Public Employees, 180

candidness, 210
Capital Works, LLC, 13*n*
Carbone, Lewis P., 280, 281*n*
Cardillo, Donna, 251
care, 290–291
career-management skills, 12
career success, and self-esteem, 46
Carey, Bridget, 99
carpal tunnel syndrome, 341
CBC, 97
cell phones, 89–92
cellphone earpiece, 91
challenge stressors, 336
channel, 64
charisma, 208–210
cheerleaders, 213
childhood experiences, 45
China, 154–155, 162, 260
civil behaviour, 244
clarification of contract, 141
clarification of the problem, 140
clarification of values, 35–36
Clark, Timothy R., 228*n*
classification of values, 33, 33*t*
cleanliness, 328–329
clichés, 75
clods, 242
closed to experience, 26
clothing, 258
clue influences on customer perceptions, 280–281, 281*f*
co-workers
   emotional support from, 283–284
   ethical workplace relationships, 314
   relationship building, 266–270, 267*f*
coaching, 210, 211–214
   characteristics of an effective coach, 214
   and mentoring, 239
   peer coaching, 211
   skills and techniques, 211–214, 212*f*
   suggestions for, 211–214
Coca-Cola, 206
cognition, 205
cognitive ability, 27–32
cognitive-behavioural approach to stress management, 343
cognitive factors, 205
cognitive fitness, 28
cognitive restructuring, 185–186
cognitive skills, 205–206
cognitive source of cultural intelligence, 159
cognitive styles, 23–27, 25*f*
cold-warm dimension, 65–66
collaboration, 121–122
collaborative style, 182
collaborative workplace, 109
Collective Brands, Inc., 250
collective efficacy, 141
collective leadership, 128
collectivism, 162
commitment, 113, 326–327
common language errors, 75
communication, 63
   see also interpersonal communication
   active listening, 75–78
   communication process, 64–65, 64*f*
   defensive communication, 72
   face-to-face communication, 63

feedback, 73
gender differences in communication style, 80–82
metacommunicate, 80
multiple-channel approach, 72–73
nonverbal communication, 66–70
overcoming communication problems and barriers, 71–82, 71*f*
persuasion, 74–75
positive attitude, 73
professional-level communication skills, 99
receiver, 64, 71–72
stressful conversations, 78–80
and values, 36
of a vision, 208–209
communication process, 64–65, 64*f*
commuting, 341
company policies, 166
compassion, 98
competition for limited resources, 176
competitive style, 181
completer-finisher, 117
compliment, 81, 99
compromise, 188
compromising style, 182
computerized calls, 288
computers, and ethical violations, 307, 308*f*
concentration, 215
concern, 290–291
concessions, 189
conciliatory, 81
conclusions, 74
Conference Board of Canada, 4, 214
confidence, 209, 256
confidential information, 99, 307
conflict, 175
   bullies in the workplace, 178–179
   competition for limited resources, 176
   cross-generational conflict, 180
   efficacy, 190
   incivility, 179–180
   inevitability of interpersonal conflict, 183
   personality clash, 178
   personality conflicts, 143
   role conflict, 176–177
   rudeness, 179–180
   sexual harassment, 190–194
   sources of interpersonal conflict in organizations, 175–180
   and teams, 114
   work-family conflict, 177–178
   workplace violence, 180
conflict of interest, 306–307
conflict resolution, 12
   and advocacy approach, 143
   bargaining, 186–190
   conflict management styles, 181–182, 181*f*
   confrontation, 183–184
   constructive handling of criticism, 184–186
   negotiating, 186–190
   problem solving, 183–184
conformity, 114, 115
confrontation, 183–184
conscientiousness, 20–21, 26
consensus, 125
constructive advice, 213
constructive criticism, 243
constructive disagreement, 265–266

constructive gossip, 269
constructive handling of criticism, 184–186
continuous learning, 239
contract, 141
coolness under pressure, 265
cooperation, 121–122
coordinator, 117
core competence, 206
core self-evaluation, 46, 201
corporate ethics programs, 314–316
"could," 213
Counseling and Mental Health Centre, 45
counselling, 239
Covey, Stephen R., 116*n*, 333*n*
creative problem solver, 117, 119
creative solutions, 58
creative subtype, 28
creativity, 204
critical, 81
critical assessments, 206
criticism, 122–125, 130, 184–186, 212, 243, 271
cross-cultural barriers, 164–166
cross-cultural relations, 12
   see also diversity
   business etiquette, 260
   cultural differences, 158–164
   cultural fluency, 161
   cultural intelligence (CQ), 159–160, 160*f*
   cultural intelligence training, 167–168
   cultural sensitivity, 158–159
   cultural training, 167
   dimensions of differences in cultural values, 161–163
   diversity training, 168–169
   language training, 168
   mentoring programs, 169–170
   overcoming cross-cultural barriers, 164–166
   political correctness, 159
   respect for all workers and cultures, 160–161
   techniques for improvement of, 166–170
cross-gender mentoring programs, 169–170
cross-generational conflict, 180
cubicles, 260
cultural differences, 158–164, 165–166
   see also cross-cultural relations
cultural fluency, 161
cultural intelligence (CQ), 159–160, 160*f*
cultural intelligence training, 167–168
cultural sensitivity, 158–159, 161
cultural training, 167
cultural values, 161–163
culturally insensitive gestures, 102
customer, adverse interaction with, 341–342
customer-centric sales process, 285
customer complaints, 294
customer dissatisfaction, 292–296
customer involvement, 295
customer needs, 284–285
customer relationship management (CRM) software, 287
customer retention attitude, 296
customer satisfaction
   abuse from customers, 283
   angry customers, 294
   bond with customer, 289–292
   care and concern, showing, 290–291

clue influences on customer perceptions, 280–281, 281f
customer complaints, dealing with, 294
customer needs, 284–285
customer service skills, 12
cycle-of-service chart, 286, 286f
dealing with customer dissatisfaction, 292–296
emotional support from co-workers, 283–284
empowerment, acceptance of, 286–287
exceptional service, 290
general principles of customer satisfaction, 281–289
and information technology, 287–288
invite the customer back, 292
involve the customer, 295
job satisfaction and, 282–283
levels of, 282f
make the buyer (customer) feel good, 291
moment of truth, positive response to, 285–286
personal relationships, 291
problem solving, focus on, 285
realistic customer retention attitude, 296
rudeness and hostility toward customers, 288–289
smile, 290
strong customer orientation, 289
survey, 293f
three components of customer experience (service), 280–281
unreasonable requests, 295–296
welcoming attitude, 290
customer service. See customer satisfaction
customer service orientation, 284
cyberbullying, 97
cycle-of-service chart, 286, 286f

D

Dale Carnegie organization, 3
Darden Restaurants, 113
data, 74
De Cremer, David, 45
deadlines, 125
deal, 244
DeBord, Grace, 65
decision making, 24, 206, 311–314
  see also group decision making
defensive communication, 72
defensiveness, 216, 273
defining moments, 308–310
Deitz, Karen A., 25n
deliberate practice, 328
Dell Computer, 210
Delp, Mark, 294
Delta Dental Plan, 129
Delta hotels, 287, 291
denial, 72
dependability, 22
Derbyshire, John, 55
derogatory information, 99, 100, 272
developmental experiences, 14
developmental need, 9–10
dictator, 240
diet, 344

difficult person, 240–245
  tactics for dealing with, 242–245
  types of difficult people, 240–242
digital devices, 11
digital lifestyle, 35
digital media, 87
digital technology
  cyberbullying, 97
  email messages, 92–93
  harassment, 97
  instant messaging, 92–93
  interpersonal skills for one-on-one interactions, 89–97
  interpersonal skills for small and large audiences, 98–104
  interpersonal skills linked to telecommuting, 103
  laptop use, 100–101
  one-on-one interactions, 89–97
  online reputation, 103–104
  personal digital assistant use, 100–101
  presentation technology, 101
  social networking by Internet, 98–100
  videoconferencing, 101–102
  webcam job interviews, 93–96
dining etiquette, 259
diplomacy, 244, 268–269
directive, 81
directness, 210
disabilities, 260
disagreeable, 26
disarming, 185
discussion boards, 100
disloyalty, 271
distracted driving, 331
distractions, 77
distributive justice, 255
diversity, 144
  in Canada, 156f
  the diversity umbrella, 155–157, 158f
  inclusion, 155
diversity training, 168–169
dominant communication, 65, 66
Druskat, Vanessa Urch, 116n
DuBrin, Andrew J., 253n
Duxbury, Linda, 338
Dyson, Esther, 329

E

Earley, Deborah, 257
Eckert, Robert A., 207
effective leader, 12
effort-to-performance expectancy, 232, 235
Egypt, 162
Einstein, Albert, 329
Electronic Frontier Foundation, 104
electronic work, 331
Elgin, Ben, 318n
email, 92–93, 94–95f, 111, 148–149
emotional arousal, 53
emotional fitness, 257
emotional intelligence, 30–31, 206–207, 254
emotional intelligence quotient, 31
emotional labour, 341–342
emotional source of cultural intelligence, 159–160
emotional stability, 20

emotional support, 213
emotionally expressive, 209–210
empathy, 71, 81, 159, 169
Employability Skills 2000+, 4
employee network (or affinity) groups, 161
employees
  common ethical problems, 303–310
  and job satisfaction, 282–283
Employment Equity Act, 190
empowerment, 286–287
Enbysk, Monte, 95n
encouragement, 239
energetic, 209
energy flow, 24
energy vampires, 236–237
ENFJ (The Communicator), 25f
ENFP (The Proponent), 25f
Enron Corporation, 114
enthusiasm, 207
The Entrepreneurial Spirit, 166
environment, 65, 67
environmental conditions, 341
environmentally conscious, 316, 317–318f
environmentally induced attention deficit disorder, 342
EQ, 31
equal status of peers, 211
equity, 305
equity, need for, 226
errors, avoidance of, 113
ESFP (The Entertainer), 24
esteem needs, 226
ethical behaviour, 12
ethical decision-making guide, 311–314
ethical screening, 311
ethics, 33
  challenges of ethical behaviour, 303–304
  common ethical problems, 303–310
  corporate ethics programs, 314–316
  defining moments, 308–310
  environmentally conscious, 316, 317–318f
  ethical decision-making guide, 311–314
  ethical workplace relationships, 314
  extent of ethical problems, 304
  frequent ethical dilemmas, 305–308, 305f
  guidelines for ethical behaviour, 310–320
  importance of business ethics, 301–303
  professional codes of conduct, 318, 319f
  questionable workplace behaviour as reported by employees, 304f
  upward ethical leadership, 319–320
  virtuousness, 310–312
ethics hotlines, 315
etiquette, 258–261
etiquette, cultural differences in, 165–166
Europe, 162
evaluation, 141
exceptional service, 290
exchange favours, 269
expectancy theory, 231–235
  basic components, 232–233, 232f
  diagnosing motivation with, 234
  effort-to-performance expectancy, 232, 235
  guidelines for applying, 234–235
  and moods, 233–234
  overview, 231–232
  performance-to-outcome expectancy, 232–233
  valence, 233

experience
　actual experience, 52
　broad experience, 217
　childhood experiences, 45
　multicultural experiences, 156
　of others, 52
expert power, 265
explaining the ropes, 239
explanatory style of optimists, 56–57
external customers, 279
extraversion, 19, 20, 22, 24, 26
extreme job, 340
extroversion, 20
eye contact, 68

F

face-saving, 190
face-to-face communication, 63
face-to-face interactions, 99
face-to-face meetings, 150
face-to-face teams, 109–110
Facebook, 46, 93, 97, 98, 100, 104, 149, 262, 270, 333
facial expressions, 68
Fairmont hotels, 287
fairness, 305–306
faking, 77–78
family-to-work conflict, 177
favours, exchange of, 269
Federal Trade Commission (U.S.), 306
FedEx, 204
feedback, 65
　on actions, 8
　and active listening, 76
　and behaviour modification, 228
　on body language, 70
　to check comprehension and feelings, 73
　coaching and, 212
　and difficult people, 242–243
　honest feedback, 130
　and self-esteem, 47
　and training, 216
feeling, 24
female bullies, 179
Fernald, Dodge, 142n
Fidelity Employer Services Division, 113
fight-or-flight response, 336
figure of speech, 76
First Nations, 344
First Nations Bank, 166
Five Factor Model, 19–22
flattery, 264
Fleet Response, 294
flexibility, 283
Florida Atlantic University, 308n
flow, 57
Ford Motor Company, 100
forgiveness, 311
formal learning, 14
four circles of intimacy, 67f
frame of reference, 72
France, 162
France Télécom, 342
Frank, Robert H., 47
frequent practice, 8
Friedman, Karen, 96
friendship, 239

Front de Libération du Québec, 208
functional clues, 281

G

g (general) factor, 27
Galatea effect, 56
Gallup Organization, 266
Gardner, Howard, 29, 30
Gardner, William L. III, 257
Garvin, David A., 143
Gates, Bill, 47
gender differences in communication style, 80–82
gender egalitarianism, 162
gender harassment, 192
General Motors Co., 206
Generation Jones, 34, 34t
Generation X, 34, 34t, 180
Generation Y, 34, 34t, 35, 180
George, Jennifer M., 333n
Germany, 157, 162, 166
gestures, 68, 70, 102
Getting Things Done (Allen), 328–329, 330
giraffe award, 229
Gladwell, Malcolm, 30
gluttony, 139
goal congruence, 36
goal-oriented, 209
goal setting, 5–7, 6f
goals, 327–328
Golden, John P., 25n
Golden Personality Type Profiler, 23–24, 23–25, 25f
Golden Rule, 37
Goldsmith, Marshall, 5, 77
Goleman, Daniel, 207
good attendance, 329
good moods, 244
Google, 104, 114, 147, 210, 330
gossip, 269
gossips, 240
Gould, Gordon, 225
grammar, 166
Grandey, Alicia A., 342
Greece, 162, 165
greed, 139
green, 316, 317–318f
Gretzky, Wayne, 123
group decision making, 11–12, 113, 137
　see also group problem solving
　collective efficacy, 141
　disagreement, management of, 142–143
　email to facilitate meetings, 148–149
　group problem-solving steps, 139–141
　guidelines for using general problem-solving groups, 139–143
　inquiry *vs.* advocacy, 143
　political decision-making model, 138–139
　rational decision-making model, 137–139
group norms, 270
group problem solving, 11–12
　see also group decision making
　being an effective meeting participant, 150
　brainstorming, 143–145
　groupware to facilitate meetings, 149
　nominal group technique (NGT), 145–147, 146f
　standup meetings, 147–148
　virtual problem solving, 149
groups. *See* group decision making; group problem solving; team
groupthink, 114
groupware, 111, 149
Grow, Brian, 318n
growth needs, 237
Gulley, Stanley M., 116n
Gutner, Toddi, 333n

H

Hall, Douglas T., 52, 211
Hallowell, Edward, 342
Hampton Inn, 286
hand gestures, 68, 70
handshake, 210
harassment, 97, 178–179, 190–194, 193f, 244
hard skills, 4
Harris Interactive, 228n
Hazen, James, 282
Health, 52n
Health Canada, 319, 340, 344
healthy diet, 344
help from others, 51
helping others, 225, 236
helping others develop and grow, 12, 99
Herbalife Ltd., 307
Hertel, Guido, 116n
Hewitt Associates, 225
Hewlett-Packard, 108–109
high expectations, 56
high-maintenance types, 242
high performance standards, 129
high productivity, 113
high-self-esteem living space, 51–52
high self-monitor, 26
hindrance stressors, 336
Hitt, William D., 218
Holiday Inn, 279
Hollenbeck, George P., 52
Holloway, Lindsay, 34n
home office, 332
honest relationships, 266–267
honesty, 310–311
hostile environment, 97
hostility, 288–289
Hudson's Bay Company, 300–301, 316
human interaction clues, 281
Human Resources Development Canada, 225
Human Rights Code, 190
human rights codes, 166
humane orientation, 162, 163
humour, 204, 244, 265
Hurd, Mark, 109
Hurst, Chalice, 46

I

IBM Canada, 257
IBM Corp., 257
identification of problem, 140
idioms, 165
Ilardie, Barbara, 51
illegal copying of software, 305, 306
image, 257
impartiality, 305

implementation plan, 141
implementer, 117
important tasks, 330–331
impression management, 255–257
impulsivity, 326
in-group collectivism, 162
in-groups, 131–132
in the zone, 57
inappropriate remarks, 192
Incalcaterra, Kara A., 116*n*
incivility, 179–180
inclusion, 155
increasing the probability, 227
independence, 80–81, 311
independent decision making, 206
indiscreet behaviour in private life, 272
individual differences, 10, 19
　in appearance, 166
　in valences, 235
　values, 33–38
individual responsibility, 114
individual values, 36–37
inductive reasoning, 28
INFJ (The Foreseer), 25*f*
informal learning, 13–14
information and communication technologies (ICT), 97
information gathering, 24
information overload, 73
information power, 264–265
information technology, 287–288, 307
INFP (The Advocate), 25*f*
inner critic, 49–50
inquiry, 143
Instagram, 98
instant messaging, 92–93, 94–95*f*, 111
integrated human being, 218
integrity, 202, 311, 313
intelligence, 27
　emotional intelligence, 30–31
　g (general) factor, 27
　multiple intelligences, 29–30
　practical intelligence, 28–29
　relating to different levels and types of intelligence, 32
　s (special) factors, 27
　traditional intelligence, 27–28
　triarchic theory of intelligence, 28, 29*f*
intention to remember, 215
interests *vs.* positions, 188
intermittent rewards, 228
internal customers, 12, 279
International Labour Organization, 180
Internet, and social networking, 98–100
Internet search skills, 332
interpersonal aspects of team play, 119–123, 121*f*
interpersonal communication, 11
　see also communication
　and relationship building, 65–66, 66*f*
interpersonal conflict. *See* conflict
interpersonal distance, 67–68
interpersonal intelligence, 30
interpersonal relations, 3
　universal training needs, 10–12
　values, 37–38
interpersonal skills
　development of, on the job, 12–13, 13*f*

for the digital world, checklist, 88–89
formal learning, 14
informal learning, 13–14
and multitasking, 96
negative interpersonal skills. *See* negative interpersonal skills
for one-on-one interactions, 89–97
for small and large audiences, 98–104
and social networking, 98–99
telecommuting, 103
interpersonal skills improvement model, 5–9, 5*f*
　action plan, 7–8
　assessment of reality, 7
　feedback on actions, 8
　frequent practice, 8
　goal or desired state of affairs, 5–7
interpersonal skills training, 4
interpretation, 213
interruptions, 77
intimacy, 67*f*
intimidating, 81
intrapersonal intelligence, 29
intrinsically motivating, 207
introductions, 259
introversion, 24, 26
Intuit, 254
intuiting-type, 26
intuition, 24, 28
Inuit, 344
invite the customer back, 292
Ireland, Karen, 309*n*
Irvine, Martha, 34*n*

J

Jacobi, Jeffrey, 68–69
Japan, 162, 340
Japanese tsunami, 35
jargon, 75
J.C. Williams Group, 137
Jekyll-and-Hydes, 242
Jett, Quintus R., 333*n*
job factors, 227, 228*f*
job factors contributing to stress, 338–343
job insecurity, 342–343
job interviews, 93–96
job loss, 342–343
job performance consequences, 336–338
job satisfaction, 113, 282–283
job search
　Internet search, as background investigation, 104
　job search skills, 12
job search skills, 12
job sources of stress, 339, 340*f*
job values, 36–37
Johnson, Abigail, 113–114
Johnson & Johnson, 113
Joshi, Aparna, 116*n*
Judge, Timothy A., 46, 56
judging, 24
Jung, Carl, 23
justice, 255, 311

K

karoshi, 340
Kent, Muhtar, 206

key leadership traits, 200–208, 200*f*
kinesthetic intelligence, 29
kissing, work-related, 193
know-it-alls, 240
knowledge base, 54–55
knowledge of the business, 206
knowledge of the task, 124
KPMG Canada, 211
Kraft Foods, 207
Kram, Kathy E., 211
Krell, Erick, 69
Kronos Incorporated, 228*n*

L

Labour Canada, 190
labour laws and practices, 166
Langred, Claus W., 116*n*
language errors, 75
language training, 168
laptops, 100–101
Latin America, 169
law of effect, 226
leader-exchange model, 131–132, 131*f*
leader-member exchange (LMX), 254–255
leadership, 126, 199
　assertiveness, 201–202
　charisma, development of, 208–210
　coaching others, 210, 211–214
　cognitive skills including critical assessments, 205–206
　collective leadership, 128
　development of leadership potential, 217–218
　effective leader, 12
　emotional intelligence, 206–207
　enthusiasm, 207
　key leadership traits, 200–208, 200*f*
　leadership efficacy, 200–201
　morality, 202–204
　participative leadership, 126
　passion, 207
　positive core self-evaluation, 201
　self-awareness, 205
　self-confidence, 200–201
　self-objectivity, 205
　self-sacrificing personality, 208
　sense of humour, 204
　shared leadership, 128
　team leadership skills, 126–132
　training others, 210, 214–216
　trustworthiness, 202–204
　upward ethical leadership, 319–320
leadership efficacy, 200–201
learning style, 216
Lebrun, Pierre, 180
Lee, Dongseop, 116*n*
lifestyle orientation, 24
Liljenquist, Katie A., 116*n*
linguistic intelligence, 29
LinkedIn, 98, 104, 262
listening
　active listening, 75–78, 78*f*
　reflective listening, 76
Livermore, Ann, 108–109
living space, 51–52
Locke, Edwin A., 310
Lockwood, Charles, 318*n*

INDEX　　373

Lockwood, Gary, 55
locus of control, 201
logical-mathematical intelligence, 29
Lovel, Pamela, 123
low neuroticism, 20
loyalty, 98
Lululemon Athletica Inc., 136–137
lying, 77–78

M

make others feel important, 267–268
make the buyer (customer) feel good, 291
making the desired response, 227
Malaysia, 162
Malhotra, Deepak, 186
managers, relationship building with, 261–266, 262f
Margolis, Joshua D., 58
Mattel, 207
Mayer, Marissa, 330
McCall, Morgan W. Jr., 14
McClure, Lynne, 180
McDonald's Corporation, 161, 288
McGill, Michael E., 218
McNatt, D. Brian, 56
meaningful contact, 99
meaningful material, 215–216
mechanical clues, 281
meditation, 345–346
medium, 64
memory, 28
men and women, relationships between, 259
mental ability, 205
mental health, 46
mentor, 237
mentoring, 237–240
　characteristics, 238
　online mentoring, 238
　specific mentoring behaviours, 238–240
　types of, 238
　virtual mentoring, 238
Merrill Lynch & Co., 267
message, 64
metacommunicate, 80
metaphors, 209
Métis, 344
Meyer, David E., 331
Michael Stern Associates, 130, 208
microinequity, 270
micromanager, 129, 213
Microsoft, 114, 210, 291
Middle East, 260
Millennials, 34t, 180
mind game, 185
minimalists, 242
mirroring, 70
misrepresentation, 307
mission, 327–328
mission statement, 128–129
mistakes, admitting, 256
modelling, 52, 213, 217–218
moment of truth, 285–286
monitor-evaluator, 117
mood, 233–234, 244
moral intensity, 303
morality, 202–204

motivation, 223
　avoidance motivation, 227
　expectancy theory, 231–235
　helping others, 225
　of interest, 215
　by mentoring, 237–240
　needs, importance of, 225–226
　negative reinforcement, 227
　by nurturing, 235–237
　of others, 12
　positive reinforcement, 226–229
　recognition, use of, 229–231
　and self-interest, 223–226
　"what's in it for me"? (WIIFM), 223–226, 233
motivational source of cultural intelligence, 159–160
motivational state, 72
Mulally, Alan, 100
multicultural experiences, 156
multiple-channel approach, 72–73
multiple intelligences, 29–30
multitasking, 96–97, 330–331
musical intelligence, 29
mutual gain, 182
Myers-Briggs Type Indicator (MBTI), 23

N

Namie, Gary, 179
napping, 344
NASA, 148
National Association for Self-Esteem, 44n
National Business Ethics Survey, 304n
naturalist, 30
Neale, Margaret A., 116n
need for achievement, 225
need for affiliation, 226
need for autonomy, 226
need for equity, 226
need for esteem, 226
need for power, 225
need for safety and security, 226
needs, 225–226
negative affectivity, 339
negative interpersonal skills
　and multitasking, 97
　and social networking, 99–100
　while text messaging, 90–92
　while using cell phones, 90–92
negative reinforcement, 227
negative self-talk, 55–56
negotiating, 186–190, 244
Nelson, Bob, 222–223
nervousness, 102
Nesbitt, Bryan, 206
networking, 261–263
New Zealand, 162
no-people, 242
noise, 65
nominal group technique (NGT), 145–147, 146f
non-hostile humour, 244
nonverbal communication, 66
　and active listening, 77
　cultural differences in, 166
　emotional expressiveness, 210
　guidelines for improvement of, 70

　modes of transmission, 67–69
　self-confidence, signals of, 210
Normen, Julie, 23
Norway, 162
numerical acuity, 28
nurturing person, 235–237
Nyberg, Anthony J., 116n

O

office cheats, 242
Olguin, Daniel, 69
Olive Garden, 113
Oliver, Kim, 159
1-800-GOT-JUNK, 42–43, 238
one-on-one interactions, 89–97
O'Neil, Sharon Lund, 73
online discussion boards, 98, 100
online mentoring, 238
online reputation, 103–104
online survey, 149
Ontario, 179, 190
Ontario Human Rights Commission, 190
Ontario Occupational Health and Safety Act, 179
open relationships, 266–267
openness to experience, 20, 21
optimism, 20, 21–22, 23, 56–57, 283
orderliness, 328–329
organizational citizenship behaviour, 22–23, 255–256
organizational politics, 251, 252f
　business etiquette, 258–261
　impression management, 255–257
　political blunders, avoiding, 271–273
　political skill, 253–255
　positive political behaviours and individual success, 261f
　relationship building with co-workers and other work associates, 266–270, 267f
　relationship building with managers and other key people, 261–266, 262f
organizational success, and self-esteem, 47
Osborn, Alex, 143
other party's perspective, 186–188
Otis, Clarence Jr., 113
out-groups, 131–132

P

paperwork, 331
paraphrase, 76–77
Parker, Glenn, 124
Parker, Polly, 211
participative leadership, 126
passion, 207
Payless ShoeSource, 250
peak performance, 57
Pearce, Craig L., 128
peer coaching, 211
peer evaluations, 131
Penney, Lisa, 179
Pentland, Sandy, 69
Penttila, Chris, 34n
people with disabilities, 260
perceived control, 339
perceiving, 24
perceptual speed, 28

perfectionism, 334–335
performance orientation, 162
performance-to-outcome expectancy, 232–233
person-role conflict, 37
personal appearance, 69, 166
personal biases and preferences, 138
personal brand, 225
personal development, 211
personal digital assistant, 100–101
personal productivity, 12, 325
    attitudes and values, 327–329
        procrastination, 325–327
        time wasters, 333–334, 333f
        work habits and skills, 330–332
personal relationships, 291
personal risks, 210
personal strengths, 48–49
personality, 19
    cognitive styles and personality types, 23–27, 25f
    combination of personality factors, 23
    conflicts, 143
    eight major personality factors and traits, 19–23
    guidelines for dealing with different personality types, 25–27
    job performance, and eight factors and traits, 22–23
    self-sacrificing personality, 208
    and stress, 338–343
    and turnover, 23
    Type A behaviour, 339
personality clash, 178
persuasion, 74–75
pessimism, 23
pests, 271
Phillips, Katherine W., 116n
physical exercise, 343–344
physical touching, 193
physiological reactions to stress, 336
Piché, Robert, 18–19, 31
pitch at end of sentences, 74
plausible demand or offer, 188–189
politeness, 81
political blunders, avoiding, 271–273
political correctness, 159
political decision-making model, 138–139
political skill, 12, 253–255
    emotional intelligence, 254
    injustice, overcoming effects of, 255
    relationship building with the leader, 254–255
    sensitivity to surroundings, 253–254
    social intelligence, 254
political tactics, 252f
poor judgment, 29
pornography, 97
positions vs. interests, 188
positive attitude, 73
positive core self-evaluation, 201
positive expectations, 283
positive gossip, 269
positive reinforcement, 226–229
positive self-esteem, 46
positive self-image, 283
positive self-talk, 55
positive visual imagery, 56
posture, 68, 95

power, 162, 163, 251, 252f
    expert power, 265
    information power, 264–265
    need for, 225
power words, 74
powerful questions, 212–213
PowerPoint, 101
practical intelligence, 28–29
practical subtype, 28
practice, 211
practise of leadership, 218
presence, 256
presentation technology, 101, 102
pride, 311
priorities, 330
Pritchett, Price, 56–57
problem solving, 183–184, 239, 285
    see also group problem solving
problem-solving steps, 139–141
Probst, Bob, 260
procedural justice, 255
procrastination, 325–327
Procter & Gamble, 217
productivity, 113, 311
    see also personal productivity
professional development, 211
proofreading, 92
protecting, 239
protégé, 237
provincial human rights code, 190
proxemics, 67
psychological harassment, 178–179
Public Health Agency of Canada, 344
punctuality, 329
Pygmalion effect, 235

Q

Quebec, 178
question-and-answer sessions, 129–130
questions, 77

R

racism, 166
RadioShack Corp., 307
Radomski, Rob, 291
Raghavan, Prabhakar, 225
RainmakerThinking Inc., 213
Ramirez, Ida, 65
rapport, 70, 80
Rath, Tom, 266
rational decision-making model, 137–139
rationality, 310
Raudsepp, Eugene, 46
realistic customer retention attitude, 296
receiver, 64, 71–72
reciprocity, 305
recognition
    and motivation, 229–231
    of others' interests and achievements, 122
recovery paradox, 294
Red Lobster, 113
referral agent, 239
reflection, 211
reflective listening, 76
reframing, 185–186
rehearsal, 95–96, 102

relationship building
    with co-workers and other work associates, 266–270, 267f
    and coaching, 211–212
    and interpersonal communication, 65–66, 66f
    with the leader, 254–255
    with managers and other key people, 261–266, 262f
relationship management, 31
relaxation, 70
relaxation response, 345–346
repetitive-strain injury, 341
reporting behaviour, 244
repulsives, 242, 243
Research in Motion (RIM), 254
resilience, 58
resource investigator, 117
respect for all workers and cultures, 160–161, 164
rest, 344
reward, 227, 228–229, 234–235
reward-performance link, 234
Rinaldi, Arlene H., 308n
risk taking, 20, 21, 26
Ritz-Carlton, 286
Roberto, Michael A., 143
Roberts, David, 318n
robocalls, 288
Rogelberg, Steven G., 150
Rogers, Kishau, 296
role, 117–119
role ambiguity, 341
role conflict, 176–177, 340–341
role model, 237, 239
role overload, 339–340
role-playing, 70, 245
Rucker, Jim, 258
rudeness, 179–180, 288–289
Russia, 162

S

s (special) factors, 27
safety jackpot, 229
safety needs, 226
Salesforce.com, 287
sandwich generation, 325, 338
SAP, 287
Saskatchewan, 179
Schoeff, Mark Jr., 243n
Schuster, Richard, 266
Schwartz, Shalom H., 33
Scudamore, Brian, 42–43
Sears, 282
Sears Canada, 319f, 319n
security needs, 113, 226
selection of alternatives, 140
self-assessment quizzes
    assertiveness scale, 203–204
    attitudes toward helping others, 236
    the blunder quiz, 272
    characteristics of an effective coach, 214
    charting your cultural dimension profile, 163
    clarifying your values, 36
    collaborative vs. competitive styles of conflict management, 176

self-assessment quizzes (continued)
  conformity quiz, 115
  cross-cultural skills and attitudes, 157
  customer-service orientation quiz, 280
  developmental needs, 11
  ethical reasoning inventory, 302
  ethical workplace relationships
    inventory, 315
  helping difficult people, 241
  how important do I make people feel?, 268
  illegal copying of software, 306
  interpersonal skills for the digital world
    checklist, 88–89
  leadership style, 126–127
  listening traps, 79
  my approach to motivating others, 224
  my problem-solving tendencies, 138
  negotiator quiz, 187
  organizational politics questionnaire,
    252–253
  presentation technology checklist of
    interpersonal behaviours, 102
  procrastination tendencies, 326
  risk-taking scale, 21
  rudeness, 289
  self-confidence, 53
  self-esteem checklist, 43–44
  team player attitudes, 110
  team player roles, 118–119
  team skills, 111
  tendencies toward perfectionism, 334–335
  voice-quality checkup, 69
self-awareness, 30, 205
self-concept, 43
self-confidence, 10
  bounce back from setbacks and
    embarrassments, 58
  development of, 54–58
  enhancement of, 54–58, 54f
  explanatory style of optimists, 56–57
  Galatea effect, 56
  high expectations, 56
  importance of, 52–53
  and leadership efficacy, 200–201
  low self-confidence, 54
  negative self-talk, avoidance of, 55–56
  non-verbal signals of, 210
  peak performance, 57
  positive self-talk, 55
  positive visual imagery, 56
  self-assessment quiz, 53
  solid knowledge base, 54–55
self-development, 218
self-effacing humour, 204
self-efficacy, 6, 52–53, 232, 339
self-esteem, 10
  and career success, 46
  childhood experiences, 45
  consequences of high self-esteem, 46–47, 46t
  development of, 45–46
  enhancement of, 47–52, 48f
  feedback, profiting from, 47
  getting help from others, 51
  and good mental health, 46
  high-self-esteem living space, 51–52
  inner critic, 49–50
  and job satisfaction, 282–283
  legitimate accomplishments, 48

  meaning of, 43
  minimization of certain situations, 50
  model behaviour of people with high
    self-esteem, 51
  needs, 113
  and organizational success, 47
  personal strengths, 48–49
  positive self-esteem, 46
  potential negative consequences, 47
  self-nurturing, 50
self-esteem calendar, 52
self-evaluation, 201
self-fulfillment, 113
self-interest, 223–226, 304
self-management, 30–31
self-monitoring of behaviour, 20, 21, 22, 26
self-nurturing, 50
self-objectivity, 205
self-oriented roles, 119
self-promotion, 210
self-rewards, 50
self-sacrificing personality, 208
Seligman, Martin, 45
Sellers, Anna, 258
sender, 64
sensation, 24
sense of humour, 204
sense of urgency, 129
sensing-type, 26
sensitivity to surroundings, 253–254
sexual coercion, 192
sexual harassment, 67, 190–194, 193f, 306
sexual implications, 192
shaper, 117
share the glory, 123
shared leadership, 128
shared whiteboard, 149
sharing challenging assignments, 239
sharing style, 182
shirking of individual responsibility, 114
"should," 213
sick building, 341
Sills, Judith, 263
Simon, Lauren S., 46
Simon, Sidney, 181
Singapore, 162, 292
situational constraint, 343
skill-building exercises
  adapting to people of different mental
    ability, 32
  applying expectancy theory, 235
  background work for the WIIFM, 226
  bonding with customers, 292
  boosting productivity through work habits
    on the Internet, 332
  brainstorming vs. brainwriting, 145
  building your self-confidence and self-
    efficacy, 57
  business etiquette, 261
  coaching a mediocre performer
    role-play, 215
  combating sexual harassment, 194
  confronting the unethical boss, 320
  creating a vision, 209
  cross-cultural relations role-play, 167
  cultural mistakes to avoid, 165
  dealing with defining moments, 310
  dealing with difficult customers, 296

  dealing with difficult people, 245
  designing a training program, 216
  developing a team mission statement, 129
  developing cultural sensitivity, 161
  developing empathy for differences, 169
  development of foreign-language skills, 168
  disarming the opposition, 185
  elevator 30-second speech, 258
  environmental audit, 318
  estimating valences for applying expectancy
    theory, 233
  ethical decision making, 314
  ethics game, 309
  flattering an influential person, 265
  general problem-solving group, 141
  getting along with co-workers role-play, 271
  habitat for the homeless, 126
  helping an intellectually challenged worker
    get started, 32
  I want a raise, 76
  the important message, 92
  interpersonal skills improvement model, 9
  justifying laptop use during a meeting, 101
  listening to a co-worker, 79
  maintaining a time log, 334
  mirroring technique, 70
  moments of truth, 286
  my personal leadership journal, 217
  negotiating a starting salary, 191
  nominal group technique, 147
  the nurturing, positive person, 237
  personal stress management action
    plan, 347
  personality role plays, 27
  positive reinforcement, 229
  recognition of team accomplishments, 130
  reframing through cognitive
    restructuring, 186
  reinforcing a positive self-image, 49
  scavenger hunt, 122
  selecting a protégé, 240
  self-esteem building club, 49
  self-esteem calendar, 52
  solving a few unusual problems, 142
  stretch your imagination, 145
  team member roles, 120
  using a mission statement and goals to
    power work habits, 328
  value-conflict role-play, 38
  visualization for stress reduction, 346
  win-win conflict resolution, 183
  the witty leader, 205
Skype, 111
Slocum, John W. Jr., 218
small concessions, 189
smile, 290
Smith, Fred, 204
Smith, Hyrum, 333n
social awareness, 31
social comparison, 52–53
social intelligence, 254
social loafing, 114
social networking, 98–100, 262
social persuasion, 53
social-support-seeking, 163
socialized charismatic, 209
soft-skill training, 4
software, copying of, 305, 306

Sorenson, Ritch, 65
source, 64
South Korea, 162
spatial intelligence, 29
spatial perception, 28
specialist, 117
splitting the difference, 182
sponsoring, 239
standup meetings, 147–148
Starbucks, 282
starting salary, 191
State Farm Insurance, 290
Statistics Canada, 156n
status, 80–81
Staybridge Suites, 291
Stern, Michael, 130, 208
Stoltz, Paul G., 58
straightforward language, 164
streamline your work, 330
stress, 335
   adverse environmental conditions, 341
   adverse interaction with customers, 341–342
   burnout, 338
   consequences of, 336–338
   emotional labour, 341–342
   environmentally induced attention deficit disorder, 342
   job factors contributing to, 338–343
   job insecurity, 342–343
   job loss, 342–343
   and job performance, 337–338, 337f
   job performance consequences, 336–338
   job sources, 339, 340f
   management of. *See* stress management
   and personality, 338–343
   physiological reactions, 336
   role ambiguity, 341
   role conflict, 340–341
   role overload, 339–340
   symptoms, 336–338, 337f
stress management, 12, 343–347
   cognitive-behavioural approach to stress management, 343
   everyday suggestions, 346–347, 346f
   healthy diet, 344
   meditation, 345–346
   physical exercise, 343–344
   rest, 344
   stressor, elimination or modification of, 343
   support network, 345
   visualization, 345–346
stressful conversations, 78–80
stressor, 335
   challenge stressors, 336
   elimination or modification of, 343
   hindrance stressors, 336
strong customer orientation, 289
style, 166
subordinate communication, 65, 66
suggestive compliments, 192
support, 239
support network, 345
Supreme Court of Canada, 191
surface acting, 342
Survey Monkey, 149
Survey on Sexual Harassment in Public Places and at Work (SSHPPW), 191–192
sustainable environment, 317–318f
Sweden, 162
symbolic consequences, 312
sympathize, 71
synergy, 112–113
Szaky, Tom, 318n

T

tact, 244
Taiwan, 284
task aspects of team play, 123–125, 123f
teaching the right skills, 239
team, 109
   advantages of group work and teamwork, 112–113
   assumption of responsibility for problems, 124
   belittling others, 123
   big picture, 124
   consensus, 125
   cooperation and collaboration, 121–122
   cultural diversity within groups, 157
   deadlines, focus on, 125
   developing teamwork, 128f
   disadvantages of group work and teamwork, 113–114
   effective teams and work groups, 116f
   face-to-face *vs.* virtual teams, 109–112
   good organizational citizen, 125
   help team members do their jobs better, 125
   helpful criticism, 122–125
   interpersonal aspects of team play, 119–123, 121f
   poor team players, 271–272
   recognition of others' interests and achievements, 122
   share the glory, 123
   task aspects of team play, 123–125, 123f
   team leadership skills, 126–132
   team member roles, 117–119
   teamwork skills, 11
   technical expertise, 124
   trust, 121
team leadership skills, 126–132
   big picture, 131
   high performance standards, 129
   honest criticism, 130
   in-groups and out-groups, 131–132
   mission statement, 128–129
   peer evaluations, 131
   question-and-answer sessions, 129–130
   recognition of each other's accomplishments, 130
   sense of urgency, 129
   shared leadership, 128
   trust, 129
team worker, 117
technical expertise, 124
teenage brain, 29
telecommuting, 86–87, 103
teleworking, 87
TELUS, 285
temperate phrasing, 80
terms of endearment, 192
text messaging, 89–92
Thailand, 162
Thain, John, 267
thinking, 24
ThisNext, 225
Thomas, Kenneth, 181, 181n
Thompson, Vince, 333n
thrill seeking, 20, 21, 26
time log, 334
time orientation, 162, 163
time wasters, 333–334, 333f
time wasting, and teams, 113–114
to-do list, 330
Toronto Parks and Recreation, 117
Toronto Stock Exchange, 178
touching, 67, 193
touching their hot buttons, 225
toxic person, 235–236
Toyota, 340
traditional intelligence, 27–28
traditional teams, 110
Traditionalists, 180
training, 210, 214–216
Treviño, Linda Klebe, 303
triarchic theory of intelligence, 28, 29f
TripAdvisor, 307
Trudeau, Pierre Elliott, 208
true stories, 210
trust, 112, 121, 129, 202, 209, 256
trusted, 239
trustworthiness, 202–204
Tschabitscher, Heinz, 95n
turnover, 23
Twitter, 51, 98, 99, 100, 230, 262, 270, 272, 333
Tyler, Kathryn, 34n
Type A behaviour, 339

U

unfair treatment, 305–306
United Kingdom, 338
United Parcel Service (UPS), 147
United States, 162, 306
universal training needs, 10–12
University of Texas, 210
University of Toronto, 179
unreasonable customer requests, 295–296
unwanted sexual attention, 192
unwritten boundaries, 263–264
upward ethical leadership, 319–320
Usana Health Sciences, Inc., 307
Useem, Michael, 218
utilitarian predisposition, 304
Utsey, Shawn O., 138

V

valence, 233, 235
value, 33
   acquisition of values, 35
   clarification of values, 35–36
   classification of values, 33, 33t
   cultural values, differences in, 161–163
   generational differences in values, 33–34
   individual and job values, 36–37
   and personal productivity, 327–329
   using values to improve interpersonal relations, 37–38
   value stereotypes for generations of workers, 34t

Vancouver Police Service, 103
Vanguard Groups of Mutual Funds, 304
verbal comprehension, 28
videoconferencing, 101–102, 111
Villeneuve, Raymond, 208
Virgin, 208
virtual mentoring, 238
virtual office, 332
virtual problem solving, 149
virtual teams, 111–112
virtuousness, 310–312
Visio, 101
vision, 208–209
visualization, 345–346
voice mail, 287–288
voice quality, 68–69
volunteering for assignments, 264

W

Wall, Eileen A., 280, 281n
Walsh, Bryan, 318n
warm, 209
Warner, Melanie, 318n
waste of company time, 307–308
Waterman, Brian, 117
webcam, 111
webcam job interviews, 93–96
Weber, Bernhard, 116n
Websmith Group LLC, 296
Weeks, Holly, 80
Welch, Jack, 177
welcoming attitude, 290
WestJet Airlines, 282
"what's in it for me"? (WIIFM), 223–226, 233
Whetton, David A., 224n
WHFM principle, 215
whiners, 242
whistleblowing, 319
WIFO principle (worst in, first out), 327
wikis, 98
Wilson, Chip, 136–137
"wimp" phrases, 74–75
win-lose approach, 181
win-win approach, 182, 183
wisdom, 29
Wolff, Steven B., 116n
women and men, relationships between, 259
word fluency, 28
words that shut down discussion, 77
work accomplishment, 113
work exhaustion, 338
work extension technology (WET), 325
work-family conflict, 177–178
work-life choices, 177–178
work orientation, 162
work overload, 340
work-related kissing, 193
work smarter, not harder, 328
work-to-family conflict, 177
workaholism, 329
workplace bullying, 178–179
Workplace Bullying Institute, 179
workplace cubicles, 260
Workplace Mental Health Promotion, 179
workplace relationships, ethical, 314
workplace violence, 180
World Vision Canada, 35

Y

Yahoo!, 225
yes-people, 242, 257
"yes response," 74
yoga, 344
YouTube, 74, 98, 100, 333

Z

Zimmerman, Matt, 104